A History of Our Time

A HISTORY OF OUR TIME

Readings on Postwar America

FOURTH EDITION

Edited by
William H. Chafe
DUKE UNIVERSITY

Harvard Sitkoff
UNIVERSITY OF NEW HAMPSHIRE

New York   Oxford
OXFORD UNIVERSITY PRESS
1995

Oxford University Press

Oxford   New York
Athens   Auckland   Bangkok   Bombay
Calcutta   Cape Town   Dar es Salaam   Delhi
Florence   Hong Kong   Istanbul   Karachi
Kuala Lampur   Madras   Madrid   Melbourne
Mexico City   Nairobi   Paris   Singapore
Taipei   Tokyo   Toronto

and associated companies in
Berlin   Ibadan

Published by Oxford University Press, Inc.,
200 Madison Avenue, New York, New York 10016

Oxford is a registered trademark of Oxford University Press

Library of Congress Cataloging-in-Publication Data
A history of our time : readings on postwar America
/ edited by William H. Chafe, Harvard Sitkoff.—4th ed.
p. cm.   Includes bibliographical references (p.).
ISBN 0-19-508277-X
1. United States—History—1945–
I. Chafe, William Henry.
II. Sitkoff, Harvard.
E742.H57   1995   973.92—dc20   94-38349

9 8 7 6 5 4 3 2 1

Printed in the United States of America
on acid-free paper

For
WILLIAM E. LEUCHTENBURG
our teacher and friend
with gratitude and affection

Preface

More than a decade-and-a-half ago, when we first contemplated putting together a collection of documents and essays on United States history since 1945, we agreed that our overriding aim was a book that addressed the *real* concerns and needs of the students we knew and taught, one lively and challenging enough to provoke discussions in the dorm room as well as the classroom. That is still our aim. Of course, much has changed in the intervening years, and this fourth edition addresses new matters of interest and new viewpoints on continuing issues of relevance. It also incorporates the suggestions of students and instructors who used earlier editions of *A History of Our Time*. We are grateful for such advice and hope to continue to receive recommendations for future editions.

As in the earlier editions, this book is structured to give students the opportunity to hear different voices of and about the past, to enable them to compare and contrast, and thus to provide a basis for asking critical questions and arriving at independent judgments on major issues. Consequently, each section of the book contains an introduction and headnotes that place the readings in historical perspective and highlight their relevance, documents that provide firsthand, and personal, analyses of postwar issues, and well-written essays that both convey the drama and "humaness" of history and reveal the diversity of themes and interpretations of the recent past. Much, of necessity, has been left out of this brief collection, and we urge those interested to consult the updated and wholly revised Suggestions for Further Reading.

The recent past is not dead; indeed, much of it is not even past. We firmly believe that the history of the last half-century still strongly influences our lives and that any conscious shaping of the future requires an understanding of this past. To that end, this collection illuminates the major political and social developments and events from the heady optimism immediately after World War II to the anxieties of the Cold War and McCarthyism, the movements for social and political change in the 1960s, the American involvement in the Vietnam War, the conservative backlash in the 1970s and 1980s, and, lastly, to the curious combination of hopefulness and uncertainty as Americans focus on the end of the Cold War; on persistent economic and environmental worries as well as on continuing inequities in matters of race, gender, and class; and on the election of the first "baby boomer" to the White House, the first president born in this postwar epoch.

We hope that readers of this volume will come away from it with a better understanding of today's headlines and of the developments that have brought us to where we are today. We hope it is of use as a guide to some unresolved questions in contemporary American life, as a map for the highway heading toward the next century.

Durham, N.C.   W. H. C.
Durham, N.H.   H. S.
July, 1994

Contents

A History of Our Time

Part 1

THE COLD WAR
ABROAD AND AT HOME

The Cold War literally defined the half-century after World War
II, marking a new era in both American and world history. It
shaped international relations around the globe and decisively affected the cultural, economic, and political lives of many peoples,
particularly Americans. In the United States, the anxieties and tensions associated with its onset helped produce the Second Red
Scare—McCarthyism—a wide-ranging anticommunist crusade at
home that paralleled the worsening contest between (according to
Americans) the Soviet-masterminded worldwide communist conspiracy against peace, democracy, and capitalism, and (according to
the Soviets) the militarized, economically aggressive United States'
effort to dominate the globe.

At its root was the transformation of the uneasy wartime collaboration between the Allies fighting Hitler's Germany into the conflict
between the United States and the Soviet Union over the nature of
the postwar world. Above all else, the Soviet Union demanded secure borders and control over those nations closest to Russia. It
sought to refashion eastern Europe in its own image. The United
States, however, clearly the strongest nation in the world and wanting to shape a new international system suited to its desires, insisted
that the war had been fought for self-determination, territorial
integrity, free trade, and traditional western freedoms. This
conflict over priorities and values would come to a head over five
critical issues.

The Polish question—the first—symbolized to both sides the primary purpose for which they had fought the war. On three occasions, western nations had invaded Russia via the Polish corridor.
Hence, a Polish government subservient, or at least friendly, to the

Soviet Union was Stalin's overriding aim. Conversely, the western Allies had gone to war with Germany over the matter of self-determination for Poland; and the right of Poland to its own democratically elected government represented, in the purest possible form, a test of the principles of the Atlantic Charter. The second issue revolved around the fate of the future governments for Greece, Rumania, and the occupied nations of eastern Europe, again pitting the Soviet Union's fears for its own security and desire to control its neighbors, versus Washington's vision of a postwar world of American-led capitalist democracies. The third involved Germany, splitting the wartime allies over such questions as whether Germany should be deindustrialized, whether it should be permanently divided, and how much it must pay in reparations. Control over atomic energy constituted a fourth point of division. Many Russians believed that the U.S. monopoly over atomic weaponry represented an American effort to intimidate the Soviet Union. The United States, however, refused to relinquish control of its nuclear secrets until the Soviet Union submitted to a comprehensive system of control and inspection by a United Nations agency. The fifth issue, relating to the economic reconstruction of Europe, found the United States and the Soviet Union at loggerheads over the specific issue of rehabilitation loans and the more general conflict between capitalism and socialism.

The first selections in Part 1 address some of the major questions of the Cold War. Robert Messer and Gar Alperovitz analyze new evidence on the "decision" to drop atomic bombs on Hiroshima and Nagasaki, and they raise vital questions about the relationship of that decision to American concerns about the Soviet Union. Henry Wallace (who preceded Truman as Roosevelt's vice president), wishing to reverse what he considered the aggressiveness of American foreign policy in 1946, calls for cooperation with the Soviet Union and an understanding of Soviet needs. Clark Clifford, Truman's personal aide, takes an opposing view in his confidential memorandum to the president in September 1946. Based largely on George F. Kennan's diplomatic cables from Moscow, Clifford's report reflects the assumptions of the developing "get tough" containment policy that the president publicly enunciates in announcing the 1947 Truman Doctrine. The massive expansion of United States military spending required by a worldwide containment policy is spelled out in the April 1950 report to the president by the

National Security Council, NSC-68. The reasoning behind the course of American actions is analyzed by Melvyn Leffler.

Reading these selections, students ought to consider such questions as Was it necessary to drop atomic bombs on Japan to end the war and to save American lives? What does "necessary" mean in this context? Were alternatives to the use of the bombs feasible? Was the use of the bombs immoral? What have been the long-term consequences of the development of atomic weaponry? To what extent was the dropping of the atomic bombs influenced by the growing rift between the United States and the Soviet Union, and what were the diplomatic consequences of the bombing? Was the Cold War inevitable? If so, what made it so? If not, how could it have been avoided? Or, at least, how could its pervasive costs have been minimized? In what areas was compromise possible? What were the sources of American and Soviet policy? Ideology? Economics? Domestic politics? Strategic and geopolitical considerations? What role did misperception play? Would it have made much difference if Roosevelt had lived and remained president until 1949? Or if Stalin had died in 1945? Finally, what light is cast on the onset of the Cold War by its recent dissolution? Compare the crucial determinants of American and Soviet foreign policies in 1990 with those of 1945.

Worsening relations with the Soviet Union after World War II provided the context in which the phenomenon we call McCarthyism grew. Americans felt apprehensive and often beleaguered as the Soviet Union asserted control over eastern Europe and tested an atomic bomb. Tension escalated when Chinese communists took control of the Chinese mainland in 1949, and troubled by disclosures that Soviet spies had secured atomic energy secrets from the United States during World War II, many Americans came to believe that only a communist conspiracy deep within the United States government itself could explain American difficulties in the world. A search for traitors and subversives, conducted by both Democrats and Republicans, both in Washington, D.C., and throughout the rest of the country, became a search for scapegoats to take the blame, a witch-hunt to ferret out and smear anyone and everyone who might be accused—fairly or unfairly—of harboring radical or even liberal sympathies.

When Senator Joseph R. McCarthy asserted to the Women's Republican Club in Wheeling, West Virginia, in February 1950 that he had a list of 205 card-carrying communists in the State Department, he carried to a new height the hysteria already gripping the nation. McCarthy had no such list. Most of his charges were fabrications. He never uncovered a single communist spy. His investigations and exposés did not lead to the successful prosecution of a single person for treasonous or disloyal acts. Yet, the very brashness of his accusations, the abrasiveness of his insinuations, the exaggerated big lie and red smear enabled McCarthy to hold center stage for four years, intimidating the innocent as well as the suspect and destroying numerous careers and lives. In late 1954, the Senate voted 67–22 to formally censure McCarthy, ending his personal effectiveness; but the larger crusade he had come to symbolize still cast a pall over the land, chilling political debate, and making it virtually impossible for yet another decade for most Americans to support any cause, domestic or international, that could possibly be distorted as sympathetic to socialism or communism.

The concluding selections in Part 1 illustrate and analyze the impact of the Cold War at home. Senator McCarthy's demagoguery is best exemplified by the words in the speech that launched his personal crusade against the Democrats for their "softness" on communism. A principled statement against McCarthy's exploitation of fear appears in the "Declaration of Conscience" by seven Republican senators and the comments of Margaret Chase Smith of Maine. The consequences of McCarthysim for those who sought to carry forward the American principles of freedom of speech and independent thought are illustrated by playwright Lillian Hellman and historian Richard Fried. Hellman, who risked going to jail by taking the position that she would inform the House Un-American Activities Committee about herself but would say nothing about other people, describes her thoughts while being interrogated; Fried surveys the devastating effect anti-communist extremism had on thousands of ordinary people.

Fried's essay also provokes thought about the origins and meaning of McCarthyism, and students should keep in mind such questions as What was the extent to which Truman himself paved the way for McCarthyism by his definition of Cold War issues? Was McCarthyism a top-down phenomenon of conservative politicians warring on their opponents or a bottom-up matter of passive politicians reflecting the hysteria welling up from the grass roots? Put another way, was McCarthyism essentially a mass movement or the tool of elite political interest groups? What allowed McCarthy to have the influence that he had? Who were his targets? How did the news media's treatment of McCarthy heighten public anxieties about communism? Could political leaders have earlier stopped or moderated the excesses of the anticommunist witch-hunt? How was it possible for so much poison to spread through the body politic in the name of patriotism and freedom? If there is any truth to the dictum "the study of history is the best guarantee against repeating it," these questions need to be carefully pondered.

The Atomic Bomb and the Origins of the Cold War

Robert L. Messer and Gar Alperovitz

The first atomic bomb, produced by the ultrasecret Manhattan Project at a cost of $2 billion, exploded in the desert near Alamogordo, New Mexico, on July 16, 1945, flashing with "the brightness of several suns at midday" and forcing a huge purplish mushroom cloud high into the atmosphere. It ushered in the atomic age. Three weeks later, on August 6, the Japanese city of Hiroshima was instantly leveled by an atomic bomb dropped from an American B-29. Some 130,000 people were killed; tens of thousands of others suffered burns, wounds, and nuclear poisoning. On August 9 another atomic bomb flattened Nagasaki, killing at least 60,000 people. Four days later the Japanese surrendered.

Assessments of the motives behind the decision to drop the atomic bombs have tended to cluster historians into opposing camps. Those labeled "traditionalist" or "orthodox" echo President Truman's and Secretary of War Henry Stimson's contentions that the bombs were used to force Japan's surrender as quickly as possible and to save American lives. They maintain that the alternatives discussed—detonating an atomic bomb on an unpopulated island with Japanese observers as witnesses; continuing to blockade and conventionally bomb Japan; encouraging the Soviet Union to declare war on Japan more quickly; pursuing Tokyo's peace feelers—would have taken too long or failed to convince the Japanese that they had to surrender at once. Contrarily, "revisionist" historians argue that the bombs were not vital to defeating Japan and that they were utilized to influence Soviet behavior. According to this interpretation, American willingness to drop atomic bombs on Japan might intimidate the Soviet Union into making concessions in eastern Europe, might serve as a deterrent against Soviet aggression, or might end the war in the

Pacific before the Soviet Union could enter and thus claim a role in the postwar management of Asia.

In the following selections, historians Messer and Alperovitz offer new evidence on President Truman's personal views, speculate on their implications, and reveal the dangers of making conclusive historical judgements on the basis of fragmentary evidence.

New Evidence on Truman's Decision

Robert L. Messer

The use of atomic bombs on Japanese cities at the end of World War II is one of the most debated and analyzed events in history. This discussion is not an attempt to explain that event. Rather, to borrow a phrase from Senator Howard Baker during the Watergate hearings, the focus is upon what the president knew and when he knew it. My purpose is not to indict President Truman, but only to clarify his role in a larger process.

The main source of information for such a clarification is not White House tape recordings, but something very nearly as candid and revealing—the president's own words. Not just his public statements, or his own writings on the subject after the fact, but Truman's private journal and letters written at the time he gave the bombing order.

The recent discovery of this evidence helps us to understand better at least some aspects of a forty-year-old issue. It reveals, for example that contrary to his public justification of the bombings as the only way to end the war without a costly invasion of Japan, Truman had already concluded that Japan was about to capitulate. Whether or not he was correct in this estimate of when the war would end, the fact that he held this view at the time he made his decision to use the bomb is clearly set down in his own hand.

This new evidence is not a "smoking gun" that settles the old issue of why the bomb was used. But it tells us more than we knew

From the *Bulletin of Atomic Scientists*. Copyright © 1985 by the Educational Foundation for Nuclear Science, 6042 South Kimbark, Chicago, IL 60637, USA. A one year subscription to the Bulletin is $30.

Endnotes omitted.

before about the timing of the bombings. It also tells us more than Harry Truman, for all his famous candor, ever told us.

In his first public statements regarding the use of the bomb, on August 6, 1945, Truman explained that this terrible new weapon represented an American victory in a life-and-death "race against the Germans." It had been dropped on a place called Hiroshima, which the president described as "a military base." It would continue to be used, he said, "until we have completely destroyed Japan's capacity to make war."

Even then there were those, although in a distinct minority, who raised questions about the bombings. What relevance to its use against Japan, they asked, was the fear that Hitler might get the bomb first? Three months before the atomic bombs fell on Japanese cities, Germany had surrendered. Months before that, Allied scientists had concluded that the worst-case scenario, which had prompted the Anglo-American atomic bomb project, was overly pessimistic. The Germans lagged far behind in the race for the bomb. Even more to the point, there had been no serious concern about a Japanese bomb. Was the bomb used then merely "because it was there," to justify its existence and its unprecedented expense?

Regarding the bomb's specific military justification, critics conceded that Hiroshima, as a major port and regional army headquarters, and Nagasaki, with its many war plants, contained legitimate military targets. We now know that those same targets could have been destroyed earlier by the sort of conventional bombing that had leveled just about every important military objective in Japan. In fact, the cities set aside as possible atomic targets were deliberately left virgin, so as not to obscure the effects of the new weapon. It soon became clear, however, that the radius of destruction of even those first-generation 13-kiloton bombs far exceeded the size of any "military base." Casualty figures varied greatly, but all showed that the overwhelming majority of those killed and wounded were civilians in their homes, not soldiers or war workers on the assembly line. For having reversed the ratio of military and unavoidable or "incidental" civilian deaths, the Hiroshima and Nagasaki bombings were condemned, even at the time, by proponents of the principles of just war as "America's atomic atrocity."

Such moral and religious outrage was confined almost exclusively to those who also had condemned conventional "obliteration" or "terror" bombing of civilians earlier in the war. By 1945 the technology of mass destruction had combined with the doctrine of total war to lower the moral threshold for all but a few dissenters. Many times brighter and hotter, the atomic fireballs over Hiroshima and Nagasaki were nonetheless dimmed when set against the precedents of the firestorms of Hamburg, Dresden, and Tokyo.

The early critics also were at a disadvantage in assailing the broader military, political, and moral justification for the bombings. The bomb was used, said Truman, "to destroy Japans' capacity to make war." Few outside government could then know to what extent that war-making capacity had been destroyed before the use of atomic weapons. Certainly the Japanese surrender within days after Hiroshima and hours after Nagasaki were bombed seemed to leave no doubt in the minds of almost all Americans: This new bomb had ended history's greatest and most destructive war; without it the war might have dragged on for many months, even years.

In announcing the bombings the president had said that they were carried out in order to "shorten the agony of war" and save "thousands and thousands of American lives." Later he would be more specific, citing the estimated 250,000 Allied casualties expected to result from the planned invasion of Japan. Added to the Allied losses were the estimates of Japanese casualties in a prolonged war. These ranged from 500,000 to 5 million. Official U.S. estimates of Japanese killed in the atomic attacks totaled about 110,000. Thus, in saving more lives than they took, the atomic bombings were justified as the lesser of two evils.[1]

At the time few could argue with such logic. Indeed, opinion polls taken immediately after the war showed that for every American who thought the bombs should not have been used (5 percent) more than four times as many (23 percent) were disappointed that more bombs had not been dropped before Japan had a chance to surrender. Predictably the majority of those polled (54 percent) backed Truman's decision to use just two bombs on cities as the proper and prudent middle course. Of course, none of these peo-

[1]After the war Truman said that he had been told that the population of the target cities was about 60,000. Hiroshima's population was in fact more than 350,000 and Nagasaki's about 280,000. Of these, nearly 200,000 were killed and 150,000 injured.

ple knew then that the entire U.S. nuclear arsenal had been expended in as rapid succession as possible, without waiting for a response to the first of the only two bombs available.

It was not long, however, before critics of the bomb decision got what seemed authoritative support for their contention that Japan was already defeated by the summer of 1945 and that therefore the use of the bomb had been an unnecessary, wanton act. The U.S. Strategic Bombing Survey's official report on the Pacific War appeared less than One year after the Hiroshima and Nagasaki bombings and on the eve of a controversial series of atomic tests at Bikini atoll.

The authors of this massive, authoritative study of Japan's warmaking capability concluded that "the Hiroshima and Nagasaki atomic bombs did not defeat Japan, nor, by the testimony of the enemy leaders who ended the war, did they persuade Japan to accept unconditional surrender." Rather, the bombs, along with conventional air power, naval blockade, Soviet intervention, and other internal and external pressures acted "jointly and cumulatively" as "lubrication" of a peace-making machinery set in motion months before the atomic attacks. The Survey's analysts concluded that "certainly prior to 31 December 1945 and in all probability prior to November 1945 Japan would have surrendered, even if the atomic bombs had not been dropped, even if Russia had not entered the war, and even if no invasion had been planned or contemplated."

Responding to a resurgence of criticism based upon the Bombing Survey's findings, Truman moved quickly to pre-empt such secondguessing of his use of the bomb. The point man for the Administration's public counteroffensive was Henry L. Stimson, former secretary of war and a key adviser on atomic matters at the time of the bomb decision. In responding to the president's urging that he "set the record straight" Stimson agreed on the need to get out in front of the issue and "satisfy the doubts of that rather difficult class of the community . . . namely educators and historians."

Sharing this concern about how future historians might judge the bomb decision, Truman lent his full support, during his years in the White House, to Stimson's writings on the subject and other such projects. After retiring to private life, he repeated—in private interviews, public statements, and his two-volume memoirs—that he had always regarded the bomb strictly as a weapon and had no thought or regret, either at the time or in retrospect or wisdom of its use against Japan. Any speculation about how things might have been done differently was based upon hindsight. Truman frequently cut off any further discussion of the subject with the observation that "any schoolboy's afterthought is worth more than all the generals' forethought."

In his off-the-record comments Truman was more blunt. To a correspondent who had questioned the propriety of the air of celebration surrounding the news of the bombings, the president responded with the observation: "When you have to deal with a beast you have to treat him as a beast." Similarly, Truman had no sympathy for anyone else who might have second thoughts. Even before Robert Oppenheimer publicly confessed to having "known sin" in helping to build the bomb, Truman dismissed him as typical of the "crybaby scientists" who thought they had blood on their hands.

Even years after wartime passions had cooled, Truman remained unapologetic. When in the 1960s the makers of a television documentary suggested that he might travel to Japan as a goodwill gesture, the former president replied in classic Trumanesque language: "I'll go . . . but I won't kiss their ass." Perhaps fortunately for all concerned the crusty old man never made the proposed trip to Hiroshima. Until his death in 1972 Truman held firm to his original justification for the bombings.

The formulation by Truman, Stimson, and other official or "orthodox" defenders of the bomb decision established the terms of the debate and held the high ground of privileged sources and classified information for many years. That defense rested upon the military necessity and therefore the lesser-of-two-evils morality of the decision. The bomb had been dropped because not to do so risked prolonging the war. By ending the war the bomb saved lives, American and Japanese. The reason for using it was strictly military—to hasten the surrender of Japan. There had been no ulterior political motives: neither domestic, in justifying a very expensive weapons development project, nor international, in regard to any power other than Japan.

In the emerging Cold War between the United States and the Soviet Union the last point was perhaps the most important. The term "atomic diplomacy" had first appeared in *Pravda* within weeks after the end of the war. The charge that the Truman Administration was attempting to use the United States' atomic monopoly to intimidate the Soviet Union was picked up by political mavericks in the United States, such as Franklin Roosevelt's former vice-president, Henry Wallace, as well as by influential voices from abroad, such as British Nobel Prize laureate in physics P. M. S. Blackett.

Blackett pointed out that the invasion of Japan, the next major U.S. military action, was not scheduled to begin until November. However, the Soviet Union, under an agreement signed by the Big Three leaders at Yalta early in 1945, was scheduled to enter the war against Japan in August, three months before the planned invasion.

After Germany's defeat, the Soviets represented Japan's last hope for a negotiated peace, and American leaders knew of Japanese peace feelers in Moscow. Why then was there the rush to use the bomb before Moscow dashed Japan's hopes by declaring war? The impact of that major diplomatic and military blow might well have brought about surrender. Why not at least wait to find out?

Blackett concluded that the timing and circumstances of the atomic bombings made sense only as an effort at atomic diplomacy directed at the Soviet Union. He put the "revisionist" cause succinctly in his observation that "the dropping of the atomic bomb was not so much the last military act of the second World War, as the first major operation in the cold diplomatic war with Russia now in progress.

The basic elements of the debate over the bomb decision remained essentially unchanged over the years. The revisionist hypothesis, largely deductive and circumstantial, won few converts beyond the left. Twenty years after the bombs fell on Japan, former State Department official-turned-historian Herbert Feis concluded that, even though we can say, with the advantage of hindsight, that the use of atomic bombs at that juncture probably was unnecessary to bring about Japan's surrender before the planned invasion, the decision-makers "ought not to be censured." Although perhaps mistaken, they acted in good faith. They sincerely believed, based upon the best evidence available to them at the time, that using this new weapon was the best, surest, and quickest way to end the war.

Feis and other orthodox defenders of the faith in U.S. leaders dismissed New Left revisionist arguments on grounds of ideological preconceptions, selective use of evidence, and shoddy scholarship.

Although in some cases deserved, such criticism of the revisionist challenge could not altogether offset the mounting evidence against the original orthodox defense.

The declassification of government documents and presidential papers, and the release of privately held manuscript sources such as Stimson's private diary forced a revision if not a total refutation of accepted orthodoxy. Drawing upon this newly available primary source material, scholars put forth analyses that were more balanced, more penetrating, and more convincing than either extreme in the previous debate over the bomb.

In the 1970s the work of Martin Sherwin, Barton Bernstein, Gregg Herken, and others revealed the early and continuing connection U.S. leaders made between the bomb and diplomacy. Recent scholarship has stressed the continuity of atomic policy from Roosevelt to Truman. Concerning the motives or objectives of this policy, by the 1980s it was generally accepted that considerations of the bomb's effect on postwar Soviet behavior had been one of the several factors contributing to what was in the end a virtually irresistible presumption in favor of using the bomb.

While it is true that dropping the bomb was virtually a foregone conclusion, it does not follow that Truman was, as General Groves described him, merely "a little boy on a toboggan." Dependent upon his advisers and far from a free agent, he was still the ultimate decision-maker. He was the only person who had the final say—not only on whether the bomb would be used at all, but when and how it would be used. With the Soviet Union about to enter the war, the decision not to tell Stalin about the bomb and the decision to drop all the available bombs in advance of Soviet entry take on major implications for our understanding of the overall decision.

Until recently the evidence of Truman's thinking at the moment he gave the order to deliver the bombs was largely circumstantial or indirect. Those "rather difficult" historians Stimson had worried about were able to reconstruct in detail the views of Truman's key advisers. We know, for example, that Truman's secretary of state, James F. Byrnes, wanted to use the bomb to end the war before Moscow "could get in so much on the kill." It is clear from his diary entries at the time that Stimson saw the bomb as the United States' "master card" in dealing, not just with Japan, but with the Soviet Union as well. But there did not seem to be comparable direct evidence about Truman's private thinking on the bomb at the time he made the decision.

The first batch of this new evidence on the bomb decision surfaced in 1979. It had been misfiled among the family records of Truman's press secretary at the Truman presidential library. This sheaf of handwritten notes made up Truman's private journal kept during his trip to the Big Three summit meeting at Potsdam outside Berlin in July 1945.

During that trip Truman first learned of the successful test explosion of a plutonium device in New Mexico, gave the order for the Hiroshima and Nagasaki bombings, and, as he sailed home, received the news that his order had been carried out. The event, he said at the time, was "the greatest thing in history."

Four years after the discovery of Truman's Potsdam diary a second batch of new evidence of Truman's contemporary thinking on matters relating to the use of the bomb turned up among his widow's private papers. These letters, written during that same Potsdam trip, along with other private correspondence between Bess and Harry Truman had been presumed destroyed years earlier. But they had somehow survived.

Taken together, these two sets of documents shed new light on how Truman came to grips with an entirely new force in human affairs and how he incorporated his understanding of the bomb into his thoughts about when, how, and on whose terms the war would end.

The first news of the successful test detonation in New Mexico reached Truman on the evening of July 16. The message gave no details about the size of the explosion. Although he makes no explicit reference to the bomb in his diary entry for that date, the news of its existence may have moved him to reflect upon the relation between technology and morality: "I hope for some sort of peace—but I fear that machines are ahead of morals by some centuries and when morals catch up perhaps there'll be no reason for any of it. I hope not. But we are only termites on a planet and maybe when we bore too deeply into the planet there'll [be] a reckoning-who knows?" Elsewhere in this diary, after the bomb's power had been made clear to him,[2] Truman wondered if this new weapon

---

[2] A full report, including vivid eye-witness accounts, arrived on the afternoon of July 21.

might "be the fire [of] destruction prophesied in the Euphrates Valley Era, after Noah and his fabulous ark." Such apocalyptic visions, however, did not keep him from using what he recognized was "the most terrible bomb in the history of the world." Perhaps he reassured himself with the observation that "it seems the most terrible thing ever discovered, but it can be made the most useful."

On July 17, still without knowing any details about the bomb test, Truman met for the first time with Stalin. In his diary account of that meeting he noted that the Soviet leader's agenda items, which included the overthrow of Franco's fascist government in Spain, were "dynamite." To this observation Truman added: "but I have some dynamite too which I'm not exploding now." Whether or not he was thinking of the bomb as his diplomatic dynamite is unclear.

But Truman then makes a very clear statement that goes to the heart of the issue of the bomb's necessity. Referring to the Soviet commitment to declare war on Japan three months after the defeat of Germany, Truman noted Stalin's reaffirmation of the agreement he had made with Roosevelt at Yalta: "He'll [Stalin] be in Jap War on August 15th." To this Truman added: "Fini Japs when that comes about." In these two brief sentences Truman set forth his understanding of how the war would end: Soviet entry into the war would finish the Japanese.

In writing to his wife the following day (July 18), the president underscored the importance of Soviet entry and its impact upon the timing of the war's end. "I've gotten what I came for—Stalin goes to war on August 15 with no strings on it. . . . I'll say that we'll end the war a year sooner now, and think of the kids who won't be killed! That is the important thing."

The implications of these passages from Truman's diary and letters for the orthodox defense of the bomb's use are devastating: if Soviet entry alone would end the war before an invasion of Japan, the use of atomic bombs cannot be justified as the only alternative to that invasion. This does not mean, of course, that having the bomb was not useful. But it does mean that for Truman the end of the war seemed at hand; the issue was no longer when the war would end, but how and on whose terms. If he believed that the war would end with Soviet entry in mid-August, then he must have realized that if the bombs were not used before that date they might well not be used at all.

This relationship between the Soviet entry, the bomb, and the end of the war is set forth in Truman's diary account for July 18. "P[rime] M[inister Churchill] and I ate alone. Discussed Manhattan [the atomic bomb] (it is a success). Decided to tell Stalin about it. Stalin had told P.M. of telegram from Jap emperor asking for peace. Stalin also read his answer to me. It was satisfactory. [I] believe Japs will fold up before Russia comes in. I am sure they will when Manhattan appears over their homeland. I shall inform Stalin about it at an opportune time." Truman apparently believed that by using the bomb the war could be ended even before the Soviet entry. The bomb would shorten the war by days rather than months. Its use would not save hundreds of thousands of lives—but it could save victory for the Americans. The race with the Germans had been won. It was now a race with Soviets.

Unaware of Soviet espionage, Truman assumed that Stalin did not know that such a race was underway. Despite his stated intention to tell Stalin about the bomb at an "opportune" time, Truman— apparently due to the urgings of Churchill and Byrnes—did not inform Stalin even of the bomb's existence, much less of the plans to use it on the eve of a major Soviet military offensive into Manchuria.

We now know that Klaus Fuchs, among others, kept Stalin well informed about progress on the bomb. But at Potsdam Truman believed he had succeeded in keeping Stalin in ignorance by a carefully staged charade, casually mentioning a "new weapon" without giving any details about it or its immediate use. Stalin showed no interest, and Truman was convinced he had fooled "Mr. Russia." The following day the order to deliver both bombs as soon as possible went out from Potsdam.

This cat-and-mouse game between the two leaders was apparently what the president had in mind when, in a letter to his wife at the end of the conference, Truman, an ardent poker player, commented on Stalin's stalling tactics: "He doesn't know it but I have an ace in the hole and another one showing—so unless he has two pairs (and I know he has not) we are sitting all right."

It can be argued that ending the war sooner rather than later, even a few days later, by whatever means at his disposal was Truman's first responsibility. It also can be argued that limiting Soviet expansion in Asia, as a bonus to ending the war as soon as possible, was in the U.S. national interest and therefore also Truman's duty.

But the point here is that the president, in justifying his use of the bomb, never made those arguments.

It is in this light that the new evidence, in both the Potsdam diary and letters to his wife, calls for a reevaluation of the old issue: why were the only two bombs available used in rapid succession so soon after testing, and on the eve of the planned Soviet entry into the war? From this unique record, in Truman's own hand, we can understand better how this relatively inexperienced leader, who had only recently first heard the words "atomic bomb," grasped this new technology, and used it as a solution for a multitude of military, political, and diplomatic problems.

The evidence of the Potsdam diary and letters does not close the book on the question why the bomb was dropped. Rather, it opens it to a previously unseen page. What appears there is by no means always clear or consistent. At times it is hard to know what to make of such statements as Truman's diary entry for July 25, in which he expresses his determination to use the bomb "so that military objectives are the target and not women and children." This extraordinary comment follows a very detailed and accurate description of the effects of the bomb test. Perhaps he really did believe that Hiroshima was just a "military base."

Elsewhere in these pages Truman seems to disprove the revisionist contention that he did not want "the Russians" in the war at all. In writing to his wife on July 18 Truman made it clear that his highest priority at the conference was getting the Soviet Union into the war against Japan. Two days later, after a "tough meeting" with Churchill and Stalin, the president noted that he had made his goals "perfectly plain" to both men: "I want the Jap War won and I want 'em both in it."

The dual objectives of assuring Soviet entry while containing Soviet expansion apparently were not contradictory to Truman. As he put it a decade later, "One of the main objectives of the Potsdam Conference [was] to get Russia in as quickly as we could and then to keep Russia out of Japan—and I did it." Although he saw the bomb as useful for ending the war before the Soviets could claim credit for the victory, Truman apparently wasn't ready to rely totally on the bomb until it was proven in combat. This lingering skepticism is revealed in his use of quotation marks in noting, on the same day he gave the bomb order, that "we 'think' we have found the way to cause a disintegration of the atom."

Truman's attitude toward "the Japs" seems clear enough in his diary references to them as "savages, ruthless, merciless and fanatic." Yet to a senator who, after the Hiroshima bombing, had urged continued attacks until the Japanese were brought "groveling to their knees," the president replied: "I can't bring myself to believe that, because they are beasts, we should ourselves at in the same manner." Indeed, after the Nagasaki bombing, Truman reportedly told his cabinet members that there would be no more such attacks because he could not bear the thought of killing "all those kids."

While these new sources, as they relate to Truman's private perspective on the bomb, contribute to our understanding, they remain fragments which by no means complete the mosaic. The point here is not that Truman single-handedly controlled the course of history. Rather, it is that as a major participant in history his attempt to mold nuclear weapons policy at the beginning of the atomic era contributes to our understanding of an event the meaning and lessons of which, after forty years, we still seek.

More on Atomic Diplomacy

Gar Alperovitz

As Robert Messer observes, the new information reveals that "contrary to his public justification of the bombings as the only way to end the war without a costly invasion of Japan, Truman had already concluded that Japan was about to capitulate." Beyond this crucial point the materials throw considerable light on two controversial historical questions:

• The first is whether there actually was anything like a "decision" to use the bombs. Some have argued that it is more accurate to say that Truman was simply carried along, on the basis of assumptions that he inherited, or by the momentum of events, or both.
• The second has to do with just how much of the decision, or assumption-decision, to use the bomb must be ascribed to political-diplomatic considerations related to the Soviet Union.

In recent years several historians, urging the assumption theory, have stressed the continuity between the Roosevelt and Truman periods. Since my own work helped initiate the case for an "assumption-based" theory, let me state now that the idea must be handled with considerable care. Even if the theory is accepted, it is all too easy to ignore crucial elements of choice in connection with Hiroshima.

For instance, it is simply not true that the use of the atomic bomb was never challenged, as Secretary of War Henry L. Stimson later wrote. Several top leaders—General Dwight D. Eisenhower, Admiral William D. Leahy, Under-secretary of the Navy Ralph A. Bard, Assistant Secretary of War John L. McCloy, Acting Secretary of

From the *Bulletin of Atomic Scientists*. Copyright © 1985 by the Educational Foundation for Nuclear Science, 6042 South Kimbark, Chicago, IL 60637, USA. A one year subscription to the Bulletin is $30.

Endnotes omitted.

State Joseph E. Grew and Stimson himself—at various points urged Truman not to use the bomb or to use other methods first.

There is also the matter of what assumptions Truman actually did inherit. There is no doubt that part of the legacy was a policy concerning international control of atomic weapons promulgated by Franklin D. Roosevelt and his top officials. This was to foster an American, and partially British, monopoly. Truman did not, however, inherit a clear policy on the use of the bomb. Rather, what evidence we have suggests that Roosevelt had doubts about using the bomb against Japan—and that in his last conversations on the subject he himself was raising the possibility of a "demonstration."

Truman, in any case, knew virtually nothing about Roosevelt's position. Moreover, while Stimson, General Leslie R. Groves, a number of scientists, and several other high officials associated with the Manhattan Project from the Roosevelt period undoubtedly assumed early on that the bomb would be used, Truman's main policy adviser, Secretary of State James F. Byrnes, was not part of that group. (And Admiral William Leahy, the chief of staff whom Truman inherited from Roosevelt and, simultaneously, presiding officer of the Joint Chiefs of Staff, was against the bombing.)

Finally, and far more important, are changes which occurred throughout the summer of 1945. Whatever assumptions Truman may have inherited, these changes presented decision-makers with a new situation.

Here the new evidence is particularly illuminating. In reviewing the history of Hiroshima, one must be extremely careful about statements and judgments made at different times between April 12, 1945, when Truman became president, and the August 6 bombing. It is almost certainly true, for instance, that American leaders assumed the bomb, like any weapon, would be used against Japan in the early summer of 1945—up to, say, the end of June. I use the qualifier "almost certainly" because there is also evidence to the contrary: At the request of the White House, Leo Szilard met with Truman's key adviser, James Byrnes, on May 28, 1945—two-and-a-half months before Hiroshima. According to Szilard, "Byrnes did not argue that it was necessary to use the bomb against the cities of Japan in order to win the war. . . . Mr. Byrnes's . . . view [was] that our possessing and demonstrating the bomb would make Russia more manageable." Admiral Leahy was also convinced that the war was essentially over by mid-June.

In any event, in the six weeks or so before Hiroshima the situation in Japan changed dramatically. First, the intensity of Japanese peace initiatives increased—in Switzerland, Sweden, and, we now know, in Portugal. As early as May 12, 1945, almost three months before Hiroshima, William Donovan, the head of the Office of Strategic Services (OSS) personally advised the president of indications that Japan might surrender if the terms included a provision that the emperor (regarded as a deity) would not be removed. Thereafter others—including, most importantly, Acting Secretary of State Joseph Grew and Stimson—urged such a change at different times. And we know from several sources that although Truman may have preferred to make no change, he had no objection in principle to the provision—, and, of course, ultimately accepted it.

The United States had also, of course, cracked the Japanese code early in the war. In mid-June, and then very actively on into July, the emperor became involved in attempting to arrange a surrender, using Moscow as the negotiating channel. The evidence on this—and U.S. leaders' knowledge of the emperor's initiative-is now well established. (Robert C. Butow's *Japans Decision to Surrender* is the classic work.) The mere fact that the emperor, traditionally aloof from politics, instigated the diplomatic move was extraordinary. We also know that Truman clearly understood what was happening; afterwards he confirmed his awareness of the main cables. The new evidence from the diaries adds to our sense of the president's personal assessment; in these pages Truman straightforwardly terms the most important intercepted message the "telegram from Jap Emperor asking for peace.

In a new edition of *Atomic Diplomacy*, I have reviewed additional intelligence and other information which helps clarify how U.S. officials understood what was happening, especially in the six or seven weeks before Hiroshima. It is enough to say here that many top officials understood that Japan's situation had changed drastically. The following (often ignored) illustrations help illuminate the shifting environment in which policy was being developed:

• Admiral Leahy's diary entry of June 18, 1945, just short of two months before Hiroshima: "It is my opinion at the present time that a surrender of Japan can be arranged with terms that can be accepted by Japan and that will make fully satisfactory provision for America's defense."

• After the war Leahy wrote: "The use of this barbarous weapon at Hiroshima and Nagasaki was of no material assistance in our war against Japan. The Japanese were already defeated and ready to surrender. . . . My own feeling is that in being the first to use It, we had adopted an ethical standard common to the barbarians of the Dark Ages. . . . I was not taught to make war in that fashion, and wars cannot be won by destroying women and children."

• General Dwight D. Eisenhower's report of his response when Stimson briefed him on the forthcoming use of the bomb:

> During his recitation of the relevant facts, I had been conscious of a feeling of depression and so I voiced to him my grave misgivings, first on the basis of my belief that Japan was already defeated and that dropping the bomb was completely unnecessary, and secondly because I thought that our country should avoid shocking world opinion by the use of a weapon whose employment was, I thought, no longer mandatory as a measure to save American lives. . . .
>
> Japan was, at that very moment, seeking some way to surrender with a minimum loss of "face". . . . It wasn't necessary to hit them with [that] awful thing.

Eisenhower met with Truman on July 20, 1945 and urged him not to use the bomb, a fact recently confirmed by the late General Omar N. Bradley, but rarely cited in studies of the period.

• Undersecretary of the Navy Ralph Bard also met with Truman, just before Potsdam, to advise another course. Bard, who resigned his official post on July 1, 1945, wrote a memo dated June 27, which included the following paragraphs:

> During recent weeks I have . . . had the feeling very definitely that the Japanese government may be searching for some opportunity which they could use as a medium of surrender. . . . This country could contact representatives from Japan . . . and make representations with regard to Russia's position and. . . . give them some information regarding the proposed use of atomic power, together with whatever assurances the President might care to make with regard to the Emperor of Japan. . . . It seems quite possible to me that this presents the opportunity which the Japanese are looking for.
>
> I don't see that we have anything in particular to lose. . . . The only way to find out is to try.

• The assistant to the Secretary of the Navy, Admiral Lewis L. Strauss (later chairman of the Atomic Energy Commission) proposed a demonstration of the new weapon over a Japanese redwood-like forest. "The war was very nearly over. The Japanese were nearly ready to capitulate."

Several other important military figures also illuminate the shifting appraisal of Japan's collapse. General Curtis LeMay, who has repeatedly declared that use of the atomic bomb was unnecessary, reportedly felt that Japan would have surrendered in two weeks (The atomic bomb "had nothing to do with the end of the war"). Army Air Force Chief, General Henry "Hap" Arnold, demanded that a statement be entered into the record of the Joint Chiefs of Staff on July 16, 1945, indicating his view that the war could easily be ended by September or October I 945 without an invasion. General Douglas MacArthur was never asked about the atomic bomb; on several occasions after the war he indicated his view that it was unnecessary. The chief British military figure, General Hastings Ismay, was filled with "revulsion" at the report that the atomic bomb had been successfully tested and could now be used: "For some time past it had been firmly fixed in my mind that the Japanese were tottering."

In many studies suggesting the near unanimity of support for using the bomb, such information is ignored or played down. Yet this information helps to clarify the way in which at least some key policy-makers viewed the situation; and, since several of them pressed their views in meetings with the president, it contributes to an assessment of what Truman must have understood. Such evidence also provides background for a consideration of other aspects of the newer materials.

The collapse of Japan during the summer of 1945—which challenged the initial assumption that the bomb would be used—must be understood in still another context: at the time, U.S. officials recognized that the Soviet Union's forthcoming declaration of war would almost certainly force Japan to surrender. The planned date for Soviet entry was August 8, 1945 (amended by one week at Postdam). Hiroshima was destroyed on August 6, 1945; Nagasaki on August 9, 1945.

We now know that after the successful Alamogordo test U.S.

leaders tried to stall Moscow's entry so that (as one official's diary put it) the Soviets would not get so much in on the kill, thereby being in a position to press for claims against China." But that is not the first point to focus upon. Rather, it is that during the summer of 1945 Japan's situation deteriorated so rapidly that Truman had available an obvious option to end the war. All he really had to do was wait a week or so for the Soviet declaration to see whether his advisers were right.

In mid-June General Marshall pointed out that "the impact of Russian entry on the already hopeless Japanese may well be the decisive action levering them into capitulation at that time or shortly thereafter if we land in Japan."

With the situation in Japan worsening, a month later the Combined U.S-U.K. Intelligence Staffs advised (as General Ismay summarized for Churchill): "If and when Russia came into the war against Japan, the Japanese would probably wish to get out on almost any terms short of the dethronement of the Emperor."

The new diary evidence confirms that Truman understood the advice he was receiving on the significance of the Soviet attack well before Hiroshima. On July 17, 1945, when Stalin told him personally that the Red Army would march, Truman's private diary shows him noting: "Fini Japs when that comes about."

And, of course, there was plenty of time. The full invasion of Japan was not scheduled until March 1946; even an initial landing on Kyushu was still three months in the future. Moreover, the invasion date could easily have been postponed. (According to Admire Leahy, Truman told him that, should negotiations take longer, time was not a major consideration if this would avoid an invasion.)

Truman's order to drop the atomic bomb at a time when he knew the war was soon likely to be over is—as Messer observes—"devastating" to the orthodox case that he took the step only because he wished to avoid a costly invasion. However, the significance extends further.

Given Truman's awareness of the Japanese peace initiatives and his understanding of the power of a Soviet declaration of war, a key question is: Why did the initial assumption that the bomb would be used continue among some people and not among others?

The evidence had become increasingly clear by early July that, from a military point of view, Japan was finished. By mid-July it was exceedingly doubtful that Truman believe the war would end by invasion. Moreover, several top military figures clearly understood this reality—and were shocked that, in these changed circumstances the bomb would still be used.

Who did not recognize the changed circumstances? Or, to put it another way, who refused to alter the early assumption? The military leaders went along with the president's decision, but they were not the source of initiative. It was Secretary of State Byrnes, Truman's chief adviser, and other officials most directly involved in diplomacy toward the Soviet Union who appeared to have been most unwilling or unable to alter their views.

Byrnes's general viewpoint is consistent and clear. He saw the atomic bomb as a way to impress the Soviets. The evidence is now massive on this point. A few of the numerous and by now well-known diary and other accounts will illustrate:

• From another report by Leo Szilard on his May 28, 1945 meeting with Byrnes:

> Byrnes . . . was concerned about Russia's postwar behavior. Russian troops had moved into Hungary and Rumania; Byrnes thought it would be very difficult to persuade Russia to withdraw her troops from these countries, and that Russia might be more manageable if impressed by American military might. I shared Byrnes's concern about Russia's throwing around her weight in the postwar period, but I was completely flabbergasted by the assumption that rattling the bomb might make Russia more manageable.

• From Ambassador Joseph Davies's diary' during the Postdam Conferences: Byrnes' attitude that the atomic bomb assured ultimate success in negotiations disturbed me more than his description of its success amazed me. . . . I told him the threat wouldn't work and might be irreparable harm."

• From Secretary of the Navy James V. Forrestal's diary: "Byrnes said he was most anxious to get the Japanese affair over with before the Russians got in, with particular reference to [the Manchurian ports of] Dairen and Port Arthur."

• From Secretary of War Stimson's diary after Potsdam: "I found that Byrnes was very much against any attempt to cooperate with Russia. His mind is full of his problems with the coming meeting of foreign ministers and he looks to having the presence of the bomb in his pocket, so to speak, as a great weapon to get through the thing."

It is also now clear that, on the basis of advice (from Stimson and—though the record is less clear—probably from Byrnes) about the bomb's importance to diplomatic relations with Moscow, Truman postponed the Potsdam meeting with Stalin until after the atomic bomb had been proven. The president wanted to have what Stimson called his "master card" in hand before negotiating on Europe. The Alamogordo test took place on July 16, 1945; the Potsdam meeting began on July 17, 1945.

We do not know for sure whether Byrnes, like Leahy and Eisenhower, clearly recognized that Japan was already finished and that the bomb was therefore not needed—but that he wanted to use it anyway. Szilard's report suggests this view. A more generous interpretation is that he and the president simply got so caught up in the assumption that the bomb would be vital to their diplomacy that they blinded themselves to information which was evident to other high-ranking officials.

However, the new evidence also calls in question the whole assumption-based theory. Since Truman had the readily available option of simply waiting for the shock of the Soviet declaration of war, the evidence suggests that he appears knowingly to have rejected this choice in favor of using the bomb first. The explanation for this decision—and decision it was—appears to have been political, not military. As a plethora of diary and other evidence powerfully suggests, he and especially Byrnes wished to avoid the Red Army's entrance into Manchuria and northern China and the enhanced Soviet political influence this would bring.

Because so many documents make it so obvious that by the end of July top U.S. officials were deeply concerned about securing U.S. objectives in Manchuria and northern China, perhaps many have ignored the fact that in so doing they were consciously rejecting what seemed the easist way to bring about surrender. If there is an unmistakable ongoing assumption, it is that, as Truman and Byrnes repeatedly stressed at Potsdam, U.S. economic and political interests in Manchuria and northern China—the "Open Door"—had to be maintained; thus, accordingly, Soviet influence had to be opposed.

Further doubts about "ongoing assumption" theories are raised by the fact that this was not a passive act; great efforts were ma e both to rush the atomic bomb project and to stall the Soviets.

Although a narrow focus on ending the war cannot be excluded as an important presidential motive, the new evidence suggests that at the decision-making level the decision or assumption that the bomb would be used appears to have been sustained—in July and early August—primarily by political considerations related to the Soviet Union. The "Soviet factor," in short, becomes central to any explanation of how the atomic bomb came to be used.

We still do not have the full story of Hiroshima. There are huge gaps, particularly in our understanding of what happened between the two key actors, Truman and Byrnes.

We do know that Truman relied heavily on the enormously prestigious Byrnes, a man who had been his senior and mentor in the Senate; that he spent the month leading up to Hiroshima with him, first on shipboard and then sharing a villa at Potsdam; that Byrnes kept other key advisers away from the President; that Truman had designated Byrnes as the lead man in connection with the bomb.

But there is much we do not know. For instance, the decision to postpone negotiations with Stalin until the bomb had been tested was a very important one. Yet we have almost no information on precisely what advice Byrnes (as opposed to Stimson) gave Truman in April and May. We do know, however, that it was Byrnes who was responsible for preparing the U.S. position for the meeting, and that he was also advising Truman about the bomb.

Throughout the summer we know that Truman and Byrnes met regularly in private, but we have almost no information on their discussions, even though the meetings between the two men both in Washington and subsequently—far more than the work of the Interim Committee, the scientists' efforts, or even top military meetings—were almost certainly where much real strategy was formulated.

Nor do we know much about the details of the many meetings between the president and his chief of staff, Admiral Leahy, who was very much against the bombing. As presiding officer of the Joint Chiefs of Staff, Leahy was in a key role, but only very sketchy and occasional diary entries exist. Allen Dulles, who was handling the Japanese negotiations through Switzerland for the OSS, was called to Potsdam, but we know little about precisely what happened there. It appears likely that, had the nuclear test failed at Alamogordo, Dulles would have been sent back to arrange a quick Japanese surrender as he had done with Italy.

It is also curious that while Eisenhower reported challenging Stimson on the decision, he never disclosed that he met with Truman and urged him not to use the bomb. Why? What considerations were expressed by the president? We do not know.

In fact, although we now know a great deal about the attitudes of many key actors during the summer of 1945, we actually know surprisingly little about how Truman himself viewed several points. The two most interesting periods—the weeks in April, May, and June which encompass the private talks with Byrnes while lie was developing atomic policy for the president but before he was officially in office, and shipboard talks between Truman, Byrnes, and possibly Leahy on the way to Postdam—are almost a complete blank. Were others as reluctant as Eisenhower to discuss very private and potentially embarrassing facts? (When doing the original research on *Atomic Diplomacy*, I interviewed Benjamin V. Cohen, the New Dealer who served as a special assistant to Byrnes; he fell silent when asked about the relationship of Byrnes's diplomacy to the Hiroshima bombing. He said he "didn't remember" in response to numerous questions which other documents reveal were at the center of attention when he was assisting Byrnes.)

One final point: We know that the Japanese did not respond positively to the Potsdam proclamation; the usual version is that they rejected it. A number of historians have noted that the term they used—*mokusatsu* be translated in several ways: "ignore," "treat with silent contempt," "take no notice of," among others. It is sometimes argued that U.S. leaders unfortunately chose to interpret the term as a full rejection—and then went ahead with the bombing.

However, we now know that Truman was advised by OSS Director William Donovan on August 2, 1945, four days before Hiroshima, that Japanese officials in Switzerland tried to clarify the meaning of their government's response. Both the Japanese chief of staff and the foreign minister in Tokyo had replied to the reports of Japanese officials in touch with the OSS operation in Switzerland. The Japanese official in Switzerland emphasized to Dulles's go-between, Per Jacobsson, that he was hoping for a "real response from Tokyo within a week unless resistance was too great. Meanwhile, the Allies should not take too seriously what was said on

Tokyo Radio concerning the Potsdam proclamation as this was merely "propaganda to maintain morale." The "real reply" would be transmitted through some "official channel," possibly the minister himself or General Okamoto in Switzerland.

Here again, we do not have much information. We do not know how Truman and his chief advisers felt about Donovan's report. On the surface it clearly reinforced other evidence—specially the cables indicating the emperor's strong initiative—of Japan's willingness to surrender, evidence we know the president had at the time.

I cite such points because nonspecialists often believe historians know and have reported the full Hiroshima story, and because I believe further caution is advisable with respect to the "ongoing-assumption" theory of the bombing. The new evidence suggests that there may well have been full awareness that the bomb was not needed, and explicit consideration of it primarily in terms of its political role vis-à-vis the Soviet Union. And privately, between Truman and Byrnes, a conscious decision may have been taken.

A modified form of the ongoing-assumption theory can still be fitted to the presently known facts. But as one who put a version of it forward originally—with, I hope, adequate caveats—let me stress that it is no longer possible to rule out the likelihood that the president knew exactly what he was doing and made a clear decision with his closest adviser. Further historical discoveries may answer the remaining questions.

Are We Only Paying Lip Service to Peace?

Henry A. Wallace

Secretary of Commerce Henry A. Wallace was deeply disturbed by what he considered the warlike drift of President Truman's foreign policy from mid-1945 to mid-1946. Wallace, who had served as secretary of agriculture from 1933 to 1941 and as vice president from 1941 to 1945, feared the consequences of reversing President Roosevelt's policy of wartime cooperation with the Soviet Union. In the following letter to the president in July 1946, he urged Truman to diminish Soviet distrust and to avoid a catastrophic arms race. The president rejected Wallace's conciliatory counsel, and following Wallace's public opposition to the administrations' policies toward the Soviet Union, Truman fired his commerce secretary in September 1946.

Wallace's views anticipate many of the arguments made by "revisionist" historians. Note particularly his emphasis on Soviet fears, the dangers of intensifying the public's anxieties, and the possibility of coexistence between competing ideologies. Compare Wallace's interpretation of postwar events with that of Clark Clifford in the next selection. How do you account for the striking differences?

I have been increasingly disturbed about the trend of international affairs since the end of the war, and I am even more troubled by the apparently growing feeling among the American people that another war is coming and the only way that we can head it off is to arm ourselves to the teeth. Yet all of past history indicates that an armaments race does not lead to peace but to war. The months just

Excerpted from a letter sent by Henry Wallace to President Truman, July 23, 1946, in Harry Truman Papers, Harry S Truman Library, Independence, Missouri.

ahead may well be the crucial period which will decide whether the civilized world will go down in destruction after the five or ten years needed for several nations to arm themselves with atomic bombs. Therefore, I want to give you my views on how the present trend toward conflict might be averted. . . .

How do American actions since V-J Day appear to other nations? I mean by actions the concrete things like $13 billion for the War and Navy Departments, the Bikini tests of the atomic bomb and continued production of bombs, the plan to arm Latin America with our weapons, production of B-29s and planned production of B-36s, and the effort to secure air bases spread over half the globe from which the other half of the globe can be bombed. I cannot but feel that these actions must make it look to the rest of the world as if we were only paying lip service to peace at the conference table.

These facts rather make it appear either (1) that we are preparing ourselves to win the war which we regard as inevitable or (2) that we are trying to build up a predominance of force to intimidate the rest of mankind. How would it look to us if Russia had the atomic bomb and we did not, if Russia had 10,000-mile bombers and air bases within a thousand miles of our coastlines, and we did not?

Some of the military men and self-styled "realists" are saying: "What's wrong with trying to build up a predominance of force? The only way to preserve peace is for this country to be so well armed that no one will dare attack us. We know that America will never start a war."

The flaw in this policy is simply that it will not work. In a world of atomic bombs and other revolutionary new weapons, such as radioactive poison gases and biological warfare, a peace maintained by a predominance of force is no longer possible.

Why is this so? The reasons are clear:

FIRST. Atomic warfare is cheap and easy compared with old-fashioned war. Within a very few years several countries can have atomic bombs and other atomic weapons. Compared with the cost of large armies and the manufacture of old-fashioned weapons, atomic bombs cost very little and require only a relatively small part of a nation's production plant and labor force.

SECOND. So far as winning a war is concerned, having more bombs—even many more bombs—than the other fellow is no longer a decisive advantage. If another nation had enough bombs to eliminate all of our principal cities and our heavy industry, it wouldn't help us very much if we had ten times as many bombs as we needed to do the same to them.

THIRD. And most important, the very fact that several nations have atomic bombs will inevitably result in a neurotic, fear-ridden, itching-trigger psychology in all the peoples of the world, and because of our wealth and vulnerability we would be among the most seriously affected. Atomic war will not require vast and timeconsuming preparations, the mobilization of large armies, the conversion of a large proportion of a country's industrial plants to the manufacture of weapons. In a world armed with atomic weapons, some incident will lead to the use of those weapons.

There is a school of military thinking which recognizes these facts, recognizes that when several nations have atomic bombs, a war which will destroy modern civilization will result and that no nation or combination of nations can win such a war. This school of thought therefore advocates a "preventive war," an attack on Russia *now* before Russia has atomic bombs.

This scheme is not only immoral, but stupid. If we should attempt to destroy all the principal Russian cities and her heavy industry, we might well succeed. But the immediate countermeasure which such an attack would call forth is the prompt occupation of all Continental Europe by the Red Army. Would we be prepared to destroy the cities of all Europe in trying to finish what we had started? This idea is so contrary to all the basic instincts and principles of the American people that any such action would be possible only under a dictatorship at home. . . .

Our basic distrust of the Russians, which has been greatly intensified in recent months by the playing up of conflict in the press, stems from differences in political and economic organization. For the first time in our history defeatists among us have raised the fear of another system as a successful rival to democracy and free enterprise in other countries and perhaps even our own. I am convinced that we can meet that challenge as we have in the past by demonstrating that economic abundance can be achieved without sacrificing personal, political and religious liberties. We cannot meet it as Hitler tried to by an anti-Comintern alliance.

It is perhaps too easy to forget that despite the deep-seated differences in our cultures and intensive anti-Russian propaganda of some twenty-five years' standing, the American people reversed their attitudes during the crisis of war. Today, under the pressure of seemingly insoluble international problems and continuing deadlocks, the tide of American public opinion is again turning against Russia. In this reaction lies one of the dangers to which this letter is addressed.

I should list the factors which make for Russian distrust of the United States and of the Western world as follows. The first is Russian history, which we must take into account because it is the setting in which Russians see all actions and policies of the rest of the world. Russian history for over a thousand years has been a succession of attempts, often unsuccessful, to resist invasion and conquest—by the Mongols, the Turks, the Swedes, the Germans and the Poles. The scant thirty years of the existence of the Soviet Government has in Russian eyes been a continuation of their historical struggle for national existence. The first four years of the new regime, from 1917 through 1921, were spent in resisting attempts at destruction by the Japanese, British and French, with some American assistance, and by the several White Russian armies encouraged and financed by the Western powers. Then, in 1941, the Soviet State was almost conquered by the Germans after a period during which the Western European powers had apparently acquiesced in the rearming of Germany in the belief that the Nazis would seek to expand eastward rather than westward. The Russians, therefore, obviously see themselves as fighting for their existence in a hostile world.

Second, it follows that to the Russians all of the defense and security measures of the Western powers seem to have an aggressive intent. Our actions to expand our military security system— such steps as extending the Monroe Doctrine to include the arming of the Western Hemisphere nations, our present monopoly of the atomic bomb, our interest in outlying bases and our general support of the British Empire—appear to them as going far beyond the requirements of defense. I think we might feel the same if the United States were the only capitalistic country in the world, and the principal socialistic countries were creating a level of armed strength far asking anything in their previous history. From the Russian point of view, also, the granting of a loan to Britain and the lack of tangible results on their request to borrow for rehabilitation purposes may be regarded as another evidence of strengthening of an anti-Soviet bloc.

Finally, our resistance to her attempts to obtain warm-water ports and her own security system in the form of "friendly" neighboring states seems, from the Russian point of view, to clinch the case. After twenty-five years of isolation and after having achieved the status of a major power, Russia believes that she is entitled to recognition of her new status. Our interest in establishing democracy in Eastern Europe, where democracy by and large has never existed, seems to her an attempt to re-establish the encirclement of unfriendly neighbors which was created after the last war, and which might serve as a springboard of still another effort to destroy her.

If this analysis is correct, and there is ample evidence to support it, the action to improve the situation is clearly indicated. The fundamental objective of such action should be to allay any reasonable Russian grounds for fear, suspicion and distrust. We must recognize that the world has changed and that today there can be no "One World" unless the United States and Russia can find some way of living together. For example, most of us are firmly convinced of the soundness of our position when we suggest the internationalization and defortification of the Danube or of the Dardanelles, but we would be horrified and angered by any Russian counterproposal that would involve also the internationalizing and disarming of Suez or Panama. We must recognize that to the Russians these seem to be identical situations. . . .

We should make an effort to counteract the irrational fear of Russia which is being systematically built up in the American people by certain individuals and publications. The slogan that communism and capitalism, regimentation and democracy, cannot continue to exist in the same world is, from a historical point of view, pure propaganda. Several religious doctrines, all claiming to be the only true gospel and salvation, have existed side by side with a reasonable degree of tolerance for centuries. This country was for the first half of its national life a democratic island in a world dominated by absolutist governments.

We should not act as if we too felt that we were threatened in today's world. We are by far the most powerful nation in the world, the only Allied nation which came out of the war without devastation and much stronger than before the war. Any talk on our part about the need for strengthening our defenses further is bound to appear hypocritical to other nations. . . .

This proposal admittedly calls for a shift in some of our thinking about international matters. It is imperative that we make this shift.

We have little time to lose. Our postwar actions have not yet been adjusted to the lessons to be gained from experience of Allied cooperation during the war and the facts of the atomic age.

It is certainly desirable that, as far as possible, we achieve unity on the home front with respect to our international relations; but unity on the basis of building up conflict abroad would prove to be not only unsound but disastrous. I think there is some reason to fear that in our earnest efforts to achieve bipartisan unity in this country we may have given way too much to isolationism masquerading as tough realism in international affairs.

The real test lies in the achievement of international unity. It will be fruitless to continue to seek solutions for the many specific problems that face us in the making of the peace and in the establishment of an enduring international order without first achieving an atmosphere of mutual trust and confidence. The task admittedly is not an easy one.

There is no question, as the Secretary of State has indicated, that negotiations with the Russians are difficult because of cultural differences, their traditional isolationism, and their insistence on a visible quid pro quo in all agreements. But the task is not an insuperable one if we take into account that to other nations our foreign policy consists not only of the principles that we advocate but of the actions we take.

Fundamentally, this comes down to the point discussed earlier in this letter, that even our own security, in the sense that we have known it in the past, cannot be preserved by military means in a world armed with atomic weapons. The only type of security which can be maintained by our own military force is the type described by a military man before the Senate Atomic Energy Commission—a security against invasion after all our cities and perhaps 40 million of our city population have been destroyed by atomic weapons. That is the best that "security" on the basis of armaments has to offer us. It is not the kind of security that our people and the people of the other United Nations are striving for.

American Firmness vs. Soviet Aggression

Clark Clifford

*To understand history requires an attitude of historical mindedness. Stu-
dents must put themselves in the position of other people in other times.
They must try to be aware of the frame of reference of others, of the
pressures on them, of the shaping influences of their thought and behavior, and of the extent and manner of their understanding of a particular
issue or development. An analysis of President Harry Truman's actions in
the Cold War, for example, in part requires an examination of how he
and his closest advisors viewed the Soviet Union and its leaders.*

*This private memorandum for the president, prepared by his special
counsel, Clark Clifford, just a year after V-J Day, summarizes the attitudes and outlook of most high level officials in the Truman administration and reveals the influence of George F. Kennan's diplomatic cables
from Moscow. It blames the Soviet Union for the developing Cold War
and urges the president to counter the direct Soviet threat to American
security by arming the United States to wage war by employing foreign
aid to build a "barrier to communism," by utilizing American economic
power to force Soviet concessions, and by "getting tough" in all negotiations with the Soviets lest they consider the United States to be weak.*

It is perhaps the greatest paradox of the present day that the leaders of a nation, now stronger than it has ever been before, should
embark on so aggressive a course because their nation is "weak."
And yet Stalin and his cohorts proclaim that "monopoly capitalism"

Excerpted from a Clark Clifford memorandum to President Truman, September 24, 1946, in Clark Clifford Papers, Harry S Truman Library, Independence, Missouri.

threatens the world with war and that Russia must strengthen her defenses against the danger of foreign attacks. The USSR, according to Kremlin propaganda, is imperilled so long as it remains within a "capitalistic encirclement." This idea is absurd when adopted by so vast a country with such great natural wealth, a population of almost 200 million and no powerful or aggressive neighbors. But the process of injecting this propaganda into the minds of the Soviet people goes on with increasing intensity.

The concept of danger from the outside is deeply rooted in the Russian people's haunting sense of insecurity inherited from their past. It is maintained by their present leaders as a justification for the oppressive nature of the Soviet police state. The thesis, that the capitalist world is conspiring to attack the Soviet Union, is not based on any objective analysis of the situation beyond Russia's borders. It has little to do, indeed, with conditions outside the Soviet Union, and it has risen mainly from basic inner-Russian necessities which existed before the Second World War and which exist today. . . .

The Kremlin acknowledges no limit to the eventual power of the Soviet Union, but it is practical enough to be concerned with the actual position of the USSR today. In any matter deemed essential to the security of the Soviet Union, Soviet leaders will prove adamant in their claims and demands. In other matters they will prove grasping and opportunistic, but flexible in proportion to the degree and nature of the resistance encountered.

Recognition of the need to postpone the "inevitable" conflict is in no sense a betrayal of the Communist faith. Marx and Lenin encouraged compromise and collaboration with non-Communists for the accomplishment of ultimate communistic purposes. The USSR has followed such a course in the past. In 1939 the Kremlin signed a nonaggression pact with Germany and in 1941 a neutrality pact with Japan. Soviet leaders will continue to collaborate whenever it seems expedient, for time is needed to build up Soviet strength and weaken the opposition. Time is on the side of the Soviet Union, since population growth and economic development will, in the Soviet view, bring an increase in its relative strength. . . .

A direct threat to American security is implicit in Soviet foreign policy which is designed to prepare the Soviet Union for war with the leading capitalistic nations of the world. Soviet leaders recognize that the United States will be the Soviet Union's most powerful enemy if such a war as that predicted by Communist theory ever comes about and therefore the United States is the chief target of Soviet foreign and military policy. . . .

The most obvious Soviet threat to American security is the growing ability of the USSR to wage an offensive war against the United States. This has not hitherto been possible, in the absence of Soviet long-range strategic air power and an almost total lack of sea power. Now, however, the USSR is rapidly developing elements of her military strength which she hitherto lacked and which will give the Soviet Union great offensive capabilities. Stalin has declared his intention of sparing no effort to build up the military strength of the Soviet Union. Development of atomic weapons, guided missiles, materials for biological warfare, a strategic air force, submarines of great cruising range, naval mines and mine craft, to name the most important, are extending the effective range of Soviet military power well into areas which the United States regards as vital to its security. . . .

The primary objective of United States policy toward the Soviet Union is to convince Soviet leaders that it is in their interest to participate in a system of world cooperation, that there are no fundamental causes for war between our two nations, and that the security and prosperity of the Soviet Union, and that of the rest of the world as well, is being jeopardized by the aggressive militaristic imperialism such as that in which the Soviet Union is now engaged.

However, these same leaders with whom we hope to achieve an understanding on the principles of international peace appear to believe that a war with the United States and the other leading capitalistic nations is inevitable. They are increasing their military power and the sphere of Soviet influence in preparation for the "inevitable" conflict, and they are trying to weaken and subvert their potential opponents by every means at their disposal. so long as these men adhere to these beliefs, it is highly dangerous to conclude that hope of international peace lies only in "accord," "mutual understanding," or "solidarity" with the Soviet Union.

Adoption of such a policy would impel the United States to make sacrifices for the sake of Soviet-U.S. relations, which would only have the effect of raising Soviet hopes and increasing Soviet demands, and to ignore alternative lines of policy, which might be much more compatible with our own national and international interests.

The Soviet government will never be easy to "get along with." The American people must accustom themselves to this thought, not as a cause for despair, but as a fact to be faced objectively and courageously. If we find it impossible to enlist Soviet cooperation in the solution of world problems, we should be prepared to join with the British and other Western countries in an attempt to build up a world of our own which will pursue its own objectives and will recognize the Soviet orbit as a distinct entity with which conflict is not predestined but with which we cannot pursue common aims.

As long as the Soviet government maintains its present foreign policy, based upon the theory of an ultimate struggle between communism and capitalism, the United States must assume that the USSR might fight at any time for the two-fold purpose of expanding the territory under Communist control and weakening its potential capitalist opponents. The Soviet Union was able to flow into the political vacuum of the Balkans, Eastern Europe, the Near East, Manchuria and Korea because no other nation was both willing and able to prevent it. Soviet leaders were encouraged by easy success and they are now preparing to take over new areas in the same way. The Soviet Union, as Stalin euphemistically phrased it, is preparing "for any eventuality."

Unless the United States is willing to sacrifice its future security for the sake of "accord" with the USSR now, this government must, as a first step toward world stabilization, seek to prevent additional Soviet aggression. . . . This government should be prepared, while scrupulously avoiding any act which would be an excuse for the Soviets to begin a war, to resist vigorously and successfully any efforts of the USSR to expand into areas vital to American security.

The language of military power is the only language which disciples of power politics understand. The United States must use that language in order that Soviet leaders will realize that our government is determined to uphold the interests of its citizens and the rights of small nations. Compromise and concessions are considered, by the Soviets, to be evidences of weakness and they are encouraged by our "retreats" to make new and greater demands.

The main deterrent to Soviet attack on the United States, or to attack on areas of the world which are vital to our security, will be the military power of this country. It must be made apparent to the Soviet government that our strength will be sufficient to repel any attack and sufficient to defeat the USSR decisively if a war should start. The prospect of defeat is the only sure means of deterring the Soviet Union.

The Soviet Union's vulnerability is limited due to the vast area over which its key industries and natural resources are widely dispersed, but it is vulnerable to atomic weapons, biological warfare, and long-range power. Therefore, in order to maintain our strength at a level which will be effective in restraining the Soviet Union, the United States must be prepared to wage atomic and biological warfare. A highly mechanized army, which can be moved either by sea or by air, capable of seizing and holding strategic areas, must be supported by powerful naval and air forces. A war with the USSR would be "total" in a more horrible sense than any previous war and there must be constant research for both offensive and defensive weapons.

Whether it would actually be in this country's interest to employ atomic and biological weapons against the Soviet Union in the event of hostilities is a question which would require careful consideration in the light of the circumstances prevailing at the time. The decision would probably be influenced by a number of factors, such as the Soviet Union's capacity to employ similar weapons, which can not now be estimated. But the important point is that the United States must be prepared to wage atomic and biological warfare if necessary. The mere fact of preparedness may be the only powerful deterrent to Soviet aggressive action and in this sense the only sure guaranty of peace.

The United States, with a military potential composed primarily of [highly] effective technical weapons, should entertain no proposal for disarmament or limitation of armament as long as the possibility of Soviet aggression exists. Any discussion on the limitation of armaments should be pursued slowly and carefully with the knowledge constantly in mind that proposals on outlawing atomic warfare and long-range offensive weapons would greatly limit United States strength, while only moderately affecting the Soviet Union. The Soviet Union relies primarily on a large infantry and artillery force and the result of such arms limitation would be to deprive the United States of its most effective weapons without impairing the Soviet Union's ability to wage a quick war of aggression in Western Europe, the Middle East or the Far East. . . .

In addition to maintaining our own strength, the United States should support and assist all democratic countries which are in any way menaced or endangered by the USSR. Providing military support in case of attack is a last resort; a more effective barrier to communism is strong economic support. Trade agreements, loans and technical missions strengthen our ties with friendly nations and are effective demonstrations that capitalism is at least the equal of communism. The United States can do much to ensure that economic opportunities, personal freedom and social equality are made possible in countries outside the Soviet sphere by generous financial assistance. Our policy on reparations should be directed toward strengthening the areas we are endeavoring to keep outside the Soviet sphere. Our efforts to break down trade barriers, open up rivers and international waterways, and bring about economic unification of countries, now divided by occupation armies, are also directed toward the reestablishment of vigorous and healthy non-Communist economies.

In conclusion, as long as the Soviet government adheres to its present policy, the United States should maintain military forces powerful enough to restrain the Soviet Union and to confine Soviet influence to its present area. All nations not now within the Soviet sphere should be given generous economic assistance and political support in their opposition to Soviet penetration. Economic aid may also be given to the Soviet government and private trade with the USSR permitted provided the results are beneficial to our interests. . . .

Even though Soviet leaders profess to believe that the conflict between Capitalism and Communism is irreconcilable and must eventually be resolved by the triumph of the latter, it is our hope that they will change their minds and work out with us a fair and equitable settlement when they realize that we are too strong to be beaten and too determined to be frightened.

The Truman Doctrine

Harry S Truman

Once President Truman decided on the containment policy advocated by his closest advisors, including Clifford and Acting Secretary of State Dean Acheson, he faced the task of persuading the Congress and the American people that this potentially dangerous and expensive new departure was necessary. Taking the advice of Republican Senator Arthur Vandenberg, the president resolved to "scare the hell out of the country." Responding to the immediate crisis brought on by Great Britain's decision that it could no longer afford to assist the governments of Greece and Turkey in their respective struggles against a communist-aided insurgent guerilla movement and against Soviet pressure for access to the Mediterranean, the president went before the Congress in March 1947 to request $400 million in military assistance to Greece and Turkey. Truman starkly depicted a communist menace that imperiled the world and threatened the United States.

I "wished to state, for all the world to know, what the position of the United States was in the face of the new totalitarian challenge," Truman later recalled about his address to Congress. "This was, I believe, the turning point in America's foreign policy, which now declared that wherever aggression, direct or indirect, threatened the peace, the security of the United States was involved." Accordingly, the Truman Doctrine came to mean that the United States had to draw the line against the spread of communism everywhere, and, that in its role of global policeman, the United States faced an almost limitless confrontation with the Soviet Union and any of its allies. The Truman Doctrine, which quickly led to the Marshall Plan and then to the North Atlantic Treaty Organization (NATO), laid the foundation for American foreign policy for much of the next four decades.

From *Public Papers of the Presidents, Harry S Truman, 1947* (Washington, D.C., 1963), pp. 176–80.

Mr. President, Mr. Speaker, Members of the Congress of the
United States:

. . . The United States had received from the Greek Government an urgent appeal for financial and economic assistance. Pre-
liminary reports from the American Economic Mission now in
Greece and reports from the American Ambassador in Greece cor-
roborate the statement of the Greek Government that assistance is
imperative if Greece is to survive as a free nation. . . .

The very existence of the Greek state is today threatened by the
terrorist activities of several thousand armed men, led by Communists, who defy the government's authority at a number of points,
particularly along the northern boundaries. A Commission appointed by the United Nations Security Council is at present investigating disturbed conditions in northern Greece and alleged border
violations along the frontier between Greece on the one hand and
Albania, Bulgaria, and Yugoslavia on the other.

Meanwhile, the Greek Government is unable to cope with the
situation. The Greek army is small and poorly equipped. It needs
supplies and equipment if it is to restore authority to the government throughout Greek territory.

Greece must have assistance if it is to become a self-supporting
and self-respecting democracy. . . .

No government is perfect. One of the chief virtues of a democracy, however, is that its defects are always visible and under democratic processes can be pointed out and corrected. The government
of Greece is not perfect. Nevertheless it represents 85 percent of
the members of the Greek Parliament who were chosen in an election last year. Foreign observers, including 692 Americans, considered this election to be a fair expression of the views of the Greek
people.

The Greek Government has been operating in an atmosphere of
chaos and extremism. It has made mistakes. The extension of aid by
this country does not mean that the United States condones everything that the Greek Government has done or will do. We have
condemned in the past, and we condemn now, extremist measures
of the right or the left. We have in the past advised tolerance, and
we advice tolerance now.

Greece's neighbor, Turkey, also deserves our attention. . . .

The British Government has informed us that, owing to its own difficulties, it can no longer extend financial or economic aid to Turkey.

As in the case of Greece, if Turkey is to have the assistance it needs, the United States must supply it. We are the only country able to provide that help.

I am fully aware of the broad implications involved if the United States extends assistance to Greece and Turkey, and I shall discuss these implications with you at this time.

One of the primary objectives of the foreign policy of the United States is the creation of conditions in which we and other nations will be able to work out a way of life free from coercion. This was a fundamental issue in the war with Germany and Japan. Our victory was won over countries which sought to impose their will, and their way of life, upon other nations.

To ensure the peaceful development of nations, free from coercion, the United States has taken a leading part in establishing the United Nations. The United Nations is designed to make possible lasting freedom and independence for all its members. We shall not realize our objectives, however, unless we are willing to help free peoples to maintain their free institutions and their national integrity against aggressive movements that seek to impose upon them totalitarian regimes. This is no more than a frank recognition that totalitarian regimes imposed upon free peoples, by direct or indirect aggression, undermine the foundations of international peace and hence the security of the United States.

The peoples of a number of countries of the world have recently had totalitarian regimes forced upon them against their will. The Government of the United States has made frequent protests against coercion and intimidation, in violation of the Yalta agreement, in Poland, Rumania, and Bulgaria. I must also state that in a number of other countries there have been similar developments.

At the present moment in world history nearly every nation must choose between alternative ways of life. The choice is too often not a free one.

One way of life is based upon the will of the majority, and is distinguished by free institutions, representative government, free elections, guarantees of individual liberty, freedom of speech and religion, and freedom from political oppression.

The second way of life is based upon the will of a minority forcibly imposed upon the majority. It relies upon terror and oppression, a controlled press and radio, fixed elections, and the suppression of personal freedoms.

I believe that it must be the policy of the United States to support free peoples who are resisting attempted subjugation by armed minorities or by outside pressures.

I believe that we must assist free peoples to work out their own destinies in their own way.

I believe that our help should be primarily through economic and financial aid which is essential to economic stability and orderly political processes.

The world is not static, and the *status quo* is not sacred. But we cannot allow changes in the *status quo* in violation of the Charter of the United Nations by such methods as coercion, or by such subterfuges as political infiltration. In helping free and independent nations to maintain their freedom, the United States will be giving effect to the principles of the Charter of the United Nations.

It is necessary only to glance at a map to realize that the survival and integrity of the Greek nation are of grave importance in a much wider situation. If Greece should fall under the control of an armed minority, the effect upon its neighbor, Turkey, would be immediate and serious. Confusion and disorder might well spread throughout the entire Middle East.

Moreover, the disappearance of Greece as an independent state would have a profound effect upon those countries in Europe whose peoples are struggling against great difficulties to maintain their freedoms and their independence while they repair the damages of war.

It would be an unspeakable tragedy if these countries, which have struggled so long against overwhelming odds, should lose that victory for which they sacrificed so much. Collapse of free institutions and loss of independence would be disastrous not only for them but for the world. Discouragement and possibly failure would quickly be the lot of neighboring peoples striving to maintain their freedom and independence.

Should we fail to aid Greece and Turkey in this fateful hour, the effect will be far reaching to the West as well as to the East. . . .

NSC-68: A Report to the National Security Council

Following the detonation of the Soviet Union's first atomic bomb and the communist victory in China in 1949, President Truman asked his advisers for a comprehensive analysis of the course of world affairs and the foreign and military policies of the United States. Largely the work of Secretary of State Dean Acheson, NSC-68 was officially a report to the National Security Council by the Departments of State and Defense in April 1950. It defined the Soviet–American conflict as global in scope and primarily military in nature. Predicting continued, perpetual conflict with international communism, NSC-68 called for a vastly enlarged military budget to counter the Soviet's alleged ambition for global domination. How to sell such an expensive, militaristic policy to a war-weary American people and a budget-minded Congress worried proponents of NSC-68. "We were sweating over it, and then—with regard to NSC-68—thank God Korea came along," recalled one of Dean Acheson's aides. Do you think Russian and/or Chinese actions as of April 1950 justified the tone and recommendations of NSC-68? What were the costs, financially and otherwise, of "the eternal vigilance" called for by NSC-68? What practical alternatives to NSC-68 did President Truman have in 1950? What were the implications of this pivotal report for the wars in Korea and Indochina?

Within the past thirty-five years the world has experienced two global wars of tremendous violence. It has witnessed two revolutions—the Russian and the Chinese—of extreme scope and intensity. It has also seen the collapse of five empires—the Ottoman, the Austro-Hungarian, German, Italian and Japanese—and

Excerpts from "NSC-68: A Report to the National Security Council," April 14, 1950, from *Foreign Relations of the United States: 1950*, I, pp. 237–92.

the drastic decline of two major imperial systems, the British and the French. During the span of one generation, the international distribution of power has been fundamentally altered. For several centuries it had proved impossible for any one nation to gain such preponderant strength that a coalition of other nations could not in time face it with greater strength. The international scene was marked by recurring periods of violence and war, but a system of sovereign and independent states was maintained, over which no state was able to achieve hegemony.

Two complex sets of factors have now basically altered this historical distribution of power. First, the defeat of Germany and Japan and the decline of the British and French Empires have interacted with the development of the United States and the Soviet Union in such a way that power has increasingly gravitated to these two centers. Second, the Soviet Union, unlike previous aspirants to hegemony, is animated by a new fanatic faith, antithetical to our own, and seeks to impose its absolute authority over the rest of the world. Conflict has, therefore, become endemic and is waged, on the part of the Soviet Union, by violent or non-violent methods in accordance with the dictates of expediency. With the development of increasingly terrifying weapons of mass destruction, every individual faces the ever-present possibility of annihilation should the conflict enter the phase of total war.

On the one hand, the people of the world yearn for relief from the anxiety arising from the risk of atomic war. On the other hand, any substantial further extension of the area under the domination of the Kremlin would raise the possibility that no coalition adequate to confront the Kremlin with greater strength could be assembled. It is in this context that this Republic and its citizens in the ascendancy of their strength stand in their deepest peril.

The issues that face us are momentous, involving the fulfillment or destruction not only of this Republic but of civilization itself. They are issues which will not await our deliberations. With conscience and resolution this Government and the people it represents must now take new and fateful decisions. . . . The fundamental design of those who control the Soviet Union and the international communist movement is to retain and solidify their absolute power, first in the Soviet Union and second in the areas now under their control. In the minds of the Soviet leaders, however, achievement of this design requires the dynamic extension of their authority and the ultimate elimination of any effective opposition to their authority.

The design, therefore, calls for the complete subversion or forcible destruction of the machinery of government and structure of society in the countries of the non-Soviet world and their replacement by an apparatus and structure subservient to and controlled from the Kremlin. To that end Soviet efforts are now directed toward the domination of the Eurasian land mass. The United States, as the principal center of power in the non-Soviet world and the bulwark of opposition to Soviet expansion, is the principal enemy whose integrity and vitality must be subverted or destroyed by one means or another if the Kremlin is to achieve its fundamental design.

The Kremlin regards the United States as the only major threat to the achievement of its fundamental design. There is a basic conflict between the idea of freedom under a government of laws, and the idea of slavery under the grim oligarchy of the Kremlin, which has come to a crisis with the polarization of power described in Section I, and the exclusive possession of atomic weapons by the two protagonists. The idea of freedom, moreover, is peculiarly and intolerably subversive of the idea of slavery. But the converse is not true. The implacable purpose of the slave state to eliminate the challenge of freedom has placed the two great powers at opposite poles. It is this fact which gives the present polarization of power the quality of crisis. . . .

Thus unwillingly our free society finds itself mortally challenged by the Soviet system. No other value system is so wholly irreconcilable with ours, so implacable in its purpose to destroy ours, so capable of turning to its own uses the most dangerous and divisive trends in our own society, no other so skillfully and powerfully evokes the elements of irrationality in human nature everywhere, and no other has the support of a great and growing center of military power. . . .

Our overall policy at the present time may be described as one designed to foster a world environment in which the American system can survive and flourish. It therefore rejects the concept of isolation and affirms the necessity of our positive participation in the world community.

This broad intention embraces two subsidiary policies. One is a policy which we would probably pursue even if there were no Soviet threat. It is a policy of attempting to develop a healthy international community. The other is the policy of "containing" the Soviet system. . . . .

A more rapid build-up of political, economic, and military strength and thereby of confidence in the free world than is now contemplated is the only course which is consistent with progress toward achieving our fundamental purpose. The frustration of the Kremlin design requires the free world to develop a successfully functioning political and economic system and a vigorous political offensive against the Soviet Union. These, in turn, require an adequate military shield under which they can develop. It is necessary to have the military power to deter, if possible, Soviet expansion, and to defeat, if necessary, aggressive Soviet or Soviet-directed actions of a limited or total character. The potential strength of the free world is great; its ability to develop these military capabilities and its will to resist Soviet expansion will be determined by the wisdom and will with which it undertakes to meet its political and economic problems. . . .

A comprehensive and decisive program to win the peace and frustrate the Kremlin design should be so designed that it can be sustained for as long as necessary to achieve our national objectives. It would probably involve:

1. The development of an adequate political and economic framework for the achievement of our long-range objectives.
2. A substantial increase in expenditures for military purposes adequate to meet the requirements for the tasks listed in Section D-1 [omitted].
3. A substantial increase in military assistance programs, designed to foster cooperative efforts, which will adequately and efficiently meet the requirements of our allies for the tasks referred to in Section D-1-*e* [omitted].
4. Some increase in economic assistance programs and recognition of the need to continue these programs until their purposes have been accomplished.
5. A concerted attack on the problem of the United States balance of payments, along the lines already approved by the President.

6. Development of programs designed to build and maintain confidence among other peoples in our strength and resolution, and to wage overt psychological warfare calculated to encourage mass defections from Soviet allegiance and to frustrate the Kremlin design in other ways.
7. Intensification of affirmative and timely measures and operations by covert means in the fields of economic warfare and political and psychological warfare with a view to fomenting and supporting unrest and revolt in selected strategic satellite countries.
8. Development of internal security and civilian defense programs.
9. Improvement and intensification of intelligence activities.
10. Reduction of Federal expenditures for purposes other than defense and foreign assistance, if necessary by the deferment of certain desirable programs.
11. Increased taxes. . . .

In summary, we must, by means of a rapid and sustained build-up of the political, economic, and military strength of the free world, and by means of an affirmative program intended to wrest the initiative from the Soviet Union, confront it with convincing evidence of the determination and ability of the free world to frustrate the Kremlin design of a world dominated by its will. Such evidence is the only means short of war which eventually may force the Kremlin to abandon its present course of action and to negotiate acceptable agreements on issues of major importance.

The whole success of the proposed program hangs ultimately on recognition by this Government, the American people, and all free peoples, that the cold war is in fact a real war in which the survival of the free world is at stake. Essential prerequisites to success are consultations with Congressional leaders designed to make the program the object of non-partisan legislative support, and a presentation to the public of a full explanation of the facts and implications of the present international situation. The prosecution of the program will require of us all the ingenuity, sacrifice, and unity demanded by the vital importance of the issue and the tenacity to persevere until our national objectives have been attained. . . .

American Cold War Policies Reexamined

Melvyn P. Leffler

The enormous, and still growing, literature on the causes and origins of the Cold War presents students with an array of conflicting, often diametrically opposed, interpretations. Historians disagree on whether mostly to blame the Soviet Union or the United States, on whether or not the Cold War was inevitable, and on which factors were the primary determinants: economics, geopolitics, atomic weaponry, domestic politics, personality, ideology, misperception, national security. In the essay excerpted below, University of Virginia diplomatic historian Melvyn Leffler, author of A Preponderance of Power *(1992), highlights the findings of recent studies and focuses on the lessons to be learned from the early years of the Cold War. In this light, reread Clark Clifford's memorandum to the president and NSC-68.*

Challenged with the greatest public relations task ever faced by a president, Truman and his advisers could not resist the temptation to simplify Soviet intentions. Throughout 1945 and early 1946 serious efforts had been made to appraise the relative importance of the strategic, economic, political, and ideological factors shaping Soviet policy. After the spring of 1946, however, these efforts ceased. George F. Kennan's assessment in the "long" telegram became the established verity, and a new prominence was given to the ideological and totalitarian character of Soviet foreign policy. This

Melvyn P. Leffler, "From the Truman Doctrine to the Carter Doctrine: Lessons and Dilemmas of the Cold War," *Diplomatic History* VII (No. 4, 1983). Reprinted by permission of Scholarly Resources Inc.

was dramatically evident in James V. Forrestal's fixation with Marxist-Leninist doctrine, in the State Department's March 1946 estimate of Soviet policy which served as a framework for military studies, and in the lengthy memorandum on U.S.–Soviet relations prepared by Clark Clifford and George Elsey for President Truman in the summer of 1946. While detailed and thoughtful assessments of Soviet short-term intentions persisted, almost always emphasizing the Kremlin's desire to avoid war, the notion that the Soviet Union sought world domination became the fundamental postulate of American national security doctrine.

Yet recent studies of Soviet foreign policy underscore the importance of examining the Kremlin's intentions and objectives with rigor, subtlety, and sophistication. The closer historians and political scientists scrutinize Soviet foreign policy in the immediate postwar era, the more difficult it becomes to generalize and simplify. Vojtech Mastny has emphasized Stalin's opportunism; Adam Ulam and William Taubman have portrayed his caution, apprehension, and circumspection; William O. McCagg has imaginatively suggested the host of institutional, economic, personal, and ideological impulses that engulfed Soviet foreign policy; and Werner G. Hahn has argued that the postwar revival of ideology within the Soviet Union had little to do with foreign policy. We now have reason to believe that Stalin was treading warily lest he provoke the West. During 1946 and early 1947 the Soviet leader probably discouraged revolutionary activity abroad. Notwithstanding his determination to dominate the Eastern European periphery, to seek opportunities in Iran and Turkey, and to orient Germany and Austria toward the East, he seemed to prefer an overall policy of détente, to use Taubman's phrase. Only after the proclamation of the Truman Doctrine, the announcement of the Marshall Plan, and the merger of the three western zones in Germany did Stalin accept the reality of the Cold War, encourage revolutionary action in Western Europe, establish the Cominform, and consolidate Soviet domination in the areas occupied at the end of World War II, particulary Hungary, Czechoslovakia, and East Germany.

If it is important to probe more deeply into Soviet intentions, it is equally imperative to develop a correct appreciation of Soviet military strength. At the time of the Truman Doctrine, American analysts recognized two critical features about Soviet military capabilities. First, the Soviet Union, because of prevailing power vacuums, could overrun in a few months all of Western Europe, much of the Middle East, and sizable chunks of Manchuria and North China. Second, the Soviet Union could not inflict serious damage on the American homeland, could not compete with a mobilized American economy, and, therefore, could not wage war successfully against the United States. Because American analysts and policymakers appreciated Soviet military weaknesses vis-à-vis the United States, they remained confident that Soviet leaders would avoid war, back down in a crisis, and succumb to demonstrations of American diplomatic determination. Kennan predicted this in his "long" telegram, and the Soviets behaved, as predicted, when they withdrew from Iran, refrained from intervention in Greece, and avoided military conflict over Berlin.

The disparity in capabilites to wage war against one another, the fundamental economic strength of the United States, and the strategic weaknesses of the Soviet Union allowed American officials to develop and implement a broad conception of national security. The overriding U.S. national security imperative, as revealed in scores of military planning documents, intelligence reports, and interagency papers, was to prevent Soviet control of the raw materials and manpower of Europe and Asia lest the Soviet Union use these resources to enhance its long-term capabilities to wage war against the United States. In other words, American officials perceived the Soviet Union as a hostile ideological foe, feared the appeal of communism, believed that Communist parties everywhere were subservient to the Kremlin, and assumed that if Communists took control anywhere in Eurasia, the latent military power of the Soviet Union would be enhanced and the economic vitality of the West would be diminished.

In early 1947 to contain Sovet/Communist power and create a stable international order conducive to U.S. economic and political interests, the Truman administration prepared to rehabilitate German industry, rebuild Western Europe, revive Japan, and implant American power on the very borders of the Soviet Union. Containment along the so-called northern tier (Greece, Turkey, and Iran) also was essential to preserve Western access to Middle East oil in peacetime and to fight more effectively in wartime should conflict unexpectedly erupt.

From the American perspective, these initiatives appeared prudent, just, and urgent; they were not designed to threaten the Soviet Union. With all sincerity Ambassador Walter Bedell Smith told Stalin in April 1946 that it was impossible for Americans to envisage any threat to the Soviet Union. Approximately one year later Secretary of State George C. Marshall expressed much the same thought to the Soviet dictator. Kennan, Clifford, and Elsey were absolutely certain that Soviet suspicions and anxieties were simply a ruse to justify the Kremlin's totalitarian control at home and/or ruthless conquest abroad.

A key lesson of the Truman Doctrine era, therefore, is for Americans to develop a better grasp of how their actions impinge upon the interests of potential adversaries and of how their own concept of security may endanger the perceived security of other powers. By mid-1947 the American security frontier stretched to the Elbe, the Dardanelles, and the Sea of Japan. More significantly, the American conception of security encompassed, among other things, the economic rebuilding of the Soviet Union's traditional enemies, Germany and Japan, and the assumption of British strategic interests in areas of long-standing Anglo-Soviet rivalry in the Middle East and Southwest Asia. If Stalin's fears of latent American power were as great as Ulam has suggested, American actions in 1947 were certain to intensify those apprehensions because these initiatives directly and indirectly influenced power relationships in areas of historic and vital interest to the Soviet Union.

There is then an enduring paradox: the policies that rehabilitated the industrial heartlands of Europe and Asia, that revitalized Western European liberalism and capitalism, and that safeguarded the petroleum resources of the Middle East were the same policies that culminated in the division of Europe, the elimination of the last vestiges of democracy in Hungary and Czechoslovakia, and the institutionalization of the Cold War. Only the disparity in the overall Soviet-American power relationship permitted the United States to exclude the Soviets from Japan, bar them from bases in the Dardanelles, and shut them out of the Ruhr-Rhineland industrial complex. Likewise, Soviet power enabled Stalin to consolidate a sphere of terror and repression in Eastern Europe.

So it might seem that Kennan's view of holding four of the five major power centers came to dominate the foreign policy of the Truman administration. Yet this was not the case. In the aftermath of World War II, vacuums of powers existed throughout Eurasia, and interest and apprehension impelled the United States to fill these vacuums. During the summer of 1946, Clifford and Elsey emphasized, with Kennan's endorsement, the need "to support and assist *all* democratic countries which are *in any way* menaced or endangered by the U.S.S.R." They specifically named China, Korea, India, the Philippines, and Southeast Asia. In preparing their studies for the Truman Doctrine, State Department officials were fully cognizant, in Joseph Jones's words, that "not just the fate of Greece was at stake. Greece was the key to a much wider situation: the freedom and security of a large part of the world." The Marshall Plan, then, accentuated the West's interest in Middle East oil. The decision to revive Japan, as Michael Schaller has shown, generated even greater concern with preserving access to the markets and raw materials of Southeast Asia.

Apprehension reinforced interest; that is, the fear that these resources might be controlled by the Kremlin reinforced U.S. determination to combat Communist efforts, particularly in Asia. This was true even in China, where, despite all the agonizing reappraisals and pervasive doubts, the United States provided almost $3 billion in aid to the Chinese nationalists from 1945 to 1949. And in mid-1949, when salvaging China was recognized as hopeless, Secretary of State Acheson instructed his trusted aide Philip Jessup to draw up programs for non-Communist Asia on the assumption that it was "a fundamental decision of American policy that the United States does not intend to permit any further communist domination on the continent of Asia or in Southeast Asia."

The definition of American interests as global was apparent in almost every important document of the Truman Doctrine era (1946–50). The Clifford/Elsey report of September 1946, Acheson and Clayton's testimony on the Truman Doctrine, NSC 7, NSC 20/4, and NSC 68 all projected American interests everywhere as did Kennan's "long" telegram and "X" article. If no financial or military commitments to Southeast Asia were made in the initial postwar years, it was not because American officials foreswore an interest in that part of the world but because they perceived no immediate threat and recognized that American resources were circumscribed. Once they perceived a threat, U.S. officials mobilized the resources to become involved. While Truman's advisers did seek to set priorities among different geographic areas, their explicit goal always was to contain Soviet/Communist influence throughout Eurasia. Hence, the propspect for American commitment, even in areas of peripheral interest, were high from the onset.

An important lesson to be learned from the Truman Doctrine era is the need to differentiate among interests, carefully identify vital interests, refrain from ideological crusades, and avoid the temptation to define all major interests as national security imperatives justifying the use of force. Once interests are defined and commitments are incurred, there is almost irresistible pressure to build up commensurate military capabilities. Truman initially hoped to limit defense expenditures. Yet once American interests were defined in global terms, an enormous gap emerged between interests and commitments on the one hand and capabilities on the other. As global instability persisted, nationalist unrest mounted, Soviet military capabilities grew, and as American prestige became vested in the maintenance of a non-Communist world order, the entire national security bureaucracy came to support a massive military buildup at home and abroad.

The accretion of American power was justified, at least in part, on the need to negotiate from strength. Presumably the failure to resolve differences was the result of Soviet negotiating intransigence and insufficient American leverage. Yet it is apparent that the stalemate in negotiations was as much the result of unreasonable American expectations as of Soviet obstinacy. Truman accepted Averell Harriman's advice that negotiations entail mutual concessions, but he expected to get his way 85 percent of the time. Stalin, Truman wrote his wife from Potsdam, "seems to like it when I hit him with a hammer." While tough, Truman's attitude was a lot more flexible than the one expressed by Acheson in March 1947 when he insisted in executive session hearings that "it is a mistake to believe that you can, at any time, sit down with the Russians and solve questions. . . ."

It was not the absence of American strength that precluded constructive negotiations; it was the inflexibility of the Soviet and U.S. negotiating positions. The Soviets were obdurate on Eastern European questions. On most other matters the United States was equally instractable. Recent books by Patricia Dawson Ward and Robert L. Messer illuminate the negotiating box in which even the malleable James F. Byrnes found himself. Gregg Herken and Larry G. Gerber demonstrate how the Baruch Plan was framed to safeguard all American interests and to place upon the Soviet Union all the initial risks of an agreement on the control of atomic energy. J. Samuel Walker has portrayed the unreceptive attitude of American officials toward negotiations in early 1948, and Ulam has lamented the unwillingness of American officials to discuss a resolution of the German problem. Conversely, throughout these years American negotiators often privately acknowledged that the Soviet position on many matters was not intransigent. Not only was this the view of Byrnes but also that of such disparate negotiators as George A. Lincoln, Lucius Clay, Ferdinand Eberstadt, and Warren Austin. But Americans did not have the patience to negotiate because European economic dislocation threatened indigenous revolution or Communist electoral victories. Either possibility seemed to portend an aggrandizement of Soviet power which American officials could no longer accept.

The foregoing is not intended to suggest that flexible negotiators could easily have resolved the momentous and contentious issues that divided Soviet and American officials. It is still not clear whether any way could have been found to safeguard legitimate American security imperatives without arousing Soviet apprehensions, jeopardizing vital Soviet interests, and eliciting Soviet countermeasures. What is clear is that by 1947 American policymakers no longer wanted to negotiate and compromise. They simplified Soviet intentions, subordinated Soviet strategic and economic concerns, focused on the ideological roots and totalitarian character of the Soviet system, and ignored the possible repercussions of their own policies on Soviet behavior. In the midst of the feverish efforts to build up situations of strength, even those officials like Kennan who sometimes preached the efficacy of nonmilitary and "asymmetrical" containment, gradually lost their influence. Any appraisal of postwar U.S. policy that seeks to establish the Truman Doctrine era as a model of successful policymaking must take note of these developments.

The Internal Communist Menace

Joseph R. McCarthy

While the debate about the deeper causes of the Second Red Scare continues—whether it was a mass movement rooted in the status resentments of lower middle-class and working-clas Americans or whether it was the result of the actions (and inactions) of both conservative and liberal political elites and interest groups—few historians doubt that Senator Joseph R. McCarthy did more than any other individual to turn the fear of internal communism into a national hysteria. His name still stirs violent emotions in those who lived through that turbulent period. The words McCarthyism *and* McCarthyite *have become a part of our language.*

McCarthy had floundered through four years in the Senate and was desperately searching for a winning reelection issue when he appeared before the Ohio County Women's Republican Club in Wheeling, West Virginia, on February 9, 1950. Following the lead of other Republican politicians, and adding his own hyperbole, McCarthy blamed American reverses in the world not on the Soviet Union but on Democratic traitors. He claimed to have a list of 205 communist spies in Truman's State Department. When later challenged to produce the evidence for his charges, McCarthy changed his accusation to "bad risks" and lowered the number to 57. The excerpt below is from the revised speech that McCarthy introduced into the Congressional Record *on February 20, 1950.*

In fact, McCarthy had no list at all. But that did not matter. In an atmosphere charged by the Truman administration's own campaign against subversion, by the communist victory in China and the successful explosion of an A-bomb by the Soviet Union, by the Hiss-Chambers confrontations, and very soon by the arrest of the Rosenbergs as atomic spies and the outbreak of war in Korea, Joe McCarthy had an issue which dominated news headlines and the Republican party had a potent weapon to pummel Democrats.

From the *Congressional Record*, 81 Congress, 2d Session, pp. 1954–57.

Five years after a world war has been won, men's hearts should anticipate a long peace, and men's minds should be free from the heavy weight that comes with war. But this is not such a period—for this is not a period of peace. This is a time of the "cold war." This is a time when all the world is split into two vast, increasingly hostile armed camps—a time of a great armaments race. . . .

Today we are engaged in a final, all-out battle between communistic atheism and Christianity. The modern champions of communism have selected this as the time. And, ladies and gentlemen, the chips are down—they are truly down. . . .

Six years ago, at the time of the first conference to map out the peace—Dumbarton Oaks—there was within the Soviet orbit 180,000,000 people. Lined up on the antitotalitarian side there were in the world at that time roughly 1,625,000,000 people. Today, only 6 years later, there are 800,000,000 people under the absolute domination of Soviet Russia—an increase of over 400 percent. On our side, the figure has shrunk to around 500,000,000. In other words, in less than 6 years the odds have changed from 9 to 1 in our favor to 8 to 5 against us. This indicates the swiftness of the tempo of Communist victories and American defeats in the cold war. As one of our outstanding historical figures once said, "When a great democracy is destroyed, it will not be because of enemies from without, but rather because of enemies from within." . . .

The reason why we find ourselves in a position of impotency is not because our only powerful potential enemy has sent men to invade our shores, but rather because of the traitorous actions of those who have been treated so well by this Nation. It has not been the less fortunate or members of minority groups who have been selling this Nation out, but rather those who have had all the benefits that the wealthiest nation on earth has had to offer—the finest homes, the finest college education, and the finest jobs in Government we can give.

This is glaringly true in the State Department. There the bright young men who are born with silver spoons in their mouths are the ones who have been the worst. . . . In my opinion the State Department, which is one of the most important government departments, is thoroughly infested with Communists.

I have in my hand 57 cases of individuals who would appear to be either card carrying members or certainly loyal to the Communists

Party, but who nevertheless are still helping to shape our foreign policy. . . .

I know that you are saying to yourself, "Well, why doesn't the Congress do something about it?" Actually, ladies and gentlemen, one of the important reasons for the graft, the corruption, the dishonesty, the disloyalty, the treason in high Government positions—one of the most important reasons why this continues is a lack of moral uprising on the part of the 140,000,000 American people. In the light of history, however, this is not hard to explain.

Is is the result of an emotional hang-over and a temporary moral lapse which follows every war. It is the apathy to evil which people who have been subjected to the tremendous evils of war feel. As the people of the world see mass murder, the destruction of defensless and innocent people, and all of the crime and lack of morals which go with war, they become numb and apathetic. It has always been thus after war.

However, the morals of our people have not been destroyed. They still exist. This cloak of numbness and apathy has only needed a spark to rekindle them. Happily, this spark has finally been supplied.

As you know, very recently the Secretary of State proclaimed his loyalty to a man guilty of what has always been considered as the most abominable of all crimes—of being a traitor to the people who gave him a position of great trust. The Secretary of State in attempting to justify his continued devotion to the man who sold out the Christian world to the atheistic world, referred to Christ's Sermon on the Mount as a justification and reason therefore, and the reaction of the American people to this would have made the heart of Abraham Lincoln happy.

When this pompous diplomat in striped pants, with a phony British accent, proclaimed to the American people that Christ on the Mount endorsed communism, high treason, and betrayal of a sacred trust, the blasphemy was so great that it awakened the dormant indignation of the American people.

He has lighted the spark which is resulting in a moral uprising and will end only when the whole sorry mess of twisted, warped thinkers are swept from the national scene so that we may have a new birth of national honesty and decency in government.

Republican Declaration of Conscience

Margaret Chase Smith

Not all Republicans applauded the accusations of treason that McCarthy hurled at the Democratic Administration. On June 1, 1950, Margaret Chase Smith of Maine presented to the Senate the Declaration of Conscience that she penned and that six other moderate Republican senators had consigned. Even handedly, it criticized the Democratic Administration's "complacency to the threat of communism here at home" while refusing to countenance Republicans who sought party victory "through the selfish political exploitation of fear bigotry, ignorance, and intolerance." Such a view, however did not represent a majority of the GOP. In the immediate years ahead Republican red-baiting increased in volume and virulence.

Mr. President, I would like to speak briefly and simply about a serious national condition. It is a national feeling of fear and frustration that could result in national suicide and the end of everything that we Americans hold dear. It is a condition that comes from the lack of effective leadership either in the legislative branch or the executive branch of our Government. That leadership is so lacking that serious and responsible proposals are being made that national advisory commissions be appointed to provide such critically needed leadership.

I speak as briefly as possible because too much harm has already been done with irresponsible words of bitterness and selfish political opportunism. I speak as simply as possible because the issue is

From *Congressional Record*, 81 Congress, 2nd Session, 1954-57.

too great to be obscured by eloquence. I speak simply and briefly in the hope that my words will be taken to heart.

Mr. President, I speak as a Republican. I speak as a woman. I speak as a United States Senator. I speak as an American.

The United States Senate has long enjoyed worldwide respect as the greatest deliberative body in the world. But recently that deliberative character has too often been debased to the level of a forum of hate and character assassination sheltered by the shield of congressional immunity.

It is ironical that we Senators can in debate in the Senate, directly or indirectly, by any form of words, impute to any American who is not a Senator any conduct or motive unworthy or unbecoming an American—and without that non-Senator American having any legal redress against us—yet if we say the same thing in the Senate about our colleagues we can be stopped on the grounds of being out of order.

It is strange that we can verbally attack anyone else without restraint and with full protection, and yet we hold ourselves above the same type of criticism here on the Senate floor. Surely the United States Senate is big enough to take self-criticism and self-appraisal. Surely we should be able to take the same kind of character attacks that we "dish out" to outsiders.

I think that it is high time for the United States Senate and its Members to do some real soul searching and to weigh our consciences as to the manner in which we are performing our duty to the people of America and the manner in which we are using or abusing our individual powers and privileges.

I think it is high time that we remembered that we have sworn to uphold and defend the Constitution. I think it is high time that we remembered that the Constitution, as amended, speaks not only of the freedom of speech but also of trial by jury instead of trial by accusation.

Whether it be a criminal prosecution in court or a character prosecution in the Senate, there is little practical distinction when the life of a person has been ruined.

Those of us who shout the loudest about Americanism in making character assassinations are all too frequently those who, by our own words and acts, ignore some of the basic principles of Americanism—

The right to criticize.

The right to hold unpopular beliefs.

The right to protest.

The right of independent thought.

The exercise of these rights should not cost one single American citizen his reputation or his right to a livelihood nor should he be in danger of losing his reputation or livelihood merely because he happens to know someone who holds unpopular beliefs. Who of us does not? Otherwise none of us could call our souls our own. Otherwise thought control would have set in.

The American people are sick and tired of being afraid to speak their minds lest they be politically smeared as Communists or Fascists by their opponents. Freedom of Speech is not what it used to be in America. It has been so abused by some that it is not exercised by others. . . .

As members of the minority party, we do not have the primary authority to formulate the policy of our Government. But we do have the responsibility of rendering constructive criticism, of clarifying issues, of allaying fears by acting as responsible citizens.

As a woman, I wonder how the mothers, wives, sisters, and daughters feel about the way in which members of their families have been politically mangled in Senate debate—and I use the word "debate" advisedly.

As a United States Senator, I am not proud of the way in which the Senate has been made a publicity platform for irresponsible sensationalism. I am not proud of the reckless abandon in which unproved charges have been hurled from this side of the aisle. I am not proud of the obviously staged, undignified countercharges which have been attempted in retaliation from the other side of the aisle.

I do not like the way the Senate has been made a rendezvous for villification, for selfish political gain at the sacrifice of individual reputations and national unity. I am not proud of the way we smear outsiders from the floor of the Senate and hide behind the cloak of congressional immunity and still place ourselves beyond criticism on the floor of the Senate.

As an American, I am shocked at the way Republicans and Democrats alike are playing directly into the Communist design of "confuse, divide, and conquer." As an American, I do not want a Democratic administration white wash or cover up any more than I want a Republican smear or witch hunt.

As an American, I condemn a Republican Fascist just as much as I condemn a Democrat Communist. I condemn a Democrat Fascist just as much as I condemn a Republican Communist. They are equally dangerous to you and me and to our country. As an American, I want to see our Nation recapture the strength and unity it once had when we fought the enemy instead of ourselves. . . .

STATEMENT OF SEVEN REPUBLICAN SENATORS

1. We are Republicans. But we are Americans first. It is as Americans that we express our concern with the growing confusion that threatens the security and stability of our country. Democrats and Republicans alike have contributed to that confusion.

2. The Democratic administration has initially created the confusion by its lack of effective leadership, by its contradictory grave warnings and optimistic assurances, by its complacency to the threat of communism here at home, by its oversensitiveness to rightful criticism, by its petty bitterness against its critics.

3. Certain elements of the Republican party have materially added to this confusion in the hopes of riding the Republican Party to victory through the selfish political exploitation of fear, bigotry, ignorance, and intolerance. There are enough mistakes of the Democrats for Republicans to criticize constructively without resorting to political smears.

4. To this extent, Democrats and Republicans alike have unwittingly, but undeniably, played directly into the Communist design of "confuse, divide, and conquer.

5. It is high time that we stopped thinking politically as Republicans and Democrats about elections and started thinking patriotically as Americans about national security based on individual freedom. It is high time that we all stopped being tools and victims of totalitarian techniques—techniques that, if continued here unchecked, will surely end what we have come to cherish as the American way of life.

Scoundrel Time

Lillian Hellman

"I cannot and will not cut my conscience to fit this year's fashions," playwright Lillian Hellman wrote to the chairman of the House Committee on Un-American Activities when called to testify in 1952. Her refusal to imitate the behavior of the "scoundrels" of the title of her book, who ruined the lives of others in their groveling appearances before the Committee, came at a particularly grim moment in the Second Red Scare. Alger Hiss had been sent to jail and the Rosenbergs condemned to death. With impunity, Joe McCarthy implicated Democratic officials for every manner of infamous behavior. And the stalemated war in Korea ground on with little hope for victory. Fear and hatred of communism were paramount. In an ugly mood, the American people apparently would brook no intefference with the congressional search for spies and scapegoats. Thus, Hellman's offer to answer all questions about herself but refusal to name others—"to bring bad trouble to people"—had an extraordinary impact at the time. Her moral courage in choosing not to hurt innocent people to save herself made it easier for others to deny the demand to name names and inspired still others to speak out for freedom of speech and thought. Although Congress, to the surprise of many, did not cite Hellman for contempt, the author paid dearly for her defiance, as her autobiographical account, Scoundrel Time, *makes painfully clear.*

DEAR MR. WOOD:

As you know, I am under subpoena to appear before your Committee on May 21, 1952.
I am most willing to answer any questions about myself. I have nothing to hide from your Committee and there is nothing in my

life of which I am ashamed. I have been advised by counsel that under the Fifth Amendment I have a constitutional privilege to decline to answer any questions about my political opinions, activities, and associations, on the grounds of self-incrimination. I do not wish to claim this privilege. I am ready and willing to testify before the representatives of our Government as to my own opinions and my own actions, regardless of any risks or consequences to myself.

But I am advised by counsel that if I answer the Committee's questions about myself, I must also answer questions about other people and that if I refuse to do so, I can be cited for contempt. My counsel tells me that if I answer questions about myself, I will have waived my rights under the Fifth Amendment and could be forced legally to answer questions about others. This is very difficult for a layman to understand. But there is one principle that I do understand: I am not willing, now or in the future, to bring bad trouble to people who, in my past association with them, were completely innocent of any talk or any action that was disloyal or subversive. I do not like subversion or disloyalty in any form, and if I had ever seen any, I would have considered it my duty to have reported it to the proper authorities. But to hurt innocent people whom I knew many years ago in order to save myself is, to me, inhuman and indecent and dishonorable. I cannot and will not cut my conscience to fit this year's fashions, even though I long ago came to the conclusion that I was not a political person and could have no comfortable place in any political group.

I was raised in an old-fashioned American tradition and there were certain homely things that were taught to me: to try to tell the truth, not to bear false witness, not to harm my neighbor, to be loyal to my country, and so on. In general, I respected these ideals of Christian honor and did as well with them as I knew how. It is my belief that you will agree with these simple rules of human decency and will not expect me to violate the good American tradition from which they spring. I would, therefore, like to come before you and speak of myself.

I am prepared to waive the privilege against self-incrimination and to tell you everything you wish to know about my views or actions if your Committee will agree to refrain from asking me to name other people. If the Committee is unwilling to give me this assurance, I will be forced to plead the privilege of the Fifth Amendment at the hearing.

A reply to this letter would be appreciated.

Sincerely yours,
LILLIAN HELLMAN

The answer to the letter is as follows:

DEAR MISS HELLMAN:

Reference is made to your letter dated May 19, 1952, wherein you indicate that in the event the Committee asks you questions regarding your association with other individuals you will be compelled to rely upon the Fifth Amendment in giving your answers to the Committee questions.

In this connection, please be advised that the Committee cannot permit witnesses to set forth the terms under which they will testify.

We have in the past secured a great deal of information from persons in the entertainment profession who cooperated wholeheartedly with the Committee. The Committee appreciates any information furnished it by persons who have been members of the Communist Party. The Committee, of course, realizes that a great number of persons who were members of the Communist Party at one time honestly felt that it was not a subversive organization. However, on the other hand, it should be pointed out that the contributions made to the Communist Party as a whole by persons who were not themselves subversive made it possible for those members of the Communist Party who were and still are subversives to carry on their work.

The Committee has endeavored to furnish a hearing to each person identified as a Communist engaged in work in the entertainment field in order that the record could be made clear as to whether they were still members of the Communist Party. Any persons identified by you during the course of Committee hearings will be afforded the opportunity of appearing before the Committee in accordance with the policy of the Committee.

Sincerely yours,
JOHN S. WOOD, *Chairman*

. . . The room suddenly began to fill up behind me and the press people began to push toward their section and were still piling in when Representative Wood began to pound his gavel. I hadn't seen the Committee come in, don't think I had realized that they were to sit on a raised platform, the government having learned from the stage, or maybe the other way around. I was glad I hadn't seen them come in—they made a gloomy picture. Through the noise of the gavel I heard one of the ladies in the rear cough very loudly. She was to cough all through the hearing. Later I heard one of her friends say loudly, "Irma, take your good cough drops."

The opening questions were standard: what was my name, where was I born, what was my occupation, what were the titles of my plays. It didn't take long to get to what really interested them: my time in Hollywood, which studios had I worked for, what periods of what years, with some mysterious emphasis on 1937. (My time in Spain, I thought, but I was wrong.)

Had I met a writer called Martin Berkeley? (I had never, still have never, met Martin Berkeley although Hammett told me later that I had once sat at a lunch table of sixteen or seventeen people with him in the old Metro-Goldwyn-Mayer commissary.) I said I must refuse to answer that question. Mr. Tavenner said he'd like to ask me again whether I had stated I was abroad in the summer of 1937. I said yes, explained that I had been in New York for several weeks before going to Europe, and got myself ready for what I knew was coming: Martin Berkeley, one of the Committee's most lavish witnesses on the subject of Hollywood, was now going to be put to work. Mr. Tavenner read Berkeley's testimony. Perhaps he is worth quoting, the small details are nicely formed, even about his "old friend Hammett," who had no more than a bowing acquaintance with him.

MR. TAVENNER: . . . I would like you to tell the committee when and where the Hollywood section of the Communist Party was first organized.

MR. BERKELEY: Well, sir, by a very strange coincidence the section was organized in my house. . . . In June of 1937, the middle of June, the meeting was held in my house. My house was picked because I had a large living room and ample parking facilities. . . . And it was a pretty good meeting. We were honored by the presence of many functionaries from downtown, and the spirit was swell. . . . Well, in addition to Jerome and the others I have mentioned before, and there is no sense in going over the list again and again. . . .

Also present was Harry Carlisle, who is now in the process of being deported, for which I am very grateful. He was an English subject. After Stanley Lawrence had stolen what funds there were from the party out here, and to make amends had gone to Spain and gotten himself killed, they sent Harry Carlisle here to conduct Marxist classes. . . . Also 'at the meeting was Donald Ogden Stewart. His name is spelled Donald Ogden S-t-e-w-a-r-t. Dorothy Parker, also a writer. Her husband Allen Campbell, C-a-m-p-b-e-l-l; my old friend Dashiell Hammett, who is now in jail in New York for his activities; that very excellent playwright, Lillian Hellman . . .

And so on.

When this nonsense was finished, Mr. Tavenner asked me if it was true. I said that I wanted to refer to the letter I had sent. I would like the Committee to reconsider my offer in the letter.

MR. TAVENNER: In other words, you are asking the committee not to ask you any questions regarding the participation of other persons in the Communist Party activities?

I said I hadn't said that.

Mr. Wood said that in order to clarify the record Mr. Tavenner should put into the record the correspondence between me and the Committee. Mr. Tavenner did just that, and when he had finished Rauh sprang to his feet, picked up a stack of mimeographed copies of my letter, and handed them out to the press section. I was puzzled by this—I hadn't noticed he had the copies—but I did notice that Rauh was looking happy.

Mr. Tavenner was upset, far more than the printed words of my hearing show. Rauh said that Tavenner himself had put the letters in the record, and thus he thought passing out copies was proper. The polite words of each as they read on the page were not polite as spoken. I am convinced that in this section of the testimony, as in several other sections—certainly in Hammett's later testimony before the Senate Internal Security Subcommittee—either the court stenographer missed some of what was said and filled it in later, or the documents were, in part, edited. Having read many examples of the work of court stenographers, I have never once seen a completely accurate report.

Mr. Wood told Mr. Tavenner that the Committee could not be "placed in the attitude of trading witnesses as to what they will testify to" and that thus he thought both letters should be read aloud.

Mr. Tavenner did just this, and there was talk I couldn't hear, a kind of rustle, from the press-section. Then Mr. Tavenner asked me if I had attended the meeting described by Berkeley, and one of the hardest things I ever did in my life was to swallow the words, "I don't know him, and a little investigation into the time and place would have proved to you that I could not have been at the meeting he talks about."

Instead, I said that I must refuse to answer the question. The "must" in that sentence annoyed Mr. Wood—it was to annoy him again and again—and he corrected me: "You might refuse to answer, the question is asked, do you refuse?"

But Wood's correction of me, the irritation in his voice, was making me nervous, and I began to move my right hand as if I had a tic, unexpected, and couldn't stop it. I told myself that if a word irritated him, the insults would begin to come very soon. So I sat up straight, made my left hand hold my right hand, and hoped it would work. But I felt the sweat on my face and arms and knew that something was going to happen to me, something out of control, and I turned to Joe, remembering the suggested toilet intermission. But the clock said we had only been there sixteen minutes, and if it was going to come, the bad time, I had better hang on for a while.

Was I a member of the Communist Party, had I been, what year had I stopped being? How could I harm such people as Martin Berkeley by admitting I had known them, and so on. At times I couldn't follow the reasoning, at times I understood full well that in refusing to answer questions about membership in the Party I had, of course, trapped myself into a seeming admission that I once had been.

But in the middle of one of the questions about my past, something so remarkable happened that I am to this day convinced that the unknown gentleman who spoke had a great deal to do with the rest of my life. A voice from the press gallery had been for at least three or four minutes louder than the other voices. (By this time, I think, the press had finished reading my letter to the committee and were discussing it.) The loud voice had been answered by a less loud voice, but no words could be distinguished. Suddenly a clear voice said, "Thank God somebody finally had the guts to do it."

It is never wise to say that something is the best minute of your life, you must be forgetting, but I still think that unknown voice made the words that helped to save me. (I had been sure that not only did the elderly ladies in the room disapprove of me, but the press would be antagonistic.) Wood rapped his gavel and said angrily, "If that occurs again, I will clear the press from these chambers."

"You do that, sir," said the same voice.

Mr. Wood spoke to somebody over his shoulder and the somebody moved around to the press section, but that is all that happened. To this day I don't know the name of the man who spoke, but for months later, almost every day I would say to myself, I wish I could tell him that I had really wanted to say to Mr. Wood: "There is no Communist menace in this country and you know it. You have made cowards into liars, an ugly business, and you made me write a letter in which I acknowledged your power. I should have gone into your Committee room, given my name and address, and walked out." Many people have said they liked what I did, but I don't much, and if I hadn't worried about rats in jail, and such. . . . Ah, the bravery you tell yourself was possible when it's all over, the bravery of the staircase.

In the Committee room I heard Mr. Wood say, "Mr. Walter does not desire to ask the witness any further questions. Is there any reason why this witness should not be excused from further attendance before the Committee?"

Mr. Tavenner said, "No, sir."

My hearing was over an hour and seven minutes after it began. I don't think I understood that it was over, but Joe was whispering so loudly and so happily that I jumped from the noise in my ear.

He said, "*Get up. Get up.* Get out of here immediately. Pollitt will take you. Don't stop for any reason, to answer any questions from anybody. Don't run, but walk as fast as you can and just shake your head and keep moving if anybody comes near you.

Life had changed and there were many people who did not call me. But there were others, a few friends, a few half-strangers, who made a point of asking me for dinner or who sent letters. That was kind, because I knew that some of them were worried about the consequences of seeing me.

But the mishmash of those years, beginning before my congressional debut and for years after, took a heavy penalty. My belief in liberalism was mostly gone. I think I have substituted for it something private called, for want of something that should be more accurate, decency. And yet certain connecting strings have outworn many knives, perhaps because the liberal connections had been there for thirty years and that's a long time. There was nothing strange about my problem, it is native to our time; but it is painful for a nature that can no longer accept liberalism not to be able to accept radicalism. One sits uncomfortably on a too comfortable cushion. Many of us now endlessly jump from one side to another and endlessly fall in space. The American creative world is not only equal but superior in talent to their colleagues in other countries, but they have given no leadership, written no words of new theory in a country that cries out for belief and, because it has none, finds too many people acting in strange and aimless violence.

But there were other penalties in that year of 1952: life was to change sharply in ordinary ways. We were to have enough money for a few years and then we didn't have any, and that was to last for a while, with occasional windfalls. I saw that coming the day the subpoena was first served. It was obvious, as I have said, the farm had to be sold. I knew I would now be banned from writing movies, that the theater was as uncertain as it always had been, and I was slow and usually took two years to write a play. Hammett's radio, television and book money was gone forever. 1 could have broken up the farm in small pieces and made a fortune—I had had an offer that made that possible—and I might have accepted it except for Hammett, who said, "No, I won't have it that way. Let everybody else mess up the land. Why don't you and I leave it alone?," a fine sentiment with which I agree and have forever regretted listening to. More important than the sale of the farm, I knew that a time of my life had ended and the faster I put it away the easier would be an altered way of living, although I think the sale of the farm was the most painful loss of my life. It was, perhaps, more painful to Hammett, although to compare the pains of the loss of beloved land one has worked oneself, a house that fits because you have made it fit thinking you would live in it forever, is a foolish guess-game.

Nightmare in Red

Richard Fried

Author of an earlier study, Men Against McCarthy *(1976), and the far-ranging account of the McCarthy era,* Nightmare in Red *(1990), from which the following selection is excerpted, Richard Fried raises a host of questions about the seeds of McCarthyism and its poisonous fruits. Note particularly his succinct commentary on the anxieties and the values that underlay American anticommunism, as well as the particular political dynamic at midcentury that made the "ism" so functional; also examine how Fried attempts to gauge the impact of anticommunist extremism on American life.*

Many Republicans in the early 1950s argued, in essence, "I don't agree with McCarthy's methods, but he is doing something that has to be done, and by golly, he gets the job done!" Do you agree? To what extent did American communists pose a danger to the United States in the postwar years? Did they constitute a significant risk to the internal security of the United States? What could and/or should the government have done to minimize that risk? How do you balance individual rights versus the needs of national security? What should the relationship between ends and means be? Do desirable goals justify despicable tactics?

For many the McCarthy era stands as the grimmest time in recent memory. Beset by Cold War anxieties, Americans developed an obsession with domestic communism that outran the actual threat and gnawed at the tissue of civil liberties. For some politicians, hunting Reds became a passport to fame—or notoriety. It was the focal point of the careers of Wisconsin Senator Joseph R. McCarthy; of Richard Nixon during his tenure as Congressman, Senator, and Vice President of the United States; of several of Nixons' colleagues on the House Committee on Un-American Activities (HUAC); of Senator Pat McCarran and other members of the Senate Internal Security Subcommittee; and of a phalanx of understudies at the national, state, and local levels.

A new vocabulary entered political discourse. "Are you now or have you ever been a member of the Communist Party?" "I refuse to answer on grounds that the answer may tend to incriminate me." "Fifth-Amendment Communist!" "Soft on communism. . . ." "Witch-hunt!" "McCarthyism!" In the barrage of accusations that rumbled through the late 1940s and early 1950s, reputations were made or ruined, careers blasted or created, lives and families shattered.

It is tempting to locate "McCarthyism" only in the realm of high politics—as the combined sum of national news headlines, noisy rhetoric, and congressional inquiries. Yet it was more than that. The anti-Communist drive touched thousands of lesser figures: a printer in the U.S. Government Printing Office, linguists and engineers at the Voice of America overseas broadcasting service, a Seattle fireman, local public housing officials, janitors, even men's room attendants. Long before the "McCarthy era," loyalty oaths affected teachers. Lawyers, other professionals, and, in Indiana, even wrestlers had to document their loyalty. Colleges policed students' political activities. Labor leaders and unions rose or fell according to their sympathy or hostility toward communism. Entertainers faced a "blacklist." Ordinary people responded to the anti-Communist fervor by reining in their political activities, curbing their talk, and keeping their thoughts to themselves.

Yet paradoxically these bleak years are also remembered as happy times. America emerged from World War II with her continental expanse untouched by the ruin visited on other lands. An "arsenal of democracy," the nation had provided materiel for a global battlefront, food and fiber for friend and conquered foe. The joblessness that haunted the 1930s vanished. Though the postwar economy had its fits and starts, and prosperity did not drizzle on every garden, pessimists were confounded as the good times persisted.

With $140 billion in pent-up wartime savings, Americans went on a buying spree. New autos rolled off assembly lines too slowly to slake demand; some customers bribed dealers in order to buy a car. Freezers, refrigerators, and soon televisions flowed out of factories and into homes. Americans bought 20,000 new TV sets a day in the mid-fifties. By the end of the decade, fifty million televisions were in use. The sprouting forests of antennas snared signals that webbed viewers in every home into the national consumer culture.

The landscape changed beyond recognition as new suburbs sprawled out from the central cities, woven to the workplace by highways. Freshly erected, moderately priced homes—such as the famous Levittown developments—sprang up like new crops in the potato fields they displaced. The family car and single-family home became the norm.

The social landscape changed as well. Though poverty persisted, affluence was far more visible. There were recessions, but no depression. Products found buyers. Buyers had jobs. Thanks to the GI Bill, veterans, many from blue-collar homes, went to college, entered professions, and attained white-collar status. They moved with their families to the thronging new suburbs and became, for good or ill, "organization men," the sociologists' term for those secure and swaddled servants of giant corporations.

For growing numbers life was comfortable. Most lived better and longer, sharing the American dream of homeownership and enjoying the fruits of social mobility. Science and technology promised to eradicate ancient problems. By 1955 Jonas Salk had perfected the vaccine that conquered the dread disease of poliomyelitis, fear of which had for years prompted parents to keep their children indoors away from beaches and crowds during the August heat. No longer.

The spokesmen for corporate America offered a sales message, both for the "free enterprise system" and for its products, that was relentlessly upbeat. "Progress is our most important product," said General Electric's TV commercials. However self-serving such slogans were, the era's prosperity did make converts even of some who had found fault with the economic system in the bleaker 1930s. The era still had its critics, though. Some argued that America's material wealth masked spiritual and civic poverty. Others lamented the tawdriness of mass culture as reflected in the American passion for automobiles—"insolent chariots," one critic called them. As government subsidized highways for autos, public transportation withered. While the family home embodied the American dream, some commentators worried that it bred privatism. On the other hand, William Levitt, pioneer of Levittown developments, ventured that no homeowner could be a Communist. "He has too much to do." Juvenile delinquency was much deplored. Some linked it to communism; others, later, to the newer menace of rock and roll. There were various national scandals. Politicians took deep freezes, vicuña coats, money. College sports and, later, TV quiz shows were blemished by cheating. A deeper blot was the nation's complacency about "race relations."

Some spokesmen thought that the cure for these ills lay in religious renewal. In the 1950s Norman Vincent Peale's *The Power of Positive Thinking* and other books with potent, if not profound, religious messages became bestsellers. The Reverend Billy Graham's monster revival meetings earned him fame and welcome at Dwight D. Eisenhower's White House. Previously unchurched, the President decided that attending Sunday service befitted his role as national leader. Congress stapled the phrase "Under God" to the Pledge of Allegiance. Hollywood star Jane Russell claimed that when you get to know God, "you find He's a Livin' Doll."

Yet beneath such froth lurked authentic anxieties that the new religiosity was bent on tranquilizing. As the Cold War jelled, particularly after 1949, the prospects of nuclear war grew worrisome. Newspapers published city maps with concentric circles showing levels of destruction expected from a nuclear blast. Schoolchildren learned in drills to crawl under their desks in the event of a bombing. Some were uneasy. In New York, Dr. Peale met a child terrified by the H-bomb. He calmed her with the simple positive thought that God would not let a bomb fall in New York. Popular magazines strove to put the new weapons in a less threatening everyday context. *Look* burbled that the H-bomb—about the size of a living room—was "one of the cheapest forms of destruction known to man."

The pulpit was not the only place, nor theology the only language, for probing flaws in Americn life. Social scientists sermonized too. Even as Americans enjoyed the bounty produced by the structured, bureaucratic corporate society in which they worked, lived, and consumed, they were its captives—or so they were told. Individual autonomy had become a casualty of the organization, which allegedly drained people's souls and sapped their independence even as it filled their bank accounts. "Organization men" chose security in a corporate womb over entrepreneurial risk, preferred a slot in Personnel ("working with people") to Sales, exalted "teamwork" and "togetherness," and disparaged lone-wolf individualism as antisocial. Lost was the spirit of adventure. Universities graduated and corporations buffed "well-rounded" people who were "other-" rather than "inner-directed" and who were guided by "radar" to pick up cues from peers rather than moved by a "gyroscope" to act according to principles or conscience. Some feared that these corporate clones, dressed alike in gray flannel suits, were dully marching toward a conformist society.

Not everyone accepted the extreme criticisms. Even William F. Whyte, Jr., whose book *The Organization Man* spread much of the critical vocabulary, warned against labeling Americans as conformists. Yet others thought the charge accurate, and many held political forces, particularly "McCarthyism," at least partly to blame for the conformity. If Dwight D. Eisenhower, the genial, grandfatherly "Ike," presided over the era's political imagery, Joseph R. McCarthy, the menacing, barrel-chested Wisconsin Senator, was an equally potent symbol. From 1950 through 1954, McCarthy personified the search for Communist influence throughout American life.

That charges of selling out to communism should be leveled against President Harry S Truman seems at first glance bizarre. After all, his administration (with "bipartisan" Republican help) had resisted Soviet expansion; sent help to Greece and Turkey in 1947 in response to the President's enunciation of the "Truman Doctrine" calling for aid to "free peoples who are resisting attempted subjugation by armed minorities or by outside pressures"; framed the Marshall Plan to save Western Europe's frail governments and economies; flown over a Soviet blockade to succor West Berlin in the 1948–49 airlift; restored the draft and joined NATO, an "entangling alliance"; built the H-bomb; planted military bases around the globe; and adopted a loyalty program to guard government from Communist infiltration. These acts, however, did not fully armor Truman and the Democrats from charges of "softness on communism." The rising fear of communism at home intertwined with the growing vexations and complexities of the struggle with communism abroad.

Scholarly debate over the Cold War's origins remains a lively art, but in the 1950s few Americans doubted whom to blame. They saw Communists in East Europe abusing rival political groups; even other leftists mysteriously vanished or were "liquidated." As the Soviets rolled back the Nazis in 1944–45, they treated ruthlessly the goods, governments, and lives of the peoples who lay in their path. Much that was not nailed down—and much that was—became "war booty" shipped back to the USSR. In Rumania, Bulgaria, and Poland, opposition parties were suppressed, civil liberties violated, the press gagged. Stalin ignored a commitment ostensibly made at Yalta to hold free elections in Poland.

Americans had not fought the war out of pure idealism; one thinks of cartoonist Bill Mauldin's weary, stubbled GIs, impatient of cant and seeking only a hot meal and dry socks. Still, a catalog of basic freedoms could be found in documents ranging from the 1941 Atlantic Charter (notably, its endorsement of self-determination, to which the Allies had adhered) to Norman Rockwell's famous *Saturday Evening Post* covers. In Eastern Europe, these basic freedoms crumbled beneath the heel of a boot.

Many historians agree that some menacing Soviet moves came as responses to real or perceived threats by the West. As precedent for its unilateral moves in Rumania, for instance, Russia could cite the West's similar dealings with conquered Italy. Disputes over reparations and Germany's future further complicated relations among the "Big Three"—the U.S., the USSR, and Great Britain. In February 1948, Czech Communists, with Soviet aid, seized control of the government. This event horrified Americans and led to the approval of Marshall Plan aid by Congress, a rearmament program, and a war scare. Yet, some have argued, the Czech coup could be seen as a defensive reaction by the Soviets, who interpreted facets of the West's "containment" policy as hostile.

Whatever the true origins of the Cold War, most Americans came to view the USSR as an aggressive power and threat to peace. Fears of Communist influence at home increasingly counterpointed the rising concern with Soviet aims abroad. Historians of the Cold War have asked whether Stalin's totalitarianism at home necessitated a "totalitarian" foreign policy. Equally one could ask whether the twin development of America's anti-Communist foreign policy and the excesses of its containment of communism at home was preordained or avoidable. It was logical, but was it inevitable?

Although chroniclers grant that the McCarthy era owed much to the Cold War, they agree on little else. Some, like Robert Griffith, in *The Politics of Fear,* have emphasized that members of the right wing of the Republican Party, "as they scrapped and clawed their way toward power," were most responsible for making anti-communism the dominant theme in American politics. These conservatives were moved by a loathing of the New Deal and a frustration at the repeated defeats their party had suffered in national elections, notably Truman's upset victory in 1948. McCarthyism not only thrived on and deepened the conflict between the two parties but also exacerbated the struggle between conservative and moderate factions in the GOP.

On the other hand, some social scientists in the 1950s (and after) attributed the virulence of the anti-Communist upsurge to social strains, to developments that made certain segments of society susceptible to McCarthyism. Some groups (Catholics, Germans, *nouveaux riches,* Texas oilmen) may have supported McCarthy because his attacks on the State Department and other institutions offered vicarious revenge upon an "Establishment" that had long kept them in their place. Or perhaps McCarthy's charges represented a form of "neo-isolationism," a means by which groups such as German- and Irish-Americans could vent their resentments against a generation of Democratic interventionist (and anti-German and pro-British) foreign policies.

More recently, some historians have said that Truman, the Democrats, and the liberals were contributors to McCarthyism, not just its victims. Did not Truman's 1947 federal loyalty program formulate language and methods that, in more extreme form, were taken up by the McCarthyites? (And further, it is suggested, the loyalty order came so soon after his Truman Doctrine address that it appeared to be a means of reinforcing to Congress the gravity of the Communist threat.) Truman and his allies also redbaited Henry A. Wallace and the Progressive Party in 1948, thus—according to the theory—legitimizing a practice that Republicans would turn upon Democrats. And Truman's strident anti-Communist rhetoric on behalf of his foreign policy created an idiom for his critics when that policy met reverses.

. . . The origins of McCarthyism lay largely among the grievances and ambitions of conservative politicians (mostly but not solely of the Republican Party). . . . McCarthyism was a political phenomenon that extended well beyond the antics of Senator McCarthy—indeed, well beyond the boundaries of conventional politics. What gave the "ism" its bite was the political dynamic that obtained at mid-century, accentuated by the anxieties germinated by the Cold War. However, anti-communism derived its persistence from a deeply rooted cluster of values shared by much of American society, a set of views antithetical to Communist doctrines and friendly to private property and political democracy (albeit sometimes oblivious to imperfections in the latter).

The once-popular sociological explanations of McCarthyism do not withstand empirical testing, but they do correctly hint at the *cultural* basis of the mid-century Red Scare. As Seymour Lipset and Earl Raab have argued, McCarthy's anti-communism "was a banner around which various segments of the population could marshal their preservatist discontents and their generalized uneasiness." Many Americans were bewildered by the deep social and political changes at work in the twentieth century. Many such changes occurring in the neighborhood, the nation, and the world could, consistent with the strength of America's anti-Communist consensus, be attributed to Communist scheming.

Thus a profound cultural aversion to communism also underlay McCarthyism. It was this detestation that gave politicians broad leeway to pursue anti-Communist endeavors. A related factor was the nation's underdeveloped appreciation of the importance of civil liberties for repudiated minorities. . . .

. . . In a sense, all anti-communism was "functional." Even true-believing politicians could build careers on it, but the blend of conviction and utilitarianism varied from case to case. Some critics of the emergent anti-communism saw deeply sinister motives. A leftist union warned of a "conspiracy . . . to identify as Communist or Communistic" anyone daring "to assert independence in thought." The "great industrial and financial monopolists" aimed to "control the economy of the United States in the interests of a few at the expense of the many, to swell profits and to beat down wages." Such goals might explain the enthusiasm of West Coast economic interests for the early efforts to deport Harry Bridges, leader of the left-wing International Longshoremen's and Warehousemen's Union (ILWU). Economics account less well for the persistence of federal officials in harassing him.

Similarly, if the thrust of Joe McCarthy's crusade had been economically oriented, he would have aimed more often at targets of directly economic rather than symbolic importance. Foreign policy can involve heavy economic stakes, but McCarthy certainly took the long way around. (If, as some historians argue, the fate of Vietnam concerned the future of American capitalism, McCarthy missed the point: in the spring of 1954, as Ho Chi Minh's forces sprang the trap at Dienbienphu, the Senator was bewitched by the question of who had promoted a Communist Army dentist.) Indeed, his critics often questioned the effectiveness of his anti-communism, though such rejoinders failed to stop him.

One might ask whether the potency of anti-communism stemmed mainly from the manipulation of public opinion by political leaders, or whether the public's latent anti-communism formed a consensus in which the elites operated and with which, in order to survive, they had to conform? Here, too, evidence is mixed. One finds labor leaders using anti-communism against union rivals (or rival unions) or corporate management happily exploiting the carnage left in the wake of inquiries by Congress. Yet the anti-communism of many unionists and politicians appears to have been ideological.

Perhaps the essential point is that there existed in Cold War America a broad anti-Communist consensus shared and seldom questioned by most liberals as well as conservatives, by intellectuals as well as plain folk, by union members as well as "bosses." This defining reality of the period, together with the weak and undeveloped civil-libertarian consciousness of most Americans, explains the ease with which anti-communism came to dominate the political scene. These circumstances were endemic. They were present even before the Cold War fixed itself upon the world. Combined with a chain of threatening developments in the Cold War and the partisan dynamic that obtained at mid-century, they were responsible for the onset of McCarthyism.

How deeply did anti-communism gouge the social and political terrain of the 1950s? With dissent defined as dangerous, the range of political debate obviously was crimped. The number of times that books were labeled dangerous, thoughts were scourged as harmful, and speakers and performers were rejected as outside the pale multiplied. Anti-Communist extremism and accomanying pressures toward conformity had impact in such areas as artistic expression, the labor movement, the cause of civil rights, and the status of minorities in American life.

For some denizens of the Right, threats of Communist influence materialized almost anywhere. For instance, Illinois American Legionnaires warned that the Girl Scouts were being spoonfed subversive doctrines. Jack Lait and Lee Mortimer's yellow-journalistic *U.S.A. Confidential* warned parents against the emerging threat of rock and roll. It bred dope use, interracialism and sex orgies. "We know that many platter-spinners are hopheads. Many others are Reds, left-wingers, or hecklers of social convention." Not every absurdity owed life to the vigilantes, however. A jittery Hollywood studio cancelled a movie based on Longfellow's "Hiawatha" for fear it would be viewed as "Communist peace propaganda."

Books and ideas remained vulnerable. It is true that the militant Indiana woman who abhorred *Robin Hood*'s subversive rob-from-the-rich-and-give-to-the-poor message failed to get it banned from school libraries. Other locales were less lucky. A committee of women appointed by the school board of Sapulpa, Oklahoma, had more success. The board burned those books that it classified as dealing improperly with socialism or sex. A spokesman claimed that only five or six "volumes of no consequence" were destroyed. A librarian in Bartlesville, Oklahoma, was fired for subscribing to the *New Republic, Nation,* and *Negro Digest*. The use of UNESCO materials in the Los Angeles schools became a hot issue in 1952. A new school board and superintendent were elected with a mandate to remove such books from school libraries.

Local sanctions against unpopular artists and speakers often were effective. In August 1950, a New Hampshire resort hotel banned a talk by Owen Lattimore after guests, apparently riled by protests of the Daughters of the American Revolution and others, remonstrated. Often local veterans—the American Legion and Catholic War Veterans—initiated pressures. The commander of an American Legion Post in Omaha protested a local production of a play whose author, Garson Kanin, was listed in *Red Channels*. A founder of *Red Channels* warned an American Legion anti-subversive seminar in Peoria, Illinois, that Arthur Miller's *Death of a Salesman*, soon to appear locally, was "a Communist-dominated play." Jaycees and Legionnaires failed to get the theatre to cancel the play, but the boycott they mounted sharply curbed the size of the audience.

Libraries often became focal points of cultural anxieties. Not every confrontation ended like those in Los Angeles or Sapulpa, but librarians felt they were under the gun. "I just put a book that is complained about away for a while," said one public librarian. Occasionally, books were burned. "Did you ever try to burn a book?" asked another librarian. "It's *very* difficult." One-third of a group of librarians sampled in the late 1950s reported having removed "controversial" items from their shelves. One-fifth said they habitually avoided buying such books.

Academics, too, were scared. Many college and university social scientists polled in 1955 confessed to reining in their political views and activities. Twenty-seven percent had "wondered" whether a political opinion they had expressed might affect their job security or promotion; 40 percent had worried that a student might pass on "a warped version of what you have said and lead to false ideas about your political views." Twenty-two percent had at times "refrained from expressing an opinion or participating in some activity in order not to embarrass" their institution. Nine percent had "toned down" recent writing to avoid controversy. One teacher said he never expressed his own opinion in class. "I express the recognized and acknowledged point of view." Some instructors no longer assigned *The Communist Manifesto*.

About a hundred professors actually lost jobs, but an even greater number of frightened faculty trimmed their sails against the storm. Episodes far short of dismissal could also have a chilling effect. An economist at a Southern school addressed a business group, his talk, titled "Know Your Enemy," assessed Soviet resources and strengths. He was denounced to his president as a Communist. Another professor was assailed for advocating a lower tariff on oranges. "If I'd said potatoes, I wouldn't have been accused unless I had said it in Idaho." Some teachers got in mild trouble for such acts as assigning Robert and Helen Lynds' classic sociological study, *Middletown*, in class or listing the Kinsey reports on human sexuality as recommended reading. A professor once sent students to a public library to read works by Marx because his college's library had too few copies. Librarians logged the students' names.

The precise effect of all this professed anxiety was fuzzy. Many liberals claimed that Americans had been cowed into silence, that even honest anti-Communist dissent had been stilled, and that basic freedoms of thought, expression, and association had languished.

The worriers trotted out appropriate comparisons: the witch trials in Salem, the Reign of Terror in France, the Alien and Sedition Acts, Know-Nothingism, and the Palmer raids. Justice William O. Douglas warned of "The Black Silence of Fear." Prominent foreigners like Bertrand Russell and Graham Greene decried the pall of fear they observed in America. On July 4, 1951, a *Madison Capital-Times* reporter asked passersby to sign a paper containing the Bill of Rights and parts of the Declaration of Independence. Out of 112, only one would do so. President Truman cited the episode to show McCarthyism's dire effects. McCarthy retorted that Truman owed an apology to the people of Wisconsin in view of that paper's Communist-line policies. Some McCarthy allies upheld the wisdom of refusing to sign any statement promiscuously offered.

McCarthy's defenders ridiculed the more outlandish laments for vanished liberties. A New York rabbi who blamed "McCarthyism" for the current spree of college "panty raids" offered a case in point. Conservative journalist Eugene Lyons was amused by an ACLU spokesman, his tonsils flaring in close-up on television, arguing "that in America no one any longer dares open his mouth." Such talk, said Lyons, led to "hysteria over hysteria." In their apologia for McCarthy, William F. Buckley and L. Brent Bozell snickered at such silliness. They found it odd that, in a time when left-of-center ideas were supposedly being crushed, liberals seemed to monopolize symposia sponsored by the major universities, even in McCarthy's home state, and that Archibald MacLeish and Bernard De Voto, two of those who condemned the enervating climate of fear, had still managed to garner two National Book Awards and a Pulitzer Prize. To Buckley and Bozell, the only conformity present was a proper one—a consensus that communism was evil and must be fought wholeheartedly.

But did such an argument miss the point? The successes enjoyed by prominent, secure liberals were one thing; far more numerous were the cases of those less visible and secure who lost entertainment and lecture bookings, chances to review books, teaching posts, even assembly-line jobs. The fight over the Communist menace had gone far beyond roistering debate or asserting the right of those who disagree with a set of views not to patronize them. People, a great number of whom had committed no crime, were made to suffer.

Rampant anti-communism narrowed the range of selection open to associations, utterances, and ideas. People were constrained by both external pressures and the inner checks with which they reactively restricted their own affairs. Fear was manifest in delicate matters of personal choice—such as what to read or think—as well as in more public behavior. In this latter respect, the collective result was a significant slowing of the momentum of change in a number of areas of American life.

In the 1930s, the civil-rights question had emerged from oblivion. FDR often ducked divisive race issues, but CIO unions, the Communist Party, and civil-rights activists pushed this American dilemma to the fore. By dramatizing the irony of battling Hitlerian racism at the same time that Jim Crow persisted, World War II heightened consciousness and hurried change. To blacks it brought occupational gains and augmented political leverage and assertiveness. Thus A. Philip Randolph's March on Washington Movement prodded FDR to create the Fair Employment Practices Commission.

This cantering change might have burst into a gallop after the war, but the rise of anti-communism inspired a new caution among mainstream civil-rights leaders. An old-time Socialist who had battled Communist efforts to infiltrate the March on Washington Movement and, earlier, the National Negro Congress, Randolph warned against dallying with the Communist conspiracy. (He also admonished that racism was a flaw vastly useful to the Soviets.) The Urban League also resisted any Communist influence in the civil-rights cause, and the 1948 national convention of the Congress of Racial Equality (CORE) went on record as opposing cooperation with Communist-front groups. In firing two professors who took the Fifth Amendment before HUAC, Fisk University proved no less timid than white colleges.

The NAACP, led by the Walter White, also preached anti-communism and worked to isolate black leaders who bucked the going trend. In 1950 its national board was authorized to expel any chapter that fell under Communist control. When in the same year the government lifted Paul Robeson's passport, the NAACP did not defend him. Its Legal Defense Fund also shunned W. E. B. Du Bois, once editor of the NAACP's journal but now linked to pro-Soviet causes. In 1951 the eighty-two-year-old Du Bois was arrested for failing to register as a leader of the Peace Information Center, an entity that aligned itself with Soviet-sponsored peace crusades. Claiming the government would successfully prove Du Bois's entanglement in conspiracy, Walter White convinced NAACP board members to remain aloof. The groundless case was later dismissed, however.

"By serving as the 'left wing of McCarthyism,'" Manning Marable has written, such leaders as Randolph and White "retarded the black movement for a decade or more." This criticism contains some truth but overlooks certain considerations. It is not clear that damn-the-torpedoes solidarity with Marxists or Popular Fronters would have advanced the civil-rights movement or that black public opinion would have supported it. As Marable notes, the Communists themselves squandered much of the sympathy they had won in the 1930s by taking pro-Soviet positions detrimental to black interests during the war. Randolph and other leaders had experienced Communists' efforts to join and exploit civil-rights groups for their own ends. CORE rejected alliance with Communists both because the latter often pursued conflicting goals and because such links would help foes to discredit CORE's cause. On balance the Communist issue operated as a retarding force, but even had it not been present, the civil-rights movement faced an uphill struggle against the tradition of American racism.

Soviet propaganda and the rise of anti-colonialism in Africa made U.S. race relations a sore point. Some American leaders came to see civil rights as at least a collateral Cold War priority. "We could not endorse a color line at home," wrote Harry Truman, "and still expect to influence the immense masses" of Asia and Africa. The greater leverage, however, lay with redbaiters and opponents of civil rights. Blacks could not, for example, use the Korean War as they had World War II as a fulcrum for change.

Feminism also traveled a rough trail in the 1950s, but most of its hardships could not be ascribed to the Red Scare: the going had been rocky since 1920. Though World War II expanded women's job prospects—as for "Rosie the Riveter"—cultural expectations changed far less. The war's end brought what one historian terms a "vicious antifeminist backlash." The term "feminism" acquired increasingly negative connotations. What remained of a feminist presence was divided against itself: an old conflict pitted feminists who sought gains through union activities and government reforms against the National Woman's Party, whose single aim was to enact the Equal Rights Amendment. Rifts in the NWP itself were so wide in the late 1940s that they prompted party founder Alice Paul to disparage the loyalty of rivals to HUAC. (Some NWP members also applauded McCarthy and pointed knowingly to the Communist Party's opposition to the ERA.)

Political conservatism in the 1950s reinforced traditional female roles. So necessary was the home as a "symbol of security and stability" in that frightsome era that few dared question the reigning "domestic ideology." TV fare made the point. The mothers, like Harriet of "Ozzie and Harriet" or Mrs. Cleaver of "Leave it to Beaver," were able, steady, but clearly maternal figures. The effervescent Lucille Ball was something of an exception. Yet a typical "I Love Lucy" episode ended with discovery of her latest escapade, followed by her red-faced, keening apology ("Oooh Ricky") and a promise to shape up. She remained a housewife and eventually became a mother. In his analysis of 1950s anti-Communist movies, Michael Rogin finds "sexual politics" often depicted by a flawed mother figure (in such films as *My Son John*), who allows communism to intrude into the family.

In the 1950s, practices deviating from the prescribed norms for family and sex were frowned on. When Alfred Kinsey's two famous studies of human sexual behavior revealed the prevalence of extramarital sex and of a great variety of sexual activity, traditionalists fumed. His *Sexual Behavior in the Human Female* (1953) impelled one cleric to detect a "fundamental kinship between that thing and Communism." A Catholic newspaper declared that the sex researcher's books "pave the way for people to believe in communism and to act like Communists." Lightheartedly, Senator Robert Kerr quipped that Dr. Kinsey and Joe McCarthy shared one trait: "They both claim to have uncovered a lot of domestic disloyalty." Morality's guardians were not amused. Congressman B. Carroll Reece's committee, which at the time was investigating charitable foundations and their support of subversive activities, assailed Kinsey's project. The general hostility to Kinsey's work, coupled with fears of what Reece might do, led the Rockefeller Foundation, already sensitive to criticisms of its funding activities, to end its grants to Kinsey.

An age leery of excessive heterosexual activity had scant sympathy for homosexuality, which indeed was commonly viewed as a source of internal weakness analogous to communism. The 1950s brought heavy pressures upon gays and lesbians, who already faced severe social sanctions. The FBI watched gay bars, and local police often declared open season on them and lesbian hang-outs. The Post Office monitored recipients of "physique magazines" and entrapped them in various ways. From 1947 on, about five homosexuals were fired per month from federal jobs under the security program; the rate rose to sixty after an official testified in February 1950 that most of the ninety-one people recently fired by the State Department on moral grounds had been homosexuals. Indeed, that agency was thought to be especially rife with "sexual perverts."

These revelations threatened to make homosexuality a political issue in 1950. Republicans demanded an inquiry. In June, as Tydings's examination of McCarthy's charges ended. Senator Clyde Hoey launched a probe of homosexuality among federal employees. Hoey's panel questioned police and medical experts. It considered homosexuals in government a threat because they were vulnerable to manipulation and blackmail by Communist intriguers. (Its only evidence was a homosexual Austrian intelligence officer whom the Russians "turned" prior to World War I.) But Hoey's inquest was tame, with testimony taken in executive session, and a victory for restraint, especially given that McCarthy was a member of the parent committee. McCarthy himself often snickered about his targets' masculinity. He labeled Dean Acheson "The Red Dean of fashion" and belittled State Department anticommunism for slapping the Reds with a lace hanky at the front door while they bludgeoned one's grandmother at the back door. (Widespread rumors that he was himself a homosexual greatly vexed Joe. In fact, many witnesses have attested to his flagrant heterosexuality.)

World War II had accelerated single-sex congregation, geographic mobility, and thus the emergence of a growing number of gays and lesbians in America. The Mattachine Society, formed in 1951, was the first ongoing organization to advocate their interests. Founders included several current and former Communists. To prevent exposure, the Society was initially kept secret and patterned after the CP's "cell" structure. This precaution was based on both Party experience and a perception that McCarthyism embodied a trend toward repression that would encompass homosexuals as well as Reds. Had the guardians of public safety known of the founders' CP background or about the model the Society followed, they would have howled in anger.

But the main threat to the originators' vision came from within the Society itself. Early organizing success brought an influx of members who were unsympathetic to the founders' radical orientation and who wanted the Society to become open and respectable. In 1953 a newspaper column critical of the Society reported that one of its leaders had taken the Fifth Amendment before HUAC. Many newer members, sensitized to the dangers of a linkage between disloyalty and homosexuality, moved to take over and reshape the Society. Conceding the inevitable, the founders yielded control. Secrecy was ended. At its convention, the Society voted down a proposed loyalty oath, but its anti-Communist position was made clear. In so doing, the Society may have purchased slight immunity against anti-communism. (The FBI still saw fit to infiltrate the Mattachines and the Daughters of Bilitis, a lesbian organization.) But the Society had surrendered much of its militancy, dynamism, and early membership gains. It thus repeated in its youth the pattern of older organizations. The times were so inhospitable, however, that quibbles about tactics or philosophy are beside the point. That, indeed, was the dilemma faced by all movements for change in this period.

Pacifists were a case in point. Having (like civil-rights activists) had disillusioning experiences, they sought to avoid links with Communists. The Cold War and especially the fighting in Korea destroyed any remaining romanticism among them about the Soviet Union. Though distancing themselves from the CP may have helped the pacifists to avert disaster, such prudence brought no appreciable gains, for at the height of the Cold War, peace groups had a hard time obtaining a hearing and were often redbaited— whether justifiably or not.

Later in the 1950s, a growing fear of radioactive fallout and of the nuclear arms race led to a rebirth of activism by peace groups. The strongest of these was SANE, the Committee for a Sane Nuclear Policy, founded in 1957. Sensitive to redbaiting, SANE's leaders adopted a resolution stating that the organization sought only members "whose support is not qualified by adherence to communist or other totalitarian doctrine." This action proved divisive and weakening—a sign itself of change—and a number of people resigned in protest at this revival of McCarthyism.

Even the cause of Indian rights was marginally vulnerable to anti-Communist assaults. Advocates of Western economic growth and conservatives generally wanted to terminate tribal trust arrangements and open Indian reservations to economic development. The Eisenhower Administration was supportive: the property of several reservations was scheduled for release from tribal control. The terminationists viewed efforts to preserve traditional Native American communities and even the Bureau of Indian Affairs itself as socialistic, bureaucratic New Deal hangovers. One proponent of termination labeled John Collier, who had led New Deal Indian reform efforts, as "the voice of Russian Communists in their plans to capture the American Indian and thus start their world wide conspiracy to communize free America." An assimilated Klamath Indian called tribal government "communistic."

Anti-communism had uses in local affairs too. For example, it was a recurrent element in the opposition to the adoption of a zoning ordinance for the city of Houston. In 1947 foes of zoning claimed that such planning "from Moscow . . . to Washington has backfired." It was a "legalistic monster, spawned in Europe and disguised in the slum-ridden eastern cities as a device to protect your homes." Oilman Hugh Roy Cullen (eventually a fervent McCarthy supporter) assailed zoning as "un-American and German." Such appeals persisted into the 1960s. In 1962 an opponent called zoning "socialized real estate." Water flouridation was also termed by some critics a communist plot.

The ease with which redbaiting discredited so many causes showed how deeply anti-Communist assumptions permeated American culture. Indeed, they were a defining, rarely questioned characteristic of that culture. By and large, the debate over anti-communism among political and intellectual elites plumbed not goal but method. Liberal critics of McCarthy and of other extremists did not question the validity of anti-communism. Rather, they often began any exposition with the phrase, "I'm anti-Communist too, but. . . ." It has been suggested that a less apologetic—indeed, less anti-Communist—orientation would have better served liberalism. But inglorious though the liberal anti-Communist posture sometimes appeared in the early 1950s, it is unlikely that a less pragmatic, more absolutist civil-libertarian position would have brought benefits. Such an argument assumes that the ultimate leverage in national politics at the Cold War's height was in the liberals' hands. Assuredly, it lay elsewhere.

Part 2

THE POLITICS OF
THE AFFLUENT SOCIETY

The 1950s and 1960s are generally seen as very different eras in American history. Under the calm, beneficent, paternal leadership of Dwight Eisenhower, America in the 1950s appeared to be enjoying a time of equanimity. After the immediate postwar tensions of inflation, strikes, and foreign policy conflicts, the era of Eisenhower seemed remarkable for its stability. The first Republican to be elected in twenty years, Eisenhower pledged moderation, peace, and an end to corruption in government. While not extending New Deal social welfare programs, neither did Eisenhower attempt to reverse them. Rather, his was an administration of consolidation. The country appeared prosperous, and happy to have a respite from conflict.

The 1960s, by contrast, represented a new cycle of reform and insurgency. Led by the presidencies of John F. Kennedy and Lyndon B. Johnson, the nation set forth to allievate persistent inequities of racial discrimination, to combat poverty, and to create a new and improved society. "We can do better," Kennedy had said in 1960. "We *will* do better," Johnson promised in 1964. At least on the surface, the two postwar eras seemed radically different, one given to complacency, quietude, and stability, the other to activism, challenge, and change.

In fact, the appearances were as deceptive as they were accurate. The struggles that brought reform in the 1960s were already emerging throughout the "quiet years of the 1950s." Moreover, the policies of the 1960s represented continuity with the past as well as an effort to generate new programs. Both eras, in fact, reflected what Godfrey Hodgson has called the "liberal consensus" in America—the belief that improvement is always possible within a fundamentally sound economic and social system, that right-minded and intelligent people can create a healthy, viable social system, that moderation is preferable to extremism, and that an economy committed to growth will provide the basis for eliminating social problems while assuring prosperity for the middle class.

Both the positive and negative aspects of that "liberal consensus" are broadly sketched in the selections that follow. Reflecting some of the vital changes wrought by the Cold War in the political culture and the economy of the United States, British journalist Godfrey Hodgson examines the basic tenets and flaws of postwar liberalism, and President Dwight Eisenhower warns of the awesome influence of the "conjunction of an immense military establishment and a large arms industry" and its direct threat to the nation's "democratic processes." Both the impact of the Cold War and the ideology of the liberal consensus are exemplified in President John Kennedy's proposal to land a man on the moon. Announcing his vision of a "Great Society" in mid-1964, President Lyndon Johnson goes considerably beyond any of his predecessors in proposing a vast array of new liberal programs to improve the quality of American life. To what extent these programs brought beneficial changes, and why they failed to bring greater fundamental changes, remain key points of contention between today's conservatives and liberals. In the final selection, Charles Murray argues that these programs failed to accomplish their objectives and, indeed, made things worse.

Many questions are raised by these selections. To what extent are we controlled by impersonal forces beyond our ability to shape? Are our political leaders capable of directing, or harnessing, these forces? What are the major assumptions of modern American liberalism? of conservatism? What accounts for the changing fortunes, of each? Whether, and how, is it possible to achieve egalitarian goals within the constraints of the existing social and political order? How do you account for today's very different popular perceptions of the Eisenhower, Kennedy, and Johnson presidencies? Did their policies owe more to the Cold War or to the unprecedented affluence of most Americans? Why did progress in the 1960s toward lessening inequalities slow and then stop? What were the major exceptions to the liberal consensus in the 1950s? What are the realistic alternatives to the liberal consensus?

The Ideology of the Liberal Consensus

Godfrey Hodgson

One of the central themes of America In Our Time, *Hodgson's probing examination of the crisis of the mind and the spirit of the United States between the inauguration of John F. Kennedy and the resignation of Richard M. Nixon, is the ideology of the liberal consensus. In the chapter from which this selection is excerpted he analyzes the main assumptions of this system of ideas and beliefs and the reasons for its widespread acceptance. Understanding its roots and the factors that enabled it to go virtually unchallenged should illuminate many aspects of American history in the 1950s and 1960s.*

It is worth considering how this consensus affected the presidencies of Eisenhower, Kennedy, and Johnson, and how its existence should inform a historical interpretation of those presidencies. It is also important to examine the accuracy of the component parts of the consensus. Did they reflect or distort the realities of the age? One may, moreover, speculate on what new myths have supplanted the old, and how erroneous assumptions today affect current ideologies.

It is always risky to try to draw the portrait of the ideas and beliefs of a society at any point in its evolution. Contradictions and crosscurrents defy generalization. Too much survives from the past, and too much anticipates the future. Usually, perhaps, the attempt is doomed to end either in superficiality or in intellectual dishonesty.

But the period from the middle of the 1950s in the United States up to the impact of the crisis of the 1960s was not usual in this respect. It was an age of consensus. Whether you look at the writings of intellectuals or at the positions taken by practicing politicians or at the data on public opinion, it is impossible not to be struck by the degree to which the majority of Americans in those years accepted the same system of assumptions. Official and semiofficial attempts were even made to codify these assumptions in such works as the report of President Eisenhower's Commission on National Goals or in the Rockefeller Brothers Fund panel reports. The crisis of the late 1960s was caused partly by the mistakes and shortcomings of this system of assumptions and partly by a series of attacks upon It

. . . At the end of the 1950s, Americans worried about their own personal lives—about health and status. At the other end of the scale of immediacy, they worried about the danger of nuclear war. But few of them doubted the essential goodness and strength of American society.

Four times between 1959 and 1961, the Gallup poll asked its sample what they regarded as the "most important problem" facing the nation. Each time, the most frequent answer (given in each case by at least close to half of the respondents and sometimes by far more than half) was "keeping the peace," sometimes glossed as "dealing with Russia." No domestic issue came anywhere close to challenging that outstanding concern.

In the presidential campaign of 1960, only two types of domestic issues were rated as critical by either candidate or by his advisers: on the one hand, atavistic ethnic issues—the Catholic vote, or Martin Luther King's arrest—and on the other hand, the behavior of the economy. And the latter, to Kennedy, at least, seemed important mainly as a prerequisite of foreign policy.

Kennedy built his appeal around the call to get the country moving again. He left a strong impression that his main reason for doing so was in order to recover lost prestige in the competition with the Soviet Union. Summing up his campaign, in Hartford, Connecticut, on the eve of polling, Senator Kennedy listed three major differences between his opponent and himself:

> first a different view of the present state of the American economy;
> secondly a different view of our prestige in the world, and therefore,

our ability to lead the free world; and thirdly, whether the balance of power in the world is shifting in our direction or that of our adversaries.

Nixon, too, had three themes. First, that Kennedy was running America down; second, that the Democrats would cause inflation; and third, that he, Richard Nixon, could speak better for America in confrontation with the Soviet leader.

When it came to sensing the issues that had a gut appeal to the electorate as a whole, that is, each candidate chose to stress foreign dangers (and glories) over domestic problems in the proportion of two to one.

The various American elites took more complicated views. A good deal of concern was expressed by intellectuals in the late 1950s about the lack of excellence in American education (especially in the context of an alleged inferiority to Soviet achievements in space science and missile technology), about the (temporarily) lagging growth rate of the economy, and in diffuse and cloudy jeremiads about the materialism of mass culture. But in the most ambitious contemporary analyses, the same dualism was the recurrent major theme: never so much hope in America, never so much danger abroad.

It was in 1956 that the Rockefeller brothers organized their special studies project to "meet and examine the most critical problems facing the nation over the next ten to fifteen years." Never before had such a prestigious team of diagnosticians gathered at the national bedside. Bipartisan and interdisciplinary, it was a roster of those men who had expounded the conventional wisdom since World War II and would remain its champions until the bitter end of the 1960s: Adolf Berle of the New Deal and John Gardner of Common Cause, Chester Bowles and Charles Percy, Edward Teller and David Sarnoff, Lucius Clay and Dean Rusk, Henry Luce and Henry Kissinger.

The reports of the various panels were published separately between January 1958 and September 1960 and as a single volume, *Prospect for America*, in 1961. Together they form a handbook of the shared assumptions of the American governmental and business elite: the two had become hard to distinguish. These were the assumptions that governed the policies of the Kennedy administration, and no one can doubt that they would have guided the Republicans if they had won in 1960.

It would not be fair to call the tone of *Prospect for America* complacent in any vulgar way. It has a muscular Christian strenuousness, rather reminiscent of Kipling's *If*, or of the sermons on the social question preached at expensive boarding schools:

> The number and the depth of the problems we face suggests that the very life of our free society may be at stake, [the report began by saying]. We are concerned that there has not been . . . enough sense of urgency throughout our nation about the mortal struggle in which we are engaged.

Yet all may not yet be lost:

> America has a notable record of responding to challenges and making the most of opportunities. With our growing population, our extraordinary record of rising productivity, the inherent dynamism in our free enterprise economy, there is every reason to face the future with all confidence.

The panel reports contained very able discussion of particular issues such as strategic policy or economic growth. But essentially they saw all the various challenges to America in terms of one big challenge: "the mortal struggle in which we are engaged," the "basic underlying Soviet danger."

The central dualism of the reports' philosophy was baldly, almost naïvely spelled out right at the beginning in a preface signed by the Rockefellers themselves:

> This project grew out of a belief that the United States in the middle of the twentieth century found itself in a critical situation.
> As a nation we had progressed in our domestic development to an extent hardly imaginable a few short decades ago. . . .
> Throughout this world alive with hope and change stalks the Communist challenge.

"Stalks" is a nice Manichaean touch. It was this very feeling that the hosts of Midian were on the prowl, that the United States was wrestling with the Evil One, and therefore needed to match the messianic beliefs of the adversary with an equivalent dogma, that made it so fashionable in the late 1950s to define the grand purposes of America. The official report on the national goals produced by the Eisenhower administration in 1960 was strikingly similar in tone and conclusions to that of the Rockefeller brothers and their experts.

The extremely distinguished panel of economists, for example— it included Paul Samuelson and Milton Friedman, Herbert Stein and Charles L. Schultze—drew almost exactly the same picture of a perfectible America threatened from without by the Communist serpent. "The American economy works well," they pronounced; "the system is highly responsive to the demands of the people." Yet, even in a discussion of the economy they felt it appropriate to add, "America and the civilization to which it belongs stand at an historic turning-point. They confront a critical danger and inspiring opportunities. The danger is indicated by the phrase 'Cold War.'"

The introduction to the National Goals report gave an official imprimatur to this same dualism. It was signed by, among others, the head of DuPont and the head of the AFL/CIO, the head of the University of California and the head of the First National City Bank of New York. At home, these Olympians thundered in unison, "We have achieved a standard of individual realization new to history." Abroad, "The nation is in grave danger, threatened by the rulers of one third of mankind."

One eminent historian was so carried away by this mood that he even projected it back into an indefinite past: "In this favored country," wrote Clinton Rossiter, "we have always found more things on which to agree than to disagree." Always? In the 1860s? Still, there could be no dissent from his next proposition: "The early 1960s appear to be a time of broad consensus on fundamentals." looking back to the same period, the late Fred Freed, one of the most thoughtful of television producers, came to much the same conclusion (it was his habit never to use capital letters):

> when i began doing my documentaries at nbc in 1961 we lived in a consensus society. those were the days of the cold war. there was an enemy outside, the communists, nikita khrushchev, the red chinese . . . back then there was general agreement in the united states about what was right and what was wrong about the country. nobody really questioned the system. . . . we had a common set of beliefs and common values.

. . . For some seven years after 1955, few fundamental disagreements, foreign or domestic, were aired in either presidential or Congressional politics. That the United States should in principle seek better relations with the Soviet Union while keeping its guard up and seeking to contain communism—this was common ground. Disagreement was relegated to issues of the second order of importance: the extent to which the United States should support the United Nations, the level of foreign aid, the speed of space development. The main lines of domestic policy were equally beyond controversy. The Eisenhower administration accepted that the federal government must continue social security and such other New Deal programs as had stood the test of public popularity. It was ready to enforce due compliance with the law in civil rights, though reluctantly and with caution. And it was prepared to use fiscal and monetary measures to maintain full employment and economic growth. Not much more, and no less, could be said of the Kennedy administration in its first two years.

The political process, it was taken for granted throughout that period, was a matter of emphasizing one nuance or another of this generally agreed program. A "liberal" congressman, as the word was then used, was one who might be expected to speak up for the particular interests of organized labor; a "conservative" would voice the reservations of corporate business or of the armed services.

Not only in Washington but in the press, on television, and—with few exceptions—in the academic community, to dissent from the broad axioms of consensus was to proclaim oneself irresponsible or ignorant. That would risk disqualifying the dissenter from being taken seriously, and indeed often from being heard at all.

A strange hybrid, liberal conservatism, blanketed the scene and muffled debate. It stretched from Americans for Democratic Action—which lay at the leftward frontiers of respectability and yet remained safely committed to anti-communism and free enterprise—as far into the board rooms of Wall Street and manufacturing industry as there could be found a realistic willingness to accept the existence of labor unions, the rights of minorities, and some role in economic life for the federal government. Since the consensus had made converts on the Right as well as on the Left, only a handful of dissidents were excluded from the Big Tent: southern diehards, rural reactionaries, the more *farouche* and paranoid fringes of the radical Right, and the divided remnants of the old,

Marxist, Left. Together, they hardly added up to a corporal's guard. And they were of course never together.

The lack of clearly opposed alternative policies was revealed, to the point of parody, by the most emotional foreign-policy issue of the time: Cuba.

"For the first and only time" in the presidential campaign of 1960, Richard Nixon wrote in *Six Crises*, he "got mad at Kennedy—personally," when Kennedy advocated support for the anti-Castro rebels. Nixon was not angry because Kennedy's position was a recipe for disaster (though it was). He was angry because Kennedy was saying in public what Nixon had been saying in private but felt bound by the obligations of national security not to reveal. He had reason to believe that Kennedy knew all along that the Eisenhower administration was secretly planning the invasion that Kennedy now, by implication, criticized it for not mounting!

After the venture duly ended in fiasco at the Bay of Pigs, Arthur M. Schlesinger, then a White House aide, was sent a cable by his former Harvard graduate students: "KENNEDY OR NIXON," it read, "DOES IT MAKE A DIFFERENCE?" The question was an unkind reference to a pamphlet with that exact title which Schlesinger had felt moved to dash off during the 1960 campaign.

Schlesinger was right, of course; it did make a difference. But this was hardly because any very distinct issues of basic policy or any sharply divergent visions of the world then lay between John Kennedy and Richard Nixon. They represented the aspirations of different categories of Americans. Their symbolic meaning—vital in the presidency—was almost antithetical. By experience and temperament, they were very different men.

The fact remains that they did share the same basic political assumptions: the primacy of foreign over domestic issues, the paramount importance of containing communism, the reign of consensus in domestic affairs, the need to assert the supremacy of the White House as the command post of a society mobilized to meet external danger. So did their staff and advisers. And so, too, did their running mates and closest rivals: Lyndon Johnson and Henry Cabot Lodge, Hubert Humphrey and Nelson Rockefeller, and everyone else who might conceivably have been nominated as a presidential candidate in that year either by the Democrats or by the Republicans. Kennedy and Nixon, wrote Eric Sevareid, Establishment liberal *par excellence* at the time, were the first two completely packaged products of the managerial revolution in politics. In politics, as in business, it was the era of imperfect competition, with candidates not just for the presidency but for most major offices hardly more different than a Chevy and a Ford, or a Pepsi and a Coke.

. . . Confident to the verge of complacency about the perfectibility of American society, anxious to the point of paranoia about the threat of communism—those were the two faces of the consensus mood. Each grew from one aspect of the experience of the 1940s: confidence from economic success, anxiety from the fear of Stalin and the frustrations of power.

Historical logic made some form of consensus likely. It was natural that the new prosperity should calm the class antipathies of the depression years. It was normal that the sense of an enemy at the gate should strengthen national unity. And a reaction was predictable after the lacerating politics of the McCarthy period. But the basis for the consensus was something more than a vague mood or a reaction to passing events. The assumptions on which it was built had an intellectual life and coherence of their own. In barest outline, they can be summarized in the following set of interrelated maxims:

1. The American free-enterprise system is different from the old capitalism. It is democratic. It creates abundance. It has a revolutionary potential for social justice.
2. The key to this potential is production: specifically, increased production, or economic growth. This makes it possible to meet people's needs out of incremental resources. Social conflict over resources between classes (which Marx called "the locomotive of history") therefore becomes obsolete and unnecessary.
3. Thus there is a natural harmony of interests in society. American society is getting more equal. It is in process of abolishing, may even have abolished, social class. Capitalists are being superseded by managers. The workers are becoming members of the middle class.
4. Social problems can be solved like industrial problems: The problem is first identified; programs are designed to solve it, by government enlightened by social science;

money and other resources—such as trained people—are then applied to the problem as "inputs"; the outputs are predictable: the problems will be solved.

5. The main threat to this beneficent system comes from the deluded adherents of Marxism. The United States and its allies, the Free World, must therefore expect a prolonged struggle against communism.

6. Quite apart from the threat of communism, it is the duty and destiny of the United States to bring the good tidings of the free-enterprise system to the rest of the world.

The germ of this intellectual system, which by about 1960 had emerged as the dominant American ideology, was a simple yet startling empirical discovery. Capitalism, after all, seemed to work.

In the early 1940s, the economist Joseph Schumpeter, at work on his last book, *Capitalism, Socialism and Democracy*, reluctantly came to the conclusion that socialism—a system about which he cherished so few illusions that he expected it to resemble fascism when it cam—was inevitable. Capitalism was doomed, he feared. Schumpeter was a conservative, though a highly original one, and he had arrived at this conclusion by his own line of argument. The modern corporation would "socialize the bourgeois mind," destroy the entrepreneurial motivation that was the driving force of capitalism, and thus "eventually kill its own roots." He was at pains to distinguish this position from what he saw as the almost universal vulgar anticapitalism of his time. "Every writer or speaker hastens to emphasize . . . his aversion to capitalist and his sympathy with anticapitalist interests."

Well under ten years later, the exact opposite would have been closer to the truth. In the United States (though nowhere else in the world), socialism was utterly discredited. The same transformation could be observed in popular attitudes and in intellectual fashion. In 1942 (the year that Schumpeter's book was published), a poll by Elmo Roper for *Fortune* found that only 40 percent of respondents opposed socialism, 25 percent said they were in favor of it, and as many as 35 percent had an open mind. By 1949, a Gallup poll found that only 15 percent wanted "to move more in the direction of socialism"; 61 percent wanted to move in the opposite direction. Making all due allowance for the respondents' possibly vague notion of what socialism means, it was a startling shift, yet not more startling than that of the intellectuals. . . .

At the root of this optimistic new political philosophy, there lay an appropriately optimistic new economic doctrine. It came to be known as the New Economics, though by the time of its triumph, in the 1960s, when its licensed practitioners monopolized the President's Council of Economic Advisers, many of its leading ideas were going on thirty years old.

There were many strands to the New Economics. But the essence of it was the acceptance in the United States of the ideas of John Maynard Keynes, *not* as first received in the 1930s but as modified by American economists in the light of the success of the American economy in the 1940s.

The nub of Keynes' teaching was that, contrary to the tenets of classical economics, savings did not necessarily become investment. This was the cause of cyclical depression and of unemployment: left to itself, the capitalist system contained forces that would tend to produce stagnation. To that extent his position was pessimistic. But Keynes was a political economist. He did not think that things should be left to themselves. He believed that governments could cure the kind of deflation that had caused the Great Depression by spending, and if necessary by deficit spending. He actually wrote a long letter to FDR, in early 1938, pleading with him to spend his way out of the recessIon. The letter was ignored. But after 1945 the university economists succeeded in persuading the more enlightened businessmen, and some politicians, that Keynes was right. Capitalism could be *made* to work. Depression and unemployment were avoidable, and it was up to government to avoid them.

From a conservative viewpoint, Schumpeter introduced ideas that matched the new Keynesian orthodoxy better than he would have liked. He stressed the unique character of American capitalism. He emphasized productivity and technological change. He argued that concentration and oligopoly, which most economists had wanted government to destroy by trust busting, actually favored invention and innovation.

Unlike Schumpeter, John Kenneth Galbraith was a Keynesian, and it was he who attempted the inevitable synthesis in *American Capitalism,* published in 1952. Galbraith also started from the observed fact that competition in American corporate capitalism was imperfect. He propounded the theory of what he called "counter-vailing power." Competition had been supposed to limit private economic power. Well, it didn't. But private power was held in check "by the countervailing power of those who are subject to it." The concentration of industry had brought into existence strong buyers—Sears Roebuck, A & P—to match strong sellers. It had also brought strong unions into existence to match strong employers.

Galbraith and Schumpeter had many disagreements. Their an-alyses were drawn from different premises and tended toward dif-ferent conclusions. Yet they shared one common perception: the empirical observation that American capitalism was a success. "It works," said Galbraith shortly on his first page, "and in the years since World War II, quite brilliantly."

> There is another fact about the social situation in the United States that has no analogue anywhere else in the world, said Schumpeter in his second edition, published in 1946, . . . namely the colossal in-dustrial success we are witnessing.

And a few pages later, he italicized a passage that condensed the gist of the new hope and the new pride:

> In the United States alone there need not lurk, behind modern programs of social betterment, that fundamental dilemma that ev-erywhere paralyzes the will of every responsible man, the dilemma between economic progress and immediate increase of the real in-come of the masses.

In practical terms, the gospel of the New Economics could be translated into exciting propositions. Government can manage the economy by using fiscal and monetary policy. The tyranny of the business cycle, which had brought economic catastrophe and the specter of political upheaval, need no longer be tolerated. De-pressions could be a thing of the past.

By changing interest rates and by increasing or decreasing the money supply—technical matters that had the added advantage of being remote from the scrutiny of everyday politics—government could flatten out fluctuations in economic activity.

The economists were emboldened to maintain that these fiscal and monetary controls could be manipulated with such precision—"fine tuning" was the phrase used—that in effect they would be able to fly the economy like an airplane, trimming its speed, course and altitude with tiny movements of the flaps and rudder. That was a later claim. The essential promise of the Keynesian system was that it would allow government to guarantee low and diminishing unemployment without inflation. It could thus banish at a stroke the worst terrors of both liberals and conservatives. At the same time, thus managed, the economy would also be able to deliver growth.

Growth was the second key concept of the new intellectual system, and the link between its strictly economic and its social and political ideas.

We are so accustomed to the idea of economic growth that it comes as a surprise to learn that it was a newer idea than Keynes' discovery of the way to beat the business cycle. Just as modern biology had to wait for the invention of the microscope and modern astronomy for the perfection of the telescope, the idea of economic growth developed only after precise techniques for measuring the gross national product became available. These were perfected only in the late 1930s, by Professor Simon Kuznets, of the University of Pennsylvania.

It is hardly possible to exaggerate the importance that the new concept assumed in the intellectual system of American liberals in the 1950s. It became the test, the aim, even the justification of free enterprise—the race, the runner and the prize.

The economic historian W. W. Rostow offered an interpretation of modern history as a contest in terms of economic growth—and called it an "anti-Communist manifesto."

The political scientist Seymour Martin Lipset came close to making it the chief criterion for judging a political system. "Prolonged effectiveness over a number of years," he suggested in his book *Political Man,* "may give legitimacy to a political system. In the modern world, such effectiveness means primarily constant economic development."

But perhaps the most lyrical description came from Walter Heller, chairman of the Council of Economic Advisers under Presidents Kennedy and Johnson. He called economic growth "the pot of gold and the rainbow."

The liberals did not worship economic growth merely as a golden calf. They saw in it the possibility of solving social problems with the incremental resources created by growth. That will be done, they hoped, without the social conflict that would be inevitable if those resources had to be found by redistributing existing wealth.

This was the hope that both Schumpeter and Galbraith had seen. Brushing aside the pessimists, Schumpeter had dared to predict in 1942 that GNP would reach $200 billion by 1950. (In the event, he was a pessimist himself: GNP in current dollars reached $284 billion by 1950.) "The huge mass of available commodities and services that this figure . . . represents," he wrote, "promises a level of satisfaction of economic needs even of the poorest members of society . . . that would eliminate anything that could possibly be described as suffering or want." And of course Schumpeter was fully aware of the ideological implications. Such a massive creation of new resources could be the key to his central dilemma. It might "annihilate the whole case for socialism so far as it is of a purely economic nature."

What Schumpeter had described as a theoretical possibility in the 1940s had become by the end of the 1950s the "conventional wisdom," and in the 1960s it was to be the foundation of public economic policy.

"Production has eliminated the more acute tensions associated with inequality," Galbraith wrote in *The Affluent Society,* a book whose title was to become a cliché to an extent that did little credit to the subtlety of its argument. "Increasing aggregate output is an alternative to redistribution."

The same idea was spelled out in the stonecutter's prose of the Rockefeller Brothers Fund's drafting committee:

> A healthy and expanding private economy means far more in terms of individual and family well-being than any reasonable expansion of government service and social programs.

No tenet of the consensus was more widely held than the idea that revolutionary American capitalism had abolished the working class, or—as approximately the same thought was sometimes expressed— that everybody in America was middle class now or that American society was rapidly approaching economic equality.

A small encyclopedia of statements to this effect can be garnered from the historians, the social scientists and the journalists of the time.

"The organizing concept of American society," wrote Peter Drucker, "has been that of social mobility . . . which denies the existence of classes."

"The union," said the editors of *Fortune,* "has made the worker, to an amazing degree, a middle class member of a middle class society."

"New Dealism," said historian Eric Goldman, ". . . found that it had created a nation of the middle class."

Yet another historian, Samuel Eliot Morison, boldly dated the abolition of the proletariat rather earlier than some would say the proletariat came into existence. He cited the observations of a Polish Communist visitor to confirm "a fact that has puzzled socialists and communists for a century: the American workman is an expectant capitalist, not a class-conscious proletarian."

Frederick L. Allen, on the other hand, wrote a best seller to prove that "the big change" in American life between 1900 and 1950 was the "democratization of our economic system."

One's first reaction is to yield to the cumulative weight of so many impassioned opinions and to conclude . . . what? For even the most cursory reading of such a miscellany raises questions. Had class stratification never existed in the United States, as Drucker seemed to think? But, then, can one imagine social mobility without class? Mobility between what? Had there never been an American proletariat, as Professor Morison seemed to believe? Or had there been a "big change"? Perhaps the proletariat had ceased to exist. But, then, which agency had earned the credit for this transformation? "Industrial enterprise," as some claimed? *Fortune*'s unions? Or Goldman's "New Dealism"? Corporate business, labor and government may work in harmony. But they are hardly synonyms.

A second reading of this miscellany of texts and of the other evidence suggests two more-modest conclusions:

1. A great many Americans, moved by the ideal of equality but perhaps also by reluctance to admit what was seen as a Marxist analysis of their own society, passionately wanted to believe that the concept of class was alien to the United States.

It suited business to believe this. It suited labor. It suited intellectuals, and it suited the press. It suited liberals, and it suited conservatives. Who was left to argue otherwise?

2. Nevertheless, something *had* happened. In the profound transformations of the 1940s the class structure of American society and its implications for politics had changed in complex and confusing ways—though not to the point of making "everybody middle class," still less of invalidating class analysis.

The mood of the country may have been relatively complacent in the late fifties and the early sixties. But this was not, as the liberal analysis assumed, because the condition of the American people left so little to be desired. It was because a number of historical factors had weakened the political unity and consciousness of the working class and deprived it of the means to perceive its own interests and to defend them.

One of these factors was the way the idea of equality had evolved in the United States. Historically, the actual condition of American society-with the two major exceptions of black and red Americans—had probably always more closely approached a condition of equality than European society. The availability of land, the unexploited resources of a "new" country of continental extent, the absence—or near absence—of an established feudal upper class with a vested interest in maintaining inequality, all tended to minimize inequality in practice. Yet in theory Americans had always been less concerned than Europeans with equality of condition. The paradox is only apparent. Because of the relative abundance of their environment, Americans could afford to think equality of condition less important than equality of opportunity. In most other cultures, people knew all too well that there would never be enough opportunities to go round.

There was a second group of reasons why American politics failed to reflect class interests or class consciousness. It is true, as Arthur Schlesinger has written, that "in spite of the current myth that class conflicts in America were a fiendish invention of Franklin Roosevelt, classes have, in fact, played a basic part in American political life from the beginning." But the horizontal class lines in American society have always been crosshatched by deep-cut vertical divisions: ethnic, sectional, and racial. Ultimately, these can be traced back to two of the great facts that set American history apart from that of all the other developed Western nations: slavery and immigration. But there were also reasons why their combined impact blurred the reality of class conflict at this particular moment in American history.

One reason was obvious.

The American working class was divided, because the feeling of belonging to a particular ethnic group often took priority over an individual's economic interests or over any sense of class solidarity. In political terms, this frequently meant that the votes of ethnically conscious low-income voters could be recruited to support politicians who, once in office, only fitfully defended the social and economic interests of their constituency. This was notoriously true of the big-city machines, which, in a decadent form, were still one of the typical forms of political organization in the fifties and, for example, played a part in the election of President Kennedy in 1960. But by the fifties the machine no longer fought for the bread-and-butter interests of its immigrant supporters as it had in its classic phase. Instead, traditional ethnic loyalties were played upon at election time to enlist the support of ethnic blocs on behalf of policies that frequently countered the real interests of lower-class voters. Ethnic antics at election time only briefly interrupted the politicians' eager cooperation with the dominant business interests.

The historical fact of immigration had another, less obvious effect. To the extent that Americans are a self-chosen people, their patriotism has always been a more self-conscious emotion than the more visceral tribal feelings of other nations. The immigrant's patriotism has tended to be compounded in roughly equal proportions of status anxiety—the desire to be assimilated as a good American—and of gratitude for his share in the abundance of American life.

Both the abundance and the anxiety were far more visible in the fifties than they had been in the thirties. In the immigrant, this desire to prove oneself a good American had often been in conflict with the impulse to protect the social and economic interests of the lower class. By the fifties, a full generation after the end of mass immigration, the drive for full assimilation was as strong as ever in second- and third-generation Americans; economic needs, as a result of the postwar prosperity, seemed far less urgent. Again, the effect was to increase the conservatism of that considerable proportion of the working class that came of relatively "new" immigrant descent. For this large group, the free-enterprise system was seen as

Americanism; social criticism, class solidarity and radical politics were rejected as "un-American."

If ethnic factors dating back to the days of mass immigration, and the preoccupation with equality of opportunity, both helped to obscure the working class's interests from its own members, the sectional and racial basis of the political system derived from the struggle over slavery was responsible for the fact that no great party of the Left was available to represent those interests. In so far as working-class interests were to be effectively represented within the two-party system, they must be represented by the Democrats. But the Democratic Party under Harry Truman and Adlai Stevenson was no party of the Left: It was not only the party of the immigrant, the Negro, the Roman Catholic, the Jew, the city dweller, and the industrial worker; it was also the party of the rural, conservative, nativist South, an element that not only accounted for a third and more of its strength in Congress but held the balance of power in presidential elections.

During the Depression, the New Deal had come closer to being a party of the Left, because the contradiction at the heart of the Democracy was partially concealed by the sheer economic need of the South. Southern Democrats could vote for and work with Roosevelt because they knew the South desperately needed the federal government's economic help. Southerners in Congress might be racial and therefore constitutional conservatives, willing to fight the national Democratic leadership if they must in defense of the South's peculiar social system; but in the New Deal period, that system was not under direct attack. The immediate issues for the South were economic. So long as that remained true, southern "economic liberals"—which often meant men who were not liberals at all except when it came to accepting federal largess—could work happily enough with northern Democrats.

The prosperity of the years after 1941, and in particular the improvement in the economic situation of the southern white working class as a result of industrialization, diminished this incentive for southern Democrats to cooperate with the national party. In spite of much picturesque mythology about their populist fervor and the wool-hats and galluses of their disciples, most of the leading Southerners in Congress in the fifties were essentially responsive to the business elites of the South. While they continued to support some liberal programs, they were not about to allow the Democratic

Party to evolve into a national party of the Left. The more racial issues supplanted economic ones in the forefront of their constituents' concern, as they did increasingly after the Brown decision in 1954, the more the sectional dilemma made any such evolution of the Democratic Party unlikely.

The Left, in short, had by the late 1950s virtually ceased to count in American political life. But this fateful eclipse was masked by the triumph of the liberals.

To draw a distinction between the Left and the liberals may sound sectarian or obscure. It is not. It is vital to understanding American politics in the age of the consensus, and therefore to understanding what happened after it.

When I say that the Left had almost ceased to exist, I am not thinking of the socialist Left, though that had indeed withered into insignificance long before the collapse of Henry Wallace's Progressive Party, in 1948.

What I mean by the "Left" is any broad, organized political force holding as a principle the need for far-reaching social and institutional change and consistently upholding the interests of the disadvantaged against the more powerful groups in the society. The liberals were never such a force.

What I mean by the liberals is those who subscribed to the ideology I have described: the ideology that held that American capitalism was a revolutionary force for social change, that economic growth was supremely good because it obviated the need for redistribution and social conflict, that class had no place in American politics. Not only are those not the ideas of the Left; at the theoretical level, they provide a sophisticated rationale for avoiding fundamental change. In practice, the liberals were almost always more concerned about distinguishing themselves from the Left than about distinguishing themselves from conservatives.

The confusion between the liberals and the Left arose partly, perhaps, because, in the 1950s, "liberal" was often used as a euphemism for "Left." In the McCarthy era, to call someone a man of the Left carried a whiff of treason with it; to call him a liberal was a graceful alternative.

A deeper reason for the confusion lay in the fact that in the very parts of American society that might have been expected to hold out as the bastions of the Left, the liberals had triumphed. Organized labor, the intelligentsia, and the universities had become the citadels of what was in effect a conservative liberalism.

There were three important developments in the American labor movement in the 1940s, said the editors of Fortune: First was the renaissance of the craft-based, politically conservative American Federation of Labor. Fighting back after a period in which it had seemed destined to be swamped by the industrial unions, the AFL doubled its membership in the 1940s and almost recovered parity with the CIO. The second was the "anti-ideological" trend in the CIO, as Fortune put it, in the Daniel Bell sense, meaning the trend toward the liberal ideology. And the third was the decline of the left wing in the labor movement generally. . . .

By the mid-1960s, the AFL-CIO was showing itself a good deal more adventurous and active in fighting communism abroad than it was in organizing unorganized workers in the U.S.A. But George Meany had always belonged to the more conservative wing of the movement. What is more surprising is that anti-communism became the shibboleth of the originally militant CIO wing to almost the same extent. At the time of the merger, Walter Reuther, the most radical and socially conscious labor leader of his generation, allowed the AFL to take the two top places in the new organization, confident that he would be the ultimate legatee of unity. Reuther had started on the left of the United Auto Workers. He was a socialist, and he spent a year in the Soviet Union in the early thirties. But when he finally emerged as the leader of the union, in the 1947 union elections, it was as the leader of the anti-communist faction, and his victory was generally reported, with approval, as "a swing to the Right." By 1948 Reuther was attacking leftist trade union officials as "colonial agents of a foreign government." At this same time, the future Supreme Court justice and member of the Johnson Cabinet Arthur Goldberg replaced the leftist Lee Pressman as general counsel of the CIO—archetypal liberal, who was to end up defending the Vietnam War to the United Nations, replacing a man of the Left. It is striking how many of the most prominent liberals of the fifties and sixties—Reuther, Goldberg, Hubert Humphrey—first came to prominence by attacking not the Right but the Left.

"Though intellectuals have not created the labor movement," wrote Joseph Schumpeter, "they have worked it up into something that differs substantially from what it would have been without them." He was right. But in the fifties the role of the intellectual was not so much to radicalize the labor movement, as Schumpeter supposed, as to divert a considerable proportion of its energies and those of what would otherwise have been the American Left, from the feelings and needs of union members and the real though complex problems of American society to a crusade against communism.

It may be that this optimistic nationalism had a special appeal to intellectuals who were, in such notable proportion, themselves the second- and third-generation children of immigrants, inheritors of the dream. It may be that, like other Americans of the same generation, they felt a need to assimilate under the pressure of the great nativist rebellion that was McCarthyism, to prove themselves good Americans and better than the book burners.

Whatever the exact causes, the intellectual ballast shifted. In 1932 those who endorsed the Communist Party's candidate for President of the United States included Ernest Hemingway, John Dos Passos, James T. Farrell, Langston Hughes, Theodore Dreiser, Erskine Caldwell, Lincoln Steffens, Richard Wright, Katherine Anne Porter, Edmund Wilson, Nathanael West and Malcolm Cowley. Twenty years later, scarcely an intellectual with a shred of reputation could be found even to raise a voice against the outlawing of that same party. The change is measured, too, by the trajectory, in hardly more than a decade, of *Partisan Review,* the most admired highbrow periodical of the time, from dutiful Stalinism through Trotskyite heresy to the bleakest Cold War anti-communist orthodoxy.

Yet it is striking, in retrospect, how central to that supposedly apolitical culture anti-communism became. The formation of Americans for Democratic Action, excluding Communists, Arthur Schlesinger thought, marked "the watershed at which American liberalism began to base itself once again on a solid conception of man and of history." Of American history? No: for Schlesinger, liberalism had virtually been created by anti-communism, apparently. "The growing necessity of checking Communism," he wrote, "by developing some constructive alternative speeded the clarification of liberal ideas in 1947 and 1948."

After World War II, in almost every department of intellectual life, the doctrine of "American exceptionalism" revived. At the same time, utilitarian doctrines, stressing that morality in politics was an illusion, undercut the moralistic basis of left-wing politics. Sociology, history, economics, political science, even theology in the hands of Reinhold Neibuhr, for example, followed parallel paths, rejecting those who argued for radical change and emphasizing the virtues of "the American way."

What role remains for the men of the Left? Seymour Martin Lipset asked in *Political Man*. Not to advocate change in the society of his own country, if he lived in "the West." Even socialists must agree, Lipset thought, that complete socialism was dangerous and that Marxism was an outmoded doctrine.

Did it follow that the Left was totally obsolete? Lipset thought not. "The leftist intellectual, the trade union leader, and the socialist politician" could still make themselves useful-abroad, where society had not yet evolved to such a fortunate state of perfection as in the United States. Such disaffected persons, no longer required at home, could "communicate and work with non-Communist revolutionaries in the Orient and Africa at the same time that they accept the fact"—it sounds like a polite way of saying "on the condition that they accept the fact"—"that serious ideological controversies have ended at home."

In the culminating chapter, that is, of one of the most admired works of political science that the age of the liberal consensus produced, it was argued as a conclusion of high academic seriousness that the only use for dissenters from the liberal ideology was as its propagandists abroad. . . .

In the great American universities, the twenty years after World War II are beginning to be remembered with nostalgia as a Golden Age. Enrollments were multiplying. Endowments were accumulating. Funds from the federal and state governments and from private foundations were becoming available on a scale undreamed of. The salaries and the social status of professors were rising. They were certainly higher, both absolutely and in relation to those of the business world, than they had been since before World War I, and perhaps higher than they had ever been, at least for men sensible enough to have specialized in some useful subject that would earn them consultancy fees from large corporations, from government, or from the armed services. At a time when the U.S. Air Force was paying (through the RAND Corporation) for a sociological study of the toilet training of the French, even that qualification need not stand in the way of a man of imagination.

But the essential reason for the intellectual excitement that blossomed in the best American universities in the late fifties was neither academic influence nor increased competition. It came from the feeling that, for the first time, the academic world seemed thoroughly integrated into the life and purposes of the nation.

To begin with, this may have owed something to the achievement of the atomic scientists. When the mightiest arm of American power was the product of research science, it was hard to dismiss any research as impractical dreaming. Physicists, mathematicians, engineers, were among the first to be accepted by government. But the social scientists were not far behind. (Indeed, one branch of social science, economics, had long moved with assurance in the world of business as well as in Washington.) The earliest big government research contracts dealt with such "nuts-and-bolts" questions as the design of unmanned satellites or the nose cones of missiles. But as early as 1948 Nathan Leites was calling on the academic techniques of textual and literary criticism to describe "The Operational Code of Politburo." It was not long before sociologists, political scientists, even historians, were being called into service by the government— all of the social sciences received from the relationship an injection of adrenalin, as well as of money.

This was the broader context in which the system of thought I have called the liberal ideology was fitted together and came to predominate not only in the universities but in government and to some extent in politics. The interaction, however, was reciprocal. The intellectuals tended to be influential only in proportion as their ideas fitted in with the needs, fears or preconceptions of their new patrons. They tended to be forced into the role of technicians. The "hot" topics of specialization were those most immediately related to the government's most urgent perplexity, or at best to the tactics of its political opponents. Either way, that generally recommended those studies which assumed the permanence and the paramountcy of the Cold War.

"It is remarkable," wrote Henry Kissinger in 1962, "that during a decade of crisis few fundamental criticisms of American policy have been offered. We have not reached an impasse because the wrong alternative was chosen in a 'Great Debate.' The alternatives have rarely been properly defined." It was indeed remarkable. The Pentagon Papers are a sustained commentary on that observation. Yet it is strange that Henry Kissinger, the future virtuoso of the Carrot and the Stick, should find it hard to understand why the alternatives did not get defined. For if the fear of being investigated had shown the intellectuals the stick during the first half of the fifties, the hope of being consulted had shown them the carrot in the second. Alternatives were not what the government wanted. It wanted solutions. It expected to get them from men who displayed a maximum of technical ingenuity with a minimum of dissent.

The liberal ideology equipped the United States with an elaborately interrelated structure of coherent and plausible working assumptions, all poised like an inverted pyramid on two fundamental assumptions, both of which happened to be diametrically wrong.

American capitalism had not, it turned out, eliminated the possibility of serious social conflict at home. Nor was the most urgent danger to the nation from communism abroad. On the contrary, the United States stood on the eve of exceptional social turmoil. Abroad, unified Communist power was breaking up, confronting the world with all the dangers of a period of fragmentation and "détente."

This error was to be pitilessly exposed, and that soon enough. Yet the effect of the liberal consensus was to be even more disastrous than the particular mistaken assumptions on which it was based. It condemned the United States to face the real dangers for too long without any fundamental debate. Thanks to the liberal triumph, the powerful emotions and interests that always work for conservative policies were not balanced by equally powerful forces and principles of the Left. Instead, they were opposed by a liberalism that was in effect hardly to be distinguished from a more sophisticated and less resolute conservatism.

The Military-Industrial Complex

Dwight D. Eisenhower

As a consequence of the Cold War, the United States gradually adopted a policy of permanent mobilization, and the military, once a tiny part of American life, waxed increasingly influential and powerful. The portion of the federal budget allocated to the military leapt from a third in 1950 to a half a decade later. By 1960, moreover, the growing military establishment was tightly interconnected with the corporate and scientific communities in a military-industrial complex that employed millions of Americans and vitally affected the economic fortunes of hundreds of American communities laden with defense plants, research facilities, and military bases. Alarmed at the enormous leverage in the councils of government exerted by this intertwined combination of interests, worried by the threat it posed to the traditional subordination of the military in American life, and fearful of the elephantine enlargement of government spending on defense and the danger it posed to the economic health of the United States, the soldier-turned-president used the occasion of his farewell address to the nation to issue a somber warning about the power and dangers of the military-industrial complex.

We now stand ten years past the midpoint of a century that has witnessed four major wars among great nations. Three of these involved our own country. Despite these holocausts, America is today the strongest, the most influential and most productive nation in the world. Understandably proud of this pre-eminence, we yet realize that America's leadership and prestige depend, not merely upon our unmatched material progress, riches and military

From *Public Papers of the Presidents of the United States: Dwight D. Eisenhower, 1960–1961* (Washington, D.C., 1961), pp. 1036–40.

strength, but on how we use our power in the interests of world peace and human betterment. . . .

Our military organization today bears little relation to that known by any of my predecessors in peacetime, or indeed by the fighting men of World War II or Korea.

Until the latest of our world conflicts, the United States had no armaments industry. American makers of plowshares could, with time and as required, make swords as well. But now we can no longer risk emergency improvisation of national defense; we have been compelled to create a permanent armaments industry of vast proportions. Added to this, three and a half million men and women are directly engaged in the defense establishment. We annually spend on military security more than the net income of all United States corporations.

This conjunction of an immense military establishment and a large arms industry is new in the American experience. The total influence—economic, political, even spiritual—is felt in every city, every State house, every office of the Federal government. We recognize the imperative need for this development. Yet we must not fail to comprehend its grave implications. Our toil, resources and livelihood are all involved; so is the very structure of our society.

In the councils of government, we must guard against the acquisition of unwarranted influence, whether sought or unsought, by the military-industrial complex. The potential for the disastrous rise of misplaced power exists and will persist.

We must never let the weight of this combination endanger our liberties or democratic processes. We should take nothing for granted. Only an alert and knowledgeable citizenry can compel the proper meshing of the huge industrial and military machinery of defense with our peaceful methods and goals, so that security and liberty may prosper together.

Akin to, and largely responsible for, the sweeping changes in our industrial-military posture has been the technological revolution during recent decades.

In this revolution, research has become central; it also becomes more formalized, complex, and costly. A steadily increasing share is conducted for, by, or at the direction of, the Federal government.

Today, the solitary inventor, tinkering in his shop, has been overshadowed by task forces of scientists in laboratories and testing fields. In the same fashion, the free university, historically the fountainhead of free ideas and scientific discovery, has experienced a revolution in the conduct of research. Partly because of the huge costs involved, a government contract becomes virtually a substitute for intellectual curiosity. For every old blackboard there are now hundreds of new electronic computers.

The prospect of domination of the nation's scholars by Federal employment, project allocations, and the power of money is ever present—and is gravely to be regarded.

Yet, in holding scientific research and discovery in respect, as we should, we must also be alert to the equal and opposite danger that public policy could itself become the captive of a scientific-technological elite.

It is the task of statesmanship to mold, to balance, and to integrate these and other forces, new and old, within the principles of our democratic system—ever aiming toward the supreme goals of our free society. . . .

The New Frontier in Space

John F. Kennedy

During his campaign for the presidency, John Kennedy repeatedly insisted that it was time to get the country moving again. Promising to provide more dynamic and vigorous leadership than had Eisenhower, Kennedy expressed the "quest for national purpose" and newfound sense of crisis that marked the late 1950s and early 1960s; and, upon entering the White House, JFK injected a spirit of adventure and urgency into political affairs. In May 1961 he went before Congress to importune that the United States commit itself to land a man on the moon before the end of the decade. Note particularly the emphasis on crisis and challenge in this excerpt, as well as the connection between foreign policy and the space program. Note, too, the aspects of this speech that illustrate what Hodgson calls the "liberal consensus."

The great battleground for the defense and expansion of freedom today is the whole southern half of the globe—Asia, Latin America, Africa and the Middle East—the lands of the rising peoples. Their revolution is the greatest in human history. They seek an end to injustice, tyranny, and exploitation. More than an end, they seek a beginning.

And theirs is a revolution which we would support regardless of the Cold War, and regardless of which political or economic route they should choose to freedom.

For the adversaries of freedom did not create the revolution; nor did they create the conditions which compel it. But they are seeking to ride the crest of its wave—to capture it for themselves.

From *Public Papers of the Presidents of the United States: John F. Kennedy, 1961* (Washington, D.C., 1962), pp. 396–98, 403–05.

Yet their aggression is more often concealed than open. They have fired no missiles; and their troops are seldom seen. They send arms, agitators, aid, technicians, and propaganda to every troubled area. But where fighting is required, it is usually done by others—by guerrillas striking at night, by assassins striking alone—assassins who have taken the lives of four thousand civil officers in the last twelve months in Vietnam alone—by subversives and saboteurs and insurrectionists, who in some cases control whole areas inside of independent nations.

With these formidable weapons, the adversaries of freedom plan to consolidate their territory—to exploit, to control, and finally to destroy the hopes of the world's newest nations; and they have ambition to do it before the end of this decade. It is a contest of will and purpose as well as force and violence—a battle for minds and souls as well as lives and territory. And in that contest, we cannot stand aside.

We stand, as we have always stood from our earliest beginnings, for the independence and equality of all nations. This nation was born of revolution and raised in freedom. And we do not intend to leave an open road for despotism. . . .

Finally, if we are to win the battle that is now going on around the world between freedom and tyranny, the dramatic achievements in space which occurred in recent weeks should have made clear to us all, as did the Sputnik in 1957, the impact of this adventure on the minds of men everywhere, who are attempting to make a determination of which road they should take. Since early in my term, our efforts in space have been under review. With the advice of the Vice President, who is Chairman of the National Space Council, we have examined where we are strong and where we are not, where we may succeed and where we may not. Now it is time to take longer strides—time for a great new American enterprise—time for this nation to take a clearly leading role in space achievement, which in many ways may hold the key to our future on earth.

I believe we possess all the resources and talents necessary. But the facts of the matter are that we have never made the national decisions or marshalled the national resources required for such leadership. We have never specified long-range goals on an urgent time schedule, or managed our resources and our time so as to insure their fulfillment.

Recognizing the head start obtained by the Soviets with their large rocket engines, which gives them many months of lead-time, and recognizing the likelihood that they will exploit this lead for some time to come in still more impressive successes, we nevertheless are required to make new efforts on our own. For while we cannot guarantee that we shall one day be first, we can guarantee that any failure to make this effort will make us last. We take an additional risk by making it in full view of the world, but as shown by the feat of astronaut Shepard, this very risk enhances our stature when we are successful. But this is not merely a race. Space is open to us now; and our eagerness to share its meaning is not governed by the efforts of others. We go into space because whatever mankind must undertake, free men must fully share.

I therefore ask the Congress, above and beyond the increases I have earlier requested for space activities, to provide the funds which are needed to meet the following national goals:

First, I believe that this nation should commit itself to achieving the goal before this decade is out, of landing a man on the moon and returning him safely to the earth. No single space project in this period will be more impressive to mankind, or more important for the long-range exploration of space; and none will be so difficult or expensive to accomplish. We propose to accelerate the development of the appropriate lunar space craft. We propose to develop alternate liquid and solid fuel boosters, much larger than any now being developed, until certain which is superior. We propose additional funds for other engine development and for unmanned explorations—explorations which are particularly important for one purpose which this nation will never overlook: the survival of the man who first makes this daring flight. But in a very real sense, it will not be one man going to the moon—if we make this judgment affirmatively, it will be an entire nation. For all of us must work to put him there. . . .

Let it be clear—and this is a judgment which the Members of the Congress must finally make—let it be clear that I am asking the Congress and the country to accept a firm commitment to a new course of action—a course which will last for many years and carry very heavy costs: 531 million dollars in fiscal '62—an estimated seven to nine billion dollars additional over the next five years. If we are to go only half way, or reduce our sights in the face of difficulty, in my judgment it would be better not to go at all. . . .

This decision demands a major national commitment of scientific and technical manpower, material and facilities, and the possibility of their diversion from other important activities where they are already thinly spread. It means a degree of dedication, organization and discipline which have not always characterized our research and development efforts. It means we cannot afford undue work stoppages, inflated costs of material or talent, wasteful interagency rivalries, or a high turnover of key personnel.

New objectives and new money cannot solve these problems. They could in fact, aggravate them further—unless every scientist, every engineer, every serviceman, every technician, contractor, and civil servant gives his personal pledge that this nation will move forward, with the full speed of freedom, in the exciting adventure of space. . . .

The Great Society

Lyndon B. Johnson

Suddenly elevated to the presidency on November 22, 1963, Lyndon Baines Johnson sought to use his powers to place his personal stamp on national politics and to secure his position in history's pantheon. Desiring to fulfill the promises of the New Deal, Fair Deal, New Frontier, and much more, Johnson assured the American people that "we have the power to shape the civilization that we want." His vision of that civilization, a Great Society of "qualitative liberalism," was proclaimed in the May 1964 address at the University of Michigan reprinted below.

Congress granted most of LBJ's far-reaching legislative requests in the next two years, but then the intensifying war in Vietnam and racial conflict at home undermined the liberal climate of opinion. Attacked by conservatives for spending too much and involving the poor themselves in reform programs, denounced by radicals for imposing middle-class values on the poor and for relying on economic growth to fund welfare benefits instead of redistributing the wealth, and deserted by middle-class Americans who believed the government was paying too much attention to the underprivileged and neglecting their own needs, the Great Society could not survive. Ironically, the president who aimed to promote harmony by concentrating on domestic reform became preoccupied with foreign affairs and significantly increased social tensions and conflict.

Worthy assessments of a presidential administration require careful distinctions between style and substance. Evaluate the presidencies of Kennedy and Johnson in this light, and consider their similarities and differences with recent presidents in matters of style and substance. How might the current president define his "great society," and how would his priorities differ from Lyndon Johnson's?

From *Public Papers of the Presidents of the United States: Lyndon B. Johnson, 1963–1964* (Washington, D.C., 1965), I, pp. 704–7.

. . . For a century we labored to settle and to subdue a continent. For half a century we called upon unbounded invention and untiring industry to create an order of plenty for all of our people.

The challenge of the next half century is whether we have the wisdom to use that wealth to enrich and elevate our national life, and to advance the quality of our American civilization.

Your imagination, your initiative, and your indignation will determine whether we build a society where progress is the servant of our needs, or a society where old values and new visions are buried under unbridled growth. For in your time we have the opportunity to move not only toward the rich society and the powerful society, but upward to the Great Society.

The Great Society rests on abundance and liberty for all. It demands an end to poverty and racial injustice, to which we are totally committed in our time. But that is just the beginning.

The Great Society is a place where every child can find knowledge to enrich his mind and to enlarge his talents. It is a place where leisure is a welcome chance to build and reflect, not a feared cause of boredom and restlessness. It is a place where the city of man serves not only the needs of the body and the demands of commerce but the desire for beauty and the hunger for community.

It is a place where man can renew contact with nature. It is a place which honors creation for its own sake and for what it adds to the understanding of the race. It is a place where men are more concerned with the quality of their goals than the quantity of their goods.

But most of all, the Great Society is not a safe harbor, a resting place, a final objective, a finished work. It is a challenge constantly renewed, beckoning us toward a destiny where the meaning of our lives matches the marvelous products of our labor. . . .

Aristotle said: "men come together in cities in order to live, but they remain together in order to live the good life." It is harder and harder to live the good life in American cities today.

The catalogue of ills is long: there is the decay of the centers and the despoiling of the suburbs. There is not enough housing for our people or transportation for our traffic. Open land is vanishing and old landmarks are violated.

Worst of all expansion is eroding the precious and time-honored values of community with neighbors and communion with nature.

The loss of these values breeds loneliness and boredom and indifference.

Our society will never be great until our cities are great. Today the frontier of imagination and innovation is inside those cities and not beyond their borders. . . .

A second place where we begin to build the Great Society is in our countryside. We have always prided ourselves on being not only America the strong and America the free, but America the beautiful. Today that beauty is in danger. The water we drink, the food we eat, the very air that we breathe, are threatened with pollution. Our parks are overcrowded, our seashores over-burdened. Green fields and dense forests are disappearing. . . .

A third place to build the Great Society is in the classrooms of America. There your children's lives will be shaped. Our society will not be great until every young mind is set free to scan the farthest reaches of thought and imagination. We are still far from that goal. . . .

In many places, classrooms are overcrowded and curricula are outdated. Most of our qualified teachers are underpaid, and many of our paid teachers are unqualified. So we must give every child a place to sit and a teacher to learn from. Poverty must not be a bar to learning, and learning must offer an escape from poverty.

But more classrooms and more teachers are not enough. We must seek an educational system which grows in excellence as it grows in size. This means better training for our teachers. It means preparing youth to enjoy their hours of leisure as well as their hours of labor. It means exploring new techniques of teaching, to find new ways to stimulate the love of learning and the capacity for creation. . . . .

For better or for worse, your generation has been appointed by history to deal with those problems and to lead America toward a new age. You have the chance never before afforded to any people in any age. You can help build a society where the demands of morality, and the needs of the spirit, can be realized in the life of the nation.

So, will you join in the battle to give every citizen the full equality which God enjoins and the law requires, whatever his belief, or race, or the color of his skin?

Will you join in the battle to give every citizen an escape from the crushing wieght of poverty?

Will you join in the battle to make it possible for all nations to live in enduring peace—as neighbors and not as mortal enemies?

Will you join in the battle to build the Great Society, to prove that our material progress is only the foundation on which we will build a richer life of mind and spirit?

There are those timid souls who say this battle cannot be won: that we are condemned to a soulless wealth. I do not agree. We have the power to shape the civilization that we want. But we need your will, your labor, your hearts, if we are to build that kind of society. . . .

So let us from this moment begin our work so that in the future men will look back and say: it was then, after a long and weary way, that man turned the exploits of his genius to the full enrichment of his life.

Losing Ground: Discredited Liberalism

Charles Murray

The extent to which Great Society programs, especially the efforts associ-ated with the War on Poverty, did or did not realize their goals remains a matter of dispute, as are the reasons they never reached their full poten-tial. Some historians focus on President Johnson's personal limitations. Others stress how the "culture of poverty" or the structural limitations of the economy hindered reform, or how the conceptual confusion and poor planning within the Johnson administration doomed chances for greater success. Still others emphasize the demise of Johnson's fragile reform coalition, the rising middle-class resistance to reform, as well as how the war in Vietnam drained resources from domestic reform.

In Losing Ground *(1984), an influential conservative critique of Johnson's welfare policies that some referred to as the Reagan adminis-tration's "bible," Charles Murray argues that the War on Poverty failed and that its failure was inherent in the strategy adopted to end poverty. Johnson's social policy, Murray concludes, encouraged the poor to behave in ways that trapped them in poverty and that produced more poor people. Consider how and why assessments of the Great Society continue to influ-ence current debates about social intervention by the federal government, especially about what the government now ought to do to end welfare and help lift people out of poverty.*

The passage of the first antipoverty bill marked a transition. Through 1964, the rationale for new social action programs was the one set by Kennedy: The government should take a more active role in helping people get on their feet. Then a new agenda, new assumptions, and a rush of events (not the least of them Vietnam) complicated the situation.

For one thing—and the importance of this must not be forgotten during the ensuing discussion—an accident of history brought a master legislator to the presidency at a moment when the other forces were converging. The antipoverty bills, Food Stamps, Medicare, Medicaid, public housing programs, manpower training, expansions of entitlements, all followed pell-mell. It was a legislative blitzkrieg, not the implementation of a master plan.

Apart from the idiosyncratic influences of Lyndon Johnson's ego and skills, a fundamental shift in the assumptions about social policy was occurring. Four forces pushed it: The economists seemed to have found the secret of lasting prosperity; policymakers and intellectuals discovered structural poverty; the civil rights movement moved north; and the original antipoverty programs failed to show the expected results. Together with other, less directly related tides in the American polity, they worked the revolution. In only three years, from 1964 to the end of 1967—what I shall refer to as the "reform period"—social policy went from the dream of ending the dole to the institution of permanent income transfers that embraced not only the recipients of the dole but large new segments of the American population. It went from the ideal of a color-blind society to the reinstallation of legalized discrimination. They were polar changes that were barely recognized as such while they were happening.

THE TRIUMPH OF THE ECONOMY

One explanation for the reforms of the 1964–67 period, and why they came then rather than earlier, is so simple that it is sometimes overlooked: 1964–67 was the first time that we thought we could afford them. We were extremely rich and extremely secure about our ability to continue getting richer. The performance of the American economy had been spectacular.

In part, it was a phenomenon that stretched back to the onset of the Second World War. In 1940, just before the war years, GNP had been less than $100 billion. Twenty-five years later, it was $685 billion, a sevenfold increase. Even after discounting for inflation, real GNP had nearly tripled.

But history alone was not the goad. During the 1964–67 period in which the shift in social welfare premises took place, Lyndon Johnson and the Congress were making decisions under the impression—based on persuasive evidence—that the boom was no longer part of an ungovernable cycle of economic expansion and contraction. The Eisenhower administration had been punctuated by two recessions, recessions that the new generation of Keynesian economists who came to Washington with Kennedy said they could avoid. Kennedy had cautiously implemented their advice. And it had worked, exactly as the economists had said it would: steady growth, no inflation. From 1961 to 1965, GNP went from $520 billion to $685 billion in increments of $40 billion, $30 billion, $42 billion, and $53 billion. The inflation rate was about 1 percent per year.

Hubris won out. "We can't prevent every little wiggle in the economic cycle," Johnson's budget director, Charles Schultze, acknowledged, but, he added confidently, "we now can prevent a major slide." Keynes was on the cover of *Time*'s last issue of 1965. "Even the most optimistic forecasts for 1965 turned out to be too low," the magazine wrote. "If the nation has economic problems, they are the problems of high employment, high growth, and high hopes."

The next two years brought more of the same—growth of $65 billion in the GNP in 1966 and $44 billion in 1967. Inflation was a bit higher, around 3 percent, but still manageable. There was no recession, no stumbling. "We are all Keynesians now," said Richard Nixon, and it seemed to be eminently reasonable to be so. It appeared that the economists were making good on translating theory into practice.

Thus we made our decisions about the poor and about social policy from what seemed at the time to be a position of impregnable economic strength. Not only were we enjoying an unprecedented boom, we now thought we had the tools to sustain it indefinitely. If there was poverty amidst plenty (a favorite phrase among writers of the time), and its solution did not come as easily as the initial optimism had projected, then there was still no good reason to back off. All the changes in policy during the 1964–67 period must be considered in light of this central fact: At the time, almost everyone thought the economic pie would grow ever larger.

THE DISCOVERY OF STRUCTURAL POVERTY

Even as the War on Poverty was beginning, its premises of self-help and open opportunities were lagging behind a new intellectual consensus that would shape policy very shortly.

To understand its power, one first must understand that poverty did not simply climb upward on our national list of problems; it abruptly reappeared from nowhere. In the prologue to this book, 1950 was described as a year in which poverty was not part of the discourse about domestic policy—indeed, as a year in which the very word "poverty" was seldom used. The silence was not peculiar to 1950. From the outset of the Second World War until 1962, little in the popular press, in political rhetoric, or in the published work of American scholars focused on poverty in America.

When poverty did get into the news before 1964, the treatment of it tended to reflect surprise that it existed at all. In November 1960, three weeks after the presidential election and the day after Thanksgiving (a deliberate juxtaposition), Edward R. Murrow broadcast a *CBS Reports* called "Harvest of Shame." It showed that tens of thousands of migrant workers were miserably paid, housed, educated, and nourished—problems that middle-class America apparently associated only with the 1930s and *The Grapes of Wrath*.

The viewing public and numerous editorial writers were shocked—a fact in itself illustrative of the obliviousness toward poverty. The more instructive reaction, however, was Murrow's own. A few months later, the day after he was sworn in as director of the United States Information Agency, one of his first acts was to try to persuade the BBC to cancel a scheduled broadcast of "Harvest of Shame." That Edward R. Murrow, the embodiment of journalistic independence, would try to stop a news show on grounds that it would be taken out of context suggests how aberrant the poverty in "Harvest of Shame" was taken to be.

In the intellectual community, phenomena such as poverty among migrant workers were seen as peripheral. Norman Podhoretz, recalling the leftist intellectual circles in which he moved during the 1950s, points out that the essential *economic* success of the American system was taken as a given even by those who were most bitterly critical of the social system. He continues:

That there were still "pockets" of unemployment and poverty, and that there was still a great spread in the distribution of income and wealth, everyone realized. But the significance of such familiar conditions paled by comparison with a situation that now seemed to defy the rule that there could be nothing new under the sun: the apparent convergence of the entire population into a single class.

Podhoretz's observation held true through the 1960 presidential campaign. Poverty was, in the terms of that campaign, something that happened mostly in Appalachia—not only in the Kennedy campaign rhetoric, but in the minds of those Democrats who considered themselves true liberals. When Arthur Schlesinger decided to proselytize among members of the liberal establishment on behalf of John Kennedy in 1960, he made his case on issues that he knew to be the ones that were exercising his friends and colleagues in the liberal wing of the party. He chose as his theme that Kennedy was the man for an era in which the struggle for material subsistence had essentially been solved.

Against this backdrop, the emergence of the structural view of the poverty problem was unexpected and rapid. As of the beginning of 1962, no one was talking about poverty; by the end of 1963 it was the hottest domestic policy topic other than civil rights. But it was not just "poverty" that was being talked about. "Structural poverty" was now at issue.

"Structural poverty" refers to poverty that is embedded within the nature of the system (or demographics) and will not be eradicated by economic growth. Its elimination, according to the proponents of this view of poverty, requires radical surgery. "The most visible structuralists," writes James Patterson, "were not social workers or government bureaucrats looking for ways to improve the situation of indivduals, but social scientists and left-wing writers who took a broad and reformist view of the functional relationship between inequality and the social system."

One such writer was Michael Harrington, who in 1962 published a book that was the most visible single reason for the sudden popularity of poverty. The book was *The Other America*. Its thesis was that a huge population of poor people—fifty million by his count—was living in our midst, ignored. They consisted of the aged, the unskilled, the women heading households with small children, and others who were bound to be bypassed no matter how much economic growth occurred, because of the way that the system distributed income.

The importance of Harrington's book was not in its details but in its central message: America was not the single-class, affluent society that a complacent intellectual establishment had assumed, but a deeply riven society in which the poor had been left to suffer unnoticed. Kennedy read *The Other America* and Dwight MacDonald's evangelizing review of it in *The New Yorker* and ordered the beginning of the staff work that Lyndon Johnson would later seize upon for his crusade.

It was a time when books became banners for causes—*Silent Spring* was published at about the same time, and *Unsafe at Any Speed* followed a few years later—and it is always difficult in such cases to determine how much was cause and how much effect. Certainly others had been forwarding a structuralist view of poverty both within and without the Kennedy administration. But even if the poor were bound to have been rediscovered in the early 1960s, Harrington was their pamphleteer, *The Other America* their *Common Sense*.

Once the argument had been made, it became very unfashionable for an intellectual in good standing to argue with it. A few, such as Irving Kristol made note of Harrington's factual inaccuracies and his reliance on dubious evidence. Later, even some of Harrington's sympathetic colleagues would dispute the centerpiece arguments about intergenerational poverty. But much of what Harrington had to say seemed indisputable. The population did include large numbers of poor people, and they didn't seem to be moving up the way that they were supposed to do. To quibble was to sound like the Chamber of Commerce.

If poverty was not an aberration, not a matter of "pockets" but structurally built into the American system, then it was necessarily true that the initial antipoverty bills represented a half-hearted and wrong-headed approach to the problem. Poverty was not going to be eradicated by a Job Corps or a few loans to small businessmen. Sweeping changes in the income distribution system were needed— a cool analytic conclusion to some, but more often a conviction held with "a passionate sense of urgency," as Jeremy Larner and Irving Howe put it. "[I]n a nation as rich as the United States," they declaimed, "it is an utter moral scandal that even the sightest remnant of poverty should remain."

In a technical sense, the structuralists made a case only for the proposition that much, not all, of American poverty derived from structural characteristics. Their message was an antidote to the folk wisdom that anyone with enough gumption could make a good living. But the "passionate sense of urgency" got in the way of balance. What emerged in the mid-1960s was an almost unbroken intellectual consensus that the individualist explanation of poverty was altogether outmoded and reactionary. Poverty was not a consequence of indolence or vice. It was not the just deserts of people who didn't try hard enough. It was produced by conditions that had nothing to do with individual virtue or effort. *Poverty was not the fault of the individual but of the system.*

For the Harringtons, it was a statement of political and economic dogma. For the politicians and policymakers and implementers of the programs, it was about to become the indispensable rationale for coping with two empirical developments that few were anticipating when the War on Poverty got under way.

THE CIVIL RIGHTS MOVEMENT MOVES NORTH

Speaking to an interviewer in 1967, Daniel Patrick Moynihan summed up in a few sentences the toils in which the social welfare experiment had wound itself when the civil rights movement moved north.

> In the South . . . there were a great many outcomes—situations, customs, rules—which were inimical to Negro rights, which violated Negro rights and which were *willed* outcomes. Intended, planned, desired outcomes. And it was, therefore, possible to seek out those individuals who were willing the outcomes and to coerce them to cease to do so.
>
> Now, you come to New York City, with its incomparable expenditures on education; and you find that, in the twelfth grade, Negro students are performing at the sixth grade level in mathematics. Find for me the man who wills *that* outcome. Find the legislator who has held back money, the teacher who's held back his skills, the school superintendent who's deliberately discriminating, the curriculum supervisor who puts the wrong books in, the architect who builds the bad schools. He isn't there!

By and large—not perfectly by any means, but by and large—the legal system outside the southern states had rid itself of designed-in racism. There were no voter "literacy" tests to get rid of, no Jim Crow laws to repeal. While northern racism might simply be more subtle, as many black leaders claimed, it provided few specific, reified targets to hit out against.

And yet equality of rights under the law had not been accompanied by equality of outcome. Blacks in the North as in the South lived in worse housing than whites, had less education, ate less nutritious food, and so on down the list of indicators that were used to measure well-being. On virtually every one, a large difference between black and white remained, and it was always to the disadvantage of the blacks. Whites were made aware of this by accounts such as Kenneth Clark's "Youth in the Ghetto," passed everywhere in mimeograph by poverty planners long before it was published. Blacks who lived in the ghetto did not need to read about it. Their response followed a pattern that could be used as a textbook example of a revolution of rising expectations.

The first phase of the civil rights movement culminated in the passage of the Civil Rights Act of 1964 on 3 July. For all practical purposes, the national legislative struggle for equality was over. The Voting Rights Bill remained to be enacted a year later, but the generalized legal cloud granted in the 1964 act was enormous: No one could with impunity deny someone *access* to the institutions of this country because of race without being liable to criminal penalties or inviting a nasty and probably losing lawsuit. The civil rights movement had triumphed—and thirteen days later came the first of the race riots, in Harlem.

The riots continued that summer in Rochester, Paterson, Philadelphia, and Dixmoor, a suburb of Chicago. They quieted during the winter, then erupted again in Watts, in August 1965, with a violence that dwarfed the disturbances of the preceding year. They would crescendo in 1967, with riots in more than thirty cities.

The riots changed, or coincided with a change in, what had until then been a movement of legal challenges, nonviolent demonstrations, and coalition-building. Writing from a Marxist perspective, some observers saw this as the trigger for the explosion in social spending that occurred during the same period: The white power structure needed to control the restiveness of blacks, and the shift from "a hand, not a handout" to income transfers was in the nature of a bribe.

A careful review of what bills passed when, with what support, casts doubt on this argument, though it retains intuitive plausibility. But the post-1964 militancy unquestionably had another and arguably more pernicious long-term effect. It tightly restricted the permissible terms of debate within academia and the government on issues involving blacks—which is to say, virtually every issue associated with social policy.

Specifically, the riots and the militancy adjoined the moral monopoly that the civil rights movement of 1964 still enjoyed. The year 1964 was not only the year when the Civil Rights Act passed and the first riots occurred. It was also the year when Martin Luther King, Jr., won the Nobel Peace Prize. It was the year when Chaney, Goodman, and Schwerner were tortured and killed in Mississippi. It was, in short, the year in which all that created the moral monopoly was most in evidence.

Black leaders blamed the riots on whites—or, coextensively, The System. Stokely Carmichael and Rap Brown said it with a rhetoric as bloody-minded and as unapologetic as the rioters. Martin Luther King said it with more elegance, thoughtfulness, and political astuteness, but said it nonetheless. "A profound judgment of today's riots," King told a convention of social scientists, "was expressed by Victor Hugo a century ago. He said, 'If a soul is left in darkness, sins will be committed. The guilty one is not he who commits the sin, but he who causes the darkness.'"

As a statement about ultimate causes, the black interpretation was nearly unarguable. But history was not the issue. The exigent question was: What do we do now, today, in response to people rioting in the streets? Devising an answer put whites in a terrible moral bind—not one that blacks were likely to have much sympathy with, but a bind nonetheless. A white who had supported the simple, purely "good" civil rights movement against the nasty southerners and now said, "Wait a minute, that doesn't mean you can start burning northern cities" was exposed as a summer soldier. Manifestly, racial discrimination continued to exist; manifestly, it was a moral perversity. Therefore. . . . And that was the hard part. What came after the "therefore"?

Whites who saw themselves as friends of the civil rights movement had to agree that the riots were regrettable but not the fault of blacks. The inevitability of the riots, even their reasonableness, had to be accepted, not as a matter of historical causation but as the basis for the white policy reaction. Of course the civil rights legislation had not forestalled violence, *Newsweek* told us. After all, "The promises of the present could not undo in a day the ugly legacy of the Negro past," the magazine wrote in its lead paragraph on the Watts riot. "A summer ago, that past exploded in a bloody war of rioting across the urban North. And last week, on a steamy, smoggy night in Los Angeles, it exploded again." A few pages later, a poll of whites' reactions to the riots divided the discussion into two paragraphs—the "intelligent" reactions, meaning those who understood that the riots were an understandable manifestation of past injustice, and those who were "less perceptive," meaning the people who said that the rioters were breaking the law and ought to be punished. The two stands were widely perceived as being mutually exclusive.

Not everybody agreed. "White backlash" was a phrase coined at about the same time as "black power." The year 1966 saw the election of an ideologically adamant conservative governor in California, Ronald Reagan, and widely publicized campaigns by racial hardliners like Boston's Louise Day Hicks. But even on Main Street, well into the riot years, a majority remained in favor of taking new steps to remedy black grievances.

Within the Establishment (for lack of a better term), a much narrower, circumscribing mindset took hold: The blame is embedded in the structure of the system, and the system must be made right.

The most vocal advocates for sweeping reform were from the left, but it would be mistaken to treat the sense of guilt as "liberal" versus "conservative." The *mea culpa* resounded everywhere, including the most unlikely places. For example:

> [W]e are creating a monster within our midst, a people being alienated from the mainstream of American life . . . [We must] cease thinking of racial relations as a nice and good thing, as one important national and local task—*among many others*—to do. American race relations today, like religion and basic ideologies historically, must have an absolute priority or we are as a nation lost! [Emphasis on the original]

Strong words—not from a political rostrum, but from the lead article in the January 1967 issue of *The American Journal of Economics and Sociology,* a sober academic journal. But they were no more unexpected than an angry editorial, entitled "Cry of the

Ghetto," complaining bitterly of "white society's stubborn refusal to admit that the ghetto is a problem it must solve, that its promises, broken and inadequate, are no longer tolerable." It appeared in *The Saturday Evening Post*—the staid, middle-American, Norman-Rockwell-covered *Saturday Evening Post*—during that bloody August of 1967.

The National Commission on Civil Disorders, headed by an ex-governor of Illinois and comprising a distinguished selection of Americans from the business and professional worlds as well as from public life, put the imprimatur of the federal government on the explanation for the riots, concluding that "[w]hite racism is essentially responsible for the explosive mixture which has been accumulating in our cities since the end of World War II." The report presented no proof for this statement, but few objected. Its truth was self-evident.

Whether the Establishment view of the black condition in the last half of the 1960s was right or wrong is not the issue that concerns us. The fact that this view was so widely shared helped force the shift in assumptions about social welfare. White America owed black America; it had a conscience to clear.

The moral agonizing among whites was strikingly white-centered. *Whites* had created the problem, it was up to *whites* to fix it, and there was very little in the dialogue that treated blacks as responsible actors. Until July 1964 most whites (and most blacks) thought in terms of equal access to opportunity. Blacks who failed to take advantage were in the same boat with whites who failed to take advantage. By 1967 this was not an intellectually acceptable way to conceive of the issue. Blacks were exempted. Once more, in a new and curious fashion, whites had put up the "Whites Only" sign.

White confusion and guilt over the turn of events in the civil rights movement created what Moynihan has called "a near-obsessive concern to locate the 'blame' for poverty, especially Negro poverty, on forces and institutions outside the community concerned." The structuralists, with their view of poverty as embedded in the American economic and social system, provided a ready-made complement to this impulse. If society were to blame for the riots, if it were to blame for the economic and social discrepancies between whites and blacks, if indeed it were to blame for poverty itself among all races, and *if society's responsibility were not put right by enforcing a formalistic legal equality*, then a social program could hardly be constructed on grounds that simply guaranteed equality of opportunity. It must work toward equality of *outcome*. A "hand" was not enough.

HARD NOSES AND SOFT DATA

The riots and black militancy constituted one of the two empirical developments that made the structural view of poverty attractive. The second was the early realization, within the ranks of the Johnson administration as well as among its critics, that the antipoverty programs were not working as expected.

For this part of the story, we return to the fall of 1964, when the first antipoverty bill had just been passed and the Office of Economic Opportunity (OEO) was being organized. Our focus shifts from the academicians, the journalists, the cabinet officers and congressional leaders to the people who did the work—the middle- and lower-echelon officials who designed and implemented the programs that constituted the War on Poverty.

They were an assortment of New Frontiersmen (Sargent Shriver at OEO being the most conspicuous example) and people who came into the bureaucracy especially to play a role in the great social reform that Johnson had launched. Few were bureaucrats, few were from the social-work tradition. They tended to see themselves as pragmatic idealists. "Hardnosed" was a favorite self-descriptor in the Kennedy years, and it carried over. The first poverty warriors did not intend to get bogged down in interminable debates about doctrine. They had a job to do and, from the accounts of people who participated in those early years of the Great Society, it was an exciting job. The recountings have the flavor of war stories—of all-night sessions preparing for crucial Senate hearings; of small, sweaty working groups designing new programs on impossibly short schedules; of meetings in Newark or Chicago or Biloxi where the people across the table were not mayors and city planners, but the heads of tenants' associations and ghetto churches and street gangs. Speaking of his staff, the director of one of the early programs wrote:

> All were the antithesis of the stereotyped bureaucrat cautiously protecting his career. Their approach right down the line was: "What

needs to be done? How can we do it best, and faster?" When the answers were clear, they were all willing to risk their careers and their health and sacrifice their personal lives, to get the job done well and quickly. Something happened to us all . . . that created a rare combination of shared dedication, excitement, and satisfaction.

Such people characterized the early years both in Washington and in the field offices. They had no serious doubts that they would have an impact on the poverty problem. It seemed obvious to them (as it did to many observers at the time) that the only reason we continued to have poverty at a time of such manifest national affluence was that nobody had really been trying to get rid of it. Once the effort was made, so their assumption went, progress would surely follow.

Their optimism had two bases. One was that the programs depended on human responses that seemed natural and indeed nearly automatic to them. The gloomy implications of the "culture of poverty" argument did not carry much weight at OEO in 1964 and 1965. A sensible, hard-working poor person would find much to work with in the opportunities offered by the initial antipoverty programs. Or to put it another way, if the people who ran the programs had suddenly found themselves poor, they probably would have been quite successful in using the antipoverty programs to rescue themselves. The early programs put chips on the table; as their advocates had promised, they did indeed give some of the poor a chance at a piece of the action, with the operative word being "chance." The staff at OEO and its companion agencies scattered around Washington did not think that the loan programs or the community development programs would transform the ghetto instantaneously, but they had no doubt that such programs would be individually successful—steps in the right direction.

In the case of the training programs such as the Job Corps, success seemed to be still more natural. The logistics of providing training were straightforward. The educational technology was adequate and in place. There were plenty of welfare recipients who said they wanted jobs and who acted as though they wanted jobs. During the 1960s, and especially after the Vietnam War heated up, jobs were available for people with the kinds of skills that could be acquired in the training programs. The training programs would work, without question. What was to stop them?

It would be important to document the successes that were about to emerge. In the spirit of cost-effectiveness that McNamara had taken to the Pentagon, the early poverty warriors were prepared to be judged on the hardest of hardnosed measures of success. The programs would be removing enough people from the welfare rolls, from drug addiction, and from crime to provide an economically attractive return on the investment.

But how was this information to be obtained? Social scientists who had been at the periphery of the policy process—sociologists, psychologists, political scientists—had the answer: scientific evaluation. The merits of doing good would no longer have to rest on faith. We would be able to *prove* that we had done good, as objectively as a scientist proves an hypothesis.

In the space of a few years, applied social science and especially program evaluation became big business. In Eisenhower's last year in office, 1960, the Department of Health, Education, and Welfare (HEW) spent $46 million on reasearch and development other than health research. It took three more years for the budget to reach $90 million, followed by sizable jumps in 1964 and 1965. Then, in a single year, 1966, the budget doubled from $154 million to $313 million. Similar patterns prevailed at the other departments, agencies, institutes, and bureaus engaged in the antipoverty struggle.

The product of all this activity and money was a literature describing what was being accomplished by the antipoverty programs. It is what scholars call a "fugitive" literature, with most reports being printed in editions of a few dozen photocopies submitted to the government sponsor. The release of a major evaluation might get a column or two on a back page of a few of the largest newspapers. But otherwise, the work of the evaluators went unread by the outside world.

Within those governmental circles where the reports *were* read, they led to a rapid loss of innocence about what could be expected from the efforts to help people escape from welfare dependency. Starting with the first evaluation reports in the mid-sixties and continuing to the present day, the results of these programs have been disappointing to their advocates and evidence of failure to their critics.

The War on Poverty had originally struck on two fronts: For depressed neighborhoods and entire communities, "community action" programs were funded in profusion, to further all sorts of objectives; for individuals, manpower programs provided training or job opportunities. We shall be discussing the substance of what the evaluators found, not only in 1964–67 but subsequently, when we examine explanations for the breakdown in progress. For now, a few examples will convey the tenor of the findings.

The Community Action Programs

The community action programs fared worst. A number of histories and case studies are available to the public at large, Moynihan's *Maximum Feasible Misunderstanding* being the best known. With the advantage of hindsight, it is not surprising that the community development programs so seldom got off the ground. Faith in spontaneity and in *ad hoc* administrative arrangements were traits of the sixties that met disillusionment in many fields besides the antipoverty programs. Surprising or not, the record they compiled was dismal. For every evaluation report that could document a success, there was a stack that told of local groups that were propped up by federal money for the duration of the grant, then disappeared, with nothing left behind.

Each project had its own tale to tell about why it failed—an ambitious city councilman who tried to horn in, a balky banker who reneged on a tentative agreement, and so on. There were always villains and heroes, dragons and maidens. But failure was very nearly universal.

The course of the projects followed a pattern. To see how this worked in practice, we have the example of the Economic Development Administrations' major employment and urban development program in Oakland, the subject of a scholarly case study. This was the sequence:

The story broke with considerable fanfare. *The Wall Street Journal* of 25 April 1966 had it on page one, under the headline "URBAN AID KICKOFF: ADMINISTRATION SELECTS OAKLAND AS FIRST CITY IN REBUILDING PROGRAM." The governor of California and the assistant secretary of commerce for economic development held a press conference announcing a program of $23 million in federal grants and loans. The program was an assortment of community-run economic development projects bankrolled by the government. Various incentives were designed to prompt private business to invest in the ghetto. In the short term, 2,200 jobs were to be provided, and more were to follow from "spinoffs." These jobs would go to the unemployed residents of the inner city.

As far as its national publicity told the story, the program was a great success. A Book (*Oakland's Not for Burning*) was in the bookstores by 1968, claiming that the program "may have made the difference" in preventing a riot in Oakland. *The New Yorker* told its readers that the program had "managed to break a longtime deadlock between the Oakland ghetto and the local business and government Establishment." Oakland was a showcase of the War on Poverty.

It was not until a year after these stories had appeared that the *Los Angeles Times* printed a follow-up story revealing that the activities described in the book and in *The New Yorker* had in actuality never gotten beyond the planning stage. All told, only twenty jobs had been created. The program was bogged down in bureaucratic infighting. The authors of the case study, writing from the perspective of four years later, concluded that the effect of the project on "despair and disillusionment" among blacks was probably to have made matters worse.

The Oakland project was not chosen for study as an example of failure; the study began while hopes were still high. The Oakland experience was representative, not exceptional, and the gradual realization of this by those connected with the poverty programs was one source of their dampened hopes for the "hand, not a handout" approach. Few of them reacted by giving up; through the rest of the 1960s and well into the 1970s, it was argued that the community action programs were slowly learning from their failures and would do better next time. But if their proponents did not give up, neither did they speak so boldly about the imminent end of the dole.

The Training Programs

The failure of the training programs was a greater surprise still. These of all programs were expected to be a sure bet. They dealt with individuals, not institutions, and teaching a person who wants to learn is something we know how to do. But starting with the first evaluation reports in the mid-sixties and conitnuing to the present day, the results failed to show the hoped-for results, or anything close to them. The programs were seldom disasters; they simply failed to help many people get and hold jobs that they would not have gotten and held anyway.

As with the community development programs, the findings varied in detail but not in pattern. In one of the most recent and technically precise studies of the Manpower Development and Training Act (MDTA), the linchpin of Kennedy's original program and one that eventually grew to a multibillion dollar effort, the final conclusion is that male trainees increased their earnings between $150 and $500 *per year* immediately after training, "declining to perhaps half this figure after five years." For the females, the study found a continuing effect of $300 to $600 per year. A panel study of the effects of vocational training found a wage increase of 1.5 percent that could be attributed to the training. The early studies of Job Corps trainees found effects of under $200 per year, and these early findings have been repeated in subsequent work. Effects of this magnitude were far from the results that had been anticipated when the programs began.

Even as the program designers and evaluators debated what to do next and how to do it better, they could not avoid recognizing some discomfiting realities. It was quickly learned that people on welfare do not necessarily enroll in job training programs once they become available. Those who enroll do not necessarily stick it through to the end of the program. Those who stick it through do not necessarily get jobs. And, of those who find jobs, many quickly lose them. Sometimes they lose them because of their lack of seniority when layoffs occur. Sometimes they lose them because of discrimination. Sometimes they lose them because they fail to show up for work or don't work very hard when they do show up. And— more often than anyone wanted to admit—people just quit, disappearing from the evaluator's scorecard.

Unable to point to large numbers of trainees who were escaping from welfare dependency, the sponsors of the training programs turned to other grounds for their justification. They found two. First, a cost-effectiveness case could be wrenched even from small increments in income. If the average trainee's earnings increase even by a few hundred dollars, sooner or later the increase will add up to more than the cost of the training, and it was this type of calculation to which the sponsors were reduced. "The average effect [on earnings] for all enrollees is quite large," we find in one evaluation of Job Corps, then read on to the next sentence, where it is revealed that the "quite large" effect amounted to $3.30 per week. It was a statistically significant gain.

Second, the training programs lent themselves to upbeat anecdotes about individual success stories: John Jones, an ex-con who had never held a job in his life, became employed because of program X and is saving money to send his child to college. Such anecdotes, filmed for the evening news, were much more interesting than economic analyses. They also were useful in hearings before congressional appropriations committees. Tacit or explicit, a generalization went with the anecdote: John Jones's story is typical of what this project is accomplishing or will accomplish for a large number of people. That such success stories were extremely rare, and that depressingly often John Jones would be out of his job and back in jail a few months after his moment in the spotlight—these facts were not commonly publicized. The anecdotes made good copy. Thus the training programs continued to get a good press throughout the 1970s. They were the archetypal "hand, not a handout" programs, and they retained much of the intellectual and emotional appeal that had made them popular in the early 1960s. To some extent, whether they worked or not was irrelevant.

We have been scanning a record that has accumulated over the years since the first antipoverty projects in the early 1960s. But the loss of innocence came early. It soon became clear that large numbers of the American poor were not going to be moved off the welfare rolls by urban development schemes or by training programs.

At another time, that might have been the end of the attempt. Or, at another time, perhaps we would have done a better job of learning from our mistakes and have developed less ambitious, more effective programs. But the demands for urban renewal programs and jobs programs and training programs were growing, not diminishing, as the disappointing results began to come in. We were not in a position to back off, and, in fact, funding for such programs continued to grow for years. Neither, however, could we depend on such programs to solve the poverty problem.

The forces converged—not neatly, not at any one point that we can identify as the crucial shift. But the intellectual analysis of the nature of structural poverty had given a respectable rationale for accepting that it was not the fault of the poor that they were poor. It was a very small step from that premise to the conclusion that it is not the fault of the poor that they fail to pull themselves up when we offer them a helping hand. White moral confusion about the course of the civil rights movement in general and the riots in particular created powerful reasons to look for excuses. It was the system's fault. It was history's fault. Tom Wicker summed up the implications for policy toward the poor:

> Really compassionate and effective reforms to do something about poverty in America would have to recognize, first, that large numbers of the poor are always going to have to be helped. Whether for physical or mental reasons, because of environmental factors, or whatever, they cannot keep pace. . . . Thus the aim of getting everyone off welfare and into "participation in our affluent society" is unreal and a pipe dream. . . . [A] decent standard of living ought to be made available not just to an eligible few but to everyone, and without degrading restrictions and policelike investigations.

The column ran on the day before Christmas, 1967. It followed by only a few months an announcement from the White House. Joseph Califano, principal aide to Lyndon Johnson, had called reporters into his office to tell them that a government analysis had shown that only 50,000 persons, or *1 percent* of the 7,300,000 people on welfare, were capable of being given skills and training to make them self-sufficient. The repudiation of the dream—to end the dole once and for all—was complete.

Part 3

THE AFRICAN-AMERICAN STRUGGLE

No domestic development has been more important to postwar American society than the struggle for racial equality. During the three-quarters of a century after the end of Reconstruction, little occurred to improve the status of African-Americans. The vast majority lived in the South, were denied the right to vote, suffered the overt and covert consequences of segregation, experienced dire poverty, and were subject—at virtually every moment—to the threat of physical intimidation and violence. Through most of that time, African-Americans strove to build the best schools, churches, and homes they could for their children and themselves. Yet in an environment shaped and defined by white supremacy, the possibilities of substantial change were minimal.

The modern civil rights struggle received a major impetus from the New Deal and World War II. Hundreds of thousands of African-Americans left the rural South to take new jobs that were opening up in the North, the West, and urban areas of the South. The number of blacks in labor unions doubled, some economic improvements occurred, and in the North especially there was the opportunity for political participation. On the other hand, both the New Deal and the war witnessed callous indifference toward racial sensibilities, the perpetuation of Jim Crow, and vicious forms of racism. African-American soldiers were not allowed to fight beside white soldiers, black blood supplies were segregated from white blood supplies, and black soldiers in southern training camps were subject to the brutality of southern white racism. Together, the New Deal and World War II brought some progress, but in a context of continued and pervasive discrimination. The combination spurred black anger and frustration, helping to galvanize a new mood of protest.

In the face of evergrowing black militancy, liberal Democrats and Republicans began to pay more attention to the issue of civil rights. Through much of the postwar era the major theme of race relations in America was the gap between promises of change and the reality of continued oppression. When African-Americans protested, whites responded with words of concern and promises of change. There then would follow years of inaction until black protest initiated the cycle once more. By the 1960s, it had become evident that only when blacks forced white institutions into action could any substantive change be anticipated.

There are two general interpretations of the developments in race relations since World War II. One emphasizes the importance of external and impersonal factors such as migration, economic progress, a shift in government policies, and the emergence of an environment more conducive toward racial justice. The second interpretation focuses more on the collective demand of African-Americans themselves for change, stressing the critical role of black protest in bringing about whatever progress has taken place. The first interpretation accentuates the role of objective and external forces; the second highlights the role of individual and collective activism. Both sources of change are clearly important, and, in most cases, only when the two complement each other does significant progress occur.

The following selections provide the basis for an assessment of the black struggle during the postwar period. Harvard Sitkoff analyzes the consequences of some of the structural changes in the economy, social values and intellectual attitudes, the law and national politics. Vincent Harding offers both a personal and historical judgment of Martin Luther King, Jr.'s role in the movement. King himself shows the powerful impact of religion in the black struggle in his "Letter from a Birmingham Jail." Critical of Kings' goals and nonviolent tactics, Malcolm X presents a revolutionary strategy for black liberation "by any means necessary." That should be contrasted with Bayard Rustin's 1965 argument in favor of a black–white progressive alliance.

Given the continuity of so much racial discrimination and segregation in American life, why did a significant civil rights movement first emerge in the 1950s and 1960s and why did it then subside? How was this movement both similar to and different from previous American movements for equality? In what ways did the movement succeed, and in what ways did it fail? Why did the strategies that had worked in the South produce such limited results in northern ghettos? What were the profound effects upon postwar race relations, both positive and negative, of television? Which groups of African-Americans responded enthusiastically to appeals for racial nationalism and separatism, and which to the dream of an egalitarian color-blind society? Why? What goals might best be achieved in a liberal coalition and what ones call for an all-black movement? Answers to these questions are crucial to understanding how we have gotten to where we are, where we need to go, and how we might get there.

The Preconditions for Racial Change

Harvard Sitkoff

Although McCarthyism and the ideology of consensus did much to mute black discontent in the first postwar decade, the African-American quest for justice and equality steadily grew more determined and insistent following the 1954 landmark decision of the Supreme Court in Brown v. Board of Education of Topeka. *In short order, thousands of black families withstood harassment, economic intimidation, and violence to desegregate their local schools; the mass of blacks in Montgomery, Alabama, boycotted city buses for 381 days to topple Jim Crow; and, in 1960, black college students in Greensboro, North Carolina, "sat in" at a white lunch counter and set off a wave of similar challenges to the Southern caste system. But the ruling that "separate educational facilities are inherently unequal," according to Harvard Sitkoff, did not cause the modern black freedom struggle. This movement, he contends, stemmed from the basic socioeconomic changes in American society set in motion by the New Deal and, especially, World War II. These structural developments set the stage for African-American activism and made possible far-reaching racial changes in national policies and legislation.*

Of the interrelated causes of progress in race relations since the start of the Great Depression, none was more important than the changes in the American economy. No facet of the race problem was untouched by the elephantine growth of the Gross National Product, which rose from $206 billion in 1940 to $500 billion in

Excerpted and revised from Harvard Sitkoff, "Race Relations: Progress and Prospects," in James T. Patterson, ed. *Paths to the Present* (Minneapolis: Burgess Publishing Co., 1975). Reprinted by permission of the author.

1960, and then in the 1960s increased by an additional 60 percent. By 1970, the economy topped the trillion dollar mark. This spectacular rate of economic growth produced some 25 million new jobs in the quarter of a century after World War II and raised real wage earnings by at least 50 percent. It made possible the increasing income of blacks; their entry into industries and labor unions previously closed to them; gains for blacks in occupational status; and created a shortage of workers that necessitated a slackening of restrictive promotion policies and the introduction of scores of government and private industry special job training programs for Afro-Americans. It also meant that the economic progress of blacks did not have to come at the expense of whites, thus undermining the most powerful source of white resistance to the advancement of blacks.

The effect of economic changes on race relations was particularly marked in the South. The rapid industrialization of the South since 1940 ended the dominance of the cotton culture. With its demise went the need for a vast underclass of unskilled, subjugated laborers. Power shifted from rural areas to the cities, and from tradition-oriented landed families to the new officers and professional workers in absentee-owned corporations. The latter had neither the historical allegiances nor the nonrational attachment to racial mores to risk economic growth for the sake of tradition. The old system of race relations had no place in the new economic order. Time and again in the 1950s and 1960s, the industrial and business elite took the lead in accommodating the South to the changes sought by the civil rights movement.

The existence of an "affluent society" boosted the fortunes of the civil rights movement itself in countless ways. Most obviously, it enabled millions of dollars in contributions from wealthy liberals and philanthropic organizations to pour into the coffers of the NAACP, Urban League, Southern Christian Leadership Conference, and countless other civil rights groups. Without those funds it is difficult to comprehend how the movement could have accomplished those tasks so essential to its success: legislative lobbying and court litigation; nationwide speaking tours and the daily mailings of press releases all over the country; the organization of mass marches, demonstrations, and rallies; constant, rapid communication and traveling over long distances; and the convocation of innumerable public conferences and private strategy sessions.

Prosperity also increased the leisure time of many Americans and enabled them to react immediately to the changing times. The sons and daughters of the newly affluent increasingly went to college. By 1970, five times as many students were in college as in 1940. What they learned helped lead to pronounced changes in white attitudes toward racial discrimination and segregation. Other whites learned from the TV sets in their homes. By the time Lyndon Johnson signed the Voting Rights Act of 1965, some 95 percent of all American families owned at least one television. The race problem entered their living rooms. Tens of millions nightly watched the drama of the Negro Revolution. The growing majority of Americans favoring racial equality and justice had those sentiments reinforced by TV shots of snarling police dogs attacking black demonstrators, rowdy white hoods molesting young blacks patiently waiting to be served at a lunch counter, and hate-filled white faces in a frenzy because of the effrontery of little black children entering a previously all-white school.

Blacks viewed the same scenes on their TV sets, and the rage these scenes engendered helped transform isolated battles into a national campaign. Concurrently, the conspicuous display of white affluence on TV vividly awakened blacks to a new sense of their relative deprivation. That, too, aroused black anger. And now something could be done about it. The growing black middle and working classes put their money and bodies on the line. In addition, because the consumer economy depended on consumer purchasing, black demands had to be taken seriously. By 1970, black buying power topped $25 billion, a large enough sum to make the threat of boycotts an effective weapon for social change. Afro-American economic advances also made blacks less patient in demanding alterations in their social status. They desired all the decencies and dignity they believed their full paycheck promised. Lastly, nationwide prosperity contributed to more blacks entering college, which stimulated higher expectations and a heightened confidence that American society need not be static.

Most importantly, changes in the economy radically affected black migration. Cotton mechanization pushed blacks off the farms, and the lure of jobs pulled them to the cities. In 1930, three-quarters of the Afro-Americans lived in or near the rural black belt. By 1973, over half the blacks lived outside the South, and nationally, nearly 80 percent resided in urban areas. Indeed, in the two decades prior to 1970, the black population in metropolitan areas rose by more than seven million—a number greater than the total immigration by any single nationality group in American history. Such a mass migration, in conjunction with prosperity, fundamentally altered the whole configuration of the race problem. First, the issue of race became national in scope. No longer did it affect only one region, and no longer could it be left in the hands of Southern whites. Second, it modified the objective conditions of life for blacks and changed their perception of what was right and how to get it. For the first time in American history the great mass of blacks were freed from the confines of a rigid caste structure. Now subject to new formative experiences, blacks developed new norms and beliefs. In the relative anonymity and freedom of the North and the big city, aggression could be turned against one's oppressor rather than against one's self; more educational and employment opportunities could be secured; and political power could be mobilized. Similarly, as expectations of racial equality increased with the size of black migration from the rural South, so the religious faith that had for so long sustained AfroAmericans working on plantations declined. The promise of a better world in the next one could not suffice. The urban black would not wait for his rewards until the afterlife.

Because blacks could vote in the North, they stopped believing they would have to wait. Enfranchisement promised all in this life that religion did in the next. The heavenly city, to put it mildly, was not achieved; but vital legislative and legal accomplishments did flow from the growing black vote. Without the presence of black political power in the North, the demonstrations in the South would not have led to the civil rights laws and presidential actions necessary to realize the objectives of those protesting against Jim Crow in Montgomery, Greensboro, Birmingham, Jackson, and Selma. Although the claim of black publicists that the concentration of Northern black votes in the industrial cities made the AfroAmerican electorate a "balance of power" in national politics was never wholly accepted by either major party, the desire of every president from Franklin Roosevelt to Lyndon Johnson to win and hold the black vote became a factor in determining public policy. And as the Democratic party became less dependent upon Southern electoral votes, and less able to garner them, it had to champion civil rights more in order to win the populous states of the North and Midwest where blacks were increasingly becoming an indispensable component of the liberal coalition.

The prominence of the United States as a world power further pushed politicians into making race relations a matter of national concern. During World War II millions of Americans became aware for the first time of the danger of racism to national security. The costs of racism went even higher during the Cold War. The Soviet Union continuously undercut American appeals to the nations of Africa and Asia by publicizing American ill-treatment of blacks. As the competition between the United States and international Communism intensified, foreign-policy makers came to recognize racism as the American's own worst enemy. President Harry Truman justified his asking Congress for civil rights legislation squarely on the world-wide implications of American race relations. Rarely in the next twenty years did a plea for civil rights before the Supreme Court, on the floor of Congress, and emanating from the White House, fail to emphasize that point. In short, fear forced the nation to hasten the redefining of the black status. The more involved in world affairs the United States became, the more imperative grew the task of setting its racial affairs in order.

The rapid growth of nationalistic independence movements among the world's colored peoples had special significance for Afro-Americans. In 1960 alone, sixteen African nations emerged from under white colonial rule. Each proclamation of independence in part shamed blacks in the United States to intensify their struggle for equality and justice, and in part caused a surge of racial pride in Afro-Americans, an affirmation of blackness. The experience of African independence proved the feasibility of change and the vulnerability of white supremacy, while at the same time aiding Afro-Americans to see themselves as members of a world majority rather than as just a hopelessly outnumbered American minority.

The decline in intellectual respectability of ideas used to justify segregation and discrimination similarly provided Afro-Americans with new weapons and shields. The excesses of Nazism and the decline of Western imperialism combined with internal developments in the academic disciplines of anthropology, biology, history, psychology, and sociology to discredit notions of inherent racial differences or predispositions. First in the 1930s, then with accelerating rapidity during World War II and every year thereafter, books and essays attacking racial injustice and inequality rolled off the presses. As early as 1944, Gunnar Myrdal in his monumental *An American Dilemma* termed the pronounced change in scholarship about race "the most important of all social trends in the field of interracial relations." This conclusion overstated the power of the word, but undoubtedly the mountain of new data, theory, and exposition at least helped to erode the pseudo-scientific rationalizations once popularly accepted as the basis for white supremacy.

In such an atmosphere, young blacks could mature without "the mark of oppression." Blacks could safely abandon the "nigger" role. To the extent that textbooks, sermons, declarations by governmental officials, advertising, and movies and TV affirmed the need to transform relationships between the races and to support black demands for full citizenship, blacks could confidently and openly rebel against the inequities they viewed as the sources of their oppression. They could publicly express the rage their parents had been forced to internalize; they could battle for what they deemed their birthright rather than wage war against themselves. Thus, in conjunction with the migration to cities, these new cultural processes helped to produce the "New Negro" hailed by essayists ever since the Montgomery bus boycott in 1956 inaugurated a more aggressive stage in the Afro-American's quest for equality.

In sum, changes in the American economy after 1940 set in motion a host of developments which made possible a transformation in race relations. The increasing income and number of jobs available to blacks and whites, and black migration and social mobility, coalesced with converging trends in politics, foreign affairs, and the mass media to endow those intent on improving race relations with both the resources and consciousness necessary to challenge the status quo. Objective conditions that had little to do with race in a primary sense thus created a context in which organizations and leaders could press successfully for racial changes. This is not to suggest that individuals do not matter in history or that the civil rights movement did not make an indispensable contribution to progress in race relations. It is, however, to emphasize the preconditions for such an endeavor to prevail. Desire and will are not enough. Significant and long-lasting alterations in society flow neither from the barrel of a gun nor from individual conversions. Mass marches, demonstrations, and rhetoric alone cannot modify entrenched behavior and values. Fundamental social change is accomplished only when individuals seize the moment to mobilize the latent power inherent in an institutional structure in flux.

Beginning in the 1930s, blacks, no longer facing a monolithic white power structure solidly arrayed against them, demanded with numbers and a unity that had never existed before the total elimination of racial inequality in American life. For three decades, the tactics and goals of the movement steadily grew more militant as the organization, protests, and power of blacks jumped exponentially. Each small triumph held out the promise of a greater one, heightening expectations and causing blacks to become ever more anxious about the pace of progress.

The first stage centered on securing the enforcement of the Fourteenth and Fifteenth Amendments. Supported mainly by white liberals and upper-middle-class blacks, the civil rights movement in the 1930s and 1940s relied on publicity, agitation, litigation in the courts, and lobbying in the halls of political power to gain the full inclusion of blacks in American life. Advances came in the legal and economic status of blacks, and in the minor social, political, and cultural concessions afforded Afro-Americans in the North, but the all-oppressive system of Jim Crow in the South remained virtually intact.

First in the court system, then in executive actions, and finally in Congress, this unceasing and mounting pressure from the civil rights movement prodded the government consistently in the direction of *real* racial equality. In the 1930s, the black movement failed to secure its two major legislative goals—anti-poll tax and anti-lynching laws—but it did manage to get Franklin D. Roosevelt and other members of his official family to speak on behalf of racial justice, to increase the numbers of blacks in government, to establish a Civil Rights Section in the Justice Department, and to ensure blacks a share of the relief and recovery assistance.

The gains during the New Deal, however, functioned primarily as a prelude to the take-off of the civil rights movement during World War II. The ideological character of the war and the government's need for the loyalty and manpower of all Americans stimulated blacks to expect a better deal from the government; this led to a militancy never before seen in black communities. Membership in the NAACP multiplied nearly ten times; the Congress of Racial Equality, organized in 1942, experimented with various forms of nonviolent direct action confrontations to challenge segregation; and A. Philip Randolph attempted to build his March-on-Washington Committee into an all-black mass protest movement. In 1941, his threat of a march on Washington, combined with the growth of the black vote and the exigencies of a foreign threat to American security, forced Roosevelt to issue Executive Order 8802 (the first such order dealing with race since Reconstruction), establishing the first President's Committee on Fair Employment Practices (FEPC). And, with increasing firmness, liberal politicians pressed for civil rights legislation and emphasized that the practices of white supremacy brought into disrepute America's stated war aims. Minimal gains to be sure, but the expectations they aroused set the stage for the greater advances in the postwar period. By 1945, Afro-Americans had benefited enough from the expansion in jobs and income, service in the armed forces and the massive migration to Northern cities to know better what they now wanted; and they had developed enough political influence, white alliances, and organizational skills to know how to go about getting their civil rights.

Equally vital, the Supreme Court began to dismantle the separate-but-equal doctrine in 1938. That year, the high court ruled that Missouri could not exclude a Negro from its state university law school when its only alternative was a scholarship to an out-of-state institution. Other Supreme Court decisions prior to World War II whittled away at discrimination in interstate travel, in employment, in judicial and police practices, and in the exclusion of blacks from jury service. During the war, the Court outlawed the white primary, holding that the nominating process of a political party constituted "state action." In other decisions handed down during the Truman presidency, the Supreme Court moved vigorously against all forms of segregation in interstate commerce, decided that states and the federal government cannot enforce restrictive racial covenants on housing, and so emphasized the importance of "intangible factors" in quality education that the demise of legally segregated schooling for students at all levels became a near certainty.

Meanwhile, the Truman administration emerged as an ally of the cause of civil rights. Responding to the growth of the black vote, the need to blunt the Soviet Union's exploitation of the race issue, and the firmly organized campaign for the advancement of blacks,

Harry Truman acted where Roosevelt had feared to. In late 1946, the President appointed a Committee on Civil Rights to recommend specific measures to safeguard the civil rights of minorities. This was the first such committee in American history, and its 1947 report, *To Secure These Rights,* eloquently pointed out all the inequities of life in Jim Crow America and spelled out the moral, economic, and international reasons for government action. It called for the end of segregation and discrimination in public education, employment, housing, the armed forces, public accommodations, and interstate transportation. Other commissions appointed by Truman stressed the need for racial equality in the armed services and the field of education. Early in 1948, Truman sent the first presidential message on civil rights to Congress. Congress failed to pass any of the measures he proposed, but Truman later issued executive orders ending segregation in the military and barring discrimination in federal employment and in work done under government contract. In addition, his Justice Department prepared *amicus curiae* briefs to gain favorable court decisions in civil rights cases, and Truman's rhetoric in behalf of racial justice helped legitimize goals of the civil rights movement. However small the meaningful accomplishment remained, the identification of the Supreme Court and the Presidency with the cause of racial equality further aroused the expectations of blacks that they would soon share in the American Dream.

No single event did more to quicken black hopes than the coup de grâce to segregated education delivered by a unanimous Supreme Court on May 17, 1954. The *Brown* ruling that separate educational facilities "are inherently unequal" struck at the very heart of white supremacy in the South. A year later, !he Court called for compliance "with all deliberate speed," mandating the lower federal courts to require from local school boards "a prompt and reasonable start toward full compliance." The end of legally mandated segregation in education started a chain reaction which led the Supreme court ever further down the road toward the total elimination of all racial distinctions in the law. For all practical purposes, the legal quest for equality had succeeded: the emphasis on legalism had accomplished its goals. Constitutionally, blacks had become first-class citizens.

But in the decade after the *Brown* decision, the promise of change far outran the reality of it. While individual blacks of talent desegregated most professions, the recessions of the Fifties caused black unemployment to soar and the gap between black and white family income to widen. And despite the rulings of the Supreme Court and the noble gestures and speeches of politicians, massive resistance to desegregation throughout the South proved the rule. This was the context for the second stage of the civil rights movement. When the nation's attempt to forestall integration and racial equality collided with both the Afro-Americans' leaping expectations and their dissatisfaction with the speed of change, blacks took to the streets in a wave of nonviolent, direct-action protests against every aspect of racism still humiliating them.

So Much History, So Much Future: Martin Luther King, Jr. and the Second Coming of America

Vincent Harding

Catapulted into national prominence by the Montgomery bus boycott of 1955–56, Martin Luther King, Jr., became the foremost symbol and spokesman for the direct action phase of the civil rights struggle that produced the Civil Rights Act of 1964 and the Voter Registration Act of 1965. With extraordinary eloquence and charisma, King communicated the essence of the black demand for freedom to white America, even as he inspired and mobilized African-Americans to join that struggle. King's articulation of nonviolence as a philosophical principle, and his reliance on the Christian doctrine of unconditional love as the starting point for his leadership, helped to make acceptable to millions of white Americans a program of change that, by previous standards of action, seemed revolutionary. At the same time, King was always in danger of not proceeding far enough or fast enough to satisfy his African-American supporters.

In this article, Vincent Harding offers a personal, as well as historical, assessment of King's journey as he sought both to respond to those who prodded him to take a more radical path, and to address the realities of white political power. With sensitivity and passion, Harding helps us to gain an inner sense of King's own struggle, and a greater awareness of what King's life meant to the values and direction of American society.

I met Martin King in 1958, twenty years ago this month, and for the ten years of his life that we knew each other he was for me, to me, a brother, comrade, neighbor, and friend. From 1961 to the time of his death he regularly encouraged me to carry out the role I had chosen for myself as one who was both an engaged participant in the movement, and at the same time a committed historian and critical analyst of its development, as one who worked at the vortex of the struggle and yet remained outside of the official structures of the main civil rights organizations. . . . I come then as Martin's friend, his brother, as one who is crazy enough still to find myself talking to him on occasion, sometimes shouting his name—along with Malcolm's, along with Fannie Lou's, along with Clarence Jordan's and Tom Merton's and Ruby Doris Smith's. (Many of these names you don't know, and if you are to get an education at this university—or any other—you must demand to know them.)

The second thing I need to indicate is probably already implicit in my first comment. In 1961, three years after first having met King, I came south from Chicago with Rosemarie Harding, my wife and comrade, to work full-time in the freedom struggle. I do not hesitate to proclaim that I am biased towards that struggle and its participants. Indeed, at the same time I seek to understand and record its past, I am totally committed to work actively towards the creation of its next, still unclear stages of development. And I expect always to maintain that partisan bias in favor of a new, more humane American society, in favor of freedom for all the men, women, and children who seek new beginnings, new opportunities to break the shackles of the many external and internal oppressive realities that still bind so many of us down to lives that are less than our best, most human selves. . . . Within that context, it is clear that we shall understand the role Martin King played in the movement only as we understand that he was at once created by the movement and a creator of some of its major thrusts. He made much history, but in doing so he was aided, limited, and defined by the struggle that was mounting all around him, making him.

This dialectic, the dynamic, ecstatic, often agonized interplay between Martin and the movement may be illustrated in many ways, at many points, but we shall choose five developments to illustrate briefly the relationship between the man and the movement and to comment on its nature and its strengths and weaknesses. Those reference points are Montgomery, Alabama, in 1955-1956; Albany,

Georgia, in 1961–1962; Birmingham, Alabama, and Washington, D.C., in 1963; Mississippi and Chicago in 1966, and the fateful, desperate road from Riverside Church, New York, on April 4, 1967, to Memphis, Tennessee, on April 4, 1968.

Let us begin at Montgomery, where black folks took the U.S. Supreme Court more seriously than the court took itself, firmly grasped the *Brown* decision, intuitively recognized its many broader implications, and began immediately to press it far beyond the limited arena of the segregated school systems. Even before he arrived in Montgomery as the new pastor of the prestigious, black middle-class dominated Dexter Avenue Baptist Church, Martin King had entered the dialectic. He was a child of one of those comfortable Atlanta black bourgeoisie, church-dominating families; but nothing could insulate him against the reality of his people's existence in the South, in America. Nothing could blind him to the fact that ever since World War II a new phase of our freedom struggle had been mounted against rugged, often savage opposition, and he knew that what we were doing, largely through the courts at first, and through early, dangerous attempts at voter registration, was somehow tied to the anti-colonial struggles being waged across the world.

Then, just a bit more than a year after he had been in Montgomery, not long after he had completed his doctoral dissertation for Boston University, while thoughts of a relatively easy life as part-pastor and part-academic danced in his head, a strong, gentle woman named Rosa Parks refused to do the usual, agonized black dance on a segregated Montgomery bus. As a result, she was arrested, and a new time was opened in the struggle . . . the new time was building on the efforts and the people of the time before, and King was initially pressed into the role by a small group of genuine local leaders who had proven themselves in the past, and in a real sense he was later anointed by the larger masses of the Montgomery black people to be the public representative of their struggle. Even then no one fully realized that the new time had really begun to come, that it was possible now to make more history than they had ever made before in Montgomery, Alabama.

Before examining that particular [moment], it will probably be helpful to remind ourselves that at the outset of the Montgomery struggle the black folk of the city established their boycott of the segregated buses for very simple goals. They did not initially demand an end to bus segregation. Indeed, as late as April 1956, four months after the beginning of the boycott, King was articulating three objectives which assured continued segregation. The three goals were:

1. More courteous treatment of black passengers.
2. Seating on a first-come, first-served basis, but with blacks continuing the current practice of filling up from the rear of the bus forward, while whites filled in from the front towards the back.
3. Hiring of black bus drivers on predominantly black lines.

That was all. That was all they asked at first, and they did not march, sit-in, or fill up the jails—they just refused to ride the buses. That was all. It seems so simple now, but it was a great step then, and it was the local context in which King began.

In the weekly mass meetings that developed as a series of increasingly politicized, religious revival sessions, King set out to put forward his evolving philosophy of Christian nonviolence. At first, it was defined primarily as a refusal to react violently to the violence of whites, as a willingness to return love for hatred, and a conviction that their action was not only constitutional but within the will of God—therefore also within the onward, righteous flow of history. So, at the first mass meeting on December 5, 1955, in his exhortation to the fearful, courageous, wondering, determined people, King said, "We are not wrong in what we are doing. If we are wrong, the Supreme Court of this nation is wrong. If we are wrong, the Constitution of the United States is wrong. If we are wrong, God Almighty is wrong. If we are wrong, Jesus of Nazareth was merely a Utopian dreamer who never came down to earth." Then he closed with one of his typically rousing and inspiring perorations: "When the history books are written in the future, somebody will have to say, 'There lived a race of people, a black people, fleecy locks and black complexion, but a people who had the marvelous courage to stand up for their rights and thereby they injected a new meaning into the being of history and of civilization.' And we are going to do that."

From that auspicious beginning, one of King's major roles was interpreter, inspirer, the prophet who saw the significance, the larger meaning of what was happening in the immediate movement. He learned that role, grew into it, made important errors in it, but it was his. . . .

So the young pastor, moving into his twenty-seventh year, had found a black community ready to take certain initial risks on behalf of a limited vision of its rights and a new determination to establish its dignity. Beginning where they were, he took the people's courage and lifted it to the highest possible level, called upon them to see themselves as far more than black men and women of Montgomery Alabama, striving for decent treatment on a bus. Instead he pressed them forward, urging them to claim their roles as actors in a great cosmic drama, one in which they were at once in unity with the best teachings of American democracy, with the winds of universal social change, and at the same time walking faithfully within the unchanging will of. . . . So, by the time the boycott had successfully ended in December 1956, by the time blacks were free to sit wherever they chose on the city buses, the possibility of an entire community of black men and women in the South taking large risks on the basis of conscience, justice, and a belief in the will of God had begun to be established. Those men and women and children of Montgomery, with their leader-spokesman, had made it possible for others to go beyond them and make even more history, create an even greater future.

Yet, once the Montgomery bus boycott had ended, King was without the base of direct mass action that he needed for the fullest, continuing development of his own role. . . . On the last day of November 1959, Martin King announced his decision to move to Atlanta by February 1, 1960. Then he said, "The time has come for a bold, broad advance of the Southern campaign for equality . . . a full scale assault will be made upon discrimination and segregation in all forms. We must train our youth and adult leaders in the techniques of social change through nonviolent resistance. We must employ new methods of struggle involving the masses of the people."

Clearly, King was speaking to himself, to the moving black community, and to the white and nonwhite world all around. Then, only two months after the announcement, on the very day of the planned move, almost as if by orchestrated agreement, an explosive response to King's vision came from the very "youth" he had hoped to train. They were not waiting for that training, and when the student sit-in movement erupted, beginning in February 1960, in Greensboro, North Carolina, it drove immediately towards the center of King's life, transforming it in ways that he had likely not quite anticipated. That was, of course, appropriate. For these neatly dressed, amazingly disciplined black young men and women, who with a few white allies began the new phase of the movement, were not only the products of the on-going school desegregation struggles of the South, they were really the children of Martin Luther King. In spite of many mixed feelings about him, they saw him as hero and model. But as is so often the case in such situations, they also went beyond him, creating what he could not create on his own, establishing the basis for the South-wide movement of massive, direct nonviolent confrontation with the segregated public facilities of the section which King had just announced. . . . They truly believed that through the power of their organized, disciplined, confrontative, nonviolent struggle, they were to be the builders of "the beloved community" in America, the harbingers of the new society Martin King had so continually evoked. Black and white together, they believed and they struggled, taking into their own flesh and spirit many of the hardest blows of white hatred and fear. . . .

But because we often create more history than we realize, because we often give birth to children that we do not understand and cannot control, it was not until the development of the Albany movement that Martin King was really able to catch up with the newest, rapid, explosive expansion of his people's struggle. What happened in this southwestern Georgia community from the fall of 1961 through the summer of 1962 was critical to the development of his role in the movement. Having moved from Montgomery to Atlanta in 1959, having developed no similar nonviolent mass action base in Atlanta, but sensing the new moment of history and its needs, King now became a kind of roving leader, responding to calls from the local movements that were springing up in hundreds of communities all over the South. . . . When in December 1961, the Albany movement invited King to come and help them, new patterns in his role began to be clear.

One of his major functions was admittedly to help inspire the local populace to greater efforts, for by now King had begun to be idolized by large sections of the black community, a development fraught with great pitfalls, of course, both for the idol and his idolizers. Nevertheless, King was their national leader, the acknowledged symbol of their struggle. And he was a great exhorter in every sense of the word. In addition, his presence was now considered a guarantee of national and even international media attention. Moreover, because Martin had begun since Montgomery to establish certain ambivalent contacts and significant influence with "liberal" white forces, especially in the religious, educational, and labor union communities, he began to be seen as the one person who could mobilize the "people of good will" (as he called them) from across the nation to come help in the struggle of local southern communities. Even more important in the minds of some persons was the fact that King seemed to have access to the Kennedy White House and its great potential power. Of course, it also came to be understood that Martin would lead marches and go to jail, and that his own organization, SCLC, with its rapidly growing staff, would provide experienced aid to those who might be new in the ways of nonviolent struggle. Albany actually was the first real testing ground for this developing role of King, the visiting leader/symbol, and SCLC, the black church-based organization, in the new phase of the southern movement.

In many ways, as one might have expected, the first experiment was an ambivalent one. In Albany, King was able with the local movement leaders to test what was essentially a new strategy, one forced upon them by the powerful thrust of the freedom movement. Rather than focusing on a single issue, such as bus desegregation, they decided to make multiple demands for changes toward racial and economic justice in their city. The internal force of the people's rush towards justice, their sense that the new time was indeed upon them, their growing understanding of the wider significance of their movement and the stubborn recalcitrance and evasiveness of the white leadership—all these pushed the black freedom fighters out of the churches, out of the train and bus stations, out of the dime stores, out into the streets.

In this motion, King was a crucial element, constantly in dynamic interaction with the force of its thrust. Through his words, his actions, and the very fact of his presence, Martin served as a great inspiration to the movement of the local black community, especially in the early weeks of their activity. Hundreds of persons for the first time in southern freedom movement history volunteered for acts of direct action civil disobedience right out on the streets—

which meant certain jailing in some of the most notorious and dangerous jails of Georgia. Out from the church mass meetings they marched, singing "We Shall Overcome," "Ain't Gonna Let Nobody Turn Me 'Round," and "This Little Light of Mine." They went to jail, singing, "I'm gonna let it shine." They sang and prayed in jail, "Paul and Silas locked in jail had nobody to go their bail, keep your eye on the prize, hold on." In the dirty jails where the memories of blood from older times were still present, they were threatened for singing and praying, and they kept on singing and praying. . . ."Over my head I see freedom in the air. There must be a God somewhere." Indeed out of the Albany jails came one of the most dynamic cultural forces of the southern movement, the SNCC freedom singers, carrying the songs of the movement across the nation and over the world, songs which were bought at a great price "Woke up this morning with my mind stayed on Freedom." . . .

But there were major problems as well. The Albany movement had not really jelled as an organization before they called on King. Thus, there were both understandable confusions in its goals and in his role. On the one hand, their sense of the need for nonviolent struggle was constantly being strained by the rush of their own motion and the violence they were meeting. On the other hand there was a temptation to see King, to encourage him to see himself as a savior—too often a peripatetic savior, one who had to leave town at various points to keep speaking and fund-raising engagements elsewhere. This created real difficulties, especially for a leader who was not essentially a day-to-day strategist in the first place. In addition, there were understandable hard feelings among the SNCC forces—who were often brilliant, brave, and sometimes foolhardy strategists. These young people were often resentful when, after their initial, lonely, and often dangerous weeks of local organizing, Martin King would arrive on the scene, trailing a coterie of supporters and a crowd of media persons behind him, and the hard, dangerous spade-work of these young freedom soldiers would tend largely to be forgotten in the aura of *Martin Luther King*. Moreover, King's leadership style, which was also SCLC's style, derived largely from the semiautocratic world of the black Baptist church, and it simply grated against the spirits of the young people from SNCC. For they were working out their own forms of sometimes anarchistic-appearing participatory democracy. . . .

Nevertheless, two final words must be spoken about Albany. First it is to King's credit that he recognized many of the problems that were built into his own new role and tried to deal with some of them, but the role of a roving leader in the midst of a mass movement spread over such a massive area, often under the glare of television cameras, was fraught with deep and intrinsic difficulties. These were especially dangerous when added to the tendency to sycophancy and adulation that was building in some of the people around him, and the tendency to psychic murder that was built into the media of mass television. Second, in spite of the mistakes of King, SCLC, SNCC, the NAACP CORE, and the Albany movement itself, Albany and its black and white people were changed and have been changed in profound, significant ways. There is no way that the black community will ever be pushed back to 1961; there is no way that white Albany will ever be the same again. But the question blacks now ask, as we must all ask, as Martin asked, is, where do we go from here?

In 1963, for King and SCLC, the geographic answer to that question was Birmingham, Alabama. But as we all knew, Birmingham, like Mississippi, was much more than a physical place. It had a bloody reputation, it was a frightening name. It was pronounced by some as "Bombingham" because of the violence whites had consistently brought against any black movements towards justice and equal rights there. And every black person in this country likely knew someone who had been run out of, beaten or killed in Birmingham, Alabama. But the Reverend Fred Shuttlesworth had not been run out, though he had been beaten more than once and almost killed, at one point with national television cameras running. It was largely at Shuttlesworth's insistence that King and SCLC came to Birmingham in the spring of 1963. . . .

By the time that King himself began to lead demonstrations—a week after they began—he was faced with the reality that a very volatile situation was at hand, the most difficult he had ever faced. Birmingham was "bigger and badder" than either Albany or Montgomery, and whites were not the only bad dudes in that town. So certain powerful contradictions began to surface. On the one hand, the "Commandments" handed out to demonstrators began, "Meditate daily on the teachings and life of Jesus," and included such additional admonitions as "walk and talk in the manner of love for God is love. . . . Refrain from violence of fist, tongue or heart."

But at the same time, Jim Bevel and other staff members were confiscating a good number of knives and other weapons from some of the brothers who had come prepared for other ways of walking and talking. Obviously, then, the tensions were there, felt more sharply, drawn more clearly than ever before. . . .

These young people of Birmingham and others like them had a powerful effect on Martin King, on the shaping of his role, on the history he was making. He saw the great forces of energy and power, black power, stored up within them, and he knew where it could lead. He realized that now they were at least potentially the children of Malcolm X as well, and he was not unmoved by that recognition. He saw them take on the dogs and the firehoses with courageous anger, and he knew that anger was not easily controlled.

So his rationale for nonviolence began to expand to account for such young men and women in Birmingham and everywhere, began to account for Malcolm and the Nation of Islam and other, even more radical and revolutionary voices abroad in the land. Now it was not simply a weapon of love. As he explained it to an increasingly perplexed white world, nonviolence was also a defense against black retaliatory violence. More explicitly than ever before, King was forced to face the stormy potential of the black young people around him, and what they meant for his own sense of the future. When forcibly given a time to rest and think in the Birmingham jail, these children, spawned out of his own body, were clearly on his mind as he wrote his famous letter. Speaking of the American blacks he said,

Consciously and unconsciously, [the Negro] has been swept in by what the Germans call the Zeitgeist, and with his black brothers of Africa, and his brown and yellow brothers of Asia, South America, and the Caribbean, he is moving with a sense of cosmic urgency toward the promised land of racial justice. Recognizing this vital urge that has engulfed the Negro community, one should readily understand public demonstrations. The Negro has many pent-up resentments and latent frustrations. He has to get them out. So let him march some times; let him have his prayer pilgrimages to the city hall; understand why he must have sit-ins and freedom rides. If his repressed emotions do not come out in these nonviolent ways, they will come out in ominous expressions of violence. This is not a threat; it is a fact of history.

From that point onward, King increasingly found himself caught between the rising rage, nationalistic fervor, and questioning of nonviolence in the black community, and the fear of the white community that would seek to hold down all those black energies, to break them up, at worst to destroy them. So while Birmingham represented the largest number of blacks ever engaged in massive direct civil disobedient action up to then, and while the agreement worked out with the city was considered a victory of sorts, King's role was clearly undergoing transition again. Forces were now at work that had long been kept in check; . . .

In a sense, Montgomery was a long, long time ago. Seen from the late spring of 1963, the bus boycott was now a time of quiet, gentle protest compared with the massive action sweeping across the South, challenging the old regime, eliciting some of its most brutal responses. This new massive direction-action pressed King more fully into another role—that of chief movement emissary to the White House. John Kennedy, who had said in January 1963, that civil rights action was not among his highest priorities, was forced to change his priorities by the whirlwind of the black movement. So White House conferences with King and others, by phone and in person, became almost *de rigueur*. But some persons soon learned— King later than some, earlier than others—that conferences with presidents may do more to divert the force of a movement than to fuel and inspire it, especially if that is one of the intentions of the president. . . . As a result, King became, partly unwarily, a tool for defusing a powerful current in a critical struggle for the future of the movement.

This is what I mean: for more than two years before Birmingham, Martin and others had talked about the development of a trained, disciplined nonviolent army that would become the spearhead for a national movement of powerful, disruptive nonviolent civil disobedience, from coast to coast. . . .

During the Birmingham demonstrations the group pressing for the development of such a nonviolent army proposed that its first action be aimed at Washington, D.C., to shut down the activities of the city until adequate civil rights legislation of many kinds was passed. Without going into the details of the transformation, it is enough to say that King allowed himself to be convinced by other more moderate black and white leaders of the civil rights coalition that such a move would be exceedingly unwise. They were convinced and were probably right that it would lose friends and anger many "neutrals" in the white community. It would certainly lose the president's supposed support for civil rights legislation specifically and racial justice generally. So, instead of a disciplined, nonviolent force—largely from the southern testing grounds—descending on Washington for an extended campaign of disruptive civil disobedience, the summer of 1963 produced the one-day, unthreatening March on Washington for Jobs and Freedom. As a result, King passed up an opportunity possibly to transform his role in the struggle, to transform the struggle itself, losing perhaps more than we can ever know. And it was not until the fiery, bloody summers of 1964-1967 had passed that he was eventually forced by the movement of his people and the larger forces of history back to the idea of an organized, national nonviolent revolutionary force. By then it would be too late-at least for that time. . . .

The issues which had been simmering, rolling the waters of the movement for a long time—sometimes pressed audaciously to the surface in the recent speeches of Adam Clayton Powell, Jr., the issues of power, the issues of racial pride, solidarity, and nationalism that had poured out anew in the North after the assassination of Malcolm X, El Hajj Malik El Shabazz; the issue of black control over the organizations of our struggle; the issue of the role of whites in the struggle; the issue of the need for black "liberation" as opposed to "integration," raised to a new level by the introduction of Frantz Fanon's *Wretched of the Earth* into the reading experience of many of the SNCC members; the concomitant rising discussion of black "revolution" as opposed to finding a place in the American status quo; the issue of the relationship between the black middle class and the masses of poor blacks, South and North; the issue of the need for the development of black leadership; the issue of sexual relations between white women and black men—all these exciting, frightening, dangerously explosive matters and many more leaped out in a compressed code from the lips of Willie Ricks of SNCC and they found their national identity in Stokely Carmichael, twenty-four-year-old veteran of the freedom rides, of the Black Panther party in Lowndes County. Alabama, of Greenwood, Mississippi.

(Always remember that Stokely at his best was no dilettante. But, like the rest of us, he was not always at his best.) *Black Power! Black Power!* Black Power had officially begun its time: June 1966, on the road from Memphis to Jackson, cities of our music and our martyrs. . . .

At many points in the fall and winter of 1966-1967, after another summer of urban rebellions, as the fierce debate over Black Power raged, as he recognized the essential failure of his heroic/quixotic foray into Chicago, as the war in Vietnam continued to expand, as white anger mounted and black criticism of his positions grew more strident, King seemed at times like a great, courageous, but deeply perplexed captain, trying desperately to control a ship that was being rocked by mutinies from within and raging storms from without.

Yet, the truth of that perilous time was even more difficult. For by then there was no longer any one entity—even symbolically speaking—which could be called the Black Freedom movement and which Martin could really lead. Indeed, the very internal power of the movement that he had done so much to create and focus, that had shaped and molded him, had now broken out in many new directions, reviving, inspiring a plethora of older black—and white—traditions. . . .

It was impossible for King—or any other single individual—to understand, much less command all the tendencies now set loose in the black communities of the land. (Of course, he knew that he was being falsely identified as an "Uncle Tom" by many northern black rhetoreticians of revolution who had never once risked their lives as King had done so many times in the cause of his people's freedom.) At the same time, Martin was trying to understand where the real, critical centers of power lay in American society, trying to understand how he could tackle the powerful forces that supported war, racism, poverty, and the internal subversion of the freedom movement's many parts.

No easy task. Still King seemed convinced that he would be unfaithful to the history he had already made with others, untrue to his forebears and his children in the struggle for justice, unless he followed what appeared to be the logic of the movement. For him, that logic, that history, that sense of integrity pressed him toward a more radical challenge than he had ever mounted before, one that would leave him more naked to his enemies than ever before. . . .

First, King decided to try to respond fully to the unspeakable agony, the terrible crime of Vietnam, defying all his critics and many of his friends, from the White House to members of his own organization and his own family. On April 4, 1967, at Riverside Church in New York City, the struggling leader-searcher addressed a major meeting sponsored by Clergy and Laymen Concerned About Vietnam. Near the beginning of his vibrant presentation, King admitted that he had not spoken clearly and early enough, but vowed that he would never make that mistake again. Justifying the connection he saw among the struggles for equal rights and economic justice in America and the demand for an end to American military involvement in Vietnam, King placed them all within the context of his commission as a minister of Jesus Christ and a Nobel Peace Prize laureate. Unflinchingly, he identified America as the essential aggressor in the war and called his nation "the greatest purveyor of violence in the world." . . .

Soon he turned from Riverside Church to forge the second prong of his militant challenge to white American power. In the summer of 1967, after two of the decade's most deadly urban uprisings—in Newark and Detroit—had stunned the nation, after a national Black Power convention had done much to stamp that variously defined slogan in the minds of black folk everywhere, King announced his plans for a major attack on America's internal structures of inequality and injustice. . . .

It was a version of the nonviolent army again, now surfacing at a far more volatile, confused, and dangerous moment in the nation's history and in King's own career. . . . By the end of 1967, King and his staff had again decided to focus this potentially revolutionary challenge in Washington, D.C., fully aware of the ugly, angry, and unreceptive mood at work in the White House and elsewhere.

At his radical best, King was determined to press the logic of his position, the movement of his people's history. Having attacked the nation's antiliberationist overseas actions, he now intended to move on the heart of the government, demanding a response to the suffering of its own semicolonized peoples. (Nor was King paving a way of welcome for his move by saying late in 1967: "I am not sad that black Americans are rebelling; this was not only inevitable but eminently desirable. Without this magnificent ferment among Negroes, the old evasions and procrastinations would have continued indefinitely." He was not paving a way, but he was indicating his own way, his own movement in the vortex of "this magnificent ferment.")

Martin was trying to be on time, trying to be faithful, trying to go forward, to create whatever openings toward the future that he could. Jamming his life against the advice of many of his black and white movement supporters, defying the angry warnings of Lyndon Johnson, King searched for his new role, for the new role of his people. In an America that seemed at times on the edge of armed racial warfare, an America increasingly torn over the Vietnam war, an America unresponsive to the deepest needs of its own people, especially its poor—in the midst of this history King was desperately searching for the connections with his past, for the openings to his and our future.

By December 1967, Martin had at least temporarily taken his new powerful and dangerous position. In a series of broadcasts for Canadian public radio, he said, "Negroes . . . must not only formulate a program; they must fashion new tactics which do not count on government goodwill." Instead he said the new tactics must be those which are forceful enough *"to compel unwilling authorities to yield to the mandates of justice."* But here at the end, at the beginning of the end, in his last major published document, King was not talking about blacks alone. The movement had grown; there was no way to "overcome" without taking on much more than we have ever taken on before. Thus he said,

> The dispossessed of this nation—the poor, both white and Negro— live in a cruelly unjust society. *They must organize a revolution against that injustice,* not against the lives of the persons who are their fellow citizens, but against the structures through which the society is refusing to take means which have been called for, and which are at hand, to lift the load of poverty.

Martin King was talking about a nonviolent revolution in America, to transform the entire society on behalf of its poorest people, for the sake of us all. Martin King was moving towards an experiment with truth and power, and he was calling for three thousand persons to join him for three months of intensive training to begin that revolution at the seat of America's political power, Washington, D.C. Martin King was shaping a new role for himself, leader of a nonviolent revolutionary army/movement, one which he also saw connecting with the oppressed peoples of other nations. . . .

Perhaps Martin King had seen and felt more than he was able to accomplish. Perhaps he could not ever be ready for this new role. Perhaps in the violent climate of America, it was impossible to be ready for such a campaign of revolutionary, nonviolent civil disobedience without an organization that was fully prepared for all the dangers, all the opportunities, and all the long, hard, preparatory work. SCLC was not that organization. Nevertheless, ready or not, King appeared to be trying to get ready—facing toward Washington, D.C.

But first there were garbage collectors to help in Memphis, and there were powerful forces at every level of American society who were determined that Martin Luther King would never be ready for the kind of revolution he had now announced. As a result, Martin never made it to Washington, never found out if he was ready or not. . . .

This man who grew from a spokesperson for his people's search for simple dignity in a medium-sized southern city to become a giant symbol of the search for justice across the globe—this man, with all his weaknesses, all his flaws," all his blindspots and all of his creative, courageous greatness, made all the history he could make. Perhaps of even more importance to us here and now, we are able to see that he helped force open the way to the possibility of a new vision, a second coming of America, an America in which justice, compassion, and humanity prevail. . . .

King helped create the possibility that all of us might break beyond our own individual and group interests and catch a vision of a new America, create a vision of a new common good in a new future which will serve us all. He saw that our needs were economic and spiritual, political *and* moral, social *and* personal, and as the end, the beginning approached, he was groping his way towards a new integration—one that had very little to do with the legalities of *Brown v. The Board of Education.*

But in the midst of this struggle, this groping, this searching, King learned some things, and the message he left was the message he had learned, the message he had been given by the earlier generations of our freedom-striving people: Freedom is a constant struggle. The message he left was that a new America cannot be created without an even more difficult, radical, and dangerous struggle than we have known up to now. The message he left is that black people can no longer make any separate peace with America, that our needs are the needs of other millions of Americans, that the entire society must be challenged with the force of revolutionary change in all its political, economic, social, and psychic structures.

Letter from a Birmingham Jail

Martin Luther King, Jr.

In the spring of 1963, the Southern Christian Leadership Conference and Martin Luther King, Jr., joined Reverend Fred Shuttlesworth's Birmingham movement to demand the desegregation of what was known as the most racist and segregated city in America. The opposition was strident and brutal, with Bull Connor's police using fire hoses and billy clubs to repel the African-American demonstrators. Even when SCLC mobilized the young people of Birmingham to lead the marches downtown, police terrorized the children, siccing police dogs on them. The pictures from those demonstrations helped galvanize Americans everywhere in support of civil rights legislation and eventually forced the Kennedy administration to take a more activist stance in support of civil rights.

In the midst of these demonstrations, King was arrested. While in jail, he responded in this letter to a statement of "moderate" white ministers in Birmingham who had asked that the demonstrations be curtailed, and who seemed to blame the victims of violence as much if not more than the perpetrators. Here, King eloquently preaches his own sermon to those ministers, calling into question a position that would use "moderation" as a means of reinforcing oppression. King's sermon is similar to an Old Testament "Jeremiad" where the prophets of Israel insisted on declaring the truth about their people.

MY DEAR FELLOW CLERGYMEN:

While confined here in the Birmingham city jail, I came across

From Martin Luther King, Jr., *Why We Can't Wait*. Reprinted by arrangement with The Heirs to the Estate of Martin Luther King, Jr., c/o Joan Daves Agency as agent for the proprietor. Copyright 1963 by the Estate of Martin Luther King, Jr. Copyright renewed 1991 by Coretta Scott King.

your recent statement calling my present activities "unwise and untimely." Seldom do I pause to answer criticism of my work and ideas. . . . But since I feel that you are men of genuine good will and that your criticisms are sincerely set forth, I want to try to answer your statement in what I hope will be patient and reasonable terms. . . .

I think I should indicate why I am here in Birmingham, since you have been influenced by the view which argues against "outsiders coming in." . . . I am here because I have organizational ties here. . . . But more basically, I am in Birmingham because injustice is here. . . .

Moreover, I am cognizant of the interrelatedness of all communities and states. I cannot sit idly by in Atlanta and not be concerned about what happens in Birmingham. Injustice anywhere is a threat to justice everywhere. We are caught in an inescapable network of mutuality, tied in a single garment of destiny.

Whatever affects one directly, affects all indirectly. Never again can we afford to live with the narrow, provincial "outside agitator" idea. Anyone who lives inside the United States can never be considered an outsider anywhere within its bounds.

You deplore the demonstrations taking place in Birmingham. But your statement, I am sorry to say, fails to express a similar concern for the conditions that brought about the demonstrations.

I am sure that none of you would want to rest content with the superficial kind of social analysis that deals merely with effects and does not grapple with underlying causes. It is unfortunate that demonstrations are taking place in Birmingham, but it is even more unfortunate that the city's white power structure left the Negro community with no alternative.

In any nonviolent campaign there are four basic steps: collection of the facts to determine whether injustices exist; negotiation; self-purification; and direct action. We have gone through all these steps in Birmingham.

There can be no gainsaying the fact that racial injustice engulfs this community. Birmingham is probably the most thoroughly segregated city in the United States. Its ugly record of brutality is widely know. Negroes have experienced grossly unjust treatment in the courts. There have been more unsolved bombing of Negro homes and churches in Birmingham than in any other city in the nation. These are the hard, brutal facts of the case. . . .

On the basis of these conditions, Negro leaders sought to negotiate with the city fathers. But the latter consistently refused to engage in good-faith negotiation. Then, last September, came the
opportunity to talk with leaders of Birmingham's economic community. In the course of the negotiations, certain promises were
made by the merchants—for example, to remove the stores' humiliating racial signs.

On the basis of these promises, the Revered Fred Shuttlesworth
and the leaders of the Alabama Christian Movement for Human
Rights agreed to a moratorium on all demonstrations. As the weeks
and months went by, we realized that we were the victims of a
broken promise. A few signs, briefly removed, returned; the others
remained.

As in so many past experiences, our hopes had been blasted, and
the shadow of deep disappointment settled upon us. We had no
alternative except to prepare for direct action, whereby we would
present our very bodies as a means of laying our case before the
conscience of the local and the national community.

Mindful of the difficulties involved, we decided to undertake the
process of self-purification. We began a series of workshops on
nonviolence, and we repeatedly asked ourselves: "Are you able to
accept blows without retaliation?" "Are you able to endure the ordeal of jail?" . . .

You may well ask, "Why direct action? Why sit-ins, marches, and
so forth? Isn't negotiation a better path?" You are quite right in
calling for negotiation. Indeed, this is the very purpose of direct
action. Nonviolent direct action seeks to create such a crisis and
foster such a tension that a community which has constantly refused to negotiate is forced to confront the issue. It seeks so to
dramatize the issue that it can no longer be ignored.

My citing the creation of tension as part of the work of the nonviolent resister may sound rather shocking. But I must confess that
I am not afraid of the word "tension." I have earnestly opposed
violent tension, but there is a type of constructive, nonviolent tension which is necessary for growth.

Just as Socrates felt that is was necessary to create a tension in the
mind so that individuals could rise from the bondage of myths and
half-truths to the unfettered realm of creative analysis and objective
appraisal, so must we see the need for nonviolent gadflies to create
the kind of tension in society that will help men rise from the dark

depths of prejudice and racism to the majestic heights of understanding and brotherhood.

The purpose of our direct-action program is to create a situation
so crisis-packed that it will inevitably open the door to negotiation. I
therefore concur with you in your call for negotiation. Too long has
our beloved Southland been bogged down in a tragic effort to live
in monologue rather than dialogue.

One of the basic points in your statement is that the action that I
and my associates have taken in Birmingham is untimely. Some
have asked: "Why didn't you give the new city administration time
to act?" The only answer that I can give to this query is that the new
Birmingham administration must be prodded about as much as the
outgoing one, before it will act. . . .

We have not made a single gain in civil rights without determined
legal and nonviolent pressure. . . . Lamentably, it is an historical
fact that privileged groups seldom give up their privileges voluntarily. Individuals may see the moral light and voluntarily give up
their unjust posture; but, as Reinhold Niebuhr has reminded us,
groups tend to be more immoral than individuals.

We know through painful experience that freedom is never voluntarily given by the oppressor. It must be demanded by the oppressed. Frankly, I have yet to engage in a direct-action campaign
that was "well timed" in view of those who have not suffered unduly
from the disease of segregation.

For years now I have heard the word "Wait!" It rings in the ear of
every Negro with piercing familiarity. This "Wait!" has almost always meant "Never." We must come to see, with one of our distinguished jurists, that 'justice too long delayed is justice denied."

We have waited for more than 340 years for our constitutional
and God-given rights. The nations of Asia and Africa are moving
with jetlike speed toward gaining political independence, but we
still creep at horse-and-buggy pace toward gaining a cup of coffee
at a lunch counter. Perhaps it is easy for those who have never felt
the stinging darts of segregation to say, "Wait."

But when you have seen vicious mobs lynch your mothers and
fathers at will and drown your sisters and brothers at whim;

when you have seen hate-filled policemen curse, kick and even
kill your black brothers and sisters;

when you see the vast majority of your twenty million Negro

brothers smothering in an airtight cage of poverty in the midst of an affluent society;

when you suddenly find your tongue twisted and your speech stammering as you seek to explain to your six-year-old daughter why she can't go to the public amusement park that has just been advertised on television, and see tears welling up in her eyes when she is told that Flintown is closed to colored children, and see ominous clouds of inferiority beginning to form in her little mental sky, and see her beginning to distort her personality by developing an unconscious bitterness toward white people;

when you have to concoct an answer for a five-year-old son who is asking, "Daddy, why do white people treat colored people so mean?";

when you take a cross-country drive and find it necessary to sleep night after night in the uncomfortable corners of your automobile because no motel will accept you;

when you are humiliated day in and day out by nagging signs reading "white" and "colored";

when your first name becomes "nigger," your middle name becomes "boy" (however old you are) and your last name becomes "John," and your wife and mother are never given the respected title "Mrs.";

when you are harried by day and haunted by night by the fact that you are a Negro, living-constantly at tiptoe stance, never quite knowing what to expect next, and are plagued with inner fears and outer resentments;

when you are forever fighting a degenerating sense of "nobodiness"—then you will understand why we find it difficult to wait.

There comes a time when the cup of endurance runs over, and men are no longer willing to be plunged into the abyss of despair. hope, sirs, you can understand our legitimate and unavoidable impatience.

You express a great deal of anxiety over our willingness to break laws. This is certainly a legitimate concern. Since we so diligently urge people to obey the Supreme Court's decision of 1954 outlawing segregation in the public schools, at first glance it may seem rather paradoxical for us consciously to break laws.

One may well ask: "How can you advocate breaking some laws

and obeying others?" The answer lies in the fact that there are two types of laws: just and unjust. I would be the first to advocate obeying just laws. One has not only a legal but a moral responsibility to obey just laws. Conversely, one has a moral responsibility to disobey unjust laws. I would agree with St. Augustine that "an unjust law is no law at all."

Now, what is the difference between the two? How does one determine whether a law is just or unjust? A just law is a man-made code that squares with the moral law or the law of God. An unjust law is a code that is out of harmony with the moral law.

To put it in the terms of St. Thomas Aquinas: An unjust law is a human law that is not rooted in eternal law and natural law. Any law that uplifts human personality is just. Any law that degrades human personality is unjust.

All segregation statutes are unjust because segregation distorts the soul and damages the personality. It gives the segregator a false sense of superiority and the segregated a false sense of inferiority. . . .

Let us consider a more concrete example of just and unjust laws. An unjust law is a code that a numerical or power majority group compels a minority group to obey but does not make binding on itself. This is *difference* made legal. By the same token, a just law is a code that a majority compels a minority to follow and that it is willing to follow itself. This is *sameness* made legal.

Let me give another explanation. A law is unjust if it is inflicted on a minority that, as a result of being denied the right to vote, had no part in enacting or devising the law. Who can say that the legislature of Alabama which set up that state's segregation laws was democratically elected?

Throughout Alabama all sorts of devious methods are used to prevent Negroes from becoming registered voters, and there are some counties in which, even though Negroes constitute a majority of the population, not a single Negro is registered. Can any law enacted under such circumstances be considered democratically structured?

Sometimes a law is just on its face and unjust in its application. For instance, I have been arrested on a charge of parading without a permit. Now, there is nothing wrong in having an ordinance which requires a permit for a parade. But such an ordinance becomes unjust when it is used to maintain segregation and to deny citizens the First-Amendment privilege of peaceful assembly and protest.

I hope you are able to see the distinction I am trying to point out. In no sense do I advocate evading or defying the law, as would the rabid segregationist. That would lead to anarchy.

One who breaks an unjust law must do so openly, lovingly and with a willingness to accept the penalty. I submit that an individual who breaks a law that conscience tells him is unjust, and who willingly accepts the penalty of imprisonment in order to arouse the conscience of the community over its injustice, is in reality expressing the highest respect for law.

Of course, there is nothing new about this kind of civil disobedience. It was evidenced sublimely in the refusal of Shadrach, Meshach, and Abednego to obey the laws of Nebuchadnezzar, on the ground that a higher moral law was at stake. It was practiced superbly by the early Christians, who were willing to face hungry lions and the excruciating pain of chopping blocks rather than submit to certain unjust laws of the Roman Empire.

To a degree, academic freedom is a reality today because Socrates practiced civil disobedience. In our own nation, the Boston Tea Party represented a massive act of civil disobedience.

We should never forget that everything Adolf Hitler did in Germany was "legal" and everything the Hungarian freedom fighters did in Hungary was "illegal." It was "illegal" to aid and comfort a Jew in Hitler's Germany. Even so, I am sure that, had I lived in Germany at the time, I would have aided and comforted my Jewish brothers. If today I lived in a Communist country where certain principles dear to the Christian faith are suppressed, I would openly advocate disobeying that country's anti-religious laws.

I must make two honest confessions to you, my Christian and Jewish brothers. First, I must confess that over the past few years I have been gravely disappointed with the white moderate. I have almost reached the regrettable conclusion that the Negro's great stumbling block in his stride toward freedom is not the White Citizen's Councilor or the Ku Klux Klanner, but the white moderate, who is more devoted to "order" than to justice; who prefers a negative peace which is the absence of tension to a positive peace which is the presence of justice; who constantly says, "I agree with you in the goal you seek, but I cannot agree with your methods of direct action"; who paternalistically believes he can set the timetable for another man's freedom; who lives by a mythical concept of time and who constantly advises the Negro to wait for a "more convenient season.

Shallow understanding from people of good will is more frustrating than absolute misunderstanding from people of ill will. Lukewarm acceptance is much more bewildering than outright rejection.

I had hoped that the white moderate would understand that law and order exist for the purpose of establishing justice and that when they fail in this purpose they become the dangerously structured dams that block the flow of social progress.

I had hoped that the white moderate would understand that the present tension in the South is a necessary phase of the transition from an obnoxious negative peace, in which the Negro passively accepted his unjust plight, to a substantive and positive peace, in which all men will respect the dignity and worth of human personality.

Actually, we who engage in nonviolent direct action are not the creators of tension. We merely bring to the surface the hidden tension that is already alive. We bring it out in the open, where it can be seen and dealt with. Like a boil that can never be cured so long as it is covered up but must be opened with all its ugliness to the natural medicines of air and light, injustice must be exposed, with all the tension its exposure creates, to the light of human conscience and the air of national opinion, before it can be cured.

In your statement you assert that our actions, even though peaceful, must be condemned because they precipitate violence. But is this a logical assertion? Isn't this like condemning a robbed man because his possession of money precipitated the evil act of robbery? . . .

We must come to see that, as the federal courts have consistently affirmed, it is wrong to urge an individual to cease his efforts to gain his basic constitutional rights because the quest may precipitate violence. Society must protect the robbed and punish the robber.

I had also hoped that the white moderate would reject the myth concerning time in relation to the struggle for freedom. . . . Actually, time itself is neutral: it can be used either destructively or constructively. More and more I feel that people of ill will have used time much more effectively than have the people of good will. We will have to repent in this generation not merely for the hateful words and actions of the bad people, but for the appalling silence of the good people.

Human progress never rolls in on wheels of inevitability: it comes through the tireless efforts of men willing to be coworkers with God, and without this hard work, time itself becomes an ally of the forces of stagnation. We must use time creatively, in the knowledge that the time is always ripe to do right.

Now is the time to make real the promise of democracy and transform our pending national elegy into a creative psalm of brotherhood. Now is the time to lift our national policy from the quicksand of racial injustice to the solid rock of human dignity.

You speak of our activity in Birmingham as extreme. At first I was rather disappointed that fellow clergymen would see my non-violent efforts as those of an extremist. I began thinking about the fact that I stand in the middle of two opposing forces in the Negro community.

One is a force of complacency, made up in part of Negroes who, as a result of long years of oppression, are so drained of self-respect and a sense of "somebodiness" that they have adjusted to segregation; and in part of a few middle-class Negroes who, because of a degree of academic and economic security and because in some ways they profit by segregation, have become insensitive to the problems of the masses.

The other force is one of bitterness and hatred, and it comes perilously close to advocating violence. It is expressed in the various black nationalist groups that are springing up across the nation, the largest and best-known being Elijah Muhammad's Muslim movement. Nourished by the Negro's frustration over the continued existence of racial discrimination, this movement is made up of people who have lost faith in America, who have absolutely repudiated Christianity, and who have concluded that the white man is an incorrigible "devil."

I have tried to stand between these two forces, saying that we need emulate neither the "do-nothingism" of the complacent nor the hatred and despair of the black nationalist. For there is the more excellent way of love and nonviolent protest. I am grateful to God that, through the influence of the Negro church, the way of nonviolence became an integral part of our struggle.

If this philosophy had not emerged, by now many streets of the South would, I am convinced, be flowing with blood. And I am further convinced that if our white brothers dismiss as "rabblerousers" and "outside agitators" those of us who employ nonviolent direct action, and if they refuse to support our nonviolent efforts, millions of Negroes will, out of frustration and despair, seek solace and security in black-nationalist ideologies—a development that would inevitably lead to a frightening racial nightmare.

Oppressed people cannot remain oppressed forever. The yearning for freedom eventually manifests itself, and that is what has happened to the American Negro. Something within has reminded him of his birthright of freedom, and something without has reminded him that it can be gained. Consciously or unconsciously, he has been caught up by the Zeitgeist, and with his black brothers of Africa and his brown and yellow brothers of Asia, South America and the Caribbean, the United States Negro is moving with a sense of great urgency toward the promised land of racial justice.

If one recognizes this vital urge that has engulfed the Negro community, one should readily understand why public demonstrations are taking place. The Negro has many pent-up resentments and latent frustrations, and he must release them. So let him march; let him make prayer pilgrimages to the city hall; let him go on freedom rides—and try to understand why he must do so.

If his repressed emotions are not released in nonviolent ways, they will seek expression through violence; this is not a threat but a fact of history. So I have not said to my people, "Get rid of your discontent." Rather, I have tried to say that this normal and healthy discontent can be channeled into the creative outlet of nonviolent direct action. And now this approach is being termed extremist.

But though I was initially disappointed at being categorized as an extremist, as I continued to think about the matter I gradually gained a measure of satisfaction from the label.

Was not Jesus an extremist for love: "Love your enemies, bless them that curse you, do good to them that hate you, and pray for them which despitefully use you, and persecute you.

Was not Amos an extremist for justice: "Let justice roll down like waters and righteousness like an ever-flowing stream." . . .

And John Bunyan: "I will stay in jail to the end of my days before I make a butchery of my conscience."

And Abraham Lincoln: "This nation cannot survive half slave

and half free." And Thomas Jefferson: "We hold these truths to be self-evident, that all men are created equal. . . .

So the question is not whether we will be extremists, but what kind of extremists we will be. Will we be extremists for hate or for love? Will we be extremists for the preservation of injustice or for the extension of justice? . . . Perhaps the South, the nation, and the world are in dire need of creative extremists.

I had hoped that the white moderate would see this need. Perhaps I was too optimistic; perhaps I expected too much. I suppose I should have realized that few members of the oppressor race can understand the deep groans and passionate yearnings of the oppressed race, and still fewer have the vision to see that injustice must be rooted out by strong, persistent, and determined action.

I am thankful, however, that some of our white brothers in the South have grasped the meaning of this social revolution and committed themselves to it. They are still all too few in quantity, but they are big in quality. Some—such as Ralph McGill, Lillian Smith, Harry Golden, James McBride Dabbs, Ann Braden, and Sarah Patton Boyle—have written about our struggle in eloquent and prophetic terms.

Others have marched with us down nameless streets of the South. They have languished in filthy, roach-infested jails, suffering the abuse and brutality of policemen who view them as "dirty nigger-lovers." Unlike so many of their moderate brothers and sisters, they have recognized the urgency of the moment and sensed the need for powerful "action" antidotes to combat the disease of segregation.

Let me take note of my other major disappointment. I have been so greatly disappointed with the white church and its leadership.

Of course, there are some notable exceptions. I am not unmindful of the fact that each of you has taken some significant stands on this issue. I commend you, Reverend Stallings, for your Christian stand on this past Sunday, in welcoming Negroes to your worship service on a nonsegregated basis. I commend the Catholic leaders of this state for integrating Spring Hill College several years ago.

But despite these notable exceptions, I must honestly reiterate that I have been disappointed with the church. I do not say this as one of those negative critics who can always find something wrong with the church. I say this as a minister of the gospel, who loves the church; who was nurtured in its bosom; who has been sustained by its spiritual blessings and who will remain true to it as long as the cord of life shall lengthen.

When I was suddenly catapulted into the leadership of the bus protest in Montgomery, Alabama, a few years ago, I felt we would be supported by the white church. I felt that the white ministers, priests and rabbis of the South would be among our strongest allies. Instead, some have been outright opponents, refusing to understand the freedom movement and misrepresenting its leaders; all too many others have been more cautious than courageous and have remained silent behind the anesthetizing security of stained-glass windows.

In spite of my shattered dreams, I came to Birmingham with the hope that the white religious leadership of this community would see the justice of our cause and, with deep moral concern, would serve as the channel through which our just grievances could reach the power structure. I had hoped that each of you would understand. But again I have been disappointed.

I have heard numerous southern religious leaders admonish their worshipers to comply with a desegregation decision because it is the law, but I have longed to hear white ministers declare: "Follow this decree because integration is morally right and because the Negro is your brother."

In the midst of blatant injustices inflicted upon the Negro, I have watched white churchmen stand on the sideline and mouth pious irrelevancies and sanctimonious trivialities. In the midst of a mighty struggle to rid our nation of racial and economic injustice, I have heard many ministers say: "Those are social issues, with which the gospel has no real concern." And I have watched many churches commit themselves to a completely otherworldly religion which makes a strange, un-Biblical distinction between body and soul; between the sacred and the secular. . . .

I hope the church as a whole will meet the challenge of this decisive hour. But even if the church does not come to the aid of justice, I have no despair about the future. I have no fear about the outcome of our struggle in Birmingham, even if our motives are at present misunderstood. We will reach the goal of freedom in Birmingham and all over the nation, because the goal of America is freedom.

Abused and scorned though we may be, our destiny is tied up with America's destiny. Before the pilgrims landed at Plymouth, we were here. For more than two centuries our forebears labored in this country, without wages; they made cotton king; they built the homes of their masters while suffering gross injustice and shameful humiliation—and yet out of a bottomless vitality they continued to thrive and develop.

If the inexpressible cruelties of slavery could not stop us, the opposition we now face will surely fail. We will win our freedom because the sacred heritage of our nation and the eternal will of God are embodied in our echoing demands.

Before closing I feel impelled to mention one other point in your statement that has troubled me profoundly. You warmly commended the Birmingham police force for keeping "order" and "preventing violence."

I doubt that you would have so warmly commended the police force if you had seen its dogs sinking their teeth into unarmed, nonviolent Negroes. I doubt that you would so quickly commend the policemen if you were to observe their ugly and inhumane treatment of Negroes here in the city jail; if you were to watch them push and curse old Negro women and young Negro girls; if you were to see them slap and kick old Negro men and young boys; if you were to observe them, as they did on two occasions, refuse to give us food because we wanted to sing our grace together. I cannot join you in your praise of the Birmingham police department.

It is true that the police have exercised a degree of discipline in handling the demonstrators. In this sense they have conducted themselves rather "nonviolently" in public. But for what purpose? To preserve the evil system of segregation.

Over the past few years I have consistently preached that non-violence demands that the means we use must be as pure as the ends we seek. I have tried to make clear that it is wrong to use immoral means to attain moral ends. But now I must affirm that it is just as wrong, or perhaps even more so, to use moral means to preserve immoral ends. . . . As T. S. Eliot has said, "The last temptation is the greatest treason: To do the right deed for the wrong reason.

I wish you had commended the Negro sit-inners and demonstrators of Birmingham for their sublime courage, their willingness to suffer, and their amazing discipline in the midst of great provocation. One day the South will recognize its real heroes. They will be the James Merediths, with the noble sense of purpose that enables

them to face jeering and hostile mobs, and with the agonizing loneliness that characterizes the life of the pioneer. They will be old,
oppressed, battered Negro women, symbolized in a seventy-two-
year-old woman in Montgomery, Alabama, who rose up with a
sense of dignity and with her people decided not to ride segregated
buses, and who responded with ungrammatical profundity to one
who inquired about her weariness: "My feets is tired, but my soul is
at rest."

They will be the young high school and college students, the
young ministers of the gospel and a host of their elders, courageously and nonviolently sitting in at lunch counters and willingly
going to jail for conscience' sake. One day the South will know that
when these disinherited children of God sat down at lunch counters, they were in reality standing up for what is best in the American dream and for the most sacred values in our Judeo-Christian
heritage, thereby bringing our nation back to those great wells of
democracy which were dug deep by the founding fathers in their
formulation of the Constitution and the Declaration of Independence.

Never before have I written so long a letter. I'm afraid it is much
too long to take your precious time. I can assure you that it would
have been much shorter if I had been writing from a comfortable
desk, but what else can one do when he is alone in a narrow jail cell,
other than write long letters, think long thoughts and pray long
prayers? . . .

Yours for the cause of peace and brotherhood,

Martin Luther King, Jr.

Message to the Grass Roots

Malcolm X

*After becoming a convert to the Nation of Islam while in prison and a
disciple of its African-American leader Elijah Muhammad, former pimp
and street hustler Malcolm Little took the name Malcolm X (the X signify-
ing that under slavery Africans had lost their true family identity). A
dynamic orator, he became the leading voice of, and major recruiter for,
the Nation of Islam, preaching the complete evilness of the white race and
the white man's responsibility for the plight of African-Americans. Espousing black nationalism and racial separatism, Malcolm X argued for
black control of black communities and urged African-Americans to fight
white racism "by any means necessary." After his break with Mohammad
in early 1964, Malcolm X modified some of his views yet still rejected
nonviolence, maintained the necessity for African-American domestic
economic and political independence, and continued to identify the struggle of African-Americans with Third World anticolonial movements.
Assassinated in February 1965, the Malcolm X who symbolized militant
defiance and racial pride then became the most significant inspiration for
and influence on the proponents of Black Power.*

*Compare the central arguments of Martin Luther King, Jr., and Mal-
colm X, and compare both with Bayard Rustin in the next selection. How
do you explain the differences in their viewpoints? Consider why different
segments of the black population believed such divergent African-
American leaders so compelling. How do you account for the shift from
integrationist to separatist sentiments in the African-American community after 1965? What is Malcolm X's legacy today?*

Malcolm X, "Message to the Grass Roots," in *Malcolm X Speaks*. Copyright
© 1965, 1989 by Betty Shabazz and Pathfinder Press. Reprinted by permission.

We want to have just an off-the-cuff chat between you and me, us. We want to talk right down to earth in a language that everybody here can easily understand. We all agree tonight, all of the speakers have agreed, that America has a very serious problem. Not only does America have a very serious problem, but our people have a very serious problem. The only reason she has a problem is she doesn't want us here. And every time you look at yourself, be you black, brown, red or yellow, a so-called Negro, you represent a person who poses such a serious problem for America because you're not wanted. Once you face this as a fact, then you can start plotting a course that will make you appear intelligent, instead of unintelligent.

What you and I need to do is learn to forget our differences. When we come together, we don't come together as Baptists or Methodists. You don't catch hell because you're a Baptist, and you don't catch hell because you're a Methodist. You don't catch hell because you're a Methodist or Baptist, you don't catch hell because you're a Democrat or Republican, you don't catch hell because you're a Mason or an Elk, and you sure don't catch hell because you're an American, because if you were an American, you wouldn't catch hell. You catch hell because you're a black man. You catch hell, all of us catch hell, for the same reason.

So we're all black people, so-called Negroes, second-class citizens, ex-slaves. You're nothing but an ex-slave. You don't like to be told that. But what else are you? You are ex-slaves. You didn't come here on the "Mayflower." You came here on a slave ship. In chains, like a horse, or a cow, or a chicken. And you were brought here by the people who came here on the "Mayflower," you were brought here by the so-called Pilgrims, or Founding Fathers. They were the ones who brought you here.

We have a common enemy. We have this in common: We have a common oppressor, a common exploiter, and a common discriminator. But once we all realize that we have a common enemy, then we unite—on the basis of what we have in common. And what we have foremost in common is that enemy—the white man. He's an enemy to all of us. I know some of you all think that some of them aren't enemies. Time will tell.

In Bandung back in, I think, 1954, was the first unity meeting in centuries of black people. And once you study what happened at the Bandung conference, and the results of the Bandung conference, it actually serves as a model for the same procedure you and I can use to get our problems solved. At Bandung all the nations came together, the dark nations from Africa and Asia. Some of them were Buddhists, some of them were Muslims, some of them were Christians, some were Confucianists, some were atheists. Despite their religious differences, they came together. Some were communists, some were socialists, some were capitalists—despite their economic and political differences, they came together. All of them were black, brown, red or yellow.

The number-one thing that was not allowed to attend the Bandung conference was the white man. He couldn't come. Once they excluded the white man, they found that they could get together. Once they kept him out, everybody else fell right in and fell in line. This is the thing that you and I have to understand. And these people who came together didn't have nuclear weapons, they didn't have jet planes, they didn't have all of the heavy armaments that the white man has. But they had unity. . . . They realized all over the world where the dark man was being oppressed, he was being oppressed by the white man; where the dark man was being exploited, he was being exploited by the white man. So they got together on this basis—that they had a common enemy.

And when you and I here in Detroit and in Michigan and in America who have been awakened today look around us, we too realize here in America we all have a common enemy, whether he's in Georgia or Michigan, whether he's in California or New York. He's the same man—blue eyes and blond hair and pale skin—the same man. So what we have to do is what they did. They agreed to stop quarreling among themselves. . . . Instead of airing our differences in public, we have to realize we're all the same family. And when you have a family squabble, you don't get out on the sidewalk. If you do, everybody calls you uncouth, unrefined, uncivilized, savage. If you don't make it at home, you settle it at home; you get in the closet, argue it out behind closed doors, and then when you come out on the street, you pose a common front, a united front. And this is what we need to do in the community, and in the city, and in the state. We need to stop airing our differences in front of the white man, put the white man out of our meetings, and then sit down and talk shop with each other. That's what we've got to do.

I would like to make a few comments concerning the difference between the black revolution and the Negro revolution. Are they both the same? And if they're not, what is the difference? What is the difference between a black revolution and a Negro revolution? First, what is a revolution? Sometimes I'm inclined to believe that many of our people are using this word "revolution" loosely, without taking careful consideration of what this word actually means, and what its historic characteristics are. When you study the historic nature of revolutions, the motive of a revolution, the objective of a revolution, the result of a revolution, and the methods used in a revolution, you may change words. You may devise another program, you may change your goal and you may change your mind.

Look at the American Revolution in 1776. That revolution was for what? For land. Why did they want land? Independence. How was it carried out? Bloodshed. Number one, it was based on land, the basis of independence. And the only way they could get it was bloodshed. The French Revolution—what was it based on? The landless against the landlord. What was it for? Land. How did they get it? Bloodshed. Was no love lost, was no compromise, was no negotiation. I'm telling you—you don't know what a revolution is. Because when you find out what it is, you'll get back in the alley, you'll get out of the way.

The Russian Revolution—what was it based on? Land; the landless against the landlord. How did they bring it about? Bloodshed. You haven't got a revolution that doesn't involve bloodshed. And you're afraid to bleed. I said, you're afraid to bleed.

As long as the white man sent you to Korea, you bled. He sent you to Germany, you bled. He sent you to the South Pacific to fight the Japanese, you bled. You bleed for white people, but when it comes to seeing your own churches being bombed and little black girls murdered, you haven't got any blood. You bleed when the white man says bleed; you bite when the white man says bite; and you bark when the white man says bark. I hate to say this about us, but it's true. How are you going to be nonviolent in Mississippi, as violent as you were in Korea? How can you justify being nonviolent in Mississippi and Alabama, when your churches are being bombed, and your little girls are being murdered, and at the same time you are going to get violent with Hitler, and Tōjō, and somebody else you don't even know?

If violence is wrong in America, violence is wrong abroad. If it is wrong to be violent defending black women and black children and black babies and black men, then it is wrong for America to draft us and make us violent abroad in defense of her. And if it is right for America to draft us, and teach us how to be violent in defense of her, then it is right for you and me to do whatever is necessary to defend our own people right here in this country.

The Chinese Revolution—they wanted land. They threw the British out, along with the Uncle Tom Chinese. Yes, they did. They set a good example. When I was in prison, I read an article—don't be shocked when I say that I was in prison. You're still in prison. That's what America means: prison. When I was in prison, I read an article in *Life* magazine showing a little Chinese girl, nine years old; her father was on his hands and knees and she was pulling the trigger because he was an Uncle Tom Chinaman. When they had the revolution over there, they took a whole generation of Uncle Toms and just wiped them out. And within ten years that little girl became a full-grown woman. No more Toms in China. And today it's one of the toughest, roughest, most feared countries on this earth—by the white man. Because there are no Uncle Toms over there.

Of all our studies, history is best qualified to reward our research. And when you see that you've got problems, all you have to do is examine the historic method used all over the world by others who have problems similar to yours. Once you see how they got theirs straight, then you know how you can get yours straight. There's been a revolution, a black revolution, going on in Africa. In Kenya, the Mau Mau were revolutionary; they were the ones who brought the word "Uhuru" to the fore. The Mau Mau, they were revolutionary, they believed in scorched earth, they knocked everything aside that got in their way, and their revolution also was based on land, a desire for land. In Algeria, the northern part of Africa, a revolution took place. The Algerians were revolutionists, they wanted land. France offered to let them be integrated into France. They told France, to hell with France, they wanted some land, not some France. And they engaged in a bloody battle.

So I cite these various revolutions, brothers and sisters, to show you that you don't have a peaceful revolution. You don't have a turn-the-other-cheek revolution. There's no such thing as a nonviolent revolution. The only kind of revolution that is nonviolent is the Negro revolution. The only revolution in which the goal is loving your enemy is the Negro revolution. It's the only revolution in which the goal is a desegregated lunch counter, a desegregated theater, a desegregated park, and a desegregated public toilet; you can sit down next to white folks—on the toilet. That's no revolution. Revolution is based on land. Land is the basis of all independence. Land is the basis of freedom, justice, and equality. . . .

Revolution is bloody, revolution is hostile, revolution knows no compromise, revolution overturns and destroys everything that gets in its way. And you, sitting around here like a knot on the wall, saying, "I'm going to love these folks no matter how much they hate me." No, you need a revolution. Whoever heard of a revolution where they lock arms, as Rev. Cleage was pointing out beautifully, singing "We Shall Overcome"? You don't do that in a revolution. You don't do any singing, you're too busy swinging. It's based on land. A revolutionary wants land so he can set up his own nation, an independent nation. These Negroes aren't asking for any nation— they're trying to crawl back on the plantation. . . .

To understand this, you have to go back to what the young brother here referred to as the house Negro and the field Negro back during slavery. There were two kinds of slaves, the house Negro and the field Negro. The house Negroes—they lived in the house with master, they dressed pretty good, they ate good because they ate his food—what he left. They lived in the attic or the basement, but still they lived near the master; and they loved the master more than the master loved himself. They would give their life to save the master's house—quicker than the master would. If the master said, "We got a good house here," the house Negro would say, "Yeah, we got a good house here." Whenever the master said "we," he said "we." That's how you can tell a house Negro.

If the master's house caught on fire, the house Negro would fight harder to put the blaze out than the master would. If the master got sick, the house Negro would say, "What's the matter, boss, *we* sick?" *We* sick! He identified himself with his master, more than his master identified with himself. And if you came to the house Negro and said, "Let's run away, let's escape, let's separate," the house Negro would look at you and say, "Man, you crazy. What you mean, separate? Where is there a better house than this? Where can I wear better clothes than this? Where can I eat better food than this?" That was that house Negro. In those days he was called a "house nigger." And that's what we call them today, because we've still got some house niggers running around here.

This modern house Negro loves his master. He wants to live near him. He'll pay three times as much as the house is worth just to live near his master, and then brag about "I'm the only Negro out here." "I'm the only one on my job." "I'm the only one in this school." You're nothing but a house Negro. And if someone comes to you right now and says, "Let's separate," you say the same thing that the house Negro said on the plantation. "What you mean, separate? From America, this good white man? Where you going to get a better job than you get here?" I mean, this is what you say. "I ain't left nothing in Africa," that's what you say. Why, you left your mind in Africa.

On that same plantation, there was the field Negro. The field Negroes—those were the masses. There were always more Negroes in the field than there were Negroes in the house. The Negro in the field caught hell. He ate leftovers. In the house they ate high up on the hog. The Negro in the field didn't get anything but what was left of the insides of the hog. They call it "chitt'lings" nowadays. In those days they called them what they were—guts. That's what you were—gut-eaters. And some of you are still gut-eaters.

The field Negro was beaten from morning to night; he lived in a shack, in a hut; he wore old, castoff clothes. He hated his master. I say he hated his master. He was intelligent. That house Negro loved his master, but that field Negro—remember, they were in the majority, and they hated the master. When the house caught on fire, he didn't try to put it out; that field Negro prayed for a wind, for a breeze. When the master got sick, the field Negro prayed that he'd die. If someone came to the field Negro and said, "Let's separate, let's run," he didn't say, "Where we going?" He'd say, "Any place is better than here." You've got field Negroes in America today. I'm a field Negro. The masses are the field Negroes. When they see this man's house on fire, you don't hear the little Negroes talking about "*our* government is in trouble." They say, "*The* government is in trouble." Imagine a Negro: "*Our* government"! I even heard one say "*our* astronauts." They won't even let him near the plant—and "*our* astronauts"! "*Our* Navy"—that's a Negro that is out of his mind, a Negro that is out of his mind.

Just as the slavemaster of that day used Tom, the house Negro, to keep the field Negroes in check, the same old slavemaster today has Negroes who are nothing but modern Uncle Toms, twentieth-century Uncle Toms, to keep you and me in check, to keep us under control, keep us passive and peaceful and nonviolent. . . .

There is nothing in our book, the Koran, that teaches us to suffer peacefully. Our religion teaches us to be intelligent. Be peaceful, be courteous, obey the law, respect everyone; but if someone puts his hand on you, send him to the cemetery. That's a good religion. In fact, that's that old-time religion. That's the one that Ma and Pa used to talk about: an eye for an eye, and a tooth for a tooth, and a head for a head, and a life for a life. That's a good religion. And nobody resents that kind of religion being taught but a wolf, who intends to make you his meal.

This is the way it is with the white man in America. He's a wolf—and you're sheep. Any time a shepherd, a pastor, teaches you and me not to run from the white man and, at the same time, teaches us not to fight the white man, he's a traitor to you and me. Don't lay down a life all by itself. No, preserve your life, it's the best thing you've got. And if you've got to give it up, let it be even-steven.

The slavemaster took Tom and dressed him well, fed him well and even gave him a little education—a *little* education; gave him a long coat and a top hat and made all the other slaves look up to him. Then he used Tom to control them. The same strategy that was used in those days is used today, by the same white man. He takes a Negro, a so-called Negro, and makes him prominent, builds him up, publicizes him, makes him a celebrity. And then he becomes a spokesman for Negroes—and a Negro leader.

I would like to mention just one other thing quickly, and that is the method that the white man uses, how the white man uses the "big guns," or Negro leaders, against the Negro revolution. They are not a part of the Negro revolution. They are used against the Negro revolution. . . .

The Negroes were out there in the streets. They were talking about how they were going to march on Washington. Right at that time Birmingham had exploded, and the Negroes in Birmingham—remember, they also exploded. They began to stab the crackers in the back and bust them up 'side their head—yes, they did. That's when Kennedy sent in the troops, down in Birmingham. After that, Kennedy got on the television and said "this is a moral issue." That's when he said he was going to put out a civil-rights bill. And when he mentioned civil-rights bill and the Southern crackers started talking about how they were going to boycott or filibuster it, then the Negroes started talking—about what? That they were going to march on Washington, march on the Senate, march on the White House, march on the Congress, and tie it up, bring it to a halt, not let the government proceed. They even said they were going out to the airport and lay down on the runway and not let any airplanes land. I'm telling you what they said. That was revolution. That was revolution. That was the black revolution.

It was the grass roots out there in the street. It scared the white man to death, scared the white power structure in Washington, D.C., to death; I was there. When they found out that this black steamroller was going to come down on the capital, they called in Wilkins, they called in Randolph, they called in these national Negro leaders that you respect and told them, "Call it off." Kennedy said, "Look, you all are letting this thing go too far." And Old Tom said, "Boss I can't stop it, because I didn't start it." I'm telling you what they said. They said, "I'm not even in it, much less at the head of it." They said, "These Negroes are doing things on their own. They're running ahead of us." And that old shrewd fox, he said, "If you all aren't in it, I'll put you in it. I'll put you at the head of it. I'll endorse it. I'll welcome it. I'll help it. I'll join it."

A matter of hours went by. They had a meeting at the Carlyle Hotel in New York City. The Carlyle Hotel is owned by the Kennedy family; that's the hotel Kennedy spent the night at, two nights ago; it belongs to his family. A philanthropic society headed by a white man named Stephen Currier called all the top civil-rights leaders together at the Carlyle Hotel. And he told them, "By you all fighting each other, you are destroying the civil-rights movement. And since you're fighting over money from white liberals, let us set up what is known as the Council for United Civil Rights Leadership. Let's form this council, and all the civil-rights organizations will belong to it, and we'll use it for fund-raising purposes." Let me show you how tricky the white man is. As soon as they got it formed, they elected Whitney Young as its chairman, and who do you think became the co-chairman? Stephen Currier, the white man, a millionaire. . . .

Once they formed it, with the white man over it, he promised them and gave them $800,000 to split up among the Big Six; and told them that after the march was over they'd give them $700,000 more. A million and a half dollars—split up between leaders that you have been following, going to jail for, crying crocodile tears for. And they're nothing but Frank James and Jesse James and the what-do-you-call-'em brothers.

As soon as they got the setup organized, the white man made available to them top public-relations experts; opened the news media across the country at their disposal, which then began to project these Big Six as the leaders of the march. Originally they weren't even in the march. You were talking this march talk on Hastings Street, you were talking march talk on Lenox Avenue, and on Fillmore Street, and on Central Avenue, and 32nd Street and 63rd Street. That's where the march talk was being talked. But the white man put the Big Six at the head of it; made them the march. They became the march. They took it over. And the first move they made after they took it over, they invited Walter Reuther, a white man; they invited a priest, a rabbi, and an old white preacher, yes, an old white preacher. The same white element that put Kennedy into power—labor, the Catholics, the Jews, and liberal Protestants; the same clique that put Kennedy in power, joined the march on Washington.

It's just like when you've got some coffee that's too black, which means it's too strong. What do you do? You integrate it with cream, you make it weak. But if you pour too much cream in it, you won't even know you ever had coffee. It used to be hot, it becomes cool. It used to be strong, it becomes weak. It used to wake you up, now it puts you to sleep. This is what they did with the march on Washington. They joined it. They didn't integrate it, they infiltrated it. They joined it, became a part of it, took it over. And as they took it over, it lost its militancy. It ceased to be angry, it ceased to be hot, it ceased to be uncompromising. Why, it even ceased to be a march. It became a picnic, a circus. Nothing but a circus, with clowns and all. . . .

No, it was a sellout. It was a takeover. When James Baldwin came in from Paris, they wouldn't let him talk, because they couldn't make him go by the script. Burt Lancaster read the speech that Baldwin was supposed to make; they wouldn't let Baldwin get up there, because they know Baldwin is liable to say anything. They controlled it so tight, they told those Negroes what time to hit town, how to come, where to stop, what signs to carry, what song to sing, what speech they could make, and what speech they couldn't make; and then told them to get out of town by sundown. And every one of those Toms was out of town by sundown. Now I know you don't like my saying this. But I can back it up. It was a circus, a performance that beat anything Hollywood could ever do, the performance of the year. Reuther and those other three devils should get an Academy Award for the best actors because they acted like they really loved Negroes and fooled a whole lot of Negroes. And the six Negro leaders should get an award too, for the best supporting cast.

From Protest to Politics

Bayard Rustin

A longtime advocate of nonviolent protest, Bayard Rustin took part in a 1947 effort to desegregate interstate bus facilities in the South, became a principal advisor to Martin Luther King, Jr., during the Montgomery bus boycott, and played a major role in organizing the 1963 March on Washington. By the mid-1960s, however, his path had diverged sharply from that of the more militant black protest leaders. He believed that the realization of true equality for African-Americans depended on their remaining part of the broad liberal coalition that had given Lyndon Johnson his landslide victory in 1964. And he feared that black campaigns of disruptive civil disobedience and militant criticism of white leaders would only alienate necessary allies in the labor movement, Congress, and the White House. In the following selection, a 1965 plea for African-Americans to turn from protest to politics, Rustin prophesied that despite civil rights victories, the plight of many African-Americans would worsen unless a black-and-white progressive force transformed the nation's most fundamental social, economic, and political institutions. Those interested in this argument will be able to see a more contemporary elaboration of some of the same ideas in William Julius Wilson's article in Part Eight.

The decade spanned by the 1954 Supreme Court decision on school desegregation and the Civil Rights Act of 1964 will undoubtedly be recorded as the period in which the legal foundations of racism in America were destroyed. To be sure, pockets of resistance ramain; but it would be hard to quarrel with the assertion that the

Bayard Rustin, "From Protest to Politics," *Commentary*, February 1965. Reprinted by permission of *Commentary* and the Estate of Bayard Rustin; all rights reserved.

elaborate legal structure of segregation and discrimination, particularly in relation to public accommodations, has virtually collapsed. On the other hand, without making light of the human sacrifices involved in the direct-action tactics (sit-ins, freedom rides, and the rest) that were so instrumental to this achievement, we must recognize that in desegregating public accommodations, we affected institutions which are relatively peripheral both to the American socioeconomic order and to the fundamental conditions of life of the Negro people. In a highly industrialized, twentieth-century civilization we hit Jim Crow precisely where it was most anachronistic, dispensable, and vulnerable—in hotels, lunch counters, terminals, libraries, swimming pools, and the like. For in these forms, Jim Crow does impede the flow of commerce in the broadest sense: it is a nuisance in a society on the move (and on the make). Not surprisingly, therefore, it was the most mobility-conscious and relatively liberated groups in the Negro community—lower-middle-class college students—who launched the attack that brought down this imposing but hollow structure.

The term "classical" appears especially apt for this phase of the civil rights movement. But in the few years that have passed since the first flush of sit-ins, several developments have taken place that have complicated matters enormously. One is the shifting focus of the movement in the South, symbolized by Birmingham; another is the spread of the revolution to the North; and the third, common to the other two, is the expansion of the movement's base in the Negro community. To attempt to disentangle these three strands is to do violence to reality. David Danzig's perceptive article, "The Meaning of Negro Strategy," correctly saw in the Birmingham events the victory of the concept of collective struggle over individual achievement as the road to Negro freedom. And Birmingham remains the unmatched symbol of grass-roots protest involving all strata of the black community. It was also in this most industrialized of Southern cities that the single-issue demands of the movement's classical stage gave way to the "package deal." No longer were Negroes satisfied with integrating lunch counters. They now sought advances in employment, housing, school integration, police protection, and so forth.

Thus, the movement in the South began to attack areas of discrimination which were not so remote from the Northern experience as were Jim Crow lunch counters. At the same time, the interrelationship of these apparently distinct areas became increasingly evident. What is the value of winning access to public accommodations for those who lack money to use them? The minute the movement faced this question, it was compelled to expand its vision beyond race relations to economic relations, including the role of education in modern society. And what also became clear is that all these interrelated problems, by their very nature, are not soluble by private, voluntary efforts but require government action—or politics. Already Southern demonstrators had recognized that the most effective way to strike at the police brutality they suffered from was by getting rid of the local sheriff—and that meant political action, which in turn meant, and still means, political action within the Democratic party where the only meaningful primary contests in the South are fought.

And so, in Mississippi, thanks largely to the leadership of Bob Moses, a turn toward political action has been taken. More than voter registration is involved here. A conscious bid for political power is being made, and in the course of that effort a tactical shift is being effected: direct-action techniques are being subordinated to a strategy calling for the building of community institutions or power bases. Clearly, the implications of this shift reach far beyond Mississippi. What began as a protest movement is being challenged to translate itself into a political movement. Is this the right course? And if it is, can the transformation be accomplished?

The very decade which has witnessed the decline of legal Jim Crow has also seen the rise of de facto segregation in our most fundamental socioeconomic institutions. More Negroes are unemployed today than in 1954, and the unemployment gap between the races is wider. The median income of Negroes has dropped from 57 percent to 54 percent of that of whites. A higher percentage of Negro workers is now concentrated in jobs vulnerable to automation than was the case ten years ago. More Negroes attend de facto segregated schools today than when the Supreme Court handed down its famous decision; while school integration proceeds at a snail's pace in the South, the number of Northern schools with an excessive proportion of minority youth proliferates. And behind this is the continuing growth of racial slums, spreading over our central cities and trapping Negro youth in a milieu which, whatever its legal definition, sows an unimaginable demoralization. Again, legal niceties aside, a resident of a racial ghetto lives in segregated housing, and more Negroes fall into this category than ever before.

These are the facts of life which generate frustration in the Negro community and challenge the civil rights movement. At issue, after all, is not *civil rights*, strictly speaking, but social and economic conditions. Last summer's riots were not race riots; they were outbursts of class aggression in a society where class and color definitions are converging disastrously. How can the (perhaps misnamed) civil rights movement deal with this problem?

Before trying to answer, let me first insist that the task of the movement is vastly complicated by the failure of many whites of good will to understand the nature of our problem. There is a widespread assumption that the removal of artificial racial barriers should result in the automatic integration of the Negro into all aspects of American life. This myth is fostered by facile analogies with the experience of various ethnic immigrant groups, particularly the Jews. But the analogies with the Jews do not hold for three simple but profound reasons. First, Jews have a long history as a literate people, a resource which has afforded them opportunities to advance in the academic and professional worlds, to achieve intellectual status even in the midst of economic hardship, and to evolve sustaining value systems in the context of ghetto life. Negroes, for the greater part of their presence in this country, were forbidden by law to read or write. Second, Jews have a long history of family stability, the importance of which in terms of aspiration and self-image is obvious. The Negro family structure was totally destroyed by slavery and with it the possibility of cultural transmission (the right of Negroes to marry and rear children is barely a century-old). Third, Jews are white and have the *option* of relinquishing their cultural-religious identity, intermarrying, passing, etc. Negroes, or at least the overwhelming majority of them, do not have this option. There is also a fourth vulgar reason. If the Jewish and Negro communities are not comparable in terms of education, family structure, and color, it is also true that their respective economic roles bear little resemblance.

This matter of economic role brings us to the greater problem—the fact that we are moving into an era in which the natural functioning of the market does not by itself ensure every man with will and ambition a place in the productive process. The immigrant who came to this country during the late nineteenth and early twentieth centuries entered a society which was expanding territorially and or economically. It was then possible to start at the bottom, as an unskilled or semiskilled worker, and move up the ladder, acquiring new skills along the way. Especially was this true when industrial unionism was burgeoning, giving new dignity and higher wages to organized workers. Today the situation has changed. We are not expanding territorially, the western frontier is settled, labor organizing has leveled off, our rate of economic growth has been stagnant for a decade. And we are in the midst of a technological revolution which is altering the fundamental structure of the labor force, destroying unskilled and semiskilled jobs—jobs in which Negroes are disproportionately concentrated.

Whatever the pace of this technological revolution may be, the *direction* is clear: the lower rungs of the economic ladder are being lopped off. This means that an individual will no longer be able to start at the bottom and work his way up; he will have to start in the middle or on top, and hold on tight. It will not even be enough to have certain specific skills, for many skilled jobs are also vulnerable to automation. A broad educational background, permitting vocational adaptability and flexibility, seems more imperative than ever We live in a society where, as Secretary of Labor Willard Wirtz puts it, machines have the equivalent of a high school diploma. Yet the average educational attainment of American Negroes is 8.2 years.

Negroes, of course, are not the only people being affected by these developments. It is reported that there are now 50 percent fewer unskilled and semiskilled jobs than there are high school dropouts. Almost one-third of the 26 million young people entering the labor market in the 1960s will be dropouts. But the percentage of Negro dropouts nationally is 57 percent, and in New York City, among Negroes 25 years of age or over, it is 68 percent. They are without a future.

To what extent can the kind of self-help campaign recently prescribed by Eric Hoffer in the *New York Times Magazine* cope with such a situation? I would advise those who think that self-help is the answer to familiarize themselves with the long history of such efforts in the Negro community, and to consider why so many foundered on the shoals of ghetto life. It goes without saying that any effort to combat demoralization and apathy is desirable, but we must understand that demoralization in the Negro community is largely a common sense response to an objective reality. Negro youths have no need of statistics to perceive, fairly accurately, what their odds are in American society. Indeed, from the point of view of motivation, some of the healthiest Negro youngsters I know are juvenile delinquents: vigorously pursuing the American Dream of material acquisition and status, yet finding the conventional means of attaining it blocked off, they do not yield to defeatism but resort to illegal (and often ingenious) methods. They are not alien to American culture: They are, in Gunnar Myrdal's phrase, "exaggerated Americans." To want a Cadillac is not un-American; to push a cart in the garment center is. If Negroes are to be persuaded that the conventional path (school, work, etc.) is superior, we had better provide evidence which is now sorely lacking. It is a double cruelty to harangue Negro youth about education and training when we do not know what jobs will be available for them. When a Negro youth can reasonably foresee a future free of slums, when the prospect of gainful employment is realistic, we will see motivation and self-help in abundant enough quantities.

Meanwhile, there is an ironic similarity between the self-help advocated by many liberals and the doctrines of the Black Muslims. Professional sociologists, psychiatrists, and social workers have expressed amazement at the Muslims' success in transforming prostitutes and dope addicts into respectable citizens. But every prostitute the Muslims convert to a model of Calvinist virtue is replaced in the ghetto with two more. Dedicated as they are to the maintenance of the ghetto, the Muslims are powerless to affect substantial moral reform. So too with every other group or program which is not aimed at the destruction of slums, their causes and effects. Selfhelp efforts, directly or indirectly, must be geared to mobilizing people into power units capable of effecting social change. That is, their goal must be genuine self-help, not merely self-improvement. Obviously, where selfimprovement activities succeed in imparting to their participants a feeling of some control over their environment, those involved may find their appetites for change whetted; they may move into the political arena.

Let me sum up what I have thus far been trying to say: the civil rights movement is evolving from a protest movement into a full-fledged *social movement*—an evolution calling its very name into question. It is now concerned not merely with removing the barriers to full *opportunity* but with achieving the fact of *equality*. From sit-ins and freedom rides we have gone into rent strikes, boycotts, community organization, and political action. As a consequence of this natural evolution, the Negro today finds himself stymied by obstacles of far greater magnitude than the legal barriers he was attacking before: automation, urban decay, de facto school segregation. These are problems which, while conditioned by Jim Crow, do not vanish upon its demise. They are more deeply rooted in our socioeconomic order; they are the result of the total society's failure to meet not only the Negro's needs, but human needs generally.

These propositions have won increasing recognition and acceptance, but with a curious twist. They have formed the common premise of two apparently contradictory lines of thought which simultaneously nourish and antagonize each other. On the one hand, there is the reasoning of the New York *Times* moderate who says that the problems are so enormous and complicated that Negro militancy is a futile irritation, and that the need is for "intelligent moderation." Thus, during the first New York school boycott, the *Times* editorialized that Negro demands, while abstractly just, would necessitate massive reforms, the funds for which could not realistically be anticipated; therefore the just demands were also foolish demands and would only antagonize white people. Moderates of this stripe are often correct in perceiving the difficulty or impossibility of racial progress in the context of present social and economic policies. But they accept the context as fixed. They ignore (or perhaps see all too well) the potentialities inherent in linking Negro demands to broader pressures for radical revision of existing policies. They apparently see nothing strange in the fact that in the last twenty-five years we have spent nearly a trillion dollars fighting or preparing for wars, yet throw up our hands before the need for overhauling our schools, clearing the slums, and really abolishing poverty. My quarrel with these moderates is that they do not even envision radical changes; their admonitions of moderation are, for all practical purposes, admonitions to the Negro to adjust to the status quo, and are therefore immoral.

The more effectively the moderates argue their case, the more they convince Negroes that American society will not or cannot be reorganized for full racial equality. Michael Harrington has said that a successful war on poverty might well require the expenditure of a $100 billion. Where, the Negro wonders, are the forces now in motion to compel such a commitment? If the voices of the moderates were raised in an insistence upon a reallocation of national resources at levels that could not be confused with tokenism (that is,—if the moderates stopped being moderates), Negroes would have greater grounds for hope. Meanwhile, the Negro movement cannot escape a sense of isolation.

It is precisely this sense of isolation that gives rise to the second line of thought I want to examine—the tendency within the civil rights movement which, despite its militancy, pursues what I call a "no-win" policy. Sharing with many moderates a recognition of the magnitude of the obstacles to freedom, spokesmen for this tendency survey the American scene and find no forces prepared to move toward radical solutions. From this they conclude that the only viable strategy is shock; above all, the hypocrisy of white liberals must be exposed. These spokesmen are often described as the radicals of the movement, but they are really its moralists. They seek to change white hearts—by traumatizing them. Frequently abetted by white self-flagellants, they may gleefully applaud (though not really agreeing with) Malcolm X because, while they admit he has no program, they think he can frighten white people into doing the right thing. To believe this, of course, you must be convinced, even if unconsciously, that at the core of the white man's heart lies a buried affection for Negroes—a proposition one may be permitted to doubt. But in any case, hearts are not relevant to the issue; neither racial affinities nor racial hostilities are rooted there. It is institutions—social, political, and economic institutions—which are the ultimate molders of collective sentiments. Let these institutions be reconstructed *today*, and let the ineluctable gradualism of history govern the formation of a new psychology.

My quarrel with the "no-win" tendency in the civil rights movement (and the reason I have so designated it) parallels my quarrel with the moderates outside the movement. As the latter lack the vision or will for fundamental change, the former lack a realistic strategy for achieving it. For such a strategy they substitute militancy. But militancy is a matter of posture and volume and not of effect.

I believe that the Negro's struggle for equality in America is essentially revolutionary. While most Negroes—in their hearts—unquestionably seek only to enjoy the fruits of American society as it now exists, their quest cannot *objectively* be satisfied within the framework of existing political and economic relations. The young

Negro who would demonstrate his way into the labor market may be motivated by a thoroughly bourgeois ambition and thoroughly "capitalist" considerations, but he will end up having to favor a great expansion of the public sector of the economy. At any rate, that is the position the movement will be forced to take as it looks at the number of jobs being generated by the private economy, and if it is to remain true to the masses of Negroes.

The revolutionary character of the Negro's struggle is manifest in the fact that this struggle may have done more to democratize life for whites than for Negroes. Clearly, it was the sit-in movement of young Southern Negroes which, as it galvanized white students, banished the ugliest features of McCarthyism from the American campus and resurrected political debate. It was not until Negroes assaulted de facto school segregation in the urban centers that the issue of quality education for *all* children stirred into motion. Finally, it seems reasonably clear that the civil rights movement, directly and through the resurgence of social conscience it kindled, did more to initiate the war on poverty than any other single force.

It will be—it has been—argued that these by-products of the Negro struggle are not revolutionary. But the term revolutionary, as I am using it, does not connote violence; it refers to the qualitative transformation of fundamental institutions, more or less rapidly, to the point where the social and economic structure which they comprised can no longer be said to be the same. The Negro struggle has hardly run its course; and it will not stop moving until it has been utterly defeated or won substantial equality. But I fail to see how the movement can be victorious in the absence of radical programs for full employment, abolition of slums, the reconstruction of our educational system, new definitions of work and leisure. Adding up the cost of such programs, we can only conclude that we are talking about a refashioning of our political economy. It has been estimated, for example, that the price of replacing New York City's slums with public housing would be $17 billion. Again, a multibillion dollar federal public works program, dwarfing the currently proposed $2 billion program, is required to reabsorb unskilled and semiskilled workers into the labor market—and this must be done if Negro workers in these categories are to be employed. "Preferential treatment" cannot help them.

I am not trying here to delineate a total program, only to suggest the scope of economic reforms which are most immediately related to the plight of the Negro community. One could speculate on their political implications—whether, for example, they do not indicate the obsolescence of state government and the superiority of regional structures as viable units of planning. Such speculations aside, it is clear that Negro needs cannot be satisfied unless we go beyond what has so far been placed on the agenda. How are these radical objectives to be achieved? The answer is simple, deceptively so: *through political power.* . . .

Neither that [the civil rights] movement nor the country's twenty million black people can win political power alone. We need allies. The future of the Negro struggle depends on whether the contradictions of this society can be resolved by a coalition of progressive forces which becomes the *effective* political majority in the United States. I speak of the coalition which staged the March on Washington, passed the Civil Rights Act, and laid the basis for the Johnson landslide—Negroes, trade unionists, liberals, and religious groups.

There are those who argue that a coalition strategy would force the Negro to surrender his political independence to white liberals, that he would be neutralized, deprived of his cutting edge, absorbed into the Establishment. Some who take this position urged last year that votes be withheld from the Johnson-Humphrey ticket as a demonstration of the Negro's political power. Curiously enough, these people who sought to demonstrate power through the nonexercise of it, also point to the Negro "swing vote" in crucial urban areas as the source of the Negro's independent political power. But here they are closer to being right: the urban Negro vote will grow in importance in the coming years. If there is anything positive in the spread of the ghetto, it is the potential political power base thus created, and to realize this potential is one of the most challenging and urgent tasks before the civil rights movement. If the movement can wrest leadership of the ghetto vote from the machines, it will have acquired an organized constituency such as other major groups in our society now have.

But we must also remember that the effectiveness of a swing vote depends solely on "other" votes. It derives its power from them. In that sense, it can never be "independent," but must opt for one candidate or the other, even if by default. Thus coalitions are inescapable, however tentative they may be. And this is the case in all but those few situations in which Negroes running on an independent ticket might conceivably win. "Independence," in other words, is not a value in itself. The issue is which coalition to join and how to make it responsive to your program. Necessarily there will be compromise. But the difference between expediency and morality in politics is the difference between selling out a principle and making smaller concessions to win larger ones. The leader who shrinks from this task reveals not his purity but his lack of political sense.

The task of molding a political movement out of the March on Washington coalition is not simple, but no alternatives have been advanced. We need to choose our allies on the basis of common political objectives. It has become fashionable in some no-win Negro circles to decry the white liberal as the main enemy (his hypocrisy is what sustains racism); by virtue of this reverse recitation of the reactionary's litany (liberalism leads to socialism, which leads to Communism) the Negro is left in majestic isolation, except for a tiny band of fervent white initiates. But the objective fact is that *Eastland* and *Goldwater* are the main enemies—they and the opponents of civil rights, of the war on poverty, of Medicare, of social security, of federal aid to education, of unions, and so forth. The labor movement, despite its obvious faults, has been the largest single organized force in this country pushing for progressive social legislation. And where the Negro-labor-liberal axis is weak, as in the farm belt, it was the religious groups that were most influential in rallying support for the Civil Rights Bill.

The durability of the coalition was interestingly tested during the election. I do not believe that the Johnson landslide proved the "white backlash" to be a myth. It proved, rather, that economic interests are more fundamental than prejudice: the backlashers decided that loss of social security was, after all, too high a price to pay for a slap at the Negro. This lesson was a valuable first step in re-educating such people, and it must be kept alive, for the civil rights movement will be advanced only to the degree that social and economic welfare gets to be inextricably entangled with civil rights. . . .

The role of the civil rights movement in the reorganization of American political life is programmatic as well as strategic. We are challenged now to broaden our social vision, to develop functional programs with concrete objectives. We need to propose alternatives to technological unemployment, urban decay, and the rest. We need to be calling for public works and training, for national economic planning, for federal aid to education, for attractive public housing—all this on a sufficiently massive scale to make a difference. We need to protest the notion that our integration into American life, so long delayed, must now proceed in an atmosphere of competitive scarcity instead of in the security of abundance which technology makes possible. We cannot claim to have answers to all the complex problems of modern society. That is too much to ask of a movement still battling barbarism in Mississippi. But we can agitate the right questions by probing at the contradictions which still stand in the way of the "Great Society." The questions having been asked, motion must begin in the larger society, for there is a limit to what Negroes can do alone.

Part 4

THE CHALLENGE TO SEXISM

Together with issues of race and class, the division of society into "masculine" and "feminine" spheres has been one of the major organizing themes of American society. To this day, whether one is born male or female has more to do with shaping one's life possibilities than almost any other factor. It determines the clothes we wear, the emotions we are taught to cultivate, the jobs we are told we should aspire to, the power we exercise—even our sense of who we are and what we are about. Through most of American history, cultural norms prescribed that women should be the tenders of the hearth, keepers of the home, rearers of children, and the moral, spiritual members of the family. Men, by contrast, were to be assertive, dominant, in control, the major source of power, influence, and income. Even though frequently these norms were not implemented in reality, they remained powerful forces in the culture. Particularly for white women of the middle and upper class, the norms defined as off-limits any active involvement in the world outside the home. Those women who worked prior to 1940 were primarily single, young, and poor. It was virtually unheard of for a married, middle-class white woman to have a job or pursue a career. For her to do so would be a repudiation of her natural role and a negative reflection of her husband's ability to provide for her. In a culture that defined success for a woman as marriage and homemaking, any deviation from that role marked failure.

As in the case of African-Americans, World War II generated significant change. Millions of women took jobs, and under the press of a wartime crisis, old definitions of women's "proper" place were set aside, at least for the moment. On the other hand, discrimination continued. Women were paid less than men, they were barred from executive positions, and despite wartime needs, day care centers were not provided in adequate numbers.

After the war, many of the advances that had occurred were reversed. What Betty Friedan called the "Feminine Mystique" be- came once again a pervasive cultural force, urging women to return to the home and to aspire to suburban domesticity. On the other hand, employment figures for women continued to increase, with more and more middle-class women taking jobs simply in order to make it possible for a family to aspire to a better life. By the late 1960s, a revitalized feminism became a powerful force in the soci- ety, exposing the contradiction between traditional definitions of women's place and the new frequency with which women were assuming roles outside the home. Questioning most of the tradi- tional definitions of masculinity and femininity, the women's libera- tion movement became one of the most significant forces of social change in the 1960s and 1970s.

In the case of the challenge to sexism, as in the black struggle, there are some who focus attention on external and impersonal sources of change, and others who emphasize the role of activists in bringing about social progress. In the following selections, William Chafe writes about some of the aggregate trends in the society that established the framework within which a revitalized feminism de- veloped. Sara Evans discusses the origins of the women's liberation movement in the civil rights struggles of the early 1960s, showing how the experience of fighting for racial equality generated a new commitment to fight for sex equality as well.

Not all women, of course, were persuaded by feminist arguments. Many black women, for example, viewed women's rights as the narrow concern of middle- and upper-class white women who oth- erwise were insensitive or indifferent to black concerns; bell hooks writes about some of these issues in the piece excerpted here. Large numbers of other women defended traditional roles and saw femi- nism as subverting the family, the community, and the sanctity of human life. Of particular concern to many of these women was the feminist position defending a woman's right to have an abortion. The Supreme Court's decision in the 1973 case of *Roe v. Wade* presents the judicial rationale for supporting women's right to choice in the matter of reproductive freedom. Rebecca Klatch then discusses the variety of issues shaping the politics of antifeminist women.

One of these issues was homosexuality and the gay rights move- ment. In the view of many lesbian feminists and gay men, sexism extended beyond the question of patriarchy and men's power over women in politics, business, and the household. It involved as well the pervasive assumption that *heterosexuality* was the only acceptable form of sexual expression. Estelle Freedman and John D'Emilio write about the origins of the gay rights movement—one of the most important offshoots of feminism—in the article excerpted here from their history of sexuality in America.

Among the questions of most interest with regard to the challenge to sexism are why it took until the middle of the 1960s for a women's liberation movement to develop; why more women did not become active feminists during and after World War II; whether the family is dependent upon traditional roles for men and women; and what the implications for the society will be of greater equality for women and men. Perhaps the largest issue is how and whether sex equality can be achieved given the values and the institutions of contemporary American society.

Social Change and the American Woman, 1940–1970

William H. Chafe

In the later years of the 1970s, feminism encountered intense resistance from the anti-ERA movement and the right-to-life groups opposing abortion. More generally, a new conservatism gained force. Many believed that progress had gone too far and that it was time to call a halt to change. Nevertheless, the feminist movement had already succeeded in increasing opportunities for women, in heightening their self-awareness, and in helping to reshape American thinking about such fundamentals as social equality, the family, and sexuality.

More difficult to ascertain than the gains of the women's movement, however, were its causes and origins. In the following analysis of the relationship between social change and the contemporary feminist movement, William Chafe focuses on the consequences of increasing female participation in the labor force. He is particularly concerned with the complicated interaction of objective conditions, such as employment patterns and income, and people's perceptions of those conditions, their attitudes and values. His account should prove he a deeper understanding of the sources and nature of women's liberation.

Although historians have largely neglected the role of women in America's past, few groups in the population merit closer study as a barometer of how American society operates. Not only do women comprise a majority of the population, but gender—together with

Excerpted from William H. Chafe, "The Paradox of Progress: Social Change Since 1930," in James T Patterson, ed. *Paths to the Present* (Minneapolis: Burgess Publishing Co., 1975). Reprinted by permission of the author.

race and class—serves as one of the principal reference points around which American society is organized. The sociologist Peter Berger has observed that "identity is socially bestowed, socially sanctioned and socially transformed," and gender has been one of the enduring foundations on which social identity has rested. It has provided the basis-for dividing up the labor of life ("breadwinning" versus "homemaking"), it has been central to the delineation of roles and authority in the family, and it has served as the source for two powerful cultural stereotypes—"masculine" and "feminine." Any change in the nature of male and female roles thus automatically affects the home, the economy, the school, and perhaps above all, the definition of who we are as human beings. . . .

The eruption of World War II made a significant dent in this pattern. The national emergency caused new industries to develop and new jobs to open up, providing an opportunity for women, like other excluded groups, to improve their economic position. . . . Hardly a job existed which women did not perform.

The statistics of female employment suggest the dimensions of the change. Between 1941 and 1945, 6.5 million women took jobs, increasing the size of the female labor force by 57 percent. At the end of 1940 approximately 25 percent of all women were gainfully employed; four years later the figure had soared to 36 percent—an increase greater than that of the previous forty years combined. Perhaps most important from a social point of view, the largest number of new workers were married and middle-aged. Prior to 1940 young and single women had made up the vast majority of the female labor force. During the war, in contrast, 75 percent of the new workers were married, and within four years the number of wives in the labor force had doubled. Although some of the new labor recruits were newlyweds who might have been expected to work in any event, the majority listed themselves as former housewives and many, including 60 percent of those hired by the War Department, had children of school and preschool age. By the time victory was achieved, it was just as likely that a wife over forty would be employed as a single woman under twenty-five. The urgency of defeating the Axis powers had swept away, temporarily at least, one of America's entrenched customs.

If women took jobs in unprecedented numbers, however, there was little evidence of a parallel shift in attitudes toward equality between the sexes. Women were consistently excluded from top policy-making committees concerned with running the war, and from higher-level management and executive positions. In addition, the war had only a minimal effect on the traditional disparity between men's and women's wages. Although the War Manpower Commission announced a firm policy of equal pay for equal work, enforcement was spotty, and employers continued to pay women less than men simply by changing the description of the job from "heavy" to "light."

The staying power of traditional values received vigorous confirmation in the postwar years. Despite effusive expressions of gratitude for women's contribution to the war effort, many Americans believed that women should return to their rightful place in the home as soon as the war had ended. In one of the most popular treatises of the postwar years, Ferdinand Lundberg and Marynia Farnham argued that female employment was a feminist conspiracy to seduce women into betraying their biological destiny. The independent woman, they claimed, was a "contradiction in terms." Women were born to be soft, nurturant, and dependent on men; motherhood represented the true goal of female life. Sounding the same theme, Agnes Meyer wrote in the *Atlantic* that though women had many careers, "they have only one vocation—motherhood." The task of modern women, she concluded, was to "boldly announce that no job is more exacting, more necessary, or more rewarding than that of housewife and mother." Most Americans seemed to agree. A series of public opinion polls taken in the postwar years showed that a large majority of people continued to subscribe to the idea of a sharp division of labor between the sexes, with husbands making the "big" decisions and wives caring for the home.

In fact, the situation was more complicated than either public opinion polls or magazine rhetoric seemed to indicate. It was one thing to focus renewed attention on traditional values, and quite another to eradicate the impact of four years of experience. As observers noted at the time, women had discovered something new about themselves in the course of the war, and many were unwilling to give up that discovery just because the war had ended. Although most of the women workers viewed their employment as temporary when the war began, a Women's Bureau survey disclosed that by war's end, 75 percent wished to remain in the labor force.

To a surprising extent, these women succeeded in their desire to remain in the job market. Although the number of women workers declined temporarily in the period immediately after the war, female employment figures showed a sharp upturn beginning in 1947, and by 1950 had once again reached wartime peaks. By 1960 the number of women workers was growing at a rate four times faster than that of men, and 40 percent of all women over sixteen were in the labor force compared to 25 percent in 1940. More important, the women who spearheaded the change were from the same groups that had first gone to work in the war. By 1970, 45 percent of the nation's wives were employed (compared to 11.5 percent in 1930 and 15 percent in 1940), and the 1970 figure included 51 percent of all mothers with children aged six to seventeen. In addition, the economic background of the women workers had shifted significantly. During the 1930s employment of married women had been limited almost exclusively to families with poverty level incomes. By 1970, in contrast, 60 percent of all families with an income of more than $10,000 had wives who worked. In short, the whole pattern of female employment had been reversed. Through legitimizing employment for the average wife and making it a matter of patriotic necessity, the war had initiated a dramatic alteration in the behavior of women and had permanently changed the day-to-day content of their lives.

But if the "objective" conditions of female employment changed so much, why did attitudes toward equality not follow suit? Why, if so many wives and mothers were holding jobs, was there so little protest about continued low pay and discrimination? Why, above all, did the woman's movement not revive in the forties or fifties instead of developing only in the late sixties? Such questions have no easy answers, but to the extent that an explanation is possible, it has to do with the context of the times. The prospect for value changes in any period depends on the frame of reference of the participants, their awareness of the possibility or need for action, and the dominant influences at work in shaping the society. When the appropriate conditions are present, change can be explosive. When they are not present, change can take on the character of an underground fire—important in the long run but for the moment beneath the surface. The latter description fits the situation of women in the forties and fifties and a consideration of the context in which their employment increased during these years is crucial to an understanding of the relationship between behavior and attitudes.

To begin with, most women in the forties and fifties lacked the frame of reference from which to challenge prevailing attitudes on sex roles. Although many women worked, the assumptions about male and female spheres of responsibility were so deeply ingrained that to question them amounted to heresy. If social values are to be changed, there must be a critical mass of protestors who can provide an alternative ideology and mobilize opposition toward traditional points of view. In the postwar period, that protest group did not exist. Feminists at the time simply had no popular support and were generally viewed as a group of cranky women who constituted a "lunatic fringe."

In such a situation, it was not surprising that most women workers exhibited little feminist consciousness. Most had taken jobs because of the benefits associated with employment, not out of a desire to compete with men or prove their equality. When a pattern of discrimination is so pervasive that it is viewed as part of the rules of the game, few individuals will have the wherewithal to protest. It takes time and an appropriate set of social conditions before a basis for ideological protest can develop. With their experience in World War II, women had gone through the first stage of a monumental change. But it would be unrealistic to think that they could move immediately into a posture of feminist rebellion without a series of intervening stages. New perceptions had to evolve; new ideas had to gain currency. And both depended to some extent on the dominant influences at work in the immediate environment.

The second reason for the persistence of traditional attitudes was that women's employment expanded under conditions which emphasized women's role as "helpmates." The continued entry of women into the labor force was directly related to skyrocketing inflation and the pent-up desire of millions of families to achieve a higher living standard. In many instances, husbands and wives could not build new homes, buy new appliances, or purchase new cars on one income alone, and the impulse not to be left behind in the race for affluence offered a convenient rationale for women to remain in the labor force. Men who might oppose in theory the idea of married women holding jobs were willing to have their own wives go to work to help the family achieve its middle-class aspirations.

But under such circumstances, the wife who held a job was playing a supportive role, not striking out on her own as an "independent" woman. The distinction was crucial. If women had been taking jobs because of a desire to prove their equality with men, their employment would probably have encountered bitter resistance. In contrast, the fact that they were thought to be only "helping out" made it possible for their efforts to receive social sanction as a fulfillment of their traditional family role.

To say that attitudes did not change, however, did not mean that behavior was without important long-range effects. Indeed, the growing employment of women offers an excellent example of the way in which changes in behavior can pave the way for subsequent changes in attitudes. As more and more wives joined the labor force after 1940, the sexual segregation of roles and responsibilities within the family slowly gave way to greater sharing. Sociological surveys showed that wherever wives held jobs, husbands performed more household tasks, especially in the areas of child care, cleaning, and shopping. In addition, power relationships between men and women underwent some change. Women who worked exercised considerably more influence on "major" economic decisions than wives who did not work. In no instance did the changes result in total equality, nor were they ideologically inspired; but sociologists unanimously concluded that women's employment played a key role in modifying the traditional distribution of tasks and authority within the family.

Similarly, the presence of an employed mother exercised a substantial impact on the socialization patterns of children. Young boys and girls who were raised in households where both parents worked grew up with the expectation that women—as well as men— would play active roles in the outside world. A number of surveys of children in elementary and junior high school showed that daughters of working mothers planned to work themselves after marriage, and the same studies suggested that young girls were more likely to name their mother as the person they most admired if she worked than if she did not work. At the same time, it appeared that these daughters developed a revised idea of what it meant to be born female. On a series of personality tests, daughters of working mothers scored lower on scales of traditional femininity and agreed that both men and women should enjoy a variety of work, household, and recreational experiences. Thus if behavioral change did not itself produce a challenge to traditional attitudes, it set in motion a process which prepared a foundation for such a challenge.

All that was required to complete the process was the development of an appropriate context, and in the early 1960s that context began to emerge. After eight years of consolidation and consensus in national politics during the Eisenhower administration, a new mood of criticism and reform started to surface in the nation. Sparked by the demands of black Americans for full equality, public leaders focused new attention on a whole variety of problems which had been festering for years. Poverty, racial injustice, and sex discrimination had a lengthy history in America, but awareness of them crystallized in a climate which emphasized the need for activism to eradicate the nation's ills. Once the process of protest had begun, it generated a momentum of its own, spreading to groups which previously had been quiescent.

Again, the experience of women dramatized the process of change. Just as World War II had served as a catalyst to behavioral change among women, the ferment of the sixties served as a catalyst to ideological change. The first major sign of the impending drive for womens liberation appeared with the publication in 1963 of Betty Friedan's best-selling *The Feminine Mystique*. Writing with eloquence and passion, Friedan traced the origins of women's oppression to a social system which persistently denied women the opportunity to develop their talents as individual human beings. "The core of the problem of women today," she wrote, "is not sexual but a problem of identity—a stunting or evasion of growth. . . ." Friedan pointed out that while men had abundant opportunities to test their mettle, women saw their entire lives circumscribed by the condition of their birth and were told repeatedly "that they could desire no greater destiny than to glory in their own femininity." If a woman had aspirations for a career, she was urged instead to find a full measure of satisfaction in the role of housewife and mother. Magazines insisted that there was no other route to happiness; consumer industries glorified her life as homemaker; and psychologists warned her that if she left her position in the home, the whole society would be endangered. The result was that she was imprisoned in a "comfortable concentration camp," prevented from discovering who she really *was* by a society which told her only what she *could be*. Although Friedan's assessment contained little that had not been said before by other feminists, her book spoke to millions of women in a fresh way, driving home the message that what had previously been perceived as only a personal problem was in fact a *woman* problem, shared by others and rooted in a set of social attitudes that required change if a better life was to be achieved.

A second—and equally important—influence feeding the woman's movement came from the burgeoning drive for civil rights. Although it was true that blacks and women had strikingly different problems, they suffered from modes of oppression which in some ways were similar. For women as well as blacks, the denial of equality occurred through' the assignment of separate and unequal roles. Both were taught to "keep their place," and were excluded from social and economic opportunities on the grounds that assertive behavior was deviant. The principal theme of the civil rights movement was the immorality of treating any human being as less equal than another on the basis of a physical characteristic, and that theme spoke as much to the condition of women as to that of blacks. In its tactics, its message, and its moral fervor, the civil rights movement provided inspiration and an organizational model for the activities of women.

Just as significant, the civil rights movement exposed many women to the direct experience of sex discrimination. Younger activists in particular found that they frequently were treated as servants whose chief function was to be sex partners for male leaders. ("The place of women in the movement," Stokely Carmichael said, "is prone.") Instead of having an equal voice in policy making, women were relegated to tasks such as making coffee or sweeping floors. Faced with such discrimination, some female activists concluded that they had to free *themselves* before they could work effectively for the freedom of others. The same women became the principal leaders of the younger, more radical segment of women's liberation, taking the organizing skills and ideological fervor which they had learned in the fight for blacks and applying them to the struggle for women.

Perhaps the most important precondition for the revival of feminism, however, was the amount of change which had already occurred in women's lives. As long as the overwhelming majority of women remained in the home, there was no frame of reference from which to question the status quo. Woman's "place" was a fact as well as an idea. With the changes which began in World War II, on the other hand, reality ceased to conform to attitudes. The march of events had already delivered a fatal blow to conventional ideas on woman's place, thereby creating a condition which made feminist arguments both timely and relevant. The experience of *some* change gave millions of women the perspective which allowed them to hear the feminists call for more change. Thus if the women who took jobs during the forties did not themselves mount an ideological assault on the status quo, they prepared a foundation which enabled the subsequent generation to take up the battle for a change in attitudes and ideas.

Women's Consciousness and the Southern Black Movement

Sara Evans

"There is no overt antifeminism in our society in 1964," observed sociologist Alice Rossi, "not because sex equality has been achieved, but because there is practically no feminist spark left among American women." The tinder existed, as Chafe describes in the preceding selection, but an acute awareness of oppression, a fiery consciousness did not. The combustion, however, would soon be provided by the young female participants in the civil rights and New Left movements. These daughters of the middle class ignited a radical critique of sexism and a mass mobilization of American women. In the voter registration campaigns of the South and in the community organizing efforts in Northern ghettos, the female volunteers found the inner strength and self-respect, the new vistas of possibility, and the political skills to pursue their own quest for equality. There they also experienced having their work minimized, even disregarded, by the men they had considered their colleagues. This shattering ordeal spun them out of the male-dominated movements and into a new one for women's liberation. Personal Politics (1979), by Sara Evans, and the following selection provocatively analyze these collective biographical roots of the revitalized challenge to sexism.

Twice in the history of the United States the struggle for racial equality has been midwife to a feminist movement. In the abolition movement of the 1830s and 1840s and again in the civil-rights revolt of the 1960s, women experiencing the contradictory expectations and stresses of changing roles began to move from individual discontents to a social movement in their own behalf. Working for racial justice, they developed both political skills and a belief in human rights which could justify their own claim to equality. . . .

Following the first wave of sit-ins in 1960, the Southern Christian Leadership Conference (SCLC), at the insistence of its assistant director, Ella Baker, called a conference at Shaw University in Raleigh, N.C., on Easter weekend. There black youth founded their own organization, the Student Nonviolent Coordinating Committee (SNCC) to provide a support network for direct action. SNCC set the style and tone of grass-roots organizing in the rural South and led the movement into the black belt. The spirit of adventure and commitment which animated the organization added new vitality to a deeply rooted struggle for racial equality.

In addition to this crucial role within the black movement, SNCC also created the social space within which women began to develop a new sense of their own potential. A critical vanguard of young women accumulated the tools for movement building: a language to describe oppression and justify revolt, experience in the strategy and tactics of organizing, and a beginning sense of themselves collectively as objects of discrimination.

Relative deprivation is an overused and overly clinical term to describe the pain, the anger, and the ambiguity of their experience.

Nevertheless, it was precisely the clash between the heightened sense of self-worth which the movement offered to its participants and the replication of traditional sex roles within it that gave birth to a new feminism. Treated as housewives, sex objects, nurturers, and political auxiliaries, and finally threatened with banishment from the movement, young white Southern women responded with the first articulation of the modern challenge to the sexual status quo. . . .

The movement's vision translated into daily realities of hard work and responsibility which admitted few sexual limitations. Young white women's sense of purpose was reinforced by the knowledge that the work they did and the responsibilities they assumed were central to the movement. In the beginning, black and white alike agreed that whites should work primarily in the white community. They had an appropriate role in urban direct-action movements where the goal was integration, but their principal job was generating support for civil rights within the white population. The handful of white women involved in the early '60s either worked in the SNCC office—gathering news, writing pamphlets, facilitating communications—or organized campus support through such agencies as the YWCA.

In direct-action demonstrations, many women discovered untapped reservoirs of courage. Cathy Cade attended Spelman College as an exchange student in the spring of 1962. She had been there only two days when she joined Howard Zinn in a sit-in in the black section of the Georgia Legislature. Never before had she so much as joined a picket line. Years later she testified: "To this day I am amazed. I just did it." Though she understood the risks involved, she does not remember being afraid. Rather she was exhilarated, for with one stroke she undid much of the fear of blacks that she had developed as a high school student in Tennessee.

Others, like Mimi Feingold, jumped eagerly at the chance to join the freedom rides but then found the experience more harrowing than they had expected. Her group had a bomb scare in Montgomery and knew that the last freedom bus in Alabama had been blown up. They never left the bus from Atlanta to Jackson, Mississippi. The arrest in Jackson was anti-climactic. Then there was a month in jail where she could hear women screaming as they were subjected to humiliating vaginal "searches."

When SNCC moved into voter registration projects in the Deep South, the experiences of white women acquired a new dimension. The years of enduring the brutality of intransigent racism finally convinced SNCC to invite several hundred white students into Mississippi for the 1964 "freedom summer." For the first time, large numbers of white women would be allowed into "the field," to work in the rural South.

They had previously been excluded because white women in rural communities were highly visible; their presence, violating both racial and sexual taboos, often provoked repression. According to Mary King, "the start of violence in a community was often tied to the point at which white women appeared to be in the civil-rights movement." However, the presence of whites also brought the attention of the national media, and, in the face of the apparent impotence of the federal law enforcement apparatus, the media became the chief weapon of the movement against violence and brutality. Thus, with considerable ambivalence, SNCC began to include whites—both men and women—in certain voter registration projects.

The freedom summer brought hundreds of Northern white

women into the Southern movement. They taught in freedom schools, ran libraries, canvassed for voter registration, and endured constant harassment from the local whites. Many reached well beyond their previously assumed limits: "I was overwhelmed at the idea of setting up a library all by myself," wrote one woman. "Then can you imagine how I felt when at Oxford, while I was learning how to drop on the ground to protect my face, my ears, and my breasts, I was asked to *coordinate* the libraries in the entire project's community centers? I wanted to cry 'HELP' in a number of ways."

And while they tested themselves and questioned their own courage, they also experienced poverty, oppression and discrimination in raw form. As one volunteer wrote:

> For the first time in my life, I am seeing what it is like to be poor, oppressed, and hated. And what I see here does not apply only to Gulfport or to Mississippi or even to the South. . . . This summer is only the briefest beginning of this experience."

Some women virtually ran the projects they were in. And they learned to live with an intensity of fear that they had never known before. By October, 1964, there had been 15 murders, 4 woundings, 37 churches bombed or burned, and over 1,000 arrests in Mississippi. Every project set up elaborate security precautions—regular communication by two-way radio, rules against going out at night or walking downtown in interracial groups. One woman summed up the experience of hundreds when she explained, "I learned a lot of respect for myself for having gone through all that."

As white women tested themselves in the movement, they were constantly inspired by the examples of black women who shattered cultural images of appropriate "female" behavior. "For the first time," according to one white Southerner, "I had role models I could respect."

Within the movement many of the legendary figures were black women around whom circulated stories of exemplary courage and audacity. Rarely did women expect or receive any special protection in demonstrations or jails. Frequently, direct-action teams were equally divided between women and men, on the theory that the presence of women in sit-in demonstrations might lessen the violent reaction. In 1960, slender Diane Nash had been transformed overnight from a Fisk University beauty queen to a principal leader of the direct-action movement in Nashville, Tennessee. . . .

Perhaps even more important than the daring of younger activists was the towering strength of older black women. There is no doubt that women were key to organizing the black community. In 1962, SNCC staff member Charles Sherrod wrote the office that in every southwest Georgia county "there is always a 'mama.' She is usually a militant woman in the community, out-spoken, understanding, and willing to catch hell, having already caught her share."

Stories of such women abound. For providing housing, food, and active support to SNCC workers, their homes were fired upon and bombed. Fannie Lou Hamer, the Sunflower County sharecropper who forfeited her livelihood to emerge as one of the most courageous and eloquent leaders of the Mississippi Freedom Democratic Party, was only the most famous. "Mama Dolly" in Lee County, Georgia, was a seventy-year-old, grey-haired lady "who can pick more cotton, slop more pigs, plow more ground, chop more wood, and do a hundred more things better than the best farmer in the area." For many white volunteers, they were also "mamas" in the sense of being mother-figures, new models of the meaning of womanhood.

Yet new models bumped up against old ones; self-assertion generated anxiety; new expectations existed alongside traditional ones; ideas about freedom and equality bent under assumptions about women as mere houseworkers and sexual objects. These contradictory forces finally generated a feminist response from those who could not deny the reality of their new-found strength.

Black and white women took on important administrative roles in the Atlanta SNCC office, but they also performed virtually all typing and clerical work. Very few women assumed the public roles of national leadership. In 1964, black women held a half-serious, half-joking sit-in to protest these conditions. By 1965, the situation had changed enough that a quarrel over who would take notes at staff meetings was settled by buying a tape recorder.

In the field, there was a tendency to assume that housework around the freedom house would be performed by women. As early as 1963, Joni Rabinowitz, a white volunteer in the southwest Georgia Project, submitted a stinging series of reports on the "woman's role."

"*Monday, 15 April:* . . . *The attitude around here toward keeping the house neat (as well as the general attitude toward the inferiority and 'proper place'* of women) *is disgusting and also terribly depressing. I never saw a cooperative enterprize (sic) that was less cooperative."*

There were also ambiguities in the position of women who had been in the movement for many years and were perceived by others as important leaders. While women increasingly became a central force in SNCC between 1960 and 1965, white women were always in a somewhat anomalous position. New recruits saw Casey Hayden and Mary King as very powerful. Hayden had been an activist since the late '50s. Her involvement in the YWCA and the Christian Faith and Life Community at the University of Texas led her to join the demonstrations which erupted in Austin in 1959. From that time on she worked full-time against segregation, sometimes through the Y, sometimes through the National Student Association or Students for a Democratic Society, but always most closely with SNCC. Mary King, daughter of a Southern Methodist minister, had visited SNCC on a trip sponsored by the Y at Ohio Wesleyan University in 1962 and soon returned to work full-time.

They and others who had joined the young movement when it included only a handful of whites knew the inner circles of SNCC through years of shared work and risk. They had an easy familiarity with the top leadership which bespoke considerable influence. Yet Hayden and King could virtually run a freedom registration program and at the same time remain outside the basic political decision-making process.

Mary King described herself and Hayden as being in "positions of relative powerlessness." They were powerful because they worked very hard. According to King, "If you were a hard worker and you were good, at least before 1965 . . . you could definitely have an influence on policy."

The key phrase is "at least before 1965," for by 1965 the positions of white women in SNCC, especially Southern women whose goals had been shaped by the vision of the "beloved community," was in steep decline. Ultimately, a growing spirit of black nationalism, fed by the tensions of large numbers of whites, especially women, entering the movement, forced these women out of SNCC and precipitated the articulation of a new feminism.

White women's presence inevitably heightened the sexual tension which runs as a constant current through racist culture. Southern women understood that in the struggle against racial discrimination they were at war with their culture. They reacted to the label

"Southern lady" as though it were an obscene epithet, for they had emerged from a society that used the symbol of "Southern white womanhood" to justify an insidious pattern of racial discrimination and brutal repression. They had, of necessity, to forge a new sense of self, a new definition of femininity apart from the one they had inherited. Gradually they came to understand the struggle against racism as "a key to pulling down all the . . . fascist notions and mythologies and institutions in the South," including "notions about white women and repression."

Thus, for Southern women this tension was a key to their incipient feminism, but it also became a disruptive force within the civil-rights movement itself. The entrance of white women in large numbers into the movement could hardly have been anything but explosive. Interracial sex was the most potent social taboo in the South. And the struggle against racism brought together young, naive, sometimes insensitive, rebellious, and idealistic white women with young, angry black men, some of whom had hardly been allowed to speak to white women before. They sat-in together. If they really believed in equality, why shouldn't they sleep together?

In many such relationships there was much warmth and caring. Several marriages resulted. One young woman described how "a whole lot of things got shared around sexuality—like black men with white women—it wasn't just sex, it was also sharing ideas and fears, and emotional support . . . My sexuality for myself was confirmed by black men for the first time ever in my life, see . . . and I needed that very badly . . . It's a positive advantage to be a big woman in the black community."

On the other hand, there remained a dehumanizing quality in many relationships. According to one woman, it "had a lot to do with the fact that people thought they might die." They lived their lives at an incredible pace and could not be very loving toward anybody. "So [people] would go to a staff meeting and . . . sleep with whoever was there."

Sexual relationships did not become a serious problem, however, until interracial sex became a widespread phenomenon in local communities in the summer of 1964. The same summer that opened new horizons to hundreds of women simultaneously induced serious strains within the movement itself. Accounts of what happened vary according to the perspectives of the observer.

Some paint a picture of hordes of "loose" white women coming to the South and spreading corruption wherever they went. One male black leader recounted that "where I was project director we put white women out of the project within the first three weeks because they tried to screw themselves across the city." He agreed that black neighborhood youth tended to be sexually aggressive. "I mean you are trained to be aggressive in this country, but you are also not expected to get a positive response."

Others saw the initiative coming almost entirely from males. According to historian Staughton Lynd, director of the Freedom Schools, "Every black SNCC worker with perhaps a few exceptions counted it a notch on his gun to have slept with a white woman—as many as possible. And I think that was just very traumatic for the women who encountered that, who hadn't thought that was what going South was about." A white woman who worked in Virginia for several years explained, "It's much harder to say 'No' to the advances of a black guy because of the strong possibility of that being taken as racist."

Clearly the boundary between sexual freedom and sexual exploitation was a thin one. Many women consciously avoided all romantic involvements in intuitive recognition of that fact. Yet the presence of hundreds of young whites from middle- and upper-middle-income families in a movement primarily of poor, rural blacks exacerbated latent racial and sexual tensions beyond the breaking point. The first angry response came not from the surrounding white community (which continually assumed sexual excesses far beyond the reality) but from young black women in the movement.

A black woman pointed out that white women would "do all the shit work and do it in a feminine kind of way while [black women] . . . were out in the streets battling with the cops. So it did something to what [our] femininity was about. We became amazons, less than and more than women at the same time." Another black woman added, "If white women had a problem in SNCC, it was not just a male/woman problem . . . it was also a black woman/ white woman problem. It was a race problem rather than a woman's problem." And a white woman, asked whether she experienced any hostility from black women, responded, "Oh tons and tons! I was very, very afraid of black women, very afraid." Though she admired them and was continually awed by their courage and strength, her sexual relationships with black men placed a barrier between herself and black women.

Soon after the 1964 summer project, black women in SNCC sharply confronted male leadership. They charged that they could not develop relationships with black men because the men did not have to be responsible to them as long as they could turn to involvement with white women.

Black women's anger and demands constituted one part of an intricate maze of tensions and struggles that were in the process of transforming the civil-rights movement. SNCC had grown from a small band of sixteen to a swollen staff of 180, of whom 50% were white. The earlier dream of a beloved community was dead. The vision of freedom lay crushed under the weight of intransigent racism, disillusion with electoral politics and nonviolence, and differences of race, class, and culture within the movement itself. Within the rising spirit of black nationalism, the anger of black women toward white women was only one element. . . .

For Southern white women who had devoted several years of their lives to the vision of a beloved community, the rejection of nonviolence and movement toward a more ideological, centralized, and black nationalist movement was bitterly disillusioning. Mary King recalled, "It was very sad to see something that was so creative and so dynamic and so strong [disintegrating]. . . . I was terribly disappointed for a long time. . . . I was most affected by the way that black women turned against me. That hurt more than the guys. But it had been there, you know. You could see it coming."

In the fall of 1965, Mary King and Casey Hayden spent several days of long discussions in the mountains of Virginia. Both of them were on their way out of the movement, though they were not fully conscious of that fact. Finally they decided to write a "kind of memo" addressed to "a number of other women in the peace and freedom movements." In it they argued that women, like blacks, "seem to be caught in a common-law caste system that operates, sometimes subtly, forcing them to work around or outside hierarchical structures of power which may exclude them. Women seem to be placed in the same position of assumed subordination in personal situations too. It is a caste system which, at its worst, uses and exploits women."

Hayden and King set the precedent of contrasting the movement's egalitarian ideas with the replication of sex roles within it. They noted the ways in which women's position in society determined women's roles in the movement—like cleaning houses, doing secretarial work, and refraining from active or public leadership. At the same time, they observed, "having learned from the movement to think radically about the personal worth and abilities of people whose role in society had gone unchallenged before, a lot of women in the movement have begun trying to apply those lessons to their own relationships with men. Each of us probably has her own story of the various results."

They spoke of the pain of trying to put aside "deeply learned fears, needs, and self-perceptions . . . and . . . to replace them with concepts of people and freedom learned from the movement and organizing." In this process many people in the movement had questioned basic institutions, such as marriage and child-rearing. Indeed, such issues had been discussed over and over again, but seriously only among women. The usual male response was laughter, and women were left feeling silly. Hayden and King lamented the "lack of community for discussion: Nobody is writing, or organizing, or talking publicly about women, in any way that reflects the problems that various women in the movement came across." Yet despite their feelings of invisibility, their words also demonstrated the ability to take the considerable risks involved in sharp criticisms. Through the movement they had developed too much self-confidence and self-respect to accept passively subordinate roles.

The memo was addressed principally to black women—long time friends and comrades-in-nonviolent-arms—in the hope that, "perhaps we can start to talk with each other more openly than in the past and create a community of support for each other so we can deal with ourselves and others with integrity and can therefore keep working." In some ways, it was a parting attempt to halt the metamorphosis in the civil-rights movement from nonviolence to nationalism, from beloved community to black power. It expressed Hayden and King's pain and isolation as white women in the movement. The black women who received it were on a different historic trajectory. They would fight some of the same battles as women, but in a different context and in their own way.

This "kind of memo" represented a flowering of women's consciousness that articulated contradictions felt most acutely by middle-class white women. While black women had been gaining strength and power within the movement, white women's position—it the nexus of sexual and racial conflicts—had become increasingly precarious. Their feminist response, then, was precipitated by loss in he immediate situation, but it was a sense of loss against the even sleeper background of new strength and self-worth which the movement had allowed them to develop. Like their foremothers in the, nineteenth century, they confronted this dilemma with the tools which the movement had given them: a language to name and describe oppression; a deep belief in freedom, equality and community to be translated into "sisterhood"; a willingness to question and engender any social institution which failed to meet human needs; the ability to organize.

It is not surprising that the issues were defined and confronted first by Southern women whose consciousness developed in a context which inextricably and paradoxically linked the fate of women and black people. These spiritual daughters of Sarah and Angelina, Grimke kept their expectations low in November, 1965. "Objectively," Hayden and King wrote, "the chances seem nil that we could start a movement based on anything as distant to general American thought as a sex-caste system." But change was in the air nd youth was on the march.

In the North there were hundreds of women who had shared in he Southern experience for a week, a month, a year, and thousands more who participated vicariously or worked to extend the struggle for freedom and equality into Northern communities. These women were ready to hear what their Southern sisters had to say. The debate within Students for a Democratic Society (SDS) which started in response to Hayden and King's ideas led, two years later, to the founding of the women's liberation movement.

Thus, the fullest expression of conscious feminism within the civil-rights movement ricocheted off the fury of black power and landed with explosive force in the Northern, white new left. One month after Hayden and King mailed out their memo, women who had read it staged an angry walkout of a national SDS conference in Champaign-Urbana, Illinois. The only man to defend their action was a black man from SNCC.

Black Women: Shaping Feminist Theory

bell hooks

When the contemporary feminist movement began, many of its proponents argued that women shared "bonds of sisterhood" across race and class lines. This "essentialist" position as it was later called, presumed that the common experience of being born female in a patriarchal social structure transcended in importance and impact the very dissimilar experiences that divided women of diverse classes and races. All too often, however, it was the experience of white, college-educated women that was being used as the basis for generalization. Controversy over this issue became a critical dividing point in the feminist movement as different groups, with distinct ideologies, sought to address the dilemma of whether gender was in fact a more important source of oppression than class or race, and the extent to which women of diverse ethnic and socioeconomic backgrounds should be expected to band together in solidarity. In the following selection, bell hooks articulates the anger of many black women toward the elitist assumptions of some white feminists.

Feminism in the United States has never emerged from the women who are most victimized by sexist oppression; women who are daily beaten down, mentally, physically, and spiritually—women who are powerless to change their condition in life. They are a silent majority. A mark of their victimization is that they accept their lot in life without visible question, without organized protest, without collective anger or rage. Betty Friedan's *The Feminine Mystique* is still heralded as having paved the way for the contemporary feminist

From bell hooks, *Feminist Theory: from margin to center* (Boston: South End Press, 1984), 1-15. Reprinted by permission.

movement—it was written as if these women did not exist. Friedan's famous phrase, "the problem that has no name," often quoted to describe the condition of women in this society, actually referred to the plight of a select group of college-educated, middle and upper class, married white women—housewives bored with leisure, with the home, with children, with buying products, who wanted more out of life. Friedan concludes her first chapter by stating: "We can no longer ignore that voice within women that says: 'I want something more than my husband and my children and my house.'" That "more" she defined as careers. She did not discuss who would be called in to take care of the children and maintain the home if more women like herself were freed from their house labor and given equal access with white men to the professions. She did not speak of the needs of women without men, without children, without homes. She ignored the existence of all non-white women and poor white women. She did not tell readers whether it was more fulfilling to be a maid, a baby-sitter, a factory worker, a clerk, or a prostitute, than to be a leisure class housewife.

She made her plight and the plight of white women like herself synonymous with a condition affecting all American women. In so doing, she deflected attention away from her classism, her racism, her sexist attitudes toward the masses of American women. In the context of her book, Friedan makes clear that the women she saw as victimized by sexism were college-educated, white women who were compelled by sexist conditioning to remain in the home. She contends:

> It is urgent to understand how the very condition of being a housewife can create a sense of emptiness, nonexistence, nothingness in women. There are aspects of the housewife role that make it almost impossible for a woman of adult intelligence to retain a sense of human identity, the firm core of self or "I" without which a human being, man or woman, is not truly alive. For women of abilIty, in America today, I am convinced that there is something about the housewife state itself that is dangerous.

Specific problems and dilemmas of leisure class white housewives were real concerns that merited consideration and change but they were not the pressing political concerns of masses of women. Masses of women were concerned about economic survival, ethnic and racial discrimination, etc. When Friedan wrote *The Feminine*

Mystique, more than one-third of all women were in the work force. Although many women longed to be housewives, only women with leisure time and money could actually shape their identities on the model of the feminine mystique. They were women who, in Friedan's words, were "told by the most advanced thinkers of our time to go back and live their lives as if they were Noras, restricted to the doll's house by Victorian prejudices."

From her early writing, it appears that Friedan never wondered whether or not the plight of college-educated, white housewives was an adequate reference point by which to gauge the impact of sexism or sexist oppression on the lives of women in American society. Nor did she move beyond her own life experience to acquire an expanded perspective on the lives of women in the United States. I say this not to discredit her work. It remains a useful discussion of the impact of sexist discrimination on a select group of women. Examined from a different perspective, it can also be seen as a case study of narcissism, insensitivity, sentimentality, and self-indulgence which reaches its peak when Friedan, in a chapter titled "Progressive Dehumanization," makes a comparison between the psychological effects of isolation on white housewives and the impact of confinement on the self-concept of prisoners in Nazi concentration camps.

Friedan was a principal shaper of contemporary feminist thought. Significantly, the one-dimensional perspective on women's reality presented in her book became a marked feature of the contemporary feminist movement. Like Friedan before them, white women who dominate feminist discourse today rarely question whether or not their perspective on women's reality is true to the lived experiences of women as a collective group. Nor are they aware of the extent to which their perspectives reflect race and class biases, although there has been a greater awareness of biases in recent years. Racism abounds in the writings of white feminists, reinforcing white supremacy and negating the possibility that women will bond politically across ethnic and racial boundaries. Past feminist refusal to draw attention to and attack racial hierarchies suppressed the link between race and class. Yet class structure in American society has been shaped by the racial politic of white supremacy; it is only by analyzing racism and its function in capitalist society that a thorough understanding of class relationships can emerge. Class struggle is inextricably bound to the struggle to end racism. Urging women to explore the full implication of class in an early essay, "The Last Straw," Rita Mae Brown explained:

> Class is much more than Marx's definition of relationship to the means of production. Class involves your behavior, your basic assumptions about life. Your experience (determined by your class) validates those assumptions, how you are taught to behave, what you expect from yourself and from others, your concept of a future, how you understand problems and solve them, how you think, feel, act. It is these behavioral patterns that middle class women resist recognizing although they may be perfectly willing to accept class in Marxist terms, a neat trick that helps them avoid dealing with class behavior and changing that behavior in themselves. It is these behavioral patterns which must be recognized, understood, and changed.

White women who dominate feminist discourse, who for the most part make and articulate feminist theory, have little or no understanding of white supremacy as a racial politic, of the psychological impact of class, of their political status within a racist, sexist, capitalist state.

It is this lack of awareness that, for example, leads Leah Fritz to write in *Dreamers and Dealers,* a discussion of the current women's movement published in 1979:

> Women's suffering under sexist tyranny is a common bond among all women, transcending the particulars of the different forms that tyranny takes. *Suffering cannot be measured and compared quantitatively.* Is the enforced idleness and vacuity of a "rich" woman, which leads her to madness and/or suicide, greater or less than the suffering of a poor woman who barely survives on welfare but retains somehow her spirit? There is no way to measure such difference, but should these two women survey each other without the screen of patriarchal class, they may find a commonality in the fact that they are both oppressed, both miserable.

Fritz's statement is another example of wishful thinking, as well as the conscious mystification of social divisions between women, that has characterized much feminist expression. While it is evident that many women suffer from sexist tyranny, there is little indication that this forges "a common bond among all women." There is much evidence substantiating the reality that race and class identity creates differences in quality of life, social status, and lifestyle that take precedence over the common experience women share—differ-

ences which are rarely transcended. The motives of materially privileged, educated, white women with a variety of career and lifestyle
options available to them must be questioned when they insist that
"suffering cannot be measured." Fritz is by no means the first white
feminist to make this statement. It is a statement that I have never
heard a poor woman of any race make. Although there is much I
would take issue with in Benjamin Barber's critique of the women's
movement, *Liberating Feminism,* I agree with his assertion:

> Suffering is not necessarily a fixed and universal experience that can
> be measured by a single rod: it is related to situations, needs, and
> aspirations. But there must be some historical and political parame-
> ters for the use of the term so that political priorities can be estab-
> lished and different forms and degrees of suffering can be given the
> most attention.

A central tenet of modern feminist thought has been the assertion that "all women are oppressed." This assertion implies that
women share a common lot, that factors like class, race, religion,
sexual preference, etc. do not create a diversity of experience that
determines the extent to which sexism will be an oppressive force in
the lives of individual women. Sexism as a system of domination is
institutionalized but it has never determined in an absolute way the
fate of all women in this society. Being oppressed means *the absence
of choices.* It is the primary point of contact between the oppressed
and the oppressor. Many women in this society do have choices (as
inadequate as they are) therefore exploitation and discrimination
are words that more accurately describe the lot of women collectively in the United States. Many women do not join organized
resistance against sexism precisely because sexism has not meant an
absolute lack of choices. They may know they are discriminated
against on the basis of sex, but they do not equate this with oppression. Under capitalism, patriarchy is structured so that sexism re-
stricts women's behavior in some realms even as freedom from
limitations is allowed in other spheres. The absence of extreme
restrictions leads many women to ignore the areas in which they are
exploited or discriminated against; it may even lead them to imagine that no women are oppressed.

There are oppressed women in the United States, and it is both
appropriate and necessary that we speak against such oppression.
French feminist Christine Delphy makes the point in her essay,

"For a Materialist Feminism," that the use of the term oppression is important because it places feminist struggle in a radical political framework:

> The rebirth of feminism coincided with the use of the term "oppression." The ruling ideology, i.e. common sense, daily speech, does not speak about oppression but about a "feminine condition." It refers back to a naturalist explanation: to a constraint of nature, exterior reality out of reach and not modifiable by human action. The term "oppression," on the contrary, refers back to a choice, an explanation, a situation that is political. "Oppression" and "social oppression" are therefore synonyms or rather social oppression is a redundance: the notion of a political origin, i.e. social, is an integral part of the concept of oppression.

However, feminist emphasis on "common oppression" in the United States was less a strategy for politicization than an appropriation by conservative and liberal women of a radical political vocabulary that masked the extent to which they shaped the movement so that it addressed and promoted their class interests.

Although the impulse toward unity and empathy that informed the notion of common oppression was directed at building solidarity, slogans like "organize around your own oppression" provided the excuse many privileged women needed to ignore the differences between their social status and the status of masses of women. It was a mark of race and class privilege, as well as the expression of freedom from the many constraints sexism places on working class women, that middle class white women were able to make their interests the primary focus of the feminist movement and employ a rhetoric of commonality that made their condition synonymous with "oppression." Who was there to demand a change in vocabulary? What other group of women in the United States had the same access to universities, publishing houses, mass media, money? Had middle class black women begun a movement in which they had labeled themselves "oppressed," no one would have taken them seriously. Had they established public forums and given speeches about their "oppression," they would have been criticized and attacked from all sides. This was not the case with white bourgeois feminists for they could appeal to a large audience of women, like themselves, who were eager to change their lot in life. Their isolation from women of other class and race groups provided no immediate comparative base by which to test their assumptions of common expression.

Initially, radical participants in the women's movement demanded that women penetrate that isolation and create a space for contact. Anthologies like *Liberation Now, Women's Liberation: Blueprint for the Future, Class and Feminism, Radical Feminism,* and *Sisterhood Is Powerful,* all published in the early 1970s, contain articles that attempted to address a wide audience of women, an audience that was not exclusively white, middle class, college-educated, and adult (many have articles on teenagers). Sookie Stambler articulated this radical spirit in her introduction to *Women's Liberation: Blueprint for the Future:*

> Movement women have always been turned off by the media's necessity to create celebrities and superstars. This goes against our basic philosophy. We cannot relate to women in our ranks towering over us with prestige and fame. We are not struggling for the benefit of the one woman or for one group of women. We are dealing with issues that concern all women.

These sentiments, shared by many feminists early in the movement, were not sustained. As more and more women acquired prestige, fame, or money from feminist writings or from gains from the feminist movement for equality in the work force, individual opportunism undermined appeals for collective struggle. Women who were not opposed to patriarchy, capitalism, classism, or racism labeled themselves "feminist." Their expectations were varied. Privileged women wanted social equality with men of their class; some women wanted equal pay for equal work; others wanted an alternative life style. Many of these legitimate concerns were easily co-opted by the ruling capitalist patriarchy. French feminist Antoinette Fouque states:

> The actions proposed by the feminist groups are spectacular, provoking. But provocation only brings to light a certain number of social contradictions. It does not reveal radical contradictions within society. The feminists claim that they do not seek equality with men, but their practice proves the contrary to be true. Feminists are a bourgeois avant-garde that maintains, in an inverted form, the dominant values. Inversion does not facilitate the passage to another kind of structure. Reformism suits everyone! Bourgeois order, capitalism, phallocentrism are ready to integrate as many feminists as will be

necessary. Since these women are becoming men, in the end it will
only mean a few more men. The difference between the sexes is not
whether one does or doesn't have a penis, it is whether or not one is
an integral part of a phallic masculine economy.

Feminists in the United States are aware of the contradictions.
Carol Ehrlich makes the point in her essay, "The Unhappy Marriage of Marxism and Feminism: Can It Be Saved?," that "feminism
seems more and more to have taken on a blind, safe, nonrevolution-
ary outlook" as "feminist radicalism loses ground to bourgeois feminism," stressing that "we cannot let this continue":

> Women need to know (and are increasingly prevented from finding
> out) that feminism is *not* about dressing for success, or becoming a
> corporate executive, or gaining elective office; it is *not* being able to
> share a two career marriage and take skiing vacations and spend
> huge amounts of time with your husband and two lovely children
> because you have a domestic worker who makes all this possible for
> you, but who hasn't the time or money to do it for herself; it is *not*
> opening a Women's Bank, or spending a weekend in an expensive
> workshop that guarantees to teach you how to become assertive (but
> not aggressive); it is most emphatically *not* about becoming a police
> detective or CIA agent or marine corps general.
>   But if these distorted images of feminism have more reality than
> ours do, it is partly our own fault. We have not worked as hard as we
> should have at providing clear and meaningful alternative analyses
> which relate to people's lives, and at providing active, accessible
> groups in which to work.

It is no accident that feminist struggle has been so easily co-opted
to serve the interests of conservative and liberal feminists since
feminism in the United States has so far been a bourgeois ideology.
Zillah Eisenstein discusses the liberal roots of North American feminism in *The Radical Future of Liberal Feminism,* explaining in the
introduction:

> One of the major contributions to be found in this study is the role of
> the ideology of liberal individualism in the construction of feminist
> theory. Today's feminists either do not discuss a theory of individu-
> ality or they unself-consciously adopt the competitive, atomistic ide-
> ology of liberal individualism. There is much confusion on this issue
> in the feminist theory we discuss here. Until a conscious differentia-
> tion is made between a theory of individuality that recognizes the

importance of the individual within the social collectivity and the ideology of individualism that assumes a competitive view of the individual, there will not be a full accounting of what a feminist theory of liberation must look like in our Western society.

The ideology of "competitive, atomistic liberal individualism" has permeated feminist thought to such an extent that it undermines the potential radicalism of feminist struggle. The usurpation of feminism by bourgeois women to support their class interests has been to a very grave extent justified by feminist theory as it has so far been conceived. (For example, the ideology of "common oppression.") Any movement to resist the co-optation of feminist struggle must begin by introducing a different feminist perspective—a new theory—one that is not informed by the ideology of liberal individualism.

The exclusionary practices of women who dominate feminist discourse have made it practically impossible for new and varied theories to emerge. Feminism has its party line and women who feel a need for a different strategy, a different foundation, often find themselves ostracized and silenced. Criticisms of or alternatives to established feminist ideas are not encouraged, for example, recent controversies about expanding feminist discussions of sexuality. Yet groups of women who feel excluded from feminist discourse and praxis can make a place for themselves only if they first create, via critiques, an awareness of the factors that alienate them. Many individual white women found in the women's movement a liberatory solution to personal dilemmas. Having directly benefitted from the movement, they are less inclined to criticize it or to engage in rigorous examination of its structure than those who feel it has not had a revolutionary impact on their lives or the lives of masses of women in our society. Non-white women who feel affirmed within the current structure of the feminist movement (even though they may form autonomous groups) seem to also feel that their definitions of the party line, whether on the issue of black feminism or on other issues, is the only legitimate discourse. Rather than encourage a diversity of voices, critical dialogue, and controversy, they, like some white women, seek to stifle dissent. As activists and writers whose work is widely known, they act as if they are best able to judge whether other women's voices should be heard. Susan Griffin warns against this overall tendency toward dogmatism in her essay, "The Way of All Ideology":

> . . . when a theory is transformed into an ideology, it begins to destroy the self and self-knowledge. Originally born of feeling, it pretends to float above and around feeling. Above sensation. It organizes experience according to itself, without touching experience. By virtue of being itself, it is supposed to know. To invoke the name of this ideology is to confer truthfulness. No one can tell it anything new. Experience ceases to surprise it, inform it, transform it. It is annoyed by any detail which does not fit into its world view. Begun as a cry against the denial of truth, now it denies any truth which does not fit into its scheme. Begun as a way to restore one's sense of reality, now it attempts to discipline real people, to remake natural beings after its own image. All that it fails to explain it records as its enemy. Begun as a theory of liberation, it is threatened by new theories of liberation; it builds a prison for the mind.

We resist hegemonic dominance of feminist thought by insisting that it is a theory in the making, that we must necessarily criticize, question, re-examine, and explore new possibilities. My persistent critique has been informed by my status as a member of an oppressed group, experience of sexist exploitation and discrimination, and the sense that prevailing feminist analysis has not been the force shaping my feminist consciousness. This is true for many women. There are white women who had never considered resisting male dominance until the feminist movement created an awareness that they could and should. My awareness of feminist struggle was stimulated by social circumstance. Growing up in a Southern, black, father-dominated, working-class household, I experienced (as did my mother, my sisters, and my brother) varying degrees of patriarchal tyranny and it made me angry—it made us all angry. Anger led me to question the politics of male dominance and enabled me to resist sexist socialization. Frequently, white feminists act as if black women did not know sexist oppression existed until they voiced feminist sentiment. They believed they are providing black women with "the" analysis and "the" program for liberation. They do not understand, cannot even imagine, that black women, as well as other groups of women who live daily in oppressive situations, often acquire an awareness of patriarchal politics from their lived experience, just as they develop strategies of resistance (even though they may not resist on a sustained or organized basis).

These black women observed white feminist focus on male tyranny and women's oppression as if it were a "new" revelation and felt such a focus had little impact on their lives. To them it was just another indication of the privileged living conditions of middle and upper class white women that they would need a theory to inform them that they were "oppressed." The implication being that people who are truly oppressed know it even though they may not be engaged in organized resistance or are unable to articulate in written form the nature of their oppression. These black women saw nothing liberatory in party line analysis of women's oppression. Neither the fact that black women have not organized collectively in huge numbers around the issues of "feminism" (many of us do not know or use the term) nor the fact that we have not had access to the machinery of power that would allow us to share our analyses or theories about gender with the American public negate its presence in our lives or place us in a position of dependency in relationship to those white and non-white feminists who address a larger audience.

The understanding I had by age thirteen of patriarchal politics created in me expectations of the feminist movement that were quite different from those of young, middle class, white women. When I entered my first women's studies class at Stanford University in the early 1970s, white women were reveling in the joy of being together—to them it was an important, momentous occasion. I had not known a life where women had not been together, where women had not helped, protected, and loved one another deeply. I had not known white women were ignorant of the impact of race and class on their social status and consciousness. (Southern white women often have a more realistic perspective on racism and classism than white women in other areas of the United States.) I did not feel sympathetic to white peers who maintained that I could not expect them to have knowledge of or understand the life experiences of black women. Despite my background (living in racially segregated communities) I knew about the lives of white women, and certainly no white women lived in our neighborhood, attended our schools, or worked in our homes.

When I participated in feminist groups, I found that white women adopted a condescending attitude toward me and other non-white participants. The condescension they directed at black women was one of the means they employed to remind us that the women's movement was "theirs"—that we were able to participate because they allowed it, even encouraged it; after all, we were needed to legitimate the process. They did not see us as equals. They did not treat us as equals. And though they expected us to provide first hand accounts of black experience, they felt it was their role to decide if these experiences were authentic. Frequently, college-educated black women (even those from poor and working class backgrounds) were dismissed as mere imitators. Our presence in movement activities did not count, as white women were convinced that "real" blackness meant speaking the patois of poor black people, being uneducated, streetwise, and a variety of other stereotypes. If we dared to criticize the movement or to assume responsibility for reshaping feminist ideas and introducing new ideas, our voices were tuned out, dismissed, silenced. We could be heard only if our statements echoed the sentiments of the dominant discourse.

Attempts by white feminists to silence black women are rarely written about. All too often they have taken place in conference rooms, classrooms, or the privacy of cozy living room settings, where one lone black woman faces the racist hostility of a group of white women. From the time the women's liberation movement began, individual black women went to groups. Many never returned after a first meeting. Anita Cornwall is correct in "Three for the Price of One: Notes from a Gay Black Feminist," when she states, "Sadly enough, fear of encountering racism seems to be one of the main reasons that so many black women refuse to join the women's movement." Recent focus on the issue of racism has generated discourse but has had little impact on the behavior of white feminists toward black women. Often the white women who are busy publishing papers and books on "unlearning racism" remain patronizing and condescending when they relate to black women. This is not surprising given that frequently their discourse is aimed solely in the direction of a white audience and they focus solely on changing attitudes rather than addressing racism in a historical and political context. They make us the "objects" of their privileged discourse on race. As "objects," we remain unequals, inferiors. Even though they may be sincerely concerned about racism, their methodology suggests they are not yet free of the type of paternalism endemic to white supremacist ideology. Some of these women place themselves in the position of "authorities" who must mediate com-

munication between racist white women (naturally they see themselves as having come to terms with their racism) and angry black
women whom they believe are incapable of rational discourse. Of
course, the system of racism, classism, and educational elitism remains intact if they are to maintain their authoritative positions.

In 1981, I enrolled in a graduate class on feminist theory where
we were given a course reading list that had writings by white
women and men, one black man, but no material by or about black,
Native American, Indian, Hispanic, or Asian women. When I criticized this oversight, white women directed an anger and hostility at
me that was so intense I found it difficult to attend the class. When I
suggested that the purpose of this collective anger was to create an
atmosphere in which it would be psychologically unbearable for me
to speak in class discussions or even attend class, I was told that they
were not angry. *I* was the one who was angry. Weeks after class
ended, I received an open letter from one white female student
acknowledging her anger and expressing regret from her attacks.
She wrote:

> I didn't know you. You were black. In class after awhile I noticed
> myself, that I would always be the one to respond to whatever you
> said. And usually it was to contradict. Not that the argument was
> always about racism by any means. But I think the hidden logic was
> that if I could prove you wrong about one thing, then you might not
> be right about anything at all.

And in another paragraph:

> I said in class one day that there were some people less entrapped
> than others by Plato's picture of the world. I said I thought we, after
> fifteen years of education, courtesy of the ruling class, might be more
> entrapped than others who had not received a start in life so close to
> the heart of the monster. My classmate, once a close friend, sister,
> colleague, has not spoken to me since then. I think the possibility that
> we were not the best spokespeople for all women made her fear for
> her self-worth and for her Ph.D.

Often in situations where white females aggressively attacked individual black women, they saw themselves as the ones who were
under attack, who were the victims. During a heated discussion with
another white female student in a racially mixed women's group I
had organized, I was told that she had heard how I had "wiped out"

people in the feminist theory class, that she was afraid of being "wiped out" too. I reminded her that I was one person speaking to a large group of angry, aggressive people. I was hardly dominating the situation. It was I who left the class in tears, not any of the people I had supposedly "wiped out."

Racist stereotypes of the strong, superhuman black woman are operative myths in the minds of many white women allowing them to ignore the extent to which black women are likely to be victimized in this society and the role white women may play in the maintenance and perpetuation of that victimization. In Lillian Hellman's autobiographical work *Pentimento,* she writes, "All my life, beginning at birth, I have taken orders from black women, wanting them and resenting then, being superstitious the few times I disobeyed." The black women Hellman describes worked in her household as family servants and their status was never that of an equal. Even as a child, she was always in the dominant position as they questioned, advised, or guided her; they were free to exercise these rights because she or another white authority figure allowed it. Hellman places power in the hands of these black women rather than acknowledge her own power over them; hence she mystifies the true nature of their relationship. By projecting onto black women a mythical power and strength, white women both promote a false image of themselves as powerless, passive victims and deflect attention away from their aggressiveness, their power (however limited in a white supremacist, male-dominated state), their willingness to dominate and control others. These unacknowledged aspects of the social status of many white women prevent them from transcending racism and limit the scope of their understanding of women's overall social status in the United States.

Privileged feminists have largely been unable to speak to, with, and for diverse groups of women because they either do not understand fully the inter-relatedness of sex, race, and class oppression or refuse to take this inter-relatedness seriously. Feminist analyses of women's lot tend to focus exclusively on gender and do not provide a solid foundation on which to construct feminist theory. They reflect the dominant tendency in Western patriarchal minds to mystify woman's reality by insisting that gender is the sole determinant of a woman's fate. Certainly it has been easier for women who do not experience race or class oppression to focus exclusively on gender. Although socialist feminists focus on class and gender, they tend to dismiss race or they make a point of acknowledging that race is important and then proceed to offer an analysis in which race is not considered.

As a group, black women are in an unusual position in this society, for not only are we collectively at the bottom of the occupational ladder, but our overall social status is lower than that of any other group. Occupying such a position, we bear the brunt of sexist, racist, and classist oppression. At the same time, we are the group that has not been socialized to assume the role of exploiter/oppressor in that we are allowed no institutionalized "other" that we can exploit or oppress. (Children do not represent an institutionalized other even though they may be oppressed by parents.) White women and black men have it both ways. They can act as oppressor or be oppressed. Black men may be victimized by racism, but sexism allows them to act as exploiters and oppressors of women. White women may be victimized by sexism, but racism enables them to act as exploiters and oppressors of black people. Both groups have led liberation movements that favor their interests and support the continued oppression of other groups. Black male sexism has undermined struggles to eradicate racism just as white female racism undermines feminist struggle. As long as these two groups or any group defines liberation as gaining social equality with ruling class white men, they have a vested interest in the continued exploitation and oppression of others.

Black women with no institutionalized "other" that we may discriminate against, exploit, or oppress often have a lived experience that directly challenges the prevailing classist, sexist, racist social structure and its concomitant ideology. This lived experience may shape our consciousness in such a way that our world view differs from those who have a degree of privilege (however relative within the existing system). It is essential for continued feminist struggle that black women recognize the special vantage point our marginality gives us and make use of this perspective to criticize the dominant racist, classist, sexist hegemony as well as to envision and create a counterhegemony. I am suggesting that we have a central role to play in the making of feminist theory and a contribution to offer that is unique and valuable. The formation of a liberatory feminist theory and praxis is a collective responsibility, one that must be shared. Though I criticize aspects of the feminist movement as we have known it so far, a critique which is sometimes harsh and unrelenting, I do so not in an attempt to diminish feminist struggle but to enrich, to share in the work of making a liberatory ideology and a liberatory movement.

Women Against Feminism

Rebecca Klatch

By an overwhelming margin, Congress passed the Equal Rights Amend-
ment (ERA) in early 1972 and submitted it to the states for ratification.
Within a year thirty states had voted in support of adding the amendment
to the Constitution. Then Phyllis Schlafly, a conservative lawyer from
Illinois who idolized Thomas Edison, Elias Howe, and Clarence Birdseye
for their contributions to the comforts of domesticity, organized a "STOP
ERA" coalition composed of fundamentalist and orthodox religious lead-
ers, conservative businessmen, radical right groups, and a growing num-
ber of women who considered themselves antifeminist. Believing that the
women's movement had gone too far, these women saw feminism as an
enemy responsible for fostering sexual permissiveness, homosexuality,
abortion, moral relativism, and what they called "secular humanism."
They feared that ERA would destroy the "special place" of women in the
home, force them to fight in combat, and mandate unisex toilets. Because
of their efforts, the deadline for ratifying ERA passed in June 1982 with
the amendment still three states short of adoption. Rebecca Klatch de-
scribes the key components of this antifeminist movement in the following
selection.

In many ways the 1960s captured the social conservative vision of
a society in decay, in chaos. The civil rights and anti-war movements, SDS and the Weathermen, the Yippies, hippies, and flower
children, all symbolize the turbulence and social conflict that ripped
apart the American dream during those tumultuous years. Signs of

moral decay pervaded the 1960s—captured in the images of the blue jeaned, beaded and bearded, long-haired youth, Timothy Leary and the LSD cult, Woodstock and communes, skinny-dipping and braless women, head shops and rock concerts, and ultimately captured in the image of a burning American flag. Further, the uprooting of traditional forms of authority also indicated "the rotting of America," as evidenced in the generation gap and the slogan "Don't trust anyone over thirty," or by the embrace of Eastern religion, yoga, Hare Krishna, and even occultism, and perhaps most radically designated by buttons declaring "God is dead" or "Question authority." Such images capture the spirit of the times and also reveal the reason behind social conservative dismay provoked by such an era. For these new images of the 1960s desecrated the sacred symbols of the social conservative world.

Yet there are two specific associations linked with the 1960s, and to feminism as well, two signs that further imply moral decay. First, the 1960s is seen as the era that initiated an attack on the American family. While the pill and the sexual revolution ate away at the traditional moral norms governing the family unit, the New Left—and later feminism—launched an ideological attack on the family. Looking back on this era, one conservative critic notes: "The New Left revived the Marxist critique of the bourgeois family, viewing it as predicated on property relations, male supremacy, and the boredom of domestic bliss." By espousing "free love," the collectivization of childcare, and the elimination of the concept of illegitimacy, the New Left promoted the collapse of the nuclear family norm so that "'Father Knows Best,' 'Leave It to Beaver,' and 'I Love Lucy' gave way to 'One Day at a Time,' 'Three's Company,' and 'Miss Winslow and Son.'"

In addition to this ideological attack on the family, erosion of family life was augmented during the 1960s by the increased number of wives and mothers entering the labor force. Pat Robertson, speaking at the Family Forum conference, explains the consequences of such a trend:

> From the mid-sixties on it was necessary for women to enter the work force, not because they necessarily wanted to, but because they were forced to [due to deficit spending because of welfare programs]. . . . What did this do to the family? Twenty-five million children under school age are being dumped into day care centers. . . . There's a lot of heady freedom to a fourteen- or fifteen-year-old who

comes home who knows that his Dada won't be home 'till later and his mother won't be home so he's got his girlfriend with him and why not? I mean after all—a little grass here, a little sex there. Six hundred thousand teenage pregnancies last year—what's happening? Well, the mothers aren't home. . . . Divorces mean children are losing their role models, they're not identifying with the proper spouse of the proper sex. You have a rise in homosexuality. You have a rise in teenage delinquencies. You've got a rise in rebellion in schools.

In short, the 1960s ushered in not only an attack on the American family by the New Left but also an internal erosion of the moral bases supporting family life, particularly with the rising divorce rate and increased number of working mothers.

The second corroding effect of the 1960s was a new emphasis on self, the ushering in of the Me Decade of the 1970s. Social conservatives attribute this elevation of the self to the predominant ethic of the 1960s, "Do your own thing." In addition, the 1960s brought with it a new emphasis on rights, as every conceivable group grabbed for its share of the pie in the name of "minority rights." This, too, culminated in a heightening of self-interest. Finally, the popularity of psychology during the 1960s, with stress on self-exploration, "I'm Okay, You're Okay," and the multitude of new therapies also added fuel to the fire of "Me-Firstism." The net result of these developments was the breeding of a culture of narcissism:

> The 1970s were characterized by an obsession with consciousness expansion, self-awareness, and a type of narcissism. The supposed new narcissism of the seventies expounded the ideas that within each individual there is a glorious talented personality, that each individual is possessed with an inner dignity that he alone can bring out in himself; each individual must think only of himself and do exactly what he or she feels like doing.

In short, the 1960s fostered conditions favorable to the advance of situation ethics and humanistic values. Increased materialism accompanied this obsession with self, as Americans sought immediate gratification and instant credit to satisfy their appetite for consumption. Everyone sought something for nothing, as a plethora of books advertising how to attain "The Joy of Sex" without guilt or how to lose weight without dieting hit the bestsellers list. Such self-gratifying trends symbolized humanism's materialistic appeal, tempting people away from the purity of spiritual belief and religious devotion.

Like the 1960s, feminism also represents moral decay. Like the 1960s, feminism is also perceived as a force attacking the American family. And, like the 1960s, feminism, too, is associated with the new narcissism, the Me Decade. In addition, feminism symbolizes a threat because it represents an attack on the status of the homemaker and the extension of Big Government.

FEMINISM AS ANTI-FAMILY

From the early days of the women's movement, feminism was perceived as a force actively working against the family. Social conservatives charge feminists with renouncing the family as a source of repression and enslavement, a tool used by men to entrap and oppress women. As one local pro-family activist puts it:

> The libbers want to abolish the family. That's what Gloria Frie—I mean Steinem says. "Women will not be liberated until marriage is eliminated." Have you seen the "Declaration on Feminism"? They state quite clearly there that they want to eliminate the family. That's why, when I hear people say they support ERA, I say to them, "Do you know what that means? Do you know what they want to do?" . . . The feminists want to abolish the family. But the family is the basis of everything. It is the foundation of our society; if that crumbles, everything else goes.

The national conference for International Women's Year (IWY) held in Houston in 1977 concretized the perception of feminism as an anti-family force. Sponsored by the United Nations, the conference brought together women from all over the country to consider "women's issues." Social conservatives were shocked by the delegates' overwhelming support for such things as ERA, gay rights, federal funding of abortion, government-sponsored childcare, and contraception for minors without parental consent, all advocated in the name of "women's rights." Angry that the taxpayer's dollar was being used to fund a convention of feminists, the meeting in fact provoked activism by many women previously uninvolved in the political arena. . . .

IWY gave birth to a network of activists and organizations that called themselves the "pro-family movement." Rosemary Thomson, a leading figure of the movement, defines pro-family as a "person or group supporting legislation protecting traditional moral values, generally opposed to a range of issues, including ERA, abortion, gay rights, federal childcare, forced busing, etc." If IWY gave birth to the pro-family movement, President Carter's 1980 White House Conference on Families (WHC)F) solidified the movement, deepening the wrath of pro-family activists and drawing in further supporters. Thomson, named national Eagle Forum coordinator for the WHCF by Phyllis Schlafly, declares: "IWY was our 'boot camp.' Now we're ready for the offensive in the battle for our families and our faith." . . .

This battle over the definition of the family is a central focus of social conservative concern. The conflict centers on what constitutes a family, where the lines are drawn. On one side stand social conservatives, defining the family as persons related by blood, marriage, or adoption; this, they contend, is the traditional definition of the family. On the other side stand the feminists and humanists, who include more diverse forms in the definition of family. In fact, Phyllis Schlafly reports that Gloria Steinem worked for months to get the White House Conference changed from "Family" to "Families" in order to include alternative lifestyles. Social conservatives reject this acceptance of multiple family forms. In a debate held during the Family Forum conference between leftist Michael Lerner and New Right leader Paul Weyrich, Weyrich argued:

> Where we disagree is in the effort to call a couple of lesbians who are bringing up a child a family, calling a couple of roommates a family calling a couple of fornicators a family. These are families . . . under your definition-garbage!! . . . It is ludicrous to call acquaintances. neighbors, live-in types, and so on families. The problem of not defining the family is that it leads to the kind of perversion of thinking which has resulted in people trying to pass off as legitimate families, illegitimate lifestyles.

This same opposition to diverse family forms, with particular animosity toward gay families, is echoed by Dr. Ronald Godwin, vice-president of the Moral Majority, who objects to the placement of "responsible, respectable kinds of families in with the homosexual families and the lesbian families and all the perverse pollutions of the definition." Yet Godwin also objects to what he calls the "pseudo-historical" approach to the family:

> You'll hear many, many feminists and anti-family spokesmen today talking about history. . . . They'll tell you that down on the Fiji Islands, somewhere down on an island of Uwunga-Bunga, there's a tribe of people who have never even practiced family life as we know it. But they also have bones in their nose and file their front teeth. And they eat rat meat for breakfast. They're some fairly strange, non-representative people. But they'll tell you about all the strange aberrations that have popped up in the human family over the centuries in various strange geographical locations. They'll tell you that in the nineteenth century in the backside of Europe such and such a thing went on. They'll deal in what is called pseudo-history. They'll try to build a historical case for the proposition that the traditional family never really was traditional and never really was a dominant force in all civilized societies.

Once again, in upholding "traditional values," in this case regarding the definition of the family, social conservatives reject the acceptance of diverse cultural forms as equally valid and acceptable moral standards by which to live. Instead, they assert one absolute standard as the only legitimate code of behavior. Looking back on the White House Conference, Thomson reflects:

> The pro-family movement was, indeed, engaged in a spiritual battle—a struggle between those who believe in Biblical principles and ungodly Humanism which rejects God's moral absolute! . . .
> Somehow, it was to the organizers of the White House Conference on Families as if the Lord had never spoken in history. As if He had never declared that taking an innocent life was forbidden. That parents were to train up a child. That sexual activity outside of marriage was fornication, and that homosexuality was an abomination to Him—sin, not gay.

In this stark black and white world, feminism is clearly intertwined with secular humanism. Both deny moral absolutes; both undermine the family. Feminism, too, is intertwined with Big Government. For it was the government-sponsored International Women's Year and White House conferences that allowed feminists and humanists to promote anti-family policies. Hence, in the battle to defend America, feminism is a threat because, like the other forces of decay, it symbolizes an attack on the sacred unit of the social conservative world.

FEMINISM AS THE NEW NARCISSISM

Inextricably bound to the association of feminism as anti-family is the perception of feminism as an extension of the new narcissism, a symbol of the Me Decade. For in condemning the family, social conservatives argue, the women's liberation movement advises women to pursue their *own* individual interest above all else. Onalee McGraw explains: "The feminist movement issued an appeal that rapidly spread through our culture urging women to liberate them-selves from the chains of family life and affirm their own self-fulfillment as the primary good." McGraw argues that the ultimate effect of such an appeal is the redefinition of the family unit:

> The humanist—feminist view of the family is that it is a biological, sociological unit in which the individual happens to reside; it has no meaning and purpose beyond that which each individual chooses to give it. Thus, the autonomous self, freely choosing and acting, must satisfy its needs. When, by its very nature, the family exercises moral authority over its members, it thereby restricts the self in its pursuit of self-fulfillment and becomes an instrument of oppression and de-nial of individual rights.

Instead of the family's being bound together by a higher moral authority, the family is reduced to a mere collection of individual interests.

Phyllis Schlafly reiterates this view of the feminist movement:

> Women's liberationists operate as Typhoid Marys carrying a germ called lost identity. They try to persuade wives that they have missed something in life because they are known by their husband's name and play second fiddle to his career. . . . As a homewrecker, women's liberation is far in the lead over "the other man," "the other woman," or "incompatibility."

Schlafly illustrates the social destruction caused by women's liber-ation by quoting Albert Martin, who wrote a book discussing his own devastation when his wife of eighteen years walked out on him and their four sons, in search of her identity:

> An extraordinary emphasis on self is happening today across our nation, and this is why we continue to tear our marriages apart, splinter our families, and raise our divorce rates to new heights every year. The very core . . . is the enshrinement of individuality, the

freedom of self, at the expense of marital union and social compromise.

Thus, in social conservative eyes, when individuality and freedom of self extend to women as well as to men, marriage, the family, and society itself are threatened. The ultimate result of such a development is what Connie Marshner labels "macho feminism":

> Feminism replaced the saccharine sentimentalizations of women and home life and projected instead a new image of women: a drab, macho feminism of hard-faced women who were bound and determined to serve their place in the world, no matter whose bodies they have to climb over to do it. This image provided the plot line for such cultural weathervanes as *Kramer vs. Kramer*. Macho feminism despises anything which seeks to interfere with the desires of Number One. A relationship which proves burdensome? Drop it! A husband whose needs cannot be conveniently met? Forget him! Children who may wake up in the middle of the night? No way! To this breed of thought, family interferes with self-fulfillment, and given the choice between family and self, the self is going to come out on top in their world. . . . Macho feminism has deceived women in that it convinced them that they would be happy only if they were treated like men, and that included treating themselves like men.

Marshner concludes: "Feminists praise self-centeredness and call it liberation."

Feminism is a threat, then, because, when women pursue self-interest, not only is the family neglected but also ultimately women become like men. Hence, "macho feminism" is destructive because if *everyone* pursues their own interest, no one is left to look out for the larger good, that is, to be altruistic, to be the nurturer, the caretaker, the mother. In short, the underlying fear expressed in this critique of feminism is the fear of a total masculinization of the world.

Further, as "the most outrageous creation of the 'me-decade'" the women's movement is seen as one of the many groups ignited by the 1960s, greedily grabbing for their rights. Feminist claims of exploitation and oppression are perceived as illegitimate, as the overreaction to common problems by another self-pitying group jumping on the bandwagon of "minority rights." As part of this "craze for equal opportunity," according to one critic, feminism is the "fight-for-your-right-to-do-anything-you-please-and-reject-all-obligations philosophy."

Carried to the extreme, this equation of feminism with total self-gratification interprets abortion as the ultimate selfish act, the placement of the mother's desires above a baby's life. Ron Godwin, speaking at the Family Forum conference, portrays abortion in these terms:

> *Roe v. Wade* in 1973 gave mothers the right to rid themselves of unwanted children. Now as I speak this morning a recurring theme is going to occur . . . and that is that all of these changes that have occurred in the last few years are based on self-centeredness, on that which is convenient, on a principle of doing one's own thing, of doing that which is pleasurable and fulfilling to the individual.

He predicts the next step will be infanticide, in which a small group of people will decide which child shall live and which shall die. Hence, at the extreme feminism represents callous self-interest, women's fulfillment at the price of human life. . . .

Besides feminism as an anti-family symbol and as a symbol of the Me Decade, there is a third association linked with feminism. In social conservative eyes, the feminist demand for self-fulfillment not only negates the traditional family but implicitly negates the role of the homemaker as well. By encouraging women to realize their full potential, feminism assumes that women are not fulfilled through meeting the needs of husband and children.

Thus, feminism represents not only a battle between a traditional and a nontraditional definition of the family but also a conflict over the very status of the homemaker. One woman interviewed, a national organizer for the Eagle Forum, explains how feminism devalues homemakers:

> The women's liberation movement really resents homemakers. There's a Chicago magazine out that gives great quotes about how they think it's an illegitimate profession being a homemaker. Now when they get a lot of media coverage saying things like that and they portray that they're working for women and they scorn the homemaker . . . , that it's not intellectually satisfying . . . and you're just a' glorified baby-sitter, et cetera, et cetera, they really caused the split to occur. They caused a resentment to grow between homemakers and working women. . . . The women who used to say, "I'm a homemaker" with pride now say, "I'm just a housewife." That's a terrible change in attitude. I don't think that's good at all. . . .

Feminism *implicitly* degrades homemakers by calling for women to seek fulfillment outside the home, which discredits those women who are fulfilled by being wives and mothers. Feminism *explicitly* belittles homemakers by labeling their work as drudgery, as mundane, as ungratifying, and as glorified baby-sitting. Feminism's call for women to go beyond the housewife role, to step into the male world of paid labor, denies the importance and the satisfaction derived by those content with their homemaker status. As one local pro-family activist explains:

> The feminists want all women to work. But all women don't want to work. I talk to women all the time around here who really want to stay home with their children. It's not because they're misled or not liberated. They honestly want to stay home with their children. I've seen women who have to work so torn up by having to leave their nine-month-old babies.

Or, in another pro-family activist's words:

> The women's liberation movement looks down on the housewife. She should he the most respected person as she is bringing up future generations. But women's liberation puts her down and says, "All she says is stay home all day and wash dirty diapers." ERA won't do anything for these women.

In this way, the conflict between feminists and homemakers is a tug-of-war between two lifestyles. There is not peaceful coexistence between those women following traditional ways and those women seeking new paths, new careers. Rather than the lifestyle of each being accepted and valued, social conservatives view feminists as promoting new roles for women at the expense of the old, thereby devaluing the homemaker's status. . . .

In social conservative eyes, it is not men who are to blame for degrading women, but feminists themselves are at fault for denying the worth of women's work in the home, for discrediting the housewife role, and for disregarding the contributions women make in rearing future generations. Accordingly, Phyllis Schlafly responds to the feminist charge that women are treated as chattel by saying, "It is too bad that some women believe such falsehoods. This is the way the women's liberation movement deliberately degrades the homemaker and hacks away at her sense of self-worth and pride and pleasure in being female."

Feminists also devalue women by measuring their worth purely in economic terms. For instance, social conservatives are appalled by feminist assessments of the monetary value of housework, believing such efforts reduce a relationship based on love to purely quantitative value. Similarly, Phyllis Schafly argues that feminists are contemptuous of volunteer services performed by women because, "in their inverted scale of values, they judge every service by money, never by love." Whereas feminists view men as taking women's voluntarism for granted, not giving it proper value, social conservatives blame feminists for judging women's volunteer activities solely in terms of the economic rewards such work yields.

This perception of feminism is evident in testimony Phyllis Schlafly gave to the U.S. House Social Security Subcommittee regarding the elimination of dependent wives' benefits. Claiming that feminists complain "it isn't fair" for a dependent wife to receive as large a Social Security benefit as a working woman, Schlafly argues that feminists reduce women's work in the home purely to cash value, without recognizing the contribution homemakers make to society. She concludes:

> The feminist movement is trying to make the dependent wife obsolete. The proposal to eliminate the wife's and widow's benefits should be identified as what it is: a radical feminist proposal to punish the woman who chooses to be a dependent wife so she can care and nurture her own children.

Feminists are viewed not only as denigrating homemakers for their lack of cash value but also as hostile toward homemakers, actively seeking to eliminate their very way of life.

In reaction, social conservatives uphold traditional values, traditional female roles, and the traditional style of life in which the homemaker is respected for the social contribution she makes. As one of the leading defenders of homemakers, Phyllis Schlafly argues that housewives make the most significant contributions to society—by rearing moral, law-abiding, industrious citizens who form strong families of their own, the foundation for the future of the nation.

Further, Schlafly argues that the homemaker role is superior to paid labor. No amount of career success compares to the joy and satisfaction of motherhood. She advises homemakers to cherish their work for the amount of control and the rewards it allows them, more than most men are allowed at their jobs:

> If you think diapers and dishes are a never-ending, repetitive routine, just remember that most of the jobs outside the home are just as repetitious, tiresome, and boring. Consider the assembly line worker who pulls the same lever, pushes the same button, or inspects thousands of identical bits of metal or glass or paper hour after weary hour. . . . The plain fact is that most women would rather cuddle a baby than a typewriter or factory machine. . . .

Yet while feminists—and not men—are blamed for attacking the status of homemakers and for degrading the traditional female role, beneath this blame is also an underlying distrust of men. This distrust is particularly evident in discussion of ERA. One reason for opposition to ERA, for example, is that ERA will abolish the requirement that a husband support his wife, thereby eliminating in one stroke women's right to be full-time homemakers. One of the most valuable property rights a woman now has is the right to be provided for by her husband: ERA will eliminate this right. Whereas now a wife has certain remedies if her husband neglects his responsibilities, such as purchasing goods on her husband's credit and letting the store handle collection of payment, ERA will destroy such options. As one anti-ERA activist put it: "Marriage as a full equal partnership is discrimination against women because the man is no longer responsible for his wife. Under the Judeo-Christian tradition, men *are* responsible. I did not get married as an equal partner."

Worst of all is the fear that men who stop loving their wives, or who find a new woman, will be freed of all responsibility to support their spouses. Phyllis Schafly warns:

> Consider a wife in her 50's whose husband decides he wants to divorce her and trade her in on a younger model. This situation has become all too common, especially with no-fault divorce in many states. If ERA is ratified, and thereby wipes out the state laws that require a husband to support his wife, the cast off wife will have to hunt for a job to support herself. . . . The most tragic effect of ERA would thus fall on the woman who has been a good wife and homemaker for decades, and who can now be turned out to pasture with impunity because a new, militant breed of liberationist has come along.

Similarly, Schlafly cautions that current Individual Retirement Accounts discriminate against homemakers because they cannot be jointly owned. Hence, the wife gets only as much retirement payment as her husband chooses to give her, "whereas he can take the full amount and then name his girlfriend or a future wife as beneficiary."

The underlying fear beneath such claims rests on a distrust of men, on the expectation that a man will pick up and leave his wife and children if no legal ties restrict him. As Mrs. Billy Graham puts it, the women's liberation movement is "turning into men's lib because we are freeing them from their responsibilities. I think we are being taken for a ride."

It is not just social conservative women who express skepticism regarding men. George Gilder speaks forcefully about the inherent unreliability of the male gender:

> This is essentially what sexual liberation is all about. It allows powerful men to leave their wives as they grow older and pursue single women, run off with their secretaries, and it allows single women open season on married men. That's the essential meaning of sexual liberation and the central meaning of the women's movement. It's a sort of alliance between powerful men who've already made it with single women on the make. . . .

The underlying image of men is of creatures with uncontrollable passions and little sense of commitment or loyalty. Only moral *and legal* authority can restrain the savagery of male nature.

Thus, when feminists remove the safety valves that currently exist to protect women, they leave homemakers particularly vulnerable to men.

> No-fault divorce laws . . . have liberated many men from the obligation to support their wives and children. Women placed in these unfortunate circumstances are touted by the feminist movement as its most valiant "heroines." However, it is the feminist movement's strident insistence on eradication of all sex-related distinctions that has contributed so greatly to the present predicament of divorced women with children who must support the family unit alone.

Besides the vulnerability of homemakers to men, one pro-family activist voiced distrust as well about the position career women face in regards to men:

All I can see is women with careers who then have to come home and clean their house, so all day Saturday or Sunday they are doing housework. All I see is women taking on men's roles, but not men helping. On one side of the feminist's mouth they call for universal daycare, and on the other they say "Don't worry. Men will help." But I don't see men helping.

Again, while feminists view this double workday as evidence of women's oppression, social conservatives blame career women for bringing on these worsened conditions through their own demands to enter the labor force.

Opposition to ERA expressed in such concerns speaks to the fear that homemakers will be left most vulnerable if legal bonds on men are lifted. With men free to "do their own thing," go their own way, with no obligations to support the family, the homemaker will be abandoned, with nothing left to hold on to.

Ironically, this same fear is voiced by feminists in recognizing that all women are just one man removed from welfare. Yet while feminists see this as the economic dependence of women, and therefore seek security through encouraging women to be independent, to be able to earn their own livelihood, social conservative women seek the same security through trying to ensure women's rights and entitlements within marriage, thereby binding men to a stable family unit. It is not, then, that social conservative women suffer from "false consciousness" in not recognizing their own self-interest as women, as some feminists charge. In fact, social conservative women are well aware of their interests as women and act in defense of these interests. The difference between social conservative women and feminists, rather, is rooted in the fundamentally different meanings each attaches to being female. Because social conservative women define femininity in terms of traditional roles of male breadwinner/female caretaker, they seek to extend and secure female rights *within* the context of marriage and the family. In this way, social conservative women are women for themselves; they act for themselves as traditional women.

FEMINISM AS BIG GOVERNMENT

Besides viewing feminism as anti-family, as narcissistic, and as attacking the status of homemakers, social conservatives see feminism as a force of moral decay because it implies Big Government. Feminism represents the extension of Big Government at the expense of the traditional authority of the church, the neighborhood, and the family. As one critic of feminism comments: "The real effect of this collective delusion of women's rights is only to reduce the once sovereign family to a support system for various governmental agencies." Similarly, Phyllis Schlafly refers to ERA as a "blank check" by which federal politicians and judges take the authority out of local hands.

Opposition to this transfer of authority is tied to a fear of the leveling effect of Big Government. The fear is that once the feminist agenda is in federal hands, the essential differences between the sexes will be eliminated, replacing diversity with uniformity. The ultimate fear in equating feminism with leveling is the fear of communism. . . .

The question inevitably arises concerning the seeming paradox of the social conservative woman. Given her adherence to traditional gender roles in which men are breadwinners and protectors and women are helpmates and caretakers, how does the social conservative woman understand her own position as a political activist involved in the public arena? How does she justify her own participation, given this ideological commitment to men's and women's separate spheres? Does her activism contradict her beliefs?

The conflict between the traditional female passive role and the vocal political leader is personified by Phyllis Schlafly. Educated at Harvard, a lawyer, an author of nine books, and twice a candidate for Congress, Schlafly is anything but passive or submissive. As past NOW president Karen DeCrow comments: "I admire her. . . . I just can't think of anyone who's so together and tough. I mean, every thing you should raise your daughter to be. . . . She's an extremely liberated woman. She sets out to do something and she does it. To me, that's liberation."

In fact, Schlafly serves as a role model of female leadership for hundreds of women every year. She holds an annual conference in order to pass on her political organizing skills to other women in the pro-family movement. One national organizer explains the importance of these efforts:

> Phyllis has done a lot to encourage and inspire and train women, give them a lot of self-confidence. I had never given a speech, written

a speech, testified, never been on radio, never been on television, never *really* done a lot of political nitty-gritty campaign management until I met Phyllis.

I think the reason she was so successful was because she encouraged her women to go for it, that there was nothing they couldn't do. You know, she has a meeting every fall where she really revs up the troops. She literally took women who were bright and talented but who *had* been very traditional women. They had gone to school; maybe some of them had gone to college. They had gotten married and they were in the process of raising families. Some of them were very talented and very organized. They could run five children, keep their house cool and do something at the church and school and do the carpools and all that good stuff. All they had to do was transfer all that organizational ability to campaigns and newsletters and learning the issue and getting it down pat. You know, if you can go study the Bible once a week, you can go study the issue of ERA once a week and get it straight and go on TV and debate.

Our women learned. Phyllis encouraged them to debate. She'd say, "No, I can't come to Virginia. *You* debate. They want somebody to debate, you do it." And then you start getting some self-confidence. You defeat a lawyer in a debate a couple of times and you start thinking, "Well, gee, that's pretty good. I didn't know I could do that."

Clearly, Phyllis Schlafly has been an inspiration to scores of women, to raise their voices, to take control, and to step into the public arena. Yet a hint of why such a position does *not* challenge traditional roles is evidenced in another comment made by this national organizer:

I think that women generally, and especially conservative women, see a role for themselves as being the power behind the throne, you know, the people who are behind the candidates. People have said to me in past years, "Well, why don't you run for the Virginia House of Delegates?" And I'd say, "Well, I can either run and maybe get myself elected or I can work in five campaigns and maybe help get five people elected who wouldn't have gotten elected." It's not that I think I'm that great. It's just that if you spend a certain amount of money in the right places and if you really organize the precincts in a legislative race, you have a big impact. I think that women will continue to do that. I think that women have a good talent for that.

When female political activism is conceptualized as the power behind the throne, women altruistically working for the benefit of a larger cause, the seeming paradox disappears. For social conservative women recognize no tension between their political activism and the traditional female role. In fact, these "new" political roles are defined within the bounds of traditional gender ideology. Social conservative ideology expands to incorporate these "new" female roles. Schlafly, for example, includes an assertive political role in her ideal of womanhood, what she terms "The Positive Woman." Because of her positive mental attitude, the Positive Woman is not crushed by life's disappointments: "To the Positive Woman, her particular set of problems is not a conspiracy against her, but a challenge to her character and her capabilities." Clearly an attack against feminists who, in Schlafly's eyes, think the world is against them, the Positive Woman looks affirmatively upon the world. She continues: "The Positive Woman accepts her responsibility to spin the fabric of civilization, to mend its tears, and to reinforce its seams. . . . God has a mission for every Positive Woman. It is up to her to find out what it is and to meet the challenge."

Pro-family leader Connie Marshner has another name for this expanded female role. In a speech to the Family Forum conference, Marshner introduces the "New Traditional Woman":

> She is the mother of the citizens of the twenty-first century. It is she who will more than anyone else transmit civilization and humanity to future generations and by her response to the challenges of life, determine whether America will be a strong, virtuous nation. . . . She is new because she is of the current era, with all its pressures and fast pace and rapid change. She is traditional because, in the face of unremitting cultural change, she is oriented around the eternal truths of faith and family. Her values are timeless and true to human nature.

In explaining the New Traditional Woman, Marshner distinguishes between conventions and traditional values. Conventions, she says, are mutable, changing with the times. For instance, the idea that women should not be educated was a convention derived from the days when survival and the maintenance of the home took all of a woman's time. As the burden of housework lightened, this convention changed, allowing women to obtain an education. On the other hand, traditional values are eternal. Traditional values are moral norms that must be followed without exception. For example, fidelity is a moral norm; adultery is always wrong. In short, Marshner argues, traditional values are non-consequentialist ethics.

The distinction between conventions and traditional values is the

framework by which Marshner understands women's "new traditional role." Certain changes in gender roles must be seen as a mere
change of conventions. For example, the fact that more women
today feel that boys should be as responsible as girls for doing the
laundry does *not* challenge traditional values; this merely indicates a
change in convention because doing laundry is a morally neutral
act. Marshner articulates the difference between conventions and
values in this way:

> I think people make the mistake, if you're talking about a traditional
> value, you're talking about mother at home with the kids which is a
> fallacy. You're talking about what they believe, what they're taught
> and what their values are. You're not talking about who cooks the
> breakfast. That's a different question. . . . It's the values that
> they're given, it's what they think is important, the policies of the
> family, if you will, more than who wipes the nose. That kind of stuff
> is fairly neutral.

While conventions may change, adapting to the times and rearranging the tasks of each sex, the underlying values must remain
untouched. Marshner gives this example:

> One traditional value is that the husband is the head of the family. A
> number of conventions have supported that value but one of the
> most widely accepted has been the general practice of the husband
> bringing home the paycheck, or at least the larger paycheck. Perhaps
> one reason for the convention is that when the husband is the eco-
> nomic provider, it is easier to accept his headship. Due to extraordi-
> nary circumstances, however, the woman may become an equal or
> chief provider. Nevertheless, the husband is still the head of the
> family. Accepting his authority may be more of a challenge for the
> woman to accept in that circumstance, but if traditional values are to
> be preserved, it must be accepted. What is moral is the fact that the
> wife accepts her husband's authority. It is not immoral that she earns
> as much or more money than he does. Who earns what is accidental,
> and not intrinsically moral or immoral.

It is moral values which root our experiences in the day-to-day
world, acting as guideposts by which to live. Women may adopt new
roles, as long as these moral values remain firmly in place. Hence,
Marshner urges women whose God-given talent is to rear children
not to be judgmental of women whose talents lie elsewhere. As long
as the husband is still the head of the household and the greater

good of the family is being served, then moral norms will be preserved.

Neither Marshner nor Schlafly sees a contradiction in the politically active social conservative woman; both interpret such involvement within the bounds of traditional gender ideology. It is, in fact, woman's role as moral gatekeeper, as protector of the moral realm, that allows her to adopt these new positions, to be a voice of righteousness in the political world. For, through such action, the social conservative woman hopes to bring moral purity to a world filled with sin. As Betsy Barber Bancroft puts it: "The concerned Christian woman who would pull on her boots and grab her mop to clean up the filth from overtaxed plumbing, can, when she has the necessary tools, rise to stem the flow of the amoral filth in which our society is awash."

Roe v. Wade, 1973

Justice Harry A. Blackmun

Few Supreme Court decisions have provoked more emotional response or societal polarization than that which ensued after the judges handed down their 7–2 ruling in Roe v. Wade *(1973). The decision held that women had an absolute right to choose an abortion through the first trimester (months one through three) of their pregnancies. Pointing out that state laws prohibiting abortions were a relatively late creation (in the second half of the nineteenth century), the majority opinion, written by Nixon appointee Justice Harry Blackmun, concluded that there was no evidence that the founders of the country meant to include unborn fetuses in their constitutional definition of "personhood." Whether or not human life began at conception or at some undefined later point, the majority reasoned, was a religious question, not a legal certitude. In that circumstance, the judges decided, a woman's right to privacy in controlling her own reproductive life took priority, at least until the health and viability of the fetus gave the state a legitimate right to intervene. The dissenting judges, on the other hand, argued that such reasoning valued "the convenience, whim or caprice of the putative mother more than the life or potential life of the fetus."*

In the years since 1973, disputes over this decision have animated profound—and intense—political debate. The Roman Catholic Church hierarchy has adamantly opposed the pro-choice position (although many Roman Catholic parishioners disagree with the church); antifeminists and the "new right" have used a "pro-life" position to rally support for their political agenda. The Supreme Court itself has modified its position several times, permitting a series of state regulations to limit the right to abortion; yet at the end of the 1990s, it seemed that the Court had decided to leave the core of the Roe v. Wade *decision intact. The brief decision that follows concisely summarizes the issues, even as it raises far more questions than it answers.*

MR. JUSTICE [HARRY A.] BLACKMUN DELIVERED THE OPINION OF THE COURT. . . .

We forthwith acknowledge our awareness of the sensitive and emotional nature of the abortion controversy, of the vigorous opposing views, even among physicians, and of the deep and seemingly absolute convictions that the subject inspires. One's philosophy, one's experiences, one's exposure to the raw edges of human existence, one's religious training, one's attitudes toward life and family and their values, and the moral standards one establishes and seeks to observe, are all likely to influence and to color one's thinking and conclusions about abortion. . . .

The Texas statutes that concern us here are Arts. 1191–1194 and 1196 of the State's Penal Code. These make it a crime to "procure an abortion," as therein defined, or to attempt one, except with respect to "an abortion procured or attempted by medical advice for the purpose of saving the life of the mother." Similar statutes are in existence in a majority of the States. . . .

Jane Roe, a single woman who was residing in Dallas County, Texas, instituted this federal action in March 1970 against the District Attorney of the county. She sought a declaratory judgment that the Texas criminal abortion statutes were unconstitutional on their face, and an injunction restraining the defendant from enforcing the statutes.

Roe alleged that she was unmarried and pregnant; that she wished to terminate her pregnancy by an abortion "performed by a competent, licensed physician, under safe, clinical conditions"; that she was unable to get a "legal" abortion in Texas because her life did not appear to be threatened by the continuation of her pregnancy; and that she could not afford to travel to another jurisdiction in order to secure a legal abortion under safe conditions. She claimed that the Texas statutes were unconstitutionally vague and that they abridged her right of personal privacy, protected by the First, Fourth, Fifth, Ninth, and Fourteenth Amendments. By an amendment to her complaint Roe purported to sue "on behalf of herself and all other women" similarly situated. . . .

The principal thrust of appellant's attack on the Texas statutes is that they improperly invade a right, said to be possessed by the pregnant woman, to choose to terminate her pregnancy. Appellant would discover this right in the concept of personal "liberty" embodied in the Fourteenth Amendment's Due Process Clause; or in personal, marital, familial, and sexual privacy said to be protected by the Bill of Rights . . . or among those rights reserved to the people by the Ninth Amendment, . . .

It perhaps is not generally appreciated that the restrictive criminal abortion laws in effect in a majority of States today are of relatively recent vintage. Those laws, generally proscribing abortion or its attempt at any time during pregnancy except when necessary to preserve the pregnant woman's life, are not of ancient or even of common-law origin. Instead, they derive from statutory changes effected, for the most part, in the latter half of the nineteenth century. . . . It is undisputed that at common law, abortion performed *before* "quickening"—the first recognizable movement of the fetus *in utero,* appearing usually from the sixteenth to the eighteenth week of pregnancy—was not an indictable offense. . . . In this country, the law in effect in all but a few States until mid-nineteenth century was the pre-existing English common law. . . .

Gradually, in the middle and late nineteenth century the quickening distinction disappeared from the statutory law of most States and the degree of the offense and the penalties were increased. By the end of the 1950s, a large majority of the jurisdictions banned abortion, however and whenever performed, unless done to save or preserve the life of the mother. . . .

It is thus apparent that at common law, at the time of the adoption of our Constitution, and throughout the major portion of the nineteenth century, abortion was viewed with less disfavor than under most American statutes currently in effect. Phrasing it another way, a woman enjoyed a substantially broader right to terminate a pregnancy than she does in most States today. At least with respect to the early stage of pregnancy, and very possibly without such a limitation, the opportunity to make this choice was present in this country well into the nineteenth century. Even later, the law continued for some time to treat less punitively an abortion procured in early pregnancy. . . .

The Constitution does not explicitly mention any right of privacy. In a line of decisions, however, . . . the Court has recognized that a right of personal privacy, or a guarantee of certain areas or zones of privacy, does exist under the Constitution. . . . This right of privacy, whether it be founded in the Fourteenth Amendment's concept of personal liberty and restrictions upon state action, as we feel it is, or, as the District Court determined, in the Ninth Amendments' reservation of rights to the people, is broad enough to encompass a woman's decision whether or not to terminate her pregnancy. . . .

We . . . conclude that the right of personal privacy includes the abortion decision, but that this right is not unqualified and must be considered against important state interest in regulation. . . .

In view of all this, we do not agree that, by adopting one theory of life, Texas may override the rights of the pregnant woman that are at stake. We repeat, however, that the State does have an important and legitimate interest in preserving and protecting the health of the pregnant woman, whether she be a resident of the State or a nonresident who seeks medical consultation and treatment there, and that it has still *another* important and legitimate interest in protecting the potentiality of human life. These interests are separate and distinct. Each grows in substantiality as the woman approaches term and, at a point during pregnancy, each becomes "compelling."

With respect to the State's important and legitimate interest in the health of the mother, the "compelling" point, in the light of present medical knowledge, is at approximately the end of the first trimester. This is so because of the now-established medical fact . . . that until the end of the first trimester mortality in abortion may be less than mortality in normal childbirth. It follows that, from and after this point, a State may regulate the abortion procedure to the extent that the regulation reasonably relates to the preservation and protection of maternal health. . . .

This means, on the other hand, that, for the period of pregnancy prior to this "compelling" point, the attending physician, in consultation with his patient, is free to determine, without regulation by the State, that, in his medical judgment, the patient's pregnancy should be terminated. If that decision is reached, the judgment may be effectuated by an abortion free of interference by the State.

With respect to the State's important and legitimate interest in potential life, the "compelling" point is at viability. This is so because the fetus then presumably has the capability of meaningful life outside the mother's womb. State regulation protective of fetal life after viability thus has both logical and biological justifications. If the State is interested in protecting fetal life after viability, it may go so far as to proscribe abortion during that period, except when it is necessary to preserve the life or health of the mother.

Measured against these standards, Art. 1196 of the Texas Penal Code, in restricting legal abortions to those "procured or attempted by medical advice for the purpose of saving the life of the mother," sweeps too broadly. The statute makes no distinction between abortions performed early in pregnancy and those performed later, and it limits to a single reason, "saving" the mother's life, the legal justification for the procedure. The statute, therefore, cannot survive the constitutional attack made upon it here.

The Emergence of Gay Liberation

Estelle Freedman and John D'Emilio

The gay rights movement of the 1970s, 1980s, and 1990s represented one of the most important social developments emerging from 1960s activism. It took great courage for feminists and civil rights protesters to march and demonstrate for their freedom. Yet once they had declared themselves, they could derive strength from their solidarity and the public crusade they were involved in. Lesbians and gay men, on the other hand, lived in a culture that discouraged them from acknowledging who they were or from doing battle against their oppressors. The pervasiveness of homophobic attitudes almost compelled living a dual life—engaging in the public pretense of being heterosexual in order to satisfy family, friends, and work associates, then in private, and often furtively, seeking out sexual partners and social companions who were gay.

Given the power of cultural norms and social prejudice, "coming out of the closet" was difficult if not impossible. It carried with it the punishment of ostracism, potential loss of employment, and vicious rumors. Thus although the Kinsey report on human sexuality asserted that as many as 10 percent of Americans were homosexual, the number of openly gay people was minimal. Suspicion of homosexuality was sufficient to bring about dishonorable discharge from the armed forces, termination of employment with the State Department (especially during the McCarthy era), and an end to any hopes of upward mobility in business or the professions.

That started to change in the postwar years, and especially in light of the feminist movement. In the movement, in an atmosphere that supposedly encouraged women to be themselves and to speak honestly, lesbian feminists felt marginalized and stifled because some feminist leaders wished to avoid any suggestion that women's rights were connected to homosexual rights. Rebelling against such control, lesbians asserted their own voices and demanded recognition that their cause—like that of other feminists—was also one of sexual subordination and oppression. At the same time, gay men became ever more angry at the harassment and intimidation directed at them. When the New York Police engaged in one of their periodic raids of Stonewall, a gay bar in New York's Greenwich Village, this anger exploded into full scale resistance. The story of how lesbian feminists and gay men shaped a new social movement for gay rights in the 1970s is recounted here in this selection by Estelle Freedman and John D'Emilio.

With the revival of feminism in the late 1960s, lesbians flocked to the cause of women's emancipation. In many ways they were a natural constituency for the movement. Closeted though they might be, they still had to move in the public world of work to support themselves and thus encountered directly the barriers women faced in the economic sphere. Without husbands to provide them a legitimate status, and uninterested in playing the part of the sexy single girl who chased men, lesbians confronted squarely the limited options available to women. At the same time, the feminist movement was offering a setting and a climate that encouraged previously heterosexual women to come out, to explore the liberating possibilities of loving other women. As Coletta Reid, an early recruit to women's liberation in Washington, D.C., explained it,

> Almost everything I was reading at the time led me toward lesbianism. If "The Myth of the Vaginal Orgasm" was true, then intercourse was not necessary or even relevant to *my* sexual satisfaction. If "Sexual Politics" was right that male sexuality was an expression of power and dominance, then I was choosing my own oppression to stay in a relationship with a man. If sex roles were an invention of society, then women—not just men—were possible people to love, in the fullest sense of that word. If I could hug and kiss a woman I loved, why couldn't I touch all of her body? Since my husband really thought men were superior, then wasn't my needing to be in a relationship with someone superior to me, self-hating and woman-hating? The conclusion seemed inescapable.

Reid was not the only one to pursue the logic of her intellectual environment. The annals of the early women's movement were filled with the stories of others who used it to move from a life as a heterosexual to lesbianism.

Their choices, and the presence of lesbians of long standing in women's organizations, did not always please their compatriots. Products of their culture, feminists were no less likely than other Americans to view lesbians with disdain, to see their sexuality as a pathological aberration at worst, or a private matter of no political consequence at best. Sensitive to the reaction that the movement was eliciting in the minds of Americans, many feminists sought to keep the issue quiet, to push lesbians out of sight. Sometimes the results were nasty. In the New York City chapter of NOW, the energy and talent of Rita Mae Brown, a young lesbian soon to achieve fame as a novelist, lifted her to a position of influence in the organization. Her insistence that lesbianism was a key feminist issue antagonized many of her associates. Although Brown left NOW of her own choosing, others were not so fortunate, as the chapter engaged in a purge of lesbian officers. Late in 1970, the worst fears of some heterosexual feminists seemed confirmed when the media picked up Kate Millett's acknowledgment of bisexuality. *Time,* hardly a friend of the movement, gave it prominent play. "Kate Millett herself contributed," the magazine commented,

> to the growing skepticism about the movement by acknowledging at a recent meeting that she is bisexual. The disclosure is bound to discredit her as a spokeswoman for her cause, cast further doubt on her theories, and reinforce the views of those skeptics who routinely dismiss all liberationists as lesbians.

Throughout the period from 1969 to 1971, women's organizations across the country were wracked by a "gay–straight" split, as tensions reached the boiling point.

Some lesbians responded to the antagonism of other feminists by leaving mixed organizations. Along with women from the nascent gay liberation movement, they formed lesbian-feminist groups of their own, fashioning in the process both a political agenda and a theory to sustain their efforts. During the early seventies, radicalized lesbians produced a body of writing that sought to reshape the contemporary understanding of same-sex relations between women and the larger issue of human sexual relations. "As the question of homosexuality has become public," wrote Charlotte Bunch, a member of the Furies collective in Washington, D.C., "reformists define it as a private question of who you sleep with in order to sidetrack our understanding of the politics of sex. For the Lesbian-Feminist, it is not private; it is a political matter of oppression, domination, and power." Heterosexuality was removed from the realm of the "natural," and reinterpreted as an ideology and an institution that kept women bound to men and blocked their struggle for full liberation. Seen from this vantage point, lesbianism became a form of political rebellion. "The Lesbian rejects male sexual/political domination; she defies his world, his social organization, his ideology, and his definition of her as inferior. Lesbianism puts women first while the society declares the male supreme. Lesbianism," Bunch continued, "threatens male supremacy at its core." Pushed to its logical conclusion this outlook implied that "feminists must become Lesbians if they hope to end male supremacy."

Not all feminists became lesbians, of course, and not all lesbians left the women's movement. Nor, for that matter, did all lesbians identify with feminism. But, as the political passions of the early seventies cooled, the goal of ending the oppression of lesbians became integrated into the agenda of mainstream feminism. Despite the resistance of liberals such as Friedan, organizations such as NOW eventually incorporated lesbian rights into their list of goals. As the gay movement of the 1970s grew and brought the issue of homosexuality into the open, a gradual healing of conflict allowed some lesbians and heterosexuals to work side by side, even as other lesbians continued to staff their own organizations and sustain an autonomous lesbian-feminist movement.

In the long run, perhaps the signal achievement of this first generation of self-conscious lesbian feminists was to put into bold relief the part that sexuality played in the subordination of women. In identifying female sexual expression so closely with the institution of marriage, modern sexual liberalism sustained an ideological construct that kept women in a domestic role, while reinforcing her inequality in the public sphere. To challenge the inevitability or naturalness of heterosexuality was to open new realms of freedom for females. As such, acceptance of lesbianism could serve as a benchmark for the whole panoply of sexual questions that the second wave of feminism raised. Whether the issue was reproductive control, rape, sexual harassment, medical anthority, prostitutes' rights, or lesbianism, feminists sought an authentic autonomy in sexual matters and an end to the gender inequality that prevented its achievement.

GAY LIBERATION

Lesbians also served as a bridge between feminism and the other sexual liberation movement that arose in the late 1960s. One of the last of the radical causes to spring from the youth rebellion of the decade, gay liberation, like feminism, took issue with some core assumptions of sexual liberalism. Rejecting the notion that marriage was the appropriate site for adult eroticism, or that heterosexuality deserved its favored status in law and custom, gay activists assaulted the structures that relegated homosexuals to an underground, hidden existence.

Few social movements can trace their birth to an event as unexpected and dramatic as the one which gave life to gay liberation. On Friday, June 27, 1969, a group of Manhattan police officers set off to close the Stonewall Inn, a gay bar in the heart of Greenwich Village. Raids of gay bars were common enough occurrences in the 1960s, and the police must have viewed their mission as a routine part of their weekend duties. But the patrons of the Stonewall Inn refused to behave according to script. As the officers hauled them one by one into police vans, a crowd of onlookers assembled on the street, taunting the cops. When a lesbian in the bar put up a struggle, the *Village Voice* reported,

> the scene became explosive. Limp wrists were forgotten. Beer cans and bottles were heaved at the windows and a rain of coins descended on the cops. . . . Almost by signal the crowd erupted into cobblestone and bottle heaving. . . . From nowhere came an uprooted parking meter—used as a battering ram on the Stonewall door. I heard several cries of "let's get some gas," but the blaze of flame which soon appeared in the window of the Stonewall was still a shock.

Although the police officers were rescued from the torched bar, their work had just begun. Rioting continued far into the night, as crowds of angry homosexuals battled the police up and down the streets of Greenwich Village. The following day, graffiti proclaiming "Gay Power" was scribbled on walls and pavements in the area. The rioting that lasted throughout the weekend signaled the start of a major social movement. Within weeks, gay men and lesbians in New York had formed the Gay Liberation Front (GLF), a self-proclaimed revolutionary organization in the style of the New Left, seeking justice for homosexuals. As word of the Stonewall riots circulated among radical gay youth and other disaffected homosexuals, the gay liberation impulse took root across the country, spawning scores of similar groups.

Dramatic as the rioting was, it was not sufficient to spark a nationwide grass-roots movement. The speed with which gay liberation grew testified to equally profound changes in the structure of gay life and the consciousness of homosexuals in the preceding years. Throughout the 1950s and 1960s, a gay subculture had been growing, providing the setting in which homosexuals might develop a group consciousness. The weakening of taboos against the public discussion of homosexuality, the pervasive police harassment of the era, and the persistent work of a small coterie of pre-Stonewall activists combined to make many lesbians and gay men receptive to the message of "gay power."

The collapse in the 1960s of strictures against the portrayal of sexual matters gave the media license to turn its attention to homosexuality. Though much of the information presented was negative—highlighting medical theories that emphasized pathology, reporting police campaigns against "deviants," or casting pitying glances at the lives of sexual outlaws—the articles in newspapers and magazines also provided welcome clues to the existence of a gay world. Magazines such as *Life* and *Look* printed photo essays of the gay subculture, alerting their audience to the concentration of homosexuals in cities such as New York, Los Angeles, and San Francisco. Series in local newspapers served much the same function as they unwittingly instructed isolated gay readers about where they might find others. A spate of Hollywood movies in the 1960s—*The Children's Hour, Advise and Consent, Walk on the Wild Side*, among others—treated gay themes. Many writers included homosexual characters and subplots in their novels, and a number of journalists published exposés of gay life in modern America. Taken together, these forays into the world of homosexuals served as mapping expeditions that made exploration and discovery easier for countless numbers of gay men and lesbians.

Meanwhile, some gay men and women were mounting a response to the repressive public policies that had characterized the Cold War era. In Los Angeles, in 1950, a group of gay men associated with the Communist party founded the Mattachine Society, a gay rights organization. A few years later, they were joined by a lesbian counterpart, the Daughters of Bilitis. During the fifties, these groups struggled to exist, as they operated with scanty resources, no models for how to proceed, and the ever-present threat of police harassment. But they did survive, establishing chapters in several cities, publishing their own magazines, and projecting, however faintly, a point of view about same-gender relationships that departed from the consensus of sin, sickness, and criminality.

During the 1960s, this pre-Stonewall generation of "homophile" leaders, as they called themselves, became bolder. Inspired by the model of the civil rights movement, activists such as Frank Kameny in New York and Barbara Gittings in Philadelphia moved beyond the task of education and shaped a more direct challenge to the laws and public policies that denied gays equality. Homophile organizations staffed picket lines around government buildings in the nation's capital to protest the ban on federal employment and the exclusion from military service. They initiated court cases to challenge discriminatory statutes, lobbied successfully to win the support of the American Civil Liberties Union, and monitored police practices. A dialogue was opened with liberal Protestant clergy, and a campaign begun within the medical establishment to have homosexuality removed from the list of mental disorders. Perhaps most importantly, these ventures made the movement newsworthy. Television cameras filmed the picketing in front of the White House, while print journalists incorporated the views of activists into their articles on gay life. By the end of the 1960s, this pioneering band had succeeded in disseminating widely a point of view that diverged sharply from the dominant consensus about homosexuality.

As consciousness within the gay subculture slowly altered, the protests of the 1960s were creating another—radicalized—gay cohort. When black power advocates proclaimed that "black is beautiful," they provided the model of an oppressed group that inverted the negative values of the society. The student movement spread

skepticism toward middle-class values among white college youth
and led to an alienation from mainstream America that encouraged
a cavalier disregard for social respectability. The hippie counterculture urged the young to drop out and "do your own thing." Finally,
the women's liberation movement launched an ideological attack on
sex-role constructs while popularizing the slogan "the personal is
political." Taken together, these movements offered another lens
through which radical gay youth, who were keeping their homosexuality secret, might view their sexual preferences. After the Stonewall riot of 1969, when some of them gathered to form the Gay
Liberation Front in New York City, they were well situated to
launch a major social movement.

The culture of protest that existed at the time provided opportunities to spread the gay liberation impulse widely. Activists appeared with gay banners at the many anti-war demonstrations that
erupted during the fall of 1969. At colleges and universities, gay
students rallied openly alongside other campus radicals. Soon,
these young gay militants were taking the message of their movement into the heart of the gay subculture. Seeing the Mafia-run bars
as oppressive institutions that reinforced self-hatred and encouraged a dehumanizing sexual objectification, gay activists in may
cities "liberated" the bars for an evening, and urged patrons to join
the struggle for freedom.

Appearing as it did at the end of the 1960s, gay liberation
adopted much of the revolutionary rhetoric of the New Left. GLF's
statement of purpose announced that "we are a revolutionary homosexual group of men and women formed with the realization
that complete sexual liberation for all people cannot come about
unless existing social institutions are abolished. We reject society's
attempt to impose sexual roles and definitions of our nature. . . .
Babylon has forced us to commit ourselves to one thing . . . revolution!" Rather than fight the ban on homosexuals in the military,
radical gays urged resistance to the Vietnam War. They marched in
solidarity with groups such as the Black Panther party, and saw
themselves as an integral part of the larger movement of oppressed
minorities seeking the overthrow of a destructive social order.

In articulating a critique of America's sexual mores, gay liberation borrowed heavily from the new literature of radical feminists.
It argued that the oppression of homosexuals stemmed from a
rigidly enforced system of heterosexual supremacy that supported

the primacy of the nuclear family and the dichotomous sex roles within it. Sex was just one more vehicle used to enforce subordination and keep the system functioning. For some, gayness itself symbolized an act of political resistance to conventional roles. "We are women and men who, from the time of our earliest memories, have been in revolt against the sex-role structure and nuclear family structure," wrote Martha Shelley of GLF. Rather than being abnormal, homosexuality was seen as a natural capacity in everyone, suppressed by family and society. Gay liberation promised an end to all that. "Gay is good for all of us," proclaimed Allen Young, a former SDS member who joined GLF in 1970.

> The artificial categories "heterosexual" and "homosexual" have been laid on us by a sexist society. . . . As gays, we demand an end to the gender programming which starts when we are born. . . . The family . . . is the primary means by which this restricted sexuality is created and enforced . . . [O]ur understanding of sexism is premised on the idea that in a free society everyone will be gay.

For Young and his associates, gayness became the sign of a sexuality freed from the hierarchical assumptions of male supremacy, and from the manipulative imagery of consumer capitalism. A sensuality based on human equality would liberate the creative potential that inhered in the erotic. In leading the way toward this utopian sexual vision, gay liberationists expected that "we are going to transform society."

As one of its chief tactics for accomplishing its goals, gay liberation adopted the notion of "coming out." In its older, original meaning, "coming out" referred to the acknowledgment of one's homosexuality to oneself and other gay people. Gay liberationists transformed it into a public avowal. A critical step on the road to freedom, coming out implied a rejection of the negative social meaning attached to homosexuality in favor of pride and self-acceptance. The men and women who took the plunge had to overcome the fear of punishment and be willing to brave the ostracism of society that might result. In the process, they would also shed much of the self-hatred that they had internalized. Thus, the act became both a marker of liberation and an act of resistance against an oppressive society. As the banner of New York GLF's newspaper exhorted, "Come Out For Freedom! Come Out Now! . . . Come Out of the Closet Before the Door Is Nailed Shut!"

This deceptively simple proposition was both a unique product of its time and an important roadmark in the history of sexuality. At a moment when the hippie counterculture was urging the young to "do your own thing," and feminists were redefining the personal as political, coming out seemed perfectly to embody both. Moreover, it was precisely adapted to the immediate constituency and needs of the movement. With the range of penalties that exposure promised to homosexuals, it was radical youth, contemptuous of the rewards that American society offered for conformity, who were most likely to rally to the banner of gay liberation. Exclusion from the military or a civil service career, ostracism by society, and the threat of arrest held little power over these self-styled revolutionaries. And, coming out promised the movement an army of permanent recruits. By discarding the protection that came from hiding, gay men and lesbians invested heavily in the successful outcome of their struggle.

But coming out signified something more. As the gay movement grew and gathered strength in the 1970s, the example of radical activists proved infectious, and many conventional homosexuals imitated this simple act of pride. Coming out of the closet was incorporated into the basic assumptions of what it meant to be gay. As such, it came to represent not simply a single act, but the adoption of an identity in which the erotic played a central role. Sexuality became emblematic of the person, not as an imposed medical label connoting deviance, but as a form of self-affirmation. No longer merely something you did in bed, sex served to define a mode of living, both private and public, that encompassed a wide range of activities and relationships. The phenomenon of coming out highlighted just how far the erotic had moved from the previous century when it was still embedded in a web of marital duties and procreative responsibilities. And the concept of gay identity placed in sharper relief alternative self-conceptions: heterosexuality or bisexuality, "straight" or "swinger." Thus gay liberation confirmed the growing significance of the erotic in modern life, even as it seemed to break with the assumptions of sexual liberalism.

As with feminism, the revolutionary expectations of the early gay liberation movement never materialized. For one, the rebellious milieu that spawned it had lost its vigor by the mid-1970s, and the nation entered a more conservative political era. Then, too, the gay movement adapted to the times, for the most part pulling back from its radical critique of the effects of sexual repression and instead recasting itself as a movement in the long tradition of American reform. Proponents spoke of fixed sexual orientation rather than polymorphous desires; they campaigned for civil rights legislation rather than a restructuring of family life and sexual socialization. Moreover, though few activists seemed aware of it, the gay movement in important ways was moving in the same direction as mainstream sexual culture. By emphasizing the centrality of sexual expression for their own well-being, they were echoing themes that the ideologues of sexual liberalism had applied to heterosexuals in marriage. And, the commercialism that came to characterize the gay male subculture of the 1970s was not different in kind from the consumerist values that had already made sex a marketable commodity.

Nonetheless, throughout the 1970s the gay movement continued to grow, sinking deeper roots into society. By 1973, almost eight hundred gay and lesbian organizations had formed; by the end of the decade their numbers reached into the thousands. Alongside the proliferating bars sprang churches, synagogues, health clinics, community centers, law offices, travel agencies, restaurants, and a host of other businesses and nonprofit services. Lesbians formed record companies to market the music they were creating; gay men formed choruses that sang in some of the most prominent performance halls in the country. In many large cities, gay men and lesbians supported their own newspapers. Gays formed Democratic and Republican clubs and ran for office. In Massachusetts Elaine Noble was elected to the state assembly; in Minnesota, Karen Clark and Allen Spear had similar successes; and in San Francisco, Harvey Milk became the city's first openly gay supervisor. Various constituencies within the gay population—blacks, Hispanics, Asians, youth, elders—staffed their own organizations. Gay teachers, nurses, doctors, bankers, and others created caucuses within their professions. In less than a decade, American society had witnessed, in the words of one commentator, "an explosion of things gay." What had been an undergroud sexual subculture increasingly came to resemble an urban community.

The gay movement also made some progress in chipping away at the institutional structures, public policies, and cultural attitudes that sustained a system of oppression. In the course of the 1970s, half the states eliminated the sodomy statute from the penal code.

In 1974, the American Psychiatric Association removed homosexuality from its list of mental disorders, and the following year the U.S. Civil Service Commission lifted its ban on the employment of gay men and lesbians. Several dozen cities, including populous ones such as Detroit, Boston, Los Angeles, San Francisco, Houston, and Washington, D.C., incorporated sexual preference into their municipal civil rights laws. Gay activists lobbied in many legislatures for similar statewide protections, and in Congress the movement found sponsors for a federal civil rights law. Candidates for elective office sought the endorsement of gay organizations; the national Democratic party, at its 1980 convention, for the first time included a gay rights plank in its platform. A number of liberal Protestant denominations created task forces on homosexuality, initiating the revision of Christian teachings that had remained fixed since the thirteenth century. In most large cities, police harassment, though not eliminated, declined sharply, allowing many gay men and lesbians greater freedom from fear than they had ever enjoyed. Newspapers, magazines, book publishers, and television offered positive portrayals of gay life. Perhaps most importantly, countless numbers of lesbians and gay men were coming out to their families, friends, co-workers, and neighbors, defusing the fear that attached to popular conceptions of homosexuality, humanizing the stereotypical images that most Americans held, and making possible a permanent alteration of attitudes. Equality had not been achieved. Indeed, by the late 1970s a vocal, well-organized resistance to gay liberation had emerged, demonstrating how deeply rooted in American culture the fear of homosexuality was. But the gay movement had set in motion profound changes in America's sexual mores.

In just a few short years, the system of sexual liberalism had come apart. The premium that it placed upon fulfillment and pleasure compromised its ability to point sexual desire toward the institution of marriage. The logic of consumer capitalism pushed the erotic beyond the boundaries of the monogamous couple as entrepreneurs played with erotic impulses and affluent youth pursued their pleasures outside the marital bond. Women's liberation attacked modern marriage as an oppressive institution, while gay liberation challenged the supremacy of heterosexual expression. A construct of the white middle class, sexual liberalism could not withstand the assaults that came from disaffected segments of its own constituency.

Although feminism and gay liberation presented radical critiques of sexual liberalism, neither movement had the strength in the short run to remake thoroughly the mores of the nation. Effective enough to challenge the hegemony of mid-twentieth-century orthodoxy, they succeeded in removing some constraints on sexual expression and refashioning how many Americans looked upon sex. Sexual behavior and meanings would change in the 1970s, though not always in the ways that these sexual revolutionaries envisioned.

Part 5

VIETNAM

The war in Vietnam represents one of the most difficult military and foreign policy experiences in American history. Each step of American involvement seemed merely a modification of past practice, an increment to existing policy, and therefore nothing that required a declaration of war or a full scale reassessment of underlying policies. Through such a process American participation in Vetnam grew from 800 troops in 1960 to 15,000 in 1963 to more than 500,000 in 1968. A civil war between the Vietnamese became an American war; the United States was perceived by most people in the world as a colonialist aggressor; and the American people themselves divided into warring factions over support or opposition to the war.

Ironically, the United States became involved in Vietnam less because of any interest in Southeast Asia itself than in order to achieve other foreign policy goals. Franklin Roosevelt had decided during World War II that colonialism should end in Southeast Asia. But after the war American officials reversed that stance. To mollify France's unhappiness over the rebuilding of Germany, the United States countenanced French policy in Southeast Asia. By 1948, the United States was providing crucial economic and political sustenance for the French occupation of Indochina.

When the French lost their own Vietnam war in 1954 and the Geneva conference divided Vietnam into two regions, the United States stepped in to provide support for the pro-western government of President Diem. This seemed a moderate enough action at the time, particularly given the fact that President Eisenhower had earlier refused a French request to use atomic weapons against the Vietnamese. But that moderate involvement in support of Diem provided the basis for ever-increasing commitments of American money and manpower. When John F. Kennedy became president,

Vietnam became a testing point of the battle against communism—again, not so much because of its own intrinsic importance as because of events elsewhere. After the debacle at the Bay of Pigs in April 1961 and Kennedy's confrontation with Khrushchev at Vienna in June 1961, the young American president wanted to find some place where he could take a stand and convey to the Russians his determination to hold firm against communism. Vietnam became such a place, and during the Kennedy years the United States significantly expanded the flow of foreign aid and military equipment to South Vietnam, increased the number of American troops engaged in the conflict to over 15,000, and launched a major effort at counterinsurgency. At the same time, however, the United States remained publicly committed to political reform in Vietnam and to the proposition that it was impossible for the United States itself to fight a war that the Vietnamese did not wish to wage.

It was Lyndon Johnson's misfortune to preside over the most massive and disastrous expansion of the war. Deeply committed to maintaining a strong military presence, fearful of abandoning Kennedy's policy, and anxious to put forward an image of strength and power, Johnson never asked the hard questions as to why we were in Vietnam, where our policy would lead, or what would happen as a consequence. As one coup d'état after another brought successive military regimes to power in South Vietnam, Johnson kept pouring more American troops and money into the country, attempting to provide, through external military support, a degree of stability that clearly was not present among the South Vietnamese themselves. The long range results are now history. The Vietnamese countryside was destroyed, millions of lives were lost, search and destroy missions became the hallmark of a senseless effort to accumulate military victories measured by body counts of Vietnamese dead, and the nation entered a downward spiral of divisiveness and mistrust.

There are various ways of interpreting American involvement in Vietnam. Some see the war as simply a logical extension of a Cold War mentality, in which any civil war or nationalist struggle was perceived as part of a communist conspiracy that must be stopped. According to that interpretation, U.S. involvement grew directly from a distorted definition of world events in which all subtleties of internal and cultural politics were lost. A second interpretation views Vietnam as the one exception to a generally successful foreign policy in the postwar world. The Vietnam experience was not the product of erroneous Cold War attitudes, but rather an unrelated mistake in which the United States became too deeply involved before it could make a correct assessment of the situation. A third interpretation is that the war represented a wise policy that went awry. According to this view, U.S. commitment to political reform in South Vietnam was intelligent, and only when America attempted to use military power in place of political persuasion did a good policy turn bad. Finally, there is the view that the policy was wise all along and was prevented from being successful only because the military was hindered by political decisions at home. According to General William Westmoreland, the war was won militarily; it was lost politically.

Whichever interpretation one accepts, there can be little question that the war was a traumatic event for America and the world. The following selections explore some of the explanations for the war, as well as the consequences it brought. John Garry Clifford places the war within the long-term framework of American foreign policy. Lyndon Johnson cogently states the reasons why Americans must fight and win. Leslie Gelb, a State Department official, analyzes the major explanations of the causes of the war and offers his own view of how and why the United States became involved so deeply. Richard Hammer describes the consequences of American policy for the Vietnamese people as well as for United States soldiers and those at home. His description of My Lai speaks as powerfully as anything to the horror of what occurred as a result of Vietnam. John Kerry, a representative of Vietnam Veterans Against the War (and now the junior Democratic Senator from Massachusetts), poignantly testifies about what he had observed and learned in the war.

Some critical questions remain. Was there ever a way that United States involvement could have led to a democratic government in Vietnam? How much racism was involved in U.S. policy? Did an episode such as My Lai represent the natural consequence of a "search and destroy" mentality, or was it a complete aberration? Finally, there is the question of how much American policy in Vietnam represented a fatal flaw in the idea that America has a moral right to tell the rest of the world how to behave.

Vietnam in Historical Perspective

John Garry Clifford

American involvement in Vietnam resulted from a series of assumptions about America's place in the world. John Garry Clifford, a diplomatic historian from the University of Connecticut, has written extensively about postwar American foreign policy. Here, he shows how the war in Vietnam reflected American ideas about the Cold War. Clifford concludes that the Vietnam experience challenged the basic tenets of American policy-makers, forcing a reassessment of how we proceed to achieve our goals. Clifford's essay accurately describes the immediate consequences of the Vietnam war. During the 1970s, Congress limited presidential power to make war without congressional approval, and circumscribed the freedom of action of the CIA. Nevertheless, students may ask whether Clifford's conclusions still hold in the 1990s.

Although it is too early to determine, the Vietnam war may well prove to have been both the logical culmination of American foreign policy since 1945 and a turning point comparable to that of World War II. Certainly on a perceptual level, in the way Americans viewed the world, the war set in motion changes that became obvious by 1970. On an institutional level, in the way government agencies connected with foreign policy defined their goals and procedures, the evidence of change by the early 1970s was less marked. One thing became certain: the options available to American diplomatists were more varied than at any other time since the fall of France in 1940.

Excerpted from John Garry Clifford, "Change and Continuity in American Foreign Policy Since 1930," in James T. Patterson, ed. *Paths to the Present* (Minneapolis: Burgess Publishing Co., 1975). Reprinted by permission of the author.

Vietnam, which Senator John F. Kennedy described in 1956 as the "cornerstone of the Free World in Southeast Asia, the Keystone to the arch, the finger in the dike," was the logical, if erroneous, culmination of Cold War perceptions. The "lessons" of the past were constantly invoked. "If we don't stop the Reds in South Vietnam," said Lyndon Johnson, "tomorrow they will be in Hawaii, and next week they will be in San Francisco." Former Undersecretary of the Air Force, Townsend Hoopes, described the thinking of Dean Rusk: "In his always articulate, sometimes eloquent, formulations, Asia seemed to be Europe, China was either Stalinist Russia or Hitler Germany, and SEATO was either NATO or the Grand Alliance of World War II." If these analogies seemed somewhat strained, intended more for public persuasion than for internal conviction, the leaders in Washington all subscribed to the belief—unquestioned since Pearl Harbor—that aggression must be deterred. Vietnam became a test of America's will. "I don't need to remind you of what happened in the Civil War," Johnson told a press conference in 1967. "People were here in the White House begging Lincoln to concede and to work out a deal with the Confederacy when word came of his victories. . . . I think you know what Roosevelt went through and President Wilson in World War I. . . . We are going to have this criticism. We are going to have this difference. . . . No one likes war. All people love peace. But you can't have freedom without defending it. . . . We are going to do whatever it is necessary to do to see that the aggressor does not succeed."

But who was the aggressor in Vietnam? The Soviet Union? As the "quagmire" deepened, observers noted that Soviet supplies indeed helped the "enemy," but that Moscow was not master-minding a world-wide Communist conspiracy. The Sino-Soviet split became so evident by the mid-1960s that even the most militant Cold Warriors had to take notice. Perhaps the "enemy" was China, and Dean Rusk conjured up the frightening image of a billion Chinese armed with hydrogen bombs. But even after President Nixon's trips to Moscow and Peking in 1972, the war continued. The suggestion persisted that it was a *civil* war, an internal conflict between two versions of Vietnamese nationality, but this reality did not gibe with Cold War perceptions. Not enough was known in Washington about the fundamental differences in Asian societies, and belief in the Domino

Theory came easily, along with visions of armed Communist hordes. Bureaucrats did not want to change their perceptions. James C. Thomson, a White House consultant during the early 1960s, recalls a conversation in March of 1964 with an Assistant Secretary of State. "But in some ways, of course, it *is* a civil war," Thomson said. "Don't play word games with me!" the official snapped.

Bureaucratic style contributed significantly to the tragedy. Part of it derived from technological superiority, which in turn gave rise to a "can do" philosophy. At one extreme, in Walter LaFeber's phrase, was "General Curtis LeMay's notion that Communism could best be handled from a height of 50,000 feet." At a more sophisticated level was the conviction that no matter how resilient the enemy proved, the United States could work its will through "smart" bombs, search and destroy tactics, electronic barriers, superior air power, or sheer economic momentum. A crazy sense of bloodlessness began to emerge. "Every quantitative measurement we have shows we're winning this war," McNamara stated in 1962. Statistics proliferated—infiltration rates, weapons-loss ratios, aircraft sorties rates, expended ammunition tonnages, allied troop contributions, enemy "body counts," friendly casualties. Bureaucratic jargon ("free fire zones," "surgical" air strikes, "threshold of pain," "slow squeeze") obscured the reality of flesh being mangled, villages devastated, ecology ruined. Describing the gradual pressure imposed by the "Rolling Thunder" bombing campaign, one State Department official said: "Our orchestration should be mainly violins, but with periodic touches of brass."

This armchair atmosphere could not be dispelled by battle reports or occasional trips to Saigon. A process of self-hypnosis seemed at work. David Halberstam has told the story of Daniel Ellsberg's return from a tour of duty in Vietnam and his attempts to tell presidential adviser Walt Rostow how badly the war was going. "No, you don't understand," said Rostow. "Victory is very near. I'll show you the charts. The charts are very good." "I don't want to see any charts," Ellsberg replied. "But, Dan, the charts are very good," Rostow insisted. Similarly, James Thomson has described his shock on returning to Harvard after several years in the State Department. He suddenly realized that "the young men, the flesh and blood I taught and saw on these university streets, were potentially some of the numbers on the charts of those faraway planners.

In a curious sense, Cambridge is closer to this war than Washington."

The imperviousness of official Washington from external dissent contributed to the debacle. The smugness that came with access to classified information was partly responsible. The experts knew the facts, the critics did not. Internal dissenters were rarer and somehow safer to government leaders. President Johnson used to greet Bill Moyers rather affectionately: "Well, here comes Mr. Stop-the-Bombing." And when the war protest became especially shrill in 1966 and 1967, Johnson, who had followed the experts into the morass, displayed his furious temper. Dissenters, he said, were "nervous Nellies," "chickenshit." "I'm the only President you have," he would say. "Why don't you get on the team?" When hawks like Bundy and McNamara began to waver, Johnson sarcastically called the former "George McBundy" and unceremoniously nominated the latter to head the World Bank. This presidential temperament reinforced the natural bureaucratic tendency to remain silent so as not to lose one's effectiveness. Townsend Hoopes has described Vice-President Hubert Humphrey's abortive dissent in 1965: "His views were received at the White House with particular coldness, and he was banished from the inner councils for some months thereafter, until he decided to 'get back on the team.'" Not until the Tet offensive of early 1968 did effective criticism penetrate the Oval Office, and then it took someone of the stature of Dean Acheson to shake Lyndon Johnson. "With all due respect, Mr. President," said the mustachioed Dean of Middletown, "the Joint Chiefs of Staff don't know what they are talking about." When the Senior Advisory Group on Vietnam corroborated Acheson's estimates a few weeks later, the President's plaintive reaction underlined the extent to which policy had been made in a vacuum. "What did you tell them that you didn't tell me?" he asked his staff. "You must have given them a different briefing."

Momentum was another reason for escalation. The men in Washington may have thought they controlled events, but in actuality the genii of war were beyond control. For all their sophisticated technology, for all their favorable statistics, for all their "can do" spirit, American leaders never understood the extent to which decisions closed options previously available, making other decisions almost inevitable. Moreover, policy decisions often resulted from compromise, as in the case of the Kennedy administration sending military advisers to South Vietnam in 1961, notwithstanding the Taylor-Rostow report which recommended 8,000 troops. These compromises represented the usual adjustment of differences between the various agencies involved: the Saigon embassy, CIA, the State Department, the White House Staff, and the Joint Chiefs. Once advisers were committed, however, pressure rose for increasing their numbers.

Similarly, in the winter of 1964–65, certain "dovish" planners in the State Department who were strongly opposed to bombing the North urged instead that ground forces be sent to the South. They thought such a move would increase bargaining leverage against the North and be a prod for negotiations. At the same time, military men determined not to fight another "land war" in Asia were calling for the air-strike option. Still other civilians seeking peace wanted to bomb Hanoi into early peace talks. Within eight months all factions were disappointed: there was a costly and ineffective air campaign against the North, a mushrooming ground commitment in the South, and negotiations farther away than before. Each step also added greater weight to the military's demands. As soon as the Army's mission had changed from advising to saving Saigon, it was inevitable that the Joint Chiefs should press for escalation. Each service had its special panaceas, and under a tacit agreement the Joint Chiefs usually spoke in unison. McNamara then scaled down their demands. The result: escalation. Even after Nixon began withdrawing ground forces in 1969, military pressure to "protect" these troops resulted in decisions to invade Cambodian sanctuaries, to mine the harbors of Haiphong and Hanoi, and to resume aerial bombardment of the North at ever-increasing rates.

Vietnam brought about an "agonizing reappraisal" in American foreign policy far more searching than anything John Foster Dulles had envisaged in the 1950s. Dissent in American wars was not a new phenomenon. New England Federalists had opposed the War of 1812, abolitionists had protested the Mexican War, and Mugwumps and anti-imperialists had been vocal in 1898. Generally these dissenters were relatively small in number, well educated, respectable (usually upper class WASP), and quite orthodox in the way they protested—pamphlets petitions, rallies, letter writing campaigns, efforts in behalf of anti-war candidates. The Vietnam war protest was different. The movement had enough diversity to include such heterogeneous spokesmen as Norman Mailer,

Muhammed Ali, Abby Hoffman, John Kenneth Galbraith, George Kennan, Jane Fonda, Joan Baez, Jeannette Rankin, Martin Luther King, Robert Kennedy, Timothy Leary, Dick Gregory, and Noam Chomsky. Protest went from genteel teach-ins, to Senator Eugene McCarthy's brash campaign for the Democratic nomination in 1968, to marches On Washington, moratoria, and violent attempts by revolutionary groups to bring the war "home" to America. Protest literature ranged from the witty to the obscene.

People opposed the war for different reasons. Some still clung to the Cold War arguments for containment, but denied that the doctrine applied to Asia, or particularly to Vietnam. Others saw the war as killing reform at home, diverting attention from desperate conditions in the cities and in race relations. A less articulate group protested the deaths of American soldiers in Asian jungles, but seemed willing to permit American aircraft to drop billions of tons of bombs on yellow peoples. Others blamed President Johnson. "We've got a wild man in the White House," said Senator McCarthy. "A desperate man who was likely to get us into war with China," warned Senator Albert Gore of Tennessee.

More and more, protest occurred because of a moral revulsion to the war. Reaction to napalm bombing and "defoliation," horror at the destruction of the city of Hue in order to "save" it, incredulity at the My Lai massacre and the shootings of students at Kent State and Jackson State in 1970—all these events called into question the ethical standards of American policy. Confused about the identity of the aggressor in Vietnam—the Viet Cong? Hanoi? China?—more and more Americans came to agree with Walt Kelly's possum, Pogo: "We have met the enemy and they are us."

By the late 1960s this moral revulsion, fueled by the obvious *practical* failure of the American effort, had prompted a reassessment of long-held assumptions. One State Department official complained in 1966: "There is a considerable sort of feeling of unhappiness here that elements in the population that used to be thought of as our 'natural constituency' are not doing yeoman service for the Department now. We do have a constituency of sorts—the Foreign Policy Association, the Council on Foreign Relations, and all the other groups like that. These people have helped us all along for years, with the United Nations, the Marshall Plan, NATO, Korea, and all the others. But they are not helping us with the American public on the Vietnam issue. When they come to town to be briefed on Vietnam, they do not leave with marching orders, as they used to." When Dean Acheson told President Johnson that the generals did not know what they were talking about, he was also serving notice that the foreign policy consensus in existence since World War II had shattered. Another symbolic confrontation occurred in the spring of 1970 following the Cambodia invasion, when a group of prominent academicians, headed by Richard Neustadt, visited Henry Kissinger and recanted their support for executive predominance in foreign policy. These defections did not mean that Nixon could not count on continued support from the "silent majority," that Congress suddenly cut off military appropriations, or that the Navy decided to convert its aircraft carriers into hospital ships. What did emerge was an eventual repudiation of the Vietnam war by a majority of the so-called "foreign policy public." "What the hell is an Establishment for, if it's not to support the President," Kissinger complained. The reaction was especially strong among academicians. The political scientist Bruce Russett wrote: "Vietnam has been to social scientists what Alamogordo was to the physicists. Few of those who have observed it can easily return to their comfortable presumptions about America's duty, or right, to fight in distant lands." . . .

Historians cannot predict the future. To suggest, however, that changes in American assumptions about the world began in the 1960s and that Watergate and Vietnam accelerated these changes, is not presumptuous. The "lower profile" of American involvement abroad, as proclaimed by the Nixon Doctrine, will result in "lower" perceptions about American power and responsibilities. The intellectual capital that financed the Marshall Plan, NATO, and Korea was expended in Southeast Asia in the 1960s. The Nixon-Kissinger policies of détente toward the Soviet Union and the People's Republic of China have in themselves altered Cold War patterns. Do these changes signal a return to the isolationism of the 1930s, as defenders of the Vietnam war sometimes suggested? In the sense that domestic needs will not automatically take second place to foreign policy, or that Congress will not rubber-stamp executive initiatives, these changes do reflect some of the concerns of the Stimson-Hoover era. Nevertheless, the huge foreign policy bureaucracy spawned by World War II and the Cold War will remain, and it will take time for new perceptions to become embedded. Public opinion, decidedly noninterventionist in Asia because of the failure of the ground war in Vietnam, may well permit intervention by means of naval and aerial bombardment in future crises. The renewal of war between Israel and the Arab states in the fall of 1973, combined with the Arab embargo of oil, raised the prospect of American intervention in the Middle East, and with it the possibility of a Soviet-American confrontation. Like all previous empires in decline, the United States will retreat reluctantly.

Nevertheless, Vietnam and Watergate have left an ambivalence which allows room for cautious optimism. As the political scientist Robert W. Tucker has observed, Pearl Harbor and the Berlin Blockade will not be automatic reference points for the coming generation of "foreign policy elites." Rather, memories of My Lai and the Cuban Missile Crisis will be much sharper. "Never again," a slogan which the Army brought out of the Korean War, ought to remain a convenient watchword. The waning of anti-Communism as a political issue, as well as the need to combat industrial pollution, to conserve energy, to revitalize public transportation, and to obtain public health insurance, should tend to "lower" profiles and "cool" American foreign policy. Gradually, one may predict, the traditional American mission of erecting a "city on the hill" and solving domestic problems will take precedence over building "democratic" governments in remote areas of the world.

John Quincy Adams said it well more than 150 years earlier:

> Wherever the standard of freedom and Independence has been or shall he unfurled, there will her [America's] heart, her benediction and her prayers be. But she goes not abroad in search of monsters to destroy. . . . She well knows that by once enlisting under other banners than her own, were they even the banners of foreign independence, she would involve herself beyond the power of extrication. . . . The fundamental maxims of her policy would change from *liberty* to *force*.

Why We Are in Vietnam

Lyndon B. Johnson

On April 7, 1965, President Johnson delivered a major address at Johns Hopkins University that he hoped might satisfy both the hawk and dove critics of his Vietnam policies. He asserted his determination to use whatever force was necessary to deter aggression as well as his readiness to begin "unconditional discussions" toward a peaceful settlement of the conflict. He even held out the promise of an American-financed billion dollar project to develop the Mekong river valley as an incentive to bring North Vietnam to the bargaining table. For the next three years, however, Johnson would talk about negotiations while continuing to escalate the war. Note the reasons he gave for the U.S. involvement, and the American objectives, in Vietnam. How realistic was his view of the stakes involved? Did he have other alternatives to the increasing use of American combat forces? If so, why were they rejected? Did Johnson think that escalation of the war was the price to be paid for preserving the Great Society programs?

Tonight Americans and Asians are dying for a world where each people may choose its own path to change.

This is the principle for which our ancestors fought in the valleys of Pennsylvania. It is the principle for which our sons fight tonight in the jungles of Vietnam.

Vietnam is far away from this quiet campus. We have no territory there, nor do we seek any. The war is dirty and brutal and difficult. And some 400 young men, born into an America that is bursting with opportunity and promise, have ended their lives on Vietnam's steaming soil.

Why must we take this painful road?

From *Public Papers of Presidents of the United States: Lyndon B. Johnson, 1965* (Washington, D.C., 1966), pp. 394–97.

Why must this Nation hazard its ease, and its interest, and its power for the sake of a people so far away?

We fight because we must fight if we are to live in a world where every country can shape its own destiny. And only in such a world will our own freedom be finally secure.

This kind of world will never be built by bombs or bullets. Yet the infirmities of man are such that force must often precede reason, and the waste of war, the works of peace.

We wish that this were not so. But we must deal with the world as it is, if it is ever to be as we wish.

The world as it is in Asia is not a serene or peaceful place.

The first reality is that North Vietnam has attacked the independent nation of South Vietnam. Its object is total conquest.

Of course, some of the people of South Vietnam are participating in attack on their own government. But trained men and supplies, orders and arms, flow in a constant stream from north to south.

This support is the heartbeat of the war.

And it is a war of unparalleled brutality. Simple farmers are the targets of assassination and kidnapping. Women and children are strangled in the night because their men are loyal to their government. And helpless villages are ravaged by sneak attacks. Large-scale raids are conducted on towns, and terror strikes in the heart of cities.

The confused nature of this conflict cannot mask the fact that it is the new face of an old enemy.

Over this war—and all Asia—is another reality: the deepening shadow of Communist China. The rulers in Hanoi are urged on by Peking. This is a regime which has destroyed freedom in Tibet, which has attacked India, and has been condemned by the United Nations for aggression in Korea. It is a nation which is helping the forces of violence in almost every continent. The contest in Vietnam is part of a wider pattern of aggressive purposes.

Why are these realities our concern? Why are we in South Vietnam?

We are there because we have a promise to keep. Since 1954 every American President has offered support to the people of South Vietnam. We have helped to build, and we have helped to defend. Thus, over many years, we have made a national pledge to help South Vietnam defend its independence.

And I intend to keep that promise.

To dishonor that pledge, to abandon this small and brave nation to its enemies, and to the terror that must follow, would be an unforgivable wrong.

We are also there to strengthen world order. Around the globe, from Berlin to Thailand, are people whose well-being rests, in part, on the belief that they can count on us if they are attacked. To leave Vietnam to its fate would shake the confidence of all these people in the value of an American commitment and in the value of America's word. The result would be increased unrest and instability, and even wider war.

We are also there because there are great stakes in the balance. Let no one think for a moment that retreat from Vietnam would bring an end to conflict. The battle would be renewed in one country and then another. The central lesson of our time is that the appetite of aggression is never satisfied. To withdraw from one battlefield means only to prepare for the next. We must say in southeast Asia—as we did in Europe—in the words of the Bible: "Hitherto shalt thou come, but no further."

There are those who say that all our effort there will be futile— that China's power is such that it is bound to dominate all southeast Asia. But there is no end to that argument until all of the nations of Asia are swallowed up.

There are those who wonder why we have a responsibility there. Well, we have it there for the same reason that we have a responsibility for the defense of Europe. World War II was fought in both Europe and Asia, and when it ended we found ourselves with continued responsibility for the defense of freedom.

Our objective is the independence of South Vietnam, and its freedom from attack. We want nothing for ourselves—only that the people of South Vietnam be allowed to guide their own country in their own way.

We will do everything necessary to reach that objective. And we will do only what is absolutely necessary.

In recent months attacks on South Vietnam were stepped up. Thus, it became necessary for us to increase our response and to make attacks by air. This is not a change of purpose. It is a change in what we believe that purpose requires.

We do this in order to slow down aggression.

We do this to increase the confidence of the brave people of South Vietnam who have bravely borne this brutal battle for so many years with so many casualties.

And we do this to convince the leaders of North Vietnam—and all who seek to share their conquest—a very simple fact:

We will not be defeated.

We will not grow tired.

We will not withdraw, either openly or under the cloak of a meaningless agreement.

We know that air attacks alone will not accomplish all of these purposes. But it is our best and prayerful judgment that they are a necessary part of the surest road to peace.

We hope that peace will come swiftly. But that is in the hands of others besides ourselves. And we must be prepared for a long continued conflict. It will require patience as well as bravery, the will to endure as well as the will to resist.

I wish it were possible to convince others with words of what we now find it necessary to say with guns and planes: Armed hostility is futile. Our resources are equal to any challenge. Because we fight for values and we fight for principles, rather than territory or colonies, our patience and our determination are unending.

Once this is clear, then it should also be clear that the only path for reasonable men is the path of peaceful settlement.

Such peace demands an independent South Vietnam—securely guaranteed and able to shape its own relationships to all others—free from outside interference—tied to no alliance—a military base for no other country.

These are the essentials of any final settlement.

We will never be second in the search for such a peaceful settlement in Vietnam.

There may be many ways to this kind of peace: in discussion or negotiation with the governments concerned; in large groups or in small ones; in the reaffirmation of old agreements or their strengthening with new ones.

We have stated this position over and over again, fifty times and more, to friend and foe alike. And we remain ready, with this purpose, for unconditional discussions.

And until that bright and necessary day of peace we will try to keep conflict from spreading. We have no desire to see thousands die in battle—Asians or Americans. We have no desire to devastate that which the people of North Vietnam have built with toil and sacrifice. We will use our power with restraint and with all the wisdom that we can command.

But we will use it.

This war, like most wars, is filled with terrible irony. For what do the people of North Vietnam want? They want what their neighbors also desire: food for their hunger; health for their bodies; a chance to learn; progress for their country; and an end to the bondage of material misery. And they would find all these things far more readily in peaceful association with others than in the endless course of battle. . . .

We often say how impressive power is. But I do not find it impressive at all. The guns and the bombs, the rockets and the warships, are all symbols of human failure. They are necessary symbols. They protect what we cherish. But they are witness to human folly.

A dam built across a great river is impressive.

In the countryside where I was born, and where I live, I have seen the night illuminated, and the kitchens warmed, and the homes heated, where once the cheerless night and the ceaseless cold held sway. And all this happened because electricity came to our area along the humming wires of the REA [Rural Electrification Administrative]. Electrification of the countryside—yes, that, too, is impressive.

A rich harvest in a hungry land is impressive.

The sight of healthy children in a classroom is impressive.

These—not mighty arms—are the achievements which the American Nation believes to be impressive.

And, if we are steadfast, the time may come when all other nations will also find it so.

Every night before I turn out the lights to sleep I ask myself this question: Have I done everything that I can do to unite this country? Have I done everything I can to help unite the world, to try to bring peace and hope to all the peoples of the world? Have I done enough?

Ask yourselves that question in your homes—and in this hall tonight. Have we, each of us, all done all we could? Have we done enough?

We may well be living in the time foretold many years ago when it was said: "I call heaven and earth to record this day against you, that I have set before you life and death, blessing and cursing: therefore choose life, that both thou and thy seed may live."

This generation of the world must choose: destroy or build, kill or aid, hate or understand.

We can do all these things on a scale never dreamed of before.

Well, we will choose life. In so doing we will prevail over the enemies within man, and over the natural enemies of all mankind. . . .

Causes of the War

Leslie Gelb

*Those who know most about the decision-making process in American
foreign policy frequently can say least about it. Officials at the State
Department and the Pentagon see a myriad of classified information
everyday. While lacking the independence and detachment of external
observers, they have a unique vantage point on how and why particular
policies are pursued. Leslie Gelb, a State Department official during the
Vietnam war years, reflects this "insider's" familiarity with all the cur-
rents and crosscurrents of advice shaping American foreign policy decisions on Vietnam. In this selection from testimony given before Congress,
Gelb assesses the relative influence of the various forces acting upon the
presidential decision-making process. Although Gelb does not cite chapter
and verse of secret memoranda supporting various positions on the war,
his is one of the most informed studies of how and why the United States
became so deeply involved in Vietnam. His conclusion that pervasive
anticommunist attitudes provide the key to our involvement in Southeast
Asia supports the argument that the Vietnam war, far from being a
deviation from postwar foreign policy, was in fact a logical extension of
the Cold War.*

Wars are supposed to tell us about ourselves. Are we a wise and just
nation? Or are we foolish and aggressive? Merciless or humane?
Well led or misled? Vital or decadent? Hopeful or hopeless? Nations
in war and after war, win or lose, try to scratch away at the paste or
glue or traditions or values that held their societies together and see
of what they are made. It is arguable whether a society should

From Leslie H. Gelb statement to the Senate Committee on Foreign Relations, May 1972.

indulge in such self-scrutiny. Societies are, as Edmund Burke wrote, "delicate, intricate wholes" that are more easily damaged than improved when subjected to the glare of Grand Inquisitors.

But in the case of our society and the war in Vietnam, too many people are seeking answers and are entitled to them, and many are only too eager to fill in the blanks. The families and friends of those who were killed and wounded will want to know whether it was worth it after all? Intellectuals will want to know "why Vietnam"? Men seeking and holding political office will demand to know who was responsible? The answers to these questions will themselves become political facts and forces, shaping the United States' role in the world and our lives at home for years to come.

CAUSES OF THE WAR: THE RANGE OF EXPLANATIONS

Central to this inquiry is the issue of causes of U.S. involvement in Vietnam. I have found eight discernible explanations advanced in the Vietnam literature. Different authors combine these explanations in various ways, but I will keep them separate for the purpose of analysis. I will, then, sketch my own position.

The Arrogance of Power

This view holds that a driving force in American involvement in Vietnam was the fact that we were a nation of enormous power and like comparable nations in history, we would seek to use this power at every opportunity. To have power is to want to employ it, is to be corrupted by it. The arrogance derives from the belief that to have power, is to be able to do anything. Power invokes right and justifies itself. Vietnam was there, a challenge to this power and an opportunity for its exercise, and no task was beyond accomplishment.

There can be no doubt about this strain in the behavior of other great powers and in the American character. But this is not a universal law. Great powers, and especially the United States have demonstrated self-restraint. The arrogance of power, I think, had more to do with our persisting in the war than with our initial involvement. It always was difficult for our leaders back in Washington and for operatives in the field to believe that American resources and ingenuity could not devise some way to overcome the adversary.

Bureaucratic Politics

There are two, not mutually exclusive, approaches within this view. One has it that national security bureaucrats (the professionals who make up the military services, civilian Defense, AID, State and the CIA) are afflicted with the curse of machismo, the need to assert and prove manhood and toughness. Career advancement and acceptability within the bureaucracy depended on showing that you were not afraid to propose the use of force. The other approach has it that bureaucrats purposefully misled their superiors about the situation in Vietnam and carefully constructed policy alternatives so as to circumscribe their superiors, thus forcing further involvement in Vietnam.

The machismo phenomenon is not unknown in the bureaucracy. It was difficult, if not damaging, to careers to appear conciliatory or "soft." Similarly, the constriction of options is a well-known bureaucratic device. But, I think, these approaches unduly emphasize the degree to which the President and his immediate advisers were trapped by the bureaucrats. The President was always in a position to ask for new options or to exclude certain others. The role of the bureaucracy was much more central to shaping the programs or the means used to fight the war than the key decisions to make the commitments in the first place.

Domestic Politics

This view is quite complicated, and authors argue their case on several different levels. The variants are if you were responsible for losing Vietnam to communism, you would: (a) lose the next election and lose the White House in particular; (b) jeopardize your domestic legislative program, your influence in general, by having to defend yourself constantly against political attack; (c) invite the return of a McCarthyite right-wing reaction; and (d) risk undermining domestic support for a continuing U.S. role abroad, in turn, risking dangerous probes by Russia and China.

There can be no doubt, despite the lack of supporting evidence in the Pentagon Papers, about the importance of domestic political considerations in both the initial commitment to and the subsequent increase in our Vietnam involvement. Officials are reluctant, for obvious reasons, to put these considerations down in writing, and scholars therefore learn too little about them. It should also be noted that domestic political factors played a key part in shaping the manner in which the war was fought—no reserve call-ups, certain limitations on bombing targeting, paying for the war, and the like.

Imperialism

This explanation. is a variant of the domestic politics explanation. Proponents of this view argue that special interest groups maneuvered the United States into the war. Their goal was to capture export markets and natural resources at public expense for private economic gain.

The evidence put forward to support this "devil theory" has not been persuasive. Certain groups do gain economically from wars, but their power to drive our political system into war tends to be exaggerated and over-dramatized.

Men Making Hard Choices Pragmatically

This is the view that our leaders over the years were not men who were inspired by any particular ideology, but were pragmatists weighing the evidence and looking at each problem on its merits. According to this perspective, our leaders knew they were facing tough choices, and their decisions always were close ones. But having decided 51 to 49 to go ahead, they tried to sell and implement their policies one hundred percent.

This view cannot be dismissed out-of-hand. Most of our leaders, and especially our Presidents, occupied centrist political positions. But Vietnam is a case, I believe, where practical politicians allowed an anti-communist world view to get the best of them.

Balance of Power Politics

Intimately related to the pragmatic explanations is the conception which often accompanies pragmatism—the desire to maintain some perceived balance-of-power among nations. The principal considerations in pursuing this goal were: seeing that "the illegal use of force" is not allowed to succeed, honoring commitments, and keeping credibility with allies and potential adversaries. The underlying judgment was that failure to stop aggression in one place would tempt others to aggress in ever more dangerous places.

These represent the words and arguments most commonly and

persuasively used in the executive branch, the Congress, and elsewhere. They seemed commonsensical and prudential. Most Americans were prepared to stretch their meaning to Vietnam. No doubt many believed these arguments on their own merits, but in most cases, I think, the broader tenet of anti-communism made them convincing.

The Slippery Slope

Tied to the pragmatic approach, the conception of balance of power, and the arrogance of power, is the explanation which holds that United States involvement in Vietnam is the story of the slippery slope. According to this view, Vietnam was not always critical to U.S. national security; it became so over the years as each succeeding administration piled commitment on commitment. Each administration sort of slid farther into the Vietnam quagmire, not really understanding the depth of the problems in Vietnam and convinced that it could win. The catchwords of this view are optimism and inadvertence.

While this explanation undoubtedly fits certain individuals and certain periods of time, it is, by itself, a fundamental distortion of the Vietnam experience. From the Korean War, stated American objectives for Vietnam were continuously high and absolute. U.S. involvement, not U.S. objectives, increased over time. Moreover, to scrutinize the range of official public statements and the private memos as revealed in the Pentagon Papers makes it difficult to argue that our leaders were deceived by the enormity of the Vietnam task before them. It was not necessary for our leaders to believe they were going to win. It was sufficient for them to believe that they could not afford to lose Vietnam to communism.

Anti-Communism

The analysts who offer this explanation hold that anti-communism was the central and all-pervasive fact of U.S. foreign policy from at least 1947 until the end of the sixties. After World War II, an ideology whose very existence seemed to threaten basic American values had combined with the national force of first Russia and then China. This combination of ideology and power brought our leaders to see the world in "we-they" terms and to insist that peace was indivisible. Going well beyond balance of power considerations, every piece of territory became critical, and every besieged nation, a potential domino. Communism came to be seen as an infection to be quarantined rather than a force to be judiciously and appropriately balanced. Vietnam, in particular, became the cockpit of confrontation between the "Free World" and Totalitarianism; it was where the action was for 20 years.

In my opinion, simple anti-communism was the principal reason for United States involvement in Vietnam. It is not the whole story, but it is the biggest part.

As of this point in my own research, I advance three propositions to explain why, how, and with what expectations the United States became involved in the Vietnam war.

First, U.S. involvement in Vietnam is not mainly or mostly a story of step by step, inadvertent descent into unforeseen quicksand. It is primarily a story of why U.S. leaders considered that it was vital not to lose Vietnam by force to Communism. Our leaders believed Vietnam to be vital not for itself, but for what they thought its "loss" would mean internationally and domestically. Previous involvement made further involvement more unavoidable, and, to this extent, commitments were inherited. But judgments of Vietnam's "vitalness"—beginning with the Korean War—were sufficient in themselves to set the course for escalation.

Second, our Presidents were never actually seeking a military victory in Vietnam. They were doing only what they thought was minimally necessary at each stage to keep Indochina, and later South Vietnam, out of Communist hands. This forced our Presidents to be brakemen, to do less than those who were urging military victory and to reject proposals for disengagement. It also meant that our Presidents wanted a negotiated settlement without fully realizing (though realizing more than their critics) that a civil war cannot be ended by political compromise.

Third, our Presidents and most of their lieutenants were not deluded by optimistic reports of progress and did not proceed on the basis of wishful thinking about winning a military victory in South Vietnam. They recognized that the steps they were taking were not adequate to win the war and that unless Hanoi relented, they would have to do more and more. Their strategy was to persevere in hope that their will to continue—if not the practical effects of their actions—would cause the Communists to relent.

One Morning in the War

Richard Hammer

More than any other single group in the population, journalists were responsible for bringing to public attention the shortcomings and contradictions of American policy in Vietnam. As early as 1963, David Halberstam, the New York Times *correspondent in Vietnam, pointed out that conventional military tactics had no place in a guerrilla war, and that a civil struggle between competing Vietnamese political factions could not be resolved by external military intervention. The contradiction between journalistic accounts of the war and official reports sent to the Pentagon and the White House continued throughout the years of American involvement in Southeast Asia.*

During the last half of the 1960s, television and newspaper reporters played a major role in turning American public opinion against the war as people saw American soldiers igniting Vietnamese thatched huts and heard an Army major say that "we had to destroy the village in order to save it." It was a journalist who first made public the atrocities committed at My Lai. In the following selection, Richard Hammer describes in searing detail one "search and destroy" mission of the war. To some, the My Lai episode represented a total aberration, with a single company going insane for one day. To others, the episode typified—in extreme form—a practice that was all too frequent. Almost everyone agrees that the My Lai tragedy dramatized the impossibility of attempting to use external military force to fight a civil war where one could not tell who was a friend and who was an enemy.

In these early days of combat, the men began to solidify their previously formed and now lasting impressions of their officers and sergeants. Medina, for one, seemed totally impervious to danger. In fact, he seemed almost to be searching for it, to test the courage of his men and of himself. At the same time, he seemed totally dedicated to the welfare of his own men, concerned about them, grieving when one of them was wounded, concerned that they be fed well, have shelter and ammunition. It was, one of the men remembers, "like he was some kind of hen taking care of her brood, if you know what I mean. If we was out in the field, one platoon going one way and another going a different way and there was some shots, then Medina'd be on the field phone right away, wanting to know what the shooting was about, if anybody was hurt, if reinforcements were needed, that kind of thing. He had to know everything that was happening everywhere in the company."

But if Medina was concerned about his own men, those who served under him noticed that he seemed utterly oblivious to the Vietnamese. On occasions when the company entered a hamlet and all was peaceful, Medina seemed bored, anxious to get moving after he had posed a few questions to the village chiefs through his interpreter, and there would be a look of weary impatience when his soldiers passed out cigarettes and canned fruit to the villagers. "I mean," one of his soldiers says, "he didn't ever talk about the gooks. He didn't call them any names, just didn't seem to care one way or another about them. . . . Except, of course, when some guy got hit, then Medina'd get real angry and talk about how we'd get ours back at them. . . ."

Calley was something different. About the best that anyone had to say for him was the summation by one corporal in his platoon: "He wasn't the best officer in the world, but then he wasn't the worst one, either."

There were others, however, who weren't quite so sure of that. . . . "It was like he was all wound up tight, just waiting to bust loose. And when he busted, everyone around him was going to be hit by the pieces. . . . Like he was a little guy, see, all puffed up, trying to make himself bigger and taller than anybody else. I guess maybe you can only do that for so long and then look out, man."

There were a number of men who pointed to an episode early in February when they were looking for some concrete evidence to back their then-vague feelings about Calley. According to James Bergthold, for one, one afternoon Calley deliberately murdered a Vietnamese civilian without any provocation. The platoon was on a routine patrol when Bergthold brought in a Vietnamese civilian, about sixty years old, whom he had just discovered in a paddy. "I brought the guy in," he said. "He was standing in a field all by himself. I brought him in, and the lieutenant asked him questions and then threw him in a well and shot him in the head. He never said why he did it." . . .

More and more as these daily patrols went on without end, the men in Task Force Barker grew to hate the dirty war they were part of, a war where everything and nothing was the enemy and fair game, where trouble could come from anyone or anything. And they began to take casualties now and again, here and there. Moving down a trail one afternoon somewhere in their district (no one is sure exactly where, as most of the men were never really sure where they were except that they were somewhere in Vietnam), a mine suddenly exploded. Three men went down, one of them dead. Just off the trail, hidden in the brush, was a fifteen year old girl, her hand still on the detonator of the mine. Simultaneously, four or five soldiers fired. The girl fell over the detonator, riddled with bullets, dead.

Another hamlet. Some of the men see a young Vietnamese girl. They grab her and pull her inside the nearest hootch. There are screams and cries from inside and then silence. Soon the men come walking out, satisfied.

The people have gathered in the center of another hamlet, smiling and greeting the Americans, milling around them while cigarettes, gum, canned fruits are passed out. A couple of the men wander casually about the settlement. They go into one hootch and emerge carrying a number of trinkets, relics and family heirlooms and start to rejoin the rest of the platoon. An old man breaks away from the group and trots after them. He bows his head, folds his hands and with a humble, obsequious smile murmurs words in Vietnamese to them and points with anguish at the souvenirs they are carrying away. It was his hootch and he would like his possessions returned. He grows tiresome and one of the soldiers turns and without a thought shoots him.

Day after day the dirty incidents of this kind, in this kind of war, mount. . . .

There was no way to tell when a fire fight might break out. The morning would start as usual, with a routine search-and-destroy mission scheduled. But sometime during the day, the VC would be waiting, the blood would be spilled on the land. Day after day it was the same thing. There was no relief. It was days out on patrol, many nights bivouacked in some field or in some hamlet, the men sleeping only from fatigue, the sentries constantly on the alert. Then it would be back to the fire base, back to LZ Dottie, back to the bunkers with no amusements, no nights off for a drink or a girl. Just the grinding fear and hate and frustration of war.

Then word came that the opportunity to strike back at the enemy in what might well be a major engagement had arrived.

At dusk that evening, Medina gathered his company together at the fire base to brief them on the operation for the next day. "I told them," he says, "that the intelligence reports indicated that the 48th VC Battalion was in the village and the intelligence reports indicated that there would be no women and children in the village, that they would have gone to market." . . .

Others, however, remember the briefing in a different way. Richard Pendleton says, "He told us there were Viet Cong in the village and we should kill them before they kill us."

It was just about seven in the morning when the first shells began to rain on Xom Lang that March 16th. Those who were still at home—most of the people in the sub-hamlet, for it was still early and many of them were just beginning breakfast—quickly sought shelter in their family bunkers. Almost every house had its bunker dug into the ground nearby. The VC when they had arrived had forced the people to build them, and from friends in other hamlets they had heard enough tales to know that in case of a bombardment, a bunker was one of the few hopes of survival. So each family dug its own.

The shells continued to thud into the ground and explode, destroying houses and gouging deep craters for about twenty minutes. The artillery barrage marched up and down the hamlet and the area around it, preparing the landing zone for the troop-carrying helicopters. Overhead, helicopter gunships hovered without any opposition, pounding the hamlet and the ground around it with rockets and machine gun fire. . . .

Captain Ernest Medina was in the lead chopper, watching the artillery and the gunships level Xom Lang. He "could see the smoke and flash of artillery" as the settlement was ripped apart. Then his helicopter settled into a paddy about a hundred and fifty meters west. Immediately the door gunners strafed the surrounding countryside with machine gun fire in case there happened to be VC waiting among the growing rice and brush.

As far as Medina could tell there was no return fire. "My instant impression," he says, "was that I didn't hear the familiar crackle of rifle bullets zinging over my head."

Accompanied by his radio operator and other company aides, Medina clambered down from the helicopter and rushed across the paddy to the edge of a small graveyard just at the edge of Xom Lang. Still there was no return fire, and all around him the other choppers were settling to the ground and the men of Company C were pouring through the doors, firing toward the houses as they emerged. It seemed to have occurred to no one at that moment that the lack of return fire might mean that this was not the hamlet where the VC was centered, that this was not "Pinkville." . . .

"When the attack started," Sergeant Charles West recalls, "it couldn't have been stopped by anyone. We were mad and we had been told that the enemy was there and we were going in there to give them a fight for what they had done to our dead buddies."

Approaching Xom Lang, "we went in shooting," West says. "We'd shoot into the hootches and there were people running around. There were big craters in the village from the bombing. When I got there I saw some of the people, some of the women and kids all torn up."

"I was just coming to the first row of houses, with five or six other guys," says another member of the platoon, "when we heard this noise behind us. Everybody was scared and on edge, and keyed up, too, to kill, and somebody turned quick and snapped off a shot. We all turned and shot. And there was this big old water buffalo, I guess that's what it was, standing in the middle of this field behind us. Everybody was shooting at it and you could see little puffs jumping out where the bullets hit. It was like something in slow motion, and finally that cow just slumped down and collapsed." His face contorted by the remembrance, he adds, "Now it seems kind of funny, but it didn't then. And once the shooting started, I guess it affected everyone. From then on it was like nobody could stop. Everyone was just shooting at everything and anything, like the ammo wouldn't ever give out."

The contagion of slaughter was spreading throughout the platoon.

Combat photographer Ronald Haeberle and Army Correspondent Jay Roberts had requested permission to accompany a combat mission in order to get both pictures and a story of American soldiers in action. They had been assigned to Charley Company and to Calley's platoon. Leaving their helicopter with about ten or fifteen other soldiers, they came upon a cow being slaughtered, and then the picture turned sickenly grisly. "Off to the right," Haeberle said, "a woman's form, a head appeared from some brush. All the other GI's started firing at her, aiming at her, firing at her over and over again."

The bullets riddled the woman's body. She slumped against a well pump in the middle of the rice paddy, her head caught between two of its poles. She was obviously already dead, but the infection, the hysteria was now ascendant. The men were oblivious to everything but slaughter. "They just kept shooting at her. You could see the bones flying in the air, chip by chip."

There were the sounds: the shots running into and over each other from inside the hamlet; it sounded as though everyone had his rifle on automatic, no one bothering to save ammunition by switching to single shot. And not drowned by the sharp bark of the rifles and duller thuds of grenades were screams; they sounded like women and children, but how can anyone tell in that kind of moment from a distance who is screaming?

Four or five Americans were outside the hamlet, moving along its perimeter. The job of their platoon was to seal it off and so prevent the VC inside from fleeing from Calley's men, to catch them in a pincer and slaughter them. Vernardo Simpson and these other soldiers were probing the bushes on the outskirts, delicately, searching for mines and booby traps. As they neared the first group of houses, a man dressed in black pajamas—the dress convinced Simpson that he must be a VC even though black pajamas were traditional peasant dress—suddenly appeared from nowhere, from some bushes and began running toward the hamlet. A woman and child popped up from the same underbrush and started "running away from us toward some huts."

"Dong lai! Dong lai!" The Americans shouted after the Vietnamese. But they kept on running. Lieutenant Brooks, the leader of this second platoon, gave the orders to shoot. If these people did not stop on command, then they must necessarily be VC. "This is what I did," Simpson says. "I shot them, the lady and the little boy. He was about two years old."

A woman and a child? Why?

"I was reluctant, but I was following a direct order. If I didn't do this I could stand court martial for not following a direct order."

Before the day was over, Simpson says, he would have killed at least ten Vietnamese in Xom Lang.

With the number killed there, his total was about the average for each soldier.

When the shelling stopped, Pham Phon crept from the bunker near his hootch. About fifty meters away, he saw a small group of American soldiers. Poking his head back into the bunker, he told his wife and three children—two sons aged nine and four, and a seven year old daughter—to come up and walk slowly toward the Americans.

Like almost all Vietnamese in the hamlets around the country, Phon and his family had learned from the three previous American visits and from the tales told by refugees who had come to Xom Lang to seek shelter after their hamlets had been turned into battle-grounds and from tales carried by others from far away, just how to act when American troops arrived.

It was imperative not to run, either toward the Americans or away from them. If you ran, the Americans would think that you were VC, running away from them or running toward them with a grenade, and they would shoot.

It was imperative not to stay inside the house or the bunker. If you did, then the Americans would think you were VC hiding in ambush, and they would shoot or throw grenades into the house or bunker.

It was imperative to walk slowly toward the Americans, with hands in plain view, or to gather in small groups in some central spot and wait for the Americans to arrive—but never to gather in large groups, for then the Americans would think the group was VC waiting to fire. It was absolutely imperative to show only ser-vility so that the Americans would know that you were not VC and had only peaceful intent.

So Phon and his family walked slowly toward the soldiers. The three children smiled and shouted, "Hello! Hello! Okay! Okay!"

Only this time, unlike the three previous American visitations, there were no answering grins, no gifts of candy and rations. The Americans pointed their rifles at the family and sternly ordered them to walk to the canal about a hundred meters away.

Inside the hamlet, the men of the first platoon were racing from house to house. They planted dynamite and explosive to the brick ones and blew them into dust. They set fires with their lighters to the thatched roofs and to the hootches, watched them flare into a ritual bonfire and then raced on to the next hootch. Some soldiers were pulling people from bunkers and out of the houses and herding them into groups. Some of the Vietnamese tried to run and were immediately shot. Others didn't seem to know what was happening, didn't understand what the Americans were doing or why. But most of them behaved as they had learned they must behave. Meekly they followed any order given.

Some of the groups were marched away in the direction of the canal, and those who straggled behind, could not keep up, were promptly shot.

There were soldiers standing outside the hootches, watching them burn, and as Vietnamese suddenly emerged from the pyres, would shoot them.

And through everything, through the sound of gunfire and through the crackling of flames, through the smoke that had begun to cover everything like a pall, came high-pitched screams of pain and terror, bewildered cries, pleading cries. All were ignored.

Michael Bernhardt remembers coming into the hamlet and seeing his fellow soldiers "doing a whole lot of shooting up. But none of it was incoming. I'd been around enough to tell that. I figured we were advancing on the village with fire power."

Inside the hamlet, Bernhardt "saw these guys doing strange things. They were doing it in three ways. They were setting fire to the hootches and huts and waiting for the people to come out and then shooting them. They were going into the hootches and shooting them up. They were gathering people in groups and shooting them."

The raging fever in the other members of his platoon stunned and shocked Bernhardt. He watched one soldier shooting at everything he saw, blazing away indiscriminately and laughing hysterically as he kept pulling the trigger, kept his finger on the trigger until all the bullets in a clip were gone, then throwing away the clip and reloading and starting again. And laughing all the time. "He just couldn't stop. He thought it was funny, funny, funny." . . . .

For Private Herbert Carter it was too much, a nightmare from which there seemed no awakening. "People began coming out of

their hootches and the guys shot them and burned the hootches—
or burned the hootches and then shot the people when they came
out. Sometimes they would round up a bunch and shoot them
together. It went on like that for what seemed like all day. Some of
the guys seemed to be having a lot of fun. They were wisecracking
and yelling, 'Chalk that one up for me.'"

When he could stand the sight no longer, Carter turned and
stumbled out of the hamlet. He sat down under a tree and shot
himself in the foot.

He was Charley Company's only casualty that morning.

When the first shells hurled their way into Xom Lang, Nguyen
Thi Nien and her family took shelter in their bunker adjacent to
their house. In the bunker with her were her eighty-year-old
father-in-law, her sister and her sister's seven-year-old daughter,
her own husband and their three children. They cowered in the
bunker for a considerable length of time. Finally they heard steady
rifle fire around them and American voices yelling: "VC di ra! VC
di ra!"—VC, get out! VC, get out!

The family crawled slowly and carefully out of the bunker, making every effort to display no hostility. But once they were out they
noticed that the Americans were still some distance away. Taking
her youngest child, still a baby, in one arm and holding her second
youngest by the hand, Nguyen Thi Nien started away, toward the
rice paddies. She did not run, but walked on steadily. Her husband
and the oldest child started to follow her. But her sister and her
sister's daughter hung back, then started in another direction. And
her father-in-law turned and started back to the house.

"I am too old," she remembers him calling after her. "I cannot
keep up. You get out and I will stay here to keep the house."

There was almost no argument. "We told him," Nguyen Thi Nien
says, "all right, you are too old. So you stay here and if the GI's
arrive you ask them not to shoot you and not to burn the house."

The old man called that that was exactly what he intended to do.
He would stand guard over the family house. But then Nguyen Thi
Nien's husband decided that he could not leave his father alone in
the house. He turned, sending the oldest child after his wife and the
other children, and went back to his father. They stood outside the
house for a brief moment arguing. The son trying to convince
the old man to get out of the house and go with them to the paddies
before the Americans arrived. The Americans were approaching

and they could hear the clatter of shots, they could see the flames licking around other houses, and the smoke.

But the old man remained adamant. He was too old, he kept insisting. He could not make it to the paddy. He refused to leave, turning from his son and starting into the house.

The Americans were almost on them; the firing was all around them now. Nien realized that he could wait no longer. If he were to escape the approaching Americans—he realized by then that this was not a friendly visit, that the Americans were hostile this time and were shooting at everything—he would have to flee immediately.

About four hundred meters away, he saw his wife and three children just ducking into the rice paddies, safe. He started after them. Ahead of him, just a few feet, was an old woman, a nearby neighbor. "But suddenly," he says, "five GI's were in front of me, about a hundred meters or so from me. The GI's saw us and started to shoot and the lady was killed. I was hit and so I lay down. Then I saw blood coming from my stomach and so I took a handkerchief and put it over my wound. I lay on the ground there for a little while and then I tried to get back to my house, to my old father and my sister-in-law and her child who must still be there. I could not walk very well and so I was crawling. On the way back to my house I saw five children and one father lying dead on the ground. When I reached my house, I saw it was on fire. Through the fire I could see the bodies of my old father, my sister-in-law and her child inside the house. Then I lost consciousness and I do not know anything more of what happened." . . .

"I was just coming into the middle of that ville," remembers one soldier, refusing to look around or to meet his questioner's eyes as he talks, "and I saw this guy. He was one of my best friends in the company. But honest to Christ, at first I didn't even recognize him. He was kneeling on the ground, this absolutely incredible . . . I don't know what you'd call it, a smile or a snarl or something, but anyway, his whole face was distorted. He was covered with smoke, his face streaked with it, and it looked like there was blood on him, too. You couldn't tell, but there was blood everywhere. Anyway, he was kneeling there holding this grenade launcher, and he was launching grenades at the hootches. A couple of times he launched grenades at groups of people. The grenades would explode, you know, KAPLOW, and then you'd see pieces of bodies flying around. Some of the groups were just piles of bodies. But I remember there was this one group a little distance away. Maybe there was ten people, most of them women and little kids, huddled all together and you could see they were really scared, they just couldn't seem to move. Anyway, he turns around toward them and lets fly with a grenade. It landed right in the middle of them. You could hear the screams and then the sound and then see the pieces of bodies scatter out, and the whole area just suddenly turned red like somebody had turned on a faucet."

Did you do anything to try to stop him?

"You got rocks or something? All you had to do was take one look at him, at his face and you knew the best thing was to leave him alone. I think if I had even said a word to him at all, he would have turned and killed me and not thought a damn thing about it." . . .

Jay Roberts and Ronald Haeberle moved about the havoc taking pictures. They came upon one group of Americans surrounding a small group of women, children and a teen-age girl. She was perhaps twelve or thirteen and was wearing the traditional peasant black pajamas. One of the Americans grabbed her by the shoulders while another began to try to strip the pajamas off her, pulling at the top of the blouse to undo it.

"Let's see what she's made of," one of the soldiers laughed.

Another moved close to her, laughing and pointing at her. "VC, boom-boom," he said. He was telling her in the GI patois that she was a whore for the VC, and indicating that if she did it for them why not for the Americans.

A third soldier examined her carefully and then turned to the others. "Jesus," he said, "I'm horny."

All around there were burning buildings and bodies and the sounds of firing and screams. But the Americans seemed totally oblivious to anything but the girl. They had almost stripped her when her mother rushed over and tried to help her escape. She clutched at the American soldiers, scratched them, clawed at their faces, screaming invectives at them. They pushed her off. One soldier slapped her across the face; another hit her in the stomach with his fist; a third kicked her in the behind, knocking her sprawling to the ground.

But the mother's actions had given the girl a chance to escape a little. She took shelter behind some of the other women in the group and tried to button the top of her blouse. Haeberle stepped in, knelt and took a picture of the scene.

Roberts remembers that at that moment, "when they noticed Ron, they left off and turned away as if everything was normal. Then a soldier asked, 'Well, what'll we do with 'em?'

"'Kill 'em,' another answered.

"I heard an M-60 go off, a light machine gun, and when we turned all of them and the kids with them were dead." . . .

Another soldier says he saw a teen-age girl running across a rice paddy, trying to hide from an American who was chasing her. As he watched, he saw this American soldier aim with his rifle and shoot. The girl gave a cry and fell down. The soldier went after her and vanished into the paddy. A few minutes later there was another shot from the area and then the soldier walked back from the field into the hamlet. . . .

A small boy, three or four, suddenly appears from nowhere on the trail in front of a group of Americans. He is wounded in the arm. Michael Terry sees "the boy clutching his wounded arm with his other hand while the blood trickled between his fingers. He was staring around himself in shock and disbelief at what he saw. He just stood there with big eyes staring around like he didn't understand what was happening. Then the captain's radio operator put a burst of 16 into him."

When Paul Meadlo came into Xom Lang, Lieutenant Calley set him and some of the other men to work gathering the people together in groups in a central location. "There was about forty, forty-five people that we gathered in the center of the village," Meadlo told an interviewer. "And we placed them in there, and it was like a little island, right there in the center of the village."

The soldiers forced the people in the group to squat on the ground. "Lieutenant Calley came over and said, 'You know what to do with them, don't you?' And I said, 'Yes.' So I took it for granted he just wanted us to watch them. And he left and came back about ten or fifteen minutes later, and said, 'How come you ain't killed them yet?' And I told him that I didn't think he wanted us to kill them, that you just wanted us to guard them. He said, 'No, I want them dead.'"

At first Meadlo was surprised by the order—not shocked or horrified, but surprised. "But three, four guys heard it and then he stepped back about ten, fifteen feet, and he started shooting them. And he told me to start shooting. I poured about four clips into the group."

A clip is seventeen rounds. Meadlo fired sixty-eight rounds into this group of people. "I fired them on automatic," he said, "so you can't . . . you just spray the area on them and so you can't know how many you killed 'cause they were going fast. So I might have killed ten or fifteen of them."

One slaughter was over, but there was more to come, and the thirst for blood had become so contagious that no one thought anything about what he was doing. "We started to gather them up, more people," Meadlo says, "and we had about seven or eight people that we was gonna put into a hootch and we dropped a hand grenade in there with them."

Then Meadlo and several other soldiers took a group of civilians—almost exclusively women and children, some of the children still too young to walk—toward one of the two canals on the outskirts of Xom Lang. "They had about seventy, seventy-five people all gathered up. So we threw ours in with them and Lieutenant Calley told me, he said, 'Meadlo, we got another job to do.' And so he walked over to the people and started pushing them off and started shooting."

Taking his cue from Calley, Meadlo and then the other members of this squad "started pushing them off and we started shooting them. So altogether we just pushed them all off and just started using automatics on them. And somebody told us to switch off to single shot so that we could save ammo. So we switched off to single shot and shot a few more rounds."

In the heat and the passion of that morning, it is almost impossible to know who is telling the real truth about any of the events or any of the people, or if there is even any real truth. And perhaps it is less than the major quest in the story of what happened and why it happened that morning in March to discover and decide just who killed whom, where and when. Many hundreds of people, most of them children, women and old men, were slaughtered at Xom Lang and Binh Dong. A mass hysteria swept over a large number of American soldiers who became executioners, indiscriminate butchers. And in the horror of it all, is there really sense and meaning in saying that one did such and such and this one did this and that? In a senseless slaughter, the attempt to fix blame for specific killings on specific people is an attempt to find sense and logic where it does not and cannot exist. The responsibility for what happened at Xom Lang lies not just with the man or the men who pulled the triggers and threw the grenades. The responsibility goes further and higher.

As darkness fell that night over Xom Lang, over Son My, over all of Vietnam, it was morning half a world away, in Washington, D.C. If the repercussions of what had happened that morning in this one corner of Vietnam had not yet reached the American capital, repercussions of Vietnam itself, of all that had led up to that morning in the war, had reached the center of government of the United States.

Senator Eugene McCarthy and his young idealists, the advocates of the "New Politics," were celebrating the victory earlier in the week over Lyndon Johnson in the New Hampshire Democratic primary. Eugene McCarthy, until then not a well-known national politician, had upset the incumbent President, the leader of his own party. The issue which he had raised to win that victory was that of the war in Vietnam.

In the caucus room of the United States Senate, Robert Francis Kennedy was about to declare that he was a candidate for his party's presidential nomination, that he, too, would take on the President, his brother's Vice President. And the quarrel which had led to this break was the war in Vietnam, what the United States under Lyndon Johnson had done to Vietnam and what it had done to itself.

In the White House, the President was in an anguished personal struggle. As a result of the war in Vietnam, the people had turned against him, had lost confidence in his ability to lead the nation. Less than four years after he had won the greatest political victory in American history as a candidate of peace, even the voters of his own party had rejected him, now identified as the candidate of war. Within two weeks, he would make his fateful decision. He would stop the bombing of North Vietnam. He would seek a beginning of peace negotiations. And he would not seek re-nomination or reelection as President of the United States. He, too, had been destroyed by the war in Vietnam.

But on that March 16, 1968, Xom Lang and Binh Dong and My Hoi, My Lai and Son My and Pinkville were names that these political leaders had never heard. They were names that most of the military in Vietnam had never heard.

There had been a minor engagement there that day. On the next day and in the days to follow, it would be hailed as a victory.

But the target of the day, the Viet Cong soldiers, had been untouched. From their camp at My Khe sub-hamlet they had heard, early in the morning, the sound of planes and guns to the west; they had heard the sounds moving across the village as the day progressed. And before the Americans came near to My Khe—My Lai (1) or Pinkville—the VC had faded from the scene, moving silently out of the hamlet and north to the sanctuary of Batangan. They would be back.

The Cambodian Incursion

Richard M. Nixon

In a televised address on May 11, 1970, President Nixon explained and defended his decision to order an "incursion" into Cambodia by American and South Vietnamese troops. By going after the Vietcong and North Vietnamese bases in Cambodia, used by the VC and NVA forces as sanctuaries from U.S. assaults and as staging areas for attacks on South Vietnam, Nixon hoped to buy time for Vietnamization; by widening the war he thought he could hasten its end. The speech sparked passionate opposition and protests by the antiwar movement. Following the killing by National Guardsmen of four students on the campus of Kent State University in Ohio during one protest, furious demonstrations and strikes erupted on scores of colleges across the nation. Two years later, however, President Nixon was overwhelmingly reelected. What aspects of this speech were received so differently by those the president called the "silent majority" and by antiwar protestors? Why? How do you account for the strong support that Nixon maintained for his Vietnam policies?

April 30, 1970

Ten days ago, in my report to the Nation on Vietnam, I announced a decision to withdraw an additional one hundred and fifty thousand American troops over the next year. I said then I was making that decision despite our concern over increased enemy activity in Laos, in Cambodia, and in South Vietnam. . . .

Cambodia, a small country of seven million people has been a

From *Public Papers of the Presidents of the United States: Richard Nixon, 1970* (Washington, D.C., 1971), pp. 405–9.

neutral nation since the Geneva Agreement of 1954—an agreement signed by the Government of North Vietnam.

American policy since then has been to scrupulously respect the neutrality of the Cambodian people. We have maintained a skeleton diplomatic mission of fewer than fifteen in Cambodia's capital since last August. For the previous four years—from 1965–1969, we did not have any diplomatic mission whatever. For the past five years, we have provided no military assistance and no economic assistance whatever to Cambodia.

North Vietnam, however, has not respected that neutrality.

For the past five years—as indicated on this map—North Vietnam has occupied military sanctuaries all along the Cambodian frontier with South Vietnam. Some of these extend up to twenty miles into Cambodia. They are used for hit-and-run attacks on American and South Vietnamese forces in South Vietnam.

These Communist occupied territories contain major base camps, training sites, logistics facilities, weapons and ammunition factories, air strips and prisoner of war compounds.

For five years, neither the United States nor South Vietnam moved against those enemy sanctuaries because we did not wish to violate the territory of a neutral nation. Even after the Vietnamese Communists began to expand these sanctuaries four weeks ago, we counselled patience to our South Vietnamese allies and imposed restraints on our commanders.

In contrast to our policy, the enemy in the past two weeks has stepped up his guerrilla actions and he is concentrating his main forces in the sanctuaries where they are building up to launch massive attacks on our forces and those of South Vietnam.

North Vietnam, in the last two weeks has stripped away all pretense of respecting the sovereignty or neutrality of Cambodia. Thousands of their soldiers are invading the country from the sanctuaries; they are encircling the Capital of Phnom Penh. Cambodia has sent out a call to the United States and a number of other nations for assistance.

If this effort succeeds, Cambodia would become a vast enemy staging area and springboard for attacks on South Vietnam along 600 miles of frontier—and a refuge where enemy troops could return from combat without fear of retaliation. . . .

This is my decision:

In cooperation with the armed forces of South Vietnam, attacks are being launched this week to clean out major enemy sanctuaries on the Cambodian-Vietnam border.

A major responsibility for the ground operations is being assumed by South Vietnamese forces. For example, the attacks in several areas including the Parrot's Beak are exclusively South Vietnamese ground operations under South Vietnamese command with the United States providing air and logistical support.

There is one area, however, where I have concluded that a combined American and South Vietnamese operation is necessary. Tonight, American and South Vietnamese units will attack the headquarters for the entire Communist military operation in South Vietnam. This key control center has been occupied by the North Vietnamese and Viet Cong for years in blatant violation of Cambodia's neutrality.

This is not an invasion of Cambodia. The areas in which these attacks will be launched are completely occupied and controlled by North Vietnamese forces. Our purpose is not to occupy the areas. Once enemy forces are driven out of these sanctuaries and their military supplies destroyed, we will withdraw.

These actions are in no way directed at the security interests of any nation. Any government that chooses to use these actions as a pretext for harming relations with the United States will be doing so on its own responsibility and at its own initiative and we will draw the appropriate conclusions.

A majority of the American people are for the withdrawal of our forces from Vietnam. The action I have taken tonight is indispensable for the continuing success of that withdrawal program.

A majority of the American people want to end this war rather than have it drag on interminably. The action I take tonight will serve that purpose.

A majority of the American people want to keep the casualties of our brave men in Vietnam at an absolute minimum. The action I take tonight is essential if we are to accomplish that goal.

We take this action not for the purpose of expanding the war into Cambodia but for the purpose of ending the war in Vietnam and winning the just peace we all desire. We have made and will continue to make every possible effort to end this war through negotiation at the conference table rather than through more fighting on the battlefield.

Let us look at the record. We have stopped the bombing of North

Vietnam. We have cut air operations by over 20 percent. We have announced the withdrawal of over 250,000 of our troops. We have offered to withdraw all of our men if they withdraw theirs. We have offered to negotiate all issues with only one condition—that the future of South Vietnam be determined not by North Vietnam, not by the United States, but by the people of South Vietnam themselves.

Their answer has been intransigence at the conference table, belligerence in Hanoi, massive military aggression in Laos and Cambodia and stepped-up attacks in South Vietnam, designed to increase American casualties.

This attitude has become intolerable. We will not react to this threat to American lives merely by plaintive diplomatic protests. If we did, the credibility of the United States would be destroyed in every area of the world where only the power of the United States deters aggression.

Tonight, I again warn the North Vietnamese that if they continue to escalate the fighting when the United States is withdrawing its forces I shall meet my responsibility as Commander-in-Chief of our Armed Forces to take the action I consider necessary to defend the security of our American men. . . .

We live in an age of anarchy both abroad and at home. We see mindless attacks on all the great institutions which have been created by free civilizations in the last five hundred years. Here in the United States, great universities are being systematically destroyed. Small nations all over the world find themselves under attack from within and from without.

If when the chips are down the U.S. acts like a pitiful helpless giant, the forces of totalitarianism and anarchy will threaten free nations and free institutions throughout the world.

It is not our power but our will and character that is being tested tonight. The question all Americans must ask and answer tonight is this: Does the richest and strongest nation in the history of the world have the character to meet a direct challenge by a group which rejects every effort to win a just peace, ignores our warning, tramples on solemn agreements, violates the neutrality of an unarmed people, and uses our prisoners as hostages?

If we failed to meet this challenge all other nations will be on notice that despite its overwhelming power the United States, when a real crisis comes, will be found wanting.

My fellow Americans: During my campaign for the Presidency, I pledged to bring Americans home from Vietnam. They are coming home.

I promised to end the war. I shall keep that promise.

I promised to win a just peace. I shall keep that promise.

We shall avoid a wider war. But we are also determined to put an end to this war.

In this room, Woodrow Wilson made the great decisions which led to victory in World War I. Franklin Roosevelt made the decisions which led to our victory in World War II. Dwight D. Eisenhower made decisions which ended the war in Korea and avoided war in the Middle East. John F. Kennedy, in his finest hour, made the great decision which removed Soviet nuclear missiles for Cuba and the Western Hemisphere.

The decision I have announced tonight is not of the same magnitude. Between those decisions and this decision, however, there is a difference that is very fundamental. In those decisions, the American people were not assailed by counsels of doubt and defeat from some of the most widely known opinion leaders of the nation.

A Republican Senator has said that this action means my party has lost all chance of winning the November elections. Others are saying today that this move against the enemy sanctuaries will make me a one-term President.

No one is more aware than I am of the political consequences of the action I have taken. It is tempting to take the easy political path: (1) To blame this war on previous Administrations and to bring all of our men home immediately regardless of the consequences; even though that would mean defeat for the United States; (2) To desert 18 million South Vietnamese people, who have put their trust in us and to expose them to the same slaughter and savagery which the leaders of North Vietnam inflicted on hundreds of thousands of North Vietnamese who chose freedom when the Communists took over North Vietnam; (3) To get peace at any price now even though I know that a peace of humiliation for the United States will lead to a bigger war or surrender later.

But I have rejected all political considerations in making this decision.

Whether my party gains in November is nothing compared to the lives of 400 thousand brave Americans fighting for our country and for the cause of peace and freedom in Vietnam. Whether I may be a one-term President is insignificant compared to whether by our failure to act in this crisis the United States proves itself to be unworthy to lead the forces of freedom in this critical period. I would rather be a one-term President than to be a two-term President at the cost of seeing America become a second rate power and see this nation accept the first defeat in its proud 190-year history. . . .

Vietnam Veterans Against the War

John Kerry

By the early 1970s the American people's initial support of the government policy in Vietnam had become a yearning for an end to what seemed an interminable and unwinnable war. Americans from all walks of life, including Vietnam veterans, now openly questioned and protested against the military effort. In the spring of 1971 disillusioned veterans came forward to denounce the war and hurl their medals onto the steps of the capitol building; then John Kerry, a representative of the Vietnam Veterans Against the War, bitterly attacked American policies in an appearance before the Senate Foreign Relations Committee that received widespread coverage in the media. Kerry expressed revulsion at the war's brutal horrors, denied that the United States was advancing the cause of freedom, disputed the government's rationale for the conflict, decried the corrupt and dictatorial regime in Saigon, and condemned American officials for deceiving the public and for deserting those they sent off to war. In 1984, Kerry was elected U.S. senator from Massachusetts and reelected in 1990.

I would like to talk on behalf of all those veterans and say that several months ago in Detroit we had an investigation at which over 150 honorably discharged, and many very highly decorated, veterans testified to war crimes committed in Southeast Asia. These were not isolated incidents but crimes committed on a day-to-day basis with the full awareness of officers at all levels of command.

From "Vietnam Veterans Against the War" statement by John Kerry to the Senate Committee on Foreign Relations, April 22, 1971.

It is impossible to describe to you exactly what did happen in Detroit—the emotions in the room and the feelings of the men who were reliving their experiences in Vietnam. They relived the absolute horror of what this country, in a sense, made them do.

They told stories that at times they had personally raped, cut off ears, cut off heads, taped wires from portable telephones to human genitals and turned up the power, cut off limbs, blown up bodies, randomly shot at civilians, razed villages in fashion reminiscent of Genghis Khan, shot cattle and dogs for fun, poisoned food stocks, and generally ravaged the countryside of South Vietnam in addition to the normal ravage of war and the normal and very particular ravaging which is done by the applied bombing power of this country.

We call this investigation the Winter Soldier Investigation. The term Winter Soldier is a play on words of Thomas Paine's in 1776 when he spoke of the Sunshine Patriots and summer time soldiers who deserted at Valley Forge because the going was rough.

We who have come here to Washington have come here because we feel we have to be winter soldiers now. We could come back to this country, we could be quiet, we could hold our silence, we could not tell what went on in Vietnam, but we feel because of what threatens this country, not the reds, but the crimes which we are committing that threaten it, that we have to speak out. . . .

In our opinion and from our experience, there is nothing in South Vietnam which could happen that realistically threatens the United States of America. And to attempt to justify the loss of one American life in Vietnam, Cambodia or Laos by linking such loss to the preservation of freedom, which those misfits supposedly abuse, is to us the height of criminal hypocrisy, and it is that kind of hyprocrisy which we feel has torn this country apart.

We found that not only was it a civil war, an effort by a people who had for years been seeking their liberation from any colonial influence whatsoever, but also we found that the Vietnamese whom we had enthusiastically molded after our own image were hard put to take up the fight against the threat we were supposedly saving them from.

We found most people didn't even know the difference between communism and democracy. They only wanted to work in rice paddies without helicopters strafing them and bombs with napalm burning their villages and tearing their country apart. They wanted everything to do with the war, particularly with this foreign presence of the United States of America, to leave them alone in peace, and they practiced the art of survival by siding with whichever military force was present at a particular time, be it Viet Cong, North Vietnamese or American.

We found also that all too often American men were dying in those rice paddies for want of support from their allies. We saw first hand how monies from American taxes were used for a corrupt dictatorial regime. We saw that many people in this country had a one-sided idea of who was kept free by our flag, and blacks provided the highest percentage of casualties. We saw Vietnam ravaged equally by American bombs and search and destroy missions, as well as by Viet Cong terrorism and yet we listened while this country tried to blame all of the havoc on the Viet Cong.

We rationalized destroying villages in order to save them. We saw America lose her sense of morality as she accepted very coolly a My Lai and refused to give up the image of American soldiers who hand out chocolate bars and chewing gum.

We learned the meaning of free fire zones, shooting anything that moves, and we watched while America placed a cheapness on the lives of Orientals.

We watched the United States falsification of body counts, in fact the glorification of body counts. We listened while month after month we were told the back of the enemy was about to break. We fought using weapons against "oriental human beings." We fought using weapons against those people which I do not believe this country would dream of using were we fighting in the European theater. We watched while men charged up hills because a general said that hill has to be taken, and after losing one platoon or two platoons they marched away to leave the hill for reoccupation by the North Vietnamese. We watched pride allow the most unimportant battles to be blown into extravaganzas, because we couldn't lose, and we couldn't retreat, and because it didn't matter how many American bodies were lost to prove that point, and so there were Hamburger Hills and Khe Sanhs and Hill 81s and Fire Base 6s, and so many others.

Now we are told that the men who fought there must watch quietly while American lives are lost so that we can exercise the incredible arrogance of Vietnamizing the Vietnamese.

Each day to facilitate the process by which the United States washes her hands of Vietnam someone has to give up his life so that the United States doesn't have to admit something that the entire world already knows, so that we can't say that we have made a mistake. Someone has to die so that President Nixon won't be, and these are his words, "the first President to lose a war."

We are asking Americans to think about that because how do you ask a man to be the last man to die in Vietnam? How do you ask a man to be the last man to die for a mistake? . . . We are here in Washington also to say that the problem of this war is not just a question of war and diplomacy. It is part and parcel of everything that we are trying as human beings to communicate to people in this country—the question of racism which is rampant in' the military, and so many other questions such as the use of weapons; the hypocrisy in our taking umbrage at the Geneva Conventions and using that as justification for a continuation of this war when we are more guilty than any other body of violations of those Geneva Conventions: in the use of free fire zones, harassment interdiction fire, search and destroy missions, the bombings, the torture of prisoners, the killing of prisoners, all accepted policy by many units in South Vietnam. That is what we are trying to say. It is part and parcel of everything.

An American Indian friend of mine who lives in the Indian Nation of Alcatraz put it to me very succinctly. He told me how as a boy on an Indian reservation he had watched television and he used to cheer the cowboys when they came in and shot the Indians, and then suddenly one day he stopped in Vietnam and he said "my God, I am doing to these people the very same thing that was done to my people," and he stopped. And that is what we are trying to say, that we think this thing has to end.

We are here to ask, and we are here to ask vehemently, where are the leaders of our country. Where is the leadership? We're here to ask where are McNamara, Rostow, Bundy, Gilpatrick, and so many others. Where are they now that we, the men they sent off to war, have returned. These are commanders who have deserted their troops. And there is no more serious crime in the laws of war. The Army says they never leave their wounded. The marines say they never leave even their dead. These men have left all the casualties and retreated behind a pious shield of public rectitude. They've left the real stuff of their reputations bleaching behind them in the sun in this country. . . .

We wish that a merciful God could wipe away our own memories of that service as easily as this administration has wiped away their memories of us. But all that they have done and all that they can do by this denial is to make more clear than ever our own determination to undertake one last mission—to search out and destroy the last vestige of this barbaric war, to pacify our own hearts, to conquer the hate and the fear that have driven this country these last ten years and more. And more. And so when thirty years from now our brothers go down the street without a leg, without an arm, or a face, and small boys ask why, we will be able to say "Vietnam" and not mean a desert, not a filthy obscene memory, but mean instead the place where America finally turned and where soldiers like us helped it in the turning.

Part 6

YEARS OF POLARIZATION

During the late 1960s American society was more profoundly divided than at any time since the Civil War. As the peaceful petitions of the nonviolent civil rights movement were replaced by black power slogans, white support for blacks plummeted. The emergence of feminism created profound divisions over traditional family roles and definitions of masculinity and femininity. The student movement began as a request for moderate changes, but with the growing crisis over Vietnam became a major challenge to the very structure of the university and government. As the protest over Vietnam grew, many cities and university campuses became domestic battlefields, with police barricades confronting student demonstrators.

The civil rights movement was crucial to the development of political activism on America's campuses. As white students and black students joined together in civil rights protests, they came face to face with the duplicity and brutality of law enforcement officials in the South. When, as frequently happened, the federal government failed to provide corrective assistance, demonstrators began to suspect that even those authorities they thought they could trust were part of the problem. What had begun as a specific protest against southern racism gradually developed into a more critical challenge to established authority generally.

When Mario Savio and others came back to campus from summer civil rights demonstrations in Mississippi in 1964, they carried their newfound criticism to university life itself. After officials at the University of California at Berkeley attempted to control distribution of political materials on a campus plaza, the Berkeley free speech movement began. Significantly, the issues were not specific, but involved protest against the "university machine" itself as a manifestation of corporate control of America. Students protested the depersonalization of the multiversity with its computerized systems, its huge classrooms, and its insensitivity to issues of human community.

By 1967 and 1968, the spirit of Berkeley had spread across the country, fueled by the fires of antiwar demonstrations. Universities were denounced for being instruments of the military-industrial complex. Students demanded the cancellation of university contracts to conduct research on weapons development. Army and Navy ROTC courses came under attack for providing a bond between the university and U.S. policy in Vietnam. When weapons manufacturers came to campus to recruit, students protested their presence, insisting that the university had no right to support the war effort—even indirectly—by making its facilities available to those who profited from the war.

Culture and politics became intermixed as long hair, marijuana, more casual attitudes toward sex, and rejection of middle-class values became associated with the antiwar movement. When students took over university buildings to protest the war, they boasted of their communal lifestyle, their hostility to monogamy, and their freedom to carve out a different lifestyle than that of their parents or elders. The so-called generation gap involved not only political disagreement, but also fundamental personal conflicts over how one would dress, what kind of language one would use, and who one would sleep with. By the end of the 1960s the moderate reformism of the Students for a Democratic Society in 1962 had given way to the militant and violent rhetoric of the Weathermen. In the meantime, reaction against youthful protest and the counterculture had spread. Commentators developed a new phrase—"Middle America"—to describe those who rejected totally the assault on middle-class values by young people of the left. And Spiro Agnew, Richard Nixon's vice president, made a cottage industry out of denouncing antiwar protestors as "ideological eunuchs" who were encouraged in their rabble-rousing "by an effete corps of impudent snobs who characterize themselves as intellectuals."

The following selections highlight some of the tensions of that era. The Port Huron statement of SDS in 1962 offers a vivid contrast to the Weatherman SDS statement of the late 1960s, illustrating how the moderation of the early years was transformed into a posture that justified the trashing of university buildings and the use of terrorism. The selection by Jerry Avorn and others on the

Columbia "Revolution" of 1968 shows how on one campus protest over the war and racism evolved, and how university response to that protest helped to radicalize the majority of "moderate" students.

Allen J. Matusow's assessment of the counterculture portrays some of the parallel shifts taking place in lifestyle, music, art, and attitudes toward sex and drugs. Although the counterculture was in some senses different from political activism, it also represented a vehicle through which the young felt they could contribute toward changing the values of the society. The counterrevolt against such changes is vividly described in Peter Schrag's portrait of "the forgotten American."

Some of the key questions that remain are why the earlier, more moderate protests of the 1960s met with such little success. Did the intransigence of those in power necessitate the shift toward a more radical position? How basic were the issues raised by political activists and supporters of the counterculture? Did they call into serious question the structures and values of the larger society? Was there a way in which young and old could have talked to each other with less hostility and intolerance? Finally, have we lost some of the valuable perspectives that that era brought, as well as its coercive divisiveness?

The Port Huron Statement

Students for a Democratic Society

To young Americans in the early 1960s, everything seemed possible. A youthful, activist President had come into office promising that "we can do better." Black students throughout the South had demonstrated through sit-ins and kneel-ins that people willing to act on their convictions could help to turn society around. Inspired by these examples and given hope by the new leadership in Washington, young white reformers came together to draw up a manifesto for social change. Those who formed Students for a Democratic Society (SDS) were deeply critical of the complacency and indifference of their society. They hoped to marshall the resources of technology, the university, corporations, and government to eliminate poverty and racism. Hence, their agenda of reform. What remains most impressive from the Port Huron Statement, however is its moderation, its faith that change can take place within the system, its conviction that social democracy could be achieved quickly and effectively, without revolution. The Port Huron Statement speaks eloquently to the idealism of a generation of student activists. Just as eloquently, it testifies to their innocence.

INTRODUCTION: AGENDA FOR A GENERATION

We are people of this generation, bred in at least modest comfort, housed now in universities, looking uncomfortably to the world we inherit.

When we were kids the United States was the wealthiest and strongest country in the world; the only one with the atom bomb,

Excerpted from Tom Hayden et al., Port Huron Statement, mimeographed (n.p., Students for a Democratic Society, 1962).

the least scarred by modern war, an initiator of the United Nations that we thought would distribute Western influence throughout the world. Freedom and equality for each individual, government of, by, and for the people—these American values we found good, principles by which we could live as men. Many of us began maturing in complacency.

As we grew, however, our comfort was penetrated by events too troubling to dismiss. First, the permeating and victimizing fact of human degradation, symbolized by the Southern struggle against racial bigotry, compelled most of us from silence to activism. Second, the enclosing fact of the Cold War, symbolized by the presence of the Bomb, brought awareness that we ourselves, and our friends, and millions of abstract "others" we knew more directly because of our common peril, might die at any time. We might deliberately ignore, or avoid, or fail to feel all other human problems, but not these two, for these were too immediate and crushing in their impact, too challenging in the demand that we as individuals take the responsibility for encounter and resolution.

While these and other problems either directly oppressed us or rankled our consciences and became our own subjective concerns, we began to see complicated and disturbing paradoxes in our surrounding America. The declaration "all men are created equal . . ." rang hollow before the facts of Negro life in the South and the big cities of the North. The proclaimed peaceful intentions of the United States contradicted its economic and military investments in the Cold War status quo. . . .

Our work is guided by the sense that we may be the last generation in the experiment with living. But we are a minority—the vast majority of our people regard the temporary equilibriums of our society and world as eternally-functional parts. In this is perhaps the outstanding paradox: we ourselves are imbued with urgency, yet the message of our society is that there is no viable alternative to the present. Beneath the reassuring tones of the politicians, beneath the common opinion that America will "muddle through," beneath the stagnation of those who have closed their minds to the future, is the pervading feeling that there simply are no alternatives, that our times have witnessed the exhaustion not only of Utopias, but of any new departures as well. . . .

Some would have us believe that Americans feel contentment amidst prosperity—but might it not better be called a glaze above deeply-felt anxieties about their role in the new world? And if these anxieties produce a developed indifference to human affairs, do they not as well produce a yearning to believe there *is* an alternative to the present, that something *can* be done to change circumstances in the school, the workplaces, the bureaucracies, the government? It is to this latter yearning, at once the spark and engine of change, that we direct our present appeal. The search for truly democratic alternatives to the present, and a commitment to social experimentation with them, is a worthy and fulfilling human enterprise, one which moves us and, we hope, others today. On such a basis do we offer this document of our convictions and analysis: as an effort in understanding and changing the conditions of humanity in the late twentieth century, an effort rooted in the ancient, still unfulfilled conception of man attaining determining influence over his circumstances of life. . . .

THE STUDENTS

If student movements for change are still rareties on the campus scene, what is commonplace there? The real campus, the familiar campus, is a place of private people, engaged in their notorious "inner emigration." It is a place of commitment to business-as-usual, getting ahead, playing it cool. It is a place of mass affirmation of the Twist, but mass reluctance toward the controversial public stance. Rules are accepted as "inevitable," bureaucracy as "just circumstances," irrelevance as "scholarship," selflessness as "martyrdom," politics as "just another way to make people, and an unprofitable one, too." . . .

Tragically, the university could serve as a significant source of social criticism and an initiator of new modes and molders of attitudes. But the actual intellectual effect of the college experience is hardly distinguishable from that of any other communications channel—say, a television set—passing on the stock truths of the day. Students leave college somewhat more "tolerant" than when they arrived, but basically unchallenged in their values and political orientations. With administrators ordering the institution, and faculty the curriculum, the student learns by his isolation to accept elite rule within the university, which prepares him to accept later forms of minority control. The real function of the educational system—

as opposed to its more rhetorical function of "searching for truth"—is to impart the key information and styles that will help the student get by, modestly but comfortably, in the big society beyond.

THE SOCIETY BEYOND

Look beyond the campus, to America itself. That student life is more intellectual, and perhaps more comfortable, does not obscure the fact that the fundamental qualities of life on the campus reflect the habits of society at large. The fraternity president is seen at the junior manager levels; the sorority queen has gone to Grosse Pointe; the serious poet burns for a place, any place, to work; the once-serious and never-serious poets work at the advertising agencies. The desperation of people threatened by forces about which they know little and of which they can say less; the cheerful emptiness of people "giving up" all hope of changing things; the faceless ones polled by Gallup who listed "international affairs" fourteenth on their list of "problems" but who also expected thermonuclear war in the next few years; in these and other forms, Americans are in withdrawal from public life, from any collective effort at directing their own affairs.

The very isolation of the individual—from power and community and ability to aspire—means the rise of a democracy without publics. With the great mass of people structurally remote and psychologically hesitant with respect to democratic institutions, those institutions themselves attenuate and become, in the fashion of the vicious circle, progressively less accessible to those few who aspire to serious participation in social affairs. The vital democratic connection between community and leadership, between the mass and the several elites, has been so wrenched and perverted that disastrous policies go unchallenged time and again.

POLITICS WITHOUT PUBLICS

The American political system is not the democratic model of which its glorifiers speak. In actuality it frustrates democracy by confusing the individual citizen, paralyzing policy discussion, and consolidating the irresponsible power of military and business interests.

A most alarming fact is that few, if any politicians are calling for changes in these conditions. Only a handful even are calling on the President to. "live up to" platform pledges; no one is demanding structural changes, such as the shuttling of Southern Democrats out of the Democratic Party. Rather than protesting the state of politics, most politicians are reinforcing and aggravating that state. . . .

THE ECONOMY

We live amidst a national celebration of economic prosperity while poverty and deprivation remain an unbreakable way of life for millions in the "affluent society," including many of our own generation. We hear glib references to the "welfare state," "free enterprise," and "shareholder's democracy" while military defense is the main item of "public" spending and obvious oligopoly and other forms of minority rule defy real individual initiative or popular control. Work, too, is often unfulfilling and victimizing, accepted as a channel to status or plenty, if not a way to pay the bills, rarely as a means of understanding and controlling self and events. In work and leisure the individual is regulated as part of the system, a consuming unit, bombarded by hard-sell, soft-sell, lies and semitrue appeals to his basest drives. He is always told that he is a "free" man because of "free enterprise." . . .

The Military-Industrial Complex

The most spectacular and important creation of the authoritarian and oligo-polistic structure of economic decision-making in America is the institution called "the military-industrial complex" by former President Eisenhower—the powerful congruence of interest and structure among military and business elites which affects so much of our development and destiny. Not only is ours the first generation to live with the possibility of world-wide cataclysm—it is the first to experience the actual social preparation for cataclysm, the general militarization of American society. . . .

Since our childhood these two trends—the rise of the military and the installation of a defense-based economy—have grown fantastically. The Department of Defense, ironically the world's largest single organization, is worth $160 billion, owns 32 million acres of

America and employs half the 7.5 million persons directly dependent on the military for subsistence, has an $11 billion payroll
which is larger than the net annual income of all American corporations. Defense spending in the Eisenhower era totaled $350 billions
and President Kennedy entered office pledged to go even beyond
the present defense allocation of 60 cents from every public dollar
spent. Except for a war-induced boom immediately after "our side"
bombed Hiroshima. American economic prosperity has coincided
with a growing dependence on military outlay—from 1911 to 1959
America's Gross National Product of $5.25 trillion included $700
billion in goods and services purchased for the defense effort,
about one-seventh of the accumulated. . . .

TOWARD AMERICAN DEMOCRACY

Every effort to end the Cold War and expand the process of world
industrialization is an effort hostile to people and institutions whose
interests lie in perpetuation of the East-West military threat and the
postponement of change in the "have not" nations of the world.
Every such effort, too, is bound to establish greater democracy in
America. The major goals of a domestic effort would be:

1. America must abolish its political party stalemate.
2. Mechanisms of voluntary association must be created
   through which political information can be imparted and
   political participation encouraged.
3. Institutions and practices which stifle dissent should be
   abolished, and the promotion of peaceful dissent should be
   actively promoted.
4. Corporations must be made publicly responsible.
5. The allocation of resources must be based on social needs.
   A truly "public sector" must be established, and its nature
   debated and planned.
6. America should concentrate on its genuine social priorities: abolish squalor, terminate neglect, and establish an
   environment for people to live in with dignity and creative-
   ness.

You Don't Need a Weatherman To Know Which Way the Wind Blows

(Submitted by Karin Ashley, Bill Ayers, Bernardine Dourn, John Jacobs, Jeff Jones, Gerry Long, Howie Machtinger, Jim Mellen, Terry Robbins, Mark Rudd and Steve Tappis)

Just seven years after the Port Huron Statement, SDS met again in national convention. In the intervening years the war in Vietnam had expanded dramatically, the integrationist petitions of the early civil rights movement had turned into demands for Black Power and a movement for student autonomy had generated massive protests on university campuses. For at least some, the primary lesson of the sixties had been the impossibility of securing change peacefully. Teach-ins at universities had not changed the government's Vietnam policy; campaigns on behalf of anti-war candidates seemed an exercise in futility; for those who were most bitter and radicalized, revolution seemed the only answer. With young people as an advance party, these activists demanded that SDS support a world-wide revolution against capitalism and imperialism. The following selection from the Weatherman Manifesto—"you don't need a weatherman to tell which way the wind is blowing"—appears, in retrospect, a hopelessly doctrinaire plea. Just one year later three of those who endorsed it blew themselves to pieces making bombs in Greenwich Village. Yet the statement also reflects just how corrosive the 1960s had been in destroying the idealism of seven years earlier.

INTERNATIONAL REVOLUTION

The contradiction between the revolutionary peoples of Asia Africa and Latin America and the imperialists headed by the United States is the

Excerpted from Karin Ashley et al. "You Don't Need a Weatherman To Know Which Way the Wind Blows," mimeographed statement, 1969.

principal contradiction in the contemporary world. The development of this
contradiction is promoting the struggle of the people of the whole world
against US imperialism and its lackeys.

Lin Piao
Long Live the Victory of Peoples War!

People ask, what is the nature of the revolution that we talk about? Who will it be made by, and for, and what are its goals and strategy,

The overriding consideration in answering these questions is that the main struggle going on in the world today is between US imperialism and the national liberation struggles against it. . . .

So the very first question people in this country must ask in considering the question of revolution is where they stand in relation to the United States as an oppressor nation, and where they stand in relation to the masses of people throughout the world whom US imperialism is oppressing. . . .

It is in this context that we must examine the revolutionary struggles in the United States. We are within the heartland of a world-wide monster, a country so rich from its world-wide plunder that even the crumbs doled out to the enslaved masses within its borders provide for material existence very much above the conditions of the masses of people of the world. The US empire, as world-wide system, channels wealth, based upon the labor and resources of the rest of the world, into the United States. The relative affluence existing in the United States is directly dependent upon the labor and natural resources of the Vietnamese, the Angolans, the Bolivians and the rest of the peoples of the Third World. All of the United Airlines Astrojets, all of the Holiday Inns, all of Hertz's automobiles, your television set, car and wardrobe already belong, to a large degree, to the people of the rest of the world. . . .

The goal is the destruction of US imperialism and the achievement of a classless world: world communism. Winning state power in the US will occur as a result of the military forces of the US overextending themselves around the world and being defeated piecemeal; struggle within the US will be a vital part of this process, but when the revolution triumphs in the US it will have been made by the people of the whole world. For socialism to be defined in national terms within so extreme and historical an oppressor nation as this is only imperialist national chauvinism on the part of the "movement."

In this context, why an emphasis on youth? Why should young people be willing to fight on the side of Third World peoples? . . .

As imperialism struggles to hold together this decaying, social fabric, it inevitably resorts to brute force and authoritarian ideology. People, especially young people, more and more find themselves in the iron grip of authoritarian institutions. Reaction against the pigs or teachers in the schools, welfare pigs or the army is generalizable and extends beyond the particular repressive institution to the society and the State as a whole. The legitimacy of the State is called into question for the first time in at least 20 years, and the anti-authoritarianism which characterizes the youth rebellion turns into rejection of the State, a refusal to be socialized into American society. Kids used to try to beat the system from inside the army or from inside the schools; now they desert from the army and burn down the schools.

The crisis in imperialism has brought about a breakdown in bourgeois social forms, culture and ideology. The family falls apart, kids leave home, women begin to break out of traditional "female" and "mother" roles. There develops a "generation gap" and a "youth problem." Our heroes are no longer struggling businessmen, and we also begin to reject the ideal career of the professional and look to Mao, Che, the Panthers, the Third World, for our models, for motion. We reject the elitist, technocratic bullshit that tells us only experts can rule, and look instead to leadership from the people's war of the Vietnamese. Chuck Berry, Elvis, the Temptations brought us closer to the "people's culture" of Black America. The racist response to the civil rights movement revealed the depth of racism in America, as well as the impossibility of real change through American institutions. And the war against Vietnam is not "the heroic war against the Nazis"; it's the big lie, with napalm, burning through everything we had heard this country stood for. Kids begin to ask questions: Where is the Free World? And who do the pigs protect at home?

THE RYM AND THE PIGS

A major focus in our neighborhood and citywide work is the pigs, because they tie together the various struggles around the state as the enemy, and thus point to the need for a movement oriented toward power to defeat it.

The pigs are the capitalist state, and as such define the limits of all political struggles; to the extent that a revolutionary struggle shows signs of success, they come in and mark the point it can't go beyond. . . . Our job is not to avoid the issue of the pigs as "diverting" from anti-imperialist struggle, but to emphasize that they are our real enemy if we fight that struggle to win.

The most important task for us toward making the revolution, and the work our collectives should engage in, is the creation of a mass revolutionary movement, without which a clandestine revolutionary party will be impossible. A revolutionary mass movement is different from the traditional revisionist mass base of "sympathizers." Rather it is akin to the Red Guard in China, based on the full participation and involvement of masses of people in the practice of making revolution; a movement with a full willingness to participate in the violent and illegal struggle. It is a movement diametrically opposed to the elitist idea that only leaders are smart enough or interested enough to accept full revolutionary conclusions. It is a movement built on the basis of faith in the masses of people.

The task of collectives is to create this kind of movement. (The party is not a substitute for it, and in fact is totally dependent on it.) This will be done at this stage principally among youth, through implementing the Revolutionary Youth Movement strategy discussed in this paper. It is practice at this, and not political "teachings" in the abstract, which will determine the relevance of the political collectives which are formed.

The strategy of the RYM for developing an active mass base, tying the city-wide fights to community and city-wide anti-pig movement, and for building a party eventually out of this motion, fits with the world strategy for winning the revolution, builds a movement oriented toward the power, and will become one division of the International Liberation Army, while its battlefields are added to the many Vietnams which will dismember and dispose of US imperialism. Long Live the Victory of People's War!

Up Against the Ivy Wall

Jerry Avorn, Robert Freedman, and Members of the Staff of the Columbia Daily Spectator

*No campus experienced greater upheaval than Columbia University in
1968. A Hollywood producer could hardly have created a scenario more
replete with typecast characters and issues. On one side stood a rigid,
conservative university president, tied through board membership to corporate America and through university contracts to government policy in
Vietnam, refusing consistently to make any concessions to student protestors. On the other stood an assortment of radicals frustrated by the
intransigence of the university and committed to finding any available
issue as a basis for confrontation. Add to the picture a black student body
intent upon acting independently of white movements, and a faculty
desperately searching for some middle ground to avoid a campus tragedy.*

*The immediate issues were simple. Columbia sought to construct a
university gymnasium in a public park overlooking Harlem, with a separate entrance at the back of the gym for community people who wished to
use the facility. A second issue involved the university's ties to the Defense
Department through research contracts that, at least indirectly, helped to
support the war. Compounding each of these was a failure of communication between students and administration. All these strands came together
in the spring of 1968. The following selection, written by the editors of the
student newspaper, highlights how a combination of university stubborn-
ness, student rebellion, and the overuse of police force resulted in the
radicalization of a significant portion of the university student body. The
Columbia story became a microcosm of what was to happen on other
campuses throughout the country, helping to create a widespread sense
that everything was coming apart, and that no institution—no matter
how venerated—was safe from radical challenge.*

"What is the singular of 'swine'?" asked Warren Goodell, vice president for administration of Columbia University, as he walked into the offices of the *Columbia Daily Spectator*.

"It must be 'pig,'" one of the editors suggested. "Why?"

"They called me one yesterday," the vice president said with a nervous smile. "They marched over to my office, and one of them yelled, 'There's another one of these swine around here,' and they came looking for me. But I wasn't in."

The incident had occurred on March 27, 1968, during a demonstration in which over one hundred members of the Columbia chapter of Students for a Democratic Society marched into Low Memorial Library, the domed-and-columned edifice that houses the offices of Columbia's top administrators. Officially the demonstration had been called to protest Columbia's affiliation with the Institute for Defense Analyses, an organization that does military research for the federal government. But beyond this it had another goal: to flout an edict, issued at the start of the academic year by Columbia President Grayson Kirk, banning all protests inside University buildings. SDS claimed that the rule was an attempt at political repression and wanted to draw the administration into a confrontation over the regulation. Inside Low, chanting "IDA Must Go!", the mass of students burst into several offices, including that of one administrator who admitted he was against the war but said he had more pressing problems. The students presented him with a petition calling for Columbia's disaffiliation from IDA, signed by more than 1,500 students and faculty. They then coursed through the building for the next fifteen minutes, chanting anti-war slogans and distracting secretaries.

Now, as Goodell spoke of the event, he grew agitated. "Take over," he murmured, "the word has gone out from national SDS—take over the universities. . . . Those students have no respect for property," the vice president said. "You should have seen the things they were doing in Low yesterday—writing on the wall, everything. I have a Picasso hanging in my office, you know. Those kids probably won't even know it's a Picasso. If they touch my Picasso they're going to the state penitentiary! . . ."

In the midst of a rapidly changing University climate, Grayson Kirk, sixty-four year old, imposing, President of Columbia University, meticulously clad in gray vest and suit, sat in his large Low Library office surrounded by his familiar mementos and objets d'art. He leaned forward in a leather chair and lit his pipe. It was five days before the uprising. His ample jowls swelling red as he puffed, Kirk explained to a small group of student editors why he had refused for eight months to make public the contents of a report he had commissioned on student life at Columbia. The report had been submitted in late August by a committee of students, faculty and administrators who had worked for nearly two years on the project. It contained an extensive set of proposals for student involvement in University decision-making, as well as rules governing student rights and protest. Kirk had finally released the report only after the student council threatened to make its copy public, and now declined to comment on any of the proposals it contained.

"For me to comment on the Student Life Report would foreclose discussion about it on campus," the President remarked with the stammer that mars much of his speech. "I would not want to say at this time in what spheres of University life the students should have a voice, because there hasn't been time to read the report carefully enough."

Discussion turned to the March 27 political demonstration inside Low Library and the disciplining of students that might follow. "The University is free to expel anyone for any reason it deems equitable," Kirk stated, "and that is as it should be. Of course, I have—under the Trustees—the final disciplinary authority." . . .

April 22, the day before it all began at Columbia, a student sent an open letter to President Kirk. It began with a quotation:

> Our young people, in disturbing numbers, appear to reject all forms of authority, from whatever source derived, and they have taken refuge in a turbulent and inchoate nihilism whose sole objectives are destruction. I know of no time in our history when the gap between the generations has been wider or more potentially dangerous.
>
> GRAYSON KIRK, APRIL 12, 1968
> Charlottesville, Va.

DEAR GRAYSON,

Your charge of nihilism is indeed ominous; for if it were true, our nihilism would bring the whole civilized world, from Columbia to Rockefeller Center, crashing down upon all our heads. Though it is not true, your charge does represent something: you call it the generation gap. I see it as a real conflict between those who run things now—you, Grayson Kirk—and those who feel oppressed by, and disgusted with, the society you rule—we, the young people.

You might want to know what is wrong with this society, since, after all, you live in a very tight self-created dream world. We can point to the war in Vietnam as an example of the unimaginable wars of aggression you are prepared to fight to maintain your control over your empire (now you've been beaten by the Vietnamese, so you call for a tactical retreat). We can point to your using us as cannon fodder to fight your war. We can point out your mansion window to the ghetto below you've helped to create through your racist University expansion policies, through your unfair labor practices, through your city government and your police. . . . You say the war in Vietnam was a well-intentioned accident. We, the young people, who you so rightly fear, say that the society is sick and you and your capitalism are the sickness.

You call for order and respect for authority; we call for justice, freedom and socialism.

There is only one thing left to say. It may sound nihilistic to you, since it is the opening shot in a war of liberation. I'll use the words of LeRoi Jones, whom I'm sure you don't like a whole lot: "Up against the wall, motherfucker, this is a stick-up."

> Yours for freedom,
> MARK [RUDD]

. . . The tactical elegance of confrontation politics lay in the fact that the radicals had a good chance of winning whether the administration gave in to their substantive demands or overcame them by repression. The use of coercive force on the part of the adversary—whether it came in the form of the University discipline or police violence—could be a powerful force to "radicalize" liberal or moderate students. For the crucial part of the SDS view is that while escalated tactics are necessary to bring pressure for change on substantive issues, the "radicalization" of large segments of the population is far more important. As Rudd said later:

> Confrontation politics puts the enemy up against the wall and forces him to define himself. In addition, it puts the individual up against the wall. He has to make a choice. Radicalization of the individual means that he must commit himself to the struggle to change society as well as share the radical view of what is wrong with society.

Shortly after the March 27 demonstration in Low the administration formulated its response to the confrontation. . . . Six students were singled out—Rudd, four other members of the SDS steering committee and the chairman of a campus draft-resistance organization—and summoned to the office of a dean to discuss their participation in the protest. . . . On April 22 the students—who came to be known as the "IDA Six"—finally agreed to meet with the dean but declined to discuss their participation in the IDA demonstration. They were summarily placed on disciplinary probation. . . .

The sun broke through a gray cloud cover shortly before noon Tuesday, April 23, 1968. Nearly one thousand Columbia students and faculty milled on Low Plaza waiting for the featured event of the afternoon—a march into Low Library sponsored by Students for a Democratic Society.

Cicero Wilson, newly elected president of the Students' Afro-American Society, stepped onto the Sundial. In a sense, Wilson's presence at the SDS rally was as significant as his speech. SDS had never been able to unite with black militants on campus and, until now, the white radicals had been unable even to get a representative of the blacks to speak at an SDS function.

"This is Harlem Heights, not Morningside Heights," Wilson told the crowd that had now grown to five hundred. Waving his fists in the air, he attacked the University's plans to build a gymnasium in Morningside Park. "What would you do if somebody came and took your property? Took your property as they're doing over at Morningside with this gym?" Wilson asked. "Would you sit still? No, you'd use every means possible to get your property back—and this is what the black people are engaged in right now." . . .

After conferring again with his fellows, Rudd mounted the Sundial. . . . Rudd looked up toward Low and saw his runner signal that the huge front door was indeed locked. "The doors are locked at Low," Rudd yelled. "We won't get in the fucking office. Maybe—"

Suddenly, before Rudd could complete his sentence, Tom Hurwitz, a radical junior sporting a revolutionary red bandana around his forehead, leapt onto the Sundial and shouted, "Did we come here to talk or did we come here to go to Low?"

Raising his right arm to the sky, Hurwitz started toward Low. The six leftist leaders who had been disciplined the day before

linked arms and pushed to the front of the crowd that was following
Hurwitz across the plaza. As the demonstrators strode swiftly up
the steps to Low, chanting "IDA Must Go! IDA Must Go!" several
administrators frantically tried to stop the surging crowd. . . .

Rudd jumped on top of a trash can just outside the security
entrance and asked for quiet so he could address the crowd. Jeff
Sokolow, a sophomore member of SDS, tugged at Rudd and said,
"Tell 'em we could have gotten in, but someone would have gotten
hurt." Rudd told the crowd just that and then once again outlined
the alternatives open to them. In the middle of Rudd's speech,
however, someone in the front of the crowd shouted, "To the gym,
to the gym site!" and nearly three hundred of the demonstrators
streamed away from Low toward a gate at Amsterdam Avenue and
117th Street. The students moved off the campus led by Cicero
Wilson and several other SAS members.

By 12:30 P.M., just one-half hour after the protest had begun at
the Sundial, students had pulled down nearly forty feet of fence
at the gym site. As protesters continued to rush down the hill toward the open gate fifteen more policemen converged on the demonstrators and started pulling people away from the fallen fence.

Several scuffles broke out between students and police. An officer
from the 24th Precinct grabbed Fred Wilson, a white student, and
tried to arrest him. A large circle of students gathered around the
pair as they struggled. The crowd began shouting, "Let him go, let
him go! Take all of us!" and pushed in around the policeman and
his prisoner. The officer slipped in the loose dirt and fell to the
ground, dragging Wilson down on top of him. The circle of demonstrators piled onto the policeman, kicking at his hands and body,
trying to free Wilson.

Robbie Roth, a thin Columbia sophomore from Queens, suggested that the entire crowd regroup at the Sundial. "We're going
to have to go back and get together," he said, "with the crowd
building, we can still salvage it." The group filed out of the gym site,
walking slowly back through the park toward the campus.

Rudd stepped onto the Sundial again. "We don't have an inco-
herent mob; it just looks that way. I'll tell you what we want to do.
We want the people under discipline to get off of discipline. We
want this guy who got busted today to get the charges dropped
against him; to get unbusted—I guess that's how you say it. We want
them to *stop* the fucking gym over there. So I think there's really

one thing we have to do and we're all together here; we're all ready to go—now. We'll start by holding a hostage."

"Where are we going to get one?" one student asked.

"We're going to hold whoever we can," Rudd said, "in return for them letting go of the six people under discipline, letting go of IDA and letting go of the fucking gym. We can't get into Low Library. We can't hold the administrators in Low hostage because we can't get in that place and, also, it's too big a place. *But*—there is one part of this administration that's responsible for what's happened today—and that's the administration of Columbia College."

Someone in front of the Sundial boomed, "SEIZE HAMILTON!" and Rudd shouted, "Hamilton Hall is right over there. Let's go!" The crowd surged along the narrow path leading to the classroom building. Within minutes the lobby of the building was overflowing with four hundred students chanting thunderously. "IDA MUST GO! IDA MUST GO!"

"Now we've got the Man where we want him," Rudd told the crowd. "He can't leave unless he gives into some of our demands." A roar rose from the demonstrators.

"Now, let me tell Dean Coleman why we're here; We're here because of the University's bullshit with IDA. After we demand an end to affiliation in IDA, they keep dong research to kill people in Vietnam and in Harlem. That's one of the reasons why we're here. We're here because the University steals land from black people, because we want them to stop building that gym. We're here because the University busts people for political stuff, as it tried to bust six of us, including myself and five other leaders of SDS for leading a demonstration against IDA. We're not going to leave until that demand, no discipline for us, is met." After sustained applause, Rudd continued, "Another demand is that our brother who got busted today—he got some sort of assault charge—that brother is released, and all the other people who have been busted for demonstrating over there. So it's clear that we can't leave this place until most of our demands are met." . . .

When it became apparent late Tuesday night that there would be no new developments at least until dawn, the Hamilton Hall demonstration turned from a sit-in to a sleep-in. As the tired speakers said their last words, the last of the tired demonstrators left the lobby for the upper floors of the building where they made temporary lodgings on corridor and classroom floors. Scattered on blankets, informal groups on each floor held bedtime parties with peanut butter and jelly sandwiches, beer, and guitars. The main classroom building of the all-male College had been transformed for one night into a coed hostel. But, though sexually integrated, the demonstration was becoming racially strained. The fragile alliance between SAS and SDS, born on the Sundial in the afternoon, was dying with the night. The blacks had segregated themselves on the third floor, leaving the remainder of the building to the whites. But the sleeping arrangements were only a sign. Though the integrated steering committee still hung together, a split over tactics was becoming more pronounced. . . .

SDS had always been concerned with mass support. "Alienating the faculty would also be dangerous," Rudd warned, "because they could approve some of our demands." The blacks, however, were not at this point concerned with the psychological impact that barricading buildings would have on the rest of the University community. They did not share the ideology of the New Left and were not obsessed with visions of mass support from the white world. While the whites wanted to radicalize the rest of the campus and use the political pressure of popular support to win their demands, the blacks preferred to rely only on the more military advantage of holding buildings, regardless of whether the campus liked it or not.

When the three white delegates to the steering committee reached the first-floor room where the blacks had been meeting, they were told, "We want to make our stand here. It would be better if you left and took your own building." Although the whites had expected all night that the break would eventually come, many were nevertheless shaken by what amounted to an order. They were even more upset when the blacks told them that there were guns in the building. Rumors had been circulating all night, but now it seemed that many blacks were prepared to make a violent stand. The prospect scared the white radicals who were becoming brazen about taking buildings but remained timid about actual violence. The blacks tried to ease the bitterness by telling the white leaders that, by leaving the building, they could act as a diversion when the police came and possibly start a second front. . . .

In an attempt to keep the demoralized group together, Rudd proposed further action. "The blacks have chosen to make *their* stand," he said; "we should—not in support, but in attack of our common enemy, the administration—go and find our own building to make a stand in."

The large center doors to Hamilton Hall were opened and the whites filed out, dazed, into the dawn. Behind them the blacks hurriedly piled desks, chairs, file cabinets and anything else that could be used to block the doors. By 6 A.M. the white exodus was over, the building barricaded and locked. . . .

Out of the confusion, a band of about two hundred students shuffled slowly across a deserted College Walk and, as if drawn by a compulsion to repeat an earlier part of their scenario, they marched to the southeast security entrance of Low Library.

Three or four students at the front of the contingent charged the security door, trying unsuccessfully to force it with their shoulders. One student spotted a board lying on a nearby bench. It was picked up and positioned in front of the large plate glass window of the door. Twice, on the verge of launching the plank through the window, the students hesitated and dropped it. On the third attempt they brought the thick board back slowly and then, in one even motion, smashed the pane. The tinkling of the glass was the only sound to crack the clammy quiet of a gray sunrise. The crowd shuddered—some because of the temperature, others because of the act. The protest had crossed another line. . . .

The students toyed with office equipment, sipped Kirk's sherry and puffed his White Owl "President" cigars. There was the President's huge mahogany desk, his sofa, his telephones, his private bathroom, his $450,000 Rembrandt "Portrait of a Dutch Admiral," his sculptured ebony lion statuette. Everything was there just as Grayson Kirk had left it. . . .

More students from the groups at the Sundial and Hamilton had entered Low, and a plan of action became necessary. The meeting of almost two hundred students was shifted from the hallway to the center of the rotunda, a place normally reserved for formal receptions and lectures by distinguished speakers. Rudd stood before the crowd and in the well-established SDS tradition, outlined the alternative actions available to the demonstrators. Suggestions to leave Low or barricade the entire building were summarily dismissed. A proposed sit-in in the rotunda was rejected for tactical reasons, after Rudd pointed out that the administration could simply lock the huge iron gates that surround the rotunda and leave them sitting there forever. At this point a runner brought news that the

New York City police had arrived on campus, were stationed in the basement of Low and would probably be ordered to clear the building. Rudd suggested that the group return to Kirk's office and barricade the doors. The plan was accepted, and the students reëntered the suite, moved into both Kirk's and Truman's private offices and placed desks, chairs and file cabinets against the three doors that lead to the hallway. They filled wastepaper baskets with water from the President's sink to be used as protection against tear gas, and they waited.

Meanwhile, as the demonstrators inside Low were deciding whether to occupy his office, Vice President Truman arrived on campus. Wearing a trench coat, his hat pulled down over his forehead, Truman paced worriedly back and forth on College Walk. The vice president, who normally smokes a pipe, chain-smoked cigarettes as he walked. Several students attempted to speak to him, but he brushed by them. . . .

At 6:50 A.M. Truman called Kirk to brief him and to ask him to come to the campus. Though Truman had argued against bringing in the police on Tuesday afternoon, with the breaking and entering into Low he changed his mind. Over the phone Kirk and Truman now agreed that it was time for the police to clear out Low.

At 7:15 A.M. a delegate from the administration was sent up to the President's office with an offer. He spoke to Rudd through the broken pane in Kirk's door and told him that if the students walked out now and turned in their identification cards they would face only University discipline and no criminal trespass charges. Rudd rejected the proposal, explaining later that it would have been foolish to accept the deal when they knew they had another way out— through the windows. . . .

Meanwhile, Truman was having trouble with the police officials. Kirk had arrived on campus, and the two were trying to arrange for the arrest of any students who remained in the President's office. As firm as they were in their decision that police should be used to clear out Low, they were also set against using the police in Hamilton, for fear of large-scale violence. . . .

The police, however, balked at this selectivity, Truman reported later, telling him that it would be impossible for them to clear out one building and not the other. It was to be all or nothing, and the dangers that could arise in Hamilton Hall convinced the administrators to do nothing. That the police were not brought in proved critical. Had they been used to clear Low, the demonstration probably would have been contained, and the administration would have had to deal only with the blacks in Hamilton. . . .

Surrounded by statues of Buddha and bodhisattvas in the Faculty Room of Low Library, Kirk told reporters:

> The University is committed to maintaining order on the campus. We insist that there be respect for the rules and conditions that make University life possible. We have exercised great restraint in the use of police and security forces, because at almost all costs, we wish to avoid physical confrontation. We have constantly tried to communicate with those students who have seized the buildings, and as late as this morning, contact was made with all of the protesting groups, but with no success. We are prepared to talk with the protesting groups, but disciplinary action will have to be taken against those students who flagrantly violated University rules. The students have had ample opportunity to leave the buildings and to engage in *lawful* protest if they so desire.

"We cannot give in on amnesty," Truman said. "This goes far beyond this University." Asked about the gym Kirk replied, "Contract obliges us to continue construction." . . .

By Friday some of the strikers' demands seemed well on their way to realization. But victories on matters such as gym construction were not the developments in which the strike leaders took most satisfaction. More significant was the change that had come over the lifestyle of the students who occupied the buildings. This transformation of the quality of life and the existential involvement of the individual were the ends toward which all of the SDS ideology pointed. The radicals saw the routinized patterns of society as repressive, manipulative and dehumanizing. The "respectable" lives of businessmen, bureaucrats and professionals to which many of them had once aspired were seen as drab, confining, cardboard existences. Now, insulated from the norms and forms of American culture by several feet of office furniture and barricades, the students inside the "liberated" buildings were able to create social patterns of their own. The takeover of the buildings had begun as a political tactic designed to bring about the goal of social reconstruction. It quickly evolved into the realization, on a small scale, of that very goal. The process of personal liberation was founded in a common existential credential—all the students in the buildings had placed their careers at Columbia in some jeopardy by joining the protest; a common tactic—confrontation; a common enemy—the administration; and a common set of immediate goals—the six demands. In addition, in the day-to-day conduct of the demonstrations each student could feel that he was in direct touch with the sources of power and decision-making within the strike apparatus. This was accomplished through participatory democracy, a central element of SDS ideology as has been noted. Students could, within the strike context, *make the decisions that affected their lives.*

Shortly before noon Saturday hopes for a peaceful mediation of the crisis suffered another setback. Members of the board of Trustees, normally distant from campus affairs, were slowly being drawn into the crisis. On Friday morning, William Petersen, president of the Irving Trust Company, who serves as chairman of the Columbia Trustees, made his first major attempt to bring peace to the Morningside campus. He phoned the Mayor of New York City. Lindsay aide Barry Gottehrer later described the conversation:

> Petersen wanted the Mayor to come up to Columbia and settle the situation. Lindsay was willing, but asked what leverage he would be given in mediating. Petersen said they would give him no leverage. He just asked the Mayor to come onto campus and walk around, talking to people, as he does in Harlem. He expected a miracle.

Lindsay never came, but Petersen continued his search for a solution. Friday evening the Trustees were called together for an informal meeting downtown to discuss what was happening to their University.

Chairman Petersen took it upon himself to issue a public statement Saturday morning stating his interpretation of the opinions expressed by the quorum of Trustees present. The Petersen statement was read to the Ad Hoc Faculty Group late Saturday morning:

> The Trustees and the University met and conferred yesterday (Friday) regarding the situation on the Morningside Heights campus. They expressed approval of the course which had been followed by the University administration. . . . In common with the administration the Trustees deplore the complete disruption of normal University operations and the illegal seizure and occupation of University buildings, perpetrated by a *small minority of students, aided and abetted by outsiders* who have injected themselves into the situation. . . .

The Trustees have advised the President that they wholeheartedly support the administration position that there shall be no amnesty accorded to those who have engaged in this illegal conduct. Moreover, they not only support the President's stand, but *affirmatively direct, that he shall maintain the ultimate disciplinary power* over the conduct of students of the University as required by the Charter and Statutes of the University.

Insofar as the gymnasium is concerned, the Trustees feel that the attempt to depict the construction of the building as a matter involving a racial issue or discrimination is an attempt to create an *entirely false issue* by individuals who are either not conversant with, or who disregard, the facts. However, the Trustees have approved the action taken by the administration *at the request of the Mayor* of New York City, on Thursday, April 25, to halt construction activities *temporarily*. This action represented an appropriate response, and *a courtesy to the chief executive of the City* at a time of tension. . . .

The Petersen statement was received with hostility in nearly every quarter of the campus and was seen as written proof that the Trustees were as out of touch with University life as everyone had imagined. Herbert Deane said later that the Petersen statement "almost blew us out of the water." The administration had announced on Thursday night that gym construction had been suspended, a partial concession to one of the Six Demands. Now on Saturday, when the gym had all but dropped out of the picture, the Trustees proclaimed that the gym was "an entirely false issue" and that construction had only been halted temporarily as a courtesy to the Mayor. Before the Petersen statement the administration had seemed ready to modify its stand on discipline by delegating some authority to the tripartite commission proposed by the Galanter committee. Now the Trustees ordered the President to "maintain the ultimate disciplinary power." . . .

If Mark Rudd had drafted the statement for the Trustees instead of Petersen it could not have made the situation more critical or the University look worse. . . . To the demonstrators a statement like Petersen's was tactically welcome, for in clearly defining the "enemy" position it further polarized the campus. And when sides were chosen few opted to be on the same team as Petersen. . . . Over the weekend it became clear that the crisis was quickly heading for one of only two possible ends—amnesty or bust.

Rumors had been circulating all Monday night that the police would arrive within hours. But the same rumors had circulated Sunday night and throughout the rest of the occupation, and few students paid much attention to them. For hours busloads of police had been unloading at five precinct centers in different parts of Manhattan. Because the Columbia operation would be on such a massive scale the men had been drawn from precincts in all boroughs of the city—Manhattan, Brooklyn, Queens, Staten Island and the Bronx. Shortly after midnight the police began gathering on the periphery of the campus. Word of the mobilization was carried on radio news broadcasts, as breathless students ran among the occupied buildings to report that at the 100th Street precinct house police buses and paddy wagons were lined up for blocks along the street.

Since the middle of the occupation the black students in Hamilton had communicated with hardly anyone, except through an occasional press release. Their secrecy had reinforced the growing image of militancy hinted at by their official statements and the conclusions of observers. With the expected police attack, most people on campus expected a small-scale Armageddon. Now, with tension higher than it had been at any other time since the crisis began, the occupants of Hamilton were addressing a rally of Harlem residents from windows overlooking Amsterdam Avenue.

More than 150 demonstrators were marching peacefully on the sidewalk carrying crudely lettered anti-Columbia placards and chanting, "Columbia goes from jerk to jerk—Eisenhower to racist Kirk." As white students joined the demonstration and the rally grew, a window opened on the fourth floor of Hamilton and Cicero Wilson leaned out over the street to deliver his first public address since April 23.

"I'd like to thank you brothers for coming out here tonight," Wilson said. "We're here to stop the gym and to get amnesty for the black students in Hamilton Hall." Teddy Kaptchuk approached a reporter standing near him in the crowd and nervously commented, "You know what he just said really doesn't matter. They're still with us. It's just a tactical thing." But, despite their protestations of unity, the white strike leaders had come to realize that Hamilton was indeed a separate decision-making unit whose actions in the next hours would be completely unpredictable. . . .

Near Low, professors and their teaching assistants pushed their way through the dense crowd that continued to accumulate outside

Kirk's offices. "Please don't stand here," they yelled, "it will be very bad if you are standing here when the police come. Go down to the Sundial where there is a rally taking place." Few students moved—most wanted to see the action firsthand. One young girl in tears, a teaching assistant in the English department, began frantically tugging at the sleeves of people she recognized, urging, "Please, go away from here. You will be badly hurt. Go to the Sundial." . . .

All the occupied buildings were not being sealed off from the inside. . . .

Tuesday, 2:10 A.M., April 30: a girl taking a drink of water in Fayerweather noticed that the fountain trickled to a stop. The water supply to the other occupied buildings was also shut off. At Strike Central a student was speaking by phone with occupied Low when the receiver went dead. Two minutes later the phones in the *Spectator* office in Ferris Booth Hall were cut off. The bust was beginning.

Mark Rudd left Strike Central with Lew Cole, Juan Gonzalez and several other strike leaders. Almost running, he crossed the Sundial and headed for Low. As he arrived a student messenger dashed to his side "They're—leaving—Hamilton—Mark," he panted. Rudd sent another runner to Hamilton to get details.

The runner sent to Hamilton now returned. "The blacks are letting themselves be taken out, Mark," the student said incredulously. No shots rang out in the air over Hamilton. No angry masses swarmed across Morningside Park from Harlem. . . .

In contrast with SDS the blacks had decided that there was nothing to gain from a bloody arrest episode. . . .

A crowd of about 250 students and faculty was standing in front of the security entrance to Low chanting, "No Violence!" and "Cops Must Go!" They tried to sing Columbia's alma mater, "Sans Souci," but after several false starts gave up because hardly anybody remembered the words. The shouting changed to cries of "STRIKE! STRIKE! STRIKE!" as a column of thirty-five Tactical Patrol Force squared off directly in front of the crowd. . . .

While the captain talked Frederick Courtney, an instructor in the Spanish department who was standing at the top of the steps, remarked to students alongside him that he had left his motorcycle helmet and camera under a hedge by St. Paul's Chapel and that he thought the helmet might be a good thing to have. He stepped down and started walking across the grassy plot between Low and the chapel. Suddenly six men leapt out of the hedges and seized him. Courtney was knocked to the ground and, as the demonstrators on the steps watched in amazement, he was punched, kicked and blackjacked. The men were plainclothesmen; some were wearing dark slacks and blue nylon windbreakers, which resembled Columbia jackets, and had looked like students in the dark. Courtney was dragged away, an officer holding each arm and leg.

As administration officials watched from a window above, another column of TPF moved into position behind the first.

The TPF captain in charge announced to the crowd, "You are obstructing police in the performance of their duty. Please move." His order was met with more cries of "No Violence!" and "No Cops!" A few athletes standing on a nearby ledge urged the police to go in and smash the demonstrators, yelling Columbia's football slogan, "Let's go, Lions!" Others yelled, "Beautiful!" and cheered as they spotted more light blue police helmets. Again the captain made his announcement: "You are blocking our progress here." Again no one moved. The captain's jovial face hardened. Suddenly the police pulled out blackjacks and flashlights and charged, ramming them into the nearest faces. Most students were merely grabbed and thrown over the low hedges onto the brick pathways out of the way of the police. Some were clubbed as they fell. The front row of resisters was hurled back and to the sides and the police now began plowing through the remaining five rows in a similar manner, throwing people onto the grass or bricks. Dean Platt, standing nearby to observe, was punched in the chest by a badgeless plainclothesman. Screaming, the crowd split; some ran north toward Avery and Fayerweather, others south to College Walk. "Is there a physician in the crowd?" someone yelled, helping a limping girl down the steps of Low Memorial Library, "we need a doctor." "Call Dr. Kirk!" an angry student shouted. The name was greeted with cries of "Butcher, Butcher!" One girl who had been in the security entrance rush now stood crying at the Sundial. "They knock you down but that's not enough, they don't let you up again. They just keep hitting. . . ." "They were pros," another student said, "those TPF guys don't even use clubs." Students returning from the confrontation reported, trembling, that girls were smashed against the stone walks when the police came in. "One guy, in uniform, grabbed me by the hair," said one student bleeding from a gash in his lips, "and said, okay, buddy, you're next. Then wham wham wham wham four times in the face." A Barnard girl who had been in the midst of the attack, nearly hysterical, kept screaming over and over, "Cops suck!" until she broke down into fits of sobbing. . . .

As the arrested students were piled into police vans on College Walk, they began chanting and shouting furiously. Choruses of "We Shall Overcome" and "Up against the wall, motherfuckers!" resounded from the metallic innards of the paddy wagons. One group of prisoners began banging rhythmically on the inside of their van, and soon the occupants of each wagon took up the new protest.

The crowd of observers on the south side of College Walk had been chanting anti-cop slogans for some time when they noticed hundreds of police marching in drill formation and regrouping on Low Plaza. Through a series of right- and left-faces and advances the policemen, mostly TPF, maneuvered to within several yards of the crowd and ordered them to move back. The group retreated grudgingly and continued to taunt the police. A group of athletes stood on the Sundial chanting "TPF! TPF!" and shouting insults at the pro-demonstration students around them. A moment later, without warning, the line of uniformed officers and plainclothes-men charged the crowd. The paddy wagons parked on College Walk swung around, their headlights spotlighting South Field and temporarily blinding the students staring up at the plaza. Flailing their clubs the police chased several hundred students onto the lawn, the glare of the bright lights on their backs as they charged. The athletes on the Sundial were overrun with the rest, their pro-police chants disregarded. The students who ran slowest in the stampede were struck with clubs, tripped or kicked. In the darker recesses of the field plainclothesmen stationed themselves near hedges and pummelled demonstrators who tried to run past them. The students who moved faster found, as they reached the south side of the campus, that all of the gates had been closed and locked. With the police sweeping across South Field, they had no place to go but inside the lobbies of the dormitories which were now filling up with the limping, the bruised and the frightened. One student running for Ferris Booth Hall was clubbed and kicked just outside the building. He lay bleeding near the door, jerking spasmodically, until he was carried away on a stretcher by volunteer medical aides.

For the next hour the police crisscrossed again and again over South Field and its environs, "clearing the campus" by chasing or clubbing the students they found. "It was the only way to disperse the crowd quickly," police spokesman Jacques Nevard explained later, "It is folly for people to stand around and watch when there is trouble. . . . Once you start using force, the chances of excessive force increase greatly."

As most police left Columbia with the coming of daylight a new armband appeared on campus. Students stood at the gates and on College Walk handing out strips of black crepe paper, signs of mourning for the death of a University. That morning *Spectator* carried a blank editorial surrounded by a black border. A new SDS flyer was hastily produced and distributed:

At 2:30 this morning, Columbia University died. . . . WE WILL AVENGE THE 139 WOUNDED MEMBERS OF THE LIBERATION. . . . DOWN WITH THE UNIVERSITY, UP WITH THE STUDENTS, UP WITH THE COMMUNITY, LONG LIVE THE FORCES OF LIBERATION AT COLUMBIA. . . .

The black armbands were also a sign of outrage. Though the liberals had previously refused to identify themselves completely with the students in the buildings, they were now forced to take sides, and it was unlikely that they would move behind the forces of "legitimate violence." Most Columbia students and faculty had never come closer to mass violence than TV news broadcasts, and the new first-hand experience of police confrontation shook them—at least temporarily—out of middle-of-the-road politics. With many students and faculty members walking around campus wearing head bandages and slings as badges of brutalization, it was hard to remain placidly uncommitted.

The protest that had been born during the occupations grew enormously in scope and support as the newly activated liberals joined its ranks. The crisis developed into its next phase: a full-scale strike against the University. The same phenomenon had occurred at Berkeley in 1964, when widespread student-faculty strike followed police clearance of a sit in in Sproul Hall. Now at Columbia the pattern was being repeated. At 7:15 A.M. Mike Nichols, executive vice president of the Columbia University Student Council, stood on Low Plaza amid reporters and shouting students and announced that the student council would support a general strike against the administration. One year ago Nicholas had appeared at a campus debate to condemn SDS and the New Left. Now he was joining forces with them against Kirk and Truman. Within hours hundreds of students joined the Strike Coördinating Committee in endorsing the strike.

Rise and Fall of a Counterculture

Allen J. Matusow

In the eyes of many Americans, the counterculture of the late 1960s represented a startling new development, threatening, in almost nihilistic fashion, every tradition and norm inherited from the past. Yet as Allen Matusow shows in this sharply written excerpt from The Unraveling of America, *many of the central themes of the counterculture went back to intellectual and cultural developments of the forties and fifties. Beatnik poets and novelists, black jazz musicians, and pioneer users of hallucinogenic drugs all helped to pave the way for the explosive rebellion of values and behavior that occurred among middle- and upper-class young people during the late sixties. Still, the confluence of cultural protests that took place in these years went beyond anything that could have been anticipated by a reader of Kerouac's* On The Road *in the fifties. At least some of the children of America's "best" families were engaging in what their parents could only see as bizarre and pathological activity—getting stoned on drugs, grooving to atonal acid rock, challenging nearly every vestige of "respectability" in social interaction, turning their backs on the Protestant ethic that had made America what it was. Here, Allen Matusow gives us a keen and precise look at the contours of that counterculture, even as he exposes its fragility and contradictions.*

America discovered hippies at the world's first Human Be-In, Golden Gate Park, San Francisco, January 14, 1967. The occasion was something special, even in a Bay Area underground long accustomed to spectacle. Political activists from Berkeley mingled with dropouts from Haight-Ashbury, ending their feud and initiating a "new epoch" in the history of man. "In unity we shall shower the country with waves of ecstasy and purification," sponsors of the Be-In prophesied. "Fear will be washed away; ignorance will be exposed to sunlight; profits and empire will lie drying on deserted beaches." . . .

Timothy Leary was there, dressed in white and wearing flowers in his hair. "Turn on to the scene, tune in to what is happening, and drop out—of high school, college, grad school, junior executive—and follow me, the hard way," said Leary, reciting his famous commercial for the synthetic hallucinogen LSD. . . . Music for the occasion was acid rock, performed by Quicksilver Messenger Service, Jefferson Airplane, and the Grateful Dead. Already an underground legend, the Dead had played Ken Kesey's notorious "acid tests," which had done so much to spread LSD and the psychedelic style throughout California a year or so before. Representing the new left was Jerry Rubin, released that very morning from jail, but not yet hip enough for this occasion. "Tune-In—Drop-Out—Take-Over." Rubin had said at a press conference prior to the event. But few at the Be-In were in a mood (or condition) to take over anything.

The real show was the crowd. "The costumes were a designer's dream," wrote music critic Ralph Gleason in the San Francisco *Chronicle,* "a wild polyglot mixture of Mod, Palladin, Ringling Brothers, Cochise, and Hells Angel's Formal." Bells tinkled, balloons floated, people on the grass played harmonicas, guitars, recorders, flutes. Beautiful girls handed out sticks of incense. A young man in a paisley parachute drifted from the sky, though no plane was in sight. An old man gave away his poems.

Newsweek was on hand to photograph the Be-In in gorgeous color and report that "it was a love feast, a psychedelic picnic, a hippie happening." Images of hip quickly began to seep into the public consciousness, provoking intense curiosity and endless analysis in the straight world. Most of the pop sociology deserved the rebuke of Bob Dylan's "Ballad of a Thin Man": "Something is happening here but you don't know what it is. Do you, Mr. Jones?" Yet understanding was imperative, for the hippie impulse that was spreading through a generation of the young challenged the traditional values of bourgeois culture, values still underpinning the liberal movement of the 1960s—reason, progress, order, achievement, social responsibility. Hippies mocked liberal politicians, scorned efforts to repair the social order, and repudiated bourgeois society. In so doing, they became cultural radicals opposed to established authority. Among the movements arrayed against him toward the end of his tenure, none baffled Lyndon Johnson more than these hippies. Somehow, in the name of liberation, they rejected everything he stood for, including his strenuous efforts to liberate the poor and the black. Clearly, liberation meant something different to liberals like him from what it meant to radicals like them.

The history of hip began with the black hipsters of the 1930s. Black folk had always constituted something of a counterculture in America, representing, at least in the white imagination, pure id. Migrating into northern ghettos after World War I, young black men used their new freedom to improvise a new variation on black deviance—the hipster-who was not only hedonistic, sensual, and sexually uninhibited, but openly contemptuous of the white world that continued to exclude him. The language that hipsters invented on Harlem street corners was jive, an action language honed in verbal duels and inaccessible to most whites. Some jive words that became part of the permanent hip lexicon were *cat, solid, chick, Big Apple, square, tea, gas, dip, flip. Ofay,* the jive word for white, meant foe in pig Latin. The hipster costume was the zoot suit, designed, as hip garb always would be, to defy and outrage conventional taste. For kicks, the hipster smoked marijuana, which heightened his sense of immediacy and helped him soar above his mean surroundings. The only bigger kick was sex.

Vital to the hipster experience was the uninhibited black music called jazz. In 1922 a writer in the *Atlantic Monthly* described jazz as the result of "an unloosing of instincts that nature wisely has taught us to hold in check, but which, every now and then, for cryptic reasons, are allowed to break the bonds of civilization." Indeed, Louis Armstrong, playing his "hot," sensual, raunchy improvisations on trumpet, was the first hipster hero. As jazz changed, the hipster persona changed with it. In the early 1940s a group of rebel black jazzmen, hostile to the commercialization of the big bands, created bebop. Bebop relied on small groups and improvisation, as before, but the sound was cool, the rhythm variable, the volume low, and the technical virtuosity of its leading performers legend. The genius of bebop was Charlie "The Bird" Parker, who lived at "the level of total spontaneity," whether he was playing alto sax or getting kicks from booze, sex or heroin. By the mid-1940s, partly because of heroin, hot was out and cool was in. Hipster dress had become more conservative; noise and brash behavior, a breach of taste; detachment, a required pose. By then, too, the hipster had ceased to be a type restricted to blacks only. In New York and other big cities, some disaffiliates among the white young found the hipster persona so expressive of their own alienation that they adopted it as their own. Thus was born, in Norman Mailer's phrase, "the white Negro," living outside the law for sex, pot, jazz, kicks—in short, for Dionysian ecstasy. . . .

What the beats added to hip was the mystic quest. In the summer of 1948, living alone in East Harlem and grieving for his departed lover Neal Cassady, Allen Ginsberg had the defining experience of his life. As he lay in bed gazing at tenement roofs with a book of William Blake's *Songs of Innocence* before him, he heard the deep voice of the poet himself reciting the "Sunflower," and he knew it was the voice of God. "Looking out the window," Ginsberg remembered, "suddenly it seemed that I saw into the depths of the universe, by looking simply into the ancient sky." Ginsberg had auditory experience of other poems that evening, and there were other visions in the days that followed, until, a week later, standing in the athletic field at Columbia, Ginsberg invoked the spirit and experienced the cosmos as monster. "The sky was not a blue hand anymore but like a hand of death coming down on me." It was years before Ginsberg would seek that void again, but in the meantime he did not forget those moments when the ego had overflowed the bounds of the self and illumination had been his. . . .

Jack Kerouac, the beat writer who shared so many of Ginsberg's adventures, also shared his mystic quest. Kerouac had gone to Columbia to play football but rebelled against the discipline, deciding instead to write novels and probe the cultural underground. Recalling the 1940s, he wrote, "Anyway, the hipsters, whose music was bop, they looked like criminals but they kept talking about the same things I liked, long outlines of personal experience and vision, nightlong confessions full of hope that became illicit and repressed by War. . . ."

Kerouac made his artistic breakthrough when he decided to write a semi-fictional account of his road experiences with Neal Cassady. Some people might have regarded Cassady as a bum. Reared on the streets of Denver by his wino father, in and out of jails mostly for stealing cars, Cassady possessed so much energy and lived so completely in the moment that the beat circle could not resist him. In April 1951 Kerouac fed a roll of teletype paper into a typewriter and let tales of Cassady flow spontaneously from his mind, in one paragraph 120 feet long. It took three weeks to write *On the Road*, six years to get it published.

On the Road portrayed Kerouac, Cassady, Ginsberg, and their hipster friends speeding across the continent in the late forties, consuming pot, jazz, and sex, envying the Negro his spontaneity, his soul, his cool. Cassady (Dean Moriarty in the book) was the natural man, the Dionysian ego, joyfully slaking his unquenchable thirst for food, sex, and life. But Kerouac saw Cassady as more than a glutton. He was "a holy con-man," "the HOLY GOOF," "Angel Dean," questing for "IT," the moment "when you know all and everything is decided forever"—that moment in jazz, Dean explained, when the man making the music "rises to his fate and has to blow equal to it." In San Francisco, deserted by Cassady and delirious from hunger, Kerouac himself (Sal Paradise) had a mystic vision, reaching "the point of ecstasy that I always wanted to reach." Eventually, as Cassady became ensnared in complication, accusation, wounds of the body, he becomes, in Kerouac's view, "BEAT—the root, the soul of Beatific." A bestseller in 1957, *On the Road* became a literary inspiration for the restless young even then preparing to scale the walls of American suburbia in search of Dionysus.

In 1955 Kerouac, still an obscure writer, bummed his way across the country to visit Ginsberg in San Francisco. Kerouac was by then deep into Buddhism. Recognizing that the beat quest for satori had more in common with Oriental than Western religion, he vowed to end suffering and achieve nirvana by overcoming desire. In California he found that in turning East he was not alone. A pinch of Zen had by now been added to the witch's brew boiling over in North Beach. . . .

By the late 1950s, a fully developed beat subculture had emerged not only in North Beach but also in Venice West (near Los Angeles), New York's Greenwich Village, and a few other hip resorts in between. The beats possessed deviant tastes in language, literature, music, drugs, and religion. Profoundly alienated from dominant American values, practicing voluntary poverty and spade cool, they rejected materialism, competition, the work ethic, hygiene, sexual repression, monogamy, and the Faustian quest to subdue nature. There were, to be sure, never more than a few thousand full-time beats, but thanks to the scandalized media, images of beat penetrated and disconcerted the middle classes. Beats, like hula hoops, were a fad. Indeed, by the early 1960s the San Francisco poets had scattered, and cops and tourists had driven the rest of the beats from their old haunts in North Beach. A remnant survived, however, and found convenient shelter in another congenial San Francisco neighborhood. It was Haight-Ashbury, a racially integrated community, forty square blocks, bordering magnificent Golden Gate Park. There, beat old-timers kept alive the hip style and the Dionysian projects, until hippies moved in and appropriated both.

In the metamorphosis from beat to hippie, hallucinogenic drugs played an indispensable part. Indians had been using peyote and magic mushrooms for sacramental purposes since before the rise of the Aztec civilization. But in industrial civilizations, knowledge of mind-altering substances had virtually disappeared. . . .

The herald of the psychedelic revolution was the British author Aldous Huxley. Swallowing some mescaline in 1953, Huxley accidentally triggered a profound mystical experience, in which he watched "a slow dance of golden lights," discovered "Eternity in a flower" and even approached the "Pure Light of the Void," before fleeing in terror from "the burning brightness of unmitigated Reality." . . .

The man who purveyed Huxley's holy message to the millions was Timothy Leary. Possessor of a Ph.D. in psychology, Leary quit his job as director of the Kaiser Foundation Hospital in Oakland, California, in 1958, convinced that conventional psychiatry did not work. Accepting a post at Harvard to pursue his unorthodox ideas, Leary was on his way to a productive scientific career until, one day in Mexico, he discovered the magic mushrooms.

Leary had retreated to a villa on Cuernavaca in the summer of 1960 to write a paper that he hoped would win him points in the academic game. He had never smoked marijuana and knew nothing about mind-altering drugs. But, when a friend procured the mushrooms from a local Indian, Leary thought it might be fun to try some. On a hot afternoon sitting around a pool, Leary and a few companions choked down a bowl of filthy, foul-tasting *crudos*. The game for Leary ended right there. "Five hours after eating the mushrooms it was all changed," he wrote. "The revelation had come. The veil had been pulled back. The classic vision. The full-blown conversion experience. The prophetic call. The works. God had spoken."

Back at Harvard in the fall, Leary secured Huxley's help in designing a scientific experiment to investigate the behavioral effects of psilocybin (synthesized magic mushrooms). Soon Leary was turning on graduate students, ministers, convicts, and stray seekers showing up at his rented mansion in suburban Boston. In truth, Leary was using science to cloak his real purpose, which was to give away the keys to paradise. And he did grow in spiritual knowledge. He learned that drugs alone could not produce a state of blessedness, that they "had no specific effect on consciousness, except to expand it." God and the Devil resided together in the nervous system. Which of these was summoned depended on one's state of mind. Leary, therefore, emphasized the importance of proper "set and setting" (candles, incense, music, art, quiet) to help the seeker experience God.

In December 1960 Leary made the connection with the hip underground in the person of Allen Ginsberg. Having met him in New York, Ginsberg spent a week at Leary's home to enlist the professor in his own crusade for mind expansion. The two hit it off from the start. On Sunday, with dogs, children, and hangers-on scattered about, Leary gave Ginsberg and Peter Orlovsky the sacred mushrooms. The poets repaired to their room, stripped naked, and played Wagner on the record player. Lying in bed, Ginsberg began to succumb to hellish visions, until Leary came in, looked in his eyes, and pronounced him a great man. Ginsberg arose, and with Orlovsky padding behind, descended to the kitchen to proclaim himself the Messiah. We will go into the streets and call the people to peace and love, Leary reports him as saying. And we will get on the phone and hook up Burroughs, Kerouac, Mailer, Kennedy, and Khrushchev and "settle all this warfare bit." . . .

Not until late 1961 did Leary try LSD—"the most shattering experience of my life." Taking him far beyond psilocybin, LSD enabled Leary to accomplish the projects of the counterculture Dionysian ecstasies, mystic and bodily. He journeyed down the DNA ladder of evolution to the single cell at the beginning of life and then outward to the cosmic vibrations where he merged with pure energy, "the white light," nothingness. He also experienced the resurrection of the body. "Blow the mind and you are left with God and life—and life is sex," he said. Leary called LSD "a powerful aphrodisiac, probably the most powerful sexual releaser known to man. . . . The union was not just your body and her body but all of your racial and evolutionary entities with all of hers. It was mythic mating." *Playboy* asked Leary if it was true that women could have multiple orgasms under LSD. He replied with a straight face, "In a carefully prepared, loving LSD session, a woman can have several hundred orgasms." . . .

If Leary spread the psychedelic revolution, Ken Kesey created the psychedelic style, West Coast version. In 1959, three years before publication of his modern classic *One Flew Over the Cuckoos Nest,* Kesey took LSD as a subject in a medical experiment, and for him, then and there, the doors of perception blew wide open. In 1964, with a group of disciples called the Merry Pranksters, he established a drug commune in rural La Honda, an hour's drive from San Francisco. One of the Pranksters was Neal Cassady. On add, Kesey and friends experienced the illusion of self, the All-in-One, the energy field of which we are all an extension. They tried to break down psychic barriers, attain intersubjectivity or group mind, and achieve synchronization with the Cosmos. And they committed themselves to a life of Dionysian ecstasy.

The Pranksters were hip, but in a new way. They were not beaten disaffiliates, warring against technology land, cursing their fate that they had not been born black. In *The Electric Kool-Aid Acid Test,* a history of Kesey in the underground, Tom Wolfe described this new hip generation, these hippies, as products of postwar affluence. Their teen years were spent driving big cars through the California suburbs, believing, like the superheroes in their Marvel comics, that anything was possible. No spade cool for them, no Zen detachment, none of Leary's "set and setting." The Pranksters used LSD to propel themselves out of their skulls toward the outer edge of Western experience. Their style was the wacko style: lurid costumes, Day-Glo paint, crazy trips in Kesey's 1939 multicolored International Harvester school bus, complete with speakers, tapes, and microphones. It was lots of kicks, of course, but it was more than kicks. For Kesey was a religious prophet whose ultimate goal was to turn America, as Michael Bowen put it, into an "electric Tibet." . . .

The Dionysian impulse in the hippie counterculture was made up in equal measures of drugs, sex, and music—not jazz music but rock and roll. When hippies moved in, the black jazz bars on Haight Street moved out. Spade jazz was now as irrelevant to hip as spade soul. Rock had once been black music too, but was so thoroughly appropriated by whites that many hip kids never knew its origins. Rock originated in the 1940s as "rhythm and blues," an urban-based blues music played with electric instruments, pounding beat, and raunchy lyrics—music by blacks for blacks. In 1952 the legendary Cleveland disc jockey Alan Freed hosted the first rhythm and blues record show for a white audience, calling the music "rock and roll." The music caught on among teenagers tired of sexless, sentimental ballads, and soon white performers fused pop and country styles with rhythm and blues to create white rock and roll. That's what Elvis Presley sang when he emerged in 1956 to become the biggest star in pop history. From the beginning, rock and roll was protest music, protest against Tin Pan Alley, protest against parental taste, protest against instinctual repression. Music of the mid-fifties rock and roll helped create a generation of cultural subversives who would in time heed the siren song of hip.

In 1958, when Elvis went into the Army, rock entered a period of decline. Meanwhile, the black sound that had inspired it was being assimilated anew by other talented musicians, this time in England, and it would return to America, bigger than before, with the Beatles. During their long years of apprenticeship, playing lowerclass clubs in Liverpool and Hamburg, John Lennon, Paul McCartney, and George Harrison explored the roots of rock and roll, even as they slowly fashioned a style of their own. By 1963 that style had fully matured. No longer just another scruffy group of Teddy Boys playing electronic guitars, they had become well-tailored professionals with a distinctive hair style (Eton long), immense stage presence, the best song-writing team in pop history (Lennon and McCartney), a fluid sound, contagious vitality, and, above all, the irrepressible beat of rock and roll. The beat helped propel the Beatles to stardom in Britain in 1963 and created Beatlemania.

Within days of its release in the United States in January 1964, "I Want to Hold Your Hand" climbed to the top of the charts, to be followed quickly by "She Loves You" and "Please, Please Me." In February the Beatles themselves arrived for a tour that began with a sensational TV performance on the *Ed Sullivan Show* and continued before hysterical teen mobs in New York, Washington, and Miami. In April all five top singles in the United States were Beatles songs and the two top albums were Beatles albums. In July the first Beatles movie, *A Hard Day's Night,* amazed critics and delighted audiences with its wit and verve. Meanwhile that year Beatles merchandise—everything from dolls to dishcloths—was grossing over $50 million. Nothing comparable to Beatlemania had ever happened in the history of pop culture. . . .

The artist who first seized the power of rock and used it to change consciousness was Bob Dylan. Born Robert Zimmerman, Dylan tried on every style of teen alienation available during the fifties in Hibbing, Minnesota. Though he wanted to be a rock and roll star, he discovered on enrolling at the University of Minnesota in 1959 that folk music was the rage on campus. In 1961 Dylan arrived in Greenwich Village, the folk capital of America, determined to become the biggest folkie of them all. A little over a year later, he was. Audiences responded to his vulnerability, the nasal whine with which he delivered his songs, and lyrics so riveting they transformed the folk art. Immersing himself in the left-liberal-civil-rights ethos permeating the Village in the early 1960s, Dylan wrote folk songs as protest. He did not compose from the headlines, as other protest singers did. He used figurative language and elusive imagery to distill the political mood of his time and place. Gambling that a poet could become a star, he won big. Two weeks after Peter, Paul, and Mary recorded his song "Blowin' in the Wind," it sold more than 300,000 copies. Songs like "A Hard Rain's Gonna Fall" were hailed as true art. And his "Times They Are A-Changin'" became a generational anthem. It was no less appropriate for Dylan to sing at the 1963 March on Washington than for Martin Luther King to deliver a sermon there.

Meanwhile, the Beatles arrived and Dylan was listening. "Everybody else thought they were for the teenyboppers, that they were gonna pass right away," Dylan said. "But it was obvious to me that they had staying power. I knew they were pointing the direction of where music had to go." In July 1965 Dylan outraged the folk world by appearing at the Newport Folk Festival, no longer the ragged waif with acoustic guitar, but as a rock and roll singer, outfitted in black leather jacket and backed by an electric band. That summer his rock single, "Like a Rolling Stone," perhaps the greatest song he ever wrote, made it all the way to number one.

Dylan took rock and made it the medium for cultural statement-folk-rock, the critics quickly labeled it. As his music changed, so did the message. Moving with his generation, Dylan now abandoned liberal politics for cultural radicalism. The lyrics he sang in the midsixties were intensely personal and frequently obscure, but taken together, they formed a stunning mosaic of a corrupt and chaotic America. It is a fact of no small social consequence that in 1965 millions of radios and record players were daily pounding Dylan's message, subliminally or otherwise, into the skulls of a generation. There was, for example, "Highway 61," which depicted America as a junkyard road heading for war; "Maggie's Farm," a dropout's contemptuous farewell to the straight world; "Desolation Row," which portrayed an insane society, governed by insane men, teetering on the brink of apocalypse; "Ballad of a Thin Man," using homosexual imagery to describe an intellectual's confusion in a world bereft of reason; and "Gates of Eden," a mystical evocation of a realm beyond the senses, beyond ego, wherein resides the timeless Real. After Dylan, a host of other rock prophets arose to preach sex, love, peace, or revolution. After Dylan rock and roll became a music that both expressed the sixties counterculture and shaped it. . . .

By the time of the Monterey International Pop Festival, June 1967, the musical energies that had been gathering in San Francisco for two years could no longer be locally contained. Some of the hippie bands performing at the festival got their first national exposure there; others had already succumbed to the lure of fat recording contracts. By summer the San Francisco Sound was making the city the new rock mecca and its performers the newest rock superstars. The big song on the top forty stations that season was the Airplane's "White Rabbit," psychedelic variations on a theme from *Alice in Wonderland,* ending with the command to "feed a head, feed a head." That summer, too, thousands of teenagers took literally Scott McKenzie's musical invitation, with its implicit promise of Dionysian revels, to come to "San Francisco (Be Sure to Wear

Flowers in Your Hair)." Ralph Gleason, San Francisco's hip music critic, understood well the cultural significance of rock. "At no time in American history has youth possessed the strength it possesses now," he wrote. "Trained by music and linked by music, it has the power for good to change the world." Significantly, he added, "That power for good carries the reverse, the power for evil."

By 1967 Haight-Ashbury had attained a population large enough to merit, at last, the designation "counterculture." . . .

Ginsberg's was the authentic voice of Haight-Ashbury. Addicted to electronic amenities, hippies merely played at being Indians, satisfied to wear Navaho jewelry and feathers. They communed with nature by picking Golden Gate Park bare of flowers; their notion of tribal harmony was to let everyone "do their own thing." As love had supposedly done for the Hopi, soit would do for them: it would conquer all. Armed with "flower power," hippies would overwhelm their enemies and live a life of ecstasy on the asphalt pavements of urban America. . . .

Emmett Grogan was perhaps Haight-Ashbury's most influential citizen. A veteran of gang wars in New York, a student of film in Italy, a draftee who was discharged from the Army in 1966 as a schizophrenic, Grogan found a home in the San Francisco Mime Troupe, which performed radical plays free on the streets. He also plunged into the city's drug culture. Grogan, however, was no ordinary head. During his first LSD session in 1965 it had come to him in a flash of illumination that property was theft. Joined by a few others from the Mime Troupe, Grogan began issuing anonymous mimeographed essays to provide the Haight with some politics. He called his essays "Digger Papers," after the seventeenth-century English radicals who appropriated common land and gave their surplus to the poor. The Digger Papers attacked hip capitalists like Thelin for hypocrisy, the hip *Oracle* for pansyness, and the psychedelic transcendentalism of Swami Bhaktivedanta as "absolute bullshit." But action counted with Grogan more than words, because action was theater, and theater could alter consciousness by altering frame of reference. In October 1966 the Diggers announced that every day at 4 P.M., at the panhandle on Ashbury Street, they would distribute free food to anyone who wanted it. And very day for the next year, serving food they begged and food they stole, the Diggers kept their promise. . . .

By the summer of 1967 the Haight's bizarre cast of characters was performing for a national audience. This was the summer when Time described the neighborhood as "the vibrant epicenter of the hippie movement," hippies estimated their full-time population nationwide at 300,000, imitation Haight-Ashburys bloomed throughout urban America, acid rock dominated the music charts, prestigious museums exhibited psychedelic posters, and doing one's own thing became the national cliche. Once school ended, San Francisco expected one to two hundred thousand kids to flood the city for the Summer of Love. But the real story that summer, unreported by the media, was that few of the thousands who did come stayed very long, Haight-Ashbury was already dying.

Its demise, so similar to the demise of hippie ghettos elsewhere, resulted from official repression, black hostility, and media hype. In San Francisco where city fathers panicked at the prospect of runaway hordes descending upon them, police began routinely roughing up hippies, health officials harassed their communes, and narcotics agents infiltrated the neighborhood. Meanwhile, black hoods from the nearby Fillmore district cruised the streets, threatening rape and violence. Blacks did not like LSD, white kids pretending to be poor, or the fact that Haight-Ashbury was, in the words of a leftover beatnik, "the first segregated Bohemia I've ever seen." Longtime residents began staying home after dark. Finally, the beguiling images of Haight-Ashbury marketed by the media attracted not only an invasion of gawking tourists, but a floating population of the unstable, the psychotic, and the criminal. By the end of the year, *reported* crime in Haight-Ashbury included 17 murders, 100 rapes, and nearly 3,000 burglaries. . . .

As the decade closed, it became clear that drugs, sex, and rock and roll lacked intrinsic moral content. The acid prophets had warned from the beginning that LSD did not inevitably produce the God experience. God and the Devil resided together in the nervous system, Leary had said. LSD could evoke either, depending on set and setting. The streets of Haight-Ashbury, even in the best days, had been littered with kids who deranged their senses on drugs— only to experience spiritual stupor. A fair number ended their trips in hospital emergency rooms, possessed of one or another demon. Satanic cults were not unknown in the Haight. One of them, the Process, apparently influenced Charles Manson, a hippie who lived in the neighborhood in 1967 and recruited confused young girls and a few men into his "family." Manson was an "acid fascist" who somehow found in the lyrics of the Beatles license to commit ritual murder. As violence in the counterculture mounted, LSD became chiefly a means to pierce the false rationality of the hated bourgeois world. The always tenuous link between drugs and love was broken. . . .

Rock and roll was the principal art of the counterculture because of its demonstrable power to liberate the instincts. At the Woodstock Music Festival, held one weekend in August 1969 at Bethel, New York, Eros ran wild. An incredible 400,000 people gathered on a farm to hear the greatest line-up of rock talent ever assembled in one place. Overcoming conditions that could conventionally be described only as disastrous, the crowd created a loving community based on drugs, sex, and rock music. But four months later at the Altamont Raceway near San Francisco, rock revealed an equal affinity for death.

The occasion was a free concert conceived by the Rolling Stones as a fitting climax to their first American tour in three years and the documentary film that was recording it. Altamont was a calamity. Because of a last-minute cancellation elsewhere, concert promoters had only one day to ready the site for a crush of 300,000 kids. Sanitary facilities were inadequate; the sound system, terrible; the setting, cheerless. Lots of bad dope, including inferior acid spiked with speed, circulated through the crowd. Harried medics had to fly in an emergency supply of Thorazine to treat the epidemic of bad trips and were kept busy administering first aid to victims of the random violence. The violence originated with the Hell's Angels. On the advice of the Grateful Dead, the Stones had hired the Angels to guard the stage for $500 worth of beer. Armed with loaded pool cues sawed-off to the length of billy clubs, high on bad dope washed down with Red Mountain vin rose, Angels indiscriminately clubbed people for offenses real or imagined. . . .

At nightfall, after keeping the crowd waiting in the cold for more than an hour, the Rolling Stones came on stage. Many critics regarded the Stones as the greatest rock and roll band in the world. Ever since their emergence, they had carefully cultivated an outlaw image—lewd, sneering, surly—to differentiate themselves from their fellow Britons, the Beatles. Their most recent music, including, notably. "Street Fighting Man" and "Sympathy for the Devil,"

reflected the growing violence of the culture of which they were
superstars. Now at Altamont there was Mick Jagger, reveling in his
image as rock's prince of evil, prancing on stage while the Angels
flailed away with their pool cues below. It was too much even for
him. Jagger stopped the music more than once to plead for order;
but when the Angels ignored him, he had no choice except to sing
on. Midway through "Sympathy for the Devil," only a few feet from
the stage, an Angel knifed a black man named Meredith Hunter to
death.

For a variety of reasons, after 1970 the counterculture faded. Eco-
nomic recession signaled that affluence could no longer be assumed
and induced a certain caution among the young. The Vietnam
War, which did so much to discredit authority, rapidly de-escalated.
And its own revels brought the hippie movement into disrepute.
Carried to the edge of sanity by their Dionysian revels, many of the
once hip retreated, some to rural communes in New Mexico or
Vermont, most all the way back to the straight world. . . .

The Forgotten American

Peter Schrag

Inevitably, the social protests of the 1960s provoked a counter-response. By the end of the decade a group, dubbed by the media as "middle-Americans," had rallied to the defense of the flag, traditional authority, and good manners. One definition of "middle-Americans" was primarily economic. Earning between $5,000 and $15,000 a year they made up 55 percent of the population. The majority were blue-collar workers, lower-echelon bureaucrats, schoolteachers, and white-collar employees. As they saw the federal government pour money into impoverished areas, they developed a sense of neglect and resentment, believing that they were being ignored while vocal protestors received all the attention. Just as important, however was a sense of crisis in cultural values, a belief that the rules were being changed in midstream. As Newsweek's *Karl Fleming observed, middle Americans felt "threatened by a terrifying array of enemies: hippies, Black Panthers, drugs, the sexually liberated, those who questioned the sanctity of marriage and the morality of work." Anti-war protests galvanized these "middle Americans" into action. From their perspective, it was blasphemy to wear the American flag on the seat of one's pants, burn one's draft card, or shout obscenities at authorities. In the following selection, Peter Schrag describes the resentments and values of middle Americans, illuminating just how profound the polarization of the 1960s was, and perceptively explaining why so many would turn from the party of the New Deal to increasingly conservative candidates.*

There is hardly a language to describe him, or even a set of social statistics. Just names: racist-bigot-redneck-ethnic-Irish-Italian-Pole-Hunkie-Yahoo. The lower middle class. A blank. The man under whose hat lies the great American desert. Who watches the tube, plays the horses, and keeps the niggers out of his union and his neighborhood. Who might vote for Wallace (but didn't). Who cheers when the cops beat up on demonstrators. Who is free, white, and twenty-one, has a job, a home, a family, and is up to his eyeballs in credit. In the guise of the working class—or the American yeoman or John Smith—he was once the hero of the civics books, the man that Andrew Jackson called "the bone and sinew of the country." Now he is "the forgotten man," perhaps the most alienated person in America.

Nothing quite fits, except perhaps omission and semi-invisibility. America is supposed to be divided between affluence and poverty, between slums and suburbs. John Kenneth Galbraith begins the foreword to *The Affluent Society* with the phrase, "Since I sailed for Switzerland in the early summer of 1955 to begin work on this book. . . . " But *between* slums and suburbs, between Scarsdale and Harlem, between Wellesley and Roxbury, between Shaker Heights and Hough, there are some eighty million people (depending on how you count them) who didn't sail for Switzerland in the summer of 1955, or at any other time, and who never expect to go. Between slums and suburbs: South Boston and South San Francisco, Bell and Parma, Astoria and Bay Ridge, Newark, Cicero, Downey, Daly City, Charlestown, Flatbush. Union halls, American Legion posts, neighborhood bars, and bowling leagues, the Ukrainian Club and the Holy Name. Main Street. To try to describe all this is like trying to describe America itself. If you look for it, you find it everywhere: the rows of frame houses overlooking the belching steel mills in Bethlehem, Pennsylvania; two-family brick houses in Canarsie (where the most common slogan, even in the middle of a political campaign, is "curb your dog"); the Fords and Chevies with a decal American flag on the rear window (usually a cut-out from the *Reader's Digest,* and displayed in counter-protest against peaceniks and "those bastards who carry Vietcong flags in demonstrations"); the bunting on the porch rail with the inscription, "Welcome Home, Pete." The gold star in the window. . . .

He does all the right things, obeys the law, goes to church and insists—usually—that his kids get a better education than he had. But the right things don't seem to be paying off. While he is making more than he ever made—perhaps more than he'd ever dreamed— he's still struggling while a lot of others—"them" (on welfare, in demonstrations, in the ghettos) are getting most of the attention. "I'm working my ass off," a guy tells you on a stoop in South Boston. "My kids don't have a place to swim, my parks are full of glass, and I'm supposed to bleed for a bunch of people on relief." In New York a man who drives a Post Office trailer truck at night (4:00 P.M. to midnight) and a cab during the day (7:00 A.M. to 2:00 P.M.), and who hustles radios for his Post Office buddies on the side, is ready, as he says, to "knock somebody's ass." "The colored guys work when they feel like it. Sometimes they show up and sometimes they don't. One guy tore up all the time cards. I'd like to see a white guy do that and get away with it."

WHAT COUNTS

Nobody knows how many people in America moonlight (half of the eighteen million families in the $5000 to $10,000 bracket have two or more wage earners) or how many have to hustle on the side. "I don't think anybody has a single job anymore," said Nicholas Kisburg, the research director for a Teamsters Union Council in New York. "All the cops are moonlighting, and the teachers; and there's a million guys who are hustling, guys with phony social-security numbers who are hiding part of what they make so they don't get kicked out of a housing project, or guys who work as guards at sports events and get free meals that they don't want to pay taxes on. Every one of them is cheating. They are underground people—*Untermenschen*. . . . We really have no systematic data on any of this. We have no ideas of the attitudes of the white worker. (We've been too busy studying the black worker.) And yet he's the source of most of the reaction in this country."

The reaction is directed at almost every visible target: at integration and welfare, taxes and sex education, at the rich and the poor, the foundations and students, at the "smart people in the suburbs." In New York State the legislature cuts the welfare budget; in Los Angeles, the voters reelect Yorty after a whispered racial campaign against the Negro favorite. In Minneapolis a police detective named Charles Stenvig, promising "to take the handcuffs off the police," wins by a margin stunning even to his supporters: in Massachusetts the voters mail tea bags to their representatives in protest against new taxes, and in state after state legislatures are passing bills to punish student demonstrators. ("We keep talking about permissiveness in training kids," said a Los Angeles labor official, "but we forget that these are our kids.")

And yet all these things are side manifestations of a malaise that lacks a language. Whatever law and order means, for example, to a man who feels his wife is unsafe on the street after dark or in the park at any time, or whose kids get shaken down in the school yard, it also means something like normality—the demand that everybody play it by the book, that cultural and social standards be somehow restored to their civics-book simplicity, that things shouldn't be as they are but as they were supposed to be. If there is a revolution in this country—a revolt in manners, standards of dress and obscenity, and, more importantly, in our official sense of what America is—there is also a counter-revolt. Sometimes it is inarticulate, and sometimes (perhaps most of the time) people are either too confused or apathetic—or simply too polite and too decent—to declare themselves. In Astoria, Queens, a white working-class district of New York, people who make $7000 or $8000 a year (sometimes in two jobs) call themselves affluent, even though the Bureau of Labor Statistics regards an income of less than $9500 in New York inadequate to a moderate standard of living. And in a similar neighborhood in Brooklyn a truck driver who earns $151 a week tells you he's doing well, living in a two-story frame house separated by a narrow driveway from similar houses, thousands of them in block after block. This year, for the first time, he will go on a cruise—he and his wife and two other couples—two weeks in the Caribbean. He went to work after World War II ($57 a week) and he has lived in the same house for twenty years, accumulating two television sets, wall-to-wall carpeting in a small living room, and a basement that he recently remodeled into a recreation room with the help of two moonlighting firemen. "We get fairly good salaries, and this is a good neighborhood, one of the few good ones left. We have no smoked Irishmen around."

Stability is what counts, stability in job and home and neighborhood, stability in the church and in friends. At night you watch television and sometimes on a weekend you go to a nice place—maybe a downtown hotel—for dinner with another couple. (Or maybe your sister, or maybe bowling, or maybe, if you're defeated, a night at the track.) The wife has the necessary appliances, often still being paid off and the money you save goes for your daughter's orthodontist, and later for her wedding. The smoked Irishmen—the colored (no one says black; few even say Negro)—represent change and instability, kids who cause trouble in school, who get treatment that your kids never got, that you never got. ("Those fucking kids," they tell you in South Boston, "raising hell, and not one of 'em paying his own way. Their fucking mothers are all on welfare.") The black kids mean a change in the rules, a double standard in grades and discipline, and—vaguely—a challenge to all you believed right. Law and order is the stability and predictability of established ways. Law and order is equal treatment—in school, in jobs, in the courts—even if you're cheating a little yourself. The Forgotten Man is Jackson's man. He is the vestigial American democrat of 1840: "They all know that their success depends upon their own industry and economy and that they must not expect to become suddenly rich by the fruits of their toil." He is also Franklin Roosevelt's man—the man whose vote (or whose father's vote) sustained the New Deal. . . .

AT THE BOTTOM OF THE WELL

American culture? Wealth is visible, and so, now, is poverty. Both have become intimidating clichés. But the rest? A vast, complex, and disregarded world that was once—in belief, and in fact—the American middle: Greyhound and Trailways bus terminals in little cities at midnight, each of them with its neon lights and its cardboard hamburgers; acres of tar-paper beach bungalows in places like Revere and Rockaway; the hair curlers in the supermarket on Saturday, and the little girls in the communion dresses the next morning; pinball machines and the *Daily News*, the *Reader's Digest* and Ed Sullivan; houses with tiny front lawns (or even large ones) adorned with statues of the Virgin or of Sambo welcomin' de folks home; Clint Eastwood or Julie Andrews at the Palace; the trotting tracks and the dog tracks—Aurora Downs, Connaught Park, Roosevelt, Yonkers, Rockingham, and forty others—where gray men come not for sport and beauty, but to read numbers, to study and dope. (If you win you have figured something, have in a small way controlled your world, have surmounted your impotence. If you lose, bad luck, shit. "I'll break his goddamned head.") Baseball is not the national pastime; racing is. For every man who goes to a major-league baseball game there are four who go to the track and probably four more who go to the candy store or the barbershop to make their bets. (Total track attendance in 1965: 62 million plus another 10 million who went to the dogs.)

There are places, and styles, and attitudes. If there are neighborhoods of aspiration, suburban enclaves for the mobile young executive and the aspiring worker, there are also places of limited expectation and dead-end districts where mobility is finished. But even there you can often find, however vestigial, a sense of place, the roots of old ethnic loyalties, and a passionate, if often futile, battle against intrusion and change. "Everybody around here," you are told, "pays his own way." In this world the problems are not the ABM or air pollution (have they heard of Biafra?) or the international population crisis; the problem is to get your street cleaned, your garbage collected, to get your husband home from Vietnam alive; to negotiate installment payments and to keep the schools orderly. Ask anyone in Scarsdale or Winnetka about the schools and they'll tell you about new programs, or about how many are getting into Harvard, or about the teachers; ask in Oakland or the North Side of Chicago, and they'll tell you that they have (or haven't) had trouble. Somewhere in his gut the man in those communities knows that mobility and choice in this society are limited. He cannot imagine any major change for the better; but he can imagine change for the worse. And yet for a decade he is the one who has been asked to carry the burden of social reform, to integrate his schools and his neighborhood, has been asked by comfortable people to pay the social debts due to the poor and the black. In Boston, in San Francisco, in Chicago (not to mention Newark or Oakland) he has been telling the reformers to go to hell. The Jewish schoolteachers of New York and the Irish parents of Dorchester have asked the same question: "What the hell did Lindsay (or the Beacon Hill Establishment) ever do for us?"

The ambiguities and changes in American life that occupy discussions in university seminars and policy debates in Washington, and that form the backbone of contemporary popular sociology, become increasingly the conditions of trauma and frustration in the middle. Although the New Frontier and Great Society contained some programs for those not already on the rolls of social pathology—federal aid for higher education, for example—the public priorities and the rhetoric contained little. The emphasis, properly, was on the poor, on the inner cities (e.g., Negroes) and the unemployed. But in Chicago a widow with three children who earns $7000 a year can't get them college loans because she makes too much; the money is reserved for people on relief. New schools are built in the ghetto but not in the white working-class neighborhoods where they are just as dilapidated. In Newark the head of a white vigilante group (now a city councilman) runs, among other things, on a platform opposing pro-Negro discrimination. "When pools are being built in the Central Ward—don't they think white kids have got frustration? The white can't get a job; we have to hire Negroes first." The middle class, said Congressman Roman Pucinski of Illinois, who represents a lot of it, "is in revolt. Everyone has been generous in supporting anti-poverty. Now the middle-class American is disqualified from most of the programs."

"SOMEBODY HAS TO SAY NO . . ."

The frustrated middle. The liberal wisdom about welfare, ghettos, student revolt, and Vietnam has only a marginal place, if any, for the values and life of the workingman. It flies in the face of most of what he was taught to cherish and respect: hard work, order, authority, self-reliance. He fought, either alone or through labor organizations, to establish the precincts he now considers his own. Union seniority, the civil-service bureaucracy, and the petty professionalism established by the merit system in the public schools become sinecures of particular ethnic groups or of those who have learned to negotiate and master the system. A man who worked all his life to accumulate the points and grades and paraphernalia to become an assistant school principal (no matter how silly the requirements) is not likely to relinquish his position with equanimity. Nor is a dock worker whose only estate is his longshoreman's card. The job, the points, the credits become property:

> Some men leave their sons money [wrote a union member to the *New York Times*], some large investments, some business connections, and some a profession. I have only one worthwhile thing to give: my trade. I hope to follow a centuries-old tradition and sponsor my sons for an apprenticeship. For this simple father's wish it is said that I discriminate against Negroes. Don't all of us discriminate? Which of us . . . will not choose a son over all others?

Suddenly the rules are changing—all the rules. If you protect your job for your own you may be called a bigot. At the same time it's perfectly acceptable to shout black power and to endorse it. What does it take to be a good American? *Give the black man a position because he is black, not because he necessarily works harder or does the job better.* What does it take to be a good American? Dress nicely, hold a job, be clean-cut, don't judge a man by the color of his skin or the country of his origin. What about the demands of Negroes, the long hair of the students, the dirty movies, the people who burn drafts cards and American flags? Do you have to go out in the street with picket signs, do you have to burn the place down to get what you want? What does it take to be a good American? *This is a sick society, a racist society, we are fighting an immoral war.* ("I'm against the Vietnam war, too," says the truck driver in Brooklyn. "I see a good kid come home with half an arm and a leg in a brace up to here, and what's it all for? I was glad to see *my kid* flunk the Army physical. Still, somebody has to say no to these demonstrators and enforce the law.") What does it take to be a good American?

The conditions of trauma and frustration in the middle. What does it take to be a good American? Suddenly there are demands for Italian power and Polish power and Ukrainian power. In Cleveland the Poles demand a seat on the school board, and get it, and in Pittsburgh, John Pankuch, the seventy-three-year-old president of the National Slovak Society, demands "action, plenty of it to make up for lost time." Black power is supposed to be nothing but emulation of the ways in which other ethnic groups made it. But have they made it? In Reardon's Bar on East Eighth Street in South Boston, where the workmen come for their fish-chowder lunch and for their rye and ginger, they still identify themselves as Galway men and Kilkenny men; in the newsstand in Astoria you can buy *Il Progresso, El Tiempo,* the *Staats-Zeitung,* the *Irish World,* plus papers in Greek, Hungarian, and Polish. At the parish of Our Lady of Mount Carmel the priests hear confession in English, Italian, and Spanish and, nearby, the biggest attraction is not the stickball game, but the *bocce* court. Some of the poorest people in America are white, native, and have lived all of their lives in the same place as their fathers and grandfathers. The problems that were presumably solved in some distant past, in that prehistoric era before the textbooks were written—problems of assimilation, of upward mobility—now turn out to be very much unsolved. The melting pot and all: millions made it, millions moved to the affluent suburbs; several million—no one knows how many—did not. The median income in Irish South Boston is $5100 a year but the community-action workers have a hard time convincing the local citizens that any white man who is not stupid or irresponsible can be poor. Pride still keeps them from applying for income supplements or Medicaid, but it does not keep them from resenting those who do. In Pittsburgh, where the members of Polish-American organizations earn an estimated $5000 to $6000 (and some fall below the poverty line), the Poverty Programs are nonetheless directed primarily to Negroes, and almost everywhere the thing called urban backlash associates itself in some fashion with ethnic groups whose members have themselves only a precarious hold on the security of affluence. Almost everywhere in the old cities, tribal neighborhoods and their styles are under assault by masscult. The Italian grocery gives way to the supermarket, the ma-and-pa store and the walk-up are attacked by urban renewal. And almost everywhere, that assault tends to depersonalize and to alienate. It has always been this way, but with time the brave new world that replaces the old patterns becomes increasingly bureaucratized, distant, and hard to control.

Yet beyond the problems of ethnic identity, beyond the problems of Poles and Irishmen left behind, there are others more pervasive and more dangerous. For every Greek or Hungarian there are a dozen American-Americans who are past ethnic consciousness and who are as alienated, as confused, and as angry as the rest. The obvious manifestations are the same everywhere—race, taxes, welfare, students—but the threat seems invariably more cultural and psychological than economic or social. What upset the police at the Chicago convention most was not so much the politics of the demonstrators as their manners and their hair. (The barbershops in their neighborhoods don't advertise Beatle Cuts but the Flat Top and the Chicago Box.) The affront comes from middle-class people—and their children—who had been cast in the role of social exemplars (and from those cast as unfortunates worthy of public charity) who offend all the things on which working class identity is built: "hippies [said a San Francisco longshoreman] who fart around the streets and don't work"; welfare recipients who strike and march for better treatment; "all those [said a California labor official] who challenge the precepts that these people live on." If ethnic groups are beginning to organize to get theirs, so are others:

police and firemen ("The cop is the new nigger"); schoolteachers; lower-middle-class housewives fighting sex education and bussing; small property owners who have no ethnic communion but a passionate interest in lower taxes, more policemen, and stiffer penalties for criminals. In San Francisco the Teamsters, who had never been known for such interests before, recently demonstrated in support of the police and law enforcement and, on another occasion, joined a group called Mothers Support Neighborhood Schools at a school-board meeting to oppose—with their presence and later, apparently, with their fists—a proposal to integrate the schools through bussing. . . .

WHEN HOPE BECOMES A THREAT

The imponderables are youth and tradition and change. The civics book and the institution it celebrates—however passé—still hold the world together. The revolt is in their name, not against them. And there is simple decency, the language and practice of the folksy cliche, the small town, the Boy Scout virtues, the neighborhood charity, the obligation to support the church, the rhetoric of open opportunity: "They can keep Wallace and they can keep Alabama. We didn't fight a dictator for four years so we could elect one over here." What happens when all that becomes Mickey Mouse? Is there an urban ethic to replace the values of the small town? Is there a coherent public philosophy, a consistent set of beliefs to replace family, home, and hard work? What happens when the hang-ups of upper-middle-class kids are in fashion and those of blue-collar kids are not? What happens when Doing Your Own Thing becomes not the slogan of the solitary deviant but the norm? Is it possible that as the institutions and beliefs of tradition are fashionably denigrated a blue-collar generation gap will open to the Right as well as to the Left? (There is statistical evidence, for example, that Wallace's greatest support within the unions came from people who are between twenty-one and twenty-nine, those, that is, who have the most tenuous association with the liberalism of labor.) Most are politically silent; although SDS has been trying to organize blue-collar high-school students, there are no Mario Savios or Mark Rudds—either of the Right or the Left—among them. At the same time the union leaders, some of them old hands from the Thirties, aren't sure that the kids are following them either. Who speaks for the son of the longshoreman or the Detroit auto worker? What happens if he doesn't get to college? What, indeed, happens when he does?

Vaguely but unmistakably the hopes that a youth-worshiping nation historically invested in its young become threats. We have never been unequivocal about the symbolic patricide of Americanization and upward mobility, but if at one time mobility meant rejection of older (or European) styles it was, at least, done in the name of America. Now the labels are blurred and the objectives indistinct. Just at the moment when a tradition-bound Italian father is persuaded that he should send his sons to college—that education is the only future—the college blows up. At the moment when a parsimonious taxpayer begins to shell out for what he considers an extravagant state university system the students go on strike. Marijuana, sexual liberation, dress styles, draft resistance, even the rhetoric of change become monsters and demons in a world that appears to turn old virtues upside down. The paranoia that fastened on Communism twenty years ago (and sometimes still does) is increasingly directed to vague conspiracies undermining the schools, the family, order and discipline. "They're feeding the kids this generation-gap business," says a Chicago housewife who grinds out a campaign against sex education on a duplicating machine in her living room. "The kids are told to make their own decisions. They're all mixed up by situation ethics and open-ended questions. They're alienating children from their own parents." They? The churches, the schools, even the YMCA and the Girl Scouts, are implicated. But a major share of the villainy is now also attributed to "the social science centers," to the apostles of sensitivity training, and to what one California lady, with some embarrassment, called "nude therapy." "People with sane minds are being altered by psychological methods." The current major campaign of the John Birch Society is not directed against Communists in government or the Supreme Court, but against sex education. . . .

CAN THE COMMON MAN COME BACK?

Beneath it all there is a more fundamental ambivalence, not only about the young, but about institutions—the schools, the churches, the Establishment—and about the future itself. In the major cities of the East (though perhaps not in the West) there is a sense that time is against you, that one is living "in one of the few decent neighborhoods left," that "if I can get $125 a week upstate (or downstate) I'll move." The institutions that were supposed to mediate social change and which, more than ever, are becoming priesthoods of information and conglomerates of social engineers, are increasingly suspect. To attack the Ford Foundation (as Wright Patman has done) is not only to fan the embers of historic populism against concentrations of wealth and power, but also to arouse those who feel that they are trapped by an alliance of upper-class Wasps and lower-class Negroes. If the foundations have done anything for the blue-collar worker he doesn't seem to be aware of it. At the same time the distrust of professional educators that characterizes the black militants is becoming increasingly prevalent among the minority of lower-middle-class whites who are beginning to discover that the schools aren't working for them either. ("Are all those new programs just a cover-up for failure?") And if the Catholic Church is under attack from its liberal members (on birth control, for example) it is also alienating the traditionalists who liked their minor saints (even if they didn't actually exist) and were perfectly content with the Latin Mass. For the alienated Catholic liberal there are other places to go; for the lower-middle-class parishioner in Chicago or Boston there are none.

Perhaps, in some measure, it has always been this way. Perhaps none of this is new. And perhaps it is also true that the American lower middle has never had it so good. And yet surely there is a difference, and that is that the common man has lost his visibility and, somehow, his claim on public attention. There are old liberals and socialists—men like Michael Harrington—who believe that a new alliance can be forged for progressive social action:

> From Marx to Mills, the Left has regarded the middle class as a stratum of hypocritical vacillating rear-guarders. There was often sound reason for this contempt. But is it not possible that a new class is coming into being? It is not the old middle class of small property owners and entrepreneurs, nor the new middle class of managers. It is composed of scientists, technicians, teachers, and professionals in the public sector of the society. By education and work experience it is predisposed toward planning. It could be an ally of the poor and the organized workers—or their sophisticated enemy. In other

words, an unprecedented social and political variable seems to be taking shape in America.

The American worker, even when he waits on a table or holds open a door, is not servile; he does not carry himself like an inferior. The openness, frankness, and democratic manner which Tocqueville described in the last century persists to this very day. They have been a source of rudeness, contemptuous ignorance, violence—and of a creative self-confidence among great masses of people. It was in this latter spirit that the CIO was organized and the black freedom movement marched.

There are recent indications that the white lower middle class is coming back on the roster of public priorities. Pucinski tells you that liberals in Congress are privately discussing the pressure from the middle class. There are proposals now to increase personal income-tax exemptions from $600 to $1000 (or $1200) for each dependent, to protect all Americans with a national insurance system covering catastrophic medical expenses, and to put a floor under all incomes. Yet these things by themselves are insufficient. Nothing is sufficient without a national sense of restoration. What Pucinski means by the middle class has, in some measure, always been represented. A physician earning $75,000 a year is also a working man but he is hardly a victim of the welfare system. Nor, by and large, are the stockholders of the Standard Oil Company or U.S. Steel. The fact that American ideals have often been corrupted in the cause of self-aggrandizement does not make them any less important for the cause of social reform and justice. "As a movement with the conviction that there is more to people than greed and fear," Harrington said, "the Left must . . . also speak in the name of the historic idealism of the United States."

The issue, finally, is not *the program* but the vision, the angle of view. A huge constituency may be coming up for grabs, and there is considerable evidence that its political mobility is more sensitive than anyone can imagine, that all the sociological determinants are not as significant as the simple facts of concern and leadership. When Robert Kennedy was killed last year, thousands of working-class people who had expected to vote for him—if not hundreds of thousands—shifted their loyalties to Wallace. A man who can change from a progressive democrat into a bigot overnight deserves attention.

Part 7

POLITICS OF
THE 1970s AND 1980s

The 1970s represented the end of an era. Throughout the thirty
years after World War II American politics had functioned on the
premise that nothing was impossible if America wished to achieve it.
We would be guardians of freedom, send a man to the moon,
conquer social injustice, eliminate poverty, develop impressive
technology—in short, control the universe. That sense of confidence and of power had been a hallmark of all political factions in
the country, even young radicals who thought that by their own
endeavors they could change the world. In the 1970s, however, a
new sense of limits struck home. The United States had suffered its
first loss in war. Richard Nixon became the first president forced to
resign in disgrace, in large part because he himself had no sense of
limits as to how far he could abuse presidential power. The oil
producing countries of OPEC quickly made Americans conscious
of their dependence on the rest of the world during the 1973–74 oil
boycott, and the sporadic shortages thereafter. When Iranian revolutionaries held American diplomats hostage for more than a year,
the sense of being subject to powers beyond one's control became a
reality reinforced by every newscast. The American tendency toward what the Greeks call *hubris*—the arrogant confidence that one
can do anything—had come face to face with the realities of human
frailty, mortality, and interdependency.

If tragedy is the working out of a fatal flaw that eventually destroys one's hopes, the Nixon administration represents perhaps
the purest example of American political tragedy. Nixon's own
political life covered the entire span of the postwar period. First
elected to Congress in 1946, he came to power through his active
participation in the anti-communist campaign of the postwar era,

and particularly his investigation of Alger Hiss. As vice president under Dwight Eisenhower, Nixon led the attack on liberals, accusing Democratic presidential-nominee Adlai Stevenson of being soft on communism. It seemed to many that Nixon's career was over after he lost the presidential election to John Kennedy in 1960 and then two years later was defeated for the governorship of California. But Nixon's most fundamental characteristic was his tenacity. One of a series of "new" Nixons emerged in the middle 1960s, and in 1968, a supposedly more mature, relaxed, and flexible Nixon offered himself to the American people with a plan to end the war in Vietnam, and to "bring us together again."

Nixon's presidency was a series of contradictions. On the one hand, he scored major triumphs in foreign policy. As only an inveterate anti-communist could do, Nixon opened the door to China, reversing three decades of anti-Chinese policy in a period of weeks. Nixon also pressed hard for a relaxation of tensions with the Soviet Union, seeking to build a world order where Europe, China, the Soviet Union, and the United States could operate in a relative balance of power. He made major strides toward stability in the Middle East, using Presidential Advisor and Secretary of State Henry Kissinger to promote exchanges between Arab countries and Israel that might provide a basis for lasting peace in that area.

But these major achievements in foreign policy were dwarfed by Nixon's abuse of power domestically and his almost inherent refusal to speak candidly of his goals. He promised to end the war in Vietnam, then expanded the war by the massive secret bombing of Cambodia. He pledged to run an open administration, then placed wiretaps on reporters and administration officials. The underlying problem was one of duplicity and pettiness. In order to disguise the illegal bombing of Cambodia, orders were given that military reports should be falsified. When former Pentagon official Daniel Ellsberg released the Pentagon Papers, an internal study of how the Vietnam war had come about, Nixon sought to discredit Ellsberg by having a secret unit of investigators—called the "plumbers"—break into Ellsberg's psychiatrist's office to get harmful information about him. Angry at antiwar demonstrators and those Democrats who supported them, the president encouraged a series of efforts, official and unofficial, to dig up information that would injure his opponents. The operation came to a head during the 1972 reelection campaign, when CREEP, the Committee to Reelect the President, sponsored break-ins and wiretaps as well as false letters and rumors to subvert the Democratic opposition. When some of CREEP's "plumbers," attempting to break in at the Democratic National Headquarters at the Watergate building, were caught, the entire web began to unravel.

The story of Watergate, like the story of Vietnam, embodies the ultimate destruction that occurs when tactics and weapons are used that go too far and stretch limits of tolerance beyond their capacity. Americans did not want to believe that My Lai had occurred, that their president had lied about the bombing of Cambodia, or that the White House had been involved in the kind of "dirty tricks" that subverted basic American freedoms and violated the law of the land. But as newspaper and congressional investigations eventually demonstrated, there was no end to the Nixon's administration's abuse of trust. America's basic faith in her political system was called into question. The country had been betrayed.

Jimmy Carter spoke directly to that sense of betrayal when in 1976 he told the American people that they deserved a government as good as they were, one based upon faith, honesty, integrity, dignity, and respect for traditional American values. Gerald Ford, Nixon's vice president, had done a superb job of healing the immediate wounds left by Watergate, but Carter offered an almost religious salve designed to reverse the damage. Running on the platform of an outsider who would bring a fresh perspective to Washington, Carter seemed to represent the simplicity and decency that would restore the faith of Americans in their political process.

The problem was that Carter knew very little about getting along in Washington. Oftentimes insensitive toward Congress, he entered into a permanent deadlock with the major institutions of the society. Although he accomplished some positive goals in foreign policy, particularly with the Camp David accords in the Middle East, he was never able to deliver on his pledge of turning the government around. While he diagnosed and articulated the crisis of confidence that existed in the American political process in the post-Nixon years, he was unable to mobilize support for constructive solutions to that crisis. The intractable problems of energy and Iran accurately reflected the sense of powerlessness that seemed to paralyze his administration.

The election of Ronald Reagan represented still another effort to recover what had been lost, this time by going back to a rhetoric and program that reminded the United States of its former power and moral leadership. Reagan possessed the genius to make people believe in simple verities. America should be strong. Communism represented a false God and the Soviet Union an "evil empire." Free enterprise worked. And every individual should be responsible for him or her self. With remarkable skill, the new president pushed through legislation to cut taxes, prune social welfare benefits, dramatically increase military expenditures, and restore conservative values. Reagan's success coincided with the rapid growth of the New Right, a congeries of single-issue groups that focused on returning the country to the bedrock values of family discipline, evangelical Christianity, and patriotism. Whether galvanized by the Equal Rights Amendment, abortion, school busing, homosexuality, or prayer in the schools, such New Right groups added a different dimension to the American political scene. For many, Ronald Reagan was a true hero. And when he scored a decisive triumph in his reelection bid in 1984, the conservative ascendancy seemed to have reached its zenith.

Yet both in 1980 and 1984, Reagan had been elected by less than 30 percent of those Americans eligible to vote. Almost half of the electorate had failed to go to the polls, dramatizing the alienation and sense of distance that millions felt toward the political process. Many of those same people who had not voted became the primary victims of Reagan's social policies, as food stamps were cut, housing subsidies reduced, and health care benefits trimmed. Even as Reagan talked about restoring America's greatness, larger and larger segments of the population seemed to have no stake whatsoever in the government that ruled them.

The following selections chronicle this story of America in the 1970s and 1980s. Jonathan Schell explores the intricacies of Watergate, giving us some flavor of the bizarre quality of the Nixon White House. Jimmy Carter's 1978 energy speech poignantly presents his ability to articulate the "malaise of the American spirit" even as it reveals his failure to come forward with effective answers, while Ronald Reagan's "The Second American Revolution" effectively conveys the buoyancy and sense of direction he brought to American politics. Kevin Phillips's article, on the other hand, describes the social cost of the Reagan revolution.

Some of the questions that remain are whether it is possible for a democracy to function when half of its people fail to vote (as opposed to voting rates of over 80 percent in most western European democracies), how successful the American political system was in dealing with the poison of Watergate, and whether it is good or bad to accept a sense of limits on America's national power. Such questions are crucial not only for understanding the 1970s and 1980s, but also for assessing what policies are appropriate for the 1990s and the twenty-first century.

Watergate

Jonathan Schell

If the decade of the 1960s is remembered for the war in Vietnam and civil rights, the decade of the 1970s will inevitbly be associated with Watergate. Through a bizarre series of events, the Nixon administration found itself in a situation where, in order to cover up high-level involvement in a burglary, it created a set of circumstances that brought down the entire administration. The ironies of the situation were endless. Nixon had such a commanding lead over his opponents that virtually no one could challenge him, yet in order to gain a still greater edge, he, or his associates, authorized a break-in at Democratic national headquarters. Even with the evidence turned up by journalists and congressional hearings, Nixon would probably have remained in office, yet the taping system he himself had installed in order to preserve history tripped him up. Perhaps appropriately, the man who sought office in order to "bring us together again" ended up accomplishing his purpose by uniting the country in revulsion against his unconstitutional actions. Jonathan Schell presents here a vivid portrait of how and why the Watergate episode occurred, revealing in the process the dangers inherent in what Arthur Schlesinger, Jr., has called "the imperial presidency."

At some point back at the beginning of the Vietnam war, long before Richard Nixon became President, American history had split into two streams. One flowed aboveground, the other underground. At first, the underground stream was only a trickle of events. But during the nineteen sixties—the period mainly de-

From *The Time of Illusion* by Jonathan Schell. Copyright © 1975 by Jonathan Schell. Reprinted by permission of Alfred A. Knopf, Inc. Originally appeared in *The New Yorker*.

scribed in the Pentagon Papers—the trickle grew to a torrent, and a significant part of the record of foreign affairs disappeared from public view. In the Nixon years, the torrent flowing underground began to include events in the domestic sphere, and soon a large part of the domestic record, too, had plunged out of sight. By 1972, an elaborate preelection strategy—the Administration strategy of dividing the Democrats—was unfolding in deep secrecy. And this strategy of dividing the Democrats governed not only a program of secret sabotage and espionage but the formation of Administration policy on the most important issues facing the nation. Indeed, hidden strategies for consolidating Presidential authority had been governing expanding areas of Administration policy since 1969, when it first occurred to the President to frame policy not to solve what one aide called "real problems" but to satisfy the needs of public relations. As more and more events occurred out of sight, the aboveground, public record of the period became impoverished and misleading. It became a carefully smoothed surface beneath which many of the most significant events of the period were being concealed. In fact, the split between the Administration's real actions and policies was largely responsible for the new form of government that had arisen in the Nixon White House—a form in which images consistently took precedence over substance, and affairs of state were ruled by what the occupants of the White House called scenarios. The methods of secrecy and the techniques of public relations were necessary to one another, for the people, lacking access to the truth, had to be told something, and it was the public-relations experts who decided what that something would be.

When the President made his trip to Russia, some students of government who had been worried about the crisis of the American Constitutional system allowed themselves to hope that the relaxation of tensions in the international sphere would spread to the domestic sphere. Since the tensions at home had grown out of events in the international sphere in the first place, it seemed reasonable to assume that an improvement in the mood abroad would give some relief in the United States, too. These hopes were soon disappointed. In fact, the President's drive to expand his authority at home was accelerated; although the nation didn't know it, this was the period in which White House operatives advanced from crimes whose purpose was the discovery of national-security leaks to crimes against the domestic political opposition. The Presidential Offensive had not been called off; it had merely been routed underground. The President spoke incessantly of peace, and had arranged for his public-relations men to portray him as a man of peace, but there was to be no peace—not in Indo-China, and not with a constantly growing list of people he saw as his domestic "enemies." Detente, far from relaxing tensions at home, was seen in the White House as one more justification for its campaign to crush the opposition and seize absolute power.

On Sunday, June 18, 1972, readers of the front page of the *Times* learned, among other things, that heavy American air strikes were continuing over North Vietnam, that the chairman of President Nixon's Council of Economic Advisers, Herbert Stein, had attacked the economic proposals of Senator George McGovern, who in less than a month was to become the Presidential nominee of the Democratic Party, and that the musical "Fiddler on the Roof" had just had its three-thousand-two-hundred-and-twenty-fifth performance on Broadway. Readers of page 30 learned, in a story not listed in the "News Summary and Index," that five men had been arrested in the headquarters of the Democratic National Committee, in the Watergate office building, with burglary tools, cameras, and equipment for electronic surveillance in their possession. In rooms that the men had rented, under aliases, in the adjacent Watergate Hotel, thirty-two hundred-dollar bills were found, along with a notebook containing the notation "E. Hunt" (for E. Howard Hunt, as it turned out) and, next to that, the notation "W. H." (for the White House). The men were members of the Gemstone team, a White House undercover group, which had been attempting to install bugging devices in the telephones of Democrats.

Most of the high command of the Nixon Administration and the Nixon reelection committee were out of town when the arrests were made. The President and his chief of staff, H. R. Halderman, were on the President's estate in Key Biscayne, Florida. The President's counsel, John Dean, was in Manila, giving a lecture on drug abuse. John Mitchell, the former Attorney General, who was then director of the Committee for the Re-Election of the President, and Jeb Magruder, a former White House aide, who had become the committee's assistant director, were in California. In the hours and days immediately following the arrests, there was a flurry of activity at the headquarters of the committee, in a Washington office building; in California; and at the White House. Magruder called his assistant in Washington and had him remove certain papers—what later came to be publicly known as Gemstone materials—from his files. Gordon Liddy, by then the chief counsel of the Finance Committee to Re-Elect the President, went into the headquarters himself, removed from his files other materials having to do with the break-in, including other hundred-dollar bills, and shredded them. At the White House, Gordon Strachan, an aide to Haldeman, shredded a number of papers having to do with the setting up of the reelection committee's undercover operation, of which the break-in at the headquarters of the Democratic National Committee was an important part. Liddy, having destroyed all the evidence in his possession, offered up another piece of potential evidence for destruction: himself. He informed Dean that if the White House wished to have him assassinated he would stand at a given street corner at an appointed time to make things easy. E. Howard Hunt went to his office in the Executive Office Building, took from a safe ten thousand dollars in cash he had there for emergencies, and used it to hire an attorney for the burglars. In the days following, Hunt's name was expunged from the White House telephone directory. On orders from John Ehrlichman, the President's chief domestic-affairs adviser, his safe was opened and his papers were removed. At one point, Dean—also said to have been acting under instructions from Ehrlichman—gave an order for Hunt to leave the country, but then the order was rescinded. Hunt's payment to an attorney for the burglars was the first of many. The. President's personal attorney, Herbert Kalmbach, was instructed by Dean and, later, by Ehrlichman, Haldeman, and Mitchell to keep on making payments, and he, in turn, delegated the task to Anthony Ulasewicz, a retired New York City policeman who had been hired to conduct covert political investigations for the White House. Theirs was a hastily improvised operation. Kalmbach and Ulasewicz spoke to each other from phone booths. (Phone booths apparently had a strong attraction for Ulasewicz. He attached a change-maker to his belt to be sure to have enough coins for his calls, and he chose to make several of his "drops" of the payoff money in them.) He and Kalmbach used aliases and code language in their conversations. Kalmbach became Mr. Novak and Ulasewicz became Mr. Rivers— names that seem to have been chosen for no specific reason. Hunt, who had some forty mystery stories published, was referred to as "the writer," and Haldeman, who wore a crewcut, as "the brush." The payoff money became "the laundry," because when Ulasewicz arrived at Kalmbach's hotel room to pick up the first installment he put it in a laundry bag. The burglars were "the players," and the payoff scheme was "the script." Apparently, the reason the White House conspirators spoke to one another from phone booths was that they thought the Democrats might be wiretapping them, just as they had wiretapped the Democrats. In late June, the President himself said to Haldeman, of the Democrats, "When they start bugging us, which they have, our little boys will not know how to handle it. I hope they will, though." Considerations like these led Kalmbach, Ulasewicz, and others working for the White House to spend many unnecessary hours in phone booths that summer.

All these actions were of the sort that any powerful group of conspirators might take upon the arrest of some of their number. Soon, however, the White House was taking actions that were possible only because the conspirators occupied high positions in the government, including the highest position of all—the Presidency. For almost four years, the President had been "reorganizing" the executive branch of the government with a view to getting the Cabinet departments and the agencies under his personal control, and now he undertook to use several of these agencies to cover up crimes committed by his subordinates. In the early stages of the coverup, his efforts were directed toward removing a single evidentiary link: the fact that the Watergate burglars had been paid with funds from his campaign committee. There was a vast amount of other information that needed to be concealed—information concerning not just the Watergate break-in but the whole four-year record of the improper and illegal activities of the White House undercover operators, which stretched from mid-1969, when the warrantless wiretaps were placed, to the months in 1972 when the secret program for dividing the Democrats was being carried out—but if this one fact could somehow be suppressed, then the chain of evidence would be broken, and the rest of it might go undetected. On June 23rd, the President met with Haldeman and ordered him to have the C.I.A. request that the F.B.I. halt its investigation into the origin of the Watergate burglars' funds, on the pretext that C.I.A. secrets might come to light if the investigation went forward. The problem, Haldeman told the President, was that "the F.B.I. is not under control, because Gray doesn't exactly know how to control it." Patrick Gray was Acting Director of the F.B.I. "The way to handle this now," he went on, "is for us to have Walters call Pat Gray and just say, 'Stay to hell out of this.'" The reference was to Vernon Walters, Deputy Director of the C.I.A. A moment later, Haldeman asked the President, concerning the F.B.I., "And you seem to think the thing to do is get them to stop?" "Right, fine," the President answered. But he wanted Haldeman to issue the instructions. "I'm not going to get that involved," he said. About two hours later, Haldeman and Ehrlichman met with C.I.A. Director Richard Helms and Deputy Director Walters, and issued the order.

The maneuver gave the White House only a temporary advantage. Six days later, on June 29th, Gray did cancel interviews with two people who could shed light on the origin of the burglars' funds. (On the twenty-eighth, Ehrlichman and Dean had handed him all the materials taken from Hunt's safe, and Dean had told him that they were never to "see the light of day." Gray had taken them home, and later he burned them.) But soon a small rebellion broke out among officials of the F.B.I. and the C.I.A. Meetings were held, and at one point Gray and Walters told each other they would rather resign than submit to the White House pressure and compromise their agencies. Several weeks after the request was made, the F.B.I. held the interviews after all. The rebellion in the ranks of the federal bureaucracy was not the first to break out against the Nixon White House. As early as 1969, some members of the Justice Department had fought Administration attempts to thwart the civil-rights laws. In 1970, members of the State Department and members of the Office of Education, in the Department of Health, Education, and Welfare, had protested the invasion of Cambodia. In 1970, too, J. Edgar Hoover had refused to go along with a White House scheme devised by a young lawyer named Tom Huston for illegal intelligence-gathering. The executive bureaucracy was one source of the President's great power, but it was also acting as a check on his power. In some ways, it served this function more effectively than the checks provided by the Constitution, for, unlike the other institutions of government, it at least had some idea of what was going on. But ultimately it was no replacement for the Constitutional checks. A President who hired and fired enough people could in time bring the bureaucracy to heel. And although a Gray, a Walters, or a Helms might offer some resistance to becoming deeply involved in White House crimes, they would do nothing to expose the crimes. Moreover, the bureaucracy had no public voice, and was therefore powerless to sway public opinion. Politicians of all persuasions could—and did—heap abuse on "faceless," "briefcase-toting" bureaucrats and their "red tape," and the bureaucracy had no way to reply to this abuse. It had only its silent rebellions, waged with the passive weapons of obfuscation, concealment, and general foot-dragging. Decisive opposition, if there was to be any, had to come from without.

With respect to the prosecutorial arm of the Justice Department, the White House had aims that were less ambitious than its aims with respect to the F.B.I. and the C.I.A., but it was more successful in achieving them. Here, on the whole, the White House men wished merely to keep abreast of developments in the grand-jury room of the U.S. District Court, where officials of the Committee for the Re-Election of the President were testifying on Watergate, and this they accomplished through the obliging cooperation of Henry Petersen, the chief of the Criminal Division, who reported regularly to John Dean and later to the President himself. Dean subsequently described the cooperation to the President by saying, "Petersen is a soldier. He played—he kept me informed. He told me when we had problems, where we had problems, and the like. Uh, he believes in, in, in you. He believes in this Administration. This Administration had made him." What happened in the grand-jury room was further controlled by the coordinating of perjured testimony from White House aides and men working for the campaign committee. As for the prosecutors, a sort of dim-wittedness—a failure to draw obvious conclusions, a failure to follow up leads, a seeming willingness to construe the Watergate case narrowly—appeared to be enough to keep them from running afoul of the White House.

While all these moves were being made, the public was treated to a steady stream of categorical denials that the White House or the President's campaign committee had had anything to do with the break-in or with efforts to cover up the origins of the crime. The day after the break-in, Mitchell, in California, described James McCord, one of the burglars, as "the proprietor of a private security agency who was employed by our Committee months ago to assist with the installation of our security system." Actually, McCord was the committee's chief of security at the moment when he was arrested. Mitchell added, "We want to emphasize that this man and

the other people involved were not operating either in our behalf
or with our consent. . . . There is no place in our campaign or in
the electoral process for this type of activity, and we will not permit
nor condone it." On June 19th, two days after the break-in, Ronald
Ziegler, the President's press secretary, contemptuously dismissed
press reports of White House involvement. "I'm not going to comment from the White House on a third-rate burglary attempt," he
said. On June 20th, when Lawrence O'Brien, the chairman of the
Democratic Party, revealed that the Party had brought a one-
million-dollar civil-damages suit against the Committee for the Re-
Election of the President and the five burglary suspects, charging
invasion of privacy and violation of the civil rights of the Democrats, Mitchell stated that the action represented "another example
of sheer demagoguery on the part of Mr. O'Brien." Mitchell said, "I
reiterate that this committee did not authorize and does not condone the alleged actions of the five men apprehended there."

Among the nation's major newspapers, only one, the Washington
Post, consistently gave the Watergate story prominent headlines on
the front page. Most papers, when they dealt with the story at all,"
tended to treat it as something of a joke. All in all, the tone of the
coverage was not unlike the coverage of the Clifford Irving affair
the previous winter, and the volume of the coverage was, if anything, less. "Caper" was the word that most of the press settled upon
to describe the incident. A week after the break-in, for instance, the
Times headlined its Watergate story "WATERGATE CAPER." When
another week had passed, and Howard Hunt's connection with the
break-in had been made known, Time stated that the story was "fast
stretching into the most provocative caper of 1972, an extraordinary bit of bungling of great potential advantage to the Democrats
and damage to the Republicans in this election year." In early
August, the Times was still running headlines like "THE PLOT
THICKENS IN WATERGATE WHODUNIT over accounts of the repercussions of the burglary. "Above all, the purpose of the break-in
seemed obscure," the Times said. "But these details are never explained until the last chapter." The President held a news conference six weeks after the break-in, and by then the story was of such
small interest to newsmen that not one question was asked concerning it.

Disavowals such as those made by Mitchell and Ziegler carried
great weight in the absence of incontrovertible evidence refuting

them. The public had grown accustomed to deception and evasion in high places, but not yet to repeated, consistent, barefaced lying at all levels. The very boldness of the lies raised the cost of contradicting them, for to do so would be to call high officials outright liars. Another effective White House technique was to induce semi-informed or wholly uninformed spokesmen to deny charges. One of these spokesmen was Clark MacGregor, a former member of Congress from Minnesota, who became reelection-campaign director early in July, when John Mitchell resigned, pleading family difficulties. A few weeks later, when Senator McGovern described the break-ins as "the kind of thing you expect under a person like Hitler," MacGregor called McGovern's remark "character assassination." The practice of using as spokesmen officials who were more or less innocent of the facts was one more refinement of the technique of dissociating "what we say" from "what we do." In this manner, honest men could be made to lend the weight of their integrity to untruths. They spoke words without knowing whether the words were true or false. Such spokesmen lent their vocal cords to the campaign but left their brains behind, and confused the public with words spoken by nobody.

On September 15th, the five men who had been caught in the Democratic National Committee headquarters were indicted—together with E. Howard Hunt and G. Gordon Liddy, who were elsewhere in the Watergate complex at the time of the break—in for the felonies of burglary, conspiracy, and wiretapping. A few days later, the seven defendants pleaded not guilty. As the case stood at that moment, their crimes were officially motiveless. The prosecutors had not been able to suggest who might have asked employees of the Committee for the Re-Election of the President to wiretap the Democratic headquarters, or why a check belonging to that committee should have found its way into the bank account of Bernard Barker. That afternoon, the President met with Haldeman and Dean, and congratulated Dean on his work. "Well," he said, "the whole thing is a can of worms. . . . But the, but the way you, you've handled it, it seems to me, has been very skillful, because you—putting your fingers in the dikes every time that leaks have sprung here and sprung there." Representative Wright Patman, the chairman of the House Banking and Currency Committee, was planning to hold hearings on the Watergate break-in, and the President, Dean, and Haldeman went on to discuss ways of "turning that off," as Dean put it. Dean reported to the two others that he was studying the possibility of blackmailing members of the Patman committee with damaging information about their own campaigns, and then the President suggested that Gerald Ford, the minority leader of the House, would be the man to pressure Patman into dropping the hearings. Ford should be told that "he's got to get at this and screw this thing up while he can," the President said. Two and a half weeks later, a majority of the members of the committee voted to deny Patman the power to subpoena witnesses. But Patman made the gesture of carrying on anyway for a while, and asked questions of an empty chair.

At the end of September—more than a month before the election—the Washington *Post* reported that John Mitchell had had control of a secret fund for spying on the Democrats. Throughout October, denials continued to pour out from the Administration. As before, some were outright lies by men who knew the facts, and others were untruths spoken by men who were simply repeating what they had been told. On October 2nd, Acting Director Gray of the F.B.I. said that it was unreasonable to believe that the President had deceived the nation about Watergate. "Even if some of us [in federal law enforcement agencies] are crooked, there aren't that many that are. I don't believe everyone is a Sir Galahad, but there's not been one single bit of pressure put on me or any of my special agents." In reality, of course, Gray had once considered resigning because the pressure from the White House to help with the cover-up had been so intense, and even as he spoke he was keeping the contents of E. Howard Hunt's safe in a drawer of a dresser at his home in Connecticut. Gray went on to say, "It strains the credulity that the President of the United States—if he had a mind to—could have done a con job on the whole American people." Gray added, "He would have to control the United States."

In the months since the election, the issue of Watergate had faded, and the papers had devoted their front pages to other news. Shortly after the trial began, however, the front-page news was that all the defendants but two had pleaded guilty. In the courtroom, Judge John Sirica, who presided, found himself dissatisfied with the questioning of witnesses by the government prosecutors. The prosecutors now had a suggestion as to the burglars' motive. They suggested that it might be blackmail. They did not say of whom or over what. At the trial, the key prosecution witness, the former F.B.I. agent Alfred Baldwin, related that on one occasion he had taken the logs of the Watergate wiretaps to the headquarters of the Committee for the Re-Election of the President. But this suggested nothing to the Justice Department, one of whose spokesmen had maintained when the indictment was handed up in September that there was "no evidence" showing that anyone except the defendants was involved. Sirica demurred. "I want to know where the money comes from," he said to the defendant Bernard Barker. "There were hundred-dollar bills floating around like coupons." When Barker replied that he had simply received the money in the mail in a blank envelope and had no idea who might have sent it, Sirica commented, "I'm sorry, but I don't believe you." When the defense lawyers protested Sirica's questioning, he said, "I don't think we should sit up here like nincompoops. The function of a trial is to search for the truth."

All the Watergate defendants but one were following the White House scenario to the letter. The exception was James McCord. He was seething with scenarios of his own. He hoped to have the charges against him dismissed, and, besides, he had been angered by what he understood as a suggestion from one of his lawyers that the blame for the Watergate break-in be assigned to the C.I.A., his old outfit, to which he retained an intense loyalty. There was some irony in the fact that McCord's anger had been aroused by an Administration plan to involve the C.I.A. in its crimes. McCord believed that Nixon's removal of C.I.A. director Richard Helms, in December of 1972—at the very time that McCord himself was being urged to lay the blame for Watergate at the door of the C.I.A.—was designed to pave the way for an attempt by the Administration itself to blame the break-in on the agency and for a takeover of the agency by the White House. He had worked for the White House, but he did not see the reorganizational wars from the White House point of view. He saw them from the bureaucrats' point of view; in his opinion, President Nixon was attempting to take over the C.I.A. in a manner reminiscent of attempts by Hitler to take control of German intelligence agencies before the Second World War. The White House, that is, belatedly discovered that it had a disgruntled "holdover" on its hands. And this particular holdover really was prepared to perform sabotage; he was prepared, indeed, to sabotage not just the President's policies but the President himself, and, what was more, he had the means to do it. McCord was putting together a scenario that could destroy the Nixon Administration. In a letter delivered to his White House contact, the undercover operative John Caulfield, McCord pronounced a dread warning: If the White House continued to try to have the C.I.A. take responsibility for the Watergate burglary, "every tree in the forest will fall," and "it will be a scorched desert." Piling on yet another metaphor of catastrophe, he wrote, "Pass the message that if they want it to blow, they are on exactly the right course. I am sorry that you will get hurt in the fallout." McCord was the first person in the Watergate conspiracy to put in writing exactly what the magnitude of the Watergate scandal was. Many observers had been amazed at the extreme hard line that the President had taken since his landslide reelection—the firings in the bureaucracies, the incomprehensible continuation of the attacks on Senator McGovern, the renewed attacks on the press, the attacks on Congress's power of the purse, the bombing of Hanoi. They could not know that at the exact moment when President Nixon was wreaking devastation on North Vietnam, James McCord was threatening to wreak devastation on him.

On February 7th, the Senate, by a vote of seventy-seven to none, established a Select Committee on Presidential Campaign Activities, to look into abuses in the Presidential campaign of 1972, including the Watergate break-in; and the Democratic leadership appointed Senator Sam Ervin, of North Carolina, the author of the resolution to establish the Select Committee, to be its chairman. Three days later, the Administration secretly convened a Watergate committee of its own, in California—at the La Costa Resort Hotel and Spa, not far from the President's estate in San Clemente, with John Dean, H. R. Haldeman, John Ehrlichman, and Richard Moore, a White House aide, in attendance. The meeting lasted for two days. Its work was to devise ways of hampering, discrediting, and ultimately blocking the Ervin committee's investigation.

The President's drive to take over the federal government was going well. By the end of March those legislators who were worried about the possibility of a collapse of the Constitutional system were in a state of near-hopelessness. It seemed that the President would have his will, and Congress could not stop him; as for the public, it was uninterested in Constitutional matters. Senator Muskie had now joined Senator McGovern in warning against the dangers of "one-man rule," and he said that the Administration's proposal for preventing the release of "classified" information, no matter how arbitrarily the "classified" designation had been applied, could impose "the silence of democracy's graveyard." Senator William Fulbright, of Arkansas, had expressed fear that the United States might "pass on, as most of the world had passed on, to a totalitarian system." In the press, a new feeling seemed to be crystallizing that Congress had had its day as an institution of American life. Commentators of all political persuasions were talking about Congress as though it were moribund. Kevin Phillips, a political writer who had played an important role in formulating "the Southern strategy," and who had once worked in John Mitchell's Justice Department, wrote, in an article in *Newsweek* called "Our Obsolete System," that "Congress's separate power is an obstacle to modern policy-making." He proposed a "fusion of powers" to replace the Constitution's separation of powers. "In sum," he wrote, "we may have reached a point where separation of powers is doing more harm than good by distorting the logical evolution of technology-era government." In *The New Republic,* the columnist TRB, who, like Senator McGovern and Senator Muskie, was worried that "one-man rule" was in prospect, wrote, "President Nixon treats Congress with contempt which, it has to be admitted, is richly deserved. We have a lot of problems—the economy, inflation, the unfinished war, Watergate—but in the long run the biggest problem is whether Congress can be salvaged, because if it can't our peculiar 18th-century form of government, with separation of powers, can't be salvaged," And he wrote, "A vacuum has to be filled. The authority of Congress has decayed till it is overripe and rotten. Mr. Nixon has merely proclaimed it." At the Justice Department, Donald Santarelli, who was shortly to become head of the Law Enforcement Assistance Administration, told a reporter, "Today, the whole Constitution is up for grabs." These observers took the undeniable fact that the Congress was impotent as a sign that the Congress was obsolete. And the executive branch, having helped reduce the Congress to helplessness, could now point to that helplessness as proof that the Congress was of no value.

The coverup and the takeover had merged into a single project. For four years, the President's anger at his "enemies" had been growing. As his anger had grown, so had that clandestine repressive apparatus in the White House whose purpose was to punish and destroy his enemies. And as this apparatus had grown, so had the need to control the Cabinet departments and the agencies; and the other branches of government, because they might find out about it—until, finally, the coverup had come to exceed in importance every other matter facing the Administration. For almost a year now, the coverup had been the motor of American politics. It had safeguarded the President's reelection, and it had determined the substance and the mood of the Administration's second term so far. In 1969, when President Nixon launched his Presidential Offensive, he had probably not foreseen that the tools he was developing then would one day serve him in a mortal struggle between his Administration and the other powers of the Republic; but now his assault on the press, the television networks, the Congress, the federal bureaucracy, and the courts had coalesced into a single, coordinated assault on the American Constitutional democracy. Either the Nixon Administration would survive in power and the democracy would die or the Administration would be driven from power and the democracy would have another chance to live. If the newly reelected President should be able to thwart investigations by the news media, the agencies of federal law enforcement, the courts, and Congress, he would be clear of all accountability, and would be above the law; on the other hand, if the rival institutions of the Republic should succeed in laying bare the crimes of his Administration and in bringing the criminals to justice, the Administration would be destroyed.

In the latter part of March, the pace of events in this area of the coverup quickened. Under the pressure of the pending sentences, two of the conspirators were breaking ranks: James McCord and Howard Hunt. McCord, who had been threatening the White House with exposure since December, now wrote a letter to Judge Sirica telling what he knew of the coverup. Hunt, for his part, was angry because he and the other defendants and their lawyers had not been paid as much money as they wanted in return for their silence. In November, 1972, he called Charles Colson to remind him that the continuation of the coverup was a "two-way street," and shortly after the middle of March he told Paul O'Brien, an attorney for the reelection committee, that if more funds weren't forthcoming immediately he might reveal some of the "many things" he had done for John Haldeman—an apparent reference to the break-in at the office of Daniel Ellsberg's psychiatrist. Shortly thereafter, O'Brien informed Dean of Hunt's demand. These events on one edge of the coverup had an immediate influence on the chemistry of the whole enterprise. On March 21st, John Dean, convinced now that the coverup could not be maintained, met with the President and told him the story of it as he knew it from beginning to end. The President's response was to recommend that the blackmail money be paid to Hunt. "I think you should handle that one pretty fast," he said. And later he said, "But at the moment don't you agree that you'd better get the Hunt thing? I mean, that's worth it, at the moment." And he said, "That's why, John, for your immediate thing you've got no choice with Hunt but the hundred and twenty or whatever it is. Right?" The President was willing to consider plans for limited disclosure, and the meeting ended with a suggestion from Haldeman, who had joined the two other men: "We've got to figure out where to turn it off at the lowest cost we can, but at whatever cost it takes."

The defection of Hunt and McCord had upset the delicate balance of roles demanded by the coverup. Information that had to be kept secret began to flow in a wide loop through the coverup's various departments. Not only Hunt and McCord but Dean and Magruder began to tell their stories to the prosecutors. The prosecutors, in turn, relayed the information to Attorney General Kleindienst and Assistant Attorney General Petersen, who then relayed it to the President, who then relayed it to Haldeman and Ehrlichman, who in this period were desperately attempting to avoid prosecution, and were therefore eager to know what was happening in the Grand Jury room. Any defections placed the remaining conspirators in an awkward position. In order to get clear of the collapsing coverup, they had to become public inquisitors of their former subordinates and collaborators. Such a transformation, however, was not likely to sit well with the defectors, who were far from eager to shoulder the blame for the crimes of others, and who, furthermore, were in possession of damaging information with which to retaliate.

Notwithstanding these new tensions, the President sought to continue the coverup. In the weeks following his meeting with Dean on March 21st, his consistent strategy was what might be called the hors d'oeuvre strategy. The President described the strategy to

Haldeman and Ehrlichman after a conversation with Dean on April 14th by saying, "Give 'em an hors d'oeuvre and maybe they won't come back for the main course." His hope was that by making certain public revelations and by offering a certain number of victims to the prosecutors he could satisfy the public's appetite, so that it would seek no more revelations and no more victims. (This technique, which Ehrlichman, on another occasion, called a "modified limited hang-out," was also what Haldeman had had in mind when he suggested that they should "turn it off at the lowest cost" they could.) Hors d'oeuvres of many kinds came under consideration. Some were in the form of scapegoats to be turned over to the prosecutors, and others were in the form of incomplete or false reports to be issued to the public. By now, the country's appetite for revelations was well developed, and in the White House it was decided that no less a man than Mitchell was needed to satisfy it.

As Ehrlichman explained the new plan to the President, Mitchell would be induced to make a statement saying, "I am both morally and legally responsible."

"How does it redound to our advantage?" the President asked.

"That you have a report from me based on three weeks' work," Ehrlichman replied, "that when you got it, you immediately acted to call Mitchell in as the provable wrongdoer, and you say, 'My God, I've got a report here. And it's clear from this report that you are guilty as hell. Now John . . . go on in there and do what you should.'"

That way, the President could pose as the man who had cracked the conspiracy.

Shortly thereafter, Mitchell was called down to the White House, and Ehrlichman proposed the plan. Mitchell did not care for it. He not only maintained his innocence but suggested that the guilt lay elsewhere; namely, in the White House. Ehrlichman told the President when Mitchell had left that Mitchell had "lobbed, uh, mud balls at the White House at every opportunity." Faced with Mitchell's refusal to play the scapegoat, the President, Haldeman, and Ehrlichman next invited Dean to step into the role. Soon after Ehrlichman's unsatisfactory experience with Mitchell, the President met with Dean and attempted to induce him to sign a letter of resignation because of his implication in the scandal.

The President approached the subject in an offhand manner. "You know, I was thinking we ought to get the odds and ends, uh

. . . we talked, and, uh, it was confirmed that—you remember we talked about resignations and so forth," he said.

"Uh huh," Dean replied.

"But I should have in hand something, or otherwise they'll say, 'What the hell did you—after Mr. Dean told you all of this, what did you do?'" the President went on.

Again Dean answered "Uh huh."

The President then related that even Henry Petersen had been concerned about "this situation on Dean," and Dean once more answered with an "uh huh."

"See what I mean?" the President asked the uncommunicative Dean.

"Are we talking Dean, or are we talking Dean, Ehrlichman, and Haldeman?" Dean finally asked.

"Well, I'm talking Dean," the President answered.

But Dean, like Mitchell before him, was talking Ehrlichman and Haldeman, too, and would not resign unless they also resigned. He did not want to be an hors d'oeuvre any more than Mitchell did. And since Dean was in possession of highly detailed information that implicated not only Haldeman and Ehrlichman but the President as well, the President was unable to "bite the Dean bullet," as he put it, until he also was willing to let Haldeman and Ehrlichman go. Their turn came quickly. By now the President was under intense pressure to act soon. If he did not, he could hardly pose as the man who had cracked the case. On April 17th, the day after the unproductive conversation with Dean, the President said to Haldeman and Ehrlichman. "Let me say this. . . . It's a hell of a lot different [from] John Dean. I know that as far as you're concerned, you'll go out and throw yourselves on a damned sword. I'm aware of that. . . . The problem we got here is this. I do not want to be in a position where the damned public clamor makes, as it did with Eisenhower, with Adams, makes it necessary or calls—to have Bob come in one day and say, 'Well, Mr. President, the public—blah, blah, blah—I'm going to leave.'" But Ehrlichman was not willing to throw himself on a sword. The person he was willing to throw on a sword was Dean. "Let me make a suggestion," he responded. It was that the President give Dean a leave of absence and then defer any decision on Ehrlichman and Haldeman until the case had developed further. However, the President pursued the point, seeming at times to favor Haldeman's and Ehrlichman's resignation, and finally Ehrlichman did what McCord, Hunt, Mitchell, and Dean had done before him. He lobbed mud balls at the White House—which in this case meant the President.

If he and Haldeman should resign, Ehrlichman observed, "we are put in a position of defending ourselves." And he went on, "The things that I am going to have to say about Dean are: basically that Dean was the sole proprietor of this project, that he reported to the President, he reported to me only incidentally."

"'Reported to the President'?" the President inquired.

A moment later, speaking in his own defense, the President said, "You see the problem you've got there is that Dean does have a point there which you've got to realize. He didn't see me when he came out to California. He didn't see me until the day you said, 'I think you ought to talk to John Dean.'"

At this point, Ehrlichman retreated into ambiguity, and said, "But you see I get into a very funny defensive position then vis-à-vis you and vis-à-vis him, and it's very damned awkward. And I haven't thought it clear through. I don't know where we come out."

On April 17th, the President made a short statement saying simply that there had been "major developments in the case concerning which it would be improper to be more specific now." He was unable to offer any diversionary reports or propitiatory victims to deflect the public's wrath at the forthcoming disclosures. He and his aides had talked over countless schemes, but all of them had foundered on the unwillingness of any of the aides to sacrifice themselves for him—or for "the Presidency," as he had asked them to do. The coverup was all one piece, and it cohered in exposure just as it had cohered in concealment.

The President had become adept at recollecting whatever was needed at a particular moment. By April of 1973, he and his aides were spending most of their time making up history out of whole cloth to suit the needs of each moment. Unfortunately for them, the history they were making up was self-serving history, and by April their individual interests had grown apart. Each of them had begun to "recollect" things to his own advantage and to the detriment of the others. As their community of interests dissolved under the pressure of the investigation, each of them was retreating into his own private, self-interested reality. The capacity for deception which had once divided them from the country but united them with one another now divided them from one another as well.

In the White House, the fabric of reality had disintegrated altogether. What had got the President into trouble from the start had been his remarkable capacity for fantasy. He had begun by imagining a host of domestic foes. In retaliating against them, he had broken the law. Then he had compounded his lawbreaking by concealing it. And, finally, in the same way that he had broken the law although breaking it was against his best interests, he was bringing himself to justice even as he thought he was evading justice. For, as though in anticipation of the deterioration of his memory, he had installed another memory in the Oval Office, which was more nearly perfect than his own, or anyone else's merely human equipment: he had installed the taping system. The Watergate coverup had cast him in the double role of conspirator and investigator. Though the conspirator in him worked hard to escape the law, it was the investigator in him that gained the upper hand in the end. While he was attempting to evade the truth, his machines were preserving it forever.

At the moment when the President announced "major developments" in the Watergate case, the national process that was the investigation overwhelmed the national process that was the coverup. The events that followed were all the more astounding to the nation because, at just the moment when the coverup began to explode, the President, in the view of many observers, had been on the point of strangling the "obsolete" Constitutional system and replacing it with a Presidential dictatorship. One moment, he was triumphant and his power was apparently irresistible; the next moment, he was at bay. For in the instant the President made his announcement, the coverup cracked—not just the Watergate coverup but the broader coverup, which concealed the underground history of the last five years—and the nation suffered an inundation of news. The newspaper headlines now came faster and thicker than ever before in American history. The stories ran backward in time, and each day's newspaper told of some event a little further in the past as reporters traced the underground history to the early days of the Administration, and even into the terms of former Administrations. With the history of half a decade pouring out all at once, the papers were stuffed with more news than even the most diligent reader could absorb, Moreover, along with the facts, nonfacts proliferated as the desperate men in the White House put out one false or distorted statement after another, so that each true fragment of the story was all but lost in a maze of deceptions, and each event, true or false, came up dozens of times, in dozens of versions, until the reader's mind was swamped. And, as if what was in the newspapers were not already too much, television soon started up, and, in coverage that was itself a full-time job to watch, presented first the proceedings of the Ervin committee and then the proceedings of the House Judiciary Committee, when it began to weigh the impeachment of the President. And, finally, in a burst of disclosure without anything close to a precedent in history, the tapes were revealed—and not just once but twice. The first set of transcripts was released by the White House and was doctored, and only the second set, which was released by the Judiciary Committee, gave an accurate account of the President's conversations.

As the flood of information flowed into the public realm, overturning the accepted history of recent years, the present scene was also transformed. The Vice-President was swept from office when his bribe-taking became known, but so rapid was the pace of events that his departure was hardly noticed. Each of the institutions of the democracy that had been menaced by the President—and all had been menaced—was galvanized into action in its turn: the press, the television networks, the Senate, the House of Representatives, and, finally, in a dispute over release of the tapes, the Supreme Court. The public, too, was at last awakened, when the President fired the Special Prosecutor whom he had appointed to look into the White House crimes. In an outpouring of public sentiment that, like so much else that happened at the time, had no precedent in the nation's history, millions of letters and telegrams poured in to Congress protesting the President's action. The time of letters sent by the President to himself was over, and the time of real letters from real people had come. No one of the democracy's institutions was powerful enough by itself to remove the President; the efforts of all were required—and only when those efforts were combined was he forced from office.

America's Crisis of Confidence

Jimmy Carter

Very early in his campaign for the presidency, Jimmy Carter established a new and successful mode of relating to the American people. Speaking partly as a moralist, partly a preacher partly a friend, he communicated a sense of caring deeply about the underlying values of the American people. When Carter came to Washington, he discovered that the same style did not work with government bureaucrats or Congressional leaders. Frustrated by his failure to win support for his plans to solve the energy crisis, Carter returned to the style of his campaign and reached over the heads of Congress to the American people. Retreating to Camp David in the Maryland mountains, Carter asked religious leaders, historians, poets, and psychiatrists to journey to Camp David and tell him what was wrong with America. The result was the speech that follows. Significantly, it traces all of America's problems to an underlying "crisis of confidence," a disease of the soul. The speech reveals both Carter's greatest strength and his greatest weakness. He successfully identifies a pervasive feeling of uncertainty and unease in the population. Yet, he failed to translate his insight into effective policy. Carter the preacher and therapist was a success. Carter the politician, was a failure.

This is a special night for me. Exactly three years ago on July 15, 1976, I accepted the nomination of my party to run for President of the United States. I promised to you a President who is not isolated from the people, who feels your pain and shares your dreams and who draws his strength and his wisdom from you.

During the past three years, I've spoken to you on many occasions about national concerns: the energy crisis, reorganizing the Government, our nation's economy and issues of war, and espe-

Excerpted from *The New York Times*, July 16, 1979.

cially peace. But over those years the subjects of the speeches, the talks and the press conferences have become increasingly narrow, focused more and more on what the isolated world of Washington thinks is important.

Ten days ago I had plans to speak to you again about a very important subject—energy. For the fifth time I would have described the urgency of the problem and laid out a series of legislative recommendations to the Congress, but as I was preparing to speak I began to ask myself the same question that I now know has been troubling many of you: Why have we not been able to get together as a nation to resolve our serious energy problem?

It's clear that the true problems of our nation are much deeper— deeper than gasoline lines or energy shortages. Deeper, even, than inflation or recession. And I realize more than ever that as President I need your help, so I decided to reach out and to listen to the voices of America. I invited to Camp David people from almost every segment of our society: business and labor; teachers and preachers; governors, mayors and private citizens.

And then I left Camp David to listen to other Americans. Men and women like you. It has been an extraordinary 10 days and I want to share with you what I heard.

ADVICE PROM THE PEOPLE

First of all, I got a lot of personal advice. Let me quote a few of the typical comments that I wrote down.

This from a Southern Governor: "Mr. President, you're not leading this nation, you're just managing the Government."

"You don't see the people enough anymore."

"Some of your Cabinet members don't seem loyal. There's not enough discipline among your disciples."

Many people talked about themselves and about the condition of our nation. This from a young woman in Pennsylvania: "I feel so far from government. I feel like ordinary people are excluded from political power." And this from a young Chicano: "Some of us have suffered from recession all our lives. Some people have wasted energy but others haven't had anything to waste." And this from a religious leader: "No material shortage can touch the important things like God's love for us or our love for one another."

Several of our discussions were on energy, and I have a notebook full of comments and advice. I'll read just a few.

"We can't go on consuming 40 percent more energy than we produce. When we import oil, we are also importing inflation plus unemployment. We've got to use what we have. The Middle East has only 5 percent of the world's energy, but the United States has 24 percent."

And this is one of the most vivid statements: "Our neck is stretched over the fence and OPEC has the knife."

These 10 days confirmed my belief in the decency and the strength and the wisdom of the American people, but it also bore out some of my long-standing concerns about our nation's underlying problems. I know, of course, being President, that Government actions and legislation can be very important.

That's why I've worked hard to put my campaign promises into law, and I have to admit with just mixed success. But after listening to the American people I have been reminded again that all the legislatures in the world can't fix what's wrong with America.

A FUNDAMENTAL THREAT

So I want to speak to you tonight about a subject even more serious than energy or inflation. I want to talk to you right now about a fundamental threat to American democracy.

I do not mean our political and civil liberties. They will endure. And I do not refer to the outward strength of America—the nation that is at peace tonight everywhere in the world with unmatched economic power and military might. The threat is nearly invisible in ordinary ways. It is a crisis of confidence. It is a crisis that strikes at the very heart and soul and spirit of our national will.

We can see this crisis in the growing doubt about the meaning of our own lives and in the loss of a unity of purpose for our nation.

The erosion of our confidence in the future is threatening to destroy the social and the political fabric of America. The confidence that we have always had as a people is not simply some romantic dream or a proverb in a dusty book that we read just on the Fourth of July. It is the idea which founded our nation and which has guided our development as a people. Confidence in the future has supported everything else—public institutions and private enterprise, our own families and the very Constitution of the United States. Confidence has defined our course and has served as a link between generations.

We've always believed in something called progress. We've always had a faith that the days of our children would be better than our own.

CLOSING THE DOOR ON OUR PAST

Our people are losing that faith. Not only in Government itself, but in their ability as citizens to serve as the ultimate rulers and shapers of our democracy. As a people, we know our past and we are proud of it. Our progress has been part of the living history of America, even the world. We always believed that we were part of a great movement of humanity itself called democracy, involved in the search for freedom. And that belief has always strengthened us in our purpose. But just as we are losing our confidence in the future, we are also beginning to close the door on our past.

In a nation that was proud of hard work, strong families, close-knit communities and our faith in God, too many of us now tend to worship self-indulgence and consumption. Human identity is no longer defined by what one does but by what one owns.

But we've discovered that owning things and consuming things does not satisfy our longing for meaning.

We have learned that piling up material goods cannot fill the emptiness of lives which have no confidence or purpose. The symptoms of this crisis of the American spirit are all around us. For the first time in the history of our country a majority of our people believe that the next five years will be worse than that past five years. Two-thirds of our people do not even vote. The productivity of American workers is actually dropping and the willingness of Americans to save for the future has fallen below that of all other people in the Western world.

As you know there is a growing disrespect for Government and for churches and for schools, the news media and other institutions. This is not a message of happiness or reassurance but it is the truth. And it is a warning. These changes did not happen overnight. They've come upon us gradually over the last generation. Years that were filled with shocks and tragedy.

We were sure that ours was a nation of the ballot, not of the bullet, until the murders of John Kennedy and Robert Kennedy and Martin Luther King, Jr. We were taught that our armies were always invincible and our causes were always just only to suffer the agony of Vietnam. We respected the Presidency as a place of honor until the shock of Watergate. We remember when the phrase "sound as a dollar" was an expression of absolute dependability until 10 years of inflation began to shrink our dollar and our savings. We believed that our nation's resources were limitless until 1973, when we had to face a growing dependence on foreign oil.

These wounds are still very deep. They have never been healed.

ISOLATION OF GOVERNMENT

Looking for a way out of this crisis, our people have turned to the Federal Government and found it isolated from the mainstream of our nation's life. Washington, D.C., has become an island. The gap between our citizens and our Government has never been so wide. The people are looking for honest answers, not easy answers, clear leadership, not false claims and evasiveness and politics as usual. What you see too often in Washington and elsewhere around the country is a system of government that seems incapable of action.

You see a Congress twisted and pulled in every direction by hundreds of well-financed and powerful special interests. You see every extreme position defended to the last vote, almost to the last breath, by one unyielding group or another.

Often you see paralysis and stagnation and drift. You don't like it. And neither do I.

What can we do? First of all, we must face the truth and then we can change our course. We simply must have faith in each other. Faith in our ability to govern ourselves and faith in the future of this nation. Restoring that faith and that confidence to America is now the most important task we face.

TURNING POINT IN HISTORY

Our fathers and mothers were strong men and women who shaped the new society during the Great Depression, who fought world wars and who carved out a new charter of peace for the world. We ourselves are the same Americans who just 10 years ago put a man on the moon. We are the generation that dedicated our society to the pursuit of human rights and equality.

And we are the generation that will win the war on the energy problem, and in that process rebuild the unity and confidence of America. We are at a turning point in our history. There are two paths to choose. One is the path I've warned about tonight—the path that leads to fragmentation and self-interest. Down that road lies a mistaken idea of freedom.

All the traditions of our past, all the lessons of our heritage, all the promises of our future point to another path: the path of common purpose and the restoration of American values. That path leads to true freedom for our nation and ourselves. We can take the first steps down that path as we begin to solve our energy problem. Energy will be the immediate test of our ability to unite this nation.

You know we can do it. We have the natural resources. We have more oil in our shale alone than several Saudi Arabias. We have more coal than any nation on earth. We have the world's highest level of technology. We have the most skilled work force, with innovative genius.

And I firmly believe we have the national will to win this war.

"The Second American Revolution"

Ronald W. Reagan

Whether political observers are hostile or friendly to Ronald Reagan, nearly every political commentator agrees that Reagan possessed extraordinary skill in articulating his point of view and rallying support for it. Although Reagan retained a level of popular backing usually reserved for "consensus" politicians of a moderate persuasion, he presented, and argued effectively for, a singularly partisan definition of America's purpose and goals. Reagan had clear ideas, many of them in deep conflict with the direction of American government and policies since the New Deal. He wished to dismantle the "welfare state," cut taxes severely, restore a laissez-faire economy, and simultaneously construct a huge new military machine. In fact, Reagan did seek a new American revolution, one that would alter dramatically the shape and substance of American politics. Here in his State of the Union Address in 1985, the dimensions of that revolution are outlined, suggesting the degree to which Reagan sought publicly to build support for his strong ideas.

Mr. Speaker, Mr. President, distinguished members of the Congress, honored guests and fellow citizens. I come before you to report on the state of our union. And I am pleased to report that, after four years of united effort, the American people have brought forth a nation renewed—stronger, freer and more secure than before.

Four years ago, we began to change—forever, I hope—our assumptions about government and its place in our lives. Out of that change has come great and robust growth—in our confidence, our economy and our role in the world. . . .

Four years ago, we said we would invigorate our economy by giving people greater freedom and incentives to take risks, and letting them keep more of what they earned.

We did what we promised, and a great industrial giant is reborn. Tonight we can take pride in 25 straight months of economic growth, the strongest in 34 years: a three-year inflation average of 3.9 percent the lowest in 17 years; and 7.3 million new jobs in two years, with more of our citizens working than ever before. . . .

We have begun well. But it's only a beginning. We are not here to congratulate ourselves on what we have done, but to challenge ourselves to finish what has not yet been done.

We are here to speak for millions in our inner cities who long for real jobs, safe neighborhoods and schools that truly teach. We are here to speak for the American farmer, the entrepreneur and every worker in industries fighting to modernize and compete. And, yes, we are here to stand, and proudly so, for all who struggle to break free from totalitarianism; for all who know in their hearts that freedom is the one true path to peace and human happiness. . . .

We honor the giants of our history not by going back, but forward to the dreams their vision foresaw. My fellow citizens, this nation is poised for greatness. The time has come to proceed toward a great new challenge—a Second American Revolution of hope and opportunity; a revolution carrying us to new heights of progress by pushing back frontiers of knowledge and space; a revolution of spirit that taps the soul of America, enabling us to summon greater strength than we have ever known; and, a revolution that carries beyond our shores the golden promise of human freedom in a world at peace.

Let us begin by challenging conventional wisdom: There are no constraints on the human mind, no walls around the human spirit, no barriers to our progress except those we ourselves erect. Already, pushing down tax rates has freed our economy to vault forward to record growth.

In Europe, they call it "the American Miracle." Day by day, we are shattering accepted notions of what is possible. . . .

We stand on the threshold of a great ability to produce more, do more, be more. Our economy is not getting older and weaker, it's getting younger and stronger; it doesn't need rest and supervision, it needs new challenge, greater freedom. And that word—freedom—is the key to the Second American Revolution we mean to bring about.

Let us move together with an historic reform of tax simplification for fairness and growth. Last year, I asked then-Treasury Secretary Regan to develop a plan to simplify the tax code, so all taxpayers would be treated more fairly, and personal tax rates could come further down.

We have cut tax rates by almost 25 percent, yet the tax system remains unfair and limits our potential for growth. Exclusions and exemptions cause similar incomes to be taxed at different levels. Low-income families face steep tax barriers that make hard lives even harder. The Treasury Department has produced an excellent reform plan whose principles will guide the final proposal we will ask you to enact.

One thing that tax reform will not be is a tax increase in disguise. We will not jeopardize the mortgage interest deduction families need. We will reduce personal tax rates as low as possible by removing many tax preferences. We will propose a top rate of no more than 35 percent, and possibly lower. And we will propose reducing corporate rates while maintaining incentives for capital formation. . . .

Tax simplification will be a giant step toward unleashing the tremendous pent-up power of our economy. But a Second American Revolution must carry the promise of opportunity for all. It is time to liberate the spirit of enterprise in the most distressed areas of our country.

This government will meet its responsibility to help those in need. But policies that increase dependency, break up families and destroy self-respect are not progressive, they are reactionary. Despite our strides in civil rights, blacks, Hispanics and all minorities will not have full and equal power until they have full economic powers. . . .

Let us resolve that we will stop spreading dependency and start spreading opportunity; that we will stop spreading bondage and start spreading freedom.

There are some who say that growth initiatives must await final action on deficit reductions. The best way to reduce deficits is through economic growth. More business will be started, more investments made, more jobs created and more people will be on payrolls paying taxes. The best way to reduce government spending is to reduce the need for spending by increasing prosperity. . . .

To move steadily toward a balanced budget we must also lighten government's claim on our total economy. We will not do this by raising taxes. We must make sure that our economy grows faster than growth in spending by federal government. In our fiscal year 1986 budget, overall government program spending will be frozen at the current level; it must not be one dime higher than fiscal year 1985. And three points are key:

First, the social safety net for the elderly, needy, disabled and unemployed will be left intact. Growth of our major health care programs, Medicare and Medicaid, will be slowed, but protections for the elderly and needy will be preserved.

Second, we must not relax our efforts to restore military strength just as we near our goal of a fully equipped, trained and ready professional corps. National security is government's first responsibility, so, in past years, defense spending took about half the federal budget. Today it takes less than a third.

We have already reduced our planned defense expenditures by nearly $100 billion over the past four years, and reduced projected spending again this year. You know, we only have a military industrial complex until a time of danger. Then it becomes the arsenal of democracy. Spending for defense is investing in things that are priceless: peace and freedom.

Third, we must reduce or eliminate costly government subsidies. For example, deregulation of the airline industry has led to cheaper airfares, but on Amtrak taxpayers pay about $35 per passenger every time an Amtrak train leaves the station. It's time we ended this huge federal subsidy.

Our farm program costs have quadrupled in recent years. Yet I know from visiting farmers, many in great financial distress, that we need an orderly transition to a market-oriented farm economy. We can help farmers best, not by expanding federal payments, but by making fundamental reforms, keeping interest rates heading down and knocking down foreign trade barriers to American farm exports. . . .

In the long run, we must protect the taxpayers from government. And I ask again that you pass, as 32 states have now called for, an amendment mandating the federal government spend no more than it takes in. And I ask for the authority used responsibly by 43 governors to veto individual items in appropriations bills. . . .

Nearly 50 years of government living beyond its means has brought us to a time of reckoning. Ours is but a moment in history. But one moment of courage, idealism and bipartisan unity can change American history forever. . . .

Every dollar the federal government does not take from us, every decision it does not make for us, will make our economy stronger, our lives more abundant, our future more free. . . .

There is another great heritage to speak of this evening. Of all the changes that have swept America the past four years, none brings greater promise than our rediscovery of the value of faith, freedom, family, work and neighborhood.

We see signs of renewal in increased attendance in places of worship: renewed optimism and faith in our future; love of country rediscovered by our young who are leading the way. We have rediscovered that work is good in and of itself; that it ennobles us to create and contribute no matter how seemingly humble our jobs. We have seen a powerful new current from an old and honorable tradition—American generosity. . . .

I thank the Congress for passing equal access legislation giving religious groups the same right to use classrooms after school that other groups enjoy. But no citizen need tremble, nor the world shudder, if a child stands in a classroom and breathes a prayer. We ask you again—give children back a right they had for a century-and-a-half or more in this country.

The question of abortion grips our nation. Abortion is either the taking of human life, or it isn't; and if it is—and medical technology is increasingly showing it is—it must be stopped. . . .

Of all the changes in the past 20 years, none has more threatened our sense of national well-being than the explosion of violent crime. One does not have to have been attacked to be a victim. The woman who must run to her car after shopping at night is a victim; the couple draping their door with locks and chains are victims; as is the tired, decent cleaning woman who can't ride a subway home without being afraid.

We do not seek to violate rights of defendants, but shouldn't we feel more compassion for victims of crime than for those who commit crime? For the first time in 20 years, the crime index has fallen two years in a row; we've convicted over 7,400 drug offenders, and put them, as well as leaders of organized crime, behind bars in record numbers.

But we must do more. I urge the House to follow the Senate and enact proposals permitting use of all reliable evidence that police officers acquire in good faith. These proposals would also reform the *habeas corpus* laws and allow, in keeping with the will of the overwhelming majority of Americans, the use of the death penalty where necessary.

There can be no economic revival in ghettos when the most violent among us are allowed to roam free. It is time we restored domestic tranquility. And we mean to do just that. . . .

Tonight I have spoken of great plans and great dreams. They are dreams we can make come true. Two hundred years of American history should have taught us that nothing is impossible. . . . Anything is possible in America if we have the faith, the will and the heart.

History is asking us, once again, to be a force for good in the world. Let us begin—in unity, with justice and love.

Thank you and God bless you.

Reagan's America: A Capital Offense

Kevin P. Phillips

When Richard Nixon ran for president in 1968, one of the political documents guiding his campaign was written by a young conservative named Kevin Phillips. Entitled The Emerging Republican Majority, *the Phillips treatise argued that by putting together the Sunbelt votes of the old Confederacy, the Southwest, and the West Coast, the Republicans could win national elections without carrying a single state of the industrial "rustbelt" in the Northeast and Midwest. Phillips's insights were prophetic, defining a new political paradigm essential to Republican dominance. Carter and Clinton, for example, were able to win in 1976 and 1992 only by breaking the Republican "Solid South," and/or winning California.*

Phillips also ensured his own reputation for sagacity. Since 1968 he has become one of the country's leading political pundits, often identifying years ahead of others the incipient political dynamics that will shape the next generation of elections. Thus, for example, he was one of the first political writers to detect the emergence of anger among middle-class voters who were riled by the way Reagan administration policies favored the rich without helping the average citizen. In this article, Phillips presents the evidence that helped shape the middle-class populism to which Bill Clinton appealed in his campaign against George Bush in 1992.

The 1980s were the triumph of upper America—an ostentatious celebration of wealth, the political ascendancy of the rich and a

Kevin P. Phillips, "Reagan's America: A Capital Offense" from *New York Times Magazine* (17 June 1990). Reprinted by permission of Kevin P. Phillips.

glorification of capitalism, free markets and finance. Not only did the concentration of wealth quietly intensify, but the sums involved took a megaleap. The definition of who's rich—and who's no longer rich—changed as radically during the Reagan era as it did during the great nouveaux riches eras of the late nineteenth century and the 1920s, periods whose excesses preceded the great reformist upheavals of the Progressive era and the New Deal.

But while money, greed, and luxury became the stuff of popular culture, few people asked why such great wealth had concentrated at the top and whether this was the result of public policy. Political leaders, even those who professed to care about the armies of homeless sleeping on grates and other sad evidence of a polarized economy, had little to say about the Republican Party's historical role: to revitalize capitalism but also to tilt power, government largess, more wealth and income toward the richest portion of the population.

The public, however, understood and worried about this Republican bias, if we can trust late 80s opinion polls; nevertheless, the Democrats largely shunned the issue in the '88 election, a reluctance their predecessors also displayed during Republican booms of the Gilded Age of the late nineteenth century and the Roaring Twenties.

As the decade ended, too many stretch limousines in Manhattan, too many yacht jams off Newport Beach and too many fur coats in Aspen foreshadowed a significant shift of mood. Only for so long would strungout $35,000-a-year families enjoy magazine articles about the hundred most successful businessmen in Dallas, or television shows about greed and glitz. Class structures may be weak in the United States, but populist sentiments run high. The political pendulum has swung in the past, and may be ready to swing again.

Indeed, money politics—be it avarice of financiers or the question of who will pay for the binges of the 80s—is shaping up as a prime theme for the 1990s. As we shall see, there is a historical cycle to such shifts: Whenever Republicans are in power long enough to transform economic policy from a middle-class orientation to capitalist overdrive, the rich get so far ahead that a popular reaction inevitably follows, with the Democrats usually tagging along, rather than leading.

But this time, the nature of the reaction against excess is likely to be different. The previous gilded ages occurred when America was on the economic rise in the world. The 1980s, on the other hand, turned into an era of paper entrepreneurialism, reflecting a nation consuming, rearranging and borrowing more than it built. For the next generation of populists who would like to rearrange American wealth, the bad news is that a large amount of it has already been redistributed—to Japan, West Germany and to the other countries that took Reagan-era I.O.U.s and credit slips.

Society matrons, Wall Street arbitrageurs, Palm Beach real-estate agents, and other money-conscious Americans picking up *USA Today* on May 22, 1987, must have been at first bewildered and then amused by the top story. In describing a Harris survey of the attitudes of upper-bracket citizens, the article summed up the typical respondent as "rich. Very. He's part of the thinnest economic upper crust: households with incomes of more than $100,000 a year."

A surprising number of 1980s polls and commentaries contributed to this naïve perception—that "rich" somehow started at $50,000 or $100,000 a year, and that gradations above that were somehow less important. The truth is that the critical concentration of wealth in the United States was developing at higher levels— decamillionaires, centimillionaires, half-billionaires and billionaires. Garden-variety American millionaires had become so common that there were about 1.5 million of them by 1989.

In fact, even many families with what seemed like good incomes—$50,000 a year, say, in Wichita, Kansas, or $90,000 a year in New York City (almost enough to qualify as "rich," according to *USA Today*)—found it hard to make ends meet because of the combined burden of Federal income and Social Security taxes, plus the soaring costs of state taxes, housing, health care and children's education. What few understood was that real economic status and leisure-class purchasing power had moved higher up the ladder, to groups whose emergence and relative affluence Middle America could scarcely comprehend.

No parallel upsurge of riches had been seen since the late nineteenth century, the era of the Vanderbilts, Morgans, and Rockefellers. It was the truly wealthy, more than anyone else, who flourished under Reagan. Calculations in a Brookings Institution study found that the share of national income going to the wealthiest 1 percent rose from 8.1 percent in 1981 to 14.7 percent in 1986. Between 1981 and 1989, the net worth of the Forbes 400 richest Americans nearly tripled. At the same time, the division between them and the rest of the country became a yawning gap. In 1980, corporate chief executive officers, for example, made roughly 40 times the income of average factory workers. By 1989, C.E.O.s were making *93 times as much.*

Finance alone built few billion-dollar fortunes in the 1980s relative to service industries like real estate and communications, but it is hard to overstate Wall Street's role during the decade, partly because Federal monetary and fiscal policies favored financial assets and because deregulation promoted new debt techniques and corporate restructuring.

Selling stock to retail clients, investment management firms or mutual funds paid well; repackaging, remortgaging or dismantling a Fortune 500 company paid magnificently. In 1981, analysts estimate, the financial community's dozen biggest earners made $5 million to $20 million a year. In 1988, despite the stock-market collapse the October before, the dozen top earners made $50 million to $200 million.

The redistribution of American wealth raised questions not just about polarization, but also about trivialization. Less and less wealth was going to people who produced something. Services were ascendant—from fast food to legal advice, investment vehicles to data bases. It is one thing for new technologies to reduce demand for obsolescent professions, enabling society to concentrate more resources in emerging sectors like health and leisure. But the distortion lies in the disproportionate rewards to society's economic, legal and cultural manipulators—from lawyers and financial advisers to advertising executives, merchandisers, media magnates and entertainers.

A related boom and distortion occurred in nonfinancial assets— art and homes, in particular. Art and antiques appreciated fourfold in the Reagan era, to the principal benefit of the richest 200,000 or 300,000 families. Similar if lesser explosions in art prices took place in the Gilded Age and in the 1920s. While the top one-half of 1 percent of Americans rolled in money, the luxuries they craved— from Picassos and eighteenth-century English furniture to Malibu beach houses—soared in markets virtually auxiliary to those in finance.

Meanwhile, everyone knew there was pain in society's lower ranks, from laid-off steelworkers to foreclosed farmers. A disproportionate number of female, black, Hispanic and young Americans lost ground in the 1980s, despite the progress of upscale minorities in each category. According to one study, for example, the inflation-adjusted income for families with children headed by an adult under 30 collapsed by roughly one-fourth between 1973 and 1986. Even on an overall basis, median family and household incomes showed only small inflation-adjusted gains between 1980 and 1988. Middle America was quietly hurting too.

While corporate presidents and chairmen feasted in the 1980s, as many as 1.5 million midlevel management jobs are estimated to have been lost during those years. Blue-collar America paid a larger price, but suburbia, where fathers rushed to catch the 8:10 train to the city, was counting its casualties, too. "Middle managers have become insecure," observed Peter F. Drucker in September 1988, "and they feel unbelievably hurt. They feel like slaves on an auction block."

American transitions of the magnitude of the capitalist blowout of the 1980s have usually coincided with a whole new range of national economic attitudes. Evolving government policies—from tax cuts to high interest rates—seem distinct, but they are actually linked.

Whether in the late nineteenth century, the 1920s or the 1980s, the country has witnessed conservative politics, a reduced role for government, entrepreneurialism and admiration of business, corporate restructuring and mergers, tax reduction, declining inflation, pain in states that rely on commodities like oil and wheat, rising inequality and concentration of wealth, and a buildup of debt and speculation. The scope of these trends has been impressive— and so has their repetition, though the two periods of the twentieth century have involved increasingly more paper manipulation and less of the raw vigor typical of the late nineteenth-century railroad and factory expansion.

Federal policy from 1981 to 1988 enormously affected investment, speculation and the creation and distribution of wealth and income, just as in the past.

The reduction or elimination of Federal income taxes was a goal in previous capitalist heydays. But it was a personal preoccupation for Ronald Reagan, whose antipathy toward income taxes dated back to his high-earning Hollywood days, when a top tax bracket of 91 percent in the 40s made it foolish to work beyond a certain point.

Under him, the top personal tax bracket would drop from 70 percent to 28 percent in only seven years. For the first time since the era of Franklin D. Roosevelt, tax policy was fundamentally rearranging its class loyalties.

Reaganite theorists reminded the country that the Harding-Coolidge income-tax cuts—from a top rate of 73 percent in 1920 to 25 percent in 1925—helped create the boom of the 20s. Back then, just as in the 80s, the prime beneficiaries were the top 5 percent of Americans, people who rode the cutting edge of the new technology of autos, radios and the like, emerging service industries, including new practices like advertising and consumer finance, a booming stock market and unprecedented real-estate development. Disposable income soared for the rich, and with it, conspicuous consumption and financial speculation. After the 1929 crash and the advent of the New Deal, tax rates rose again; the top rate reached 79 percent by 1936 and 91 percent right after the war. In 1964, the rate fell in two stages, to 77 percent and then to 70 percent.

Under Reagan, Federal budget policy, like tax changes, became a factor in the realignment of wealth, especially after the 1981–82 recession sent the deficit soaring. The slack was made up by money borrowed at home and abroad at high cost. The first effect lay in who received more Government funds. Republican constituencies—military producers and installations, agribusiness, bondholders and the elderly—clearly benefited, while decreases in social programs hurt Democratic interests and constituencies: the poor, big cities, housing, education. Equally to the point, the huge payments of high-interest charges on the growing national debt enriched the wealthy, who bought the bonds that kept Government afloat.

Prosperous individuals and financial institutions were beneficiaries of Government policies in other ways. Starting in the Carter years, Congress began to deregulate the financial industry; but the leap came in the early 1980s, when deposit and loan interest ceilings were removed. To attract deposits, financial institutions raised their interest rates, which rose and even exceeded record postwar levels. The small saver profited, but the much larger gain, predictably, went to the wealthy. (The benefits of high interest were intensified, of course, by the declining maximum tax rate on dividend and interest income. The explosion of after-tax unearned income for the top 1 percent of Americans was just that—an explosion.)

The savings and loan crisis weighing on American taxpayers [in 1990] also had roots in deregulation. Before 1982, savings and loan associations were required to place almost all their loans in home mortgages, a relatively safe and stable class of assets. But in 1982, after soaring interest rates turned millions of low-interest mortgages into undesirable assets, a new law allowed savings and loans to invest their funds more freely—100 percent in commercial real-estate ventures if they so desired. Like banks in the 1920s, many thrifts proceeded to gamble with their deposits, and by 1988, many had lost. Gamblers and speculators enriched themselves even as they stuck other Americans with the tab.

Reagan's permissiveness toward mergers, antitrust enforcement and new forms of speculative finance was likewise typical of Republican go-go conservatism. Unnerving parallels were made between the Wall Street raiders of the 1980s—Ivan Boesky and T. Boone Pickens—and the takeover pools of the 1920s, when high-powered operators would combine to "boom" a particular stock. For a small group of Americans at the top, the pickings were enormous.

As egregious misperception of late twentieth-century politics is to associate only Democrats with extremes of public debt. Before 1933, conservatives—Federalists, Whigs and Republicans alike—sponsored Government indebtedness and used high-interest payments to redistribute wealth upward.

In addition, Republican eras were noted for a huge expansion of private debt. In the 1920s, individual, consumer and corporate debt kept setting record levels, aided by new techniques like installment purchases and margin debt for purchasing securities. In the kindred 80s, total private and public debt grew from $4.2 trillion to more than $10 trillion. And just as they had sixty years earlier, new varieties of debt became an art form.

Government fiscal strategists were equally loose. In part to avoid the deficit-reduction mandates of the Gramm-Rudman-Hollings Act, they allowed Federal credit programs, including student and housing loans, to balloon from $300 billion in 1984 to $500 billion in 1989.

In contrast to previous capitalist blowouts, the fast-and-loose Federal debt strategies of the 80s did not simply rearrange assets within the country but served to transfer large amounts of the nation's wealth overseas as well. America's share of global wealth expanded in the Gilded Age and again in the 1920s. The late 1980s,

however, marked a significant downward movement: one calculation, by the Japanese newspaper *Nihon Keizai Shimbun*, had Japan
overtaking the United States, with estimated comparative assets of
$43.7 trillion in 1987 for Japan, versus $36.2 trillion for the United
States.

The United States was losing relative purchasing power on a
grand scale. There might be more wealthy Americans than ever
before, but foreigners commanded greater resources. On the 1989
Forbes list of the world's billionaires, the top twelve, with the exception of one American, were all foreigners—from Japan, Europe,
Canada and South Korea. Dollar millionaires, once the envy of the
world, were becoming an outdated elite.

This shift reflected the ebb of America's postwar-eminence. Yet
the same Reagan policies that moved riches internally also accelerated the shift of world wealth, beginning with the budget deficits of
the early 1980s but intensifying after the ensuing devaluation of the
dollar from 1985 to 1988.

If the devalued dollar made the Japanese, French, and Germans
relatively richer, it also increased their purchasing power in the
United States, turning the country into a bargain basement for
overseas buyers. This is the explanation for the surging foreign
acquisition of properties, from Fortune 500 companies to Rockefeller Center in Manhattan and a large share of the office buildings in
downtown Los Angeles.

The dollar's decline also pushed per capita gross national product and comparative wages in the United States below those of a
number of Western European nations. The economist Lester C.
Thurow summed up the predicament: "When it comes to wealth,
we can argue about domestic purchasing power. But, in terms of
international purchasing power, the United States is now only the
ninth wealthiest country in the world in terms of per capita G.N.P.
We have been surpassed by Austria, Switzerland, the Netherlands,
West Germany, Denmark, Sweden, Norway and Japan."

Not everyone looked askance at foreign wealth and investment.
American cities and states welcomed it. From the textile towns of
South Carolina to the rolling hills of Ohio, foreigners were helping
declining regions to reverse their fate. Yet as Warren Buffett, the
investor, said: "We are much like a wealthy family that annually sells
acreage so that it can sustain a life style unwarranted by its current
output. Until the plantation is gone, it's all pleasure and no pain. In

the end, however, the family will have traded the life of an owner for the life of a tenant farmer."

Nowhere was Japanese investment more obvious than in Hawaii, where real-estate moguls from Tokyo pronounced the property they were grabbing up "almost free." An economist at a Hawaiian bank warned that the state was "a kind of test lab for what's facing the whole country." Indeed, in 1988, broader foreign ambitions were apparent. The author Daniel Burstein quoted Masaaki Kurokawa, then head of Japan's Nomura Securities International, who raised with American dinner guests the possibility of turning California into a joint U.S.-Japanese economic community.

Public concern over America's international weakness had been a factor in Ronald Reagan's election back in 1980. Voters had wanted a more aggressive leader than Jimmy Carter. For various reasons, the great things promised were not delivered. Reagan could re-create a sense of military prowess with his attacks on Grenada and Libya. But in the global economy he took a country that had been the world's biggest creditor in 1980 and turned it into the world's largest debtor. Despite opinion polls documenting public concern about this erosion, surprisingly little was made of the issue in the 1988 Presidential campaign, possibly because the Democrats could not develop a coherent domestic and international alternative.

Much of the new emphasis in the 1980s on tax reduction and the aggressive accumulation of wealth reflected the Republican Party's long record of support for unabashed capitalism. It was no fluke that three important Republican supremacies coincided with and helped generate the Gilded Age, the Roaring Twenties and the Reagan-Bush years.

Part of the reason survival-of-the-fittest periods are so relentless, however, rests on the performance of the Democrats as history's second-most enthusiastic capitalist party. They do not interfere with capitalist momentum, but wait for excesses and the inevitable popular reaction.

In the United States, elections arguably play a more important cultural and economic role than in other lands. Because we lack a hereditary aristocracy or Establishment, our leadership elites and the alignment of wealth are more the product of political cycles than they are elsewhere. Capitalism is maneuvered more easily in the United States, pushed in new regional and sectoral directions. As a result, the genius of American politics—failing only in the Civil

War—has been to manage through ballot boxes the problems that less-fluid societies resolve with barricades and with party structures geared to class warfare.

Because we are a mobile society, Americans tolerate one of the largest disparities in the industrial world between top and bottom incomes, as people from the middle move to the top, and vice versa. Opportunity has counted more than equality.

But if circulating elites are a reality, electoral politics is an important traffic controller. From the time of Thomas Jefferson, the nation has undulated in 28- to 36-year waves as each watershed election puts a new dominant region, culture, ideology or economic interest (or combination) into the White House, changing the country's direction. But after a decade or two, the new forces lose touch with the public, excessively empower their own elites and become a target for a new round of populist reform. Only the United States among major nations reveals such recurrent electoral behavior over two centuries.

The Republicans rode such a wave into office in 1968, as a middle-class, anti-elite correction, successfully squelching the social permissiveness and disorder of the 60s. Significantly, each Republican coalition—from Lincoln's to Nixon's—began by emphasizing national themes and unity symbols, while subordinating commercial and financial interests.

But it is the second stage—dynamic capitalism, market economics, and the concentration of wealth—that the Republican Party is all about. When Republicans are in power long enough, they ultimately find themselves embracing limited government, less regulation of business, reduced taxation, disinflation and high real interest rates. During America's first two centuries, these policies shaped the three periods that would incubate the biggest growth of American millionaires (or, by the 1980s, billionaires). History suggests that it takes a decade or more for the Republican party to shift from broad middle-class nationalism into capitalist overdrive, and the lapse of twelve years between the first Nixon inauguration in 1969 and the first Reagan inauguration repeats this transformation.

Nixon, like the previous Republican nationalist Presidents Abraham Lincoln and William McKinley, was altogether middle class, as was his "new majority" Republicanism. He had no interest in unbridled capitalism during his 1969–74 Presidency.

In fact, many of the new adherents recruited for the Republican coalition in 1968 and 1972 were wooed with the party's populist attacks on inflation, big government, social engineering and the Liberal Establishment. Many Republican voters of that era embraced outsider and anti-elite values, and like similar participants in previous Republican national coalitions, they would become uneasy in the 1980s as Reagan or Bush Republicanism embraced Beverly Hills or Yale culture and the economics of leveraged buyouts, not of Main Street.

Besides this uneasiness, reflected in opinion polls, a second sign that a conservative cycle is moving toward its climax has been the extent to which Democratic politics has been cooperative: when wealth is in fashion, Democrats go along. The solitary Democratic President of the Gilded Age, Grover Cleveland, was a conservative with close Wall Street connections. In the 20s, the Democratic Presidential nominees in both 1920 (James Cox, an Ohio publisher) and 1924 (John W. Davis, a corporate lawyer) were in the Cleveland mold. Alfred E. Smith, who ran in 1928, would eventually oppose Roosevelt and the New Deal. In the 20s, Congressional Democrats competed with Republicans to cut upper-bracket and corporate taxes.

Fifty years later, Jimmy Carter, the only Democratic President to interrupt the long Republican hegemony after 1968, was accused by the historian Arthur M. Schlesinger Jr. of an "eccentric effort to carry the Democratic Party back to Grover Cleveland." Despite his support for substantial new Federal regulation, Carter clearly deviated from his party's larger post–New Deal norm. He built foundations that would become conservative architecture under Reagan: economic deregulation; capital-gains tax reduction and the tight-money policies of the Federal Reserve. (The Fed's chairman, Paul A. Volcker, was a Carter appointee.) Congressional Democrats echoed their policies of the 1920s by colluding in the bipartisan tax-bracket changes of 1981 and 1986.

Thus, the Democrats could hardly criticize Reagan's tax reductions. For the most part, they laid little groundwork for an election-year critique in 1988, leaving the issue to Jesse Jackson, whose appeal was limited by his race and third-world rhetoric, and to noncandidates like Mario M. Cuomo. Michael S. Dukakis was obviously uncomfortable with populist politics. Though several consultants and economists urged him to pick up the theme of economic inequality, Dukakis made competence, not ideology, his initial campaign issue. Only in late October, with his campaign crumbling, did the Democratic candidate reluctantly convert to a more traditional party line. It came too late.

Republican strategists could hardly believe their luck. Said Lee Atwater, Bush's campaign manager, after the election: "The way to win a Presidential race against the Republicans is to develop the class-warfare issue, as Dukakis did at the end—to divide up the haves and the have nots and to try to reinvigorate the New Deal coalition and to attack."

On the surface, this was a missed Democratic opportunity. But the lesson of history is that the party of Cleveland, Carter and Dukakis has rarely rushed its anti-elite corrective role. There would be no rush again in 1988—nor, indeed, in 1989.

Early in his presidency, George Bush replaced the Coolidge portrait hung by Ronald Reagan in the White House with one of Theodore Roosevelt, reflecting Bush's belief in T.R.'s commitment to conservation, patrician reform, and somewhat greater regulatory involvement.

Yet there has not been too much evidence of a kinder, gentler America beyond softer, more conciliatory rhetoric. The budget remained unkind to any major expansion of domestic programs, and Bush's main tax objective was a reduction in the capital gains rate, a shift that critics said would continue to concentrate benefits among the top 1 percent of Americans.

By spring 1990, Washington politicians confronted the most serious debt- and credit-related problems since the bank failures, collapsed stock prices, farm foreclosures and European war debt defaults of the Great Depression. From the savings and loan associations bailout to junk bonds, from soaring bankruptcies and shaky real-estate markets to Japanese influence in the bond market, Federal policy makers were forced to realize that a crucial task—and peril—of the 1990s would involve cleaning up after the previous decade's credit-card parties and speculative distortions. . . .

Whether the populist reactions that followed past boom periods recur in the 90s no one can know. But there could be no doubt that the last decade ended as it had begun: with a rising imperative for a new political and economic philosophy, and growing odds that the 1990s will be a very different chapter than the 1980s in the annals of American wealth and power.

Part 8

WHERE DO WE GO FROM HERE?

As America prepares to enter a new century, issues that developed as an outgrowth of World War II continue to shape our national agenda, even as dramatic changes in the world suggest the emergence of a whole new series of challenges. From 1945 until the present, the American economy has functioned with extraordinary power. Yet since the mid-1970s, it has become increasingly clear that the United States is no longer solely in control, but rather has become as dependent on the economies of other countries as *they* are on the economy of America. Japan and Germany, reindustrialized by the United States after World War II, now set the standard for productivity and per capita income. Those countries have been joined by nations on the Pacific Rim, from Korea to Thailand to China, as the new high growth sectors of the world. Developing countries in Latin America, Africa, and Asia compete for the same jobs—jobs that are now leaving America and other "first world" countries.

As this interdependency grows, it inevitably diminishes the extent to which America stands as the sole repository of prosperous democratic capitalism. When good jobs leave, workers' wages decline, consumer patterns alter, trade deficits grow, and living standards deteriorate. As Kevin Phillips indicated in his article on the Reagan revolution, American society has become more and more bifurcated, with "two tiers" of people—those that prosper because of their education and technological skills, and those who barely survive in minimum-wage jobs, crippled by their lack of education and skills. As high school dropout rates increase, so too do the welfare rolls, the number of female-headed households, and the ranks of those now referred to as the "underclass"—people permanently outside the employment structure, who constitute a vivid refutation of America as an "equal opportunity" society.

In the meantime, the structure of world geopolitics has undergone its own transformation. Nearly three quarters of a century after coming into existence, the Soviet Union has disappeared. The Cold War, which for nearly half a century shaped American foreign policy and profoundly influenced its domestic policy as well, suddenly came to an end, with the United States occupying the unanticipated position of being declared the undisputed "winner," now the only superpower of the world. As freedom—and capitalism—coursed through the streets of Moscow, Prague, Budapest, and Warsaw, the world took on a new shape.

At the same time, a new administration took over in Washington. Reflecting the changes in the world order, the Bill Clinton presidency became the first in nearly half a century to focus primarily on domestic issues. During the Cold War, it had been impossible to debate some issues because of the domestic ramifications of anti-communism. During the 1940s and 1950s, for example, ideas like national health insurance were denounced as "socialized medicine," hence automatically ruled out of consideration. Now, Congress debated seriously for the first time whether America should enter the ranks of other industrial nations where health care was assumed to be a governmental and societal responsibility.

Yet changes in the way the world had once been organized did not necessarily bring peace or stability. New international problems proliferated, with ethnic nationalism, indigenous civil wars, and religious jihads taking over where once there had reigned what now seemed, in retrospect, a "golden age" of stability associated with the Cold War. How was it possible to determine what was morally correct or politically advantageous when the choices in international affairs were so murky and muddled?

Nor were the issues only those of geopolitics. World environmental concerns exploded, even as the ability of nations to come together and work cooperatively to solve them seemed to diminish. What happened to the World's oceans, to its water supplies, to its atmosphere as a consequence of uncontrolled development, reckless consumerism, wanton disregard for waste disposal, and short-sighted destruction of fossil fuel supplies?

The world also faced the outbreak of perhaps the worst health epidemic since the bubonic plague. The AIDS virus spread through Africa and Asia, decimating whole populations. In many Western and industrial nations, a commitment of resources adequate for fighting a plague became hostage to debates among politicians and religious leaders over whether the AIDS virus should be seen as primarily a problem of homosexuals, and hence less deserving of attention. By this bizarre reasoning, homosexuals were a different order of being than heterosexuals. Even as the epidemic threatened to reach uncontrollable proportions, politicians still worried over whether to acknowledge its presence. In one more instance, forces of division around cultural and political issues threatened to prevent people and nations from coming together around their common humanity.

The following selections address some of these issues. Robert Reich's article on the world economy emphasizes the crisis America faces if it does not recognize the impact of global economic shifts by addressing the inequities in our own social and economic infrastructure. Commenting on the impact of some of these same changes, William Julius Wilson analyzes the plight of the urban underclass in an advanced industrial society and argues that its amelioration requires broad economic reforms rather than "race-specific" antidiscrimination policies. Vice President Al Gore comments on the way our assault on the environment has put at risk our survival as an ecologically viable planet. In his speech to the Congress on the State of the Union in 1994, and in particular the importance of national health care reform, President Bill Clinton offers a vision of his presidency and what he hopes to accomplish. The end of the Cold War began a new era of world affairs—with unanticipated developments, unexpected crises, and much confusion about the goals and manner of American foreign policy. As the essay by Daniel Deudney and G. John Ikenberry explains, moreover, the Cold War's finish also has a profound impact on the domestic affairs of the United States. And Jeffrey Schmalz, a reporter for the *New York Times,* provides an analysis, published after his death from AIDS, on how and why federal policy toward the AIDS epidemic has fallen so far short of the mark.

In all of this, the challenges facing a new generation begin to take shape and definition, suggesting that as difficult and tumultuous as the issues of the post–World War II world were, they may well pale beside those of the post–Cold War world.

As the World Turns

Robert B. Reich

When the Arab oil embargo of 1973 caused American automobile and homeowners to panic because of lack of fuel, it was the first visible indication to the American public that the United States no longer was in economic charge of the world. Since then the message has become unavoidable. Not only has the standard of living in America fallen below that of several other industrial countries, we know, from the brand names of our stereos and TV's as well as the "made in China" label on our clothes, that the goods we consume and the technology we use, more often than not, come from outside our own borders.

The consequences of this change are fundamental. In the early 1950s, there were still more blue-collar workers in America than white-collar workers. Today, factory jobs have plummeted, and experts predict that every new job created will be in the service sector of the economy. The implications of this shift are staggering—for wages, quality of life, possibilities for home ownership, and a sense of social cohesion, among other things. In the following article, Robert Reich, a political economist at the Kennedy School of Government at Harvard, explores some of the challenges posed by these world economic changes for our society and its sense of shared values.

Between 1978 and 1987, the poorest fifth of American families became eight percent poorer, and the richest fifth became 13 percent richer. That leaves the poorest fifth with less than five percent of the nation's income, and the richest fifth with more than 40 percent. This widening gap can't be blamed on the growth in single-parent lower-income families, which in fact slowed markedly after the late 1970s. Nor is it due mainly to the stingy social policy of

Reprinted from *The New Republic* (May 1, 1989), by permission.

the Reagan years. Granted, Food Stamp benefits have dropped in real terms by about 13 percent since 1981, and many states have failed to raise benefits for the poor and unemployed to keep up with inflation. But this doesn't come close to accounting for the growing inequality Rather, the trend is connected to a profound change in the American economy as it merges with the global economy. And because the merging is far from complete, this trend will not stop of its own accord anytime soon.

It is significant that the growth of inequality shows up most strikingly among Americans who have jobs. Through most of the postwar era, the wages of Americans at different income levels rose at about the same pace. Although different workers occupied different steps on the escalator, everyone moved up together. In those days poverty was the condition of *jobless* Americans, and the major economic challenge was to create enough jobs for everyone. Once people were safely on the work force escalator, their problems were assumed to be over. Thus "full employment" became a liberal rallying cry, while conservatives fretted over the inflationary tendencies of a full-employment economy.

In recent years working Americans have been traveling on two escalators—one going up, the other going down. In 1987 the average hourly earnings of non-supervisory workers, adjusted for inflation, were lower than in any year since 1966. Middle-level managers fared much better, although their median real earnings were only slightly above the levels of the 1970s. Executives, however, did spectacularly well. In 1988 alone, CEOs of the hundred largest publicly held industrial corporations received raises averaging almost 12 percent. The remunerations of lesser executives rose almost as much, and executives of smaller companies followed close behind.

Between 1978 and 1987, as the real earnings of unskilled workers were declining, the real incomes of workers in the securities industry (investment bankers, arbitrageurs, and brokers) rose 21 percent. Few investment bankers pocket anything near the $50 million lavished yearly upon the partners of Kohlberg, Kravis, Roberts & Company, or the $550 million commandeered last year by Michael Milken, but it is not unusual for a run-of-the-mill investment banker to bring home comfortably over a million dollars. Partners in America's largest corporate law firms are comparatively deprived, enjoying average yearly earnings of only $400,000 to $1.2 million.

Meanwhile, the number of impoverished *working* Americans climbed by nearly two million, or 23 percent, between 1978 and 1987. The number who worked full time and year round but were poor climbed faster by 43 percent. Nearly 60 percent of the 20 million people who now fall below the Census Bureau's poverty line are from families with at least one member in full-time or part-time work.

The American economy, in short, is creating a wider range of earnings than at any other time in the postwar era. The most basic reason, put simply, is that America itself is ceasing to exist as a system of production and exchange separate from the rest of the world. One can no more meaningfully speak of an "American economy" than of a "Delaware economy." We are becoming but a region—albeit still a relatively wealthy region—of a global economy, whose technologies, savings, and investments move effortlessly across borders, making it harder for individual nations to control their economic destinies.

By now Washington officials well understand that the nation's fiscal and monetary policies cannot be set without taking account of the savings that will slosh in or slosh out of the nation in consequence. Less understood is the speed and ease with which new technologies now spread across the globe, from computers in, say, San Jose, to satellite, and then back down to computers in Taiwan. (America's efforts to stop the Japanese from copying our commercial designs and the Soviets from copying our military designs are about equally doomed.) And we have yet to come to terms with the rise of the global corporation, whose managers, shareholders, and employees span the world. Our debates over the future of American jobs still focus on topics like the competitiveness of the American automobile industry or the future of American manufacturing. But these categories are increasingly irrelevant. They assume the existence of a separate American economy in which all the jobs associated with a particular industry, or even more generally with a particular sector, are bound together, facing a common fate.

New technologies of worldwide communication and transportation have redrawn the playing field. American industries no longer com-pete against Japanese or European industries. Rather, a company with headquarters in the United States, production facilities in Taiwan, and a marketing force spread across many nations competes with another, similarly ecumenical company. So when General Motors, say, is doing well, that probably is good news for a lot of executives in Detroit, and for GM shareholders across the globe, but it isn't necessarily good news for a lot of assembly-line workers in Detroit, because there may, in fact, be very few GM assembly-line workers in Detroit, or elsewhere in America. The welfare of assembly-line workers in Detroit may depend, instead, on the health of corporations based in Japan or Canada.

More to the point: even if those Canadian and Japanese corporations are doing well, these workers may be in trouble. For they are increasingly part of an international labor market, encompassing Asia, Africa, Western Europe—and perhaps, before long, Eastern Europe. Corporations can with relative ease relocate their production centers, and alter their international lines of communication and transportation accordingly, to take advantage of low wages. So American workers find themselves settling for low wages in order to hold onto their jobs. More and more, your "competitiveness" as a worker depends not on the fortunes of any American corporation, or of any American industry, but on what function you serve within the global economy. GM executives are becoming more "competitive" even as GM production workers become less so, because the functions that GM executives perform are more highly valued in the world market than the functions that GM production workers perform.

In order to see in greater detail what is happening to American jobs, it helps to view the work Americans do in terms of functional categories that reflect the real competitive positions of workers in the global economy. Essentially, three broad categories are emerging. Call them symbolic-analytic services, routine production services, and routine personal services.

1. *Symbolic-analytic services* are based on the manipulation of information: data, words, and oral and visual symbols. Symbolic analysis comprises some (but by no means all) of the work undertaken by people who call themselves lawyers, investment bankers, commercial bankers, management consultants, research scientists, academics, public relations executives, real estate developers, and even a few creative accountants. Also: advertising and marketing specialists, art directors, design engineers, architects, writers and editors, musicians, and television and film producers. Some of the manipu-

lations performed by symbolic analysts reveal ways of more efficiently deploying resources or shifting financial assets, or of otherwise saving time and energy. Other manipulations grab money from people who are too slow or naive to protect themselves by manipulation in response. Still others serve to entertain the recipients.

Most symbolic analysts work alone or in small teams. If they work with others, they often have partners rather than bosses or supervisors, and their yearly income is variable, depending on how much value they add to the business. Their work environments tend to be quiet and tastefully decorated, often within tall steel-and-glass buildings. They rarely come in direct contact with the ultimate beneficiaries of their work. When they are not analyzing, designing, or strategizing, they are in meetings or on the telephone—giving advice or making deals. Many of them spend inordinate time in jet planes and hotels. They are articulate and well-groomed. The vast majority are white males.

Symbolic analysis now accounts for more than 40 percent of America's gross national product, and almost 20 percent of our jobs. Within what we still term our "manufacturing sector," symbolic-analytic jobs have been increasing at a rate almost three times that of total manufacturing employment in the United States, as routine manufacturing jobs have drifted overseas or been mastered by machines.

The services performed by America's symbolic analysts are in high demand around the world, regardless of whether the symbolic analysts provide them in person or transmit them via satellite and fiber-optic cable. The Japanese are buying up the insights and inventions of America's scientists and engineers (who are only too happy to sell them at a fat profit). The Europeans, meanwhile, are hiring our management consultants, business strategists, and investment bankers. Developing nations are hiring our civil and design engineers; and almost everyone is buying the output of our pop musicians, television stars, and film producers.

It is the same with the global corporation. The central offices of these sprawling entities, headquartered in America, are filled with symbolic analysts who manipulate information and then export their insights via the corporation's far-flung enterprise. IBM doesn't export machines from the United States; it makes machines all over the globe, and services them on the spot. IBM world head-quarters, in Armonk, New York, just exports strategic planning and related management services.

Thus has the standard of living of America's symbolic analysts risen. They increasingly find themselves part of a global labor market, not a national one. And because the United States has a highly developed economy, and an excellent university system, they find that the services they have to offer are quite scarce in the context of the whole world. So elementary laws of supply and demand ensure that their salaries are quite high.

These salaries are likely to go even higher in the years ahead, as the world market for symbolic analysis continues to grow. Foreigners are trying to learn these skills and techniques, to be sure, but they still have a long way to go. No other country does a better job of preparing its most fortunate citizens for symbolic analysis than does the United States. None has surpassed America in providing experience and training, often with entire regions specializing in one or another kind of symbolic analysis (New York and Chicago for finance, Los Angeles for music and film, the San Francisco Bay area and greater Boston for science and engineering). In this we can take pride. But for the second major category of American workers—the providers of routine production services—the laws of supply and demand don't bode well.

2. *Routine production services* involve tasks that are repeated over and over, as one step in a sequence of steps for producing a finished product. Although we tend to associate these jobs with manufacturing, they are becoming common in the storage and retrieval of information. Banking, insurance, wholesaling, retailing, health care—all employ hordes of people who spend their days processing data, often putting information into computers or taking it out.

Most providers of routine production services work with many other people who do similar work within large, centralized facilities. They are overseen by supervisors, who in turn are monitored by more senior supervisors. They are usually paid an hourly wage. Their jobs are monotonous. Most of these people do not have a college education; they need only be able to take directions and, occasionally, undertake simple computations. Those who deal with metal are mostly white males; those who deal with fabrics or information tend to be female and/or minorities.

Decades ago, jobs like these were relatively well paid. Henry Ford gave his early production workers five dollars a day, a remarkable sum for the time, in the (correct) belief that they and their neighbors would be among the major buyers of Fords. But in recent years America's providers of routine production services have found themselves in direct competition with millions of foreign workers, most of whom are eager to work for a fraction of the pay of American workers. Through the miracle of satellite transmission, even routine data processing can now be undertaken in relatively poor nations, thousands of miles away from the skyscrapers where the data are finally used. This fact has given management-level symbolic analysts ever greater bargaining leverage. If routine producers living in America don't agree to reduce their wages, then the work will go abroad.

And it has. In 1950 routine production services constituted about 30 percent of our national product and well over half of American jobs. Today such services represent about 20 percent of national product and one-fourth of jobs. And the scattering of foreign-owned factories placed here to circumvent American protectionism isn't going to reverse the trend. So the standard of living of America's routine production workers will likely keep declining. The dynamics behind the wage concessions, plant closings, and union-busting that have become commonplace are not likely to change.

3. *Routine personal services* also entail simple, repetitive work, but, unlike routine production services, they are provided in person. Their immediate objects are specific customers rather than streams of metal, fabric, or data. Included in this employment category are restaurant and hotel workers, barbers and beauticians, retail sales personnel, cabdrivers, household cleaners, day-care workers, hospital attendants and orderlies, truck drivers, and—among the fastest-growing of all—custodians and security guards.

Like production workers, providers of personal services are usually paid by the hour, are carefully supervised, and rarely have more than a high school education. But unlike people in the other two categories of work, these people are in direct contact with the ultimate beneficiaries of what they do. And the companies they work for are often small. In fact, some routine personal-service workers turn entrepreneurial. (Most new businesses and new jobs in America come from this sector—now constituting about 20 percent of GNP and 30 percent of jobs.) Women and minorities make up the bulk of routine personal-service workers.

Apart from the small number who strike out on their own, these workers are poorly paid. They are sheltered from the direct effects of global competition, but not the indirect effects. They often compete with illegal aliens willing to work for low wages, or with former or would-be production workers who can't find well-paying production jobs, or with labor-saving machinery (automated tellers, self-service gas pumps, computerized cashiers) dreamed up by symbolic analysts in America and manufactured in Asia. And because they tend to be unskilled and dispersed among small businesses, personal-service workers rarely have a union or a powerful lobby group to stand up for their interests. When the economy turns sour, they are among the first to feel the effects. These workers will continue to have jobs in the years ahead and may experience some small increase in real wages. They will have demographics on their side, as the American work force shrinks. But for all the foregoing reasons, the gap between their earnings and those of the symbolic analysts will continue to grow.

These three functional categories—symbolic analysis, routine production and routine personal service—over at least three out of four American jobs. The rest of the nation's work force consists mainly of government employees (including public schoolteachers), employees in regulated industries (like utility workers), and government-financed workers (engineers working on defense weapons systems), many of whom are sheltered from global competition. One further clarification: some traditional job categories overlap with several functional categories. People called "secretaries," for example, include those who actually spend their time doing symbolic-analytic work closely allied to what their bosses do; those who do routine data entry or retrieval of a sort that will eventually be automated or done overseas; and those who provide routine personal services.

The important point is that workers in these three functional categories are coming to have a different competitive position in the world economy. Symbolic analysts hold a commanding position in an increasingly global labor market. Routine production workers hold a relatively weak position in an increasingly global labor market. Personal-service workers still find themselves in a national labor market, but for various reasons they suffer the indirect effects of competition from workers abroad.

How should we respond to these trends? One response is to accept them as inevitable consequences of change, but try to offset their polarizing effects through a truly progressive income tax, coupled with more generous income assistance—including health insurance—for poor working Americans. (For a start, we might reverse the extraordinarily regressive Social Security amendments of 1983, through which poor working Americans are now financing the federal budget deficit, often paying more in payroll taxes than in income taxes.)

A more ambitious response would be to guard against class rigidities by ensuring that any talented American kid can become a symbolic analyst—regardless of family income or race. Unlike America's old vertically integrated economy, whose white-collar jobs were necessarily limited in proportion to the number of blue-collar jobs beneath them, the global economy imposes no particular limit upon the number of Americans who can sell symbolic-analytic services. In principle, all of America's routine production workers could become symbolic analysts and let their old jobs drift overseas. In practice, of course, we can't even inch toward such a state anytime soon. Not even America's gifted but poor children can aspire to such jobs until the government spends substantially more than it does now to ensure excellent public schools in every city and region to which talented children can go, and ample financial help when they are ready to attend college.

Of course, it isn't clear that even under those circumstances there would be radical growth in the number of Americans who became research scientists, design engineers, musicians, management consultants, or (even if the world needed them) investment bankers and lawyers. So other responses are also needed. Perhaps the most ambitious would be to increase the numbers of Americans who could apply symbolic analysis to production and to personal services.

There is ample evidence, for example, that access to computerized information can enrich production jobs by enabling workers to alter the flow of materials and components in ways that generate new efficiencies. (Soshana Zuboff's recent book *In the Age of the Smart Machine* carefully documents these possibilities.) Production workers who thus have broader responsibilities and more control over how production is organized cease to be "routine" workers—becoming, in effect, symbolic analysts at a level very close to the production process. The same transformation can occur in personal-service jobs. Consider, for example, the checkout clerk whose computer enables her to control inventory and decide when to reorder items from the factory.

The number of such technologically empowered jobs, of course, is limited by the ability of workers to learn on the job. That means a far greater number of Americans will need good health care (including prenatal and postnatal) and also a good grounding in mathematics, basic science, and reading and communicating. So once again, comfortably integrating the American work force into the new world economy turns out to rest heavily on education.

Education and health care for poor children are apt to be costly. Since poorer working Americans, already under a heavy tax load, can't afford it, the cost would have to be borne by wealthier American—who also would have to bear the cost of any income redistribution plans designed to neutralize the polarizing domestic effects of a globalized economy. Thus a central question is the willingness of the more fortunate American citizens—specially symbolic analysts, who constitute the most fortunate fifth, with 40 percent of the nation's income—to bear the burden. But here lies a Catch-22. For as our economic fates diverge, the top fifth may be losing the sense of connectedness with the bottom fifth, or even the bottom half, that would elicit such generosity.

The conservative tide that has swept the land during the last decade surely has many causes, but these economic fundamentals should not be discounted. It is now possible for the most fortunate fifth to sell their expertise directly in the global market, and thus maintain and enhance their standard of living and that of their children, even as that of other Americans declines. There is less and less basis for a strong sense of interclass interdependence. Meanwhile, the fortunate fifth have also been able to insulate themselves from the less fortunate, by living in suburban enclaves far removed from the effects of poverty. Neither patriotism nor altruism may be sufficient to overcome these realities. Yet without the active support of the fortunate fifth, it will be difficult to muster the political will necessary for change.

George Bush speaks eloquently of "a thousand points of light" and of the importance of generosity. But so far his administration has set a poor example. A miniscule sum has been budgeted for education, training, and health care for the poor. The president says we can't afford any more. Meanwhile, he pushes a reduction in the capital gains tax rate—another boon to the fortunate fifth.

On withdrawing from the presidential race of 1988, Paul Simon of Illinois said, "Americans instinctively know that we are one nation, one family, and when anyone in that family hurts, all of us hurt." Sadly, that is coming to be less and less the case.

The Urban Underclass in Advanced Industrial Society

William Julius Wilson

Many Americans in the 1980s came to believe, along with Ronald Reagan, that black Americans had totally won their civil rights and now enjoyed equal opportunity. Impressed by the prosperity and family togetherness featured on televisions "Bill Cosby Show, "they could feel comfortable about the progress America had made in eliminating poverty and discrimination. Too few people realized that the poverty rate in America had increased during the 1980s to include one out of every seven people in this country. Or that one-third of all black and Hispanic families lived below the poverty line, with the percentages growing year by year. Nor did the average American know that one out of every five children lives in poverty—and one out of every two children in inner city areas—where jobs are scarce, and female-headed households account for more than 60 percent of the black and Hispanic population.

Many scholars have commented on this growing development of an "underclass"—people condemned to live in poverty from generation to generation. Some blame the phenomenon exclusively on continued racism; others see a more insidious blending of race, class, and gender oppression. In this selection, William Julius Wilson, harkening back to Bayard Rustin (see Part Four), takes a structural approach to the existence of the underclass, emphasizing the necessity of color-blind, fundamental economic reforms y economic and social stability are to be restored in America.

Excerpted from William Julius Wilson, "The Urban Underclass in Advanced Industrial Society," in Paul E. Peterson, ed., *The New Urban Reality* (Washington, D.C.: The Brookings Institution, 1985). Reprinted by permission.

Footnotes and tables omitted.

The social problems of urban life in the United States are, in large measure, associated with race. The rates of crime, drug addiction, teenage pregnancies, female-headed families, and welfare dependency have risen dramatically in the last several years, and they reflect a noticeably uneven distribution by race. Liberal social scientists, journalists, policy-makers, and civil rights leaders have nonetheless been reluctant to face this fact. Often analysts make no reference to race at all when discussing issues such as crime and teenage pregnancy, except to emphasize the deleterious effects of racial discrimination or of the institutionalized inequality of American society.

Indeed, in an effort to avoid the charge of racism or of "blaming the victim," some scholars have refrained from describing any behavior that might be construed as stigmatizing or unflattering to particular racial minorities. Accordingly, the increase among blacks in crime, female-headed families, teenage pregnancies, and welfare dependency has not received careful and systematic attention.

Such neglect is relatively recent. During the mid-1960s scholars such as Kenneth B. Clark, Lee Rainwater, and Daniel Patrick Moynihan forthrightly examined the cumulative effects of racial isolation and class subordination on life and behavior in the inner city. As Clark described it: "The symptoms of lower class society afflict the dark ghettos of America—low aspiration, poor education, family instability, illegitimacy, unemployment, crime, drug addiction and alcoholism, frequent illness and early death. But because Negroes begin with the primary affliction of inferior racial status, the burdens of despair and hatred are more pervasive." In Clark's analysis of psychological dimensions of the ghetto and Rainwater's and Moynihan's examinations of ghetto family patterns, the conditions of ghetto life "that are usually forgotten or ignored in polite discussions" were vividly described and systematically analyzed.

All of these studies linked discussions of the experiences of inequality to discussions of the structure of inequality. In other words, they attempted to show the connection between the economic and social environment into which many blacks are born and the creation of patterns and norms of behavior that, in the words of Clark, took the form of a "self-perpetuating pathology." The studies by Clark and Rainwater in particular not only sensitively analyzed those structural conditions, including changing economic relations, that combined with race-specific experiences to bring about these features.

One of the reasons social scientists have lately shied away from this line of research may perhaps be the virulent attacks on the "Moynihan report" concerning the Negro family in the latter half of the 1960s. There is no need here for detailed discussion of the controversy surrounding the report, which like so many controversies over social issues raged in great measure because of distortions and misinterpretations. However, it should be pointed out that various parts of Moynihan's arguments had been raised previously by people such as Clark, E. Franklin Frazier, and Bayard Rustin. Like Rustin, Moynihan argued that as anti-discrimination legislation breaks down barriers to black liberty, issues of equality will draw attention away from issues of liberty; in other words, concerns for equal resources enabling blacks to live in material ways comparable to whites will exceed concerns of freedom. The simple removal of legal barriers will not achieve the goal of equality, he maintained, because the cumulative effects of discrimination make it very nearly impossible for a majority of black Americans to take advantage of opportunities provided by civil rights laws. He observed, in this connection, that "the Negro community is dividing between a stable middle-class group that is steadily growing stronger and more successful, and an increasingly disorganized and disadvantaged lower-class group."

Like Clark, Moynihan emphasized that family deterioration—as revealed in urban blacks' rising rates of broken marriages, female-headed homes, out-of-wedlock births, and welfare dependency—was one of the central problems of the black lower class. And as had Frazier, Moynihan argued that the problems of the black family, which present major obstacles to black equality, derive from previous patterns of inequality that originated in the slavery experience and have been maintained and reinforced by years of racial discrimination. He concluded his report by recommending a shift in the direction of federal civil rights activities to "bring the Negro American to full and equal sharing in the responsibilities and rewards of citizenship" and thereby to increase "the stability and resources of the Negro American family."

The vitriolic criticism of the Moynihan report, which paid far more attention to Moynihan's unflattering depiction of the black family in the urban ghetto than to his historical analysis of the black family's special plight or to his proposed remedies, helped to create an atmosphere that discouraged many social scientists from researching certain aspects of lower-class black life. This atmosphere was enhanced by the emergence of a "black solidarity" movement in the second half of the 1960s that, among other things, profferred a new definition of the black experience in the United States as the "black perspective." This new definition was popularized by militant black spokesmen during the mid-1960s and was incorporated as a dominant theme in the writings of young black intellectuals by the early 1970s. Although the black perspective represented a variety of views on racial matters, the trumpeting of black pride and black self-affirmation was a characteristic feature of the speeches and writings that embodied the intellectual component of the black solidarity movement. Accordingly, the emphasis on the positive aspects of the black experience led to the uniform rejection of earlier arguments, which asserted that some aspects of ghetto life were pathological, in favor of those that accented strengths in the black community. And arguments extolling the "strengths" and "virtues" of black families replaced those that described the deterioration of black families. In fact, features of ghetto behavior characterized as pathological in the studies of the mid-1960s were reinterpreted or redefined as functional because, argued some black perspective proponents, blacks were displaying the ability to survive and even flourish in an economically depressed environment. Ghetto families were described as resilient and capable of adapting creatively to an oppressive, racist society. In short, these revisionist studies purporting to "liberate" the social sciences from the influence of "racism" effectively shifted the focus of social science analysis away from discussions of the consequences of racial isolation and economic class subordination to discussions of black achievement.

Also consistent with the dominant theme of racial solidarity in the writings of the black perspective proponents was an emphasis on "black" versus "white" and "we" versus "they." Since the focus was overwhelmingly on race, neither the social and economic differences within the black community nor the economy's problems received major attention. Thus the promising move to outline programs of economic reform by describing the effects of American economic organization on the minority community in the early and mid-1960s was cut short by calls for "reparations," or "black control of institutions serving the black community" in the late 1960s. This is why Orlando Patterson lamented, in a later analysis, that black ethnicity had become "a form of mystification, diverting attention from the correct kinds of solutions to the terrible economic condition of the group," thereby making it difficult for blacks to see "how their fate is inextricably tied up with the structure of the American economy."

Meanwhile, during this period of black glorification, significant developments were unfolding in ghetto communities across the United States that profoundly affected the lives of millions of blacks and dramatically revealed that the problems earlier described by Clark, Moynihan, and others had reached catastrophic proportions. To be more specific, one-quarter of all black births were outside of marriage in 1965, the year Moynihan wrote his report on the Negro family, and by 1980 over half were; in 1965 nearly 25 percent of all black families were headed by women, and by 1980 41 percent were; and, partly as a result, welfare dependency among poor blacks has mushroomed. And perhaps the most dramatic indicator of the extent to which social dislocations have afflicted urban blacks is crime, especially violent crime, which has increased sharply in recent years. Finally, these growing social problems have accompanied increasing black rates of joblessness.

Although these problems are heavily concentrated in urban areas, it would be a serious mistake to assume that they afflict all segments of the urban minority community. Rather, these problems disproportionately plague the urban underclass—that heterogeneous grouping of inner-city families and individuals who are outside the mainstream of the American occupational system. Included in this population are persons who lack training and skills and either experience long-term unemployment or have dropped out of the labor force altogether; who are long-term public assistance recipients; and who are engaged in street criminal activity and other forms of aberrant behavior.

THE TANGLE OF PATHOLOGY IN THE INNER CITY

When figures on black crime, teenage pregnancy, female-headed families, and welfare dependency are released to the public without sufficient explanation, racial stereotypes are reinforced. And the tendency of liberal social scientists either to ignore these issues or to address them in circumspect ways does more to reinforce than to undermine racist perceptions.

These problems cannot be accounted for simply in terms of racial discrimination or in terms of a culture of poverty. Rather, they must be seen as having complex sociological antecedents that range from demographic changes to problems of economic organization. But before turning to these explanatory factors, I should like to sketch the growing problems of social dislocation in the inner city, beginning first with violent crime.

Race and Violent Crime

Only one of nine persons in the United States is black; yet in 1980 nearly one of every two persons arrested for murder and non-negligent manslaughter was black, and 44 percent of all victims of murder were black. As Norval Morris and Michael Tonry indicate, "Homicide is the leading cause of death of black men and women aged 25 to 34." Furthermore, nearly 60 percent of all persons arrested for robbery and 36 percent of those arrested for aggravated assault in 1980 were black. Moreover, the rate of black imprisonment in 1979 was $8^{1}/_{2}$ times greater than the rate of white imprisonment.

The disproportionate involvement of blacks in violent crime is clearly revealed in the data on city arrests collected by the Federal Bureau of Investigation (FBI). Blacks constitute 13 percent of the population in cities, but they account for nearly half of all city arrests for violent crimes. More than half of those arrested for murders and nonnegligent manslaughter, more than half of those arrested for forcible rape, and 61 percent of those arrested for robbery are black. The rate of black crime is even greater in large urban areas where blacks constitute a larger percentage of the population. Although the FBI does not provide data on arrest by size of city and race, the magnitude and social significance of the problems of violent black crimes in large metropolises can perhaps be revealed by examining data on murder rates provided by the Chicago Police Department. . . .

In Chicago, like other major urban centers, blacks are not only more likely to commit murder, they are also more likely to be victims of murder. During the 1970s, eight of every ten murderers in Chicago were black, as were seven of every ten murder victims. In

1979, 547 blacks, 180 Hispanics, and 120 whites (other than Hispanic) were victims of murder; and 573 of the murders were committed by blacks, 169 by Hispanics, and 64 by whites. In 1970 only 56 of the murder victims were Hispanic, compared with 135 white and 607 black victims. Age changes in the Hispanic population accounted in large measure for their increased involvement in violent crimes—a matter that will be discussed later in greater detail. Homicides in Chicago were overwhelmingly intraracial or intraethnic. During the 1970s, 98 percent of black homicides were committed by other blacks, 75 percent of Hispanic homicides were committed by other Hispanics, and 51.5 percent of white homicides were committed by other whites.

In examining the figures on homicide in Chicago it is important to recognize that the rates vary significantly according to the economic status of the community, with the highest rates of violent crime associated with the communities of the underclass. More than half the murders and shooting assaults in Chicago in the first ten months of 1980 were concentrated in seven of the city's twenty-four police districts, the areas with a heavy concentration of low-income black or Latino residents.

The most violent area is the overwhelmingly black Wentworth Avenue police district on the South Side of Chicago. "Within this four-square-mile area an average of more than 90 murders and 400 shooting assaults occur each year; and one of every 10 murders and shooting assaults in Chicago occurred there during the 1970s. Through mid-November of 1980, Wentworth saw 82 murders (almost 12 percent of the citywide total) and 309 shooting assaults (11.3 percent of the city total.)"

The Wentworth figures on violent crime are high partly because the Robert Taylor Homes, the largest public housing project in the city of Chicago, is located there. Robert Taylor Homes is a complex of twenty-eight sixteen-story buildings covering ninety-two acres. The official population in 1980 was almost 20,000, but, according to a recent report, "there are an additional 5,000 to 7,000 adult residents who are not registered with the housing authority." In 1980 all of the more than 4,200 registered households were black and 72 percent of the official population were minors. The median family income was $4,925. Women headed 90 percent of the families with children, and 81 percent of the households received aid to families with dependent children (AFDC). Unemployment was estimated to be 47 percent in 1980. Although only a little more than 0.5 percent of Chicago's more than 3 million people live in Robert Taylor Homes, "11 percent of the city's murders, 9 percent of its rapes, and 10 percent of its aggravated assaults were committed in this project."

Robert Taylor Homes is by no means the only violent large housing project in Chicago. For example, Cabrini-Green, the second largest, experienced a rash of violent crimes in early 1981 that prompted Chicago's former mayor, Jane Byrne, to take up residence there for several weeks to help stem the tide. Cabrini-Green includes eighty-one high- and low-rise buildings covering seventy acres on Chicago's near North Side. In 1980 almost 14,000 people, almost all black, were officially registered there; but like Robert Taylor Homes, there are many more who reside there but do not appear in the records of the Chicago Housing Authority (CHA). Minors were 67 percent of the registered population; 90 percent of the families with children were headed by women; 70 percent of the households were on welfare in 1980; and 70 percent received AFDC. In a nine-week period beginning in early January 1981, ten Cabrini-Green residents were murdered; thirty-five were wounded by gunshots, including random sniping; and the Chicago police confiscated more than fifty firearms, "the tip of an immense illegal arsenal," according to the police.

Family Dissolution and Welfare Dependency

What is true of the structure of families and welfare dependency in Robert Taylor Homes and Cabrini-Green is typical of all the CHA housing projects. In 1980, of the 27,000 families with children living in CHA projects, only 11 percent were married-couple families, and 67 percent of the family households received AFDC. But female-headed families and welfare dependency are not confined to public housing projects. The projects simply magnify these problems, which permeate ghetto neighborhoods and to a lesser extent metropolitan areas generally.

The increase in the number of female-headed families in the United States was dramatic during the 1970s. Whereas the total number of families grew by 12 percent from 1970 to 1979, the number of female-headed families increased by 51 percent. Moreover, the number of families headed by women with one or more of their children present in the home increased by 81 percent. If the change in family structure was notable for all families in the 1970s, it was close to phenomenal for blacks and Hispanics. Families headed by white women increased by 42 percent; families headed by black and Hispanic women grew by 73 and 77 percent, respectively.

In 1965 Moynihan expressed great concern that 25 percent of all black families were headed by women. That figure rose to 28 percent in 1969, 37 percent in 1976, and a startling 42 percent in 1980. By contrast, only 12 percent of white families and 22 percent of Hispanic families were headed by women in 1980, even though each group recorded a significant increase in female-headed families during the 1970s. . . .

Even if a female householder is employed full time, her earnings are usually substantially less than that of a male worker and are not likely to be supplemented with income from a second full-time employed member of the household. For women who head families and are not employed (including those who have never been employed, have dropped out of the labor force to become full-time mothers, or are employed only part-time), the economic situation is often desperate. In 1980 the median income of female-headed families ($10,408) was only 45 percent of the median income of husband-wife families ($23,141); and the median income of families headed by black women ($7,425) was only 40 percent of the median income of husband-wife black families ($18,592). In 1978, of the roughly 3.2 million families who recorded incomes of less than $4,000, more than half were headed by women. . . .

Economic hardship has become almost synonymous with black female-headed families: only 30 percent of all poor black families were headed by women in 1959, but by 1978 the proportion reached 74 percent (though it dipped to 70 percent in 1981). By contrast, 38 percent of all poor white families were headed by women in 1978. Reflecting the growth of black female-headed families, the proportion of black children in married-couple families dropped significantly, from 64 percent in 1970 to 56 percent in 1974 and 49 percent in 1978. Moreover, 41 percent of black children under 18 years of age resided in families whose incomes were below the poverty level in 1978, and three-fourths of those were in families headed by females.

The rise of female-headed families among blacks corresponds

closely with the increase in the ratio of out-of-wedlock births. Only 15 percent of all black births in 1959 were out of wedlock. This figure jumped roughly 24 percent in 1965 and 53 percent in 1978, six times greater than the white ratio. Indeed, despite the far greater white population, the number of black babies born out of wedlock actually exceeded the number of illegitimate white babies in 1978. Although the proportion of black births that are outside of marriage is, in part, a function of the general decline in fertility among married blacks (a point discussed below), it is also a reflection of the growing prevalence of out-of-wedlock births among black teenagers. In 1978, 83 percent of the births to black teenagers (and 29 percent of the births to white teenagers) were outside of marriage.

These developments have significant implications for the problems of welfare dependency. In 1977 the proportion of black families receiving AFDC slightly exceeded the proportion of white females, despite the great difference in total population. It is estimated that about 60 percent of the children who are born out of wedlock and are alive and not adopted receive welfare. A study by the Urban Institute pointed out that "more than half of all AFDC assistance in 1975 was paid to women who were or had been teenager mothers."

I focus on female-headed families, out-of-wedlock births, and teenage pregnancy because they have become inextricably connected with poverty and dependency. The sharp increase in these and other forms of social dislocations in the inner city (including joblessness and violent crime) offers a difficult challenge to policymakers. Because there has been so little recent systematic research on these problems and a paucity of thoughtful explanations for them, racial stereotypes of life and behavior in the urban ghetto have not been adequately challenged. The physical and social isolation of residents in the urban ghetto is thereby reinforced. The fundamental question is: why have the social conditions of the urban underclass deteriorated so rapidly since the mid-1960s?

TOWARD A COMPREHENSIVE EXPLANATION

There is no single explanation for the racial or ethnic variations in the rates of social dislocations I have described. But I would like to suggest several interrelated explanations that range from the fairly obvious to ones that most observers of urban processes overlook altogether. In the process, I hope to be able to show that these problems are not intractable, as some people have suggested, and that their amelioration calls for imaginative and comprehensive programs of economic and social reform that are in sharp contrast to the current approaches to social policy in America, which are based on short-term political considerations.

The Effects of Historic and Contemporary Discrimination

Discrimination is the most frequently invoked explanation of social dislocations in the urban ghetto. However, proponents of the discrimination thesis often fail to make a distinction between the effects of historic discrimination, that is, discrimination before the middle of the twentieth century, and the effects of discrimination following that time. They therefore find it difficult to explain why the economic position of poor urban blacks actually deteriorated during the very period in which the most sweeping antidiscrimination legislation and programs were enacted and implemented. And their emphasis on discrimination becomes even more problematic in view of the economic progress of the black middle class during the same period.

There is no doubt that contemporary discrimination has contributed to or aggravated the social and economic problems of the urban underclass. But is discrimination greater today than in 1948, when black unemployment was less than half the 1980 rate, and the black-white unemployment ratio was almost one-fourth less than the 1980 ratio? Although labor economists have noted the short-comings of the official unemployment rates as an indicator of the economic conditions of groups, these rates have generally been accepted as one significant measure of relative disadvantage. It is therefore important to point out that it was not until 1954 that 2:1 unemployment ratio between blacks and whites was reached, and that since 1954, despite shifts from good to bad economic years, the black-white unemployment ratio has shown very little change. There are obviously many reasons for the higher levels of black unemployment since the mid-1950s (including the migration of blacks from a rural subsistence economy to an urban economy with protected labor markets), but to suggest contemporary discrimination as the main factor is to obscure the impact of economic and demographic changes and to leave unanswered the question of why black unemployment was lower not after but before 1950. . . .

It should also be emphasized that, contrary to prevailing opinion, the black family showed signs of significant deterioration not before, but after, the middle of the twentieth century. Until the publication of Herbert Gutman's impressive historical study on the black family, scholars had assumed that the current problems of the black family could be traced back to slavery. "Stimulated by the bitter public and academic controversy" surrounding the Moynihan report, Gutman presented data that convincingly demonstrated that the black family was not particularly disorganized during slavery or during the early years of blacks' first migration to the urban North, beginning after the turn of the century. The problems of the modern black family, he suggests, are a product of more recent social forces.

But are these problems mainly a consequence of present-day discrimination, or are they related to other factors that may have little or nothing to do with race? If contemporary discrimination is the main culprit, why did it produce the most severe problems of urban social dislocation during the 1970s, a decade that followed an unprecedented period of civil rights legislation and ushered in the affirmative action programs? The problem, as I see it, is unraveling the effects of present-day discrimination, on the one hand, and historic discrimination, on the other.

My own view is that historic discrimination is far more important than contemporary discrimination in explaining the plight of the urban underclass, but that a full appreciation of the effects of historic discrimination is impossible without taking into account other historical and contemporary forces that have also shaped the experiences and behavior of impoverished urban minorities.

The Importance of the Flow of Migrants

One of the legacies of historic discrimination is the presence of a large black underclass in central cities. Blacks constituted 23 percent of the population of central cities in 1977, but they were 46 percent of the poor in these cities. In accounting for the historical developments that contributed to this concentration of urban black poverty, I would like to draw briefly upon Stanley Lieberson's work.

On the basis of a systematic analysis of early U.S. censuses and other sources of data, Lieberson concluded that in many spheres of life, including the labor market, blacks were discriminated against far more severely in the early twentieth century than were the new white immigrants from southern, central, and eastern Europe. The disadvantage of skin color, in the sense that the dominant white population preferred whites over nonwhites, is one that blacks shared with the Japanese, Chinese, and other nonwhite groups. However, skin color per se "was not an insurmountable obstacle." Because changes in immigration policy cut off Asian migration to America in the late nineteenth century, the Chinese and Japanese populations did not reach large numbers and, therefore, did not pose as great a threat as did blacks. Lieberson was aware that the "response of whites to Chinese and Japanese was of the same violent and savage character in areas where they were concentrated," but he emphasized that "the threat was quickly stopped through changes in immigration policy." Furthermore, the discontinuation of large-scale immigration from China and Japan enabled those already here to solidify networks of ethnic contacts and to occupy particular occupational niches in small, relatively stable communities.

If different population sizes accounted for much of the difference in the economic success of blacks and Asians, they also helped to determine the dissimilar rates of progress of urban blacks and the new European arrivals. The dynamic factor behind these differences, and perhaps the most important single contributor to the varying rates of urban racial and ethnic progress in the twentieth century United States, is the flow of migrants. After the changes in immigration policy that halted Asian immigration to America came drastic restrictions on new European immigration. However, black migration to the urban North continued in substantial numbers for several decades. The sizable and continuous migration of blacks from the South to the North, coupled with the curtailment of immigration from eastern, central, and southern Europe, created a situation in which other whites muffled their negative disposition toward the new Europeans and directed their antagonisms against blacks. According to Lieberson, "the presence of blacks made it harder to discriminate against the new Europeans because the alternative was viewed less favorably."

The flow of migrants also made it much more difficult for blacks to follow the path of both the new Europeans and the Asian-Americans in overcoming the negative effects of discrimination by finding special occupational niches. Only a small part of a group's total work force can be absorbed in such specialties when the group's population increases rapidly or is a sizable proportion of the total population. Furthermore, the continuing flow of migrants had a harmful effect on the urban blacks who had arrived earlier. Lieberson points out:

> Sizable numbers of newcomers raise the level of ethnic and/or racial consciousness on the part of others in the city; moreover, if these newcomers are less able to compete for more desirable positions than are the longer-standing residents, they will tend to undercut the position of other members of the group. This is because the older residents and those of higher socioeconomic status cannot totally avoid the newcomers, although they work at it through subgroup residential isolation. Hence, there is some deterioration in the quality of residential areas, schools, and the like for those earlier residents who might otherwise enjoy more fully the rewards of their mobility. Beyond this, from the point of view of the dominant outsiders, the newcomers may reinforce stereotypes and negative dispositions that affect all members of the group.

The pattern of rural black migration that began with the rise of urban industrial centers in the North has been strong in recent years in the South. In Atlanta and Houston, to illustrate, the continuous influx of rural southern blacks, clue in large measure to the increasing mechanization of agriculture, has resulted in the creation of large urban ghettos that closely resemble those in the North. The net result in both the North and the South is that as the nation entered the last quarter of this century its large cities continued to have a disproportionate concentration of low-income blacks who were especially vulnerable to recent structural changes in the economy.

A reason for optimism is that black migration to urban areas has been minimal in recent years. Indeed, between 1970 and 1977 there was actually a net outmigration of 653,000 blacks from the central cities. In most large cities the number of blacks increased only moderately or declined. Increases in the urban black population during the 1970s were mainly due to births. This would indicate that for the first time in the twentieth century the ranks of central-city blacks are no longer being replenished by poor migrants. This strongly suggests that, other things being equal, the average socioeconomic status of urban blacks will in time steadily Improve, including a decrease in joblessness, crime, out-of-wedlock births, teenage pregnancy, female-headed homes, and welfare dependency. Just as the Asian and newer European immigrants benefitted from a cessation of migration, so too is there reason to expect that the cessation of black migration to the central city will help to improve the socioeconomic status of urban blacks. There are other factors that affect the differential rate of ethnic progress at different periods, such as discrimination, structural changes in the economy, and size of the population. But one of the major obstacles to urban black advancement—the constant flow of migrants—has been removed.

Hispanics, on the other hand, appear to be migrating to urban areas in increasing numbers. The comparative status of Hispanics as an ethnic group is not entirely clear because comparable data on their types of residence in 1970 are not available. But data collected since 1974 indicate that their numbers in central—cities are increasing rapidly because of both immigration and births. Indeed, in several large cities, including New York, Los Angeles, San Diego, San Francisco, Denver, and Phoenix, "they apparently outnumber American blacks." Although the Hispanic population is diverse in nationalities and socioeconomic status—for example, in 1979 the median income of Mexicans and Cubans was significantly greater than that of Puerto Ricans—they are often identified collectively as a distinct ethnic group because of their common Spanish-speaking origins. Accordingly, the rapid growth of the urban Hispanic population, accompanied by the opposite trend for the urban black population, could contribute significantly to different outcomes for these two groups in the last two decades of the twentieth century. More specifically, whereas urban blacks could very well record a decrease in their rates of joblessness, crime, teenage pregnancy, female-headed homes, and welfare dependency, Hispanics could show a steady increase in each. Moreover, blacks could experience a decrease in the ethnic hostility directed toward them, but Hispanics, with their growing visibility, could be victims of increasing ethnic antagonisms.

However, Hispanics are not the only ethnic group in urban America experiencing a rapid growth in numbers. According to the U.S. Census Bureau, Asians, who constitute less than 2 percent of the nation's population, were the fastest-growing American ethnic group in the 1970s. Following the liberation of U.S. immigration policies, the large influx of immigrants from Southeast Asia and, to a lesser degree, from South Korea and China has been associated with reports of increasing problems, including anti-Asian sentiments, joblessness, and violent crime. According to one report, the nation's economic woes have exacerbated the situation as the newcomers have competed with black, Hispanic, and white urban workers for jobs. Moreover, the steady inpouring of immigrants from Taiwan, Hong Kong, and China has disrupted the social organization of Chinatowns. Once stable and homogeneous, Chinatowns are now suffering from problems that have traditionally plagued innercity black neighborhoods, such as joblessness, school dropouts, overcrowding, violent street crime, and gang warfare.

The Relevance of Changes in the Age Structure

The flow of migrants also affects the average age of an ethnic group. For example, the black migration to urban centers—the continual replenishment of urban black populations by poor newcomers—predictably skewed the age profile of the urban black community and kept it relatively young. The higher the median age of a group, the greater its representation in higher income categories and professional positions. It is therefore not surprising that ethnic groups such as blacks and Hispanics, who on average are younger than whites, also tend to have high unemployment and crime rates. . . .

In the nation's central cities in 1977, the median age for whites was 30.3, for blacks 23.9, and for Hispanics 21.8. One cannot overemphasize the importance of the sudden growth of young minorities in the central cities. The number of central-city blacks aged 14 to 24 rose by 78 percent from 1960 to 1970, compared with an increase of only 23 percent for whites of the same age. From 1970 to 1977 the increase in the number of young blacks slackened off somewhat, but it was still substantial. For example, in the central cities the number of blacks aged 14 to 24 increased by 21 percent from 1970 to 1977 and the number of Hispanics by 26 percent, while whites of this age group decreased by 4 percent.

On the basis of these demographic changes alone one would expect blacks and Hispanics to contribute disproportionately to the increasing rates of social dislocation in the central city, such as crime. Indeed, 55 percent of all those arrested for violent and property crimes in American cities in 1980 were under 21 years of age.

Youth is not only a factor in crime; it is also associated with out-of-wedlock births, female-headed homes, and welfare dependency. Teenagers accounted for nearly half of all out-of-wedlock births in 1978, and 80 percent of all illegitimate black births in that year were to teenage and young adult women. The median age of female householders has decreased substantially in recent years; and the explosion of teenage births has contributed significantly to the rise in the number of children on AFDC, from 35 per 1,000 children under 18 in 1960 to 113 per 1,000 in 1979.

In short, much of what has gone awry in the inner city is due in part to the sheer increase in the number of young people, especially young minorities. However, as James Q. Wilson has pointed out in his analysis of the proliferation of social problems in the 1960s (a period of general economic prosperity), "changes in the age structure of the population cannot alone account for the social dislocations" of that decade. He argues, for example, that from 1960 to 1970 the rate of unemployment in the District of Columbia increased by 100 percent and the rate of serious crime by over 400 percent, yet the number of young persons between 16 and 21 years of age rose by only 32 percent. Also, the number of murders in Detroit increased from 100 in 1960 to 500 in 1971, "yet the number of young persons did not quintuple."

Wilson states that the "increase in the murder rate during the 1960s was more than ten times greater than what one would have expected from the changing age structure of the population alone" and "only 13.4 percent of the increase in arrests for robbery between 1950 and 1965 could be accounted for by the increase in the numbers of persons between the ages of ten and twenty-four." Speculating on this problem, Wilson advances the hypothesis that an abrupt rise in the number of young persons has an "exponential effect on the rate of certain social problems." In other words, there may be a "critical mass" of young persons in a given community such that when that mass is reached or is increased suddenly and substantially, "a self-sustaining chain reaction is set off that creates an explosive increase in the amount of crime, addiction, and welfare dependency."

This hypothesis seems to be especially relevant to densely populated inner-city neighborhoods and even more so to those with large public housing projects. Opposition from organized community groups to the construction of public housing in their neighborhoods has "led to massive, segregated housing projects, which become ghettos for minorities and the economically disadvantaged." As the earlier description of Robert Taylor Homes and Cabrini-Green in Chicago suggests, when large poor families were placed in high-density housing projects in the ghetto, both family and neighborhood life suffered. High crime rates, family dissolution, and vandalism flourished in these projects. In St. Louis, the Pruit-Igoe project, which included about 10,000 adults and children, developed serious problems five years after it opened "and it became so unlivable that it was destroyed in 1976, 22 years after it was built."

Wilson's critical mass theory would seem to be demonstrated convincingly in densely populated ghetto neighborhoods with large concentrations of teenagers and young adults. As Oscar Newman has shown, the population concentration in these projects, the types of housing, and the surrounding neighborhood populations have interactive effects on the occurrence and types of crimes. In other words, the problems of crime, generally high in poor inner-city neighborhoods, are exacerbated by the conditions in the housing projects. In the past two decades the population explosion of young minorities in the already densely settled ghetto neighborhoods has created a situation whereby life throughout ghetto neighborhoods has come close to approximating life in the housing projects.

In both the housing projects and other densely settled inner-city neighborhoods, residents have difficulty identifying their neighbors. They are, therefore, less likely to engage in reciprocal guardian behavior. Events in one part of the block or neighborhood tend to be of little concern to those residing in other parts. These conditions of social disorganization are as acute as they are because of the unprecedented increase in the number of younger minorities in these neighborhoods, many of whom are jobless, not enrolled in school, and a source of delinquency, crime, and unrest.

The cessation of black in-migration to the central cities and the steady out-migration to the suburbs will partially relieve the population pressures in the inner city. Perhaps even more significant, there were 6 percent fewer blacks aged 13 and under in metropolitan areas in 1977 than in 1970, and 13 percent fewer in the central cities. White children in this age category also decreased during this period by even greater percentages: 17 percent in metropolitan areas and 24 percent in the central cities. By contrast, Hispanic children increased from 1970 to 1977 by 16 percent in metropolitan areas and 12 percent in the central cities. Thus, just as the change in migration flow could affect the rates of ethnic groups involvement in certain types of social problems, so too could changes in the age structure. Whereas whites and blacks—all other things being equal—are likely to show a decrease in problems such as joblessness, crime, out-of-wedlock births, teenage pregnancy, family dissolution, and welfare dependency in the near future, the growing Hispanic population, due to rapid increases in births and migration, is more likely to experience increasing rates of social dislocation.

The Impact of Basic Economic Changes

The population explosion among minority youths occurred at a time when changes in the economy posed serious problems for unskilled individuals, both in and out of the labor force. Urban minorities have been particularly vulnerable to structural economic changes, such as the shift from goods-producing to service-producing industries, the increasing polarization of the labor market into low-wage and high-wage sectors, technological innovations, and the relocation of manufacturing industries out of the central cities. These economic shifts point out the fact that nearly all of the large and densely populated metropolises experienced their most rapid development during an earlier industrial and transportation era. Today these urban centers are undergoing an irreversible structural transformation from "centers of production and distribution of material goods to centers of administration, information exchange, and higher-order service provision," as John D. Kasarda points out. The central-city labor market has been profoundly altered in the process.

Roughly 60 percent of the unemployed blacks in the United States reside within central cities, mostly within the cities' low-income areas. There is much more dispersion among unemployed whites; approximately 40 percent reside in suburban areas and an additional 30 percent live in non-metropolitan areas. Furthermore, the percentage of black men employed as laborers and service workers is twice that of white workers. The lack of economic opportunity for low-income blacks means that they are compelled to remain in economically depressed ghettos and their children are forced to attend inferior ghetto schools. This leads into a vicious cycle, as ghetto isolation and inferior opportunities in education reinforce their disadvantaged position in the labor market and contribute to problems of crime, family dissolution, and welfare dependency.

Indeed, the problems of joblessness among blacks, especially low-income blacks, are more severe than those of any other large ethnic group in America. Heavily concentrated in inner cities, blacks have experienced a deterioration of their economic position on nearly all the major labor-market indicators. . . .

Blacks, especially young males, are dropping out of the labor force in significant numbers. The severe problems of joblessness for black teenagers-and young adults are seen in the figures on changes in the male civilian labor force participation rates. The percentage of black males in the labor force fell sharply between 1960 and the end of 1983 for those aged 16 to 24, and somewhat less for those aged 25 to 34. Black males began dropping out of the labor force in increasing numbers as early as 1965, while white males either maintained or increased their rate of participation until 1977. Sharp declines in the three younger age categories took place from 1977 through 1983—a period plagued by a deep recession.

But even these figures do not reveal the severity of joblessness among younger blacks. Only a minority of non-institutionalized black youth are employed. The percentage of black male youth who are employed has sharply and steadily declined since 1955, whereas among white males it increased slightly for teenagers and virtually held steady for those aged 20 to 24 between 1955 and 1973. However, the years of recession after 1978 probably took their toll on white workers, evidenced by the noticeable increase in joblessness for all the age categories by 1983. The fact that only 55 percent of all black young adult males, 31 percent of all black males aged 18 to 19, and 14 percent of those aged 16 to 17 were employed in 1983 reveals a problem of joblessness for young black men that has reached catastrophic proportions.

Finally, the discouraging employment situation for young blacks is further demonstrated by the data on work experience. The percentage of young blacks obtaining any work experience at all has generally declined. The proportion of white male teenagers with work experience changed very little from 1966 to 1977, but the proportion of black male teenagers with work experience decreased from 67 to 47 percent during the same period.

The combined indicators of labor force participation, employment-population ratios, and work experience reveal a disturbing picture of black joblessness, especially among younger blacks. If the evidence presented in recent longitudinal research is correct, joblessness during youth will have a long-term effect on later success in the labor market. Increasing joblessness during youth is a problem primarily experienced by lower-income blacks—those already in or near the underclass. . . . Of the unemployed teenagers living at home in 1977, 67 percent were from families with incomes below $10,000. And among those unemployed teenagers living at home and not enrolled in school, 75 percent were from families with less than $10,000 income and 41 percent from families with less than $5,000.

The changes associated with the cessation of black migration to the central city and the sharp drop in the number of black children under age 13 may increase the likelihood that the economic situation of urban blacks will improve in the near future. However, the current problems of black joblessness are so overwhelming that it is just as likely that only a major program of economic reform will be sufficient to prevent a significant proportion of the urban underclass from being permanently locked out of the mainstream of the American occupational system.

The Role of Ethnic Group Culture

. . . A well-founded sociological argument is that different ethnic behavior and outcomes are largely due to different opportunities and external obstacles against advancement—which were determined by different historical and material circumstances, including different times of arrival and patterns of settlement in the United States. Furthermore, even if one were able to show that different ethnic group behavior is related to differences in values, mobility, and success, this hardly constitutes an adequate explanation. Uncovering cultural differences is only the first step in a proper sociological investigation. The analysis of their social and historical roots represents the succeeding and more fundamental step.

In short, cultural values do not ultimately determine behavior or success. Rather, cultural values emerge from specific circumstances and life chances and reflect one's position in the class structure. Thus, if underclass blacks have low aspirations or do not plan for the future, it is not ultimately the result of different cultural norms but the product of restricted opportunities, a bleak future, and feelings of resignation originating from bitter personal experiences. Accordingly, behavior described as socially pathological and associated with lower-class minorities should be analyzed not as a cultural aberration but as a symptom of class inequality.

As social and economic opportunities change, new behavioral solutions originate, develop into patterns, and are later complemented and upheld by norms. If new situations emerge, both the behavior patterns and the norms eventually undergo change. As Herbert Cans states: "Some behavioral norms are more persistent than others, but over the long run, all of the norms and aspirations by which people live are nonpersistent: they rise and fall with changes in situations."

CONCLUSION

To hold, as I do, that changes in economic and social situations will lead to changes in behavior patterns and norms, raises the issue of what public policy can deal effectively with the social dislocations that have plagued the urban underclass for the past several years. Any significant reduction of joblessness and related problems of crime, out-of-wedlock births, teenage pregnancies, single-parent homes, and welfare dependency requires a far more comprehensive program of economic and social reform than Americans have generally deemed appropriate or desirable. In short, it would require a radicalism that neither the Democratic nor the Republican party has been bold enough to propose.

A shift away from the convenient focus on "racism" would probably result in a greater understanding and appreciation of the complex factors associated with the recent increases in the rates of social dislocation among the urban underclass. Although present-day discrimination undoubtedly has contributed to their economic and social woes in the last twenty years, I have argued that these problems have been due far more to shifts in the American economy from manufacturing to service industries, which have produced extraordinary rates of joblessness in the inner city and exacerbated conditions generated by the historic flow of migrants, and to changes in the urban minority age structure and consequent population changes in the central city.

For all these reasons, the urban underclass has not benefitted significantly from "race-specific" antidiscrimination policy programs, such as affirmative action, which have helped so many trained and educated blacks. If inner-city blacks are to be helped, they will be aided not by policies addressed primarily to poor minorities, but by policies designed to benefit all of the nation's poor. These will need to address the broader problems of generating full employment, developing sustained and balanced urban economic growth, and achieving effective welfare reform. Unless such problems are seriously faced, there is little hope for the effectiveness of other policies, including race-specific ones, in significantly reducing social dislocations among the urban underclass.

I am reminded in this connection of Bayard Rustin's plea during the early 1960s that blacks ought to recognize the importance of *fundamental* economic reform (including a system of national economic planning along with new education, manpower, and public works programs to help reach full employment) and the need for a broad-based coalition to achieve it. And since an effective political coalition will in part depend upon how the issues are defined, it is essential that the political message underline the need for economic and social reform that benefits all groups in the United States, not just poor minorities. Politicians and civil rights organizations, as two important examples, ought to shift or expand their definition of America's racial problems and broaden the scope of suggested policy programs to address them. They should, of course, continue to fight for an end to racial discrimination. But they must also recognize that poor minorities are profoundly affected by problems in America that go beyond racial considerations. The dislocations that follow these problems have made the underclass a reality of urban life, and if left alone they will continue to do so.

The Global Environment Crisis

Albert Gore, Jr.

George Bush promised to be "the environmental president." Initially, he reversed the policy of the Reagan administration, increasing appropriations for the Environmental Protection Agency, appointing a crusader for stronger antipollution measures to head it, and signing the Clean Air Act of 1990. But as the economy faltered, Bush allowed the Justice Department to overrule the EPA when it sought to prosecute large corporate polluters and created the Council on Competitiveness, which undercut regulations requiring businesses to control emissions of sulfur dioxide and nitrogen oxides on the grounds that they impeded economic growth and cost jobs. In 1992 at the United Nations' Earth Summit in Rio de Janeiro, moreover, Bush was the only one of the hundred heads of state attending who refused to sign a biological diversity treaty to conserve millions of plant and animal species. In response, the president's chief environmental critic in the Senate, Albert Gore, Jr., of Tennessee, author of Earth in the Balance: Healing the Global Environment *(1992), repeatedly accused the Bush administration of bowing to corporate interests and blocking actions to improve the quality of the environment.*

Taking most political observers by surprise, Bill Clinton eschewed the practice of balancing the ticket and in July 1992 selected Senator Gore, a fellow border-state moderate, Baptist, and baby boomer, as his running mate. In the speech below, given at the United Nations in June 1993, Vice President Gore outlines the dangers to the global environment and how the crisis can be met.

It is a year since Rio.

And while we usually focus on the ideas expressed during the official proceedings of the Earth Summit, I remember a lot more.

Excerpted from the Keynote Address to the United Nations Commission on Sustainable Development by Vice President Al Gore, June 14, 1993.

For the great riches of human creativity were on full display in Rio: that giant "tree of life" decorated with messages written in crayon on paper leaves from children around the world; representatives of indigenous peoples like the Kayapao, Yanomami, Inuit and Penan presenting impassioned defenses of the endangered remnants of wilderness within which their ancient cultures are struggling to survive.

Scientists displayed startlingly beautiful computer images of every square inch of the earth—as seen from space. Artists crafted spectacular sculptures, paintings, music, graphics and films.

And they all seemed more alike than different: the indigenous person and the artist, the scientist and the child, the tourist and the diplomat. All seemed to share a deeper understanding—a recognition that we are all part of something much larger than ourselves, a family related only distantly by blood but intimately by commitment to each other's common future.

And so it is today. We are from different parts of the globe. . . .

But we are united by a common premise: that human activities are needlessly causing grave and perhaps irreparable damage to the global environment.

The dangers are clear to all of us.

The earth's forests are being destroyed at the rate of one football field's worth every second. An enormous hole is opening in the ozone layer, reducing the earth's ability to protect life from deadly ultraviolet radiation. Living species die at such an unprecedented rate that more than half may disappear within our lifetimes. More and more chemical wastes seep down to poison groundwater—and up to destroy the atmosphere's delicate balance. Degradation of land, forests and fresh water—individually and synergistically—play critical roles in international instability. Huge quantities of carbon dioxide, methane, and other greenhouse gases dumped in the atmosphere trap heat and raise global temperatures.

You know this. Our shared sense of urgency has brought us here, today. Would that everyone saw things the same way.

They don't.

A few weeks ago, Harvard Professor Edward Wilson, writing in the *New York Times,* summarized the notions of those who have a different view.

"Population growth? Good for the economy—so let it run. Land shortages? Try fusion energy to power the desalting of sea water, then reclaim the world's deserts . . . by towing icebergs to coastal pipelines. . . .

"Species going extinct? Not to worry," the skeptics say. "That is nature's way. Think of humankind as only the latest in a long line of exterminating agents in geological time. Resources? The planet has more than enough resources to last indefinitely."

Wilson called this group the "exemptionalists" because they hold that humans are so transcendent in intelligence and spirit that they have been exempted "from the iron laws of ecology that bind all other species."

The human race is not exempt.

The laws of ecology bind us, too. . . .

In fact, from the vast array of problems about which it is possible to be pessimistic, let me mention two.

First, population growth.

It is sobering to realize what is happening to the world's population in the course of our lifetimes.

From the beginning of the human species until the end of World War II, when I was born, it took more than 10,000 generations to reach a world population of a little more than 2 billion. But in just the past forty-five years, it has gone from a little over 2 billion to 5½ billion.

And if I live another forty-five years, it will be 9 or 10 billion.

The changes brought about by this explosion are not for the distant future. This is not only a problem for our grandchildren.

The problems are already here.

Soil erosion. The loss of vegetative cover. Extinction. Desertification. Famine. The garbage crisis.

The population explosion, accompanied by wholesale changes in technology, affects every aspect of our lives, in every part of the globe.

Now, sometimes, developing countries feel the population argument is one made by wealthy countries who want to clamp down on their ability to grow.

Let me answer that.

Sometimes the developing countries are right.

So I say this to citizens of the developed nations: we have a disproportionate impact on the global environment. We have less than a quarter of the world's population—but we use *three* quarters of the world's raw materials and create three quarters of all solid waste.

One way to put it is this: a child born in the United States will have thirty times more impact on the earth's environment during his or her lifetime than a child born in India.

The affluent of the world have a responsibility to deal with their disproportionate impact.

But population growth affects everyone. By the year 2000, thirty-one low-income countries will be unable to feed their people using their own land.

At the Second Preparatory Committee Meeting for the International Conference on Population and Development, the United States pledged its commitment to help promote international consensus around the goal of stabilizing world population growth.

We called for a comprehensive approach built around three areas: the environment, development—and the rights and needs of women.

Is population growth only a problem of birth control? Of course not. Paradoxically, reducing infant mortality is important as well. Several decades ago, Julius Nyerere put this matter cogently: "The most powerful contraceptive is the confidence by parents that their children will survive."

More recently, a doctor in India put the matter a slightly different way, as he explained the success of programs in Kerala that have dramatically reduced birth rates. "The most enduring contraception is female education," he said. "Women realize they have a conscious choice and that hopes and dreams for their children are not unrealistic."

Slowing population growth is in the deepest self-interest of all governments. It is a responsibility for rich and poor countries alike.

Rapid population growth is only one of the causes of a profound transformation in the relationship between human civilization and the ecological system of the earth. The emergence of extremely powerful new technologies which magnify the impact each of us can have on the global environment has also played an important role.

Most significant of all, many people now think about our relationship to the earth in ways that assume we don't have to concern ourselves with the consequences of our actions—as if the global environment will forever be impervious to the rapidly mounting insults to its integrity and balance. But the evidence of deterioration is all around us.

Take, for example, the threat to our supply of fresh water.

There is a lot of water on earth. But there isn't very much fresh water—only about 2.5 percent of all water on earth is fresh and most of that is locked away as ice, say, in Antarctica, or Greenland, or other areas.

Furthermore, much of that water is used inefficiently. It also may be polluted by toxics and human waste. Meanwhile, by the year 2000, eighteen of the twenty-two largest metropolitan areas in the world—those with more than 10 million people—will be in developing countries. By 2025, 60 percent of the world's population will live in cities—that's more than 5 billion people. They will urgently need fresh water and water sanitation.

And not just to drink. Water affects industrial development. It is the medium necessary for heat exchange, processing and transport. It affects the world's ability to produce food; 76 percent of global water use is agricultural. A significant change in the availability of fresh water supply can trigger massive human migrations.

Because we know how precious drinkable water is, our ways of supplying it have become justly celebrated as triumphs of human ingenuity, whether the first irrigation networks along the Nile, to the monumental system of tunnels that bring water to this city so you could brush your teeth in the hotel room this morning.

We will need all our ingenuity to prevent that supply from drying up. Rapid growth itself is a threat to our supply of fresh water, whether in Mexico City where the water level of the main aquifer drops as much as eleven feet a year, or in any of the approximately eighty countries which already suffer from serious water shortages.

Meanwhile, the World Health Organization estimates that contaminated water causes at least 25 million deaths in developing nations each year. Hundreds of millions more suffer from debilitating water-borne diseases. In fact, about eighty percent of all diseases and over one-third of all deaths in developing countries are caused by the consumption of contaminated water. More than 3 million infants die each year from diarrhea alone, due to contaminated drinking water and inadequate sanitation.

What is the reason for the great popular indifference to these crises?

I sometimes like to remind people of the old science experiment involving a frog. Put the frog into a pot of boiling water and it jumps right out. It recognizes the danger.

But put the same frog into a pot of lukewarm water and bring it slowly to a boil. It'll just sit there until it is rescued (I've learned over the years that it's important to rescue the frog in the middle of the story).

The point of this story is that when the process of change seems gradual we have trouble recognizing it. From day to day, the lives of most of us seem not to change all that much. It is only when we lift our gaze beyond the next few days or years that we see the truth.

Similarly, even though our worldwide civilization confronts an unprecedented global environmental crisis, we can go from day to day without confronting the rapid change now underway. We must recognize the extent to which we are damaging the global environment, and we must develop new ways to work together to foster economic progress without environmental destruction.

How do we do it?

Let me dispose of a few myths.

No matter what this Commission does, it can't do everything by itself.

Archimedes said if he had the right lever and a firm place to stand, he could move the world. This Commission should seek to exert leverage on other institutions which can help us accomplish our task.

Second, the industrial countries do not have a monopoly on ideas. In fact, last year at Rio many developing countries showed the way.

Third, we must once and for all abandon the idea that economic development and environmental responsibility are incompatible. Economic development is no excuse for environmental vandalism. Rich countries cannot impose limits on poor countries or deny them the right to achieve wealth. At the same time there is increasing recognition that the fastest growing markets are in developing countries—countries where the demand for environmentally responsible technologies is also growing rapidly.

Economic progress without environmental destruction. That's what sustainable development is all about.

Two principles must guide us as we set about the pursuit of sustainable development.

First, the principle of *national responsibility*.

After all, the role of this Commission is primarily catalytic. It can focus attention on issues of common interest. It can serve as a forum for raising ideas and plans. It can help resolve issues that arise as nations proceed in their sustainable development agendas. It can monitor progress.

It can help shift the multilateral financial institutions and bilateral assistance efforts towards a sustainable development agenda.

It can help revitalize the United Nations system to ensure that sustainable development is a central theme in each organization.

Indeed, this Commission, through its focus on sustainable development, can enhance United Nations' efforts to maintain peace, stability and prosperity in this post–Cold War world.

But it can do none of these things unless each country makes a strong commitment to change. This Commission will simply be a meeting about meetings if the members fail to bring to the table a strong sense of national responsibility.

Will the United States show that sense of commitment?

We can. We will.

That's why we'll announce a plan to move forward on climate change by August—a detailed outline for action that will continue the trend of reduced emissions past the next seven years.

That's why we've established a National Biological Survey to protect our own biodiversity.

That's why we're moving immediately to reduce toxic releases in federal facilities.

That's why we're buying energy-efficient technologies, including alternative fuel vehicles for federal fleets.

That's why we will soon announce a new management plan for federal forests.

That's why President Clinton, in his first full day in office, changed the so-called "Mexico City" policy and acted to promote access to the full range of quality reproductive health care for women everywhere.

And that's just the start.

But just as each nation must assume national responsibility, so must we all act together.

If sustainable development is to become a reality, the second principle we must follow is that of *partnership*.

There are still those who think the wealthy countries on this

planet have a monopoly on technology and insight. That's nonsense. We can all learn from each other. That's why this Commission must encourage partnership *among* countries—especially between North and South. . . .

National responsibility.

Partnership.

Can we actually translate these ideas, the staple of political rhetoric, into reality?

I don't blame those who are pessimistic.

In fact, a few months ago I was going through the solutions for
our environmental crisis for a group of scientists. And at the end,
one of them raised his hand and said, "You know, I agree with
everything you've said, but I know enough about politics to tell you
that it's not likely to occur. The momentum towards continuing our
current way of doing things is just too powerful."

There's something to that.

But what if four or five years ago we had said that in the next few
months all of the Communist countries in Eastern Europe will suddenly become democracies and choose free market capitalism?

What if we had said that all the statues of Lenin would be torn
down and that we would have a chance to remake the world in the
aftermath of the Cold War?

What if we had said that Nelson Mandela would be free, and
F. W. de Klerk would announce the end of apartheid, and together
they would set out on the road to reconciliation in South Africa?

None of those seemed likely.

We can assume change is impossible. Or we can be part of the
solution.

We can assume our enemies are too powerful—or we can assume
the urgency of our mission is more powerful.

I believe there is every reason for hope.

Part of the reason is this group, from every part of the planet,
committed to the idea of sustainable development.

But that's not the only reason.

For there are millions who believe as we do. Some are working in
government, attending meetings like this one. But there are countless others whose work goes uncelebrated.

A woman in Kenya's Greenbelt movement plants a tree, then
organizes a meeting about family planning. An engineer in Detroit
comes up with a way to use less gasoline. A scientist in Antarctica

drilling through the ice finds clues to the history of our planet. A teacher in Brazil leads a class full of children in a discussion about the rainforests.

These are the men and women who give us hope.

In the next few days, as we plan the future of this Commission, let us remember the spirit animating our meeting, thousands of miles to the South, exactly a year ago.

Remember how we achieved unity of purpose out of diversity. And let that memory of past success give us confidence that we will succeed in the future—and *for* the future.

The State of the Union, 1994

William Jefferson Clinton

Bill Clinton came to the White House with a clear sense of what he wished to accomplish. One of a breed of "new Democrats," as they were called, he recognized the need to contain deficit spending, employ new technologies, and devise creative approaches to intransigent problems such as welfare reform. Clinton broke from the traditional liberal mold when he fought for NAFTA, the free trade pact with Canada and Mexico, which trade unionists were against since they thought it would cost American jobs; he also took a hard stance against crime, pairing that position with ardent and successful support for gun control legislation.

But the heart of the Clinton presidency was the issue of health care. Clinton risked everything on this issue. He also broke new ground by asking Hillary Rodham Clinton, the first lady and a political personage frequently described as his equal or superior in policy matters, to be in charge of the health care program.

This speech succinctly distills the Clinton program on taxes, deficit reduction, technology, welfare reform, and the health care issue. In its conclusion, it also highlights Clinton fondness for the role of being a national preacher, seeking to rally people as members of a national family around issues of safety, security, and protecting the next generation.

Throughout the 1992 campaign, a sign hung in Clinton headquarters screaming the message, "THE ECONOMY, STUPID," thereby reminding Clinton and his staff that domestic issues were what mattered. Readers might want to ask whether that remains the case—and whether, by the standards set forth in this speech, Clinton has been a success or a failure. They might also want to consider whether the 1994 Congressional triumph of Republicans means that the American people have rejected Clinton's concern with these domestic issues or simply the way he has approached them, and what all this means for the 1996 presidential election.

Mr. Speaker, Mr. President, members of the 103rd Congress, my fellow Americans:

. . . We gather tonight in a world of changes so profound and rapid that all nations are tested.

Our American heritage has always been to master change, to expand opportunity at home, and provide leadership abroad.

But for too long, and in too many ways, that heritage was abandoned and our country drifted.

For thirty years, family life in America has been breaking down. For twenty years, the wages of working families have been stagnant or declining. For twelve years of trickle-down economics, we tried to build a false prosperity on a hollow base. Our national debt quadrupled. From 1989 to 1992, we experienced the slowest growth in a half century.

For too many families, even when both parents are working, the American dream has been slipping away.

In 1992, the American people demanded change. One year ago I asked you to join me and accept responsibility for the future of our country. Well, we did. We replaced drift and deadlock with renewal and reform.

I want to thank all of you who heard the American people, broke girdlock, and gave them the most successful teamwork between a president and a Congress for thirty years.

This Congress produced:

- A budget that cut the deficit by half a trillion dollars, cut spending and raised income taxes only on the very wealthiest Americans.
- Tax relief for millions of low-income workers to reward work over welfare.
- NAFTA.
- The Brady bill—which is now the Brady law.
- Tax cuts to help nine our of ten small businesses invest more and create jobs.
- More research and treatment for AIDS.
- More childhood immunizations.
- More support for women's health research.
- More affordable college loans for the middle class.
- A new national service program for those who want to

give something back to their community and earn money
for higher education.
- A dramatic increase in high-tech investments to move us
from a defense to a domestic economy.
- A new law, the motor voter bill, to help millions of people
register to vote.
- Family and medical leave.

All passed. All signed into law with no vetoes. These accomplishments were all commitments I made when I sought this office, and
they were all passed by this Congress. But the real credit belongs to
the people who sent us here, pay our salaries and hold our feet to
the fire.

What we do here is really beginning to change lives. I will never
forget what family and medical leave meant to one father who
brought his little girl to visit the White House last year.

After we talked and took a picture, he held on to my arm and
said, "My little girl is really sick, and she's probably not going to
make it. But because of the family and medical leave law I can take
time off without losing my job. I have had some precious time with
my child, the most important time I have ever had, without hurting
the rest of my family. Don't you ever think that what you do up here
doesn't make a difference."

Though we are making a difference, our work has just begun.
Many Americans still haven't felt the impact of what we have done.
The recovery has still not touched every community or created
enough jobs. Incomes are still stagnant. There is still too much
violence and not enough hope. And abroad, the young democracies
we support still face difficult times and look to us for leadership.

And so tonight, let us continue our journey of renewal: to create
more and better jobs, guarantee health security for all, reward work
over welfare, promote democracy abroad and begin to reclaim our
streets from violent crime and drugs and renew our own American
community.

Last year, we began to put our house in order by tackling the
budget deficit that was driving us toward bankruptcy. . . .

Because the deficit was so large and because they had benefited
from tax cuts in the 1980s, we asked the wealthy to pay more to
reduce the deficit. So April 15th, the American people will discover
the truth about what we did last year on taxes. Only the top 1.2

percent of Americans will face higher income tax rates. Let me
repeat: only the wealthiest 1.2 percent of Americans will face
higher income tax rates, and no one else will.

The naysayers said our plan wouldn't work. Well, they were
wrong.

When I became president, the experts predicted next year's deficit would be $300 billion. But because we acted, the deficit is now
going to be less than $180 billion—40 percent lower than predicted.

Our economic program has helped to produce the lowest core
inflation rate and the lowest interests rates in twenty years. And
because those interest rates are down, business investment in equipment is growing at seven times the pace of the previous four years.

Auto sales are way up. Home sales are at a record high. Millions
have refinanced their homes. And our economy has produced 1.6
million private-sector jobs in 1993—more than were created in the
previous four years combined. The people who supported this economic plan should be proud of its first results. . . .

Our economic plan also bolsters America's strength and credibility around the world.

Once we reduced the deficit, and put the steel back in our competitive edge, the world echoed with the sound of falling trade
barriers.

In one year, with NAFTA, GATT, our efforts in Asia and the
national export strategy, we did more to open world markets to
American products than at any time over the last two generations.
That will mean more jobs and rising living standards for the American people.

Low deficits, low inflation, low interest rates, low trade barriers
and high investment—these are the building blocks of our recovery. But if we want to take full advantage of the opportunities
before us in the global economy, we must do more. . . .

We must transform America's outdated unemployment system
into a re-employment system. The old system just kept you going
while you waited for your old job to come back; but we have to have
a new system to move people into new and better jobs, because most
people don't get their old jobs back.

The only way to get a real job with a growing income is to have
real skills and the ability to learn new ones. We simply must stream-
line today's patchwork of training programs and make them a
source of new skills for people who lose their jobs. Re-employment,

not unemployment, will be the centerpiece of our program for economic renewal, and I urge you to pass it this year.

Just as we must transform our unemployment system, we must also revolutionize our welfare system. It doesn't work. It defies our values as a nation.

If we value work, we cannot justify a system that makes welfare more attractive than work.

If we value personal responsibility, we cannot ignore the $34 billion in child support that absent parents ought to be paying to millions of mothers and children.

If we value strong families, we cannot perpetuate a system that penalizes those who stay together. Can you believe that a child who has a child gets more money from the government for leaving home than for staying with a parent or a grandparent?

That's not just bad policy; it is wrong. And we must change it.

I worked for years on this welfare problem, and I can tell you: the people who most want to change welfare are the very people on it. They want to get off welfare, and get back to work, and support their children.

Last year, we began. We gave the states more power to innovate—because we know that great ideas can come from outside Washington—and many states are using it.

Then, we took a dramatic step. Instead of taxing people with modest incomes who are working their way out of poverty, we dramatically increased the earned income tax credit to lift them out of poverty, to reward work over welfare, to make it possible for people to be successful workers and successful parents.

But there is much more to be done.

This spring, I will send you comprehensive welfare reform legislation that builds on the Family Support Act and restores the basic values of work and responsibility.

We will say to teenagers, "If you have a child out of wedlock, we will no longer give you a check to set up a separate household. We want families to stay together."

To absent parents who aren't paying child support, we'll say: "If you're not providing for your children, we'll garnish your wages, we'll suspend your license, we'll track you across state lines, and if necessary, we'll make some of you work off what you owe. People who bring children into this world can't just walk away."

And to all those who depend on welfare, we offer this simple compact: we will provide the support, the job training, the child care you need for up to two years. But after that, anyone who can work must work—in the private sector if possible, in community service if necessary. We will make welfare what it ought to be: A second chance, not a way of life.

We must tackle welfare reform in 1994, yes, as we tackle health care. A million people are on welfare today are there because it's the only way they can get health care coverage. Those who choose to leave welfare for jobs without health benefits find themselves in the incredible position of paying taxes that help pay for health coverage for those who choose to stay on welfare. No wonder many people leave work and go back on welfare to get health care coverage. We must solve the health care problem to solve the welfare problem.

Health care.

This year, we will make history by reforming our health care system. This is another issue where the people are way ahead of the politicians.

The first lady has received almost a million letters from people all across America and all walks of life. Let me share one of them with you.

Richard Anderson of Reno, Nevada, lost his job and, with it, his health insurance. Two weeks later, his wife Judy suffered a cerebral aneurysm. He rushed her to the hospital, where she stayed in intensive care for twenty-one days.

The Andersons' bills exceeded $120,000. Although Judy recovered and Richard went back to work, at $8 an hour, the bills were too much for them. They were forced into bankruptcy by high medical costs.

"Mrs. Clinton," he wrote to Hillary, "no one in the United States of America should have to lose everything they have worked for all their lives because they were unfortunate enough to become ill."

It was to help the Richard and Judy Andersons of America that the first lady and so many others have worked so hard on the health care issue, and we owe them our thanks.

There are others in Washington who say there is no health care crisis. Tell that to Richard and Judy Anderson. Tell it to the 58 million Americans who have no coverage at all for some time each year that there is no health care crisis. Tell it to the 81 million

Americans with "pre-existing" conditions who are paying more, can't get insurance or can't change jobs.

Tell it to the small businesses burdened by the skyrocketing cost of insurance. Tell it to the 76 percent of insured Americans whose policies have lifetime limits—and who can find themselves without any coverage just when they need it most—tell them there is no health care crisis. You tell them—because I can't.

The naysayers don't understand the impact of this problem on people's lives. They just don't get it. We must act now to show that we do.

From the day we began, our health care initiative has been designed to strengthen all that is good about our health care system. The world's best health professionals. Cutting-edge research and research institutions. Medicare for older Americans. None of this should be put at risk.

We're paying more and more money for less and less care. Every year fewer and fewer Americans even get to choose their doctors. Every year doctors and nurses spend more time on paperwork and less on patients because of the bureaucratic nightmare the present system has become. The system is riddled with inefficiency, abuse and fraud.

In today's health care system, insurance companies call all the shots.

They pick and choose whom they cover. They can cut off your benefits when you need your coverage most. They are in charge.

And so every night, millions of well-insured Americans go to bed just an illness, an accident or a pink slip away from financial ruin. Every morning millions more go to work without health insurance for their families. And every year, hard-working people are told to pick a new doctor because their boss picked a new plan, and countless others turn down better jobs because they fear losing their insurance.

If we let the health care system continue to drift, Americans will have less care, fewer choices and higher bills. Our approach protects the quality of care and people's choices.

It builds on what works today in the private sector. To expand the employer-based system and guarantee private insurance for every American—something proposed by President Richard Nixon more than twenty years ago. That's what we want: guaranteed private insurance.

Right now, nine out of ten people who have private insurance get it through employers—and that must continue. And if your employer is providing good benefits at reasonable prices—that must continue, too.

Our goal is health insurance you can depend on: comprehensive benefits that cover preventive care and prescription drugs; health premiums that don't jump when you get sick or get older; the power, no matter how small your business is, to choose dependable insurance at the same rates government and big companies get; one simple form for people who are sick; and, most of all, the freedom to choose a health plan and the right to choose your own doctor.

Our approach protects older Americans. Every plan before Congress proposes to slow the growth of Medicare. The difference is this: we believe those savings should be used to improve health care for senior citizens. Medicare must be protected, and it should cover prescription drugs. And we should take the first steps toward covering long-term care. To those who would cut Medicare without protecting seniors, I say: the solution to today's squeeze on middle-class working people is not to put the squeeze on middle-class retired people.

When it's all said and done, insurance must mean what it used to mean.

You pay a fair price for security and, when you get sick, health care is always there. No matter what.

Along with the guarantee of health security, there must be more responsibility. Parents must take their kids to be immunized; we all should take advantage of preventive care; and we all must work together to stop the violence that crowds its victims into our emergency rooms. People who don't have insurance will get coverage—but they'll have to pay something.

The minority of business that provide no insurance and shift the costs to others, will have to contribute something. People who smoke will pay more for a pack of cigarettes. If we want to solve the health care crisis in this country, there can be no more something for nothing.

In the coming months, I want to work with Democrats and Republicans to reform our health care system by using the market to bring down costs and to achieve lasting health security.

For sixty years, this country has tried to reform health care. President Roosevelt tried. President Truman tried. President Nixon

tried. President Carter tried. Every time, the powerful special interests defeated them. But not this time.

Facing up to special interests will require courage. It will raise
critical questions about the way we finance our campaigns and how
lobbyists peddle their influence. The work of change will never get
easier until we limit the influence of well-financed interests who
profit from the current system. So I call on you now to finish the job
you began last year by passing tough, meaningful campaign finance
reform and lobbying reform this year.

This is a test for all of us. The American people provide those of
us in government service with great benefits—health care that's
always there. We need to give every hard-working, tax-paying
American the same health care security they give us.

Hear me clearly. If the legislation you send me does not guarantee every American private health insurance that can never be taken
away, I will take this pen, veto that legislation and we'll come right
back here and start over again.

But I believe we're ready to do it right now. If you're ready to
guarantee to every American health care that can never be taken
away, now is the time to stand with the people who sent you here.

As we take these steps together to renew America's strength at
home, we must also continue our work to renew America's leadership abroad.

This is a promising moment. Because of the agreements we have
reached, Russia's strategic nuclear missiles soon will no longer be
pointed at the United States, nor will we point ours at them. Instead
of building weapons in space, Russian scientists will help us build
the international space station.

There are still dangers in the world: arms proliferation; bitter
regional conflicts; ethnic and nationalist tensions in many new democracies; severe environmental degradation; and fanatics who
seek to cripple the world's cities with terror. . . .

Ultimately, the best strategy to ensure our security and build a
durable peace is to support the advance of democracy. Democracies
do not attack each other; they make better partners in trade and
diplomacy.

That is why we have supported the democratic reformers in
Russia and in the other states of the former Soviet bloc. I applaud
the bipartisan support this Congress provided last year for our

initiatives to help Russia, Ukraine, and other states through their epic transformations.

Our support of reform must combine patience and vigilance. We will urge Russia and the other states to continue with their economic reforms. And we will seek to cooperate with Russia to solve regional problems, while insisting that if Russian troops operate in neighboring states, they do so only when those states agree to their presence, and in strict accord with international standards. . . .

We will also work for new progress toward peace in the Middle East. Last year, the world watched Yitzakh Rabin and Yasser Arafat at the White House in their historic handshake of reconciliation. On the long, hard road ahead, I am determined to do all I can to help achieve a comprehensive and lasting peace for all the peoples of the region.

There are some in our country who argue that with the Cold War over, America should turn its back on the rest of the world. Many around the world were afraid we would do just that. But I took this office on a pledge to keep our nation secure by remaining engaged in the world.

And this year, because of our work together—enacting NAFTA, keeping our military strong and prepared, supporting democracy abroad—we reaffirmed America's leadership and increased the security of the American people.

While Americans are more secure from threats abroad, we are less secure from threats here at home.

Every day, the national peace is shattered by crime. In Petaluma, California, an innocent slumber party gives way to agonizing tragedy for the family of Polly Klass. An ordinary train ride on Long Island ends in a hail of 9-millimeter rounds.

A tourist in Florida is nearly burned alive by bigots simply because he is black. Right here in our nation's capital, a brave young man named Jason White—a policeman, the son and grandson of policemen—is ruthlessly gunned down.

Violent crime and the fear it provokes are crippling our society, limiting personal freedom and fraying the ties that bind us. The crime bill before Congress gives you a chance to do something about it—to be tough and smart.

First, we must recognize that most violent crimes are committed by a small percentage of criminals, who too often break the laws even on parole. Those who commit crimes must be punished, and those who commit repeated violent crimes must be told: commit a third violent crime and you'll be put away, and put away for good. Three strikes and you're out.

Second, we must take steps to reduce violence and prevent crimes, beginning with more police officers and more community policing. We know that police who work the streets, know the folks, have the respect of the kids and focus on high-crime areas, are more likely to prevent crime as well as catch criminals. . . .

That's why we must hire 100,000 new community police officers, well trained and patrolling beats all over America; a police corps; and move retiring military personnel into police forces across America. We must also invest in safe schools, so that our children can learn to count and read and write without also learning how to duck bullets.

Third, we must build on the Brady bill, and take further steps to keep guns out of the hands of criminals. When it comes to guns, let me be clear: hunters must always be free to hunt, and law-abiding adults should be free to own guns and protect their homes. I respect that part of American culture. I grew up in it.

But I want to ask sportsmen and others who lawfully own guns to join us in a common campaign to reduce gun violence. You didn't create this problem, but we need your help to solve it. There is no sporting purpose on Earth that should stop us from banishing the assault weapons that outgun our police and cut down our children. So, I urge you to pass an assault weapons ban.

Fourth, we must remember that drugs are a factor in an enormous percentage of crimes. Recent studies indicate that drug use is on the rise again among young people. The crime bill contains more money for drug treatment for criminal addicts and boot camps for youthful offenders. The administration budget contains a large increase in funding for drug treatment and drug education. I hope you will pass them both.

The problem of violence is an American problem. It has no partisan or philosophical element. Therefore, I urge you to set aside your partisan differences and pass a strong, smart, tough crime bill now.

But, further, I urge you: As we demand tougher penalties for those who choose violence, let us also remember how we came to this sad point. In America's toughest neighborhoods, meanest streets and poorest rural areas, we have seen a stunning breakdown of community, family and work—the heart and soul of civilized society.

This has created a vast vacuum into which violence, drugs and gangs have moved. So, even as we say no to crime, we must give people—especially our young people—something to say yes to.

Many of our initiatives—from job training to welfare reform to health care to national service—will help rebuild distressed communities, strengthen families and provide work. But more needs to be done.

That is what our community empowerment agenda is all about: challenging businesses to provide more investment through empowerment zones; insuring that banks make loans in the same communities their deposits come from; and passing legislation to unleash the power of capital through community development banks to create jobs, opportunity and hope where they are needed most.

Let's be honest. Our problems go way beyond the reach of any government program. They are rooted in the loss of values, the disappearance of work, and the breakdown of our families and our communities.

My fellow Americans, we can cut the deficit, create jobs, promote democracy around the globe, pass welfare reform and health care reform and the toughest crime bill in history, and still leave too many of our people behind. The American people must want to change within, if we are to bring back work, family and community.

We cannot renew our country when within a decade more than half of our children will be born into families where there is no marriage.

We cannot renew our country when thirteen-year-old boys get semi-automatic weapons and gun down nine-year-old boys—just for the kick of it.

We cannot renew our country when children are having children and the fathers of those children are walking away from them as if they don't amount to anything.

We cannot renew our country when our businesses eagerly look for new investments and new customers abroad, but ignore those who would give anything to have their jobs and would gladly buy their products if they had the money to do it right here at home.

We cannot renew our country unless more of us are willing to join the churches and other good citizens who are saving kids, adopting schools, making streets safer.

We cannot renew our country until we all realize that governments don't raise children, parents do—parents who know their children's teachers, turn off the TV, help with the homework and teach right from wrong—can make all the difference.

Let us give our children a future.

Let us take away their guns and give them books. Let us overcome their despair and replace it with hope. Let us, by our example, teach them to obey the law, respect our neighbors and cherish our values. Let us weave these sturdy threads into a new American community that can once more stand strong against the forces of despair and evil and lead us to a better tomorrow.

The naysayers fear we will not be equal to the challenges of our time, but they misread our history, our heritage, and even today's headlines. They all tell us we can and we will overcome any challenge.

When the earth shook and fires raged in California, when the Mississippi deluged the farmlands of the Midwest, when a century's bitterest cold swept from North Dakota to Newport News, it seemed as though the world itself was coming apart at the seams.

But the American people came together. They rose to the occasion, neighbor helping neighbor, strangers risking life and limb to save strangers, showing the better angels of our nature.

Let us not reserve those better angels only for natural disasters, leaving our deepest problems to petty political fights. Let us instead be true to our spirit—facing facts, coming together, bringing hope, moving forward.

Tonight, we are summoned to answer a question as old as the Republic itself. My fellow Americans, what is the State of the Union? It is growing stronger. But it must be stronger still. With your help and with God's, it will be.

Thank you. May God bless America.

After the Long War

Daniel Deudney and G. John Ikenberry

The end of the Cold War that had dominated world politics since the closing days of World War II, along with the collapse of communism in eastern Europe and in the newly fragmented Soviet states, terminated a historical era. The emerging new age brought relief from old difficulties and a host of unanticipated and unforeseen crises, raising vital questions about the role of the United States in world affairs at the end of the twentieth century. President George Bush spoke of a "new world order," but as a blueprint for action it remained blurred and bereft of clear guidelines; and President Bill Clinton, in his first two years in office, similarly failed to articulate a definition of American interests, values, and goals as he faced complex troubles from Somalia to Haiti, and from North Korea to Bosnia. At the same time, behind the headlines, the end of the Cold War has had, and will continue to have, a decisive impact on American politics and society. The domestic consequences of a half-century of Cold War, and the likely effects of its conclusion, are outlined in the selection that follows. Carefully consider Deudney's and Ikenberry's premises, and speculate about the developments that might radically alter their deductions.

When the Cold War ended, one era of American history closed and a new one dawned. While the features of the new era remain un-clear, Americans across the political spectrum generally welcome the turn of events. On the Right and the Left, the end of the Cold War has been seen as a triumph—a vindication of each side's efforts. For others, the Cold War's finish has been seen as a welcome opportunity to redirect resources and attention to long-neglected domestic needs. The emerging debate over the domestic implications of the end of the Cold War has focused on reallocating the federal budget and restructuring defense. To most Americans, the disappearance of the Soviet threat promises both improved security and a hefty peace dividend.

American politics after the Cold War, however, may not be so benign; the end of the East-West conflict holds deeper implications for the American polity than is generally recognized. Despite the widespread expectation that relations *among* the Western democracies would be disrupted by the end of the Cold War, the reality is that relations *within* those democracies have been more profoundly disturbed. . . . The Cold War's conclusion weighed heavily in the failed reelection bid of George Bush, the quintessential Cold War president, whose foreign policy accomplishments were unable to prevent his fall from unprecedented popularity to electoral defeat in less than a year. With the Soviet threat gone, domestic political coalitions have begun to unravel, as seen most dramatically in the United States in the strongest third-party presidential showing since 1912. Such political fragmentation is likely to be reinforced by major post–Cold War foreign policy controversies such as the North American Free Trade Agreement (NAFTA). Unlike the Soviet threat, which stimulated national unity, the North American trade pact and the evolving politics of global trade and finance pit region against region, class against class, and fracture existing party alignments. The end of the Cold War is not the source of such troubles, but it removes a powerful counterforce to them.

The diplomatic historian John Lewis Gaddis has dubbed the Cold War era "the long peace," the longest period of general peace in Europe in modern times. But for the American polity, it has been "the long war." Since the late 1930's the United States has sustained a nearly continuous military mobilization for global war, an effort that profoundly shaped and changed the American polity. In the flush of triumph and optimism, it is easy to overlook the fact that the great half-century struggle with fascism and communism made it easier—perhaps even possible—to cope with a wide array of domestic problems. The long war mobilization created a new model for relations between the state and society, between the institutions of government, and between the parties as it reshaped the national identity.

Foreign struggle paradoxically brought great domestic benefit for the United States. Sustained mobilization for global conflict required a "social bargain" that effectively modernized and democratized American institutions. It is easy to forget that before World War II the American political system had reached an impasse in responding to the demands of industrialization and state building. The permanence and pervasiveness of international conflict, beginning in the 1940s, made it necessary and possible for the United States to build a strong state, manage an industrial economy, reduce social inequalities, and foster national cohesion. Ironically, it was the fascist and communist challenges from abroad that pushed the development of American capitalism in a more progressive direction.

The end of the Cold War threatens to unravel those accomplishments and return the United States to the impasses of the 1920s and 1930s. If modernization and democratization at home were accidental side effects of the global struggle, then sustaining the institutional legacy of the process may well be beyond the capacity of the American political system. The unraveling social bargain will have to be rewoven. The tasks ahead are not simply to reorder budget priorities, but rather to reconstitute the consensus for an activist state, the provision of social welfare, and a sense of national identity. That reweaving of a consensus will inevitably reshape the political parties and the presidency. The future holds not a return to some mythical halcyon normalcy, but a divisive struggle over the basic principles of the American political and economic order.

To understand the domestic impact of the Cold War, it is necessary to recall the trajectories and dilemmas of U.S. political development before global engagement. Since the middle of the nineteenth century, American institutions, like those of Germany, Japan, and Russia, have had to adapt to the spread of industrialization. First, the capitalist cycles of boom and bust generated demands for elaborate and powerful mechanisms for state intervention and management of the economy. Second, the emergence of a mass urban working class produced social problems and the need for a social safety net of labor laws, unemployment insurance, retirement income, and welfare provisions. Third, industrial societies tended to become much more occupationally and socially stratified while at the same time more densely linked and compressed, thus generating the need for new forms of national identity and cohesion.

In the United States, efforts to cope with those dilemmas ran against the grain of the American system. In some respects, the United States was better equipped to deal with its obstacles than were countries with feudal social and autocratic political systems such as Germany, Russia, and Japan, all of whom experienced revolutionary upheaval. But the twin pillars of American politics—individualism and limited government—imposed formidable constraints. Emerging in the late nineteenth and early twentieth centuries, the populist and progressive reform movements met with only modest success in mobilizing suffcient political power to restructure American institutions.

In the decade immediately before World War II, the United States faced chronic economic stagnation, class warfare, and political disarray. The first New Deal programs had lost momentum by the mid-1930s. Although the populist-progressive coalition had a working majority, entrenched opposition to modern state-building had blocked important institutional change.

The ultimate sources of that impasse were a late–eighteenth century constitution designed to limit central government activity and balance competing political forces and an early–nineteenth century capitalist system that absolutized private property rights and eschewed government economic management. Without external pressures, those factors prevented the creation of a modern state and the realization of progressive social goals.

A half century of global engagement profoundly altered America's domestic political order. Beginning with the rearmament in anticipation of World War II, intensifying during war with the Axis powers, and continuing during four decades of Cold War struggle, American politics took a new direction. America's rise to global preeminence and activism required major institutional innovation—innovation that broke the impasse on political development and accomplished much of the progressive agenda. Fifty years of global engagement produced changes in four domestic areas: the strength of the state apparatus, economic management, social equity and welfare, and national identity. In effect, without needing to mobilize a political consensus for domestic modernization, the United States reaped the benefits of such change. The long war forged a social bargain, but an accidental one.

War and state building are intimately connected throughout history, and the United States is no exception. As political critic Randolph Bourne observed "war is essentially the health of the state." From the Declaration of Independence through the beginning of World War II, war played a crucial role in the episodic expansion of central state power in America. The need for a central government able to fend off European economic and military predations was, as historian Frederick Marks III has noted, the decisive argument in the close-fought effort to ratify the Constitution of 1787.

During the Civil War the strength of the central government grew with the establishment of the federal banking system, conscription, direct taxation of individuals, the transcontinental railroad, and the Homestead Act. The presidency itself was also strengthened within the national government. Moreover, as sociologist Theda Skocpol recently argued, the pension system for Civil War veterans was the first major federal income maintenance program, a prototype for the subsequent welfare state. The demands of World War I led to further growth in the powers and resources of the central government. The return to normalcy after both wars was marked by only a partial dismantlement of war-born powers and institutions.

In the twentieth century, America's struggle to maintain the world balance of power greatly altered the domestic balance of power as well. The demands of war enhanced the power and prestige of the federal government in relation to the states. Within the national government, the power of the executive grew at the expense of the judicial and legislative branches. War transformed the president from the chief administrative officer of a federated and balanced system into a paramount leader—or what historian Arthur Schlesinger called the "imperial presidency." As leader of the free world and sole commander-in-chief of American nuclear forces, the president gained an almost monarchical aura. Often that concentration of power could be brought to bear on domestic agendas—particularly if they could be connected, however tenuously, to national security goals.

Continuous global engagement also required centralized economic management. In the conditions of total war in the 1940s, it was politically possible for the federal government to manage labor and capital effectively in the pursuit of maximum economic output. As war raged abroad, the fear of class struggles at home gave way to an administered peace. After World War II, the actual system of wage and price controls was ended, but the techniques of Keynesian macroeconomic management and the federal commitment to maximum employment were maintained. During the longer Cold War struggle, direct federal involvement was concentrated on technological sectors with military import. In the cases of atomic energy, aeronautics, and space, the federal government called whole industries into existence and dramatically quickened innovation. During the 1950s, government-sponsored construction of the interstate highway system and improvements in science and math education were justified as national defense imperatives.

The long war's impact on equity, class, and social welfare was equally significant, if less direct. Growth in defense spending and related manpower requirements led to programs and institutions that advanced social equity and the mobility of citizens. Veterans' benefits, particularly the G.I. Bill, opened the door to the middle class for millions of Americans. The post-*Sputnik* commitment to bolster education broadened social opportunity. Moreover, the initial success of racial integration within the armed services gave impetus to integration within society at large.

The peculiar character of the Soviet Union and communism as America's antagonists heightened American sensitivity to social and class issues. Unlike the Japanese and German threats in World War II, the communist challenge had an ideological edge: to build a worker's paradise as well as a great military power. Thus, particularly in the 1950s and 1960s, the performance of American capitalism in providing full employment, health care, and adequate housing took on added significance. The willingness of political and economic elites to make concessions to improve working conditions and take care of society's less-fortunate was increased by competition with the communist movement. At the same time, the threat posed by a communist state delegitimized more radical programs or truly comprehensive agendas for change. Ironically, the struggle with Soviet communism helped American capitalism overcome many of the flaws and instabilities so manifest in the 1930s.

Finally, the semi-permanent mobilization against communism strengthened the national identity of Americans. That unifying dynamic helped overcome ethnic and sectional differences and the ideological heritage of individualism. The long war was particularly important in integrating the South and the West into the national economy and society. The existence of a total adversary greatly strengthened the ability of leaders to mobilize public support for national goals. Moreover, U.S. leadership of the "free world" and its role as a model for peoples elsewhere infused American citizens and leaders with a sense of high purpose and responsibility for domestic as well as international actions.

The net result of fifty years of global struggle was the forging of a social bargain that met many progressive goals but did not depend upon the establishment of a domestic progressive consensus. The stimulative effect of that competition was greatest between the late 1930s and the mid-1960s and had already begun to wane in the subsequent decades. The Cold War made it easier and at times possible to realize many progressive goals, though some accomplishments—such as civil rights gains in the 1960s—had mainly domestic origins. Nonetheless, the long war has left a substantial imprint on the American polity. Because of this conflict, it was more democratic and more cohesive. The inability of a domestic consensus to modernize American political institutions was overcome by the need to rise to global challenges. The crusade against communism abroad inadvertently had the side-effect of furthering the partial modernization of the American political system and the partial realization of the progressive agenda.

The end of the Cold War raises a far-reaching question about American politics: Can the accidental social bargain be sustained without the circumstances that led to its formation? Nothing is inevitable in politics, but several signs indicate that the domestic Cold War order is coming undone, ushering in a period of political decay. Such decay and the tasks that come with it will pose daunting new challenges for parties and presidents and increasingly define the fault lines in American politics.

Unfortunately, this default scenario, in which the country returns to the impasses experienced by the American polity before World War II, is the most likely. Decay is already manifest in four areas.

First, power at the political system's center is eroding. Increasingly, the president will be the big loser. The powers of the presidency are greatest in foreign and military policy, but without an overriding concern for such issues, the salience of the presidency will decline. Outside of foreign and military policy, there is no presumption of presidential preeminence and strong domestic forces and interests impede action. Similarly, the overall importance of the federal government within the country will wane. Even if the federal government remains large because of domestic social spending, its political complexion will be transformed. Institutions designed for foreign and military activity aim to give political leaders room for choice and decisive action, whereas institutions oriented to domestic needs leave little room for creative or bold use of executive power.

Second, the justification for federal support for technological innovation and industrial development will be weakened, and the state's capacity for economic management generally could be diminished. Without a Cold War warrant, it will be necessary to promote industrial policies supporting promising technologies on their own merits. The Advanced Research Projects Agency and other national security units have played a comparable role to Japan's Ministry of International Trade and Industry in stimulating high-tech development, but they have only an incidental role in assisting the civilian sector. American industrial policy must now move into an open political debate where the cacophony of corporate, sectional, and ideological divisions bode ill for its survival. Without the cloak of national security secrecy, decisions on technology funding become more contentious and difficult to resolve.

Third, the Cold War's absence will make the achievement of internal social equity and welfare more difficult, reinvigorating class divisions. The major military threat gone, the size of the military will continue to decline, shrinking an important vehicle for social mobility. The political costs of severe social inequity will also decline with the ideological challenge to capitalism vanquished. Without an adversary claiming to represent the universal interests of the poor, concern for equity loses part of its rationale and constituency. Domestic concern for social equity will be further eroded as the relevant standard of comparison shifts to Third World countries teeming with cheap labor, blighted by severe class divisions, and bereft of even rudimentary social programs. The American welfare state, already under fiscal pressure and lacking a strong constituency, is thus further weakened by the new global environment. Finally, the end of the long Cold War will also erode national political cohesiveness as ethnic and sectional differences come to the fore. If, as conventional wisdom holds, we are shifting from an age of geopolitics to one of geoeconomics, then national unity is sure to decline as sectional economic differences rooted in geography reassert themselves. It is much easier to generate a national consensus against a powerful military adversary threatening the entire country than it is to build one on trade policy among Northern shoe manufacturers, Midwestern wheat farmers, or Western computer makers. Also, the fissiparous nature of multicultural population will increasingly lack a national counterbalance, thereby eroding a common collective identity. The military's declining salience in the country's life will likewise weaken an important institution for national acculturation.

That is a bleak scenario, but is it the entire story? Skeptics will raise doubts. First, the social bargain may have gained suffcient momentum to endure without the conditions that generated it. Habits and institutions tend to persist and create their own constituencies. That perspective is probably true in one regard: It will probably slow the decay. But it is unlikely to prevent it, particularly in an era of tight curbs on government spending.

A second possibility is that a new foreign threat will arise to breathe new life into institutions of the long war. The most likely candidates are America's capitalist trading partners in Europe and Asia. It is those states that seem to put American prosperity at risk and that call for a major government response. Conflict among capitalist states may escalate; but the lines of conflict will not be as clear-cut as those in the Cold War. Alliances *across* national borders (by class, sector, or region) are as likely as those along them. Barring the unlikely degeneration of intra-capitalist disputes into military confrontation, such conflicts will not elicit measures of the sort needed to underpin the social bargain struck in the long war.

Inherited momentum and rising foreign threats will slow the decay, but they are not strong enough to arrest it. Taken together, the four tendencies of decay are likely to reinforce each other— making all the more likely the unraveling of the accidental bargain and a return to the conflicts that once plagued American politics.

The passing of the Cold War is also likely to profoundly alter the balance of power between the parties and their respective abilities to win the White House. Since the 1940s, the Republican party has dominated presidential elections in large measure because of its hard-line stance toward the Cold War. Faced with an ominous foreign threat, Republican presidents seemed to excel at acting tough but responsible. The Cold War–era president was first and foremost the leader of the Western alliance—the man with the finger on the button. Candidates for the office were judged accordingly. The first post–Cold War election in 1992 offered a glimpse of a new dynamic among the political parties. Bush was not one of the stronger Republican candidates in accomplishment or appeal; nevertheless, the 1992 election points to a deep crisis for the Republican party after the long war.

Columnist George Will has observed that the Democrats are the party of government, but it is equally true that the Republicans—at least when it comes to foreign policy—are the party of the state. Although usually opposed to a strong state in domestic affairs, the Republicans have been the most vigorous proponents of the national security establishment. Despite their smaller bloc of registered voters, Republicans captured the White House in seven of eleven races during the Cold War. In all seven victories (Dwight Eisenhower twice, Richard Nixon twice, Ronald Reagan twice, and Bush once) the Republicans were clearly positioned to the right on the issue of anticommunism. Republican contenders lost in 1948, 1960, and 1976 when the Democrats appeared to be at least as anticommunist, if not more, than the GOP. The election of 1964 was an anomaly: Lyndon Johnson, a hawkish Texas Democrat, defeated the even more harshly anticommunist Barry Goldwater, who seemed threateningly irresponsible. During the Cold War, anticommunism served the Republican party in much the same way as the ghost of Herbert Hoover worked for the Democrats after the Great Depression and "waving the bloody shirt" worked for the Republicans after the Civil War.

By contrast, the prominence of anticommunism tended to divide the Democratic party. Cold War–era Democrats captured the White House only briefly, and only then usually by being more loudly anticommunist that the Republicans. Many conservative Democrats, such as Henry Jackson, Sam Nunn, Walter George, and James Schlesinger, have played important roles in the Cold War security establishment. But they have stood outside the mainstream of their party, and their insistence that the Democrats emulate the Republicans on foreign and military policy has been a perennial source of Democratic division. The Korean and Vietnam wars were more divisive to the Democrats that to the Republicans.

The 1992 election brought the first defeat of an elected incumbent Republican president since Herbert Hoover's defeat sixty years earlier. Like previous postwar Republican presidents, Bush's strong suit was foreign and military affairs. He believed that the Operation Desert Storm would sustain popular support, but found that the impact quickly faded. Saddam Hussein may have looked like Hilter, but the American people saw that his threat was of a different caliber. Without a sufficient foreign threat, the election turned on domestic issues that had long been overshadowed.

Reading from the traditional Republican script, Bush hammered away on the issue of seasoned judgment and foreign policy experience, but with little consequence. Ross Perot's candidacy was made more plausible because the public did not judge him by the old Cold War standard of calm crisis leadership in the shadow of nuclear war. That Perot's legendary volatility and his long record of gun-slinging hyper-nationalism were hardly mentioned—let alone disqualifying—revealed just how little the American public remembered the standards by which it had so carefully considered previous candidates.

Republican liabilities became Democratic opportunities. Questions over Bill Clinton's character and military service record were much debated, but they lacked the punch they might have had in previous elections. Further, despite Bush's efforts, Clinton was able to largely ignore foreign and military policy during the campaign at little political cost. In general, the Democratic found that its divisions on foreign policy had become far less relevant and that its traditional focus on nitty-gritty domestic issues had renewed appeal.

The end of the Cold War has created a fundamental crisis for the Republican party by eliminating its electoral trump card. Not only must the GOP find a new foreign policy, but it may also find that foreign policy has lost its recent importance. A return to prewar Republicanism is out of the question. The older Republican orthodoxy featured America-first isolationism, with occasional bursts of opportunistic imperialism. The party center, exemplified by Ohio senator Robert Taft, was anchored in an inward-looking business class. Despite strident Republican voices like that of Pat Buchanan urging a return to isolationism, the political foundations for that view have now been undermined. Over that last fifty years, there has been a decisive shift within the American business community

away from the inward-looking, Main Street–style capitalism toward
a multinational, free-trade orientation. That the most active support for NAFTA comes from the mainstream business community
reveals how difficult it would be for the Republicans to return to a
nativist, protectionist stance.

Such changes present opportunities and constraints for the Clinton
administration. The powers and tasks of the president, as well as
public expectations, are being transformed after the long war.

Clinton inherits an office poorly designed for pursuing a domestic agenda. The powers of the office of the president are not fungi-
ble. The capability to wage global war against the Soviet Union does
not readily lend itself to cleaning up the environment, providing
health care, or controlling street crime. There will be a strong temptation to view domestic problems through lenses left from the Cold
War—declaring a "war on drugs" or proclaiming environmental
degradation a national security threat. When national security is at
stake, resources can be more easily mobilized and a consensus attained. Unfortunately, the national security rationale does not
travel well. As the gridlock over energy policy in the 1970s demonstrated, it is very diffcult to resolve complex internal problems even
when they can be credibly linked to traditional national security.

Public expectations of presidents and the standards for measuring their performance left over from the long war will now weigh
heavily. During the Cold War, the president was first and foremost
expected to lead the anticommunist alliance. Central to a successful
presidency was the display of toughness and resolve on the world
stage. Beyond that, the expectations on the president were relatively low. Thus, the powers of the presidency were those necessary
to meet public expectations of presidential performance. If the
public continues to judge the president by wartime standards, presidents will appear chronically deficient. That gap between ingrained public expectations and actual presidential power will hob-
ble even the most skilled leader. . . .

The success of presidents in the post–Cold War era will hinge on
their ability to recast public expectations about their performance
in new directions, while redeploying presidential energy toward
foreign opportunities linked to domestic economic problems. Presidents must learn new ways to harness and deploy their power, but
they must also redefine how the public sees and judges them.

Without the overriding mission of the long war, American politics is undergoing fundamental change, as are the politics of the other Western industrial democracies. The Cold War helped forge and modernize many vital U.S. institutions. As the long war fades into history, there is reason to worry about the ability of parties and presidents to build coalitions for managing a modern society and economy.

The current debate about domestic renewal misses this deep-seated problem that strikes at the heart of the American polity. In effect, what the United States faces is another deficit—a political deficit. For forty-five years, the American political system benefited from public institutions whose formation did not require an explicit consensus. Now America's politics must confront the gap between the institutions it depends on and the political support undergirding them. The challenge for presidents and other leaders is to build a new basis of support for an activist state and a progressive political agenda without the help of an external threat: A new social bargain must be forged. Only then will the long war really give way to a long peace.

Whatever Happened to AIDS?

Jeffrey Schmalz

Ronald Reagan was president of the United States when AIDS was first discovered and publicized as a disease in 1981. Initially, it was spoken about only in whispers. Identified in the first instance as an illness that struck only homosexual men and was transmitted only through sexual contact, there existed almost a conspiracy of silence around the disease. Many, if not most, members of the New Right and Moral Majority viewed AIDS as a fitting punishment for what they saw as the sin of homosexuality. In part because of Reagan's political alignment with such forces, he and his administration practiced a policy of "benign neglect" toward the growing epidemic.

But slowly the horror of AIDS began to enter public consciousness. Movie star Rock Hudson died of AIDS, and Hollywood stars like Elizabeth Taylor and Barbra Streisand initiated national campaigns to raise money to fight the disease. Ryan White, a young boy with hemophilia, also succumbed to the AIDS virus, transmitted through a blood transfusion. By the time Ervin "Magic" Johnson, one of America's athletic heroes, announced that he had contracted the HIV virus through heterosexual contact, it was no longer possible to ignore the existence of the disease or the degree to which it threatened everyone. In 1992, both the Republican and Democratic conventions featured dramatic speeches by people infected by AIDS.

Yet as Jeffrey Schmalz reveals in this dramatic selection published after his own death from AIDS, there was still no adequate program responding to the disease. The Clinton presidency was far more sensitive than its predecessors; but nothing approaching the kind of mobilized scientific effort that produced the atom bomb was in the offing. Jeffrey Schmalz had covered the AIDS crisis for the New York Times. *Here, he conveys his frustration at the failure to forge a bold and imaginative policy toward the AIDS epidemic, even as he wonders whether the sense of crisis over the disease is dissipating in the face of other news items of greater interest to the media.*

I have come to the realization that I will almost certainly die of AIDS. I have wavered on that point. When the disease was first diagnosed in early 1991, I was sure I would die—and soon. I was facing brain surgery; the surgeons discovered an infection often fatal in four months. I would shortly develop pneumonia, then blood clots. I was hospitalized four times over five months. But by the end of that year, I thought differently. My health rebounded, almost certainly because of AZT. I was doing so well; I really might beat it.

Now, it is clear I will not. You can beat the statistics only so long. My T-cell count, which was only 2 when I got my diagnosis, has never gone above 30—a dangerously low level. I have lived longer than the median survival time by ten months. The treatments simply are not there. They are not even in the pipeline. A miracle is possible, of course. And for a long time, I thought one would happen. But let's face it, a miracle isn't going to happen. One day soon I will simply become one of the ninety people in America to die that day of AIDS. It's like knowing I will be killed by a speeding car, but not knowing when or where. I used to be the exception in my H.I.V. support group, the only one of its eight members who was not merely infected with the virus but who had advanced to full-blown AIDS. Now, just a year and a half later, the exception in my group is the one person who does not have AIDS. All the rest of us have deteriorated with the hallmarks of the disease—a seizure, Kaposi's sarcoma, pneumonia. Our weekly meetings simmer with desperation: We are getting sicker. *I* am getting sicker. Time is running out.

Once AIDS was a hot topic in America—promising treatments on the horizon, intense media interest, a political battlefield. Now, twelve years after it was first recognized as a new disease, AIDS has become normalized, part of the landscape. It is at once everywhere and nowhere, the leading cause of death among young men nationwide, but little threat to the core of American political power, the white heterosexual suburbanite. No cure or vaccine is in sight. And what small treatment advances had been won are now crumbling. The world is moving on, uncaring, frustrated and bored, leaving by the roadside those of us who are infected and who can't help but wonder: Whatever happened to AIDS? As a journalist who has written about this disease for five years, and as a patient who has had it for nearly as long, I went out looking for answers.

THE DISEASE AND THE DOCTORS

Dr. Anthony S. Fauci speaks with a hint of a Brooklyn accent, which is out of sync with the elegance of his appearance—well tailored, tidy, trim. At fifty two, he is scientist-cum-celebrity, ridiculed by Larry Kramer in the play "The Destiny of Me," lionized by George Bush in the 1988 Presidential debate as a hero.

Being the Government's point man on AIDS has made Tony Fauci (rhymes with OUCH-ee) famous. He professes to be solely the scientist. But in fact, he is very much the star and the politician, one year defending modest Reagan-Bush AIDS budget proposals as adequate, the next defending generous Clinton proposals as necessary. He is the activist's enemy—"Murderer!" Kramer once called him in an essay published in The Village Voice. He is the activist's friend, a comrade in arms, showing up last October at the opening of the Kramer play wearing a red AIDS ribbon.

Fauci's starring AIDS role comes from the many hats he wears—among them director of the National Institute of Allergy and Infectious Diseases and director of the National Institutes of Health's Office of AIDS Research.

"Fauci deserves a lot of the blame for where we are on AIDS," said Peter Staley of TAG, the activist Treatment Action Group. But others say that is not fair. "You can't blame any one person," said Gregg Gonsalves, who wrote TAG's report on the status of AIDS research. "We've gotten to the edge of a scientific cliff."

Whatever Fauci's faults, I have never doubted his commitment. Still, he is the face of the AIDS scientific community, and twelve years into the disease there are only temporary treatments that work for a few years at most. AIDS remains a fatal illness. Approximately a million Americans are believed to be infected with the human immunodeficiency virus, the key component of AIDS, and virtually all of them are expected to develop the disease eventually. Close to half a million Americans are expected to have full-blown AIDS by the end of next year; more than 200,000 have already died. Roughly 350,000 will have died by the end of 1994. The World Health Organization puts the number infected worldwide at more than 13 million adults and additional 1 million or more children.

So far, the only treatments are nucleoside analogues, drugs like, AZT, DDC, and DDI. A fourth nucleoside analogue, D4T, is expected to be approved by the spring [of 1993]. Fauci has focused national research efforts on these analogues, which slow the virus by fooling it with a decoy of genetic material it needs to reproduce. But the analogues have problems. They are highly toxic, and the virus, which mutates rapidly, eventually catches on to the deception.

Everyone knew going into the international AIDS conference in Berlin in June [1993] that the nucleoside analogues were of limited use, but the horrible surprise was just *how* limited. A report issued just before the meeting—the Concorde Study, conducted in England, France and Ireland—found that, contrary to the recommendations of the United States Government, use of AZT before the onset of AIDS symptoms did not necessarily prolong life. (In an extraordinary action, a United States Government panel has since pulled back the earlier recommendation. AZT is still recommended for those with full-blown AIDS. But the panel left it for patients and their doctors to decide on earlier use.)

A subsequent Australian study, published in July, found that AZT, used early, did prolong life. I have always felt that it has prolonged mine. Still, what makes the fuss over AZT so stunning is not just the the drug has shortcomings—almost everyone knew that from the start. It is that AZT, flawed as it was, had become the Gold Standard of treatment, against which other therapies were being measured. The chilling message of the AZT dispute is this: Things are not just failing to get better; they are getting worse. We are losing ground.

"The fallout from Berlin has been devastating," said Martin Delaney, founding director of Project Inform, an AIDS treatment information and lobbying group. "There were no surprises. But the risk now is that AIDS gets put up on the shelf alone with a lot of other long-term unresolved problems. We lose the urgency for money and the scientific momentum." The bad news has left drug companies scrambling. Last spring things were so desperate that a group of fifteen announced they would pool research data. Many scientists—and activists—are fed up with the drug companies, which seem hellbent on pursuing more nucleoside analogues when the real future of AIDS treatment probably lies with gene therapy. The idea is to alter the genetic structure of cells to make them inhospitable to H.I.V. But the problem is, no one knows how to translate the occasional test-tube success into a workable treatment. In addition, most of the gene therapies are being developed by small biotechnology companies that will take years to get into full production.

So, was all the time and money spent on the nucleoside analogues wasted? Fauci, who obviously has an investment in the answer, was emphatic that it wasn't. "People say the Berlin meeting was so depressing, nothing's happening," Fauci said in his office overlooking the N. I. H. campus in Bethesda, Maryland. "I say that's not the way science works. There are little steps, building blocks. What's important is whether you're going in the right direction, and I am convinced that we are.

"Was it grossly inappropriate to do the extensive studies of AZT and DDI?" he continued. "No. Should we have done more with other drugs? If we had them, one could say, yes."

"Let's say a year and a half from now, nevirapine isn't working," Fauci said of an experimental drug undergoing trials in combination with the nucleoside analogues. "Somebody's going to say, 'Why did you waste all that time with it?' But you don't know it doesn't work until you test it."

If Fauci is defensive, it may be because he is still smarting from a political bruising. His Office of AIDS Research has been reorganized by the Clinton Administration and he has been, in effect, ousted—done in by the AIDS activists through their Democratic friends in Congress. And while some of his time is being diverted to playing politics, in his own laboratory research he has now returned to basics—Square 1—where many AIDS researchers are working. Fauci is studying the pathogenesis of the disease, its route through the body.

I asked him the obvious: twelve years into the disease—shouldn't we know that already? "More effort looking at pathogenesis might have been appropriate in retrospect," Fauci responded. "But we were constantly being diverted—by the activists, by Congress. It was: 'What can you give me right now? Get those drugs out there as quickly as you can.'"

Not so long ago we believed that if we just could find enough money, we could make the disease manageable, like diabetes. But in a further sign of how little hope exists these days in the scientific community, money isn't seen as the main issue anymore.

"Certainly, there are more scientific opportunities than there are resources to fulfill them," Fauci said, echoing the views of other scientists. "But should we dump billions into AIDS research now? I think we'd reach a point of diminishing returns."

Fauci presents a front of optimism, at least for me. After all, there is no cure for any virus, only vaccines to prevent them—measles is an example. By the year 2000, he predicted, "We'll be into vaccine trials that show a vaccine is much more feasible than we thought, though we may not have the best vaccine by then."

Other scientists are unconvinced. They point out that the rapid mutation of the AIDS virus and its many strains make development of a vaccine difficult.

"The public is frustrated; it says, 'You've been working on this for ten years,'" said Dr. Irvin S. Y. Chen, director of the AIDS Institute at the University of California at Los Angeles. Chen bemoaned the lack of money for biomedical research in general, which he said was discouraging the best and the brightest from entering the field.

"We're in that in-between stage," said Dr. Merle A. Sande, an AIDS expert at the University of California at San Francisco; he was head of the Government panel on AZT use. "We know a lot about the virus, but we just don't seem able to translate that knowledge into significant treatment advances. It's incredibly frustrating."

Still, the frustration of the public and the scientists is nothing compared with the frustration of those of us living with AIDS or H.I.V. Will people still be dying of AIDS in the year 2000? Fauci didn't hesitate for a second before replying. "I don't think there's any question that will be the case."

THE ACTIVISTS AND THE GOVERNMENT

Tim Bailey was one of the Marys, and that's as close to the Act Up royalty as anybody can get.

The Marys are a subgroup of Act Up, the group involved in the more radical demonstrations, like disrupting services at St. Patrick's Cathedral. When Bailey died in June at 35, stipulating that he wanted a political funeral in Washington, Act Up was obliged to comply.

So on a drizzly Thursday at 7 A.M., two buses filled with Act Up members set out from New York. They were to rendezvous with the body in Washington, then carry the open coffin through the streets from the Capitol to the White House. They would show Bill Clinton the urgency of AIDS. They would bring one of its carcasses to his doorstep.

But it was not to be. The police would not let them march, and the day turned into a sodden fiasco, as the police and activists quarreled over the body, shoving the coffin in and out of a van parked in front of the Capitol. The rage was there, but the organization was not. And when the police said no, whom did Act Up members run to for help but the White House, the very target of their protest, getting Bob Hattoy, a White House staff member with AIDS, to intervene. In the end, Act Up members gave up and went home, taking the body with them.

It was a perfect metaphor for the state of AIDS activism—raging in desperate but unfocused anger, one foot on the inside, one on the outside.

The AIDS movement was built on grass-roots efforts. Now those efforts are in disarray. Many Act Up leaders have died. The group's very existence was based on the belief that AIDS could be cured quickly if only enough money and effort were thrown at it—something that now seems increasingly in doubt. Besides, it is hard to maintain attacks against a Government that is seeking big increases in AIDS spending. Much of the cream of Act Up has fled, forming groups like TAG and joining mainstream AIDS organizations like the Gay Men's Health Crisis and the American Foundation for AIDS Research.

Those left behind are Act Up's hard core. Act Up was always part theater, part group therapy. Now, sadly, Act Up is increasingly reduced to burying its dead.

To say all that is not to belittle the accomplishments of the group. One reason for Act Up's decline is that it has got so much of what it wanted. Act Up forced AIDS into the Presidential race, dogging candidates. Because of Act Up the price of AZT is lower. Drugs are approved more quickly. Today it is a given that the communities affected by a disease have a voice, and must be consulted. To a great extent, Act Up deserves much of the credit for the increasing political power of the entire gay rights movement. But now even the gay movement has pushed AIDS to the sidelines.

Anyone questioning how AIDS ranks as an issue among gay groups need only look to the march on Washington on April 25. Six years earlier, in 1987, a similar gay march had one overriding theme: AIDS. If there was a dominant theme last April, it was homosexuals in the military. To be sure, AIDS was an element of the march, but *just* an element. Speaker after speaker ignored it.

"It's like they are waiting for us to die so they can get on with their agenda," said Dr. Nicholas A. Rango, the director of New York State's AIDS Institute, a gay man who himself has AIDS and watched the march on C-Span from his Manhattan hospital bed. [He died on November 10.]

Torie Osborn, formerly executive director of the National Gay and Lesbian Task Force, argued that the shift was inevitable with the election of a Democratic President, renewed attacks from the right wing and just plain burnout. Increasingly, many homosexuals, especially those who test negative for H.I.V. do not want a disease to be what defines their community. "There is a deep yearning to broaden the agenda beyond AIDS," she said. "There's a natural need for human beings who are in deep grieving to reach for a future beyond their grieving.

"It's one thing to be fighting for treatment, believing you're going to get a cure that will have everyone survive," continued Osborn, who recently buried three friends who had died of AIDS. "But it's an incredibly depressing truth that AIDS has become part of the backdrop of gay life."

What is to some a broadening of the gay agenda, however, is to others desertion. "It's one thing for the politicians to abandon AIDS," Kevin Frost, a TAG member, said. "But for our own community to abandon the issue. . . . Who brought this issue of gays in the military out in the open? A couple of flashy queers with checkbooks. Well, what about AIDS?"

What *about* AIDS? Perhaps the greatest development affecting Act Up, the activist community and the entire AIDS care world is the changing face of the disease. Homosexual sex still accounts for the majority of cases, 57 percent. But that number is dropping, down from 61 percent in 1989. Meanwhile, the percentage of cases tied to intravenous drug use is beginning to climb. It is now at 23 percent, up from 21 percent in 1989.

Black and Hispanic groups are clamoring for a greater role in running AIDS care organizations. Their intentions seem genuine—what do gay groups know of inner-city drug use?—but also seem driven in part by a desire for money and power. In an age of Government cutbacks, AIDS is where the money is—"today's equivalent of the Great Society programs of the 60s" as Rango put it.

In Washington and Houston, gay groups and black and Hispanic groups are bickering over who should control the money and the programs. In New York, the largest AIDS care organization, the Gay Men's Health Crisis, is trying valiantly to be all things to all constituencies—it contributed $25,000 to the lobbying effort to allow homosexuals in the military even as it was helping to expand legal services in Harlem. Inevitably, focus is lost.

G.M.H.C. has recently changed executive directors, as have many of the more than 3,500 AIDS organizations in the United States. The average executive director of an AIDS service group lasts less than two years, burned out by depression and exhausted by the bickering among AIDS constituencies.

"We should be fighting the virus, not each other," said Dan Bross, the executive director of the AIDS Action Council. "We're eating our young."

Mary Fisher, who addressed the Republican National Convention in Houston as a woman infected with H.I.V., whom I interviewed at the time and who has since become a friend, also believes the AIDS movement is adrift. She was sitting at lunch in Manhattan with Larry Kramer, both of them bemoaning the state of AIDS activism.

"We need to agree on the goals," Fisher said.

"That's just rhetoric," Kramer shot back. "The goal is to find a cure."

Fisher see AIDS entering a dangerous never-never land, with the day fast approaching when *no one* will be carrying the AIDS banner.

"The gay community is going to stop screaming," she said. "It is already stopping."

"I'm very despondent," Kramer said. "You don't know where to yell or who to yell at. Clinton says all the right things, then doesn't do anything."

Indeed, the Clinton Administration does say all the right things, at times coming close to being patronizing about it.

"I have a real understanding that the people who feel the strongest about this, they don't have time," Carol H. Rasco, the President's top domestic policy adviser, said in defense of the zealotry of Act Up. "When a bomb is ticking inside you, you have to keep pushing."

Where once Washington doors were closed to AIDS activists, they are now open. Indeed, perhaps the single biggest AIDS change in Washington under the Clinton Administration has been one of tone. AIDS sufferers are no longer treated as immoral lepers. David Barr, director of treatment education and advocacy for the Gay Men's Health Crisis, recalled a May meeting with Donna E. Shalala, the Secretary of Health and Human Services.

"She agreed to everything we wanted," Barr said. "I was amazed. We're so used to doing battle. But is it a ploy?"

Certainly Bill Clinton is a vast improvement over George Bush. The President proposed a major increase in spending on AIDS research, about 20 percent, coming up with an additional $227 million. That would raise the total N.I.H. spending on AIDS research to $1.3 billion. In aid for outpatient care, the White House proposed a giant increase in what is known as Ryan White money, named for the Midwestern teen-ager who died of AIDS in April 1990. The current appropriation is $348 million, which the Administration proposed to nearly double by adding $310 million. The House didn't add the entire amount, just a $200 million increase, but it still brought the total to $548 million. The Senate was slightly more generous, and the final appropriation was $579 million.

But is more money enough? AIDS activists say they want leadership, but they are not sure anymore what that means.

"It was much easier," said Torie Osborn, "when we could hate George Bush and Ronald Reagan, when we thought we had evil genocidal Republican Presidents who weren't doing what needed to be done to get a cure."

Still, as is so often the case with Bill Clinton, he is victim of his own lofty campaign rhetoric. He spoke eloquently about AIDS in his pitches for the gay vote. He insisted that people infected with the AIDS virus, Bob Hattoy and Elizabeth Glaser, speak at the Democratic National Convention. On Election Night, he mentioned AIDS high in his victory speech. It all seemed so promising. David B. Mixner, a Clinton friend who helped rally the gay vote, exclaimed in the flush of a Clinton victory, "I believe thousands of my friends who wouldn't make it, who would die of AIDS, might make it now because Bill Clinton is President."

There it is: the man from Arkansas was to be not just President but savior. He's not. Bogged down early on in a battle over homosexuals in the military, Clinton has grown wary of anything that the public might perceive as a gay issue. He delayed fulfilling his campaign pledge to name an AIDS czar, finally naming her five months into his term—and only when the National Commission on AIDS was about to attack him for not providing leadership on the epidemic.

More than anything else, what the AIDS community wants from Bill Clinton is a sense of urgency. Carol Rasco maintains that Clinton is committed. "Health-care reform and AIDS are the only things I've worked on every day since I got here," said the domestic policy adviser. But others, even in the Administration, think Clinton is doing little to help.

"Other than myself, who lives with AIDS every day, there's no one at the White House for whom this is their first-tier issue," said Bob Hattoy, who, after serving six months as a White House aide often critical of the Administration's AIDS policies, was shifted to the Interior Department. He praised the President and Mrs. Clinton for having "a profoundly sensitive awareness about AIDS," but at the staff level, he said, "AIDS is not on the radar screens at the White House every day." And the political advisers? Hattoy scoffed. "I don't think they'll address AIDS until the Perot voters start getting it."

THE CZAR AND THE PRESS

There was a time when it was thought that the solution to the AIDS crisis could be found in two words: AIDS czar. One omnipotent public figure with the power to marshal funds, direct research, cut through the bureaucracy—in short, to lead a Manhattan Project-size effort to force a cure for AIDS. Kristine M. Gebbie doesn't look like a czar, and she doesn't think of herself as one either. At fifty, she has the air of the head nurse. There is something at once no-nonsense and fussy about her—her erect posture, her precise and proper answers, her tendency to correct an interviewer's questions. She is what she is—a nurse who worked her way up through the public-health bureaucracy, a divorced mother of three children, who has willed herself to a better lot in life. In 1978 she became the chief health officer of Oregon and then, eleven years later, the chief health officer of Washington State. Her experience with AIDS is primarily as a bureaucrat, as chairman of the Centers for Disease Control's advisory panel on H.I.V. prevention and as a member of the National Commission on AIDS.

Now, she is the AIDS czar—a far cry from the stellar names that AIDS activists had fantasized about: H. Norman Schwarzkopf, Jimmy Carter, C. Everett Koop.

"We wanted 'Jurassic Park,' and we got 'Snow White,'" Larry Kramer likes to say.

"The activists wanted a war on AIDS," Gebbie said, shaking her head. "I am not one of the big names. I am someone who has struggled with systems around this epidemic since the beginning. I think I have a feel for what it takes to bring people together."

Indeed, asked to give her job description, she responded, "consensus builder."

Gebbie, whose offical title is national AIDS policy coordinator, sees her job as exactly that—coordinating the various Federal agencies like Defense and Housing and Education in terms of prevention, care and research. Her goal is to have the agencies themselves take over the assault on AIDS, so she sees hers as a short-term job—three or five years, "ten years tops." She expects to take no role in research other than, again, as a coordinator, but not one who independently sets priorities.

And what happened to the eagerly awaited Manhattan Project?

"Manhattan Project?" Gebbie said. "I don't know what that means. Both the Manhattan Project and the Man-on-the-moon project involved, I think, a much more targeted goal. We know where we'd like to go—fix AIDS—but I'm not sure we can conceptualize what it would take to do that. On the other hand, if what 'Manhattan Project' conveys is: 'The Government is behind you,' well, if I do my job right, we will target and have energy and direction. What we won't have is somebody in general's stripes who can walk around and order people, 'Drop what you're doing and work on H.I.V.'"

Gebbie advocates distributing condoms to sexually active teenagers, though not necessarily in the schools. She supports supplying clean needles to drug addicts. She backs "in extreme cases and only as a very last resort" the isolation of people infected with H.I.V. who continue to be sexually irresponsible. "It might be in a hospital or a group home," she said. And she advocates, in theory, and with full civil rights protection, the reporting of names of those with H.I.V. as a public-health technique for making sure connections are made to their partners for counseling and possible treatment.

Kristine Gebbie was not at the top of the Administration's list of candidates for AIDS czar. Most of the medical and private-sector leaders who were approached said they had withdrawn their names for personal reasons. Yet it was clear that they did not regard the post as the all-powerful one it might have been.

"There's this contradiction," said Dr. Mark D. Smith, a San Francisco AIDS expert who discussed the job with the Administration but eventually withdrew, "between the public perception of great responsibility and the reality of no real organizational authority."

Most of those considered said, however, that they might have taken the job as AIDS adviser to the President if Clinton himself had called to convince them. But he didn't. The $112,000-a-year position, which does not require Senate confirmation, was offered to Gebbie in a phone call from Rasco. Gebbie never met the President until the morning of the June 25 news conference to announce her appointment.

To be fair, on that sunny Friday in the Rose Garden when he announced the appointment of Gebbie, the President sounded like the old Bill Clinton, the one in the campaign. He finally did what the activists wanted—he spoke out on AIDS as President. He labeled the virus "one of the most dreaded and mysterious diseases humanity has ever known" and "an epidemic that has already claimed too many of our brothers and sisters, our parents and children, our friends and colleagues."

But the trouble was, no one was listening. Newspapers and the networks reported the naming of Gebbie. But few carried the President's comments on AIDS. *Newsweek* magazine, in a week-in-the-life-of-the-President piece, didn't even mention the Gebbie announcement. At the news conference, there was only one question on AIDS, and that was directed to Gebbie about her qualifications. Reporters were eager to move on to the real news, like the budget and homosexuals in the military.

AIDS, it seems, had become old news.

"In the early days of AIDS, when knowledge was expanding, there were lots of very compelling things to write about," said Marlene Cimons, who covers AIDS and Federal health policy out of the Washington bureau of *The Los Angeles Times*. "We were in the infant stages of making policy decisions about AIDS that had unique social and political ramifications. Now it's become harder to find angles. We've written to death most aspects of the disease: AIDS in the classroom, AIDS in the workplace. Testing. They filled the front pages. Now there's a vacuum."

Stuart Shear, a reporter for *The MacNeil/Lehrer Newshour* who covers AIDS, said the conflicts that had made for good stories—the fights between Republican Administrations and AIDS advocates—were gone.

"It's become a pure science story," he said. "When it gets down to the clinical nitty-gritty, that's not what we look at. It's hard to get people to come on and complain about an Administration that's increasing funding."

For her part, Gebbie, who has a budget of just under $3 million and a staff "of four or five"—with fifteen to twenty others, she said, in another office—seems to prefer being in the shadows. Her office will not be in the White House but in a building across the street that houses a McDonald's. "My guess," she said, "is that the choice of me makes clear that this isn't intended to be somebody who spends all their time outside rousing people up, but somebody who is prepared to spend a lot of time inside making it work.

"It's very clear how many people really did expect miracles," Gebbie said. "When I give what I know are appropriate answers, I know I sound like a bureaucratic stick-in-the-mud: 'This lady is not worth two bits to us; she talks about coordination and cooperation. Blah!'

"But part of my mission," Gebbie said mater-of-factly, "is to help people keep their expectations within reality."

Gebbie needn't worry. Expectations could hardly be lower. "People are weary and hopeless and sad—the researchers, the activists, the care-givers," John H. Templeton, director of AIDS educational services at Grady Memorial Hospital in Atlanta, told me. "There is this sense that no matter what you do, it's all going to turn out the same in the end."

THE PATIENT AND JOURNALIST

In my interviews for this article and others, I always ask people with AIDS if they expect to die of the disease. One reason for that is a genuine reporter's curiosity; the answer is part of the profile of who they are. But I am also searching for hope for myself. Increasingly, the answers come back the same, even from the most optimistic of Act Up zealots: Yes, we will die of AIDS.

I thought about that the other day in the emergency room at Lenox Hill Hospital. I had taken my boyfriend there for a blood transfusion to offset the anemia caused by the chemotherapy for his Kaposi's sarcoma. I realized on that Sunday morning in the emergency room that the moment of crisis wasn't coming tomorrow or the next day for my boyfriend. It was here today. And it will soon be here today for me, too.

Does that make me angry? Yes. I had such hope when I interviewed Bill Clinton about AIDS and gay issues for *The New York Times* in August 1992. He spoke so eloquently on AIDS. I really did see him as a white knight who might save me. How naïve I was to think that one man could make that big a difference. At its core, the problem isn't a government; it's a virus.

Still, in interviews with researchers and Administration officials, it was clear that we are talking from different planets. I need help now, not five years from now. Yet the urgency just wasn't there. Compassion and concern, yes; even sympathy. But urgency, no. I felt alone, abandoned, cheated.

I asked Gebbie what she says to someone with AIDS—in other words, what she says to me. And for one brief moment, there was a glimmer of realization that delay means death.

"I say, 'I hear you and I appreciate the frustration and the sorrow and the loneliness,'" she said. "That can sound trite, but it is genuine. It's inappropriate for me to hold out a false promise to you. It would be easy to say: 'There, there. It will be better soon.' That's a disservice, so I have to be honest with you. We don't have quick answers. I can't tell you when we're going to have a cure."

I am on the cutting edge of drug testing, in a trial at New York Hospital for a new combination therapy: AZT, DDI and nevirapine. That is the combination that drew so much publicity last February when researchers in Boston declared that they had found the combination was effective in inhibiting the virus. But at the Berlin conference, the formulator of the concept, Yung-Kang Chow, a Havard medical student, reported a flaw in part of the original study. Other researchers challenged the findings after they were unable to confirm the results.

I was surprised at how jealous many of my fellow members of the support group were when I got into the trial—1 of only 25 people accepted out of more than 400 applicants. The group members felt that I had used influence. I had not. Yet admission to these trials is not purely luck, either—a point driven home when a number of leading researchers called, offering to get me into one of the nevirapine trials. I did not take them up on it. If my doctors used influence to get me in, it was not with my knowledge. But I am grateful if they did. The ship is beginning to sink; the water is lapping onto the deck. I am eager for any lifeboat, however leaky.

The letters pour in from readers who know I have AIDS, which I wrote about in this newpaper last December. A Florida woman wrote detailing her son's agonizing death from AIDS. Halfway through the letter, she caught herself, suddenly blurting out, "I don't know why I am writing this to you." Like so many of the letters, it was really not so much for me as for the writer, an excuse to open up her heart and let out the pain. She ended with a line I think of often, a line as much for her dead son, also named Jefffrey, as for me. "I intend this letter," she wrote, "as a mother's hug."

Hardly a day goes by without my getting a letter or call from someone who has the cure for AIDS. Many are crackpots. But others, I'm not so sure. Perhaps I will soon be desperate enough to pursue them.

More and more of the letters are nasty, even cruel. They are still the minority, but they make clear how deep the resentment runs against the attention given AIDS.

"As an average American," a man from Brooklyn wrote in a letter to the editor that made its way to me, "I cannot feel compassion for those who contracted AIDS through the pleasures of homosexuality, promiscuity or drug injection. The advent of the AIDS sickness in the world breaks my heart—but only for those who contracted it from blood transfusion, medical skin pricks or birth. The insipid news stories and other media accounts of AIDS pain, pneumonias and cancers attempt to reach me, but they only turn me off. And I, in turn, turn them off, as I suppose that millions of your readers do. Let's permit these pleasure seekers of the flesh to live out their years in hospices or homes at minimal cost and then die."

Am I bitter? Increasingly, yes. At the Act Up funeral for Bailey in Washington, I thought of how much the anger of the activists mirrored my own. I, too, wanted to shout—at no one really, just to vent the rage. I am dying. Why doesn't someone help us?

I didn't shout. I couldn't. All I could think about on that rainy Thursday afternoon was that a political funeral is not for me. It is at once very noble and very tacky.

What, then, is for me? I usually say that my epitaph is not a phrase but the body of my work. I am writing it with each article, including this one. But actually, there is a phrase that I want shouted at my funeral and written on the memorial cards, a phrase that captures the mix of cynicism and despair that I feel right now and that I will almost certainly take to my grave: *Whatever happened to AIDS?*

Suggestions For Further Reading

Conflicting assessments of the decision to drop the atomic bombs appear in G. Alperovitz, *Atomic Dipolmacy: Hiroshima and Potsdam* (rev. ed., 1985); H. Feis, *The Atomic Bomb and the End of World War II* (1966); M. Sherwin, *A World Destroyed: The Atomic Bomb and the Grand Alliance* (1975); L. Sigal, *Fighting to a Finish* (1988); and John Ray Skates, *The Invasion of Japan, Alternative to the Bomb* (1994). Also see G. Herken's comprehensive *The Winning Weapon: The Atomic Bomb in the Cold War, 1945–1950* (1982); J. Hershberg, *James B. Conant: Harvard to Hiroshima and the Making of the Nuclear Age* (1993); and two stimulating analyses of the cultural and psychological impact of the atomic weaponry: P. Boyer, *By the Bomb's Early Light* (1985), and A. Winkler, *Life Under a Cloud* (1993). On the origins and course of the Cold War consult J. Gaddis, *The United States and the Origins of the Cold War* (1972), *The Long Peace* (1987), and *Russia, the Soviet Union, and the United States* (2d ed., 1990); and for a more critical view, T. J. McCormick, *America's Half Century: United States Foreign Policy in the Cold War* (1992). Other explanations include J. Gormly, *The Collapse of the Grand Alliance, 1945–1948* (1987); F. Harbutt, *The Iron Curtain: Churchill, America and the Origins of the Cold War* (1986); M. Hogan, *The Marshall Plan* (1987); W. LaFeber, *America, Russia, and the Cold War* (6th ed., 1991); V. Mastny, *Russia's Road to the Cold War* (1979); R. Pollard, *Economic Security and the Origins of the Cold War* (1985); H. Thomas, *Armed Truce: The Beginnings of the Cold War* (1987); and L. Wittner, *American Intervention in Greece, 1943–1949* (1982). Of particular interest are M. Leffler's prizewinning *A Preponderance of Power* (1992); R. Maddox's controversial *From War to Cold War: The Education of Harry S. Truman* (1988); T. Paterson's revisionist *Meeting* the Communist Threat: Truman to Reagan (1988), and On Every Front: The Making and Unmaking of the Cold War (1992). Opposing interpretations of the Korean War are in R. Appleman, Disaster in Korea (1992); R. Foot, A Substitute for Victory (1990); J. Halliday and B. Cumings, Korea: The Unknown War (1989); and C. A. MacDonald, Korea (1987). Also see S. G. Zhang, Deterrence and Strategic Culture: Chinese-American Confrontations, 1949–1958 (1993). For the thinking of key American cold warriors, see W. Isaacson and E. Thomas, The Wise Men (1986); R. Messer, The End of an Alliance (1982); W. D. Miscamble, George F. Kennan and the Making of American Foreign Policy (1992); H. Schaffer, Chester Bowles: New Dealer in the Cold War (1993); M. Schaller, Douglas MacArthur (1989); and S. Talbott, The Master of the Game: Paul Nitze and the Nuclear Peace (1988). Compare with H. W. Brands, The Devil We Knew: American and the Cold War (1993), and J. S. Walter, Henry A. Wallace and American Foreign Policy (1976).

An excellent introduction to the meaning of McCarthyism is R. Fried, Nightmare in Red (1990). Fascinating full-scale accounts are J. Kovel, Red Hunting in the Promised Land (1994); D. Oshinsky, A Conspiracy So Immense: The World of Joe McCarthy (1983); and T. Reeves, The Life and Times of Joe McCarthy (1982). Clashing interpretations appear in D. Caute's biting The Great Fear: The Anti-Communist Purge Under Truman and Eisenhower (1978); R. Griffith, The Politics of Fear: Joseph R. McCarthy and the Senate (rev. ed., 1987); E. Latham, The Communist Controversy in Washington: From the New Deal to McCarthy (1966); M. Rogin, The Intellectuals and McCarthy: The Radical Specter (1967); and A. Theoharis's revisionist Seeds of Repression: Harry S Truman and the Origins of McCarthyism (1971). Also see A. Bloom's enlightening The New York Intellectuals: The Rise and Decline of the Anti-Stalinist Left (1987); H. Brick, Daniel Bell and the Decline of Intellectual Radicalism (1986); W. Graebner, The Age of Doubt: American Thought and Culture in the 1940s (1991); R. Pells, The Liberal Mind in a Conservative Age (1985); M. McAuliffe, Crisis on the Left: Cold War Politics and American Liberals (1978); G. May, Un-American Activities: The Trials of William Remington (1994); L. May, ed., Recasting America: Culture and Politics in the Age of Cold War America (1989); E. Schrecker, No Ivory Tower: McCarthyism and the Universities (1986); A. Theoharis and J. S. Cox, The Boss: J. Edgar Hoover and the Great American Inquisi-

tion (1988); and the provocative S. Whitfield, *The Culture of the Cold War* (1987).

Postwar American politics and social movements are broadly surveyed in J. M. Blum, *Years of Discord* (1991); W. H. Chafe, *The Unfinished Journey, America since World War II* (2d ed., 1991); D. Chidester, *Patterns of Power: Religion and Politics in American Culture* (1988); J. Diggins, *The Proud Decades: America in War and Peace* (1988); D. Halberstam, *The Fifties* (1993); M. Jezer, *The Dark Ages* (1982); W. O'Neill, *American High: The Years of Confidence* (1988); and G. Reichard's analytical *Politics as Usual* (1988). On the Truman presidency, see A. Dunar, *The Truman Scandals and the Politics of Morality* (1984); A. Hamby, *Beyond the New Deal: Harry S Truman and American Liberalism* (1973); M. Lacey, ed., *The Truman Presidency* (1989); D. McCullough's vivid *Truman* (1992); and W. Pemberton, *Harry S Truman: Fair Dealer and Cold Warrior* (1989). For Eisenhower: P. Brendon, *Ike* (1986); R. Burk, *Dwight D. Eisenhower: Hero & Politician* (1986); C. Pach, Jr., and E. Richardson, *The Presidency of Dwight D. Eisenhower* (1991); and N. Rae, *The Decline and Fall of the Liberal Republicans* (1989). Also see S. Gillon's perceptive *The ADA and American Liberalism* (1987); E. T. May, *Homeward Bound: American Families in the Cold War Era* (1988); B. Schulman, *From Cotton Belt to Sunbelt* (1991); and E. Taylor's challenging *Prime-Time Families: Television Culture in Postwar America* (1989). The Kennedy administration is best aproached in I. Bernstein's highly sympathetic *Promises Kept: John F. Kennedy's New Frontier* (1991); T. Brown, *JFK: History of an Image* (1988); D. Burner, *John F. Kennedy and a New Generation* (1988); J. Giglio, *The Presidency of John F. Kennedy* (1991); and T. Reeves's critical *A Question of Character: A Life of John F. Kennedy* (1991). The range of interpretations appears in K. Thompson, ed., *The Kennedy Presidency* (1985). For foreign policies, see M. Beschloss, *The Crisis Years* (1991). G. Posner, *Case Closed: Lee Harvey Oswald and the Assassination of JFK* (1993) is the most recent salvo fired in this continuing battle of theories. V. Bornet, *The Presidency of Lyndon B. Johnson* (1983); P. Conkin, *Big Daddy from the Pedernales: Lyndon Baines Johnson* (1986); R. Dallek's balanced *Lone Star Rising: Lyndon Johnson and His Times* (1990); R. Divine, ed., *The Johnson Years* (1987); and D. Kearns's insightful *Lyndon Johnson and the American Dream* (1976) examine LBJ's life and presidency. Also see E. Berkowitz and K. McQuaid, *Creating the Welfare State* (1992); W. Leuchtenburg, *In the Shadow of FDR, From Harry Truman to Ronald Reagan* (1983); A. Matusow, *The Unraveling of America: A History of Liberalism in the 1960s* (1984); G. O'Brien, *Dream Time* (1988); T. Schactman, *Decade of Shocks: Dallas to Watergate* (1983); and T. White, *America in Search of Itself: The Making of the President, 1954–1980* (1982). Conflicting assessments of 1960s' liberalism appear in Charles Murray, *Losing Ground* (1984); J. Patterson, *America's Struggle Against Poverty* (1981); L. Meade, *Beyond Entitlement* (1986); J. Schwarz, *America's Hidden Success* (1983); and D. Zarefsky, *President Johnson's War on Poverty: Rhetoric and History* (1986).

The literature on the African-American freedom struggle continues to multiply rapidly, with insightful reminiscences and reflections as well as thoughtful monographs. An updated and comprehensive overview of the movement is H. Sitkoff, *The Struggle For Black Equality, 1954–1992* (rev. ed., 1993). Also see H. Hill and J. Jones, eds., *Race in America: The Struggle for Equality* (1993); R. King, *Civil Rights and the Idea of Freedom* (1992); R. Weisbrot, *Freedom Bound* (1991); and the photographic essay by D. Lyon, *Memories of the Southern Civil Rights Movement* (1992). On King, see T. Branch's dramatic *Parting the Waters, America in the King Years, 1954–63* (1988); J. Colaiaco, *Martin Luther King, Jr.: Apostle of Militant Nonviolence* (1993); D. Garrow, *Bearing the Cross* (1986); J. Ralph, Jr., *Northern Protest: Martin Luther King, Chicago, and the Civil Rights Movement* (1993); and the essays in P. Albert and R. Hoffman, eds., *We Shall Overcome: Martin Luther King, Jr. and the Black Freedom Struggle* (1990). Key monographs include C. Carson's sensitive analysis, *In Struggle: SNCC and the Black Awakening of the 1960s* (1981); W. H. Chafe, *Civilities and Civil Rights: Greensboro, North Carolina, and the Black Struggle for Freedom* (1980); D. Chappell, *Inside Agitators: White Southerners in the Civil Rights Movement* (1994); E. C. Clark, *The Schoolhouse Door: Segregation's Last Stand at the University of Alabama* (1993); D. Nieman, *Promises to Keep, African-Americans and the Constitutional Order, 1776 to the Present* (1991); R. Norrell, *Reaping the Whirlwind: The Civil Rights Movement in Tuskegee* (1985); M. Stern, *Calculating Vision: Kennedy, Johnson, and Civil Rights* (1992); J. Ralph, *Northern Protest: Martin Luther King, Jr., Chicago, and the Civil Rights Movement* (1993); and

W. L. Van Deburg's illuminating *New Day in Babylon: The Black Power Movement and American Culture* (1992). Major surveys include D. Goldfield, *Black White, and Southern: Race Relations and Southern Culture* (1990); and S. Lawson, *Running for Freedom: Civil Rights and Black Politics in America since 1941* (1991). On the women of the freedom struggle, see M. King, *Freedom Song: A Personal Story of the 1960s Civil Rights Movement* (1987); K. Mills, *This Little Light of Mine: The Life of Fannie Lou Hamer* (1993); and G. Wade-Gayles, *Pushed Back to Strength: A Black Woman's Journey Home* (1993). Vital first-person accounts are R. Abernathy, *And The Walls Came Tumbling Down* (1989); E. Brown, *A Taste of Power: A Black Woman's Story* (1992); J. Forman, *The Making of Black Revolutionaries* (1972); and D. Hilliard and L. Cole, *This Side of Glory: The Autobiography of David Hilliard and the Story of the Black Panther Party* (1993). In addition to Malcom X, as told to Alex Haley, *The Autobiography of Malcolm X* (1965), see the essays on Spike Lee's feature film *Malcolm X* by N. Painter and G. Horne in the *American Historical Review* (April 1993).

The rebirth of feminism is analyzed in W. H. Chafe, *The Paradox of Change* (1991) and *Women and Equality* (1977); A. Echols, *Daring to be Bad: Radical Feminism in America, 1965–1975* (1989); S. Evans's controversial and important, *Personal Politics: The Roots of Women's Liberation in the Civil Rights Movement and the New Left* (1978); R. Gatlin, *American Women Since 1945* (1987); C. Harrison's carefully argued *On Account of Sex: The Politics of Women's Issues, 1945–1968* (1988); E. Klein, *Gender Politics* (1984); and S. Lynn, *Progressive Women in Conservative Times: Racial Justice, Peace, and Feminism, 1945 to the 1960s* (1992). M. Faux, *Roe v. Wade* (1988), and K. Luker, *Abortion and the Politics of Motherhood* (1984), are sensitive studies. Also see R. Petchesky, *Abortion and Women's Choice* (1984). Analyses of the campaign for the Equal Rights Amendment include M. Berry, *Why the ERA Failed* (1986); J. Hoff-Wilson, *Rites of Passage: The Past and Future of the ERA* (1986); J. Mansbridge, *Why We Lost the ERA* (1986); and J. Sherron Dehart and D. Mathews, *The Equal Rights Amendment and the Politics of Cultural Conflict* (1988). Sexism and the color line is the subject of P. Cleage, *Deals With the Devil, and Other Reasons to Riot* (1993); P. Giddings, *When and Where I Enter: The Impact of Black Women on Race and Sex in America* (1984); and M. Wallace, *Black Macho and the Myth of the Superwoman*

(1979). Supplement with E. DuBois and V. Ruiz, eds., *Unequal Sisters: A Multicultural Reader in Women's History* (1990). An indispensable fictional account of women in the African-American freedom struggle is A. Walker, *Meridian* (1976). Other enlightening studies include B. Bailey, *From Front Porch to Back Seat: Courtship in Twentieth-Century America* (1988); S. Coontz, *The Way We Never Were* (1992); J. D'Emilio and E. Freedman's well-researched *Intimate Matters: A History of Sexuality in America* (1988); L. Faderman, *Odd Girls and Twilight Lovers, A History of Lesbian Life in Twentieth-Century America* (1994); E. Marcus, *Making History: An Oral History of the Struggle for Gay and Lesbian Civil Rights, 1945–1990* (1992); E. T. May, *Homeward Bound: American Families in the Cold War Era* (1988); and A. Skolnick, *Embattled Paradise* (1991). On the importance of gender as a historical subject, consult "Gender Histories and Heresies," special issue of *Radical History Review* 52 (Winter 1992).

The most useful histories of the United States intervention in Vietnam are E. Bergerud, *The Dynamics of Defeat* (1991); W. Gibbons, *The U. S. Government and the Vietnam War* (1986); G. Herring's forthright *America's Longest War* (2d ed., 1986); G. Hess's compelling *Vietnam and the Unites States* (1990); S. Karnow, *Vietnam* (rev. ed., 1991); G. Kolko, *Anatomy of a War: Vietnam, The United States, and the Modern Historical Experience* (1986); A. Short, *The Origins of the Vietnam War* (1989); and M. Young's revisionist *The Vietnam Wars* (1991). For the origins of American involvement see D. Anderson, *Trapped by Success* (1991); J. Arnold, *The First Domino* (1991); L. Gardner's insightful *Approaching Vietnam* (1988); and A. Rotter, *The Path to Vietnam* (1987). The escalation of the war is explained by L. Berman, *Lyndon Johnson's War* (1989); L. Cable, *Unholy Grail* (1991); D. Shapley, *Promise and Power: The Life and Times of Robert McNamara* (1993); and B. VanDerMark, *Into the Quagmire* (1991). Classic analyses still worth consulting are F. Fitzgerald, *Fire in the Lake: The Vietnamese and the Americans in Vietnam* (1972), and D. Halberstam, *The Best and the Brightest* (1972), on one side, and G. Lewy, *America in Vietnam* (1978), and N. Podhoretz, *Why We Were in Vietnam* (1982), on the other. Also see C. Appey, *Working Class War* (1992); A. Krepinevich, Jr., *The Army and Vietnam* (1986); T. Schoenbaum, *Waging Peace and War* (1988); and N. Sheehan, *A Bright Shining Lie: John Paul Vann and America in Vietnam* (1988). Helpful assessments of the lessons and legacies of the conflict include L. Baritz's intriguing *Backfire: A History of How American Culture Led Us into Vietnam and Made Us Fight the Way We Did* (1985); J. Hellman, *American Myth and the Legacy of Vietnam* (1986); D. Levy, *The Debate over Vietnam* (1991); T. J. Lomperis, *The War Everyone Lost—and Won* (1984); M. MacPherson, *Long Time Passing: Vietnam and the Haunted Generation* (1984); and J. Rowe and R. Berg, eds., *The Vietnam War and American Culture* (1991). The behavior and policies of the presidents are analyzed in D. L. Anderson, ed., *Shadow on the White House: Presidents and the Vietnam War* (1993). Opposition to the war is analyzed in C. DeBenedetti and C. Chatfield, *An American Ordeal: The Antiwar Movement of the Vietnam Era* (1990); K. Heineman, *Campus Wars* (1993); M. Small and W. Hoover, eds., *Give Peace a Chance: Exploring the Vietnam Antiwar Movement* (1992); T. Wells, *The War Within* (1994); and N. Zaroulis and G. Sullivan, *Who Spoke Up? American Protests Against the War in Vietnam* (1984). More broadly, the revolt of the young in the 1960s is discussed by such former activists as W. Breines, *Community and Organization in the New Left, 1962–1968* (rev. ed., 1989); T. Gitlin, *The Sixties: Years of Hope, Days of Rage* (1987); T. Hayden, *Reunion* (1988); M. Isserman, *If I Had a Hammer . . . : The Death of the Old Left and the Birth of the New Left* (1987); J. Miller, *"Democracy Is in the Streets": From Port Huron to the Siege of Chicago* (1987); and W. J. Rorabaugh, *Berkeley at War: The 1960s* (1989). Also see D. Dellinger, *From Yale to Jail, The Life Story of a Moral Dissenter* (1993); A. Jamison and R. Eyerman, *Seeds of the Sixties* (1994); C. Levitt, *Children of Privilege: Student Revolt in the Sixties* (1984); and the scholarly collection, D. Farber, ed., *The 1960s: From Memory to History* (1994). A scathing look at the New Left and the protest movements is P. Collier and D. Horowitz, *Destructive Generation: Second Thoughts About the Sixties* (1989); a positive interpretation is W. H. Chafe, *Never Stop Running: Allard Lowenstein and the Struggle to Save American Liberalism* (1993). Fascinating accounts of the counterculture include S. Booth, *Dance With the Devil: The Rolling Stones and Their Times* (1984); M. Dickstein, *Gates of Eden: American Culture in the Sixties* (1977); C. Perry, *The Haight-Ashbury* (1984); J. Stevens, *Storming Heaven: LSD and the American Dream* (1987); and J. Weiner, *Come Together: John Lennon in His Time* (1984). They should be supplemented with C. Reich, *The Greening of America* (1970); T. Roszak, *The Making of a*

Counter Culture (1969); and P. Slater, *The Pursuit of Loneliness* (rev. ed., 1976). The year of shocks is analyzed by D. Farber, *Chicago '68* (1988); L. Gould, *1968: The Election That Changed America* (1993); C. Kaiser, *1968 in America* (1988); and I. Unger and D. Unger, *Turning Point: 1968* (1988). The years after are traced by B. Epstein, *Political Protest and Cultural Revolution: Nonviolent Direct Action in the 1970s and 1980s* (1991), and P. Carroll, *It Seemed Like Nothing Happened: America in the 1970s* (1990).

Important studies of the Nixon presidency and Watergate include S. Ambrose, *Nixon*, 3 vols. (1987–1991); S. Kutler, *The Wars of Watergate: The Last Crisis of the Nixon Presidency* (1990); K. McQuaid, *The Anxious Years: America in the Vietnam-Watergate Era* (1989); R. Morris, *Richard Milhous Nixon* (1990); H. Parmet, *Richard Nixon and His America* (1990); J. Schell, *Observing the Nixon Years* (1989); and T. Wicker, *One of Us* (1991). The turn to the right is analyzed by W. C. Berman, *America's Right Turn, From Nixon to Bush* (1994); S. Blumenthal, *The Rise of the Counter-Establishment* (1986); T. Edsall and M. Edsall, *Chain Reaction* (1991); T. Ferguson and J. Rogers, *Right Turn: The Decline of the Democrats and the Future of American Politics* (1986); J. D. Hunter, *Culture Wars, The Struggle to Define America* (1991); and D. Reinhard, *The Republican Right Since 1945* (1983). Also see J. R. Greene, *The Limits of Power: The Nixon and Ford Administrations* (1992); B. Kaufman, *The Presidency of James Earl Carter, Jr.* (1993); and A. J. Reichley, *Conservatives in an Age of Change: The Nixon and Ford Administrations* (1981). Key questions are raised by P. Arnold, *Making the Managerial Presidency* (1986), and W. Grover, *The President as Prisoner: A Structural Critique of the Carter and Reagan Years* (1990). Contemporary interpretations of the Reagan and Bush administrations are S. Blumenthal, *Our Long National Daydream* (1988); P. Boyer, ed., *Reagan as President* (1990); C. Campbell and B. A. Rockman, eds., *The Bush Presidency: First Appraisals* (1991); L. Cannon, *President Reagan: A Role of a Lifetime* (1991); M. Duffy and D. Goodgame, *Marching in Place: The Status Quo Presidency of George Bush* (1992); L. Freedman and E. Karsh, *The Gulf Conflict 1990–1991* (1993); H. Johnson, *Sleepwalking Through History: America in the Reagan Years* (1991); W. Niskanen, *Reaganomics* (1988); K. Phillips, *The Politics of Rich and Poor* (1990); M. Rogin, *Ronald Reagan the Movie, and Other Episodes in Political Demonology* (1987); M. Schaller, *Reckoning with*

Reagan (1992); and J. K. White, *The New Politics of Old Values* (1988). Interesting journalistic accounts of politics in the 1990s include E. J. Dionne, *Why Americans Hate Politics* (1992); W. Greider, *Who Will Tell the People* (1992); K. A. Jamieson, *Dirty Politics* (1992); K. Phillips, *Boiling Point: Republicans, Democrats, and the Decline of Middle-Class Prosperity* (1993); and R. Teixeira, *The Disappearing American Voter* (1992). A valuable guide for researchers is W. Hixson, Jr., *Search for the American Right Wing: An Analysis of the Social Science Record, 1955–1987* (1994).

Looking toward the new century, racial and immigration matters are analyzed in J. Cockcroft, *Outlaws in the Promised Land: Mexican Immigrant Workers and America's Future* (1986); S. Cornell, *The Return of the Native: American Indian Political Resurgence* (1988); R. Daniels, *Coming to America* (1990); M. Davis, *Mexican Voices, American Dreams* (1990); R. Farley and W. Allen, *The Color Line and the Quality of Life in America* (1987); L. Fuchs, *The American Kaleidoscope: Race, Ethnicity and the Civic Culture* (1990); L. Kessler, *Stubborn Twig: Three Generations in the Life of a Japanese American Family* (1993); N. McCall, *Make Me Wanna Holler, A Young Black Man in America* (1994); P. MacDonald with T. Schwarz, *The Last Warrior* (1993); D. Reimers, *Still the Golden Door: The Third World Comes to America* (1985); P. J. Rutledge, *The Vietnamese Experience in America* (1992); L. Sigelman and S. Welch, *Black American's Views of Racial Inequality* (1991); S. Terkel, *Race: How Blacks and Whites Think and Feel About the American Obsession* (1992); and V. Yans-McLaughlin, ed., *Immigration Reconsidered: History, Sociology, and Politics* (1990). Class and the economy are treated in D. Bartlett and J. Steele, *America: What Went Wrong* (1992); B. Bluestone and B. Harrison, *The Deindustrialization of America* (1982); D. Ellwood, *Poor Support: Poverty in the American Family* (1988); C. Jencks, *Rethinking Social Policy: Race, Poverty, and the Underclass* (1992); F. Levy, *Dollars and Dreams: The Changing American Income Distribution* (1987); K. Newman, *Falling from Grace: The Experience of Downward Mobility in the American Middle Class* (1988); G. Pappas, *The Magic City: Unemployment in a Working-Class Community* (1989); L. Thurow, *The Zero-Sum Society: Distribution and the Possibilites for Economic Change* (1980); and W. J. Wilson, *The Truly Disadvantaged: The Inner City, the Underclass, and Public Policy* (1987). M. Katz, *The Undeserving Poor: From the War on Poverty to the War on Welfare* (1989) is vital.

For continuing gender issues, see S. Evans and B. Nelson, *Wage Justice: Comparable Worth and the Paradox of Technocratic Reform* (1989); S. Faludi, *Backlash: The Undeclared War Against American Women* (1991); A. R. Hochschild, *The Second Shift: Working Parents and the Revolution at Home* (1989); and R. Sidel, *Women and Children Last* (1986). Further examinations of related issues are L. Gordon, *Heroes of Their Own Lives: The Politics and History of Family Violence* (1988); L. Gordon, ed., *Women, the State, and Welfare* (1990); S. A. Hewlett, *When the Bough Breaks: The Cost of Neglecting Our Children* (1991); J. Kozol, *Rachel and Her Children: Homeless Families in America* (1988); and E. F. Torrey, *Nowhere to Go: The Tragic Odyssey of the Homeless Mentally Ill* (1988).

Thoughtful approaches to some of today's vital environmental issues include B. Commoner's influential *The Closing Circle* (1971) and *Making Peace with the Planet* (rev. ed., 1990); M. D'Antonio, *Atomic Harvest* (1993); D. Day, *The Environmental Wars* (1989); D. Fisher, *Fire & Ice: The Greenhouse Effect, Ozone Depletion, and Nuclear Winter* (1990); D. Ford, *Three Mile Island* (1982); S. P. Hays, *Beauty, Health, and Permanence: Environmental Politics in the United States, 1955–1985* (1987); C. Manes, *Green Rage: Radical Environmentalism* (1990); M. Melosi, *Garbage in the Cities: Refuse, Reform, and the Environment* (1981); R. Nash, *The Rights of Nature: A History of Environmental Ethics* (1989); R. Paehlke, *Environmentalism and the Future of Progressive Politics* (1989); M. Reisner, *Cadillac Desert: The American West and Its Disappearing Water* (1986); R. Vietor, *Energy Policy in America Since 1945* (1984); L. Winner, *The Whale and the Reactor: A Search for Limits in an Age of High Technology* (1986); and D. Worster's thoughtful *Rivers of Empire: Water, Aridity and the Growth of the American West* (1985). Also see D. Worster, ed., *The Ends of the Earth: Perspectives on Modern Environmental History* (1988), as well as the perceptive speculations: J. Chace, *The Consequences of Peace* (1992); O. Graham, *Losing Time: The Industrial Policy Debate* (1992); and N. Mills, *Culture in an Age of Money: The Legacy of the 1980s in America* (1990).